THE AGE OF ROOSEVELT

The Crisis of the Old Order

1919–1933

BOOKS BY
ARTHUR M. SCHLESINGER, JR.

Orestes A. Brownson:
A Pilgrim's Progress

The Age of Jackson

The Vital Center

The General and the President
(with Richard H. Rovere)

The Age of Roosevelt
I. The Crisis of the Old Order, 1919-1933
II. The Coming of the New Deal
III. The Politics of Upheaval

The Politics of Hope

A Thousand Days:
John F. Kennedy in the White House

The Bitter Heritage:
Vietnam and American Democracy, 1941-1966

The Crisis of Confidence:
Ideas, Power and Violence in America

The Imperial Presidency

Robert Kennedy and His Times

The Cycles of American History

The American Heritage Library

THE AGE OF ROOSEVELT

THE CRISIS OF THE OLD ORDER

1919–1933

Arthur M. Schlesinger, Jr.

Houghton Mifflin Company · Boston

For information about permission to reproduce selections
from this book, write to Permissions, Houghton Mifflin Company,
2 Park Street, Boston, Massachusetts 02108.

Library of Congress Cataloging-in-Publication Data

Schlesinger, Arthur Meier, date.
    The crisis of the old order, 1919-1933 / Arthur M. Schlesinger, Jr.
        p.   cm. — (The American Heritage library)   (The Age of Roosevelt)
    Bibliography: p.
    Includes index.
    ISBN 0-395-48903-2 (pbk.)
    1. United States—History—1919-1933. 2. Depressions—1929—
United States. I. Title. II. Series. III. Series: Schlesinger, Arthur
Meier, date.   Age of Roosevelt.
E784.S36 1988 88-8210
973.91—dc19 CIP

Printed in the United States of America

S 10 9 8 7 6 5 4 3 2 1

FOR REINHOLD NIEBUHR

"Every revolution was first a thought
in one man's mind."

EMERSON

Foreword to
the American Heritage Library Edition

THE FIRST THREE VOLUMES of *The Age of Roosevelt*, now reissued in the American Heritage Library, were published a generation ago: *The Crisis of the Old Order* in 1957, *The Coming of the New Deal* in 1958, and *The Politics of Upheaval* in 1960. These volumes cover the life and times of Franklin Roosevelt through the election of 1936. Their emphasis, reflecting FDR's own priorities during these years, is on the New Deal and domestic affairs.

The next volume was scheduled to deal with FDR and foreign affairs in the 1930s. But in 1960 many essential foreign policy documents were under official lock and key, protected by government classification from scholarly inquiry. I saw no choice but to suspend *The Age of Roosevelt* until I could gain access to the files. Then, for a number of years thereafter, I was drawn into other matters, political and scholarly.

In these years also the American and British archives were gradually opened to the end of the Second World War (and now well beyond). The fourth volume of *The Age of Roosevelt*, covering FDR and the coming of the war, is at last in the making. More volumes will follow in due course. I regret the delay but take solace in the example of my putative ancestor George Bancroft, who published the first volume of his *History of the United States* in 1834 and, after spirited and interesting digressions into politics and public service, published the tenth (and final) volume in 1874 — and then added a two-volume *History of the Formation of the Constitution of the United States* in 1882 (at the age of eighty-two).

When I wrote *The Crisis of the Old Order*, FDR had been dead for hardly more than a decade. His presidency had stirred vivid and intense emotions. Like all great American presidents, he had been a divisive figure in his own time. Most Americans revered him. Some detested and reviled him. Change always provokes resentment and anger, especially on the part of those who benefit from the old order. The passions of the 1930s had not much abated by the 1950s. Many Americans still actively loved Roosevelt. A not inconsiderable number still actively hated him.

Moreover, the 1950s, like the 1920s thirty years before and the 1980s thirty years after, fell in the conservative phase of the political cycle. (In the same way, times of liberalism, reform, and affirmative government come along every thirty years: Theodore Roosevelt and the Progressive era in 1901, FDR and the New Deal in 1933, John Kennedy and the New Frontier in 1961.) The reputation of liberal presidents declines in conservative swings of the cycle, as the reputation of conservative presidents declines in liberal swings.

In any case, presidential reputations tend to be at low ebb in the years shortly after a president's death. When I went to college in the 1930s, Theodore Roosevelt, who died in 1919, and Woodrow Wilson, who died in 1924, were only beginning to emerge from the fashionable judgment that one was an adolescent braggart and the other a Presbyterian fanatic. The combination of the conservative phase of the cycle with the recency of FDR's death accounts for the somewhat defensive tone the reader may find in the foreword to *The Crisis of the Old Order*.

Today, nearly half a century after Roosevelt's death, the bitter passions of the 1930s and 1940s have pretty well subsided. Periodic polls of historians and political scientists routinely rank Roosevelt as one of the three greatest American presidents, with Lincoln and Washington. FDR reshaped scholarly conceptions and popular expectations about the presidency, and his towering personality and astute management of the office have haunted all his successors, as William Leuchtenburg reminded us in his excellent book of 1985, *In the Shadow of FDR*. Even during the conservative 1980s, when the most conservative president since Herbert Hoover mounted a counterrevolution against FDR's New Deal, Ronald Reagan nevertheless spoke with affection and respect of Franklin Roosevelt himself, perhaps because, when younger and possibly wiser, he had cast his first *four* presidential votes for FDR.

But history should never be an exercise in reverence. Franklin

Roosevelt had superb qualities of leadership, superb instincts for the crucial problems of his age, superb ability to select and manage vigorous subordinates, enormous skill as a public educator, and enormous ability to lift the spirits of the republic and to mobilize national energies. He was, however, far from infallible. He made mistakes both in policy and in politics. He had his moments of deviousness, craftiness, vanity, undue casualness, and insouciant cruelty. He combined soaring idealism with tough and sometimes petty realism. He was, in other words, a human being, somewhat larger than life but hardly exempt from human infirmity, frailty, and error.

Those vigorous subordinates in FDR's supporting cast add color and excitement to the age of Roosevelt. When these volumes were first published, their names and personalities—Hopkins, Ickes, Wallace, Hull, Morgenthau, Frankfurter, Tugwell, Berle, Frances Perkins, Tom Corcoran and Ben Cohen, Jimmy Byrnes and Jesse Jones, Robert Jackson and Francis Biddle, Sumner Welles and David Lilienthal—were still well known. What a formidable and dashing group they were! Few of them, alas, are household words today. Still I trust that these pages contain enough about their characters and contributions to explain their impact on those turbulent and agitated times. I had the great luck to know and interview a good many of them, and I hope that their testimony will impart a certain directness to the narrative.

Indeed, the determination to take advantage of living witnesses was an important motive in my decision to attempt *The Age of Roosevelt*. When I was preparing to write *The Age of Jackson*, I benefited greatly, as have all Jackson scholars, from James Parton's wonderful *Life of Andrew Jackson*. In his preface Parton discussed the problems of discovering information "respecting a man whom two thirds of his fellow-citizens deified, and the other third vilified, for a space of twelve years or more." To find out what Jackson was like, Parton, conducting his research a decade after Jackson's death, "conversed with politicians of the last generation, who have now no longer an interest in concealing the truth." He roamed around the country eliciting "the recollections of men and women, bond and free, who knew him well, knew him at all periods of his life, lived near him, and with him, served him and were served by him. . . . Thus it was that contradictions were reconciled, that mysteries were revealed, and that the truth was made apparent."

I cannot pretend to the journalistic skills or literary graces of James Parton. But I was struck by his methods. I was struck too by the frustrations that attend those methods, for the questions Parton asked of his witnesses were not always the questions to which future historians have sought answers. At any rate, I was inspired by his example to talk to FDR's friends, associates, and adversaries (no one was more generous and helpful than the fine man he trounced in 1936, Alfred M. Landon). I do not suppose that I was any more successful than James Parton in asking the questions that will interest scholars of the future, but I hope that at least testimony may have been preserved that might otherwise have perished with the witnesses.

Since these books were published, a very considerable literature has appeared on many facets of the age of Roosevelt. I do not believe that the outpouring of scholarly books, monographs, and articles changes the main outline of the story told in these volumes, but some float ingenious theories and others add valuable details. I will take account of this rich literature in the volumes of *The Age of Roosevelt* yet to come.

The Roosevelt years were above all a battlefield of ideas—ideas about the American past and the American future; ideas about the role of government in guaranteeing the economy and protecting the forgotten man (and woman); ideas about isolationism and internationalism and America's relationship to the world beyond; ideas articulated with uncommon vehemence and ardor and often with authentic brilliance; ideas that intersected with power and helped shape the destiny of the United States and the world.

Today, I believe, a new cyclical change impends in American politics. If the rhythm holds, the nation can be expected to move from the energetically conservative 1980s into an energetically progressive new decade. I would like to think that in this coming period new generations will find power and resonance in the memory of Franklin Roosevelt and the New Deal. Of course the problems of the 1990s will be very different from the problems of the 1930s. But the spirit of experiment, idealism, and concern with which the republic defeated the worst depression and won the greatest war in American history remains, I think, a precious resource as we confront the darkly unpredictable future.

ARTHUR M. SCHLESINGER, JR.

May 21, 1988

Foreword

THE AGE OF FRANKLIN DELANO ROOSEVELT covered much more than the dozen years of his Presidency. The events of 1933–45 climaxed half a century of American life. The nation, in responding to the bitter challenges of depression and war, summoned up the resources, moral and intellectual, of an earlier progressivism, an earlier war effort, and a decade of business leadership. Roosevelt's administration must be understood against this background of a generation's ideas, hopes, and experience.

This is, I suppose, a bad time to be writing about Franklin Roosevelt. As historians well know, the reputation of a commanding figure is often at its lowest in the period ten to twenty years after his death. We are always in a zone of imperfect visibility so far as the history just over our shoulder is concerned. It is as if we were in the hollow of the historical wave; not until we reach the crest of the next one can we look back and estimate properly what went on before. Theodore Roosevelt and Woodrow Wilson, for example, have only recently emerged from the season of comparative disfavor to which the passing of time temporarily condemned them.

This book claims no capacity to transcend these limitations. No one knows better than the author the inadequacy of the present perspective for any sort of lasting judgment. There are, however, compensating advantages in writing so soon — in particular, the opportunity to consult those who took part in great events and thus to rescue information which might otherwise elude the written record. Again, this book lays no claim to completeness on this score. The author will greatly welcome any corrections or amplifications for possible future editions.

My obligations in this undertaking are manifold. My father Arthur M. Schlesinger has, as ever, been a constant source of wisdom, guidance, and inspiration. To him and to my mother Elizabeth Bancroft Schlesinger I am indebted for a careful reading of the manuscript, and for much else. I owe a special debt to my friends Seymour E. Harris and J. Kenneth Galbraith, who have borne patiently through the years with my ignorance on economic matters and who saved me many errors through their critical reading of the text — a fact that does not, however, convict them of responsibility for the errors which may remain. My fellow Roosevelt scholars Herman Kahn, Frank Freidel, Basil Rauch, and John M. Blum have been generous in suggestion and counsel. A number of friends have read part or all of the manuscript and vastly improved it by their criticism: Emily Morison Beck, Ruth Harris, Barbara Wendell Kerr, Mary McCarthy, Richard H. Rovere, Morton G. White. Paul Brooks, Helen Phillips, and Anne Barrett of Houghton Mifflin have made valuable suggestions.

I want to express special acknowledgment to the Franklin D. Roosevelt Library, to Herman Kahn, who, as director, has shown with spectacular success how a library can serve the cause of scholarship, and to George Roach, William J. Nichols, and the rest of the admirable staff. I am also greatly in debt to the staff of the Harvard University Library, the National Archives, and the Oral History Project at Columbia University for many courtesies. I am grateful to Adolf A. Berle, Jr., Mary W. Dewson, Anna Roosevelt Halsted, Henry Morgenthau, Jr., Rexford G. Tugwell, and McGeorge Bundy (for the Henry L. Stimson estate) for permission to examine and quote from personal papers, as well as for counsel on many points.

A grant from the Guggenheim Foundation enabled me to begin work on this project; and grants from the Milton Fund at Harvard were of material assistance at later stages. My obligation to my secretary Julie Armstrong Jeppson is immeasurable, not only for typing and retyping the manuscript and checking references but even more for her inexhaustible patience, good humor, and generosity. And the work could never have been completed without the indispensable collaboration of my wife Marian Cannon Schlesinger, who improved the manuscript by crisp and thoughtful criticism and, more than that, tolerated and sustained her husband during the course of composition.

ARTHUR M. SCHLESINGER, JR.

February 25, 1956

Contents

THE AGE OF ROOSEVELT

The Crisis of the Old Order

1919 – 1933

1. Prologue: 1933

THE WHITE HOUSE, midnight, Friday, March 3, 1933. Across the country the banks of the nation had gradually shuttered their windows and locked their doors. The very machinery of the American economy seemed to be coming to a stop. The rich and fertile nation, overflowing with natural wealth in its fields and forests and mines, equipped with unsurpassed technology, endowed with boundless resources in its men and women, lay stricken. "We are at the end of our rope," the weary President at last said, as the striking clock announced the day of his retirement. "There is nothing more we can do." [1]

Saturday, March 4, dawned gray and bleak. Heavy winter clouds hung over the city. A chill northwest wind brought brief gusts of rain. The darkness of the day intensified the mood of helplessness. "A sense of depression had settled over the capital," reported the *New York Times*, "so that it could be felt." In the late morning, people began to gather for the noon ceremonies, drawn, it would seem, by curiosity as much as by hope. Nearly one hundred thousand assembled in the grounds before the Capitol, standing in quiet groups, sitting on benches, watching from rooftops. Some climbed the bare, sleet-hung trees. As they waited, they murmured among themselves. "What are those things that look like little cages?" one asked. "Machine guns," replied a woman with a nervous giggle. "The atmosphere which surrounded the change of government in the United States," wrote Arthur Krock, "was comparable to that which might be found in a beleaguered capital in war time." The colorless light of the cast-iron skies, the numb

faces of the crowd, created almost an air of fantasy. Only the
Capitol seemed real, etched like a steel engraving against the dark
clouds.[2]

On the drive from the White House to the Capitol, the retiring
President, his eyes lowered, his expression downcast, did not try
to hide his feelings. The nation which had helped him rise from
a poor Iowa farm to wealth and power, which he had repaid with
high-minded and unstinted service, had rejected him. "Democracy
is not a polite employer," Herbert Hoover later wrote. "The only
way out of elective office is to get sick or die or get kicked out." [3]

It was customary for the retiring President to ask his successor
for dinner on the night of the third of March; but Hoover had
declined to issue the usual invitation. At length, the White House
usher insisted that the President-elect must be given the opportunity to pay his respects. Instead of the traditional dinner, a tea
was arranged for the afternoon of the third. It had been a strained
occasion in the Red Room, complicated by fruitless last-minute
discussions about the banking crisis. Finally the President-elect,
recognizing that Hoover was not in the mood to complete the
round of protocol, politely suggested that the President need not
return the visit. Hoover looked his successor in the eye. "Mr.
Roosevelt," he said coldly, "when you are in Washington as long
as I have been, you will learn that the President of the United
States calls on nobody." Franklin Delano Roosevelt, hurrying
his family from the room, returned to the Mayflower Hotel visibly
annoyed. "It was . . ." a close friend later reported, "one of the
few times I have ever seen him really angry." [4]

Now Hoover sat motionless and unheeding as the car moved
through crowded streets toward the Capitol. Doubtless he assumed
the occasional cheers from the packed sidewalks were for Roosevelt
and so not his to acknowledge. But for Roosevelt, sitting beside
him in the open car, these last moments belonged to the retiring
President; it was not for the President-elect to respond to the
faint applause. On they drove in uncomfortable silence. Passing
the new Commerce Building on Constitution Avenue, Roosevelt
hoped that at least this sight might tempt the former Secretary of
Commerce into an exchange of amiabilities. When a friendly remark produced only an unintelligible murmur in reply, the Presi-

dent-elect suddenly felt that the two men could not ride on forever
like graven images. Turning, he began to smile to the men and
women along the street and to wave his top hat.[5] Hoover rode on,
his face heavy and expressionless.

The fog of despair hung over the land. One out of every four
American workers lacked a job. Factories that had once darkened
the skies with smoke stood ghostly and silent, like extinct volcanoes.
Families slept in tarpaper shacks and tin-lined caves and scavenged
like dogs for food in the city dump. In October the New York
City Health Department had reported that over one-fifth of the
pupils in public schools were suffering from malnutrition. Thousands of vagabond children were roaming the land, wild boys of
the road. Hunger marchers, pinched and bitter, were parading
cold streets in New York and Chicago. On the countryside unrest
had already flared into violence. Farmers stopped milk trucks along
Iowa roads and poured the milk into the ditch. Mobs halted mortgage sales, ran the men from the banks and insurance companies
out of town, intimidated courts and judges, demanded a moratorium
on debts. When a sales company in Nebraska invaded a farm and
seized two trucks, the farmers in the Newman Grove district
organized a posse, called it the "Red Army," and took the trucks
back. In West Virginia, mining families, turned out of their
homes, lived in tents along the road on pinto beans and black
coffee.[6]

In January, Edward A. O'Neal, an Alabama planter, head of the
Farm Bureau Federation, bluntly warned a Senate committee,
"Unless something is done for the American farmer we will have
revolution in the countryside within less than twelve months."
Donald Richberg, a Chicago lawyer, told another Senate committee
a few weeks later, "There are many signs that if the lawfully constituted leadership does not soon substitute action for words, a
new leadership, perhaps unlawfully constituted, will arise and
act." William Green, the ordinarily benign president of the
ordinarily conservative American Federation of Labor, told a third
committee that if Congress did not enact a thirty-hour law, labor
would compel employers to grant it "by universal strike." "Which
would be class war, practically?" interrupted Senator Hugo Black.
"Whatever it would be," said Green, "it would be that. . . . That

is the only language that a lot of employers ever understand — the language of force." [7] In the cities and on the farms, Communist organizers were finding a ready audience and a zealous following.

Patrick J. Hurley, Hoover's Secretary of War, ordered a transfer of troops from a small Texas post to Kentucky. Tom Connally of Texas, rising in the Senate, accused the War Department of deliberately concentrating its armed units near the larger cities. "The Secretary of War, with a glitter of fear in his eye," Connally reported, "referred to Reds and possible Communists that may be abroad in the land." The mayor of New York, newly inaugurated, sought to reassure his city: "You're going to have a Mayor with a chin and fight in him. I'll preserve the Metropolis from the Red Army." But the next week a group of Communists shoved their way though a police line before the brownstone house on East 65th Street where Franklin D. Roosevelt was making his plans for the future. Eleven Democratic leaders were having their picture taken on the front steps; they stepped nervously into the house as the Communists shook their fists and shouted, "When do we eat? We want action!" (Among the politicians were Cordell Hull and James F. Byrnes; they would have more to do with Communists before they were through.) The police with a flourish of nightsticks cleared the street.[8]

Elmer Davis reported that the leading citizens of one industrial city — it was Dayton, Ohio — had organized a committee to plan how the city and the country around could function as an economic unit if the power lines were cut and the railroads stopped running. Over champagne and cigars, at the Everglades in Palm Beach, a banker declared the country on the verge of revolution; another guest, breaking the startled silence, advised the company to "step without the territorial boundaries of the United States of America with as much cash as you can carry just as soon as it is feasible for you to get away." "There'll be a revolution, sure," a Los Angeles banker said on a transcontinental train. "The farmers will rise up. So will labor. The Reds will run the country — or maybe the Fascists. Unless, of course, Roosevelt does something." [9]

But what could he do? In February 1933, the Senate Finance Committee summoned a procession of business leaders to solicit their ideas on the crisis. Said John W. Davis, the leader of the

American bar, "I have nothing to offer, either of fact or theory." W. W. Atterbury of the Pennsylvania Railroad: "There is no panacea." Most endorsed the thesis advanced by the permanent elder statesman Bernard Baruch: "Delay in balancing the Budget is trifling with disaster." And, as they spoke their lusterless pieces, the banks began to close their doors. "Our entire banking system," said William Gibbs McAdoo in exasperation, "does credit to a collection of imbeciles." [10]

But bankruptcy of ideas seemed almost as complete among the intellectuals. "My heartbreak at liberalism," wrote William Allen White, "is that it has sounded no note of hope, made no plans for the future, offered no program." On the eve of the inaugural, a leading American theologian pronounced an obituary on liberal society. His essay was written, said Reinhold Niebuhr, on the assumption that "capitalism is dying and with the conviction that it ought to die." Let no one delude himself by hoping for reform from within. "There is nothing in history to support the thesis that a dominant class ever yields its position or its privileges in society because its rule has been convicted of ineptness or injustices." Others, in their despair, could only yearn for a savior. Hamilton Fish, the New York congressman, spoke for millions when he wrote to Roosevelt late in February that in the crisis we must "give you any power that you may need." [11]

The images of a nation as it approached zero hour: the well-groomed men, baffled and impotent in their double-breasted suits before the Senate committee; the confusion and dismay in the business office and the university; the fear in the country club; the angry men marching in the silent street; the scramble for the rotting garbage in the dump; the sweet milk trickling down the dusty road; the noose dangling over the barn door; the raw northwest wind blasting its way across Capitol plaza.

In the Capitol, the President-elect waited in the Military Affairs Committee Room. Sober and white-faced, he sat in silence, glancing at the manuscript of his inaugural address. Huey Long, the senator from Louisiana, glimpsed him and started to sweep into the room; then paused at the threshold and tiptoed away. Ten minutes before noon Roosevelt started down the corridor toward the Senate, only to be stopped. "All right," he said, "we'll go back and wait some more." When the moment arrived, he was to ride in his wheelchair to the east door; then walk thirty-five yards to the speaker's stand.

A few moments before, in the Senate Chamber, the new Vice-President, John Nance Garner of Texas, had taken his oath of office. There followed a rush from the Senate to the inaugural stand outside. The mass of people, swarming into the narrow exit from the east doors of the Capitol, blocked the runway. In a moment the congestion was hopeless. Garner and the retiring Vice-President, Charles Curtis of Kansas, had meanwhile reached the stand. The Texan, with no overcoat, shivered in the harsh wind; he borrowed a muffler and wrapped it around his neck. Near him Curtis disappeared into the depth of his fur coat, looking steadily at the floor, apparently lost in memory. Gradually, invited guests began to force their way through the jam: members of the new cabinet, half a dozen senators, the new President's wife, his mother, his tall sons. Eventually Charles Evans Hughes, the Chief Justice of the United States, made his appearance, erect and stately, a black silk skullcap on his head, his white beard stirred by the wind and his black robe fluttering about his legs. In a leather-upholstered chair to the left of the lectern sat Herbert Hoover.

The tension in the crowd mounted steadily with the delay. Presently a Supreme Court attendant arrived bearing the family Bible of the Roosevelts. Then, at last, the bugle sounded; and Franklin Delano Roosevelt, intensely pale, leaning on the arm of his eldest son James, walked slowly up the maroon-carpeted ramp. The Marine Band, in its scarlet jackets and blue trousers, finished the last bars of "Hail to the Chief." There was a convulsive stir in the crowd, spread over forty acres of park and pavement; then cheers and applause. Mrs. Woodrow Wilson waved a handkerchief. Bernard Baruch leaped upon a bench and swung his black silk hat. Josephus Daniels, the new President's old chief, his eyes wet with tears, pounded vigorously with his cane. A few rays of sunshine broke for a moment through the slate clouds upon the inaugural stand.

The Chief Justice read the oath with dignity and power. Instead of returning the customary "I do," Roosevelt repeated the full oath. ("I am glad," Hughes had written when the President-elect suggested this. ". . . I think the repetition is the more dignified and appropriate course." [12]) The family Bible lay open to the thirteenth chapter of the First Corinthians. "For now we see through a glass, darkly; but then face to face: now I know in part; but then shall I know even as also I am known. And now abideth faith, hope, charity, these three; but the greatest of these *is* charity."

Six days before, Roosevelt in his Hyde Park study, writing with pencil on a lined, legal-sized yellow pad, had made a draft of his inaugural address. Waiting in the Senate committee room on inauguration day, he added a new opening sentence to his reading copy: "This is a day of consecration." But, as the great crowd quieted down, the solemnity of the occasion surged over him; he said, in ringing tones, "This is a day of national consecration." [13]

Across the country millions clustered around radio sets. The new President stood bareheaded and unsmiling, his hands gripping the lectern. The moment had come, he said, to speak the truth, the whole truth, frankly and boldly. "Let me assert my firm belief that the only thing we have to fear is fear itself — nameless, un-reasoning, unjustified terror which paralyzes needed efforts to convert retreat into advance." The speaker flung back his head. "In every dark hour of our national life a leadership of frankness and vigor has met with that understanding and support of the people themselves which is essential to victory."

The bounty of nature, he continued, was undiminished. "Plenty is at our doorstep, but a generous use of it languishes in the very sight of the supply." Why? Because the rulers of the exchange of mankind's goods "have failed through their own stubbornness and their own incompetence, have admitted their failure, and have abdicated. . . . They have no vision, and when there is no vision the people perish. The money changers have fled from their high seats in the temple of our civilization." The crowd delivered itself of its first great applause. "There must be an end," Roosevelt went on, "to a conduct in banking and in business which too often has given to a sacred trust the likeness of callous and selfish wrong-doing." Again the crowd shouted.

"This Nation asks for action, and action now. . . . We must act and act quickly. . . . We must move as a trained and loyal army willing to sacrifice for the good of a common discipline, because without such discipline no progress is made, no leadership becomes effective." "It may be," he said, "that an unprecedented

demand and need for undelayed action may call for temporary
departure from that normal balance of public procedure." If
Congress should fail to enact the necessary measures, if the
emergency were still critical, then, added Roosevelt solemnly, "I
shall ask the Congress for the one remaining instrument to meet
the crisis — broad Executive power to wage a war against the
emergency, as great as the power that would be given to me if we
were in fact invaded by a foreign foe." The crowd thundered
approval in a long, continuing demonstration — the loudest applause of the day.

Roosevelt — "his face still so grim," reported Arthur Krock,
"as to seem unfamiliar to those who have long known him" — did
not acknowledge the applause. Nor, indeed, did all share the
enthusiasm. Some who watched the handsome head and heard
the cultivated voice mistrusted what lay behind the charm and the
rhetoric. "I was thoroughly scared," the retiring Secretary of State,
Henry L. Stimson, wrote in his diary. ". . . Like most of his past
speeches, it was full of weasel words and would let him do about
what he wanted to." Edmund Wilson, covering the inaugural for
the *New Republic,* saw "the old unctuousness, the old pulpit
vagueness," the echoes of Woodrow Wilson's eloquence without
Wilson's glow of life behind them. "The thing that emerges most
clearly," wrote Wilson, "is the warning of a dictatorship."

But the unsmiling President showed no evidence of doubt. "We
do not distrust the future of essential democracy," he said in summation. "The people of the United States have not failed. In
their need they have registered a mandate that they want direct,
vigorous action. They have asked for discipline and direction
under leadership. They have made me the present instrument of
their wishes. In the spirit of the gift I take it." Herbert Hoover
stared at the ground.

The high clear note of the cavalry bugles announced the inaugural parade. Franklin Roosevelt, in the presidential car, waved
greetings to the crowd along the way — men and women now
curiously awakened from apathy and daze. The horsemen wheeled
into line, and the parade began.

In Washington the weather remained cold and gray. Across the
land the fog began to lift.

I

The Golden Day

2. Darkness at Noon

LLOYD GEORGE rose in the House of Commons. "I hope we may say," he said, with emotion, "that thus, this fateful morning, came to an end all wars." [1]

Many men on that November day in 1918 cherished no less magnificent a vision of the future. If the shock of world war had warned of a civilization on the edge of disaster, then the experience of victory now suggested that men had within them the resources for salvation. For, if war meant slaughter and destruction, it also meant the common dedication to an end larger than self or profit. In such a spirit civilization could be reborn.

War thus offered hope. And it offered in addition a vast release of energy — the release that came from the breaking of molds, the diversion of lives from accustomed channels. When boys who should have been at school held in their hands the power of life and death, what could they not now do to rebuild the tormented world? The atmosphere trembled everywhere with anticipation of change. It was the moment of revolution in Russia and imminent revolution in Germany, of Wells and Shaw and the Webbs and the Fabian hope, of ferment and faith. It seemed a time of illimitable possibility.

And nowhere was it felt more a young man's world than at Versailles, where in the spring of 1919 the victors gathered to make the peace. The old men might retain the power of decision, but the young believed that they could propose the plans and define the choices. The official exegesis for Woodrow Wilson's Fourteen Points had been prepared by Walter Lippmann, aged 30. Joseph C. Grew, aged 39, was secretary-general of the American Commission; Norman H. Davis, aged 40, its financial adviser. The reparations provision of the settlement was in the charge of John Foster Dulles, aged 31, and his younger brother Allen, aged 26, was a key member of the American secretariat. William C. Bullitt, aged 28, was chief of intelligence for the American delegation, while Adolf A. Berle, Jr., aged 24, was acting chief of the Russian section. Edwin M. Watson, aged 35, was President Wilson's military aide. As counsel for the American Zionists, Benjamin V. Cohen, aged 25, was working to secure a homeland for the Jews.

The young men circulated on the periphery of power. If, as realists, they were fascinated by its exercise, they were as idealists passionately concerned that it create a world adequate to the needs of mankind. Bill Bullitt was characteristic, though more explosive than the rest. In his career in these bitter months, the idealism of youth clashed most sharply with the disillusionment of age and the necessity of nations.

II

Born in Philadelphia, reared in Rittenhouse Square, educated at Yale, Bullitt was rosy-cheeked, bright, restless, charming, and willful. He had traveled widely and had a talent for historic moments. One night in July 1914, when he was visiting Moscow with his mother, he had been awakened by an uproar in the streets. From his window in the Hotel National he watched the angered crowd stream down the avenue from the Kremlin, shouting for war. Later the Philadelphia *Public Ledger* sent him back to Europe on Henry Ford's Peace Ship; and, from there, Bullitt, accompanied by his wife, moved on to cover the war from inside Germany. "We feared to go to sleep lest we talk indiscreetly," Ernesta Drinker Bullitt noted in her diary when they arrived in Hamburg. "That a dictograph was hidden in the heater was a certainty, in Billy's mind." The dictograph in the heater would always be a certainty for Billy, the symbol of the romantic and conspiratorial temper which lay just under his urbanity and fun. (But it represented too an accurate foreboding of an age when, all too often, the dictograph would really be in the heater.) [2]

Bullitt returned from Germany convinced that the Central Powers presented a mortal threat to the United States. But war could be justified only as a means to peace, and peace only if it were founded on justice. Bullitt avidly followed the news from Russia. He read with excitement the speech in which Woodrow Wilson launched the Fourteen Points. The voice of the Russian people, Wilson said, seemed to him "more thrilling and more compelling than any of the many moving voices with which the troubled air of the world is filled." The treatment accorded Russia by her sister nations, the President continued, must be the "acid test" of their good will.[3]

Determined to share in the great work of peace, skilled, confiding, and useful, Bullitt won the support of Colonel House and an assignment at Versailles. The question of Russia loomed over the peace conference; and Bullitt suggested that the best way to find out whether the Bolsheviks would enter the concert of Europe would be to ask them. Early in 1919, Bullitt, under orders from Wilson and Lloyd George, set out to see whether terms could be negotiated. In his party was Lincoln Steffens, the veteran American muckraker; also a male secretary, with whom, throughout the trip, Bullitt wrestled and tumbled, as Steffens said, "like a couple of bear cubs along the Arctic Circle."

The mission succeeded beyond expectation. Bullitt obtained from Lenin terms far more favorable to the Allies than anyone could have expected. It was Steffens after this mission who replied, when Bernard Baruch asked him what Russia was like, "I have been over into the future, and it works." But Bullitt, if less epigrammatic, was no less impressed. He wrote Wilson that "no government save a socialist government can be set up in Russia today except by foreign bayonets" and that "the Lenin wing of the communist party is to-day as moderate as any socialist government which can control Russia."

Bullitt returned to Paris brimming with enthusiasm. He reported to Colonel House, who congratulated him; then, Wilson not being immediately available, he breakfasted with Lloyd George and told him the news. But Wilson, whether because of pique that Bullitt had talked to House and Lloyd George first or for other reasons, declined to see him. New forces conspired against a settlement with the Bolsheviks. The conservative press in London and Paris denounced the idea; and, when in April the White divisions of Admiral Kolchak seemed to be pushing the Reds back, the Bullitt proposals dropped out of the picture. Questioned in Commons, Lloyd George casually said, "I know nothing of a journey some young Americans were reported to have made to Russia." [4]

III

On a May night in a private room at the Crillon, the "young Americans" gathered to discuss the emerging shape of the peace. Steffens was the only older man present. For the rest, there were Bullitt, Berle, Samuel Eliot Morison, Christian A. Herter, and others. Bullitt saw nothing ahead but disaster. He said here, perhaps for the first time (though not for the last), that he planned to go to the Riviera to lie on the sand and watch the world go to hell. Most of the company agreed. The proposed treaty was a betrayal; this was no new order, but rather the evil old conspiracy of naked force; youth had once again been done in by age.

Bullitt, Berle, and Morison advocated resigning from the delegation. Someone asked what this would accomplish. Such an act, it was suggested, had the futile gallantry of mosquitoes charging a battleship. Berle replied hotly that in the long run force was bound to be temporary, that idealism was "America's sharpest sword" and would determine history. Over the coffee (as Berle remembers it) Bullitt took up flowers from the table, awarding red roses, badges of honor, to those who would resign; to those who would not, he contemptuously tossed yellow jonquils. It was late in the evening before the party broke up. The young Americans, a little sad and lonely, dispersed in the blue haze of the Place de la Concorde.[5]

Berle and Morison on May 15, 1919, sent dignified letters to Grew, protesting the treaty as a flagrant abandonment of Wilson's pledges. Two days later Bullitt addressed a letter, more grandly, to the President of the United States. "I am sorry," he wrote, "that you did not fight our fight to the finish and that you had so little faith in the millions of men, like myself, in every nation who had faith in you." His words were bitter. "Our Government," he concluded, "has consented now to deliver the suffering peoples of the world to new oppressions, subjections and dismemberments — a new century of war." [6]

IV

And so the springtime hope began to fade. Herbert Hoover, the director of American relief in Europe, awakened at four in the morning by a messenger with the treaty draft, read it with mounting anxiety. Unable in his concern to sleep, he walked the empty streets in the Paris dawn, until he encountered General Smuts, similarly distressed.[7] Later in the day they met with an English economist, whose exquisite Cambridge superiority could not conceal a brilliant intelligence. Like the young Americans, John Maynard Keynes soon resigned from his delegation. During the summer and fall, he composed a prophetic and gloomy tract, *The Economic Consequences of the Peace.*

As for Bullitt, he returned to America, ready to punish the President in whom he had recently invested such faith. In September 1919, Senator Henry Cabot Lodge called Bullitt to the hearings on the Versailles Treaty before the Senate Foreign Relations Committee. Before gratified senators, Bullitt produced official papers, memoranda of private conversation, and other confidential matter to support a tale of betrayal. No doubt he exceeded strict bounds of propriety and even of truth. Robert Lansing, Wilson's Secretary of State, called his conduct "despicable and outrageous," and Philip Kerr, Lloyd George's secretary, known to a later generation as Lord Lothian, described Bullitt's account of talks with Lloyd George and himself as "a tissue of lies." But there could be no doubt about his impact. "We are very much obliged to you indeed, Mr. Bullitt," said Senator Lodge.

Four days before Bullitt's testimony, Woodrow Wilson said at Omaha, "I tell you, my fellow citizens, I can predict with absolute certainty that within another generation there will be another world war if the nations of the world do not concert the method by which to prevent it." [8] And thirteen days afterward, the President, gray and exhausted, still pleading for the League, now in Pueblo, Colorado, suffered his first collapse.

And the dream collapsed too. The golden moment became an illusion of the shining Paris spring. By fall Keynes wrote, "We are at the dead season of our fortunes." The power of feeling beyond the immediate questions of one's own well-being, he said, was spent. "We have been moved already beyond endurance, and need rest. Never in the lifetime of men now living has the universal element in the soul of man burnt so dimly." [9]

3. The New Nationalism

But in America the universal element still burned in the soul. There the hope of 1919 was no sudden impulse of enthusiasm. "Democracy is infectious," the *New Republic* had proclaimed in 1917. "It is now as certain as anything human can be that the war . . . will dissolve into democratic revolution the world over." [1]

In the United States the democratic revolution had been gathering strength for thirty years. The Populist challenge to business rule in the 1890's had ushered in a new stage in American reform. Breaking sharply with the Jeffersonian past, the Populists renounced the old faith that that government was best which governed least. "We believe," their platform declared in 1892, "that the powers of government — in other words, of the people — should be expanded . . . to the end that oppression, injustice, and poverty shall eventually cease in the land." [2] The Populist uprising had its ambiguous elements. In part a justified protest by poor farmers against excessive levies by banks, railroads, and processors, it was in part too an irrational upsurge of frustration and spite, tending to interpret the world in terms of a conspiracy of international bankers controlled by Wall Street and the House of Rothschild. But, for all the rancor of Populism, the Populist platform was rich in political and economic invention. The Populist demands — a rudimentary farm-price support system, a graduated income tax, the secret ballot, the direct election of senators, the initiative and referendum, and the government ownership of railroads, telephone, and telegraph — defined the objectives of reform for the next generation.

In 1896 the Populist spirit captured the Democratic party and

created William Jennings Bryan. In the later nineties the rise in
farm prices diminished the radicalism of the countryside; but the
reform impulse only took other forms, the cities becoming the new
source of reform energy. Where Populism was driven by a sense of
panic over what the farmers took as conspiratorial business domination, Progressivism emerged rather from the feelings of distress
experienced by settled community leadership now threatened by a
crude and grasping class of *nouveau riche*. Middle-class in its outlook, moralistic in its temper, moderate and resourceful in its approach to problems of policy, Progressivism originated less than
Populism. But it executed much more.

The Progressive era was an unprecedented time of popular education. The muckrakers in press and magazines disclosed the techniques of political and business corruption. And political leaders
sought to show how honesty and intelligence might provide the
remedy. Thus there arose Robert M. La Follette of Wisconsin,
Charles Evans Hughes of New York, Hiram Johnson of California,
James M. Cox of Ohio — typical Progressive governors, some Republicans, some Democrats, but all standing for the enforcement of
middle-class standards of civic decency against greedy wealth and
crooked politics. The greatest of them all in his public impact was
Theodore Roosevelt of New York.

II

Roosevelt transfixed the imagination of the American middle class
as did no other figure of the time. With his squeaky voice, his gleaming teeth, his overpowering grin, and his incurable delight in self-
dramatization, he brought everything he touched to life. His capacity for moral indignation was unlimited; his energy cascaded everywhere. He gathered into himself the mounting discontent with
which Americans were contemplating business rule. By offering this
discontent release in melodrama, he no doubt reduced the pressure
behind it for accomplishment. La Follette and others complained
of his "rhetorical radicalism." His cannonading back and forth, La
Follette said, filled the air with noise and smoke, but, when the
battle cloud drifted by, little had been achieved.[3] Yet Roosevelt's
personality gave the reform movement a momentum it could hardly

have obtained from economics alone. He stirred the conscience of America. Young men followed him in the service of the commonweal as they had followed no American since Lincoln.

Theodore Roosevelt, indeed, was more complicated than he sometimes seemed. He sensed with brilliant insight the implications of America's new industrial might. At home, the industrial triumph had rendered acute the problems of economic justice and social peace. Abroad, it was thrusting America irrevocably into world power politics. With all the boisterousness of his personality, Roosevelt sought to awaken the nation to a recognition of new responsibilities. And the only way these responsibilities — domestic or foreign — could be met, he deeply believed, was by establishing a "powerful National government" and thus affirming national purpose as the guiding force in public policy.

Ancestry and outlook equipped Roosevelt peculiarly for this revival of a sense of national purpose. Coming from a well-born family in New York, inheriting wealth and independence, he considered himself above class allegiances. In particular, he looked with disdain on the business community. "I do not dislike," he wrote, "but I certainly have no especial respect or admiration for and no trust in, the typical big moneyed men of my country. I do not regard them as furnishing sound opinion as regards either foreign or domestic policies." There was absolutely nothing to be said, he continued, for "government by a plutocracy, for government by men very powerful in certain lines and gifted with 'the money touch,' but with ideals which in their essence are merely those of so many glorified pawnbrokers." He stood equally, he declared, against government by a plutocracy and government by a mob.[4]

He was fortified by the conviction that he was restoring an older tradition of national purpose — the tradition of the Federalists, about which he had written with such ardor as a young historian. His admiration for Hamilton's conception of government was qualified only by regret over Hamilton's skepticism toward democracy. Jefferson, even though he was right about the plain people, was hopelessly wrong about the role of the state. As Roosevelt's younger friend Henry L. Stimson liked to put it, government was not "a mere organized police force, a sort of necessary evil, but rather an affirmative agency of national progress and social betterment." [5]

For national government to do its job, it had to be stronger than any private group in society. Instead of regarding the state as a possible tyrant, "as Jefferson did," said Stimson, "we now look to executive action to protect the individual citizen against the oppression of this unofficial power of business." [6] From very nearly the start of his presidency, Roosevelt was engaged in battles to vindicate the national will against its boldest domestic challengers — the trusts and combines, the court favorites of earlier Republican rule.

III

Roosevelt's warfare against the trusts was neither very consistent nor very effective. But his uncertainty derived less from political expediency than from the fact that he had a more complex vision of the problem than the old-fashioned trust busters. For a man like La Follette, with his ruthless simplicities, the Sherman Antitrust Act remained "the strongest, most perfect weapon which the ingenuity of man could forge for the protection of the people against the power and sordid greed of monopoly." [7] But for Roosevelt, who discerned an evolutionary necessity in economic concentration, the Sherman Act was an exercise in nostalgia.

Herbert Croly's *The Promises of American Life,* published in 1909, the year when Roosevelt left the Presidency, added little to Roosevelt's program. But it gave his instinct for national assertion a persuasive setting in political philosophy. In a thoughtful reconsideration of the national experience, Croly saw the essence of the American faith in the careless belief that the nation was "predestined to success by its own adequacy." The promise of American life had been too long considered somehow self-fulfilling; the same automatic processes which had taken care of the past would take care of the future. Croly sharply challenged this whole spirit of optimism and drift. The traditional American confidence in individual freedom, he said, had resulted in a morally and socially undesirable distribution of wealth under which "the ideal Promise, instead of being automatically fulfilled, may well be automatically stifled." The only hope was to transform the national attitude toward social development, to convert the old unconscious sense of national destiny into a conscious sense of national purpose, to replace drift by management. What this meant, Croly said, was that the national state would have to take an active and detailed responsibility for economic and social conditions. It meant a "more highly socialized democracy," a "new nationalism." The theory of the Sherman Act, he added, operated as a "fatal bar" to national planning.[8]

Croly was more interested in affirming a viewpoint than in designing a program; but others were ready to give the New Nationalism its economics. George W. Perkins of J. P. Morgan and Company, himself one of the great trust organizers, felt that modern technology had revolutionized the world and rendered old-style competition obsolete. "What underlies ruthless competitive methods?" Perkins asked. "The desire to supply the public with better goods at a lower price? Is that the moving, impelling force behind it? Nonsense!" Competition, he said, was simply a struggle for power at the expense of everything else. "The entire path of our industrial progress is strewn with the white bones of just such competition." What had given us exploitation, evil working conditions, unemployment, low wages? Competition! "The Congressman who stands for a literal enforcement of the Sherman Act," declared Perkins, "stands for the sweat shop and child labor." Competition had become "too destructive to be tolerated. Co-operation must be the order of the day."

The national government, Perkins said, had first undertaken the supervision of the states, then of the banks, then of the railroads; now, he said, it must undertake the supervision of big business. Let the government license all interstate corporations; and let the licensing system enforce federal standards with respect to capitalization, trade practices, prices, and labor policy. As for corporations, they must recognize that they had obligations to labor and to the public as well as to their stockholders. Let them work out plans for co-partnership; let them, as he put it in a clumsy but expressive phrase, "people-ize" modern industry; let them devise plans for profit-sharing, for social insurance, for old-age pensions. In true co-partnership, said Perkins, there would be "socialism of the highest, best and most ideal sort" — socialism, in other words, which preserved the right of private property.[9]

Perkins was sincerely impressed by the advantages of the German cartel system — for social security, for economic stability, for industrial growth, for national unity — and he wanted to propel American economic development in the same direction. In 1910 he left Morgan's and went up and down the country, preaching the gospel to any group that would listen. In 1912 he gave over $250,000 to Roosevelt's campaign. As for T.R., he valued Perkins's ideas as much as his money.

T.R. discovered further stimulus in a book published in the spring of 1912 — *Concentration and Control: A Solution of the Trust Problem in the United States,* written by Charles R. Van Hise, a classmate of La Follette's at the University of Wisconsin and later the university's president. Agreeing with Perkins about the inevitability of concentration, Van Hise asserted even more strongly the indispensability of control. "If we allow concentration and co-operation," he wrote, "there must be control in order to protect the people, and adequate control is only possible through the administrative commission." 10

As his own thought clarified, and as his resentment of William Howard Taft, his successor in the Presidency, grew, Roosevelt became increasingly specific. Trust busting seemed to him madness — "futile madness." "It is preposterous to abandon all that has been wrought in the application of the cooperative idea in business and to return to the era of cut-throat competition." But acceptance of bigness could not be allowed to mean surrender to bigness: this was the test of democratic government. "The man who wrongly holds that every human right is secondary to his profit," Roosevelt declared, "must now give way to the advocate of human welfare, who rightly maintains that every man holds his property subject to the general right of the community to regulate its use to whatever degree the public welfare may require it." 11 *To whatever degree:* this was strong language, even for Teddy Roosevelt.

IV

One other force contributed vitally to Roosevelt's developing philosophy. Mastery of private bigness was only half the job; the other half was help for the individual cast adrift in the great society. Here the New Nationalism absorbed the new experience of social work as well as the new teachings of the Social Gospel.

Both the Social Gospel and social work had arisen in the late nineteenth century as nonpolitical responses to the miseries and injustices of the industrial order. Socially-minded ministers began to remind their parishioners that Christians had duties toward their fellow men, that Christian morality was relevant to slums and sweatshops, and that the Christian task would not be completed until the social order itself had been Christianized. "The Christian law," said Dr. Washington Gladden, "is meant to live by, to do business by, to rule politics." When society was transformed by Christian faith, "rotten politics and grinding monopolies would shrivel and disappear; under its banner light and beauty, peace and plenty, joy and gladness would be led in."

This goal, the advocates of the Social Gospel reckoned, could be achieved within history; the Kingdom of God would, in due time, realize itself on earth. But it could not be achieved by the churches alone. "There is a certain important work to be done," wrote Gladden, "which no voluntary organization can succeed in doing — a work which requires the exercise of the power of the state." Nor was this likely to be the existing state, controlled as it was by the business class. "If the banner of the Kingdom of God is to enter through the gates of the future," said Walter Rauschenbusch, the most searching theologian of the Social Gospel, "it will have to be carried by the tramping hosts of labor." [12]

Gladden and Rauschenbusch, in rousing the conscience of modern Protestantism, thus predisposed it both toward an affirmative theory of the state and toward a belief that the power of business must be offset by the power of labor. The formation of such organizations as the Methodist Federation for Social Service in 1907 and the Federal Council of Churches in 1908 signaled the spread of the Social Gospel through the Protestant churches.

v

What was faith for the apostles of the Social Gospel became works for the men and women of the settlement houses. The first heroine of social work was Jane Addams of Hull-House on Halsted Street in Chicago. Soon after, Lillian Wald set up the Henry Street Settlement in New York. Hull-House, Henry Street, and their counterparts in other cities gave the middle class its first extended contact with the life of the working class — with the sweatshops, the child labor, the unsanitary working conditions, the long hours, the starvation wages, the denial of the right to organize. Relinquishing comfortable middle-class homes, the social workers moved to the city slums and labored to create a breathing-space of hope for the poor, the immigrant, and, above all, for the slum-born children.

This middle-class mission to the poor coincided with the release of energy which came from the new emancipation of women. Hull-House and Henry Street, in particular, produced an extraordinary group of women whose vitality and compassion reshaped American liberalism. From Hull-House came Florence Kelley, who became the driving force in the National Consumers' League. The idea of the United States Children's Bureau was Lillian Wald's, and its first two chiefs — Julia Lathrop and Grace Abbott — were from Hull-House. The same hopes and ideals fired many younger women — Josephine Goldmark, Frances Perkins, Mary Dewson, Mary Anderson, Edith Abbott. These were the "dedicated old maids." Social work not only relieved their middle-class conscience. It also provided an outlet for their energy in a field which women could make their own.

More than anyone else, Florence Kelley devised the new techniques of social reform. The daughter of W.D. ("Pig-Iron") Kelley, the protectionist congressman, she was a socialist, a friend of Friedrich Engles, and a whirlwind of courage, vigor, and, in Frances Perkins's phrase, "blazing moral indignation." The National Consumers' League had been established in 1899 on the belief that the customer who bought sweatshop goods was as much the employer of sweated labor as the boss of the shop. Under Florence Kelley's direction, the League battled against home manufacturers in tenements, against child labor, against night work and excessive hours for women. The League's investigations turned up facts to stir the public conscience. Then the League's lawyers drafted bills, and the League's lobbyists sought to push them through legislatures. The League thus initiated the fight for minimum-wage laws and worked out a model statute, soon enacted in thirteen states and the District of Columbia. When the law was challenged in the courts, Florence Kelley rushed up to Boston to ask Louis D. Brandeis to argue its constitutionality. For this purpose Brandeis invented the famous "Brandeis brief," which introduced the heresy that the facts as well as the law were relevant to determinations of community health and welfare.

Organizations like the Women's Trade Union League and the Association for Labor Legislation carried on other aspects of the fight for decent labor standards. It was from these middle-class groups, and not from the trade unions, that the first demand came for the abolition of child labor, for maximum-hour and minimum-wage laws, and for social insurance. And the opposition these reformers met from many businessmen — an opposition often camouflaged as solicitude for the "freedom" of women to work twelve hours a day or of seven-year-old children to strip tobacco leaves or twist artificial flowers in slum tenements — deepened suspicion of business motives.

Hull-House, Henry Street, the Consumers' League, and the other organizations educated a whole generation in social responsibility. Henry Morgenthau, Jr., Herbert Lehman, and Adolf A. Berle, Jr., all worked at Henry Street; Frances Perkins, Gerard Swope, and Charles A. Beard at Hull-House (where John Dewey was an early member of the board of trustees); Sidney Hillman at both Hull-House and Henry Street; Joseph B. Eastman at Robert A. Woods's South End House in Boston; an Iowa boy coming east from Grinnell College in 1912 went to work at Christadora House on the lower East Side of New York; his name, Harry Hopkins. Through Belle Moskowitz the social work ethos infected Alfred E. Smith; through Frances Perkins and others, Robert F. Wagner; through Eleanor Roosevelt, active in the Women's Trade Union League and a friend of Florence Kelley's and Lillian Wald's, Franklin D. Roosevelt.

And, for all the appearance of innocence and defenselessness the social workers' apparatus wielded power. "One could not overestimate," observed Wagner, "the central part played by social workers in bringing before their representatives in Congress and state legislatures the present and insistent problems of modern-day life." The subtle and persistent saintliness of the social workers was in the end more deadly than all the bluster of business. Theirs was the implacability of gentleness.[13]

VI

Among politicians, no one responded more alertly than Theodore Roosevelt. In the early eighties he had led the fight in the New York legislature against cigar-making in tenement houses. As President, he hailed the Consumers' League as early as 1907; and his White House conference on children gave social work, said Jane Addams, "a dignity and a place in the national life which it never had before." Nor was the alliance unnatural. The inner logic of social work was, to a considerable degree, *noblesse oblige* and paternalistic; the bias was more toward helping people than toward enabling them to help themselves. The caseworker often felt she knew best. T.R. always knew best too.

In the meantime, the Progressives in the Republican party were pressing their battle against the Taft administration. La Follette had been their original candidate; but early in 1912 Roosevelt announced his availability. When the Republican convention renominated Taft, Roosevelt decided to quit the party. Before his own convention, he met with a group of leading social workers and adopted a program recently drawn up by the National Conference of Social Work. "Our best plank," he later wrote of the Progressive platform, "the plank which has really given our party its distinctive character, came from them. . . . [The social workers] are doing literally invaluable work." At the convention, Jane Addams was among those seconding his nomination.[14]

Roosevelt's movement reached its climax at Chicago in August. Before a crowd gone mad, T.R., strong as a bull moose, challenged his followers to stand at Armageddon and battle for the Lord. Across the nation young men rose to his call: Gifford Pinchot of Pennsylvania; Harold Ickes and Donald Richberg of Illinois; William Allen White and Alfred M. Landon of Kansas; George W. Norris of Nebraska; Frank Knox of Michigan; Henry A. Wallace of Iowa; Felix Frankfurter and Norman Thomas of New York; Francis Biddle of Pennsylvania; John G. Winant and Charles W. Tobey of New Hampshire; Dean Acheson of Connecticut.

4. The New Freedom

FOR THEIR PART, the Democrats in 1912 nominated Woodrow Wilson, the governor of New Jersey. Wilson brought qualities as unusual as those of Theodore Roosevelt to American politics. The two men had much in common: cultivation, knowledge, literary skill, personal magnetism, relentless drive. But, where Roosevelt was unbuttoned and expansive, Wilson was reserved and cool; no one known to history ever called him "Woody" or "W.W." Both were lay preachers, but where Roosevelt was a revivalist, bullying his listeners to hit the sawdust trail, Wilson had the severe eloquence of a Calvinist divine. Roosevelt's egotism overflowed his personality; Wilson's was a hard concentrate within. Roosevelt's power lay in what he did, Wilson's in what he held in reserve.

Erect in bearing, quick in movement, tidy in dress, with sharp eyes and a belligerent jaw, Wilson, when not overcome by self-righteousness or moral fervor, had humor and charm. For all his professorial background, he showed considerable aptitude for politics. He was, in particular, a powerful orator — as the nation discovered in 1912 when he outlined his alternative to the New Nationalism in a series of notable speeches. Declaring "a new social age, a new era of human relationships . . . a new economic society," Wilson summoned his countrymen to the task of liberating the nation from the new tyranny of concentrated wealth. "When we undertake the strategy which is going to be necessary to overcome and destroy this far-reaching system of monopoly," he said, "we are rescuing the business of this country, we are not injuring it; and when we separate the interests from each other and dismember these communities of connection, we have in mind . . . that vision which sees that no society is renewed from the top but that every society is renewed from the bottom." This was the New Freedom.

Wilson vigorously rejected theories of the paternal state. Hamilton had no charm for him: "a great man, but, in my judgment, not a great American." The philosophy of America was equal rights for all and special privileges for none — "a free field and no favor." "I do not want to live under a philanthropy," Wilson said. "I do not want to be taken care of by the government. . . . We do not want a benevolent government. We want a free and a just government."

He cherished the Jeffersonian dream. Yet he began to give his Jeffersonianism significant new inflections. As he had read the "spirit of Jefferson" as late as 1906, it had enjoined him to eschew nearly all forms of public intervention in the economy. But the very goal of dismantling the system of special privilege called for action by the state. In the end, he set the Jeffersonian theory of the state on its head: "I feel confident that if Jefferson were living in our day he would see what we see. . . . Without the watchful interference, the resolute interference of the government, there can be no fair play." And his experience as governor soon increased his tolerance of governmental power. Political ambition at the same time sharpened his sensitivity to popular discontents; and contacts with William G. McAdoo and Louis D. Brandeis in the 1912 campaign completed the transformation of his Jeffersonianism from a counsel of inaction to a doctrine with a cutting edge. Under the pressure of responsibility, he was coming to see that if he aspired to Jeffersonian ends he might have to relinquish Jeffersonian means.[1]

II

In McAdoo, Wilson found a businessman with a free-wheeling operator's animus toward Wall Street and with developed ideas about business reform. A Georgian by birth, a New Yorker by residence, a lawyer by training, a promoter by temperament, McAdoo, who was forty-nine years old in 1912, had built the first tunnel under the Hudson and was now president of the Hudson and Manhattan Railroad Company. Tough and energetic, he observed insistently to the business community that corporations must be the servants, not the masters, of the people; that "the public be damned" approach had to be replaced by "the public be pleased." His reading of America's economic development was diametrically opposite to that of George W. Perkins. Where Perkins wrote that the modern corporation's underlying cause was "not the greed of man for wealth and power, but the working of natural causes — of evolution," McAdoo rejoined, "These great combinations are not the *natural* outgrowth of new economic conditions and complex civilization. They are more likely the artificial product of the unrestrained activities of ambitious men of highly-developed acquisitive power."

What could be done about them? "For my part," replied McAdoo, "I believe that all the powers of the nation should be exerted to preserve competitive conditions." Regulation could be attempted; but regulation was only possible through commissions; and the real question was, Who would control the commissions? "Unregulated competition is better than regulated monopoly," said McAdoo early in 1911, thrusting some new phrases into the controversy, "but regulated competition is better than either." [2]

Louis D. Brandeis carried the analysis a few steps farther. Born in 1856 in Louisville, Kentucky, Brandeis had graduated from the Harvard Law School and then settled down to an immensely successful law practice in Boston. His analytical brilliance and his tenacious advocacy won him the clients who could pay most for these talents. By 1907 Brandeis was a millionaire. But, for an idealist, bred in the tradition of the Revolution of 1848, material success was hardly enough. Beginning in the nineties, he had developed a second career — this time as a "people's lawyer," working without fee in the public interest, moving from local problems (streetcar franchises) to state (savings bank life insurance) and then to regional (the New Haven railroad). Starting in 1907, he came to national attention as counsel for the Consumers' League in a series of notable tests of hours and wages legislation.

He was a tall, stooped figure, with longish gray hair, deep-set eyes, a face of melancholy nobility and brooding wisdom, and something of the aspect of a Jewish Lincoln. In combat, his wrath aroused, he displayed the stern righteousness of an Old Testament prophet; this sometimes made it hard for him to believe that his opponents, too, had honest motives. But, in relaxation, talking among friends, a tinge of Kentucky drawl still in his voice, he had rare serenity of spirit.

For Wilson, Jeffersonianism had been a faith; Brandeis seemed to transform it into a policy. He bluntly denied the major premise of the New Nationalists. Economic bigness, he said, was not inevitable. It did not come from the necessities of the machine age. It was not the inescapable result of the movement toward efficiency. It was the creation, not of technology, but of finance. It sprang from the manipulations of the bankers, eager to float new securities and water new stocks.

The mania for consolidation, Brandeis believed, could end only in the strangling of freedom: J. P. Morgan was the socialists' best friend, because, after he was through with his work, socialism would have so little left to do. "Just as Emperor Nero is said to have remarked in regard to his people that he wished that the Christians had but one neck that he might cut it off by a single blow of his sword, so they say here: 'Let these men gather these things together; they will soon have them all under one head, and by a single act we will take over the whole industry.'"

Where Croly was concerned with the morale of the nation, Brandeis was concerned with the morality of the individual. The curse was bigness: "we are now coming to see that big things may be very bad and mean." For, though business and government might increase indefinitely, men would always remain the same size. Excessive power was the great corrupter. To bestow more power on men than they could endure was to change the few into tyrants, while it destroyed the rest. Centralization enfeebled society by choking off experiment and draining talent from the community into the center. Nor could one pin faith on government regulation: "remedial institutions are apt to fall under the control of the enemy and to become instruments of oppression." In the end responsibility was the only developer — the institutions of the state and the economy must be proportioned to the capabilities of man. The growth of the individual, Brandeis concluded, was "both a necessary means and the end sought." [3]

III

Here was the reformulation of Jeffersonianism toward which Wilson had been groping. His first meeting with Brandeis in August 1912 was an instant success. The problem, Wilson agreed, was not to regulate monopoly but to regulate competition; and he soon asked Brandeis for a program. Competition, Brandeis replied, could and should be maintained in every branch of private industry. Where monopoly could not be avoided, industry should be "owned by the people and not by the capitalists." Government regulation of monopoly, he continued, was a delusion; either break the power up or take it over. The nation must choose between industrial absolutism, tempered by government control, and industrial liberty.[4]

Thus the New Freedom, and to this summons, too, young men rallied — W. G. McAdoo and Franklin Delano Roosevelt of New York, Cordell Hull of Tennessee, John N. Garner and Sam Rayburn of Texas, Homer Cummings of Connecticut, Dan Roper of North Carolina, Joseph E. Davies of Wisconsin.

5. Nationalizing the New Freedom

THE PARTISANS of 1912 had no doubt that they were debating fundamentals. To the followers of Wilson, the New Nationalism was a menacing tyranny, in which the twin giants of business and government would grind the individual to sand. To the followers of Roosevelt, the New Freedom harked back impotently to the Jeffersonian past — Jeffersonianism restated, to be sure, in terms of finance capitalism, but obsolete nonetheless in the assumption that the system, once reformed, could run by itself. Wilson and Roosevelt thus raged at each other over the trust issue as if they stood on opposite sides of an impassable abyss.

"This difference in the economic policy of the two parties," declared Brandeis in 1912, "is fundamental and irreconcilable." [1] The New Nationalists could not agree more. Nor did Wilson's election and his initial policies reassure them. As late as 1914 Croly dismissed Wilson's program as a mere "revival of Jeffersonian individualism," lacking in a sense of national purpose, oblivious to the fact that "the nationalism of Hamilton, with all its aristocratic leaning, was more democratic, because more constructively social, than the indiscriminate individualism of Jefferson." The young historian Charles A. Beard, fresh from his bold researches into the origins of the Constitution, concurred: agrarian democracy had been Jefferson's futile ambition, "just as the equally unreal and unattainable democracy of small business is Wilson's goal." The acute and fluent journalist Walter Lippmann, only lately resigned from the Socialist party, contrasted the Wilsonian policy of drift with the Rooseveltian policy of mastery. As George

Perkins summed it up with scorn, the "New Freedom had better be called the Old Bondage." [2]

But the gap soon turned out to be less impassable than it had first appeared. Roosevelt did not — as Wilson charged — want to make monopoly universal, any more than Wilson — as Roosevelt replied — wanted to break up every corporation in the country. In abusing each other and misrepresenting each other's views, they obscured the fact that their agreements were actually greater than their differences. Whether the objective was to regulate monopoly or competition, the method was to meet the power of business by expanding the power of government. The New Nationalism and the New Freedom alike affirmed the necessity of active intervention in economic life by the state.

Wilson had already accepted this as the logic of twentieth-century Jeffersonianism when he had shifted from his do-nothing position of 1906 to his activism of 1912. "The program of a government of freedom," he said, "must in these days be positive." [3] Even Brandeis, for all his fear of bigness, wanted the state not only to break up the trusts but to carry out an extensive program on behalf of labor and social security.

Others of Wilson's associates looked even more genially on the state. Colonel E. M. House, the quiet and self-effacing Texan, soon to become the new President's confidential adviser, had published in 1912 *Philip Dru, Administrator,* a utopian fantasy in which the hero, fearful in the year 1920 that organized wealth was about to end American freedom, seized power and proclaimed himself dictator. Dru had to divest himself, House noted, of early states-rights predispositions; but he quickly established a strong central regime, put corporations under stringent national control (while declining to limit their size), abolished holding companies, socialized the telephone and telegraph, enacted full employment legislation, decreed federal old-age and unemployment insurance, and in general set up a nationalism so comprehensive that it might even have given Theodore Roosevelt pause.[4] Yet, by 1918, Franklin K. Lane, Wilson's Secretary of the Interior noted, "All that book has said should be, comes about slowly, even woman suffrage. The President comes to *Philip Dru* in the end." [5]

II

Still, it was less advice than circumstance which caused Wilson
to begin to bridge the abyss. The first pressure came from the
radical wing of the southern Democrats. Southerners of a more
genteel stripe, like Carter Glass of Virginia and Oscar W. Under-
wood of Alabama, were well satisfied with the New Freedom of
1912. But some of their colleagues had a more active conception
of government. Congressman Cordell Hull wanted a federal income
tax. Congressman Sam Rayburn, with Brandeis's assistance, had
drawn up a bill to control the marketing of railroad securities.
And, for the agrarian Democrats of the Bryan school, champions of
the cracker and the redneck, haters of Wall Street, the first New
Freedom seemed especially meager. It was not enough they felt,
to whittle down class legislation for the business community. The
Wilson Administration, they believed, had a positive obligation to
the poor. It must balance Republican favoritism for big business
by doing something itself for small business and the farmers. The
southern radicals had their first triumph when they helped Bryan,
Brandeis, and McAdoo force a basic revision of Carter Glass's bill
for a Federal Reserve system. Then they made another breach in
the conservative conception of the New Freedom by tacking on to
the Federal Reserve bill provisions for short-term credits for farmers.
Wilson soon found himself accepting what was, by his theory of
1912, class legislation.[6]

At the same time, Wilson began to move in strange new directions
in the critical field of antitrust policy. Brandeis, who in 1912 had
felt regulation to be worse than useless, now took up the New
Nationalist idea of a federal commission to supervise corporations.
As a result came the laws of 1914 establishing the Federal Trade
Commission and giving it regulatory powers. Worse, Brandeis
soon recommended for appointment as chairman of the Commission on Industrial Relations the same Charles Van Hise whose
Concentration and Control had been T.R.'s bible two years earlier.
The "fundamental and irreconcilable" differences of 1912 had lost
their sting by 1914.

As the election of 1916 approached, Wilson completed his acceptance of the main lines of the Progressive program of 1912. He

now stood clearly for strong government, for administrative regulation, for some intervention on behalf of the farmer and the worker — in short, for affirmative federal action aimed to produce equality of opportunity. In a basic respect, Roosevelt seemed to have been right: the people's government had to be stronger than business if popular rule were to be effective.

III

While Wilson was appropriating its platform, the Progressive party, already set back by the elections of 1914, was fighting for its life. Its adored leader callously showed his new opinion of his old crusade by suggesting that it might make Henry Cabot Lodge its candidate in 1916. George W. Perkins, the party's angel, had also come to feel that the Bull Moose had outlived its usefulness. Whether the party was killed by Perkins, as Harold Ickes believed, or by Wilson, its 1916 convention showed that its time had passed.

As for the men and women who had battled for the Lord, many now found to their surprise that the New Nationalism was fulfilled in the New Freedom. As Walter Lippmann put it, Wilson's Democratic party was "the only party which at this moment is national in scope, liberal in purpose, and effective in action." Herbert Croly, repenting his earlier skepticism, announced his support for Wilson. Progressives like Bainbridge Colby and Frederic C. Howe, Edward P. Costigan and Amos Pinchot, Jane Addams, Lillian Wald, and Washington Gladden turned to Wilson.[7]

And Roosevelt? "Like you, I am a radical," he wrote to Harold Ickes in December 1915. "I stand for every particle of our platform in 1912; but overwhelmingly my chief interest at present is in the relationship of the United States to the present European situation." The old radicalism still had moments of life. In March 1918, T.R. moved far ahead of the Wilson administration and set new goals for American liberalism in demanding a system of old-age, sickness, and unemployment insurance, public housing, and other reforms. But more and more in these years foreign policy consumed and, in the end, exhausted him. Bitter because Wilson refused to use him in the war, bitter more essentially because of wasted years since 1908, sick, tired, and unhappy, he died in the first month of 1919.

"Something went out of my life that has never been replaced," Ickes said a quarter-century later of the moment when he heard of Roosevelt's death. "I could only press my face into the pillow," wrote Donald Richberg, receiving word on a sickbed in Chicago. "and cry like a child." [8]

6. Euphoria and Collapse

WAR COMPLETED Wilson's conversion. The requirements of mobilization made him, in the end, the best New Nationalist of them all. To meet the needs of war, central direction of the economy proved necessary; and war itself, by creating clear and definite priorities, supplied the criteria that made the rational organization of industry possible. For a moment Washington became the unchallenged economic capital of the nation. Through the War Industries Board, the government mobilized industrial production. Through the War Food Administration, it sought to control the production and consumption of food. Through the Capital Issues Committee, it tried to regulate private investment. Through the War Finance Corporation, it directed and financed industrial expansion. It took over the railroads and the telephone and telegraph systems. It set up independent public corporations in diverse fields from the United States Housing Corporation to the Shipping Board Emergency Fleet Corporation, from the Sugar Equalization Board to the Spruce Production Corporation. The national government had never gone so far in the operation and conduct of business. "War," as Randolph Bourne said in his pacifist discontent, "is the health of the State." [1]

The War Industries Board was the central experiment in economic planning. With Bernard Baruch as its chairman and Alexander Legge of International Harvester as its driving force, assisted by such men as Brigadier-General Hugh S. Johnson, George N. Peek, and Gerard Swope, the WIB soon began to realize the nationalist vision of Roosevelt and Croly. Almost the first thing

to go, to Roosevelt's delight, was the antitrust act. "If the Sherman
Law hurts our production and our business efficiency in war time,"
T.R. said, "it hurts it also in peace time, for the problems . . . are
no different." Through the priority system, as Baruch wrote almost
in the language of Croly, the economy could be "made to move
in response to a national purpose rather than in response to the
wills of those who had money to buy." [2]

By later wartime standards, the central control of 1918 was
rudimentary. For all the talk of subordination to a "national purpose," the civilian automobile business, for example, was permitted
to come of age, while the American government still depended for
tanks and planes on European factories. Yet the WIB experience
gave a hint of the economic power which collective action might
generate. Summing up, Baruch, a South Carolina Democrat, was
obliged to dismiss the philosophy of the Sherman and Clayton
Acts as an effort to make business conform to "the simpler principles
sufficient for the conditions of a bygone day." War had forced the
trades to organize into national associations, each responsible for
its member companies, each under government supervision. Businessmen had experienced for the first time "the tremendous
advantages, both to themselves and to the general public, of combination, of cooperation and common action, with their natural competitors." Why not, Baruch suggested, develop the trade associations
in peacetime so that industry, under government supervision, could
carry out its own programs of self-coordination? [3]

If the War Industries Board, in Baruch's words, was "inspired
by a picture of our industry so mobilized, and with all conflicting
efforts so synchronized" that it could meet all social needs, it was
hard to blame the editors of the New Republic for writing that
the United States was entering the war in "far more nearly the
morale of a cooperative commonwealth than of a nation in arms." [4]
Cooperative commonwealth: the phrase had embodied the dream
of American radicalism for thirty years. Never, for a moment, did
that dream seem so near fulfillment. What mattered was not just
the influx of the young liberals to Washington to work in the war
effort, or to engage in conversations with President Wilson or
Colonel House, or to spend gay evenings with other young men at
the residence on 19th Street which Mr. Justice Holmes called the

"House of Truth." It was even more the sense that the spirit of national sacrifice and the gestures toward national planning were the American expression of a grand historical movement toward social justice.

II

No one uttered this conviction more earnestly than John Dewey, already accepted by the intellectual community as the philosopher of American liberalism. What impressed Dewey most in 1918 was what he called "the social possibilities of war" — the use of technology for communal purposes, the subordination of production for profit to production for use, the organization of the means for public control. War, he said, had given the old belief in the sacredness of private property a blow from which it could never recover. "No matter how many among the special agencies for public control decay with the disappearance of war stress," said Dewey, "the movement will never go backward." [5]

For the progressives, war was administering the *coup de grâce* to the old capitalism. "The truth is," observed Donald Richberg, "that no man of any political intelligence and economic vision has been able to defend the existing economic order since the World War laid bare its utter inadequacy and its insane consequences." Feeling that T.R.'s progressivism had not gone far enough, Richberg called broadly, if obscurely, for the "democratization of industry." Walter Weyl of the *New Republic* was equally sanguine. "What we have learned in war," he wrote, "we shall hardly forget in peace. . . . The new economic solidarity, once gained, can never again be surrendered." It is little wonder that J. P. Morgan could remark in the anxious winter of 1917–18 that the country was approaching the condition of Russia. "Legislation is aimed and boastfully aimed against business and [for] the destruction of values," said the great financier moodily. "But nobody can say anything or do anything at the present time. Sentiment has got to run its course." [6]

Wilson himself sounded the call for social reconstruction. In a message to the special session of Congress, cabled from Paris in May 1919, the President declared that the question of capital and labor "stands at the front of all others in every country." To meet this question, Wilson continued, America must move on to "a new organization of industry," a "genuine democratization of industry," a "cooperation and partnership based upon a real community of interest and participation in control." He spoke of the rights of workers to share "in some organic way in every decision" which affected their welfare. The vision was vague, but it was clearly a long stride from the Jeffersonian simplicities of 1912, with their faith in the economy's automatic harmonies.[7]

Government was plainly to be a major instrument of reform; and, within the government, the energies of reform were centering increasingly in McAdoo as the Secretary of the Treasury. A widower, McAdoo had climaxed his lively career by marrying Wilson's young daughter Eleanor at a White House wedding in 1914. As a sort of putative crown prince, he looked with unbounded self-confidence on the paternal estate. "What is Government for?" he said in a moment of wrath in 1915. "Is it something in a strait-jacket? Is it sitting in a corner like a thing with palsied hands afraid to act, or is it something vital?"[8] No one doubted his own answer to these questions. In 1917 McAdoo persuaded Wilson to take over the railroads, had himself appointed administrator, and carried out the job with dash and dispatch. A few weeks after the armistice McAdoo suggested the possibility of extending federal control over the railroads until 1924 to test unified operation in peacetime.

There were other proposals for new government activity. Josephus Daniels, the Secretary of the Navy, impressed by the potentialities of wireless communications, presented a plan for the federal ownership and operation of international radio. And such official projects were only a pale reflection of the thinking of enthusiasts in the nation. William Allen White, defining the program of the western progressives for Lord Bryce in 1917, spelled out the radical creed: railroad nationalization; federal old-age pensions; public operation "along socialistic lines" of the natural resources — oil, water, power, forests, mines; and the "genuine redistribution of the wealth of the country." A year later, White thought wartime price control should be made permanent, and in another year he advocated a constitutional amendment giving Congress "unlimited powers" over industry and commerce, with a national minimum wage and guaranteed full employment.[9]

By 1919 popular radicalism was at full tide. Glenn E. Plumb, a Chicago lawyer, worked out for the railroad brotherhoods a proposal for the nationalization of the railroads. The American Federation of Labor in its Denver convention called for the extension of the Plumb plan to other industries. The United Mine Workers voted for the nationalization of the mines. And in the background was an immense wave of strikes; never in American history had so many workers been involved. A general strike shut down Seattle in February. By autumn, the surge of strikes in the basic industries — especially steel and coal — suggested that the American labor movement, so long dormant, was at last awake.

As in Paris, possibilities, for a wild moment, appeared illimitable. Hardly a fortnight passed without an essay in the liberal weeklies on the imminence of a new social order. Talk of "revolution" — constitutional and peaceful, of course — was everywhere in the air. For young men climbing out of their uniforms, the world never seemed more alive. Any spring was a time of overturn, as John Dos Passos later wrote, but there were never such currents of excitement breaking out on every side as in the spring of 1919, when he and thousands of other young Americans came back from France. Imperial America, Dos Passos remembered, was all shiny with the new idea of Ritz. Whenever you went to the movies, you saw Charlie Chaplin. In every direction the countries of the world stretched out, starving and angry, ready for anything turbulent and new.[10]

IV

And yet, even as Wilson and the others talked most glowingly of reconstruction, their projects began to crumble before their eyes. War had produced a season of moral dedication. With peace, selfishness returned. "It was," wrote Donald Richberg, "as though a hard frost overnight had killed the rank growth of war emotions and ideals." On every side he could hear the brittle rustling of falling leaves.[11] Disillusion began to be epidemic in 1919, not only with Bullitt and Berle and Keynes in Paris, but in Washington, in New York, soon in every city of the country.

Wilson's "democratization of industry" was the first to go. In February 1919 he set up the Industrial Board, under George Peek and Hugh S. Johnson, to extend War Industries Board controls through the transition period. But by May the Peek board, lacking enforcement powers, lacking — what was more important — support in the now fast unraveling national morale, began to break up. McAdoo, who was tired of government and wanted to make money, resigned from the Treasury immediately after the armistice. Wilson soon announced the return of the railroads to private ownership. Congress rejected Daniels's plan for radio as a government monopoly. In one field after another government contracted its activities. The only important wartime agency to last was another McAdoo project, the War Finance Corporation, where energetic Eugene Meyer planned to use easy credit to help the economy through the vicissitudes of reconversion. But Meyer had to fight hard for the WFC against the conservative views of McAdoo's successors in the Treasury, Carter Glass and David F. Houston.[12]

From one field only did the government not recede; that was the field of thought and expression. Randolph Bourne had been right: war was indeed the health of the state. To give government the power to do good, it now seemed, might be also to give the power to do evil, and in 1919 the power to do evil survived. Attorney-General A. Mitchell Palmer, it is true, had grounds for concern; he had narrowly escaped death in the spring of 1919 when a bomb blew in the front of his house. But he generalized his own experience into a national emergency. Looking back at the situation a year later, he swelled to his theme: "Like a prairie-fire, the blaze of revolution was sweeping over every American institution of law and order a year ago. It was eating its way into the homes of the American workman, its sharp tongues of revolutionary heat were licking the altars of the churches, leaping into the belfry of the school bell, crawling into the sacred corners of American homes, seeking to replace marriage vows with libertine laws, burning up the foundations of society." [13]

On New Year's Day 1920, the Attorney-General ordered simultaneous raids on radical centers through the country. Palmer's agents captured over 6000 individuals, but only three revolvers and no dynamite at all — not quite the raw material for a great conspiracy. Yet his alarming noises did succeed in spreading a contagion of fear. In Hartford, Connecticut, for example, visitors at the jail inquiring after friends caught in the raid were themselves arrested on the ground that this solicitude was prima facie evidence of Bolshevik affiliation. . . . At one cabinet meeting, early in 1920, the President, trembling and ghostlike, turned to his Attorney-General. "Palmer," he said, "do not let this country see red." [14]

v

But it was too late. As Clemenceau slew the liberal dream in Paris, so Palmer slew it in America; and, in each case, Woodrow Wilson was the accomplice. To the liberals who had opposed the war, all was coming about as they had foretold: war had destroyed progressivism. Wilson had silenced some critics by putting them in jail, commented Harold Stearns — others by putting them in the government. To Stearns the liberal collapse was the laboratory demonstration of the refusal of liberalism to pursue its analysis whenever the results became embarrassing. He called it the "technique of liberal failure." [15]

The pro-war liberals began to lose their confidence. The veteran reformer Frederic C. Howe — who had fought the progressive fight since the turn of the century, who had worked with Tom Johnson and Newton Baker for municipal reform in Cleveland and had stood with T.R. at Armageddon, who had served as Wilson's Commissioner of Immigration at Ellis Island and had dealt with T. E. Lawrence and Feisal on Near Eastern questions at Versailles — saw the New Nationalism in a fresh perspective. The liberals, he observed, were now persecuted by the state they loved so much more fervently than did the federal agents who spied upon them;

and this persecution was the result of a war which had promised democracy to all the world. If but a few had actual indictments hanging over them, "all felt a sentence suspended over their enthusiasms, their beliefs, their innermost thoughts." As he stood in the wreck of the progressive movement, Howe saw his faith in big government fall away; "I became distrustful of the state." Many reformers shared Howe's disillusion. Even Harold Ickes, who had called for the war in the best T.R. style and who rarely confessed error, was convinced by Hiram Johnson in 1919 that he had been wrong.[16]

For a moment Johnson seemed to offer a last chance. Square, thick-set, hard, dry, brimming over with resentment and gloom, Johnson had stood out bravely against the hysteria. He had been an excellent liberal governor of California; he had been Roosevelt's running mate in 1912; he was tough and masterful and radical. The Republican Progressives gathered in Chicago in the summer of 1920, hoping against hope that they could put Johnson over. But the convention chose (or had chosen for it) Warren G. Harding, the affable conservative from Ohio; Johnson turned down the vice-presidential nomination; and the designation of Calvin Coolidge of Massachusetts for the second place perfected the most standpat ticket the Republicans had put up for twenty years.

Dejectedly, the Progressives met for a last time after the convention — Gifford Pinchot, William Allen White, Ickes, Donald Richberg, a few others. Someone suggested that they should continue to keep in touch as a group. Ickes, who had the mailing list, silently resolved to call it a day. The Bull Moose crusade was over. (During the campaign Josephus Daniels observed that the Republicans were supposed to have swallowed the Bull Moose. "If so," he said, "they will have more brains in their belly than they have in their head.") [17]

The Democrats tried to keep their spirits up. Their convention, held in remote San Francisco, opened to a stirring defense of Wilson and the League by Homer Cummings, the party's national chairman. As a great oil portrait of the President was unveiled on the stage, a mood of affirmation began to come over the hall. One delegation after another rose to take part in a marching demonstration. Only the disgruntled braves of Tammany Hall sat silent, till suddenly the tall figure of the Assistant Secretary of the

Navy arose to seize the New York banner. For a moment, there was scuffling; then Franklin D. Roosevelt broke free and, holding the standard high, joined the marching parade.

In Washington, Wilson pathetically cherished the hope that he might run for a third term. After the demonstration, it was only with difficulty that Bainbridge Colby, the Secretary of State, could be restrained from calling for Wilson's nomination by acclamation. But the professionals believed that there was a deep revulsion against Wilson through the country. After forty ballots, they nominated James M. Cox, who had been a good reform governor of Ohio. To complete the ticket, they chose for Vice-President the Democratic Roosevelt, who had done a first-class job in the Navy Department and had shown himself a liberal in state politics. Cox and Roosevelt put up a gallant fight. But Keynes was right: the liberals were at the dead season of their fortunes. In November the people chose Harding and Coolidge.

Washington, 1920, Hiram Johnson talking to a newspaperman. "The war has set back the people for a generation. They have bowed to a hundred repressed acts. They have become slaves to the government. They are frightened at the excesses in Russia. They are docile; and they will not recover from being so for many years. The interests which control the Republican party will make the most of their docility."

"In the end, of course," Johnson added, "there will be a revolution, but it will not come in my time." [18]

II

The Politics of Prosperity

7. Main Street in the White House

ON FRIDAY, February 1, 1919, Edward L. Doheny, the oil million-aire, was holding forth in his splendid suite on the S.S. *Aquitania*. The great danger to America, Doheny said, was socialism — social-ism and its offsprings, Communism and Bolshevism. "A majority of the college professors in the United States," he said, "are teach-ing socialism and Bolshevism. . . . William Boyce Thompson is teaching Bolshevism and he may yet convert Lamont of J. P. Mor-gan and Co. Vanderlip is a Bolshevist, so is Charles R. Crane. . . . Henry Ford is another and so are most of those one hundred his-torians Wilson took abroad with him." [1]

On Friday, March 4, 1921, Doheny should have felt better. The Bolshevists were now gone from Washington; and the new ad-ministration was one in which men like Doheny, who had con-tributed $25,000 to its arrival, felt at home. The change from Woodrow Wilson to Warren Gamaliel Harding, from the high-minded and lofty-visioned intellectual to the handsome small-town sport, could not have been more reassuring.

Why Harding? The Republican party had far abler men in 1920. But somehow these men — General Leonard Wood and Governor Frank Lowden, Hiram Johnson and Herbert Hoover — canceled one another out. In February 1920, Harding's intimate friend Harry Daugherty had predicted that ten or twenty weary politi-cians, sitting around a table in the last days of a deadlocked con-vention, would finally agree on Harding; and so it came to pass. The nation, fatigued with the higher idealism, accepted the de-cision.

Wilson, living on in Washington, watched Harding with supreme contempt. It was reported that the former President had coined the phrase "the bungalow mind" to describe his successor. And, indeed, it was not inappropriate that the year in which Sinclair Lewis published his famous novel saw Main Street take over 1600 Pennsylvania Avenue. For Harding exuded the atmosphere of a sleepy Ohio town — the shady streets, the weekly lodge meetings, the smoking-room stories, golf on Sunday morning, followed by a fried chicken dinner and an afternoon nap. Alice Roosevelt Long-worth, the daughter of another Republican President and the wife of the Speaker of the House, could never forget a typical White House scene — the President's study filled with cronies; cards and poker chips on the table; whisky and tall glasses on the trays; the air thick with cigar smoke; a general atmosphere of unbuttoned vests, feet on the desk, and spittle in the cuspidor. "Harding was not a bad man," observed Alice Longworth. "He was just a slob." [2]

Harding was not a bad man. He was kindly and amiable, devoted in friendship and without malice in antagonism. Where Wilson refused to release the Socialist Eugene Debs from his Atlanta cell, Harding had no hesitation about commuting Debs's sentence. Terre Haute and Marion, after all, were much the same. "We understand each other perfectly," exclaimed Debs, after a visit to the White House. [3] And Harding had no illusions about himself. He was a joiner, a booster, a glad-hander. This was the life he loved, and he wanted no other. But relentlessly his wife — "the Duchess," he called her — pushed her Warren on; and in the end, against his pathetic wisps of better judgment, he found himself President of the United States.

While he drank and gambled in the presidential mansion, while he played the stock market from the presidential study (he died owing a Cleveland brokerage house $180,000), while his back-slapping friends from Ohio lined their pockets, Harding still somehow sensed the dignity of the Presidency — and sensed too his own inability ever to achieve it. In 1922, in an off-the-record speech at the National Press Club, he recalled that his father had once said to him that it was a good thing that he had not been born a girl: "you'd be in the family way all the time. You can't say No." "My God, this is a hell of a job!" Harding complained to William Allen

White. "My God-damn friends, White, they're the ones that keep me walking the floor nights!" Again: "This White House is a prison. I can't get away from the men who dog my footsteps. I am in jail." And, again, to Nicholas Murray Butler, "I am not fit for this office and should never have been here." [4]

II

The Presidency was more than a man. It was an institution, making its own decisions, generating its own momentum, living its own life. No matter how many afternoons the President spent on the golf course, how many evenings at the card table, the business of the Presidency went on. And in Charles Evans Hughes as Secretary of State, in Andrew Mellon as Secretary of the Treasury, in Henry C. Wallace as Secretary of Agriculture, in Herbert Hoover as Secretary of Commerce, Harding had men around him of ability and character.

But Harry Daugherty, his Attorney-General, was a small-time fixer, shrill in the field of policy, dissolute in the field of morals. When the railroad shopmen struck in 1922, Daugherty convinced himself that it was a Communist attempt to overthrow the government of the United States. "It *is* civil war," he told Harding, civil war instigated by Moscow; and he secured a sweeping injunction charging the strikers with 17,000 crimes. Hughes and Hoover found the injunction so outrageous that they attacked it in Cabinet; but when Senator Burton K. Wheeler of Montana protested publicly, the Attorney-General of the United States was quick to denounce him as "the Communist leader in the Senate." [5] And while Daugherty labored to save the republic from such Bolsheviki as Wheeler and Donald Richberg, who was counsel for the striking unions, he applied himself with even greater diligence to manipulating the Department of Justice on behalf of old Ohio friends in the Little Green House on K Street.

The Secretary of the Interior was of similar stripe. To William Allen White, the unkempt and ill-visaged Albert B. Fall looked like a patent-medicine vendor — "a cheap, obvious faker. I could hardly believe my eyes." [6] But Harding, who greatly admired Fall, wanted to make him Secretary of State; and Edward L. Doheny found him so irresistible that on November 30, 1921, he conveyed to Fall a satchel containing $100,000 in cash — a "loan," conceived out of fondness for an old friend, absolutely unconnected, Doheny later testified under oath, with Fall's decision to give Doheny a lease on the naval oil reserves at Elk Hills in California. Doheny at last had found a public official who was indisputably not a Bolshevist.

Daugherty and Fall were without shame. In time rumors began to spread around Washington. Then a member of the Ohio gang committed suicide just before Harding left on a trip to Alaska in the summer of 1923. The President himself began perhaps to have a sense of impending disaster. He suddenly invited his Secretary of Commerce, Herbert Hoover, to join the trip. Possibly Harding thought for a moment he wanted Hoover's counsel, but it soon seemed as if it was rather because Hoover was a good bridge player. Certainly the President played bridge compulsively in smoky, overheated rooms, from breakfast to midnight, seeking distraction in the everlasting fall of the cards. When dummy, the Secretary rushed to ship decks or observation cars to fill his lungs with fresh air.

Harding had never seemed more restless. "I cannot hope to be one of the great presidents," he said to Charles Michelson of the New York *World,* "but perhaps I may be remembered as one of the best loved." One day he finally took Hoover aside and asked him vaguely what he should do if, say, there were scandals in the administration. The apprehensions were indefinite but obsessive. By now the party was back in the Pacific Northwest, where the President, worn and haggard, resumed his speaking schedule. Soon he was sick, laid low, it was stated, by bad crabmeat (though no crabmeat was to be found on the official menu). For a day or so he seemed to rally. Then, on August 3, while his wife was reading him an article about himself from the *Saturday Evening Post,* he turned pale and gave a shudder. In a few moments he was dead. (An Associated Press reporter scored a beat on the story; his name was Steve Early, and he had worked for Franklin Roosevelt in the 1920 campaign.) The Alaska trip gave Herbert Hoover a permanent distaste for bridge. He never played again.[7]

Slowly the funeral train made its way back to Washington, the nation struck for a moment with genuine grief, hushed crowds watching the train roll by, schoolchildren singing "Nearer My God to Thee" at stations and crossroads along the way. Harding's body lay in the East Room, a simple coffin with four wreaths of flowers standing in the center of the great room. One August night, at two in the morning, Florence Harding came down to look in the open coffin, where her husband, rouged and lipsticked, had in the dimness almost the color of life. The Duchess called for a chair and sat by him, speaking softly to him, her face close to his. "Warren," she said, "the trip has not hurt you one bit." And then: "No one can hurt you now, Warren." [8]

8. The Ethos of Normalcy

IT WAS after midnight in Plymouth, Vermont. The white cottage by the side of the road was dark, the little town still, when the clatter of an automobile suddenly broke through the night. In a moment, a Western Union messenger from Bridgewater was beating on the door of the Coolidge house. Calvin Coolidge's father sleepily lit a kerosene lamp and turned to open the telegram. In a few moments the Vice-President, hurriedly awakened, began to put on his best black suit. Soon Secretary Hughes was urging him by long-distance telephone to come to Washington for the swearing in. But Coolidge always knew what he wanted. His father was a notary public; the house had its family Bible; and, at 2.47 by the rococo Victorian clock on the mantel, Calvin Coolidge took the presidential oath.[1]

Coolidge arrived at the Presidency at a propitious time. No one yet knew how far the corruption had gone. It was only clear that the country needed leadership which could inspire moral respect. After the slackness and indolence of Harding, it needed "character." Who could supply it better than a Vermont Yankee, reared in thrift and frugality, a fanatic for the old-fashioned virtues?

The concept of "character" was basic in the morality of conservatism. J. P. Morgan had stated the principle at the Pujo hearings just before the First World War. The committee counsel asked him whether commercial credit was not based primarily on property. "No, sir," Morgan replied. "The first thing is character." Before money or property? "Before money or anything else. Money cannot buy it." [2] Nor was "character" a nonexistent phenomenon, even if its definition sometimes seemed restricted. In business, it was what distinguished a Morgan from a Jim Fisk, a Dwight Morrow from a Doheny or an H. F. Sinclair; in politics, an Elihu Root, a Henry Cabot Lodge, an H. L. Stimson from a Blaine, a Foraker, or a Harding. The men of character had culture, responsibility, a feeling of *noblesse oblige,* a sense of standards.

They had once dominated both business and politics. But in the postwar years they lost considerable ground. Not entirely: foreign affairs were still considered their province, since it suited their urbanity, their knowledge of languages, their taste for foreign travel. So a Charles Evans Hughes could become Secretary of State, or a Henry L. Stimson Governor-General of the Philippines. But few cared about foreign affairs. "I was an outsider," wrote Stimson wryly years later. "I had been 'skylarking' in the Far East while America was doing business." [3] Where things mattered, the high-minded conservatives counted less and less. The typical big moneyed men, whom Theodore Roosevelt twenty years before found so boring and absurd, were now the insiders.

And, to a considerable degree, the men of character cheered on the new dispensation. During the 1920's Henry Cabot Lodge commended Harding to his personal friends in Boston; and he wrote so enthusiastically to Theodore Roosevelt of Albert Fall that he later found the references embarrassing and struck them out before publishing the correspondence. Similarly, when Fall resigned from the Interior Department, the virtuous Herbert Hoover sent him a cordial note, expressing hope for a quick return to public life and adding rashly, "In my recollection, that department has never had so constructive and legal a headship as you gave it." This was written before the Fall scandals came out; but it was addressed to a man whom Charles Evans Hughes found a long-winded bore, and whose humbuggery seemed so patent that William Allen White could not believe his eyes. (And, as early as March 1922 — a year before the Hoover letter — Secretary Wallace had called attention to the transfer of the naval oil leases.) As for Daugherty, William Howard Taft, whom Harding made Chief Justice of the United States, called him "one of the finest fellows I know." [4]

Thus the high-minded men contributed to their own degradation. Hughes, frosty and clearheaded, remained an exception. In private, at least, he had few illusions. But Hughes was more un-approachable than ever in these genial days. Except for Wallace, he had no personal friends in the cabinet. Even Hoover complained that Hughes was "the most self-contained man I ever knew. . . . He simply had no instinct for personal friendship that I could ever discover." [5] Most of the rest, whether because of mistaken loyalties to party, or because of naïveté about people, carelessly relaxed their standards. Like Chief Justice Taft, they described Harry Daugherty as "loyal, hard-working, disinterested, honest and courageous," a veritable Eagle Scout in politics; while Thomas J. Walsh and Burton K. Wheeler, who exposed the Harding graft, were scandalmongers and socialists.

Still, in time, not even the Tafts could reject Senator Walsh's facts; and acceptance constituted a blow to the moral confidence of the nation. It was this damage which Coolidge seemed so qualified to repair. Indeed, the situation had almost been foreseen. No banking house better represented the cult of character than J. P. Morgan; and in 1920 one of the two members of the firm who most embodied this virtue wrote a letter to the other. "In looking ahead in the next four or eight years," said Dwight Morrow to Thomas W. Lamont, "I think what America needs more than anything else is a man who will in himself be a demonstration of character. I think Coolidge comes more nearly being that man than any other man in either party." [6]

II

Morrow had known Coolidge since their college years at Amherst in the nineties. Not everyone rated Coolidge so highly. Yet no one could deny that this neat, well-brushed, immaculate little Yankee, so laconic in public, so garrulous in private, so self-centered and so self-satisfied, so wickedly humorous, so thin-lipped and so sharp-eyed, had the authentic tang of personality.

He had moved far from his rural Vermont childhood — "I never saw a man," exclaimed the British Ambassador, "who looked less like the son of a farmer." Entering law and politics in Massachusetts, he had always been competent, taciturn, and safe. The Boston police strike gave him as governor an accidental reputation for swift decision and made him Vice-President. But he had had little impact on Washington. According to a young Republican editor in Michigan named Arthur H. Vandenberg, Coolidge was "so unimpressive" that he would probably have been denied renomination.

His speeches offered his social philosophy in dry pellets of aphorism. "The chief business of the American people," he said, "is business." But, for Coolidge, business was more than business; it was a religion; and to it he committed all the passion of his arid nature. "The man who builds a factory," he wrote, "builds a temple. . . . The man who works there worships there." He felt these things with a fierce intensity. William Allen White, who knew him well, called him a mystic, a whirling dervish of business, as persuaded of the divine character of wealth as Lincoln had been of the divine character of man, "crazy about it, sincerely, genuinely, terribly crazy."

As he worshipped business, so he detested government. "If the Federal Government should go out of existence, the common run of people would not detect the difference in the affairs of their daily life for a considerable length of time." The federal government justified itself only as it served business. "The law that builds up the people is the law that builds up industry." And the chief way by which the federal government could serve business was to diminish itself; "the Government can do more to remedy the economic ills of the people by a system of rigid economy in public expenditure than can be accomplished through any other action." Economy was his self-confessed obsession; it was "idealism in its most practical form"; it was the "full test of our national character."

As President, he dedicated himself to inactivity. "No other President in my time," said the White House usher, "ever slept so much." In his dozen or so waking hours, he did as little as possible. In his *Autobiography* he singled out one rule as more important than any other: "It consists in never doing anything that someone else can do for you." In practice, he added another rule: say as little as possible. "The things I don't say," he would dryly remark, "never get me into trouble." Silence was the best defense; it baffled and defeated the outside world. Nine-tenths of the White House callers, he told Hoover, want something they ought not to have. "If you keep dead-still they will run down in three or four minutes. If you even cough ,or smile they will start up all over again." When a senator charged in one day demanding that something be done, Coolidge, his feet on the desk, said, "Don't you know that four-fifths of all our troubles in this life would disappear if we would only sit down and keep still?"

The main social events at the White House in Coolidge's time were his breakfasts: pancakes with Vermont maple syrup, served promptly at eight, his large white collies wandering about the room or licking the sugar out of the bottom of his coffee cup. On other mornings, he ate breakfast in his bedroom while a valet rubbed his head with Vaseline. When his faith was not involved, he watched life with a quizzical air. His humor was mordant and unpredictable. His eyes sometimes shone with the peculiar gleam of a parrot about to give someone a tweak; and then deadly remarks snapped out of compressed lips; or, in a mood of aimless mischief, he might press all the bells in his room at once and disappear to fool the servants, or he might play unfunny practical jokes on the Secret Service men. He could be irascible and nasty, straining all the understanding of his gracious wife. In the memory of the White House usher, Theodore Roosevelt in his worst rage was placid compared with Coolidge.[7]

To some his aphoristic self-confidence represented homely folk wisdom; to others, intolerable smugness. To some his inaction was masterly restraint; to others, it was the complacent emptiness of a dull and lazy man. To some his humor was innocent fun; to others, it was sadistic meanness. To some his satisfaction with his purpose represented "character"; to others, it seemed a bankruptcy of mind and soul. To some he was the best in the American middle class. To others he was almost the worst.

William Allen White called him "a Puritan in Babylon." His frugality sanctified an age of waste, his simplicity an age of luxury, his taciturnity an age of ballyhoo. He was the moral symbol the times seemed to demand.

III

And he moved to make the symbolism good. As the disclosures of the Walsh investigation roused public opinion, Coolidge dismissed Daugherty as Attorney-General and began to tidy up the administration. At the same time, he quietly established his control of the Republican party — or, rather, permitted his friend William Morgan Butler to establish control on his behalf.

The rise of Butler, a Massachusetts businessman, president of the Hoosac and Quissett Mills and the West End Thread Corporation, was symptomatic. In the past, business influence in the party had been at one remove. Politicians like Henry Cabot Lodge and Boies Penrose had negotiated with business leaders as equals. Lodge, indeed, had the contemptuous feeling that businessmen were worse in politics than men of any other class; "the businessman dealing with a large political question is really a painful sight." [8] But the North Shore patrician had not anticipated the new age. He had served the Republican party for nearly half a century; he had been permanent chairman of the convention a quarter of a century before; he had gone farther than most of his class in coming to terms with the men of trade. Yet he went to his last convention in 1924 an ordinary delegate, little noticed, never consulted, while the New Bedford textile manufacturer, backed by the cunning middle-class lawyer from Northampton, ran the show. Lodge sat through his humiliation with proud, expressionless face, aristocrat to the last, denying his enemies the satisfaction of seeing how much they had hurt him.

The Republican convention of 1924 went like clockwork. The delegates, showing no undue emotion (except when confronted by Secretary Mellon, one of the richest men in America), nominated Coolidge by virtual acclamation. After William E. Borah rejected the vice-presidential nomination ("At which end?" Borah was supposed to have said), it went to Brigadier-General Charles Gates Dawes of Illinois; and the delegates dispersed, serenely confident that the nation shared their determination to keep cool with Coolidge.

When the Democrats, after their bitter convention, nominated John W. Davis of New York, by now a conservative corporation lawyer, many liberals of both parties looked to old Bob La Follette to provide an alternative. He did so, under the standard of a new Progressive party; and it was the Progressive challenge to business supremacy, weak as this challenge was, which supplied the theme for the Republican campaign. The issue, as General Dawes declared in ringing tones, "is whether you stand on the rock of common sense with Calvin Coolidge, or upon the sinking sands of socialism with Robert M. La Follette." If this were the issue, there was no question how the American people stood.

"It was a famous victory," said William Howard Taft, meditating the results a few days after the election. Whenever the American people understand that the issue is between radicalism and conservatism, mused the Chief Justice, the answer will always be the same. "This country is no country for radicalism. I think it is really the most conservative country in the world." [9]

9. The Economics of Republicanism

In 1925, *Nation's Business*, the organ of the United States Chamber of Commerce, called the American businessman "the most influential person in the nation." The businessman now occupied, *Nation's Business* observed, "a position of leadership which the businessman has never held before." "Never before, here or anywhere else," added the *Wall Street Journal*, "has a government been so completely fused with business." From his side, Calvin Coolidge confirmed the alliance. "This is a business country," he said, ". . . and it wants a business government." [1]

This was the essence of the Republican experiment; and, as Secretary of the Treasury, Andrew Mellon incarnated the new unity. Seventy years old in 1925, Mellon had seen in his own lifetime the transformation of a rural and colonial economy into the greatest industrial power in the world. He had entered the banking business in Pittsburgh in 1874; the great business leaders who had wrought the miraculous transformation were his contemporaries; and, as a man who remembered Bryan and Roosevelt and Wilson, he felt a shy satisfaction at the passing away of the old distrust and the national acceptance of business leadership. His own appointment to the Treasury, unthinkable in an earlier epoch, seemed to symbolize the revolution in popular attitudes.

Slight and frail, with prominent cheekbones in a grave face, he had a gentle Edwardian formality of manner and dress. His suits were dark, sober, and luxurious, with carefully buttoned coat and black tie; his hats were soft and gray. He was most himself, perhaps, among fine wines, rich cigars, antique china, and beautiful paintings. But his public face was one of perpetual weariness and worry. With a cold smile and querulous voice, he never ceased to call for government economy.[2]

"The Government is just a business," said Mellon, "and can and should be run on business principles." The first necessity, accordingly, was to balance the budget, and the second to pay off the debt. But Mellon's greater interest, it soon developed, was somewhat inconsistently in the reduction of tax rates, especially in the highest brackets. Existing surtax rates, he felt, were intolerable. A man with an income of $1,000,000 had to pay an income tax of nearly $300,000. The consequences, he declared, were already visible on every side; everyone knew "of businesses which have not been started, and of new projects which have been abandoned, all for one reason — high surtaxes." There was a difference, he warned, between taxation and confiscation; and, to restore that difference, he proposed to establish a maximum surtax rate of 25 per cent. No one, however much money he made, should be required to pay more than one quarter of his income in surtax; otherwise it would be the end of American initiative.[3]

A tax bill which concentrated on cutting taxes for millionaires could not command unreserved enthusiasm, even in the nineteen twenties. John Nance Garner, the wily congressman from Texas, licked Mellon's tax proposals in 1924 and forced Coolidge to sign a somewhat stiffer bill. But Mellon, ever tenacious, kept chipping away each year at rates in the upper brackets. His opponents remained notably lacking in sympathy. "Mr. Mellon himself," as George W. Norris of Nebraska observed of the Mellon bill of 1925, "gets a larger personal reduction than the aggregate of practically all the taxpayers in the state of Nebraska." [4] But such insinuations could not daunt Mellon's crusade.

Nor was tax reduction Mellon's only resource. What he could not reduce, he could often refund — a process which had the advantage of taking place behind closed doors. Not until Garner forced the revelation of the figures in 1930 did the country know what Mellon had done. In his first eight years at the Treasury, the Secretary dispensed $3.5 billion in the shape of cash refunds, credits, and abatements. The size of these disbursements mounted steadily during the period, except in 1927 and 1930, when congressional grumbling forced the Treasury to hold back. Several million dollars went to Mellon's own companies; other millions, as Garner took pleasure in pointing out, went where they promised to do the most good to the Republican party. Thus each of the seventeen individuals contributing $10,000 to the Republican campaign in 1930 had been beneficiaries of Mr. Mellon's official generosity.[5]

Meanwhile, Mellon himself continued an active life of speculation. Through family corporations, the Mellons shared in the grand barbecue. The *New York Times* reported in 1926 that the Secretary of the Treasury's relatives had made $300 million in the bull market on aluminum and Gulf Oil alone. Nor did this exhaust the possibilities of family corporations. "Pursuant to your request for a memorandum setting forth the various ways by which an individual may legally avoid tax," wrote the Commissioner of Internal Revenue to the Secretary of the Treasury, "I am pleased to submit the following." The following consisted of ten possible methods of tax avoidance, five of which Mellon in time admitted under oath he actually employed. The Commissioner also sent Mellon a tax expert to help prepare the Secretary's income tax return; the expert soon showed up on Mellon's personal payroll, where he turned to the Secretary's private account the knowledge accumulated in the public service. It was this expert who set up more family corporations and, through paper losses in stock sales to and among them, enabled the Secretary to slash his tax payments at the very time when in his official capacity, Mellon was appealing to the taxpayers to pay their own income taxes.[6]

II

The Mellon tax program had — at least in the minds of skeptical observers — its contradictions in equity and ethics. And it had contradictions in economics too. For, if debt reduction and budget balancing might have constituted a useful sedative for the nervous economy, the Mellon penchant for tax reduction served to make more money available for speculation. "A decrease of taxes," as Mellon said, "causes an inspiration to trade and commerce."[7] With this he injected a few more billion dollars into a boom which hardly needed to be further inspired.

Yet it was what the business community thought it wanted; and, across the board, this was the new test for economic policy. So Coolidge similarly cherished the high wall of protection for American industry erected in the Republican tariff of 1922. At the same time he backed Secretary of Commerce Hoover in his vigorous program to promote the sale of American manufactures abroad. Woodrow Wilson had naïvely thought a high tariff and a flourishing export trade to be incompatible. In his last official act as President, vetoing a bill to raise tariff rates, Wilson had argued that the United States was now a creditor nation, and that foreign nations could buy American goods only in three ways — through borrowing dollars from America, or selling gold to it, or selling goods to it. Wilson had rejected the first two methods. "If we wish to have Europe settle her debts," he had concluded, ". . . we must be prepared to buy from her." [8] But Hoover, indifferent to Wilson's quandary, was content to rear the American export trade on the basis of American foreign loans. This was a project with which New York bankers were glad to cooperate. Through the twenties, billions of American dollars went abroad in private loans to subsidize the role of American goods abroad.

President Coolidge was prepared further to attest his trust in business leadership by weakening the instrumentalities through which past national governments had sought to regulate business. The regulatory commissions, inherited from more suspicious days, were quickly infused with the new spirit of unity. To the Tariff Commission, for example, were sent men who acted almost as open representatives of protected industries. When the Commission's minority, led by E. P. Costigan of Colorado, began to object that members were sitting on cases in which they or their relatives were known to have financial stakes, Coolidge upbraided them for raising prudish scruples. After all, who were better qualified to sit in such cases than men equipped by special interests with superior judgment and knowledge? In the same spirit, the White House slipped W. W. Atterbury, the president of the Pennsylvania Railroad, advance copies of the President's special message to Congress on railroad consolidation.[9]

Coolidge, wholly honest himself, perceived no conflict of interests, and he set the model for his administration. In the years since the New Freedom, the Federal Trade Commission had been a central agency of government regulation. But, with the appointment of W. E. Humphrey in 1925, a new era began. Humphrey denounced the Wilsonian FTC as "an instrument of oppression and disturbance and injury instead of a help to business"; no longer, he said, would the Commission serve as a "publicity bureau to spread socialistic propaganda." He soon brought about drastic changes in policies and procedures. Where the FTC had been set up to discourage monopoly, it now espoused the cause of the self-regulation of business and sponsored conference after conference to encourage industry-wide agreements on trade practices.[10]

Washington thus began to smile upon tendencies toward economic concentration, which for the better part of the century it had, in theory at least, disapproved. Hoover, recalling the War Industries Board experience, threw his Commerce Department behind the trade association movement. With Commerce Department aid, trade associations worked out "codes," which were then endorsed by the FTC and adopted by the industry. Though dedicated to the elimination of "unfair" trade practices, the codes gradually began to spill over into such questions as price-cutting and, in some cases, provided fronts behind which businessmen fraternally conspired to evade the antitrust law.

More overt forms of concentration thrived equally. Holding companies moved into the utility and transportation fields, chain stores into retail distribution; in all areas, big firms swallowed small firms and merged with other big ones. By 1930 the two hundred largest nonbanking corporations, after growing during the decade at a rate two to three times as fast as the smaller nonbanking corporations, controlled about half the total corporate wealth of the country.[11] And from the viewpoint of government, private economic power could not have collected in more responsible hands.

III

Nor was this a wholly unreasonable point of view. If the merit of an economic structure was to be judged by its surface performance, then the American economy of the early twenties ranked high. The living standards of the nation steadily rose; economic opportunities steadily expanded; the flow of consumer goods steadily increased. The imagination of the American capitalist and the ingenuity of the American engineer were never more apparent in the life of the people. For a time, the country seemed to be on the edge of a new abundance.

Yet the very processes of plenty created new problems. The decisive economic fact was the extraordinary increase in technological efficiency and productivity. The output per man-hour in industry rose about 40 per cent during the decade. The central economic challenge was to distribute the gains of productivity in a manner that would maintain employment and prosperity.

By the rules of orthodox economics, the reduction in production costs should have brought about either a reduction in prices or a rise in wages, or both. But the rigidities in the economy, in part the result of the process of concentration, seemed to have anaesthetized the market. The price system, so exquisitely sensitive in classical theory, was turning out to be sluggish in practice.

Denied outlet in lower prices because of accumulating rigidities, the gains of technological efficiency were equally denied outlet in higher wages or in higher farm prices because of the bargaining feebleness of the labor movement and of the farm bloc. As a result, these gains were captured increasingly by the businessmen themselves in the form of profits. Through the decade, profits rose over 80 per cent as a whole, or twice as much as productivity; the profits of financial institutions rose a fantastic 150 per cent.[12]

The increase in profits naturally pushed up the prices of corporate securities; and, as securities rose in value, corporations found that the easiest way to obtain new cash was to issue new securities. This was cheap money, because there was no need to pay a return on stock issues as one would pay interest on bank loans. In turn, the corporations used the cash to expand plant, thereby increasing the flood of goods into an already crowded market; or, as time passed, they funneled their funds more and more into speculation. The result was to push stocks up again, repeating the whole process at a higher level. As the twenties proceeded, the stock market sucked off an increasing share of the undistributed gains of industrial efficiency.

The stock market boom in its early phases was by no means artificial. For a time it reflected solid industrial expansion. The automobile industry, in particular, had energized basic sectors of the economy — steel, machine tools, petroleum, rubber, roads, and public construction — and had encouraged innovation and research. But the very excess profits which were stimulating the boom were at the same time shortening its life. For the diversion of the gains of efficiency into profits was bound to result in a falling off of the capacity of the people as a whole to buy. The Mellon tax policy, placing its emphasis on relief for millionaires rather than for consumers, made the maldistribution of income and oversaving even worse. By 1929, the 2.3 per cent of the population with incomes over $10,000 were responsible for two-thirds of the 15 billion dollars of savings. The 60,000 families in the nation with the highest incomes saved almost as much as the bottom 25 million.[13] The mass of the population simply lacked the increase in purchasing power to enable them to absorb the increase in goods.

The rural depression further distorted the structure of demand. The farmers had lost their foreign markets after the war; and the resulting sag in agricultural income built a basic imbalance into the economy. But the Republican administration could not get so excited over the predicament of farmers as over the predicament of business. "Farmers have never made money," Coolidge remarked philosophically to the chairman of the Farm Loan Board. "I don't believe we can do much about it." [14] The farmers, many of them living in privation, most of them under the shadow of mortgages, were less philosophical. But when they devised measures to do for them what the protective tariff did for the manufacturer, they found no sympathy in Washington. As a result, the agricultural half of the economy could not do its share in maintaining demand.

As for city people, whose wages failed to keep pace with productivity, they found no more support in Washington than the farmers. While businessmen talked a good deal in public about the American faith in high wages, in practice they let the percentage rise of wages lag behind the rise of output and profit. Between 1923 and 1929, output per man-hour in manufacturing rose almost 32 per cent, while hourly wages rose but slightly over 8 per cent.[15] Nor did anyone in authority see any economic value in a strong labor movement.

The unsatisfactory level of wages and of farm income meant that "prosperity" was steadily less able to generate buying power in sufficient volume to meet the steadily rising productive capacity — or, in time, to carry already available goods off the market. Still, even with a better distribution of purchasing power, the economy might have faltered as soon as the first growth of the automotive industry began to slacken. And deep structural weaknesses, especially in the banking system and on the security exchanges, rendered the future even more dubious.

IV

Yet Wall Street and Washington had few qualms. By the middle twenties, the whole economic process began to focus on a single point — the ticker-tape machine with its endless chatter of stock market quotations. The torrent of excess money, pouring into the market, swept stock prices ever upward. And the leaders of the business community, now heedless of caution in their passion for gain, promoted new investment trusts, devised new holding companies and manipulated new pools, always with the aim of floating new securities for the apparently insatiable market. In 1923 capital issues amounted to $3.2 billion, and the annual sum rose steadily, reaching nearly $10 billion by 1927. A similar increase occurred in the volume of sales, from 236 million shares on the New York exchange in 1923 to 577 million in 1927 and 1125 in 1928. The market value of all shares on the New York Stock Exchange soared from $27 billion in 1925 to $67 billion in 1929. The net private debt of the nation climbed from $106 billion in 1920 to $162 billion in 1929.[16]

In time it would appear that even the leaders of business could not decipher the intricate financial structures they were erecting. But for the moment everyone understood that here was an endless source of money and power, a roulette wheel at which no one lost. More and more the nation's passions centered on the feverish trading in the narrow streets at the lower tip of Manhattan Island. The American people learned a new vocabulary. "Brokers' loans" were loans made by the broker to the customer; they enabled customers to speculate far beyond their supply of cash. "Buying on the margin" meant that in using brokers' loans in the market the customer had to supply only a fixed proportion of the value of the shares purchased. When brokers' loans were at a 25 per cent margin, the customer's hard dollar was worth, in effect, four on the stock market. With the market steadily rising, who could lose?

Government officials meanwhile watched the speculative boom with affable approval. A decade earlier, Wilson had established the Federal Reserve System as a means of steadying the economy. The System had two chief instruments of credit policy in the twenties. Through open-market operations, it used the purchase or sale of government securities to alter the reserves of member banks and thus enlarge or contract the base of the money supply. Through the discount rate, it made the money supply tight or easy by raising or lowering the rate at which banks borrowed from the Federal Reserve.

No doubt in the twenties many exaggerated the power of monetary policy. But such power as the Federal Reserve System had was used, in the main, on the side of easy money. In part this was in deference to the situation in Europe. By keeping interest rates low and credit cheap, for example, the Board both discouraged the import of gold from Europe and made more American money available for foreign loans. Thus it believed it aided the task of European reconstruction. In the same spirit, Benjamin Strong, the vigorous governor of the Federal Reserve Bank in New York, and Montagu Norman of the Bank of England were responsible for a critical decision in the summer of 1927 to reduce the discount rate from 4 to 3.5 per cent. This act was designed to keep Britain on the gold standard to which Chancellor of the Exchequer Winston S. Churchill had rashly committed it two years earlier, and thus to avert a world-wide deflation. But the easy-money policy had the effect of accelerating the inflation in the United States. And in 1928, an election year, it was impossible to get a firm decision to check the upward spiral.[17]

Sober businessmen began to regard the situation with discomfort. Occasionally these doubts found public expression, causing faint tremors of anxiety. But whenever the market faltered, someone in the administration could be relied on to speak words of encouragement. Nor could it be supposed that the White House or the Treasury were badly informed; for the business leaders of the country were President Coolidge's guests for lunch and dinner; and everyone knew that Secretary Mellon was himself deep in the market through his family corporation.

The doubts sometimes broke through to the President. Secretary Hoover, for example, objected periodically (though not publicly) to the buoyant Federal Reserve policy. But Coolidge's stock reply was to insist that the Board was independent of the Treasury and beyond the scope of the Executive, while Mellon seemed to dismiss his colleague's intermittent concern as much ado about nothing.

Early in 1927 William Z. Ripley, a Harvard professor, called at the White House. Ripley, who was in the tradition of Brandeis and Thorstein Veblen, though he presented his thought in a more genial vein, was much exercised by the process in which the economy was at once dispersing ownership and concentrating control. While stocks and bonds flowed from Wall Street to Main Street, power flowed from Main Street to Wall Street; and the consequence, Professor Ripley felt, was to encourage corporate secrecy and deceit — "double-shuffling, honey-fugling, hornswoggling and skulduggery." The President, his feet on his desk, a cigar clamped between his teeth, listened in increasing gloom; finally he asked, "Is there anything we can do down here?" Ripley, who did not then consider securities regulation a federal responsibility, replied, "No, it's a state matter." The President looked up, his face grateful with relief.[18]

By the end of 1927 brokers' loans went nearly to the $4 billion mark. To many this seemed a wobbling basis for the superstructure of inflated values. Then on January 7, 1928, President Coolidge again came to the rescue. The increase in brokers' loans, he said, was a natural expansion of business in the securities market; he saw nothing wrong in it. A few weeks later, Roy Young of the Federal Reserve Board, the good friend of Secretary Hoover, told a congressional committee that he could not say whether brokers' loans were too low or too high; but "I am satisfied they are safely and conservatively made." [19] And so the market continued to rise.

10. The Age of Business

IF THE BUSINESS of America was business, then business meant much
more to Americans than the making of money. There had been, in
the words of Dr. Julius Klein, a leading official of Herbert Hoover's
Department and a minor prophet of the New Era, an "amazing
transformation in the soul of business"; business had become "a
thing of morals." In this process, business had purged itself of the
gross and greedy qualities of its earlier existence. Capitalism had
transcended its individualism and materialism, becoming social and
spiritual. Yet it had miraculously retained the spur of profit, without which all social schemes were utopian. "Long before this,"
Garet Garrett, another lesser prophet, wrote with wonder, "a state
of society had been imagined in which the desire for private gain
as the paramount economic motive should yield to the idea of
social function. But nobody had ever imagined it would really
pay." [1]

The new faith permeated the churches, the courts, the colleges,
the press. It created a literature of complacency, of which Edgar A.
Guest was, no doubt, the poet laureate. It developed an economics
of success and a metaphysics of optimism. For some of its followers — as for Calvin Coolidge — the process went even farther:
the factory was the temple, work was worship, and business verged
on a new religion. For the true believer, its commandment was
Service, its sacrament the weekly lunches of fellowship at Kiwanis
or Rotary, its ritual the collective chanting of cheerful songs, its
theologian a New York advertising man named Bruce Barton. In
his best-selling book of 1925, *The Man Nobody Knows,* Barton as-

similated Jesus Christ into the new cult, observing admiringly of
the Son of God that He had "picked up twelve men from the bottom ranks of business and forged them into an organization that
conquered the world." [2]

Salvation was to be measured by success; and success thus became
the visible evidence of spiritual merit. The individuals who made
good deserved the gratitude of all mankind. "Without these great
minds," remarked a business writer, "the multitude would eat their
heads off, and, as history proves, would lapse into barbarism. . . .
The masses are the beneficiaries, the few, the benefactors." And,
if individual effort were the road to salvation, then the resort to
government was a lure of the devil. The president of the National
Association of Manufacturers ticked off the satanic litany in his
1925 address: "Listen to the strange philosophies of the living wage,
the check-off system, the minimum wage, government controlled
children, the closed union shop, and the socialistic redistribution
of wealth."

The federal government, even under Coolidge's light rein, appeared a particular threat. James M. Beck, who had been Solicitor-
General under Harding, could entitle his book of 1926 *The Vanishing Rights of the States.* That same year, in the House of Representatives, Ogden Mills, a sharp and able conservative, earnestly
declared that federal centralization was "striking at the very corner-
stone of our institutions," and that "the most important need in
the country today" was the strengthening of local government.[3]

II

The Darwinian conception of character as forged in the competitive struggle was modified in the twenties to include new
sentiments of business responsibility. The public was no longer
altogether to be damned; it was to be pleased, and to be served.
Emphasis was shifting from production and competition to distribution, consumption and cooperation. The self-reliant manufacturer, surrounded by his turbines or his blast-furnaces, was less
the culture hero than the promoter, the traveling salesman, or the
business statesman.

Owen D. Young of General Electric, RCA, and the Federal

Reserve Bank of New York was an influential voice of the new mood. His thesis was that the unbridled pursuit of profit was giving way to a sense of trusteeship. "One no longer feels the obligation to take from labor for the benefit of capital, nor to take from the public for the benefit of both, but rather to administer wisely and fairly in the interest of all." [4]

There were others like Young. But, in a sense, the most influential of all business leaders was Henry Ford; and Ford was the more revealing, because, while a great producer in the old tradition, he nonetheless led the whole business community to think in the new terms of promotion, of distribution, and of statesmanship. A man of genius, he was at the same time narrow, ignorant, and mean-spirited. He carried a gun, believed in reincarnation, and hated bankers, doctors, Jews, Catholics, fat men, liquor, tobacco, prisons and capital punishment. His impulses were vagrant and confused, and too often he acted on them. In 1916 he had sent the Peace Ship to Europe in order to end the First World War; in 1918, at Woodrow Wilson's personal request, he was a Democratic candidate for the United States Senate; and in 1920 he began to publish the Protocols of the Elders of Zion in the *Dearborn Independent.* He believed always that God was with him: "I'm guided," he told his friends, pointing to his head. "I'm guided." [5]

Yet, for all his zaniness, Ford had a compelling vision of a new age. Modern mass production, he was convinced, had created an economy that was capable of anything; the fact of abundance must therefore revolutionize the philosophy of business. High output, low prices, and high wages must be the new objectives. Only by steadily raising wages and reducing prices could the business community maintain the buying power of the people. "These fundamentals," he liked to add, "are all summed up in the single word 'service.'" If business did not serve, it would not survive. [6]

Ford's spotlighting of purchasing power brought a wholly new element into business economics. For businessmen of an earlier generation, as Edward A. Filene put it, buying power had "just happened"; in the New Era, businessmen had the responsibility of producing it — or the system would break down. The task was to keep the stream of demand flowing. Now that the problem of production had been solved, in the words of Garet Garrett, "people may ruin themselves by saving instead of spending." The nation must realize, Garrett warned, that, rigorously practiced, thrift becomes "economically disastrous." [7]

III

This was the official philosophy of the New Era — character, service, and high wages; the desire for private gain yielding to the idea of social function, with the profits still rolling in. But the new faith did not quite carry total conviction. Of course, the professional critics could be expected to jeer at the businessman's effort to dignify his occupation. "He is the only one," wrote H. L. Mencken, "who always seeks to make it appear, when he attains the object of his labors, *i.e.*, the making of a great deal of money, that it was not the object of his labors." [8] But others too retained doubts. Somehow the new business idealism, so much of it so devoted and sincere, had not wholly transmuted the acquisitive impulse underneath.

Perhaps it was the gap between principle and action: the men who talked of character in their clubs while they plotted to get on preferred lists and into insiders' pools; or who spoke eloquently of service at Rotary while cursing out farmers, workers, foreigners, and intellectuals in the locker room. "What a God-damned world this is!" exclaimed William Allen White, recollecting an earlier idealism. " . . . If anyone had told me ten years ago that our country would be what it is today . . . I should have questioned his reason." [9] Despite the noble words and the lofty hope, to many the New Era seemed at heart only a stampede to make money.

General Billy Mitchell began in these years his fight for American air power. Looking back a decade later, he told a committee of Congress why he had failed. "When the merchants get hold of our government," he said, "we might as well stop work." What do you mean, merchants? someone asked. "People who have something to sell," the General grimly replied. And so it seemed: the single motive had been nurtured until it drove out all others. Joseph B. Eastman, a distinguished Wilson appointment to the Interstate Commerce Commission, protested in 1925 against the prevalent philosophy. The pursuit of private gain did not seem to him, he said, as it evidently did to Coolidge, "the only impelling force in human beings" which could produce desirable results; "indeed, I would go so far as to say that the most important services to mankind have been the products of higher motives." But only a few were left to heed such sentiments — to feel, with the old Wilsonian, Daniel C. Roper, that the ideals of the Founding Fathers had been forgotten.

The whole nation, Dan Roper lamented, was caught up in the "money madness" — churches, schools, homes, everything. Instead of trying to help their fellow men, Americans were trying to make money out of them. "It is scarcely metaphorical to say that we had become Children in the Wilderness." George Norris remarked that he could not recall meeting a single really happy man since the war ended. "Europe was devastated by war," observed Brandeis, "we by the aftermath." [10]

IV

Even devotees of the business cult showed traces of misgiving. They were starved for something; their idealism needed an outlet — some fairer object of adoration than the complacent Coolidge or the capricious Ford or the brokers or the salesman. How profound this need was became clear for a moment in the spring of 1927. The hopes and fears of the nation were suddenly centered with devout intensity on a young man of whom most Americans a few days before had never heard — a kid, out by himself in a lonely monoplane, suspended between sky and sea, in a mad effort to fly the Atlantic Ocean. Millions held their breath, wept, prayed, while they waited for the news. When he made Le Bourget, a whole nation went wild. Nothing could have seemed more fitting than President Coolidge's action in dispatching a cruiser to bring him back. At last the twenties had a hero.

Charles A. Lindbergh, Jr., was a symbol of redemption. He personified all that the twenties passionately wanted to admire — adventure in a time of calculation, faith in a time of expediency, youth in a time of gross middle age. He carried people away from the furies that consumed them back to motives deeper and higher than the pursuit of private gain. For a moment, many Americans seemed merchants no longer. They wiped away their tears, not knowing whether to be proud or ashamed. They wanted to leap recklessly into adventures that might mean disaster for the individual but everything for humanity. "People set down their glasses in country clubs and speak-easies," said Scott Fitzgerald, "and thought of their old best dreams." [11]

Lindbergh's marriage to the daughter of Dwight Morrow was an appropriate dynastic alliance. But Lindbergh was only a boy, and he wished nothing more than to be left alone. He could not satisfy the need for national leadership — for a man who could elicit the potentialities for spiritual good which people believed were locked away in the excitement of prosperity. Americans searched more than ever for the man who could transform the money madness into the benevolent order of service they dreamed of in their moments of exaltation.

11. Prophet of the New Era

MORE AND MORE in the twenties, one American emerged as the man who might bridge the gap between the ideals and the realities of the New Era. Herbert Clark Hoover was both Secretary of Commerce and a Quaker. His job placed him in the very center of economic life, while his faith identified him with the highest aspirations of service. His whole life, moreover, had been the realization of an American dream. More than anyone else in this decade, he articulated — as his career already exemplified — the ethic of American individualism, not the savage individualism of the ruthless past, but the hopeful individualism of a cooperative future.

Born in 1874 at West Branch, Iowa, Hoover had enjoyed the innocent pleasures of a classic small-town boyhood: in summer, fishing with willow poles and angleworms; in autumn, stalking pigeons and prairie chickens with bow and arrow and cooking them over a campfire; in the freezing winter dawn, tracking rabbits across snowy fields. In later years these recollections brought out a strain of unexpected lyricism in him, a memory of security. But the idyll soon came to an end. By the time he was eight years old, both his parents were dead. Soon after, he left Iowa to live with relatives in Oregon.

Something in his teens spurred him to become an engineer, and he seized the chance of training at the new university that Leland Stanford was founding in California. Finishing Stanford in 1895, a big man on campus, he set out to seek his fortune. By 1897, when twenty-three years old, he had already made his local name. The

British mining firm of Bewick, Moreing and Company sent word
to California that they needed an American engineer with gold-
mining experience for their Australian interests. Young Hoover
got the job.

His was the first generation of Americans to fan out in force
across the world: the years that followed were like a series of adventures out of Richard Harding Davis. Hoover went first to
Western Australia; then on to China, where, now twenty-five years
old, he became chief engineer for the Chinese Bureau of Mines at
$20,000 a year, helped make the natural resources of China, includ-
ing the great Kaiping coal mines, safe for foreign investment, and
was caught in an eddy of the Boxer Rebellion. The home office
in London was quick to recognize the driving qualities of this
remarkable young American. When he was only twenty-seven,
Bewick, Moreing offered him a junior partnership. His business
life now centered in London; but Hoover himself continued to
work largely in the field, surveying mining properties, organizing
new companies and syndicates, spending days and weeks on trains
and steamships, a new sheaf of cables awaiting him at every stop.
He traveled endlessly, from Mandalay to the Transvaal, from Egypt
to the Malay States, from a turquoise mine at Mount Sinai to the
foggy, gas-lit streets of the City of London.

It was a Richard Harding Davis life, but Hoover was hardly a
Richard Harding Davis hero. Contained, wary, enormously capable and efficient, with round face, hazel eyes, straight mouse-colored
hair, and broad shoulders, he transmuted all adventure into business, as a Davis hero would transmute all business into adventure.
His manner, except among old friends to whom he had given his
confidence, was forbidding; and, even among old friends, he remained reserved. Will Irwin, who had known him intimately since
Stanford days, wrote in 1928: "I cannot remember that I have ever
heard him laugh 'out loud.'" Something seemed to separate
Hoover from human irrationality. Perhaps it was his dispassionate
engineer's intelligence, concerned with solving problems rather
than with relieving feelings; perhaps it was a protective coldness
which an initially warm heart had to acquire at a time and in
places where economic progress was purchased at such a cost in
human misery.

As his reputation grew, Hoover was soon spending less and less time in actual engineering, more and more as the organizer and promoter of companies. His rise during these years could hardly have been more spectacular. The road from West Branch, Iowa, to the Red House, Hornton Street, Campden Hill, London, had been traversed with extraordinary speed. And, though he was far better known in the City of London than in Wall Street, in Rangoon and Johannesburg than in Washington, he took care to keep up his American connections. In 1907 he bought a cottage on the Stanford campus. In 1909 he joined the National Republican Club (in West Branch the only Democrat had been the town drunkard).[1] In 1912 he contributed to Theodore Roosevelt's campaign.

By 1908 Hoover had laid the basis for a personal fortune. He decided now to strike out on his own as consulting engineer. In a short time he had offices from San Francisco to Petrograd and was a dominant figure, openly or in the shadows, in a dozen of the great international Edwardian undertakings — Russo-Asiatic Consolidated, the Inter-Argentine Syndicate, the Inter-Siberian Syndicate, Northern Nigeria Tin Mines, and many others. His interests spread from the Yukon to Tierra del Fuego and from the Altai Mountains and the Irtysh River to the Sierras. "My aggregate income from professional activities in various countries," he said of himself in 1914, "probably exceeded that of any other American engineer."

These were happy years for Hoover. Engineering and company management presented him with concrete problems that he could master with his impersonal force and intelligence. And life was rich and satisfying. "Pre-war England," he later wrote, "was the most comfortable place in which to live in the whole world"; and, again, "the happiest period of all humanity in the Western World in ten centuries was the twenty-five years before the First World War." But, alas, this idyll was to be spoiled too. Hoover was in his London offices in the tense month of August 1914. War in his view was unthinkable. When it came, it appeared, he wrote, "like an earthquake. The substance and bottom seemed to go out of everything." [2]

II

From the start, Hoover's organizing talent was in demand, first to take care of Americans stranded in Europe, then to administer relief in Belgium. With infinite patience and resourcefulness, he tackled the Belgian situation, negotiating problems of food, transport, finance, and diplomacy. Trips back to the United States began to re-establish him in the American scene. He made a significant impression in Washington. Wilson found him orderly and reassuring. To Brandeis he seemed "the biggest figure injected into Washington life by the war."

A few found him disconcertingly impersonal. "He told of the big work in Belgium," said Josephus Daniels, "as coldly as if he were giving statistics of production. From his words and his manner he seemed to regard human beings as so many numbers. Not once did he show the slightest feeling or convey to me a picture of the tragedies that went on." When he left, with a cold shake of the hand, Daniels felt that either Hoover had no heart or that his heart had been atrophied by his experience. But no one, not even Daniels, could gainsay Hoover's ability. As War Food Administrator, he took over in Washington with impressive mastery. "When you know me better," Hoover told General Peyton C. March, "you will find that when I say a thing is a fact it is a fact." By 1918 he was a household name in the United States. The end of the war did not terminate his responsibilities. The emphasis now shifted to the problem of averting famine and chaos abroad.

Before the war Hoover had loved the art, the literature, the magnificent cities and historic cathedrals of Europe. But war, he felt, had transformed the old continent into a "furnace of hate." Was he wrong now to perceive in the glare certain underlying European realities — forces of nationalism and imperialism, age-old hates, revenges, fierce distrusts, anxieties, fears? He did not know; he thought perhaps that the idealism of war could yet produce a European regeneration. Crossing the Atlantic from America in late 1918, Hoover, with Robert A. Taft, Lewis L. Strauss and other members of his staff, talked with anticipation. This seemed, perhaps, the moment when Europe might break with its past, when civilization itself could be reborn in the crucible of destruction.

Soon after arrival, disillusion began. Hoover attended a meeting of the Allied Ministers. They seemed to ooze, he later wrote, intrigue, selfishness, and heartlessness from every pore. As the weeks passed, it became increasingly apparent that war had not clarified the European mind or purified the European soul. Hoover fought valiantly to do his job. His representatives brought sustenance and hope to the far corners of Europe. In the discussions at Versailles, Hoover employed all his insistent force to make the statesmen forget the clash of national interest and face up to the essential facts of the European situation. He was, wrote John Maynard Keynes, "the only man who emerged from the ordeal of Paris with an enhanced reputation."

But at every turn he kept running up against emotion, prejudice, self-interest. He now succumbed to moods of deep pessimism — moods that deepened as his projects had to depend on the cooperation, not of slide rules or of hired hands, but of human equals. "He is simply reveling in gloom," wrote Colonel House to Wilson after a talk with Hoover in 1919. The treaty itself came as the shattering climax; then the troubled walk in the Paris sunrise and the meetings with Smuts and Keynes.

For Hoover the returns were in. Europe could not redeem itself, nor could America redeem it; the American destiny was separate and unique. For a long time, it was hard for him to speak of Europe without loathing. Nearly twenty years passed before he even set foot again on the European continent.[3]

III

When Hoover returned to America in September 1919, he found himself a national political figure. Men of good will everywhere saw in him the largeness of character and vision which could pull the country together for the transition to peace. "I am 100 percent for him," said Brandeis in February 1920. "High public spirit, extraordinary intelligence, knowledge, sympathy, youth, and a rare perception of what is really worth-while for the country, would, with his organizing ability and power of inspiring loyalty, do wonderful things in the Presidency."[4] On this question, at least, Herbert Croly agreed with Brandeis; and the New Republic launched a campaign for Hoover. A number of younger Democrats, recalling Hoover's appeal in 1918 for a Congress that would support Wilson, assumed he was one of themselves and began to agitate for his nomination.

Prominent in this group was the Assistant Secretary of the Navy, Franklin D. Roosevelt, who, after talking to Hoover late in 1919, reported with enthusiasm, "He is certainly a wonder and I wish we could make him President of the United States. There could not be a better one." According to his later memory, Roosevelt and Franklin Lane even tried to lay out a political timetable for an interested Hoover [5] but to no avail; after a period of vacillation, Hoover decided to return to Republicanism.

Whether Hoover miscalculated in 1920 or whether he had no serious desire for either nomination is not clear from the evidence. In any case, he found no difficulty in supporting Harding; and, believing that Harding was for the League, he declared at Indianapolis that support of "the principle of an organized association of nations for the preservation of peace" was the "test of the entire sincerity, integrity and statesmanship of the Republican Party." [6] Harding rewarded him with a choice of the Commerce or Interior Departments. Hoover chose Commerce on condition that he would have a voice in all important economic policies, whether in the field of business or labor, agriculture or finance or foreign affairs.

It is not to be supposed that Hoover made this condition out of passion for power. His return to America had precipitated in his mind a philosophy of American society — a philosophy that he felt needed expression throughout the national government. This philosophy animated the rest of his public career. In 1922 he gave it utterance in his small but important book, *American Individualism*.

IV

American Individualism had its roots in his wartime disillusion. Hoover wished to repudiate the selfish, caste-ridden individualism of Europe. This was "individualism run riot," and it brought inequality and injustice in its train. And he wished equally to repudiate the philosophy of socialism which had arisen as Europe's answer to its arrogant individualism. This leveling equalitarianism had begun with "the claptrap of the French Revolution"; it had gained momentum with the expansion of the state during the war and "the dreamy social ferment of war emotion." Hoover had no doubt that socialism had already wrecked itself "finally" upon the rocks of "destroyed production and moral degeneracy"; look at "the ghastly failure of Russia." Still, the dangers of radicalism should not be ignored; its "destructive criticism" might well lead to revolution. Above all, beware the crowd! "The crowd only feels: it has no mind of its own which can plan. The crowd is credulous, it destroys, it consumes, it hates, and it dreams — but it never builds."

America, Hoover urged, must reject both European reaction and European radicalism; and he went on to define at length the unique mission of the new "progressive individualism" of the United States. American individualism did not have as its end "the acquisition and preservation of private property — the selfish snatching and hoarding of the common product." We had neutralized the selfish tendencies in individualism, he said, by affirming two great moral principles — the principles of equality of opportunity and of service. Equality of opportunity meant that people rose in society on their own merits. As for the "rising vision of service," which had evolved during the recent years of suffering, this great mystical force had infused society with a new sense of cooperation. Together these principles gave American individualism its spiritual setting and its moral purpose.

As Hoover looked out at America in 1922, he found that American society had already made great progress toward its ethical fulfillment. It was easy to point to undernourished and undereducated children on the one hand, petted and privileged children on the other; "but if we take the whole thirty-five millions of children of the United States, it would be a gross exaggeration to say that a million of them suffer from any of these injustices." Business organization had once been controlled by arbitrary individual ownership; now, as people acquired stock, ownership was being diffused among the population, so that "100,000 to 200,000 partners in a single concern are not uncommon." As a result, directors and managers were developing community responsibility; and business organization was "moving strongly toward cooperation." [7]

This eloquent vision supplied an agreeable moral framework in which to interpret current tendencies toward economic concentration, increase in securities flotation, indifference to social reform, repression of radicalism. As a social philosopher, Hoover had gone far to reconcile practice and principle in the business community of the twenties. As Secretary of Commerce, he now proposed to complete the process of reconciliation.

Hoover moved into the Commerce Department as he might have into a bankrupt mining company a decade earlier. At a time when the federal government tended to languish and wither, Commerce burst into rich and vivid flower. Hoover, said S. Parker Gilbert, the banker and reparations agent, was "Secretary of Commerce and Under-Secretary of all other departments." [8]

His greatest activity was in the foreign field. He turned the Department into a machine for promoting American sales abroad; and, with private American loans funneling dollars into foreign countries, American export trade was able for a few years to give a lively impression of prosperity. Though he expanded research in trade problems and supported the first adequate balance of payments studies, Hoover remained curiously myopic on the subject of the tariff and saw no relation between the dollar resources of foreign nations and their ability to sell in the American market. As he explained to Henry Hazlitt after the passage of the Fordney-McCumber Tariff of 1922, facts were more important than theories; and the fact was that an increasing percentage of our imports were entering duty-free. The related fact that this was because a higher tariff necessarily reduced the import of dutiable articles — that an absolutely prohibitive tariff on dutiable articles would have meant that all American imports would be duty-free — did not disturb his calculations.[9]

In the domestic field, he sought wherever he could to give substance to his vision of service. A revolution, he felt, was taking place in our economic life: "we are passing from a period of extremely individualistic action into a period of associational activities." [10] In the interests of this revolution, he encouraged the trade association as well as the simplification and standardization of machines and specifications; in other ways he tried to mobilize the business community into collective action against waste, "over-reckless competition" and unfair trade practices.

V

The boldest expression of his "progressive individualism" came in his approach to the business cycle. In the midst of the postwar slump of 1921, Hoover persuaded Harding to call a President's Conference on Unemployment. Harding opened the Conference by saying that the depression was inevitable, that anyone who thought planning might have averted it was deluding himself, and that, in particular, any plan involving government spending would only increase the trouble. The Conference itself declared flatly that unemployment was primarily a "community problem." Yet, for all these pieties, the Conference nonetheless ventured into new fields, ending with a series of recommendations about the use of public works as a stabilizing factor in the economy. Hoover, in summation, emphasized that methods had to be devised to level out the business cycle; "there is," he insisted, "a solution somewhere."

The search for a solution led to a series of basic economic studies — one, directed by Wesley C. Mitchell, on business cycles; one on stability in the construction industry; and a third, in 1928–29, on recent economic changes in America. Otto T. Mallery of the Pennsylvania State Industrial Board had been largely responsible for inducing the Conference to back the theory of a public works reserve; and in the business cycle volume he worked out his argument in greater detail. The construction study lent further support to the stabilization theory. It had been backed by the American Construction Council, whose president, Franklin D. Roosevelt, ardently supported the notion of spreading construction work through good and bad periods. We are trying, Roosevelt wrote in 1923, "to eliminate the harmful peaks of inflation, and the resulting equally harmful valleys of extreme depression. This can be done only by collective action and by the education of the public as to the facts."

In 1921 and 1923 Hoover sought with mild success to use government construction for contra-cyclical purposes, accelerating public works in the period of depression, postponing them in the period of inflation. In the meantime, Senator W. S. Kenyon of Iowa and Representative F. N. Zihlman of Maryland introduced bills in Congress calling for the expansion of public works as the remedy for periodic unemployment. Though Hoover backed these bills, they got nowhere; and two bills introduced in 1928 by Senators Wesley Jones of Washington and Robert F. Wagner of New York, both of which went farther than earlier proposals in laying down procedures for the timing of construction decisions, did no better.[11]

The climax of these endeavors came at the Governors' Conference in New Orleans in November 1928. Governor Ralph Owen Brewster of Maine (he had not yet abandoned his first name), announcing that he was speaking on Hoover's behalf, unfolded a federal-state-municipal program for the use of public works as the balance wheel in the economy. With an annual $7 billion expenditure on construction, Brewster said, "America is in a position to stabilize prosperity to a most remarkable extent. . . . With the facts in hand, the expenditure of comparatively few millions in useful work may easily head off a depression that would cost a billion."

The Brewster plan — or the "Hoover plan," as it came to be known — differed from earlier proposals in two particulars. In the first place, while it professed to be concerned only with the timing — acceleration or postponement — of necessary public works, it contemplated a reserve fund of $3 billion, which was far larger than anything seriously suggested up to that point. In the second place, it proposed that the funds for government spending in depression should come not from tax revenues, but from government borrowing. In both these respects, it showed the imprint of the economic argument of William Trufant Foster and Waddill Catchings, whose enormously popular volume *The Road to Plenty* had come out earlier in the year. Professor Foster actually accompanied Governor Brewster to New Orleans to answer questions about the plan. But, after lengthy debate, the Governors' Conference voted to table the proposal.[12]

Hoover's private attitude toward these ideas is hard to estimate. He gave them nominal support; but his active interest seems to have declined after the nation recovered from the postwar recession. The public works reserve schemes required, for example, rather elaborate statistical data; but Hoover did little in Commerce to set up studies on such questions as national income. He permitted the launching of the Brewster plan in his name in 1928; but nothing was heard of it thereafter, and he did not even mention the incident in his memoirs. Yet such plans seemed a further example of his constructive approach to national issues and of the new maturity he was bringing to business thought. They identified him all the more in the public mind with the idea of wisdom and foresight.

VI

There were other forces assisting this identification. Hoover had by no means forsaken politics. He was the first President, Walter Lippmann later wrote, "whose whole public career has been presented through the machinery of modern publicity." [13] Every item released by the Department of Commerce enhanced the picture of the master organizer, the irresistible engineer, the omniscient economist. This incessant activity did not particularly commend itself to President Coolidge, who disapproved in principle of Hoover's energy and in practice of his ambition. The President used to refer to his Secretary of Commerce sarcastically as "the wonder boy" or "the miracle worker." [14] But he interposed no obstacles to Hoover's policies; and, as for Hoover's politics, Coolidge's objections were too feeble and oblique to have much effect.

No one knows precisely what Coolidge had in mind when he remarked cryptically in the Black Hills, "I do not choose to run for President in 1928." He may have intended to take himself out of the running; he may have hoped to shut out the other candidates by provoking a party draft for himself; or, most likely, he may with Vermont prudence have been closing the door on renomination — about three-quarters of the way. When a newspaperman asked him after his Black Hills statement whether he would be glad to retire to private life, Coolidge looked at him keenly for a few moments and then replied, "No." But whatever his intention, the effect of his delphic words was to clear the way for Hoover.

By the spring of 1928, it was evident that the Secretary of Commerce was outdistancing all rivals. It was evident too, however, that the President was increasingly unhappy about his heir-apparent. To his Secretary of Agriculture, Coolidge remarked in May of the Secretary of Commerce, "That man has offered me unsolicited advice for six years, all of it bad!" But when Senator Butler, Secretary Mellon, and others sought a go-ahead signal from him, the President relapsed into dour silence.

Three weeks before the convention, Jim Watson of Indiana made a final plea. Coolidge demurred. "The basic fact remains that I do not want the nomination," he said, as Watson remembered it. "I think I know myself very well. I fitted into the situation that existed right after the war, but I might not fit into the next one. . . . From this time on, there must be something constructive applied to the affairs of government," he continued surprisingly, "and it will not be sufficient to say, 'Let business take care of itself.' " Watson persisted. Would the President accept renomination? "Well," said Coolidge, "that is a matter for the Convention to decide." And, when it became clear three weeks later how the convention was deciding, Coolidge, hearing the news in visible distress, refused lunch and threw himself despairingly across his White House bed.[15]

VII

No American in 1928 could have provided a fairer test of the capacity of the business community to govern a great and multifarious nation than Herbert Hoover. And Hoover fully understood his responsibility. He had said with pride in the campaign that the Republican administration had "introduced a new basis in government relation with business." The result, he believed, was visible on every side. "Without the wise policies which the Republican Party has made effective during the past seven and one-half years the great prosperity we now enjoy would not have been possible." If the nation wanted the prosperity to last, "a continuation of the policies of the Republican Party is fundamentally necessary to the further advancement of this progress."

There were threats to prosperity, of course — above all, Democratic policies in agriculture and in public power which portended government in business, state socialism. The American people,

Hoover said, had a fundamental conflict to resolve: American individualism, "rugged individualism" versus the philosophy of government operation and control. But Americans would not be beguiled from the path so clearly marked out for them by the Republicans. Confident in the wisdom of the past ("never has a political party been able to look back upon a similar period with more satisfaction"), exultant over the future ("no one can rightly deny the fundamental correctness of our economic system"), Hoover spoke repeatedly, almost ecstatically, of "the abolition of poverty."

"We in America today," said Herbert Hoover on August 11, 1928, "are nearer to the final triumph over poverty than ever before in the history of any land. The poorhouse is vanishing from among us. We have not yet reached the goal, but, given a chance to go forward with the policies of the last eight years, we shall soon with the help of God be in sight of the day when poverty will be banished from this nation." [16]

On November 6, 1928, the American people gave Herbert Hoover the chance he sought.

III

Outside Looking In

12. The Politics of Frustration

THE PEOPLE had made their choice, but not all the people. From the start of the decade, there had been another view of the New Era. In May 1921, Franklin K. Lane, Woodrow Wilson's Secretary of the Interior, the close friend of Franklin D. Roosevelt, lay in his room at the Mayo Clinic, wondering about death. "If I had passed into that other land, whom would I have sought — and what should I have done?" A parade of images passed through his mind. "For my heart's content in that new land, I think I'd rather loaf with Lincoln along a river bank." His thoughts drifted to the life he was leaving. "Yes, we would sit down where the bank sloped gently to the quiet stream and glance at the picture of our people, the negroes being lynched, the miners' civil war, labor's hold ups, employers' ruthlessness, the subordination of humanity to industry, — " His scrawl broke off. The next day they found him dead.[1]

The old Wilsonians watched the New Era in indignation and contempt. They were men who had known the exaltation of idealism. They had dared to act greatly and risk greatly. They saw after 1920 a different America moved, as they conceived it, by ignoble motives. Nowhere was resentment greater than in the house on S Street in Washington where Woodrow Wilson lived on, a ghost still lingering at the Republican feast. At times Wilson seemed to regard himself as a possible Democratic candidate in 1924; he certainly saw himself still as the intellectual leader of the party. He used to meet regularly with Brandeis, Baruch, Newton D. Baker, Norman Davis, and others in an effort to formulate a

Democratic manifesto. After many revisions, the draft called for regulation of railroads, fuel supply, and electrical power "to the utmost limit of the constitutional power of the federal government." But it lacked inspiration and was never made public.[2]

Instead Wilson issued a personal testament. The Russian Revolution seemed to him the symbol of the discontent of the age, and he began to consider its implications. Its cause, he wrote, was the systematic denial to the Russian people of the rights that all normal men desired. And it was notable too, he said, that the discontented classes everywhere were drawing their indictment against capitalism. Nor was this indictment altogether false. "Is it not, on the contrary, too true that capitalists have often seemed to regard the men whom they used as mere instruments of profit, whose physical and mental powers it was legitimate to exploit with as slight cost to themselves as possible, either of money or of sympathy?"

"The world has been made safe for democracy," said Wilson. But "democracy has not yet made the world safe against irrational revolution. That supreme task, which is nothing less than the salvation of civilization, now faces democracy, insistent, imperative. There is no escaping it, unless everything we have built up is presently to fall in ruin about us; and the United States, as the greatest of democracies, must undertake it."

The road away from revolution, Wilson said, was social justice — the willingness to forego one's own self-interest to promote the happiness of all. "This is what our age is blindly feeling in its reaction against what it deems the too great selfishness of the capitalistic system."[3] In the end, he seemed to conclude, the international order must begin in economic reform. The dream of the League of Nations was giving way to the older dream of the New Freedom. Six months later Wilson was dead.

II

But his conviction that the Democratic party had to be the progressive party survived. His son-in-law, W. G. McAdoo, gave this conviction an agrarian slant. Facile and plastic, McAdoo was making himself over in the image of William Jennings Bryan. A corporation lawyer, he freely attacked Wall Street and the monopolies, even while accepting a retainer from E. L. Doheny. He became, like Bryan, a strong prohibitionist. He deferred to the religious passions of the Bible belt. He even adopted a cautious agnosticism toward the Ku Klux Klan. In March 1922, moving from New York to California, he was emerging as the unquestioned leader of southern and western Democrats.

The Democratic gains in the congressional elections later that year filled him with hope. With Cordell Hull of Tennessee as chairman of the National Committee, a reinvigorated Democratic party picked up seventy-three seats in the House of Representatives. "What a wonderful victory we won in November!" McAdoo wrote to Franklin D. Roosevelt of New York. "But this is a mere circumstance to what we can do to the Republican reactionaries and standpatters in 1924 if the Democratic Party convinces the country during the next two years that it is truly a liberal and progressive Party." 4

But McAdoo had opted for Bryan too late. The character of the nation had changed since 1896. The 1920 census disclosed, for the first time in American history, that more people were living in cities than in the countryside. And New York, the greatest of cities, was giving the urban democracy an effective spokesman.

Alfred E. Smith, fifty-one years old, was completing his second term as New York's governor in 1924. Born on the third floor of an East Side tenement, he grew up near the Battery, swam with the gang in the East River, attended parochial school, and worked during his teens from dawn to sunset as a checker at the Fulton Fish Market. The city was in his rolling walk, in the nattiness of his dress, in the nasal twang of his voice, in the tilt of his head and the breezy impudence of his wisecracks. He was, among other things, a talented amateur actor; and this heightened the arresting impression he gave of the American cockney.

With his lively wit and his affable personality, Smith drifted easily into politics. In 1903 he was sent to the state Assembly at Albany; by 1911 he was the Democratic leader. The legislative experience at first dismayed him. But, with his exceptional practical intelligence, he began to attain a striking mastery of state affairs. At the same time, he began to take the lead in working toward new social programs for the Democratic party. The city organization had always been more or less "for the people" by instinct and function. It had to serve them to survive, and serve them it did — by finding them jobs in good times, paying their rent in bad, interceding for them with the police or the priest, and remembering them at Thanksgiving and Christmas. But the machine could not cope with such problems as wages, hours, and working conditions. Legislative action by the state was necessary to fill this gap.

In the spring of 1911 nearly 150 girls died in a fire at the Triangle Shirtwaist Factory, suffocating in the narrow space behind locked doors, or leaping, screaming, to the streets below. The disaster shocked the public into protest. A citizens' committee on safety was formed; Henry Stimson and Henry Morgenthau, Sr., were at various times its chairmen, McAdoo was one of its members, and its secretary was a social worker named Frances Perkins, who had actually watched the Triangle Fire.

The state legislature was quick to respond. In June 1911, it set up a Factory Investigating Commission. Its chairman was Robert F. Wagner, an earnest young German from the upper East Side, who had become Democratic leader in the Senate; Al Smith, the Irishman, was vice-chairman. Both Smith and Wagner understood from their own experience something of the helplessness of immigrant laborers in American industry. When someone once cited Wagner's own rise from the slums as proof of the opportunities for the poor, Wagner replied, "That is the most God-awful bunk. I came through it, yes. That was luck, luck, luck. Think of the others." Yet neither Wagner nor Smith had fully realized before the aching hours of labor in dark lofts, the filth and stink in the washrooms and toilets, the callous use of child labor. Frances Perkins, as an investigator for the Commission, took Smith to see the thousands of women, pale and exhausted, coming off the ten-hour night shift on the ropewalks in Auburn. In one factory she made Bob Wagner crawl through the tiny hole in the wall, marked "Fire Escape," to the steep iron ladder covered with ice and ending twelve feet above the ground. She got the Commission up at dawn to watch six- and seven-year-old children snipping beans and shelling peas at a Cattaraugus County cannery. Neither Smith nor Wagner ever forgot what he then learned.[5]

III

The result was a more purposeful direction for Democratic legislative policies. In the past, all the persistence of the social workers and the Consumers' League had been necessary to get social measures on to the floor. But many Democratic legislators, who knew poverty by birthright, were sympathetic; and the bosses were now acknowledging the political appeal of reform. Charles F. Murphy, the boss of Tammany Hall, had opposed a bill limiting the work week for women to fifty-four hours. When Frances Perkins subsequently asked his support for a new welfare measure, he said, "It is my observation that that bill made us many votes. I will tell the boys to give all the help they can."

For men like Smith and Wagner, it was a labor of conscience and of love. Smith, who had demonstrated his grasp of state problems in the Constitutional Convention of 1915 ("of all the men in the convention," said Elihu Root, its president, "Alfred E. Smith was the best informed on the business of the State"), was elected Governor in 1918. The social work ethos, as interpreted by his close friend Belle Moskowitz, guided his executive policies. Defeated in the Republican sweep of 1920, he was re-elected in 1922, and his program received new vindication.

Where Bryan and McAdoo and the agrarian Democrats stood for an economic pseudo-radicalism, prickling with fulminations against Wall Street and monopoly, Smith stood for a social welfare liberalism, indifferent to the concentration of wealth, uninterested in basic change, but concerned with protecting the individual against the hazards of industrial society. Smith's message to the legislature in January 1920 summed up his program: a minimum-wage law; eight-hour day for women; maternity insurance; extension of workmen's compensation; state doctors and nurses in rural communities. He also favored the state ownership of hydroelectric power, and he had a profound faith in civil liberties — a faith that led him to oppose reckless legislative investigations of radicalism and attempts to censor books and films.

Smith excelled as a public administrator. He used experts with skill and confidence; but the court of last resort was his own sturdy and equable instinct for government. "He has a marvelous faculty," said Franklin Roosevelt in 1924, "for cutting the Gordian knots of argument and counter-argument with the sharp sword of common sense." And Smith knew that reform would not endure except on the basis of popular understanding. His programs succeeded in the end because he saw politics as an educational process.[6]

IV

Rural America was digging in for its rearguard stand in the twenties. In the Eighteenth Amendment, it made one last effort to impose its mores on the cities. Through the Ku Klux Klan, it sought to maintain racial purity against the city immigrants. In a series of smaller actions, of which the Scopes case in Dayton, Tennessee, was the most spectacular, it tried to protect the dogmas of traditional faith against urban heresy. When Democrats gathered for the convention of 1924, McAdoo and Smith were more than rival candidates. They were antagonistic symbols for the emotions of agrarianism, prohibitionism, fundamentalism, and xenophobia. And this year the convention met in New York — for Al Smith home, and for Bryan "the enemy's country."

There were moments in the long sessions at Madison Square Garden when the city-country tension lifted. One was when Franklin D. Roosevelt, the vice-presidential candidate four years before, approached the rostrum to nominate Smith. Crippled in 1921 by an attack of poliomyelitis, Roosevelt was making his return to national politics. He was wheeled to the platform in a chair; then, leaning on crutches, he walked to the speaker's desk. The galleries went wild when he hailed Smith as "the 'Happy Warrior' of the political battlefield." The speech, Walter Lippmann wrote to Roosevelt, was "a moving and distinguished thing. I am utterly hard-boiled about speeches, but yours seems to me perfect in temper and manner and most eloquent in its effect." In the corridors delegates talked with regret about Roosevelt's unavailability.[7]

Another such moment came when Newton D. Baker called for an endorsement of the League of Nations. Tears in his eyes, Baker spoke of his duties as Secretary of War: "The acceptance of a strange and perverse fate called upon me who loved the life of youth . . . to come to your houses and ask you to give me your sons that I might send them into those deadly places. And I watched them and shivered and shrank with fearful fear and I welcomed the living back, oh, with such unutterable relief and joy, and I swore an obligation to the dead that in season and out, by day and by night, in church, in political meeting, in the market-place, I intended to lift up my voice always and ever until their sacrifices were really perfected." For a moment the exaltation of 1919 was renewed. But Baker spoke to the conscience of the convention, not to its calculations, and the delegates, cheering his speech to the echo, voted down his resolution.[8]

The motion to denounce the Ku Klux Klan by name in the platform brought the deeper issues to the surface. For months McAdoo had been importuned to come out against the Klan. Instead, under the embarrassment of the disclosure of his Doheny connection, McAdoo talked darkly when he arrived for the convention about the "sinister, unscrupulous, invisible government which has its seat in the citadel of privilege and finance in New York City." The Klan was the cutting edge of rural protest; and McAdoo could not reject it. As a bitter debate proceeded, William Jennings Bryan finally rose to speak against the motion. The galleries, packed by Tammany, shouted and booed. On the floor southern and western delegates watched in cold anger as their hero faced the urban scorn. Bryan waited for the storm to subside; then the melodious voice rang out, and he tried to call the convention back to the issues in factory and farm. "My friends," he added, "it requires more courage to fight the Republican Party than it does to fight the Ku Klux Klan." But his immense dignity could only still the galleries; it could not persuade them. Finally the convention rejected by a single vote the proposal to name the Klan.[9]

The fight between Smith and McAdoo dragged on, ballot after weary ballot, the delegates meeting in caucuses and answering rollcalls through the humid session, then retiring for snatches of sleep in steaming hotel rooms. Two-thirds was necessary for victory, by the ancient rule of the Democratic party; but neither Smith nor McAdoo could win even a majority. Each day of deadlock reduced the value of the nomination. Finally a steady drift of exasperated delegates to John W. Davis of West Virginia brought his nomination on the one hundred and third ballot. With even less enthusiasm, the convention picked Bryan's younger brother, Governor Charles W. Bryan of Nebraska, to complete the ticket. . . . A newspaperman congratulated Davis. "Thanks," said Davis with a wry smile, "but you know how much it is worth." 10

Yet, for all the chaos of the convention, few men were better qualified for the Presidency than the man it eventually chose. Davis had served in Congress, where he helped draft the Clayton Act and had a generally progressive record. He had been a brilliant Solicitor-General under Wilson, and, at the age of forty-five, had become Ambassador to Great Britain. Wilson had opposed the suggestion of his nomination in 1920; but in many respects Davis was the perfect heir of the New Freedom that Wilson had expounded in 1912. Born the same day as Thomas Jefferson, Davis was unqualified in his literal Jeffersonian devotion. "I think Jefferson was the greatest political thinker this country has produced, and I expect to die in that faith." His program was tariff reduction, tax reduction, and economy. "Above all," he said, "as the keynote of all Democratic policy, in passing upon any question, let the controlling aim and ambition be to keep the road open for private enterprise and personal initiative." 11

But he was vulnerable as a candidate. On leaving the government service in 1921, he had become a Wall Street lawyer. For many progressives, the choice between W. M. Butler's crony and J. P. Morgan's counsel was bitter. To radicals of both parties, one man stood out as the incorruptible champion of the public welfare — Robert M. La Follette of Wisconsin.

v

Where T.R. and Wilson had walked down the path of nationalism and war, where Bryan had succumbed to Chautauqua evangelism and Florida real estate, La Follette, austere and mistrustful, had kept the faith. Under his leadership Wisconsin had established the first modern income tax law, the first effective workmen's compensation law, the first modern labor legislation, the first legislative drafting service. In the complacent twenties, he was now demanding increased inheritance taxes, an excess profits tax, public ownership of railroads and water power, and abolition of the labor injunction. He was particularly exercised about the Supreme Court — "the actual ruler of the American people," he called it in 1922 — and he suggested that Congress be given power to re-enact statutes nullified by the Court.[12]

Insurgency had been bubbling up elsewhere in the farm belt since the war. In North Dakota the Nonpartisan League, with its Socialist organizers and editors, had begun moving through the grain states demanding state-owned elevators, flour mills, and packinghouses; by 1920 Nonpartisan Leaguers helped found the Farmer-Labor party in Minnesota. And organized labor too was discontented: in 1922 the fifteen railroad brotherhoods called a Conference for Progressive Political Action in Cleveland. Out of the spreading unrest there were emerging the materials for a third party.

But the war had bred new perils for American liberalism. The American Workers' party, operating under orders from the Comintern in Moscow, saw its opportunity in the La Follette enthusiasm. The Communist-dominated Farmer-Labor Federation accordingly called a convention to nominate La Follette in the spring of 1924. But the grizzled old fighter had no illusions about the Communists. Their only purpose in joining the Progressive movement, he said, was to further the chaos they required for their ultimate aims. "I believe, therefore, that all Progressives should refuse to participate in any movement which makes common cause with any Communist organization." [13]

The Progressive convention in July was a reunion of a generation of reform. From General Jacob Coxey on, they came to Cleveland, New Nationalists and New Freedomites, social workers and social gospelers, trade unionists, Nonpartisan Leaguers and Socialists. La Follette received the nomination by acclamation; and Burton K. Wheeler, the radical Democratic senator from Montana, joined him on the ticket. "Between Davis and Coolidge," said Wheeler, "there is only a choice for conservatives"; during the campaign he called them the "Gold Dust Twins." The convention platform stood pretty much in its proposals for western radicalism of the old antimonopoly type. In its affirmations (contributed by the Bull Mooser Donald Richberg), it spoke in the accents of the New Nationalism, condemning "the principle of ruthless individualism and competition" and backing "the progressive principle of cooperation." [14]

The Progressive ticket won the support of the Scripps-Howard press, the American Federation of Labor, and most of the reformers. La Follette concentrated largely on the monopoly issue, though he added enough attacks on Wilson's war policy to alienate many Wilsonians and attract many German-Americans. But, despite the Progressives, it was a listless campaign. The combination of Coolidge and prosperity was invincible. Together the Progressives and the Democrats polled about two million fewer votes than the Republicans. La Follette while carrying Wisconsin and beating Davis in a few other states ran about three and a half million votes behind him in the nation.

The Progressive party of 1924 had even less future than the Progressive party of 1912. The railroad brotherhoods pulled out early in 1925, leaving the organization to a tug-of-war between the western agrarians and the Socialists. Someone saw La Follette early in 1925, lying on the couch in his office, his face lined and anxious, puffing at his pipe. "I believe in democracy," the old man said, "but will it ever work?" With his death a few months later, his party crumbled away. It had no center of faith or doctrine to hold its parts together — nothing but the scraps of thirty years of agitation. "Throughout this period," said Donald Richberg, looking back a few years later, "the progressive forces in American political life had only the vaguest ideas of where they were going." [15]

VI

As for the Democrats, they were little better off. McAdoo's anti-Wall Street rhetoric could not conceal his lack of ideas about financial concentration. Smith had an excellent social program on the state level, but few larger conceptions. No doubt agitated him, for example, about the soundness of the economic order; as Walter Lippmann noted in 1928, he was "the most powerful conservative in urban America." [16] And the national party organization was in hopeless disrepair.

In December 1924 Franklin Roosevelt addressed a circular letter to the delegates at the recent convention. The Republican party, he observed, stood "for conservatism, for the control of the social and economic structure of the country by a small minority of hand-picked associates"; but the Democratic party as "the party of progress and liberal thought" could not realize its potentialities until it had achieved party efficiency and unity. What might be done to revive the party organization? [17]

The replies amounted to an inquest on a party in defeat. Some, like Carter Glass of Virginia, argued that the party was getting too tainted with "La Follette-ism and Bryan-ism"; Albert C. Ritchie, the governor of Maryland, wanted to assert states rights against Republican policies of centralization. Others, like Governor William E. Sweet of Colorado and Clarence C. Dill of Washington, thought the party too conservative. Some described the party as merely an aggregation of local interest, incapable of affirmative purpose. Some said that little could be done so long as the press was closed to the Democrats; as Homer Cummings of Connecticut put it, "We are really up against what might be called a 'ruling class' proposition." Many appeared to sympathize with the melancholy observation of Harry T. Rainey of Illinois: "We can do nothing except wait for the Republican party to blow up." A number expressed wistful interest in Roosevelt as a possible candidate in 1928.[18]

Roosevelt next suggested a party conference to consider issues of organization. But the national chairman was unhappy about this proposal; influential New York Democrats, like Baruch and Norman Davis, opposed it; Bryan and the McAdoo supporters, remembering Roosevelt as Smith's manager in 1924, were suspicious. In the end, the conference dwindled to a series of dinner meetings in Washington between Roosevelt and leading Democratic senators and congressmen.

Roosevelt continued to emphasize in his incessant correspondence that the Democratic party must make itself "by definite policy, the Party of constructive progress, before we can attract a larger following." Ever since 1920, he wrote in 1925, "we have been doing nothing — waiting for the other fellow to put his foot in it." The other fellow had put his foot in it, Roosevelt continued, with the Harding scandals and the Mellon tax plan; but the Democrats could not even carry the Congress. The trouble lay in the fact that "in the minds of the average voter the Democratic Party has today no definite constructive aims."

In November 1925 Roosevelt read Claude Bowers's *Jefferson and Hamilton.* Reviewing it for the New York *World,* he contrasted Hamilton, backed by the well-organized forces of wealth, birth, commerce, and the press, with Jefferson, who could count only "on the scattered raw material of the working masses, difficult to reach, more difficult to organize." Roosevelt wrote that when he laid down the book, he had a breathless feeling of what the republic might be like if Hamilton had won. "I have a breathless feeling too," he said, "as I wonder if, a century and a quarter later, the same contending forces are not again mobilizing."

"Hamiltons we have today," said Franklin D. Roosevelt. "Is a Jefferson on the horizon?" [19]

13. Protest on the Countryside

THE AMERICAN FARMERS had risen nobly to the challenge of war. In the decade after 1910, they had increased the aggregate acreage harvested by nearly 15 per cent. American food saved much of Europe from hunger and revolution. But prosperity had induced expansion of output; and, when European farms resumed production after the war, the export market for American agricultural products began to decline. While businessmen in the cities marveled at having solved the secret of prosperity, the farmers, in gloom and indignation, watched gross agricultural income fall from $17.7 billion in 1919 to $10.5 billion in 1921. The farm price index fell in the same period from 215 to 124; and farm land values capsized everywhere. As prices dropped, the burden of taxation and debt grew. Interest charges per acre more than doubled between 1916 and 1923. The countryside's terms of trade with the city turned sharply for the worse.[1]

Discontent produced protest. The crisis gave new life to the Grange and the Farmers' Union and unexpected scope to the new and aggressive American Farm Bureau Federation. Where the Progressive party of 1912 had barely mentioned the farmer until the seventy-second paragraph of its interminable platform, the Progressive party of 1924 centered its whole appeal around the farmer's sense of inequality. As early as 1921, agricultural senators and representatives began to huddle together in the so-called Farm Bloc. "Under the policy of protection we have built up a great industrial nation," said Senator Arthur Capper of Kansas in 1922, "and the same protection cannot now be withheld from agriculture if we would preserve the balance between industrial and agricultural growth." [2]

But the problem remained to work out this protective principle in legislation. An answer soon came, not from farmers, but from two executives fresh from the War Industries Board, a farm machinery manufacturer named George N. Peek, and a retired cavalry brigadier-general named Hugh S. Johnson, now president and general counsel of the Moline Plow Company in Illinois.

Early in 1922 Peek and Johnson circulated an unsigned pamphlet entitled *Equality for Agriculture.* They proposed a two-price plan for American farm output: a protected price for the American market, and a world price for the surplus thrown on the world market. The American price would be determined by what the authors called the "fair exchange value" of the crop — that is, a price bearing the same relation to the general price index, as the average crop price for the ten prewar years bore to the average general price index for the same period. (*Wallace's Farmer* in Des Moines promptly dubbed this concept "parity.") As for the surplus, a federal export corporation would buy it at the American price and dump it abroad for whatever the market would bring. The loss to the government would be made up by an assessment imposed upon the owners of the commodity benefited; this assessment was known as the "equalization fee." [3]

The Peek-Johnson plan ignored such long-range problems as reduction of costs, technical reorganization, and soil conservation. But it did offer a mechanism that would prevent the surplus from toppling the whole structure of farm prices. An unrelenting advocate, Peek devoted an increasing amount of his time after 1922 popularizing the equalization fee idea. And in Henry C. Wallace, Harding's Secretary of Agriculture, Peek found a sympathetic listener.

II

Wallace, who had been for many years editor of *Wallace's Farmer,* knew the worries of the grain belt. But he discovered himself almost alone in this concern in the Harding administration. "The farmers of America," reported Senator Capper bitterly in 1922, "found themselves being opposed instead of aided, by business groups which should be the best friends of agriculture." The appointed voice of business in the cabinet was, of course, Secretary Hoover; and Hoover had ideas of his own about what he persisted in calling "the agricultural industry." In 1920 the Washington representative of the Grange had pronounced him, of all the presidential possibilities, "the most objectionable to the farmers of this country." "His dealings with hog and milk and beef producers," said Wallace the same year in reference to the War Food Administration, "gave evidence of a mental bias which causes farmers to thoroughly distrust him. They look upon him as a typical autocrat of big business." [4]

Hoover felt that the Department of Agriculture should confine itself to telling the farmer what he should grow, while Commerce should tell him how he should dispose of it. But Wallace had no intention of resigning functions he deemed so indispensable to the farmer's prosperity. He tried to strengthen the Department, particularly by organizing the Bureau of Agricultural Economics; but his effort to gain a voice for agriculture in the business administration was an uphill job. "Unless farmers as a class get busy and *fight* for their rights," he told an adviser, "we in the Department will not long be able to take a national point of view because the point of view of other interests will dominate us." [5]

Early in 1923 Wallace directed the preparation of a draft bill based on the Peek-Johnson plan. In January 1924, Senator Charles McNary of Oregon and Representative Gilbert N. Haugen of Iowa introduced the bill into Congress. But Hoover opposed the McNary-Haugen bill with violence. Even thirty years later, he called Wallace "a fascist" for favoring the measure. And in 1924 an alliance between the agricultural South and the business community defeated the bill in the House. Still, its advocates were quick to rally. Peek organized the American Council of Agriculture to coordinate the fight; Bernard Baruch supplied funds and encouragement; and Wallace called on Chester C. Davis, farm editor and Montana Commissioner of Agriculture, to come to Washington to work for the bill.

The Secretary's energy, though, was beginning to ebb. Worn by Hoover's incessant opposition, racked by sciatica, Wallace labored beyond his strength in the McNary-Haugen fight and on a book of his own about the farm crisis. In October he went to the hospital for an operation. A week later he was dead. "Many said that the situation in Washington killed Wallace," wrote a close associate. "Others made it more definite and personal." Coolidge promptly offered the vacant Agriculture job to Hoover. Hoover turned it down; the post went instead to W. M. Jardine, who admired the Commerce Department and, as Hoover laconically wrote, "established at once full cooperation with us." [6]

III

Hoover was now in control. But the McNary-Haugenites were undiscouraged; and they had a new Wallace to assist them. The Secretary's son, Henry Agard Wallace, lanky, awkward, tousled, and deeply sincere, a brilliant experimental geneticist and a talented farm economist, had taken over the editorship of *Wallace's Farmer* during his father's absence in Washington.

In a book of 1920, *Agricultural Prices*, young Wallace had placed the farm problem in a broad historical context. He was skeptical of the "idealistic social workers, representatives of organized labor, and many farmers [who] would like to do away with the speculative system of registering prices, substituting price-fixing legislation." But he emphasized that the only way for the farmer to maintain income in a free market was to reduce the size of his crop at strategic moments. As Wallace wrote, in accents reminiscent of Thorstein Veblen, whom he greatly admired, farmers "will find it necessary to practice sabotage in the same scientific, businesslike way as labor and capital." And when the farmers succeeded in this, when capital, labor, and farmers were all placed in equally powerful bargaining position, then, said Wallace, would there not be the possibility that all might come to see "the futility of sabotage as a price-sustaining force?" [7]

In the meantime, he was ready to offer the farmer temporary expedients. In 1921 he urged voluntary acreage reduction: "less corn, more clover, more money." He advocated governmental crop insurance and, as early as 1922, began to talk about an "ever-normal granary." And he sharply criticized Republican farm policies. (Hoover used to complain to Harding and Coolidge about disrespectful editorials in *Wallace's Farmer*. On one occasion, according to a much told story, Coolidge asked Hoover why a man who had been so long in public life worried about such attacks. "Don't you?" said Hoover, mentioning an article on Coolidge by Frank Kent in the *American Mercury*. "You mean that one in the magazine with the green cover?" replied Coolidge. "I started to read it, but it was against me, so I didn't finish it." As for Secretary Wallace, he bore patiently with his son's strictures on his colleagues; only once did he say to young Henry, "Have a heart.") [8]

Young Wallace also had a shrewd political sense. The farmers' hope, he was coming to feel, lay in what he called "a marriage of corn and cotton." [9] Chester Davis worked particularly hard on developing a West-South alliance. Their efforts were aided by southern fears of a cotton surplus in 1926. In 1927, with mounting southern support, the McNary-Haugen bill passed both houses of the Congress. Coolidge — on the same day that he issued a proclamation increasing the tariff on pig iron 50 per cent — vetoed the bill in an unwontedly wrathful message. A year later, Congress passed the bill once more, and Coolidge snapped back with another veto.

In the meantime, other nations were building defenses against the unloading of farm surpluses. That spring in Washington Chester Davis told Peek, "George, this is the last heat I trot. We can't dump surpluses over the sort of tariff walls they're rearing over the water now." "The hell we can't!" Peek said shortly.[10]

The McNary-Haugen bill had other defects. It would probably have been difficult to administer; and, worst of all, it had no means of stopping its higher prices from creating even greater surpluses. After the 1928 veto, enthusiasm for it began to wane. The National Grange turned to the export debenture plan, which proposed to subsidize crop exports by a system of bounties on export products; but this plan, while administratively simpler than the McNary-Haugen bill, also had no means of preventing surpluses and assumed that dumping would be indefinitely feasible as a solution. Young Henry Wallace and others agreed with Davis that the rise of economic nationalism was rendering both McNary-Haugen and the export debenture plan obsolete.

IV

The hard question, it now appeared, was how to raise farm prices without calling new acreage into production. In the early twenties John D. Black of the University of Minnesota and M. L. Wilson of Montana State College had begun to put forward the idea of agricultural adjustment — that is, of some kind of planned relationship between planting and demand. In 1927 a Department of Agriculture economist, W. J. Spillman, in a book called *Balancing the Farm Output,* contended that the answer lay in limiting the amount of crop for which the farmer was to have protection and thus making it hard for the farmer to profit by increasing his acreage of a protected crop.

Spillman's scheme involved a complicated system of "limited debentures." But in the late twenties Beardsley Ruml of the Laura Spelman Rockefeller Foundation, impressed by a program of agricultural control he observed in operation in Germany, asked John Black, now at Harvard, to investigate its adaptability to the American farm problem. In 1929 Black worked out the details of what he christened the voluntary domestic allotment plan — so called because it was based on the principle of allotments to individual producers of rights to sell the domestic part of their crop in the domestic market at the protected price. Since output beyond the allotment contract would not receive price protection, the probable effect, it was argued, would be to discourage surpluses; as a consequence, dumping was far less important than in the competing schemes. The farmer, in short, would receive a subsidy in return for a tacit agreement to limit his output.[11]

For men like H. A. Wallace and Chester Davis, already moving beyond McNary-Haugenism, the domestic allotment plan began to hold out some hope. M. L. Wilson read Black's statement of the plan with excitement out in Montana. "The problem of immediate farm relief," wrote Professor Rexford G. Tugwell of Columbia, "is then, that of limiting production, not to the nation's or the world's needs, but to the buying capacity of the farmers' market." [12] In 1928 domestic allotment still seemed an academic proposition. Yet, in the meantime, the struggle over the McNary-Haugen bill had had a powerful educational impact on both the farmer and the country. The farmer was now beginning to think in national terms, and economists as well as politicians were at last regarding agriculture as a national problem.

14. The Stirrings of Labor

THE NEARLY eleven million Americans engaged in agriculture in 1920 were not the only group outside the orbit of the business classes. Three times as many men and women worked for daily or weekly wages. Like the farmers, the workers as a class had prospered during the war; like the farmers, they watched their fortunes slump badly in the postwar depression, when aggregate payrolls dropped over one-third in a single dismal year. For the rest of the decade, however, labor made a better recovery than agriculture.

It was not, accordingly, a time of marked labor discontent. Yet real wages, while improving steadily, still lagged dangerously behind the even greater increases in productivity. And average wages were hardly high enough to sustain the illusion that labor was a full partner in the boom. Estimates of minimum "health-and-decency" budgets ran from $1820 to $2080 a year; but average earnings of workers never rose above $1500 at any point in the decade. And there were many below the average. In 1922 the average hourly wage for a male weaver in Alabama was 25 cents, for a female frame spinner, 17 cents. Nor could it be said that labor was paid off in increased leisure. The average work week remained around 50 hours, and in some industries it was longer. Even at the end of the decade, tens of thousands of steelworkers were working seven days a week and thousands were working 84 hours. In southern textile mills, women and children worked from 54 to 60 or 70 hours a week. And business leaders were generally hostile to proposals for a five-day week. "Nothing breeds radicalism more

quickly than unhappiness unless it is leisure," said the president
of the National Association of Manufacturers in 1929.[1]

But the trade union movement, consisting essentially of skilled
and relatively well paid workers, showed little interest in the
overworked, underpaid mass-production industries. Union membership itself declined from its all-time high in 1920 of over 5
million to 3.4 million in 1929 — from 12 per cent of the labor force
in 1920 to 7 per cent at the end of the decade.[2] And labor leadership grew increasingly cautious and conservative. Thus the United
Mine Workers had been in 1920 the largest union in the country;
its membership of nearly 500,000 included almost 60 per cent of the
miners. When the coal depression and internal feuds began to
weaken the organization, rebels sought to revitalize the union with
new economic ideas and new organizing drives. But John L. Lewis,
the UMW's powerful and crafty president, a believer in free enterprise and the Republican party, beat off his progressive critics and
established firm control. By 1930 the union was less than half its
size of a decade earlier. "He killed more than the leaders of our
union," a miners' group said that year of Lewis. "He killed its
very soul."[3]

Stagnation spread through the labor movement. The once
powerful railroad unions did not quickly recover from the exhausting strikes of 1921 and 1922. Textile unionism was nearly extinct,
even in the North. Iron and steel, machine tools and metals, were
less organized than they had been during the war. The expanding
automobile industry wholly resisted unionization. Unions grew
stronger in the garment trades, but in important centers like New
York their growth was racked by troubles with gangsters and
Communists. Only in the building trades did unions flourish. At
the beginning of the decade, this most conservative group included
about one-fifth of the total A.F. of L. membership; by the end,
nearly one-third.

The A.F. of L. was more than ever an exclusive movement of the
skilled crafts, representing a small minority of American workers.
When Samuel Gompers, for nearly half a century its leader, died
in 1925, the scramble for succession resulted in the triumph of the
lowest common denominator among the contenders — an ex-miner
named William Green. A comfortable man with the air of a small-

town banker, rimless glasses on a placid face, a large gold watch-chain in his vest, and a diamond ring on his finger, an Odd Fellow and an Elk, Green brought the Harding virtues to the leadership of American labor.

II

But it was not only internal stagnation that accounted for the decline of the labor movement. External opposition played as large a role. Businessmen broke unions, smashed strikes, and everywhere asserted the sacred principle of the open shop. They held up unionists to community disdain: thus when a few Detroit ministers invited labor people to occupy their pulpits during the A.F. of L. convention in 1926, the Board of Commerce had most of the invitations revoked. (A young pastor in a working-class parish named Reinhold Niebuhr defied the edict; at the same time, he was baffled by the fear of the labor leaders, who, Niebuhr wrote, "impressed me as having about the same amount of daring and imagination as a group of village bankers.") [4]

The courts meanwhile gave business sentiment the force of law. As the Chief Justice of the United States said of the American labor movement in 1922, "That faction we have to hit every little while." [5] Under Taft's leadership, the Supreme Court proceeded to hit labor whenever it could. In the Bailey case, the Court struck down a congressional attempt to prohibit child labor. In the Adkins case, it struck down a District of Columbia law setting minimum wages for women and children, thereby rejecting a brief prepared by Felix Frankfurter and Molly Dewson for the Consumers' League. And courts fairly regularly approved the "yellow-dog" contract, which compelled the worker to agree not to join a union if he wished to hold his job, as well as the labor injunction, to which business freely resorted as a means of stopping strikes.

The adverse court decisions in the early twenties were largely responsible for organized labor's flier in politics. But the La Follette campaign seemed to exhaust labor's political energies. The Railway Labor Act of 1926, drafted by Donald Richberg, helped bind the wounds of the railroad brotherhoods. By 1928 labor leadership could hardly have been less rebellious. John L. Lewis, describing Secretary Hoover as "the foremost industrial statesman of modern times," declared his election an imperative necessity "so that the unprecedented industrial and business prosperity which he inaugurated may be properly developed and stabilized." [6]

III

Non-labor people continued to fight labor's battles. "It is significant," said Abraham Epstein, the champion of social insurance, "that most of the labor legislation already on the statute books is largely the result of individual efforts of organizations made up of but few union card men and with little or no financial support from the labor movement." [7] And accident occasionally enlisted new recruits. Senator George W. Norris of Nebraska, campaigning in Pennsylvania in 1926, was driven about a company town by a wreck of a man, whose head was jammed out of shape, his skin seared black, a survivor of an explosion in the mines. He told Norris about the miner's life, about the company towns, about the workers in debt to company stores. He showed him in a neglected cemetery a tombstone with the chiseled epitaph:

> For forty years beneath the sod
> With pick and spade I did my task
> The coal king's slave, but now, thank God,
> I'm free at last.

On his return to Washington, Norris began his fight for the abolition of the yellow-dog contract and for the limitation of the labor injunction. With the assistance of such lawyers as Frankfurter, Richberg, and Professor Herman Oliphant of Johns Hopkins, he drafted a bill to achieve these purposes. In the House of Representatives, the volatile representative from New York City, Fiorello La Guardia, introduced a companion bill.[8]

Labor benefited from such efforts. But the A.F. of L. played little role in initiating them, preferring rather to place its trust in the foremost industrial statesman of modern times. Yet, underneath, new currents were stirring. Toward the end of the twenties, a series of strikes, especially in the needle trades and in the textile mills, showed a defiance not yet smothered by the boom.

IV

Gastonia, North Carolina, called itself the combed-yarn center of the South. Men, women, and children from the poverty-stricken Carolina backcountry crowded into flimsy shacks on the outskirts of town to take jobs in the mills. In the largest mill, they received an average wage of less than $9 for a full work week of 66 hours. Many women had to work on night shifts. Fourteen-year-old girls, operating two spinning frames with four sides, on their feet 11 hours a day, 6 days a week, received $4.95 a week. Perpetually in debt to the company store, the Gastonia workers were growing resentful and ready for leadership. The stagnation in the A.F. of L. left a vacuum for bolder men to fill.

When Communist organizers came to Gastonia in 1929, they found the workers, deeply religious Anglo-Saxon and Scotch-Irish mountaineers, ready to embrace the union with almost evangelical fervor. But the attempt to organize provoked company retaliation and then a strike. Ella May Wiggins became a familiar figure on the picket line. She was twenty-nine years old, the mother of nine children, and she had worked on the night shift in the mills. When her babies came down with whooping cough, she no longer dared leave them in the care of her eleven-year-old daughter. But the foreman refused to put her on the day shift so that she could tend the children herself. Ella May quit her job. With no money for medicine, she watched four of her children die. From her grief, Ella May Wiggins began to speak to the mill workers. Her face was wrinkled, her cheeks sunken, but her untaught voice rang out, clear and true, in the melancholy cadences of the mountain ballads.

> We leave our homes in the morning,
> We kiss our children good-bye,
> While we slave for the bosses,
> Our children scream and cry.

In September, as the strike was entering its sixth month, Ella May rode on a truck to a union meeting. An armed mob forced the truck off the road. One of the mob raised his gun and fired.

Ella May gasped with incredulity, "My God, they have shot me!"
and dropped to the bottom of the truck.

> It is for our little children
> That seem to us so dear,
> But for them nor us, dear workers,
> The bosses do not care.

The rain drizzled down on the open grave. The workers huddled
in silence, Ella May's five little children stood in terrible loneliness,
while the cheap casket was lowered into the ground. As the first
clods of red earth fell on the coffin, a friend completed Ella May's
song.

> But listen to me workers,
> A union they do fear;
> Let's stand together, workers,
> And have a union here.[9]

15. The Struggle for Public Power

As FOR the liberals, they too were remote from power. In the eras of the first Roosevelt and of Wilson, Presidents had read their books, sought their advice, and solicited their support. But the business community dismissed them as starry-eyed idealists, when it did not denounce them as dangerous Bolsheviks. And, to their resentment over their fall, the liberals added the conviction that business supremacy was degrading the nation they loved.

Many issues crystallized this apprehension, but none, perhaps, so much as natural resources. From the day of Theodore Roosevelt, conservation had been a leading tenet in the liberal faith. "Of all the questions which can come before this nation, short of the actual preservation of its existence in a great war," Roosevelt said, "there is none which compares in importance with the great central task of leaving this land even a better land for our descendants than it is for us." For Roosevelt and for his Chief Forester, Gifford Pinchot, conservation meant above all the development of resources "for the benefit of the many, and not merely for the profit of the few." The land, the water, the forests, the minerals of the United States could not be sacrificed to the quest for profit. "Life is something more than a matter of business," wrote Pinchot. "No man can make his life what it ought to be by living it merely on a business basis. There are things higher than business." [1]

The fight between Pinchot and Taft's Secretary of the Interior, Richard A. Ballinger, dramatized the fact that conservation programs were never secure; and Taft's repudiation of Pinchot exposed him — at least in the eyes of the Progressives — as an agent of greed.

Conservationist rule was restored during Wilson's administration, only to suffer a new setback when Harding appointed Albert B. Fall as the Secretary of the Interior.

In the meantime, the issue of hydroelectric power was growing in importance. Until the Forest Service was created in 1905, Congress had been giving away the right to erect power dams on navigable streams without compensation and without time limit — "in other words," said Pinchot, "for ever and for nothing." Pinchot instituted a policy of granting permits for limited periods in exchange for the payment of fees. This policy outraged the private power companies. But Pinchot responded that if a few men ever succeeded in controlling the sources of power they would eventually control all industry and thus the whole nation as well. Roosevelt, backing him up, described the power monopoly "as the most threatening which has ever appeared" in the history of the nation.[2]

II

What had been an apprehension in 1910 was an actuality in 1925. Though the establishment of the Federal Power Commission in 1920 had given the government new authority to regulate interstate hydroelectric development, the Commission was hardly disposed to exercise its powers in the New Era. State regulation through public utility commissions, embarked on so confidently before the war, was floundering. Overshadowing the feeble mechanisms of regulation stood the complex and impenetrable structure of the private utility systems.

Never had the architects of corporate finance built with such craft and mystification. As electric power sales more than doubled through the decade, the utilities field attracted the attention of the nation's most ingenious financiers. By the end of the twenties, ten great utility systems had absorbed about three-fourths of the total electric light and power business of the nation. But, unlike the industrial field, where centralization often sprang from a desire to integrate production, the units in the utility networks were ordinarily wholly disconnected. The impulse behind the holding company was thus not operating integration. It was rather the temptation to exploit the quirk in corporate finance which enabled a man, by pyramiding his investment, to control an empire with an infinitesimal commitment of his own cash. With bond and nonvoting stock carrying most of a company's corporate assets, 50 per cent or even less of the common stock gave power over a lot for a little.

A further charm of the holding company lay in its immunity to regulation. "A Holding Company," said Will Rogers, "is a thing where you hand an accomplice the goods while the policeman searches you." [3] Operating companies were subject to state regulation for their stock and bond issues as well as for their rates to consumers; but holding companies were relatively free to water their stocks and overvalue their assets as the market permitted. Through new security issues, holding companies could pay for their investment in the operating companies; and since the holding company ordinarily paid less in interest on its own issues than it received from its investment in the operating companies, its financial basis seemed foolproof. Once one level of holding company organization had been exploited, another level could be built upon it, each new layer creating a new bonanza for the promoters.

So profitable was this traffic in operating companies that holding companies bid up their price far beyond their actual worth. The result was to inflate the value of the securities out of all proportion to the value of the plant. The consequent burden of overcapitalization, passed along to the operating companies, was eventually discharged onto the consumers through higher rates. And, as the utility empires grew in complexity, they grew in irresponsibility. The first effect of the corporate sleight of hand was to disenfranchise the already bewildered stockholders. As the fast shuffle accelerated, so too did the confusion. In the end, only sheer momentum — or the will of a dominant personality — could hold the structure together.

III

The two largest utility groups — United Corporation and Electric Bond and Share — were sustained chiefly by momentum. The third largest — the Insull group — expressed the unlimited ambition of its founder, Samuel Insull of Chicago. Insull's talent was partly his superior knowledge and daring, partly his astute use of the devices of incorporation, partly his ruthless managerial skill. Once when asked on the witness stand whether more humane policies in his gas plant might not result in greater efficiency, Insull characteristically replied, "My experience is that the greatest aid to efficiency of labor is a long line of men waiting at the gate."

When the utility boom of the twenties commenced, Insull rode upon it with cool confidence. As he had multiplied plants before the war, he now multiplied holding companies. By 1930 the gross assets of his group amounted to almost $2.5 billion; it produced nearly one-eighth of the country's electric power. But the structure of his systems was increasingly beyond belief. In his fantastic financial improvisation, no motive now remained but the immediacies of profit and power. Owen D. Young of General Electric, the most enlightened of the utility magnates, later testified on the Insull group before a committee of Congress. "I confess to a feeling of helplessness," said Young, who had reorganized the finances of Europe without a tremor, "as I begin to examine in February, 1932, the complicated structure of that organization." There were operating utilities, Young said, with holding companies superimposed on them, and more holding companies superimposed on the holding companies, and more investment companies and affiliates on the fringe: it was, Young surmised, "impossible for any man, however able, really to grasp the real situation." Young paused a moment. "I should like to say here," he added, "that I believe Mr. Samuel Insull was very largely the victim of that complicated structure, which got even beyond his power, competent as he was, to understand it." [4]

Insull's ideas extended far beyond his own utilities system. From his estate in Libertyville, he dominated Chicago, bribing the state utilities commission, affably encouraging the corruptions of local politics, even building an opera house. For the Chicago reformers — Harold Ickes and Donald Richberg — Insull was the enemy; and they sniped constantly at his well-fortified outposts. To meet the threat of criticism, Insull set up the Illinois Committee on Public Utility Information. Soon various private utilities combined to establish the National Electric Light Association to do the job for the nation.

IV

The NELA and its affiliates distributed literature to newspapers, libraries, schools, and fraternal orders. They dispatched speakers to clubs, forums, even to churches. They buttonholed legislators and public officials. College professors, students, editors, lecturers, were secretly placed on the utilities payroll. Research was subsidized, and university funds replenished. Textbooks that told the truthful history of utilities finance were censored, and more agreeable writings procured in their place. A relentless campaign was conducted against the Bolshevik heresy of public ownership. Rarely in American history had business organized so powerful a propaganda offensive; and the final brilliance lay in the fact that the expenses were borne by the people themselves when they paid their electric light bills.[5]

The federal government did not require much pressure. In articles and speeches, Hoover contended that the power magnates were men of vision, moved by the spirit of service, and that the state regulatory commissions were assuring the consumer all the protection he could possibly desire. "The majority of men who dominate and control the electrical utilities," he said, "themselves belong to a new school of public understanding as to the responsibilities of big business to the people." Insull praised Hoover's work, and the NELA distributed his speeches. When Hoover's two chief advisers on power questions left the Commerce Department, one became the NELA's managing director, and the other went to work for a utility lobby.[6]

Even Hoover conceded that certain engineering projects — like the Boulder Dam on the Colorado River — could be undertaken only by the federal government; and that, in such circumstances, the government might generate electric power. But it must sell this power at the dam; government distribution of the power it generated was in Hoover's view "pure socialism." [7] And, in cases, like Muscle Shoals in Tennessee, where the government owned power capacity built during the First World War, the chief Republican desire was to dispose of it as quickly as possible to private enterprise. Liberals in Congress, headed by George N. Norris of Nebraska, succeeded in blocking such proposals. But Norris's own bills for federal development of Tennessee power were doomed by presidential veto.

V

Of all the men in politics, no one cared more about public power than this smallish man, with his white stiff collar and black string tie, who had represented Nebraska in the Senate since 1913. Norris was getting to be an old man; he was sixty-five in 1926. Born on an Ohio stump farm of parents barely able to write their names, he was three years old when his father died. "I never heard a song upon the lips of my mother," Norris wrote later. "I never even heard her hum a tune." But the family was warm and devoted, held together by a woman determined that her children should have the opportunities she had missed. Young Norris, sleeping in an unfinished loft, where in winter the snow sifted in over his bed, was fired with his mother's ambitions for the future. On one warm spring afternoon when she sweated in the sun to plant an apple tree, Norris asked why she worked so hard: "You will be dead long before this tree comes into bearing." She paused and replied, "I may never see this tree in bearing, Willie, but somebody will." 8

As a young man Norris taught school until he earned enough money to study law. In 1885 he moved west to the Beaver valley of Nebraska. A fanatical Republican, he opposed the Populists in 1892, became a prosecuting attorney and then a district judge, and in 1903 went to Washington as a congressman. Increasingly influenced by Roosevelt Progressivism, Norris began in time to chafe under Republican orthodoxy. "Clearly and with absolute certainty," he said, "I was compelled to abandon my belief in the lofty character of the Republican party." 9 Doggedly devoted to principle, Norris saw no alternative to an independent course. His first target was Joe Cannon, whose power as Speaker enabled him to rule the House of Representatives like a czar.

With his plain black clothes and his humble manners, Norris was an easy man to underrate. He led a successful revolt against Cannon. Then, elevated to the Senate in 1913, he continued to walk his own path. He was one of six senators who opposed the declaration of war in 1917. During the twenties he fought against the labor injunction and the yellow-dog contract; he strove for a constitutional amendment to end the lameduck session, where members of Congress who failed of re-election could still make the laws of the nation; and he devoted himself above all to the battle for public control of the natural resources and against the power trust.

Norris's liberalism was of an austere and fundamentalist type. Born to frugality, he had, for all his sweetness, a puritan's suspicion of luxury. "No man can stick his legs under the tables of the idle rich every night," he said, "and be fit the next day to sit in judgment on those who toil." He bore scars of personal tragedy: the death of his father, his first child born dead, his first wife dying after the birth of their third daughter, his twin sons by his second wife born dead. The dark shadow rarely lifted from him; and at times he seemed to withdraw altogether behind a veil of patient skepticism or of brooding melancholy.

"I am on the downhill side," he remarked in 1930, " — sometimes, I think, traveling rapidly. The end cannot be very many years in advance. I think I have, to a great extent, run my race." The old man, his white hair brushed straight back in a crest, his arched eyebrows unexpectedly black, his skin fresh and pink, continued in his mild, midwestern voice, "I am not conscious of having a single selfish ambition. Neither money nor office holds any enchanting allurements. . . . I have received all the honor I can ever expect. I should like to repay the people by an unprejudiced and unbiased service in their behalf, I have no other ambition." [10]

For all his pessimism, George Norris had a poetic vision of the possibilities of American life. "We are living," he liked to say, "in the dawn of an electric age." Every stream in America, tumbling "from the mountains through the meadows to the sea," was a potential power source; every drop of running water, "from the snows, the springs, and the rain," might make life better for future generations. He saw America as a shining land of turbines, generators, and transmission lines, white dams brilliant in the sun with sparkling blue water behind, power flowing to the people at a price that all could afford. "This is a property," Norris said, "which belongs to all of us, a source of human happiness." Its development, he declared, ought always to be under public ownership and public operation.

All Norris's disgust consequently went for those who would deny Americans their heritage.

The power trust is the greatest monopolistic corporation that has been organized for private greed. . . . It has bought and sold legislatures. . . . It has managed to infest farm organizations; it has not hesitated to enter the sacred walls of churches and religious organizations. . . . With its slimy fingers it reaches into every community and levies its tribute upon every fireside. There is no avenue of human activity that it has not undertaken to control. It has undertaken to poison the minds of our boys in the Boy Scout organization. It has undertaken to bribe the minister in the pulpit, and with its sinister stealthy tread, it has even entered our public schools and tried to poison the minds of our children.[11]

As utilities propaganda became more insistent and the utility structure more nightmarish, many liberals felt that public power, more than any other question, summed up the larger issue between the business community and the people. "The power issue," said John Dewey, "is the most weighty single issue in the political field." "Hydroelectric power," Felix Frankfurter wrote Franklin Roosevelt in 1929, "raises without a doubt the most far-reaching social and economic issues before the American people, certainly for the next decade." [12] As governor of Pennsylvania, Gifford Pinchot resumed his old fight and in 1923 established the Giant Power Survey which laid the basis for the idea of public rural electrification. Nebraska, under Norris's influence, set up its public electric power system. In New York Al Smith called for state ownership and operation of water power. One community after another conducted local fights for municipal power.

The utilities denounced such proposals as socialistic and un-American. "This water power program of the Democratic Party is socialistic, if you like," replied Franklin Roosevelt in 1928; but the postal system of the United States was socialistic in the same sense and for the same reason. "We are willing to have the Government of the United States carry on certain kinds of business for us, if the Government can do it better than anybody else, and that is why I want the Government of this State to develop the power sites of this State, because the Government can do it better than anybody else." [13]

16. The Campaign of 1928

IN TIME, the streams of discontent began to converge: the farmers' concern for income, the social workers' for welfare, the trade unionists' for organization, the liberals' for the restraint of business power. The opposition party provided the natural outlet; and in that party Governor Smith of New York, well identified with social justice, public power, and civil liberties, seemed by the winter of 1927 the appointed leader. His re-election as Governor in 1926 made him more than ever an attractive political figure. Meanwhile McAdoo announced in September 1927 that he was not a presidential candidate.

In the national convention at Houston the next year, the brawlers of 1924 could hardly be recognized in the happy family of 1928. When Franklin D. Roosevelt, completing his nominating address, offered "one who has the will to win — who not only deserves success but commands it. Victory is his habit — the happy warrior," the delegates roared in a gratifying demonstration of solidarity.[1] Smith received an easy first-ballot nomination, with Senator Joseph Robinson of Arkansas as his running mate.

The problem was now the strategy of the campaign. Smith had obvious choices. He might, like La Follette in 1924, draw a sharp issue with business rule. As the former New York Democratic State Chairman, Herbert Claiborne Pell, a Tuxedo aristocrat with contempt for businessmen, suggested in January 1928, "Under the Coolidge administration the rich have declared war on the poor. Let them beware of the retaliation of those that they despise today."[2] But Smith chose rather to try to persuade business that

it could trust the Democrats. To run his campaign he selected
John J. Raskob, a Republican industrialist prominent in Du Pont
and General Motors who had actually hoped to vote for Coolidge
in 1928. Like Smith, Raskob was a Catholic and a wet and thereby
not a national chairman calculated to improve Democratic chances
in the Bible belt. But Smith, assuming that he would get southern
and liberal votes anyway, calculated that his best chance lay in
splitting the business-minded Northeast. To assist Raskob in this
project, Smith appointed four more millionaires — James W.
Gerard, Herbert H. Lehman, Jesse Jones, and Senator Peter G.
Gerry — to top places in the campaign organization. The Democrats spent over $7 million in the campaign — only $2 million
less than the Republicans.[3]

Raskob gave more money than anyone else and became a dominating figure in the party. Bashful and uneasy, with an inaudible
speaking voice, he had worked his way up from a lowly start as a
stenographer. Experience had persuaded him that a society in
which such a rise was possible was ideal; and, except for the repeal
of the prohibition amendment, he had no desire for social change.
Neither business in government nor bigness in business, nor even
the euphoria of the stock market, disturbed his sleep. His dictum
that a blue-chip stock should sell at fifteen times its corporation's
earnings rather than at the old-fashioned ten had already given
Wall Street a new access of energy. In the summer of 1929 he wrote
an article for a women's magazine entitled, with disarming directness, "Everybody Ought to be Rich." The New Era had no more
devoted follower.[4]

II

The first effect of the Raskob appointment was to reopen the
wounds of 1924 which, for a moment, had seemed healed by
Houston. The Bryan-McAdoo wing of the party felt its suspicion
of the urban Democracy return in full force. As George Fort
Milton of Tennessee wrote McAdoo in July, the Smith design was
obviously to appeal "to the aliens, who feel that the older America,
the America of the Anglo-Saxon stock, is a hateful thing which
must be overturned and humiliated; to the northern negroes, who

lust for social equality and racial dominance; to the Catholics
who have been made to believe that they are entitled to the White
House, and to the Jews who likewise are to be instilled with the
feeling that this is the time for God's chosen people to chastise
America yesteryear." "If the dominance of such groups represents
the new America which Smith is seeking to arouse," Milton concluded, "the Old America, the America of Jackson, and of Lincoln
and Wilson, should rise up in wrath and defeat it."

The Raskob appointment also dismayed all Democrats who
hoped for a campaign along progressive lines. Franklin D. Roosevelt told his friends it was "a grave mistake," adding his fear that
it would "permanently drive away a host of people in the south and
west and rural east who are not particularly favorable to Smith,
but who up to today have been seeping back into the Party." A
fortnight later Roosevelt wrote confidentially, "Frankly, the campaign is working out in a way which I, personally, should not have
allowed and Smith has burned his bridges behind him." At that
point — late July — Roosevelt felt that he would stay out altogether; but eventually he was prevailed upon to head the Division
of Commerce, Industry, and Professional Activities at Democratic
headquarters, where he loyally wrote, or signed, letters to businessmen telling them that they had more to fear from Hoover than
from Smith. ("Some of Mr. Hoover's regulatory attempts are undoubtedly for the good of our economic system," ran one of these
documents, "but I think the policy of Governor Smith to let businessmen look after business matters is far safer for our country.") [5]

In his campaign, Smith dumped the traditional Democratic tariff
policy, came out for protection, and sought in other ways to reassure the business community. At the same time, his loyalty to
the New York welfare programs kept him the support of the social
workers; and his defense of public power won him the backing
of George Norris. Acknowledging the discontent in the farm belt,
he vaguely endorsed the broad purposes of McNary-Haugenism,
thereby inducing George Peek, Chester Davis, young Henry Wallace,
and a few other farm leaders to swing behind his candidacy. Under
attack for his religion, he missed few opportunities to affirm his
faith in civil and religious freedom.

Still his impact was less as a conservative or even as a liberal than as the candidate embodying the dynamism of the city. He threw himself into the role with his actor's zest. The band played "The Sidewalks of New York"; and Al Smith appeared on the back platform with his familiar accessories, the brown derby on his head, the big cigar rolling in his mouth, the vibrant city voice, ringing out across the crowd. His speeches were direct, practical, and energetic — above all, they were alive. Smith talked from notes on the back of envelopes, wagging his head and waving his arms as he approached his climax. He drew immense crowds, larger than Hoover's. Many were attracted just by curiosity about the city man, however, and a few were drawn by uglier emotions. As the train approached Oklahoma City, Smith could see the fiery crosses of the Klan burning on the countryside. That night, referring with characteristic nonchalance to the cross which symbolized their fanaticism and his faith, he denounced the Klan.[6]

But as his campaign was too liberal for the business community, it was too mild for the more ardent reformers. Led by Professor Paul H. Douglas of the University of Chicago, a group of liberal educators assailed the "sterile and corrupt groups" behind Smith as well as Hoover and called for support of Norman Thomas, the Socialist candidate.[7] Smith's appeal to the farm belt was offset by Senator William E. Borah of Idaho, who unexpectedly used his vast prestige to rally the farmers for Hoover. Raskob's political incompetence led to frightful misdirection of effort, such as spending great sums in the vain hope of carrying Pennsylvania, which Hoover won by a million votes. And beneath the surface maneuvers of the campaign was a slanderous undercurrent of religious bigotry — whispers that Smith's election would bring the Pope to America, that all Protestant marriages would be annulled and all Protestant children declared bastards. Above all else, there was the issue of prosperity, the New Era — the chicken in every pot and the two cars in every garage, the vanishing poorhouse: "given a chance to go forward with the policies of the last eight years, we shall soon with the help of God be in sight of the day when poverty will be banished from this nation."

III

On election day Smith received 87 electoral votes, Hoover 444. The Republican victory tore gaping holes in the Solid South. Smith lost not only every border state but also five of the old Confederate states. He did not even carry his own state of New York. Hoover polled 58 per cent of the popular vote as against Smith's 40.7 per cent.

Actually analysis of the returns might have cheered the Democrats. Smith received nearly twice as many popular votes as John W. Davis in 1924; indeed, he polled 6 million votes more than any Democratic presidential candidate in history. In 1924 the Republicans had carried the dozen largest cities by 1.3 million votes; in 1928, for all the heady Republican success in the electoral college, the Democrats carried the same cities by a small but symptomatic margin. Hoover may have split the Democratic South; but Smith dented the Republican North. And there were even consolations in the agricultural vote. In Iowa, for example, the Democrats nearly doubled their percentage of votes on the farms and increased their percentages markedly in the towns and cities.[8]

But neither Republican nor Democrat read the portents. Instead, one group looked to permanent power; the other, in spite of itself, to permanent frustration. Franklin D. Roosevelt, who had survived the sweep to win as Governor of New York, remained buoyant. But he struck little response among party leaders. "In my judgment," John W. Davis wrote Roosevelt in early 1929, "there is little that can be done at the moment along lines of party regeneration. A beaten army must be permitted to lie in its rest billets and nurse its wounds." In a few months, a former publicity director of the Democratic National Committee wrote a despondent article entitled "Will the Democrats Follow the Whigs?"[9] Many joined, some merrily, some dolefully in speculating whether the Democrat was indeed a vanishing species, doomed to early extinction.

17. The Philosophy of Liberalism

THE LIBERALISM of 1919 had broken in two after the return of normalcy in 1920. Its more practical half found intermittent embodiment in such issues as public power, farm relief, and social legislation; here men like Norris, La Follette, and Smith kept up the punishing day-to-day fight for limited gains. The ideological residue fell to the intellectuals, less interested now in solving immediate problems than in formulating a new liberal philosophy. John Dewey, Herbert Croly, Thorstein Veblen, and Charles A. Beard were the dominant thinkers in this undertaking. Dewey's instrumentalism gave the liberal synthesis its philosophy; Croly's progressivism its politics; Veblen's institutionalism its economics; and Beard's history its sense of the past and its conviction of the future. Together the four men completed the job of reorganizing the liberal mind and reconstructing the liberal tradition.[1]

Dewey established the framework for the new synthesis. Before the war, a generation of intellectuals had rebelled against the orthodoxies of the 1890's. The impulse behind the uprising was a distaste for syllogism, for deduction, for abstraction — a belief that not just the life of the law but all life was, in Oliver Wendell Holmes's phrase, not logic but experience. Morton White has called it "the revolt against formalism." It began by shifting attention from theory to fact, from word to substance, from ideology to actuality. Even if it ended by creating a new scholasticism of its own, it subjected older assumptions along the way to mordant criticism, and it introduced for a season a new sense of reality into philosophical and social discourse. Dewey was not its most exciting figure, but he was its most thoughtful and dogged systematizer. His signal contribution was to define the logic of the revolt. His writings made clear to insurgents across the board — whether in philosophy or history, economics or jurisprudence or politics — what they were doing and what they were seeking. He extracted from their controversies a common thesis and a common faith.

For Dewey, the ultimate authority was experience; and he made of experience a far more organized concept than it had been in the more brilliant philosophy of William James. For James experience was provisional, personal, individual; for Dewey it was, in some sense, public and collective. In socializing James's pragmatism, Dewey developed its bearings for society in ways that James could hardly have anticipated. The logic of action, Dewey suggested, must be the logic of experiment and education; it must be based on a faith in man's capacity to respond to reason; it must understand the role of social learning and collective inquiry. A thoroughgoing philosophy of experience, framed in the light of science and technology, could produce an organized social intelligence; and the organized social intelligence, Dewey believed, could direct the processes of social change into a rational and beatific future.

His book of 1922, *Human Nature and Conduct,* emphasized the malleability of human nature. The instincts of man, Dewey wrote, were the most plastic things about him, the "most readily modifiable through use, most subject to educative direction." [2] In *The Public and Its Problems* he sought to show how his analysis of human nature and his instrumental method applied to social questions. There was no point, he said, in further dalliance with the tired old abstractions — freedom vs. authority, the individual vs. society, and the rest. Let us investigate questions, he urged, not by metaphysics, but by inquiry into practical consequences. Through science, through education, above all through participation in the creative experience of democracy, the inchoate mass could become a responsible public, capable of defining itself, teaching itself, and evolving rational plans for the future.

By 1929, in *Individualism Old and New,* Dewey was ready to become specific. The old ideal of individualism — presumably the ideal celebrated by Hoover in *American Individualism* — had been perverted, Dewey wrote, "to conform to the practices of a pecuniary culture." What was now necessary was to liberate individualism from its pecuniary bondage. The first step in this liberation, he said, was the realization that we had already entered "the collective age." The choice lay between the anarchic collectivism of business conducted for profit and the planned collectivism of public authority. The means to a responsible solution lay through the scientific method. But the introduction of responsibility into the business system, Dewey warned, would seal "the doom of an exclusively pecuniary-profit industry." He sometimes doubted whether the scientific method could be employed against the opposition of those "who use it for private ends and who strive to defeat its social application for fear of destructive effects upon their power and profit." Yet his deeper hope was that a national economic council representing government, business, and labor might put America voluntarily on the collective road which the Soviet Union was traveling with so much coercion. Only democratic collectivism, Dewey said, could create the conditions for a new and authentic American individualism.[3]

II

Where Dewey was led by philosophy and psychology, Croly was inclined by the study of history and politics. Twenty years earlier, *The Promise of American Life* had given the idea of national management both emotional force and historical vindication. But Croly's successive disillusionments with Theodore Roosevelt and Wilson had discouraged him about the prospects of realizing the Promise. As an admirer of social engineering, he thought for a moment in 1919 that Hoover might have the disinterested technical intelligence to organize the future; Hoover even seemed interested in buying stock in the *New Republic*. But the Hoover hope washed out too, and in 1920 Croly was reduced to the sad expedient of supporting the presidential candidacy of Parley P. Christensen on the Farm-Labor ticket. The failure of La Follette in 1924 was the final blow. After 1924, Croly lost interest in politics. The job of liberalism, he now thought, was to gain "an increasing knowledge of human behavior and how it can be modified, economized and

utilized." Like Dewey, Croly conceived the field to be social education: the strategy, social learning; the means, the experimental
method and creative experience.[4]

Croly became increasingly indifferent to program, perhaps because of the quasi-religious mysticism which welled up in his
thought during the last years before his death in 1930. Yet he
shared this programmatic vagueness with the nonmystical Dewey.
This common fuzziness may have been due to a faith in experimentalism so deep that neither was willing to prejudice the experiments by anticipating the results. Today's program, they both
believed, would infallibly be tomorrow's orthodoxy; so that it was
wiser now to concentrate not on program but on process. Faith
in human nature, in the organized scientific intelligence and in
creative experience convinced them that central social planning
was possible at the same time that it diminished their interest in
the details of the plans.

Beard, the historian, approached the planning goal from another direction. His earlier work had cut through abstract liberal
idealism by identifying what Beard regarded as the basic economic
factors in history and showing that the conflict between democracy
and property went back to the first days of the republic. In 1927
his *Rise of American Civilization* traced the course of American
development up to the Machine Age, where society, as he depicted
it, now trembled between integration and catastrophe. The Machine Age, Beard thought, had its own inner logic; and, in editing
his symposium of 1928, *Whither Mankind,* he sought to show that
in society as in nature man had no choice but "to reduce the confusion of the modern age to principles of control." Technological
civilization, founded on science and power-driven machinery, must
"extend its area and intensify its characteristics" until its concepts
of order ruled even public policy." [5]

Whither Mankind challenged a group of engineers in New York
to answer Beard's call for a social technology. Editing the results
in *Toward Civilization* in 1930, Beard enlarged his conception of
social engineering. The machine process, he declared, imposed
rationality on politics. "By inherent necessity it forces upon society
an ever larger planned area of conduct." He had a rhapsodic vision
of "the imperative necessity of planning. . . . Controlling unlimited

power, mastering the nature of materials, adapting them to mankind and mankind to them, conscious rationality triumphant." [6]

Beard thus gave an historian's support to the thesis that the new liberalism should rest on national planning. But planning remained still a faith rather than a program. Could the liberals enlist the economists in the cause of "conscious rationality?"

III

The twenties were not an unfruitful decade in economic thought. Men in the classical liberal tradition — F. W. Taussig may serve as an example — were presenting thoughtful arguments for lower tariffs, for improved budgetary practices, for better utilities regulation. Others were striking out on fresh tangents: Irving Fisher was making brilliant inquiries into monetary theory; Wesley Mitchell was breaking new paths with his study of business cycles; John R. Commons and his followers were proposing specific reforms in labor policy, in social insurance and a dozen other fields; Paul H. Douglas was conducting his valuable investigations into the theory and facts of wages; Arthur Altmeyer in Wisconsin and Abraham Epstein in Pennsylvania were working out programs of social security; W. Z. Ripley was questioning the processes and practices of corporate financing; talented journalists like Stuart Chase, George Soule, and John T. Flynn were examining all aspects of the economic process from Wall Street to the corner grocery; and William Trufant Foster and Waddill Catchings were proposing audacious new policies to maintain economic growth and stability.

Foster and Catchings had in some respects the most striking insights of any American economists of the decade. Foster, who had formerly been president of Reed College, and Catchings, an iron manufacturer and soon a partner in Goldman, Sachs, made the most sustained effort in the period to work out the economic logic of the purchasing-power theory. Henry Ford's faith in high wages seemed to them all right so far as it went; but it did not go nearly far enough. In *Business Without a Buyer* in 1927, and in *The Road to Plenty* the following year, Foster and Catchings indicated how much farther they thought it necessary to go.

The Road to Plenty was a triumph of seductive economic explanation. Casting their argument in the form of a group discussion, the authors amiably led their readers into what soon turned out to be a fundamental assault on classical economics and particularly on that long impregnable bastion, Say's Law of Markets. According to Say's Law — for a century a foundation of orthodox economic theory — the total demand for goods must in the end equal the total supply; or, in other words, the financing of production automatically created enough purchasing power to move all the goods produced. Take care of production, in short, and consumption will take care of itself.

According to Foster and Catchings, this whole theory was a delusion. It did not correspond to business experience. It overlooked, for example, the innumerable lags and leakages in the flow of money. "As industry increases its output," they pointed out, "it does not, for any length of time, proportionately increase its payments to the people." In consequence, the flow of money to the consumer could not keep pace with the flow of consumers' goods. In addition, Say's Law overlooked what they called the Dilemma of Thrift. Both corporations and individuals had to save; yet every dollar saved was a dollar subtracted from the flow to the potential consumer, and the result of saving was inevitably to increase the shortage of consumer demand. In the end this process would cause depression — unless government found a way to offset the deficiencies in demand created by oversaving.

How to account then for the existing prosperity? Ford's formula — high wages — was no answer; never in a single year, Foster and Catchings noted, had Ford himself paid out enough in wages to buy the cars that rolled off his assembly line. The secret of prosperity lay rather in the fact that the volume of money had expanded sufficiently, in connection both with new capital investment and with government spending for public works, "to make up the deficit in consumer buying due to savings." But in the future these private and public outlays could not be left to chance. Government, they said, must make it a main objective of policy to maintain an adequate flow of money income to consumers. It must found its policies on the principle of "putting more money into consumers' hands when business is falling off, and less money when inflation is under way."

They summed up their antidepression policy in a single slogan: "When business begins to look rotten, more public spending." But would not this increase the national debt? Only in times of depression, they replied; and, in any case, debt increase was hardly an irreparable disaster. "It means scarcely more than that the people of the United States collectively owe themselves more money," while the nation gains in real wealth and spares itself the "greatest waste of all . . . the waste of idle plants and idle workers." [7]

These ideas roused interest in some quarters. Many businessmen, reading *The Road to Plenty* idly, construed it as a demonstration that prosperity could be made permanent by consumer spending. Governor Brewster of Maine made it the basis of his stabilization program. A few liberals shared Henry A. Wallace's hope that hundreds of thousands of people might read the book. But professional economists, while engaging happily in the competition set by the authors who offered large cash prizes to anyone detecting errors in their reasoning, were mostly put off by the cavalier treatment of Say's Law; and a good liberal Democrat like Franklin Roosevelt scrawled in his copy of *The Road to Plenty:* "Too good to be true — You can't get something for nothing." [8]

And the liberal sages — Dewey, Croly, Beard — seemed unaware of the existence of Foster and Catchings. For it was the pride of Foster and Catchings that their policy involved no change in the essentials of the established order. "It leaves," they said, "individual initiative, responsibility, and rewards, throughout the whole domain of commerce and finance, exactly where they are to-day." [9] Men who wanted to reorganize social institutions required something more sustaining than fiscal policy.

IV

Official liberalism discovered what it needed rather in the new school of institutionalist economics — a school which found its inspiration in Simon Patten and Thorstein Veblen and their damaging attack on the methods and assumptions of classical economics.

For Patten the central fact of economics was the momentum of the machine. Modern technology, he felt, was placing the world on the edge of a new historic era. The age of economic deficit was giving way to the age of surplus; and the impending economy of abundance would bring about a transvaluation of economic ideas and institutions. Instead of the destructive competition of old, Patten said, there would be emphasis on cooperation and the role of the state; instead of abstinence and thrift, recognition that "the non-saver is now a higher type of man than the saver"; instead of "a morality of restraint," "a morality of activity." "Disease, oppression, irregular work, premature old age, and race hatreds characterized the vanishing age of deficit; plenty of food, shelter, capital, security and mobility of men and goods define the age of surplus." [10]

Patten died early in the twenties. But his confident belief that intelligent planning could abolish the nonsense of scarcity had impressed a generation of students at the Wharton School of Finance and Commerce of the University of Pennsylvania, among them Rexford G. Tugwell and Frances Perkins. Thorstein Veblen was going even farther in mounting a direct attack on economic orthodoxy. For Veblen, classical equilibrium economics was fundamentally wrong. The models which balanced out so perfectly in the textbooks bore, he declared, no relation to what actually happened in the market place. If economists could not account for concrete economic institutions and economic behavior, then, in Veblen's mind, they were futile; worse, they were helping the exploiting class conceal from its victims the true nature of the system.

In a series of books over the first quarter of the century, Veblen tried to identify the true characteristics of the free-market economy. In *The Theory of Business Enterprise* he offered his cardinal distinction between "industry" and "business." Where industry found fulfillment in production, business found fulfillment in profit; and the struggle between the two — between technology and capitalism — seemed to Veblen the key to American society. Veblen kept his greatest ferocity for the price system, which he regarded as the device by which capitalism sabotaged production and business thwarted the potentialities of industry. "In any community that is organized on the price system," he wrote, ". . . habitual unemployment of the available industrial plant and workmen, in whole or in part, appears to be the indispensable condition."

Veblen's pose was that of a dispassionate observer, a visitor from

another world, amused by the everlasting spectacle of human im-
becility. Yet beneath the ironic detachment there remained a
moralist's passion to realize the possibilities of the new technology.
In 1921, in *The Engineers and the Price System,* he sketched the
design of an economy by which industry could be organized "as
a systematic whore." He embroidered the scheme with his usual
satiric gibes; but its main element remained clear — the abolition
of the price system in favor of a soviet of technicians with power
to allocate resources directly through the economy. Of course, business would go; indeed, ex-businessmen would be excluded under
some kind of loyalty system from "all positions of trust and executive responsibility." [11]

Veblen's technocratic manifesto influenced his fellow economists
much less than his broad emphasis on economic institutions. Inspired by his insights, while tempering his extravagance, the "institutionalist" school began to emerge in the twenties. Its leading
younger member was Wesley C. Mitchell, who had studied with
Dewey as well as with Veblen. In Mitchell's hands, institutionalism
tended to become statistical and descriptive, though Mitchell retained an interest in central economic planning. Other institutionalists — especially R. G. Tugwell and Gardiner C. Means of
Columbia, Isador Lubin of Brookings and Walton H. Hamilton
of Brookings and Yale — were more prepared to develop the ideological bearings of their doctrine. Most accepted the Veblen of
The Theory of Business Enterprise. But few took the Veblen of
The Engineers and the Price System very seriously.

The intellectuals, on the other hand, tended to swallow Veblen
whole. His sociological and literary patter gave his economics an
appearance of readability, and many of his stinging phrases passed
quickly into the liberal vocabulary. His distinction between business and industry, in particular, brought a new approach to discussions of social reorganization. It simplified life by implying
that if only business — the price system and the profit motive —
could be eliminated, then industry would automatically give birth
to the planned society. The planning thesis thus seemed to receive
the endorsement not only of the most brilliant of professional economists but of the new technology itself.

And impulses from an earlier period — especially the traditions of social work and of the Social Gospel — gave further strength to the planning thesis. Social workers and social pastors had long agreed that reason, education, and cooperation were (or ought to be) the decisive agents of social change, that human nature interposed no serious obstacle, and that before long the Kingdom of God, in one sense or another, could be realized on earth. As these traditions had prepared people for the planning idea, so in the twenties Dewey and Croly instilled specific confidence in the power of man to plan, Veblen asserted the technical feasibility of a planned economy, Beard gave planning the stamp of historic necessity. By the end of the decade, the liberal synthesis was becoming clear. And one of its results was to mark off the liberals with greater clarity than ever from the devotees of the New Era.

v

In the meantime, business civilization itself was accentuating the sense of estrangement. Businessmen did not seek to hide their contempt for the reformers. Silas Strawn, chairman of the board at Montgomery Ward, midway in 1929 between his presidency of the American Bar Association and his presidency of the United States Chamber of Commerce, could qualify as a representative leader. Addressing the National Association of Manufacturers, he expressed his desire to deport "those creatures" who "in the role of 'parlor socialists,' while enjoying all the luxuries and pleasures which are so easily available and which generally have come to them by the industry and economy of their ancestors, complain about conditions obtaining here instead of trying to do something helpful or constructive." Yet the liberals, even at the risk of being condemned as knockers and crepe-hangers, could not feel that Bruce Barton and Rotary International exhausted the spiritual possibilities of American life. When Herbert Hoover, defying Sinclair Lewis, remarked that "it is from Main Street and its countryside that the creative energies of the nation must be replenished," this merely confirmed their impression of Mr. Hoover.[12]

One episode above all perfected liberal doubts about the existing order. In May 1920, following the murder of a paymaster in South Braintree, Massachusetts. Brockton police picked up two Italians in an automobile filled with the innocent and febrile literature of anarchistic propaganda. These were the days of the red scare: Nicola Sacco and Bartolomeo Vanzetti, not knowing why they had been stopped, hardly able to understand English, acted confused and guilty. Eventually brought to trial on the murder charge, they stood little chance as confessed radicals, aliens, and draft-dodgers in a time of hysteria. The trial judge, who soon boasted of what he had done to "those anarchistic bastards," completed the design of Massachusetts justice. So in 1921 Sacco and Vanzetti were sentenced to death — two obscure immigrants about whom no one cared.

Yet a few people in Massachusetts cared about the system of justice — about the thinness of the evidence, the gaps in the testimony, the predilections of the judge. New lawyers came into the case, with new motions, new appeals. Gardner Jackson, a Boston newspaperman, directed the efforts of a defense committee. The matter dragged on, year after year. In March 1927 Professor Felix Frankfurter of the Harvard Law School summed up the case and Judge Thayer's role in it in a powerful article for the *Atlantic Monthly*.

Sacco was a sturdy, inconspicuous man, whirled into the case by the accident of his friendship with Vanzetti. Vanzetti was the more striking figure, a philosophical anarchist in the Italian manner, with large mustaches, unruly hair, and penetrating eyes. Judge Thayer, when he pronounced final sentence in 1927, visibly flinched from looking the men in the face. Vanzetti said: "What we have suffered during these seven years no human tongue can say, and yet you see me before you, not trembling, you see me looking in your eyes straight; not blushing, not changing color, not ashamed or in fear." Sacco said: "I never knew, never heard, even read in history anything so cruel as this court."

Thayer, after passing sentence, said to the newspapermen, "Boys, you know I've often been good to you. Now see what you can do for me." Nobody answered him.

By 1927 the Sacco-Vanzetti case was a world concern. It had stabbed through the gaiety and indifference of the twenties like a knife into the liberal conscience. As the day of execution approached, tension radiated from Beacon Hill around the globe.

On that hot August night, public buildings were under guard, the streets were heavily patrolled, the Charlestown prison armed and garrisoned as if in preparation for a siege, its walls lined with searchlights and machine guns. When at last the telephone bell rang twice in the defense committee office, a newspaperman's signal that the execution had taken place, the tension broke into grief. But the last moment truly belonged to Sacco and Vanzetti: their agony was their triumph. "Our words — our lives — our pains — nothing! The taking of our lives . . . all!"

The case of Sacco and Vanzetti was a traumatic experience for American liberalism. The execution, said Edmund Wilson, made liberals "lose their bearings." Edna St. Vincent Millay, who had walked weary hours as a picket, thought that she never again could find peace in a road through the woods or a stretch of shore. "The beauty of these things can no longer make up to me for all the ugliness of man, his cruelty, his greed, his lying face." "Don't you see the glory of this case," said a character in Upton Sinclair's *Boston*, "it kills off the liberals!" "It forced me," wrote Robert Morss Lovett, "to accept a doctrine which I had always repudiated as partisan tactics — the class war." "America our nation," said John Dos Passos, "has been beaten by strangers who have turned our language inside out who have taken the clean words our fathers spoke and made them slimy and foul." "All right," said Dos Passos, "all right we are two nations."

"The momentum of the established order," said Robert Lincoln O'Brien, publisher of the conservative Boston *Herald*, "required the execution of Sacco and Vanzetti, and never in your life or mine, has that momentum acquired such tremendous force." All right, they were two nations.[13]

VI

In 1927, the year of the Sacco-Vanzetti execution, a number of American liberals, among them Dewey, Tugwell, Paul H. Douglas, and Stuart Chase, visited the Soviet Union. None was converted by the Communist theology or impressed by the exportability of the Communist solution. But several were struck by the demonstration in Russia of the power of the collective will. It was hard,

Dewey wrote, "not to feel a certain envy for the intellectual and educational workers in Russia" because "a unified religious social faith brings with it such simplification and integration of life. . . . They are organized members of an organic going movement." Tugwell, seeing Communism in Veblenian terms as "the experiment of running industry without the mechanism of business," felt himself inclining to the slightly sententious belief that "the humanly achieved industrial balance in Russia is more likely to attain the objective of 'necessities for all before luxuries for any' than in our own competitive system." Chase similarly subdued doubts to guess "under a sort of dizzy conviction" that the Gosplan might really work.[14]

Others went much farther in finding the Soviet Union a pleasurable alternative to the America that executed Sacco and Vanzetti. Social Gospel ministers, notably Harry Ward and Sherwood Eddy, saw Communism as an experiment in practical Christianity. A flurry of literary people circulated around the American Communist Party. And old Russian hands like Lincoln Steffens did not falter in their faith. If Steffens was finding a new hero in Mussolini, Fascism came to him as additional evidence that liberalism was "unscientific," and that, if America wanted a decent society, it would have to discover "something like the Russian-Italian method" of getting it.[15]

VII

Even the most hopeful advocates of liberalism began to feel discouragement toward the end of the decade. The margin of the Hoover victory in 1928 was a blow. When Paul Douglas organized the League for Independent Political Action in 1929 as a means of fulfilling Dewey's *The Public and Its Problems,* he found meager response. The suspicion was spreading, even among liberals, that the theorists of the New Era might be right — that business leadership was not only stronger but wiser than ever before, that the next step might really be, as Mr. Hoover had promised, the abolition of poverty. "The more or less unconscious and unplanned activities of business men," wrote Walter Lippmann in 1928, "are for once more novel, more daring, and in general more revolutionary, than the theories of the progressives." By 1929 even Steffens, who a decade earlier had reported that he had seen the future and it worked, moved to reconsider. "Big business in America," he wrote, "is producing what the Socialists held up as their goal; food, shelter and clothing for all. You will see it during the Hoover administration." And the once bright hope of Communism? "The unconscious experiment this country is making in civilization and culture," declared Steffens, "is equal to that of Soviet Russia. The race is saved, one way or the other and, I think both ways." [16]

So few clung to the faith. "What has become of this movement that promised so much twenty years ago?" cried Fred Howe. "What has become of the pre-war radicals?" They gave so much; they led so many; now most of them have laid down their arms. "Was the fight too hard? Did youth burn itself out? . . . May it be — as some of them feel — that there is little for liberals to do?"

Howe's question provoked a confusion of answers. Some liberals had lost their illusions. "It was during those grilling years that I put in trying to establish the innocence of Mooney and Billings," said Fremont Older, "that I learned my lesson about human nature and discovered that practically the only difference between the poor classes and the rich classes was that one had money and the other had not." Some blamed the impotence of liberalism on prosperity. "You cannot dramatize the injustices of the present situation," said William Allen White. "Hence the reformer's occupation is gone." "The old reformer," said Norman Thomas, "has become the Tired Radical and his sons and daughters drink at the fountain of the *American Mercury*." Some blamed the war. "I have no doubt," said Clarence Darrow, "but what the world war is largely responsible for the reactionary tendency of the day." "We have discovered," said John Haynes Holmes, "that America is no longer, probably never was, the country that we loved. The liberals of the last generation believed passionately in America as a country unique. . . . Then came the War — and America was seen to be . . . just one more cruel imperialism." Some were driven to radical conclusions. "Political liberalism is dead," said Roger Baldwin. ". . . The only power that works is class power."

"Few indeed," wrote Donald Richberg in 1929, "are the progressives of my generation who have survived the bludgeoning of these years. Death and defeat and discouragement have taken most of them." Young Bob La Follette, talking with Steffens on a California veranda through a summer afternoon and evening the same year, said that among the liberal crowd there was nothing but cynicism, disillusionment, and "what's the use?" A few days later, Thorstein Veblen, unappeased and unappeasable to the end, died in obscurity in California, and his ashes were scattered in the Pacific. Those whom the New Era could not convert it outlived.

William Allen White and Louis D. Brandeis exchanged thoughts in this climactic year of the boom.

"Shall we soon have another 'great rebellion'?" asked Brandeis.

"Probably not, I should say," White answered.[17]

18. The Revolt of the Intellectuals

BUT THE intellectual malaise went deeper than simply the exhaustion of liberalism. Only a minority of intellectuals, and those mostly the older, earnest men who remembered the New Nationalism and the New Freedom, retained much concern about America as a democratic society. The new generation had grown up, their spokesman said, "to find all Gods dead, all wars fought, all faiths in man shaken"; all they knew, wrote Scott Fitzgerald, was that "America was going on the greatest, gaudiest spree in history." It was an era of enchantment, where everything was rosy and romantic, where diamonds were as big as the Ritz, where for a brief decade, as Fitzgerald saw it, the wistful past and the fulfilled future seemed mingled in a single gorgeous moment.[1]

"It was characteristic of the Jazz Age," said Fitzgerald, "that it had no interest in politics at all." It was an age of art, of excess, of satire, of miracle; but who was to care about economics, when business policy seemed so infallible? Or about politics, when business power seemed so invincible? If pressed, the young writer might confess himself an anarchist, devoted to the freedom of the individual, hostile to censorship and prohibition and Babbittry; but politics — So what, Oh yeah, No, Nah. "I decline to pollute my mind with such obscenities," said George Jean Nathan. ". . . If all the Armenians were to be killed tomorrow and if half the Russians were to starve to death the day after, it would not matter to me in the least." "If I am convinced of anything," said H. L. Mencken, "it is that Doing Good is in bad taste." Sending money to starving children in Europe, suggested Joseph Hergesheimer, was "one of the least engaging ways in which money could be spent." "I burn with generous indignation over this world's pig-headedness and injustice," said James Branch Cabell, "at no time whatever." [2]

It was not that they had any use for the business civilization. They hated it; but, while hating it, they accepted it basically at the businessman's own evaluation — accepted it, that is, as a successful system, believed that it was working. Yet it remained for them stifling and repellent. The money madness, as a Chicago advertising man named Sherwood Anderson put it, was "beastly unclean." "America," wrote Kenneth Burke, a representative young intellectual of 1923, "is the purest concentration point for the vices and vulgarities of the world." [3] Such a culture demanded defiance; but defiance took the form not of a challenge to its politics or economies, but of an explosion of creative energy.

There were various styles of accommodation. Some chose physical flight — to Greenwich Village, or to the primitivism of Mexico, or to the sophistication of Paris. And those who stayed in the United States had their own forms of flight. On a common level there was the pose of ineffectuality, the average man's defense against an aggressive social order, expressed in the popular images on which the people unloaded their humors and their doubts: Krazy Kat, happy and hopeful, but everlastingly hit by the inevitable brick; Harold Lloyd, ever beset; Keaton, ever baffled; above all, Chaplin as lonesome humanity defying a world which must eventually all but overwhelm him.

On a more literary level, the technique of accommodation through comedy produced satire and fantasy — Lardner, Kaufman, and Hart, or, in a different vein, Cabell, Hergesheimer. The greatest satirical *fantaisiste* of them all, Sinclair Lewis, created a Middle West, stocked it with unforgettable symbols of business domination, and fixed the image of America, not just for the intellectuals of his own generation, but for the world in the next half-century. Or accommodation through escape found Hemingway and Fitzgerald seeking images of grace, courage, and love in the money-ridden world. Or accommodation through revolt — Dreiser, filled with clumsy pity, or Dos Passos, laying bare American life with shallow strokes of a shining surgical knife.

II

The novel was the most available means of resolving sensitive man's relationship to insensitive society; and, in the nonpolitical atmosphere of the twenties, it had a special attraction. Even men whose happier medium was politics now turned to literature. Donald Richberg, it is true, had published novels before. "Writing down an incoherent revolt tends to strengthen it and to make it real," he once said; thus his book of 1911, *The Shadow Men,* a melodramatic indictment of speculation, helped start him on his reform career. But his book of 1922, *A Man of Purpose,* was far more troubled and unhappy, with its bitter attack on business and its pathetic hope for some spiritual infusion, some nobility of purpose, in American life.[4]

William C. Bullitt was another fugitive from politics in fiction. Too restless to lie long on the Riviera, Bullitt had married the widow of John Reed, the Harvard Communist, and plunged into the excitement of the twenties. Between consulting with Freud in Vienna, living magnificently by the Bosporus, and returning occasionally to see the New Era at first hand, he settled old scores in Philadelphia by publishing *It's Not Done* in 1926. It was an agreeable exercise in the comedy of manners, filled with aristocratic contempt for postwar life, where success was defined as futility on the upgrade. "I seem to see," observes one character, "a capering virgin heifer with a blue face, a yellow back, and a buttoned-down tail who nevertheless exudes perpetually a stream of immaculately conceived milk and answers to the name: America." In the end, one character observes, "All we have to look forward to is Raoul's world, I suppose, Communism." The next year Bullitt's fellow townsman Francis Biddle in his graceful novel *The Llanfear Pattern* drew a scathing picture of life "without gaiety and without earnestness, mechanical, content, indifferent."[5] And Biddle could not even console himself with Bullitt's expectations of the future.

III

But this mood of gentlemanly resignation was not enough for the younger generation. They found the stimulus they sought much more in Henry L. Mencken and his comedy of revolt. With his magnificent nonchalance, his superb polemical style, and his uproarious contempt for the business culture, Mencken expressed what they wished they could have thought up about the impossibility of American life. There emerged the portrait of a nation in which the businessman and the farmer — in Menckenese, the booboisie and the Bible belt — had enthroned puritanism and hypocrisy; where the man who liked *potage créole*, Pilsener beer, Rühlander 1903, Brahms, pretty girls, and serious fiction was being suffocated between the Rotarian and the peasant.

It was all very splendid and liberating. But there was in it, not fully perceived, a deeper implication. The cultural pressures against which Mencken inveighed in the name of individual liberty appeared to him on closer examination inseparable from democracy itself. His essays turned into sustained ridicule of the very idea of self-government. Prohibition, censorship, the Klan, whether backed by the swinish rich or by the anthropoid rabble, were the inevitable consequence of the democratic theory.

Democracy, after all, in the end came to nothing but the mob, which was sodden, brutal, and ignorant. "Politics under democracy," said Mencken, "consists almost wholly of the discovery, chase and scotching of bugaboos. The statesman becomes, in the last analysis, a mere witch-hunter, a glorified smeller and snooper, eternally chanting 'Fe, Fi, Fo, Fum.'" Democracy's dominating motive was envy, given the force and dignity of law; the technique was government by orgy, almost by orgasm; in essence, democracy was a combat between jackals and jackasses. "It has become a psychic impossibility for a gentleman to hold office under the Federal Union, save by a combination of miracles that must tax the resourcefulness even of God." Urging more gentlemen to enter politics made no more sense, said Mencken, than to argue that the remedy for prostitution was to fill the bawdyhouses with virgins.

Mencken's typical congressman? "A knavish and preposterous nonentity, half way between a kleagle of the Ku Klux Klan and a grand worthy of the Knights of Zoroaster. It is such vermin who make the laws of the United States." The civil service? "A mere refuge for prehensile morons." Public opinion? The immemorial fears of the mob, "piped to central factories . . . flavoured and coloured, and put into cans." Democratic morality? "When one has written off cruelty, envy and cowardice, one has accounted for nine-tenths of it." The great democratic leaders? These were the most intolerable of all: Bryan, the "Fundamentalist Pope"; T.R., the "national Barbarossa"; Wilson, "the self-bamboozled Presbyterian, the right-thinker, the great moral statesman, the perfect model of the Christian cad." Democracy as a theory? "All the known facts lie flatly against it." [6]

The example of Mencken was devastating. He made interest in social questions ludicrous and unfashionable, democracy itself defensible only as farce. And, while Mencken provoked violent opposition, very little of it concerned itself with his assault on democracy. Indeed, his most formidable critics were, if anything, more vehement than he in their repudiation of democracy. These were the New Humanists, who, rejecting equally the anarchic natur-alism of Mencken, the sentimentality of the liberals, and the philis-tinism of the business community, sought to evoke for the Coolidge era an aristocratic philosophy of self-discipline, standards, *appa-mada*, the "inner check."

Irving Babbitt, the most influential of the New Humanists, ob-jected to the whole modern movement of democracy. He doubted whether universal suffrage was compatible with the degree of safety for property which civilization required; and he had no use for the "sickly sentimentalizing over the lot of the underdog." A real states-man, said Babbitt, would have "died in his tracks" rather than sign, as had Wilson, the Adamson Act establishing an eight-hour day for railroad labor. Laissez faire was little better, making mill operatives mere cannon fodder in the industrial warfare. "The remedy for the evils of competition," said Babbitt, "is found in the moderation and magnanimity of the strong and the successful." And, while he did not pretend to be happy about the choice, circum-stances might well arise, he said, "when we may esteem ourselves fortunate if we get the American equivalent of a Mussolini; he may be needed to save us from the equivalent of a Lenin." [7]

IV

What began as an alienation from business culture was ending in some cases as an alienation from democracy itself. And it was an alienation that provoked no exploration of social alternatives; for there seemed little point in seeking alternatives when the existing order seemed so permanent. Never before in American history had artists and writers felt so impotent in their relation to American society. The business culture wanted nothing from the intellectual, had no use for him, gave him no sustenance. And, once the first gust of creative revolt had blown out, writers themselves began to feel that their sources of vitality were drying up. By 1927, reported Fitzgerald, a widespread neurosis began to be evident; by 1928 even Paris seemed stifling, and the lost generation began to look homeward.

T. S. Eliot, the American poet who had moved to England, a Harvard classmate of Walter Lippmann and John Reed, of Heywood Broun and Hamilton Fish and Bronson Cutting, had perceived the tendency earlier in the decade.

> What are the roots that clutch, what branches grow
> Out of this stony rubbish? Son of man,
> You cannot say, or guess, for you know only
> A heap of broken images, where the sun beats,
> And the dead tree gives no shelter, the cricket no relief,
> And the dry stone no sound of water. . . .
> I will show you fear in a handful of dust.[8]

Was this modern man's destiny — life in the valley of dying stars? shape without form, shade without color, gesture without motion? Two books of 1929 said that it was, and that modern man must come to terms with it.

Walter Lippmann had in his own life described the arc of American liberalism, from Socialism to the New Nationalism to the New Freedom to urbane analyses of public opinion and political psychology. It was a journey away from conviction; and the first chapter of *A Preface to Morals* was appropriately entitled "The Problem of Unbelief." The acids of modernity, Lippmann said, had destroyed the faith that human destiny was in the charge of an omnipotent deity. The test of maturity, he suggested, was when man understood this "vast indifference of the universe to his own fate"; and the problem was how mankind, now deprived of the great fictions, could meet the deep human needs which had made those fictions necessary.

His answer was a personal one — the recovery of moral insight, to be achieved first by disentangling virtue from the traditional religious and metaphysical sanctions, then by encouraging that growth into maturity which would render an authoritarian morality unnecessary. The mature man must take the world as it comes. He "would be strong, not with the strength of hard resolves, but because he was free of that tension which vain expectations beget." Defeat and disappointment would not touch him, for he would be "without compulsion to seize anything and without anxiety as to its fate." Renouncing desire, he would renounce disillusion; renouncing hope, he would renounce despair. In the last sentences of the book, Lippmann summarized his ideal of modern man. "Since nothing gnawed at his vitals, neither doubt nor ambition, nor frustration, nor fear, he would move easily through life. And so whether he saw the thing as comedy, or high tragedy, or plain farce, he would affirm that it is what it is, and that the wise man can enjoy it." [9]

With less eloquence but with even more implacable logic, Joseph Wood Krutch reached similar conclusions. What preoccupied him in *The Modern Temper* was the evident disappearance of animal vitality in modern civilization. Somehow mind itself had reasoned away, one by one, all those fixed points with reference to which life could be organized; science had destroyed faith in moral standards, in human dignity, in life itself. In the view of modern man, wrote Krutch, "there is no reason to suppose that his own life has any more meaning than the life of the humblest insect that crawls from one annihilation to another." For races have been enfeebled by civilization as though by a disease; human virtues could be biologic vices. "Civilizations," said Krutch, "die from philosophical calm, irony and the sense of fair play quite as surely as they die of debauchery."

Krutch was more pessimistic than Lippmann. When civilization became decadent, its hope of rejuvenation lay with the barbarians, who might restore a primitive instinct for survival; possibly the Communists might be the modern equivalent of the Goths and Vandals and, in destroying civilization, would give it the vital energy to rise again. But such hopes would mean little to modern men. "The world may be rejuvenated in one way or another, but we will not. Skepticism has entered too deeply into our souls ever to be replaced by faith." [10]

IV

The Valley of Darkness

19. Crash

BUT THE New Era knew no skepticism. The nation had reached, it seemed, a permanent plateau of prosperity. Business was expanding. Foreign trade was growing. The stock market was continuing to rise. And national leadership could not now be in more expert or safer hands. "For the first time in our history," wrote Foster and Catchings, "we have a President who, by technical training, engineering achievement, cabinet experience, and grasp of economic fundamentals, is qualified for business leadership." "I have no fears for the future of our country," said Herbert Hoover in his inaugural address in March 1929. "It is bright with hope." [1]

There remained a few discordant voices, anxious in the main over the stock market boom. But the President regarded agricultural relief and tariff revision as the more pressing questions. In the spring of 1929, he summoned a special session of the Congress to deal with these issues. The session was not a success. Hoover's agricultural program did not satisfy the farm bloc, though Congress, after vehement debate, adopted the President's recommendations and set up a new agency, the Federal Farm Board. The Board's purpose was to control the flow of commodities to the market; one provision authorized the establishment of stabilization corporations as a means of controlling temporary surpluses. Then the session, after wrangling from April to November, adjourned without taking action on the tariff.

In other respects, Hoover as President tried to apply the policies he had developed as Secretary of Commerce. In August 1929, he moved into the conservation field, proposing that the unreserved public lands, as well as all new reclamation projects and related irrigation matters, be withdrawn from national control. The states, he said, were "more competent to manage much of these affairs than is the Federal Government," and his aim was to place the local communities — and presumably the strongest interests in them — in control of their own natural resources. "Well," remarked one newspaper, "conservation was a pretty dream while it lasted." [2]

The President's attitude toward utilities regulation was similar. Certain that state regulation and private responsibility were enough, he had no misgivings about making the statutory appointment of the Secretary of War, James W. Good, the former counsel for the Alabama Power Company, as head of the Federal Power Commission. When the Commission was reorganized in 1930, staff members whose zeal had irritated the utilities were discharged; one of them, the former solicitor of the Commission, told the press that Hoover had personally intervened to prevent the rigorous application of the Federal Water Power Act to the private companies. [3]

II

Yet most Americans remained more interested in the stock market than in any other economic question; and for a few interest was now beginning to turn into concern. Early in 1929, the Federal Reserve Board, under continuing pressure from the New York Federal Reserve Bank, finally consented to warn member banks that they should not lend money for speculative purposes. But this reliance on moral suasion did not satisfy conservative members of the financial community, like Dr. Adolph Miller of the Board, Paul M. Warburg of Kuhn, Loeb, and Russell Leffingwell of Morgan's. Such men wanted the Board to slow down the boom by raising the discount rate to 6 per cent.

Expansionists like Foster and Catchings, however, argued that a restrictive policy might well induce deflation. The Board had already, they felt, created "a state of mind which breeds depression." [4] And it was certainly true that reducing the interest rate was a clumsy way of combatting the boom. So long as the stock market offered the highest returns, it was bound to have first call on funds. In the short run, a higher interest rate might thus slow down real investment faster than speculation. And in the longer run, a higher interest rate would tend, through the capitalization process, to bring down the prices of all capital assets and thus to discourage real investment even further. And so the debate continued through the spring and summer. The President, preoccupied with other issues and not clear in his own mind whether he wanted to stop the easy-money policy, did little but watch the Board in its vacillating course.

By the summer of 1929 some danger signs were apparent — for example, the startling decline in building contracts. Net investment for residential construction for the entire year sank to $216 million, over a billion dollars less than 1928. At the same time, there was an alarming growth in business inventories, more than trebling from $500 million in 1928 to $1800 million in 1929. Concurrently, the rate of consumer spending was slackening; it had risen at a rate of 7.4 per cent in 1927–28 but slowed down to an inauspicious 1.5 per cent in 1928–29.[5]

By midsummer 1929, these developments began to be discernible in production and price indexes. Industrial production reached its height in June and dropped off in July; employment rose till July, building began to fall off, and, week after week, wholesale commodity prices dropped with ominous regularity. In August the Federal Reserve Board strengthened deflationary tendencies by finally agreeing to raise the discount rate to 6 per cent.

But the stock market, riding on the impetus of half a dozen years of steady increase, paid little attention to the indexes. Early in September Stock Exchange price averages reached their highest point of all time. A.T. & T. was up to 304; General Electric up to 396, having more than tripled its price in eighteen months. By the beginning of October, brokers' loans — an index of margin buying — topped the $6 billion mark. Business leaders meanwhile competed with each other in expressions of optimism, and Washington displayed no concern.

III

September saw some minor setbacks. Yet through October brokers looked optimistically ahead to the moment when stocks would resume their upward climb. Then on Wednesday, October 23, there was an unexpected and drastic break, with securities suddenly unloaded in quantity, prices falling, and acute pressure on margin traders. For a moment, Wall Street was shaken, and the anxiety was suddenly infectious. The next day, selling orders began to stream down on the Stock Exchange in unprecedented volume, and prices took a frightening plunge. For a few ghastly moments the Exchange saw stocks on sale for which there were no buyers at any price. As panic spread, the Exchange decided to close the visitors' gallery; among the observers that morning had been the former British Chancellor of the Exchequer, Winston S. Churchill. The tickers fell helplessly behind in recording transactions on the floor; and, as the confusion communicated itself through the country, the instinct to unload threatened to turn into a frenzy. Down, down, down: how long could the market take it?

Around noon a group of worried men gathered in the office of Thomas W. Lamont of Morgan's; it included four of New York's great bankers (among them, Charles E. Mitchell of the National City Bank and Albert H. Wiggin of the Chase). Each was prepared to contribute $40 million on behalf of their banks to bolster the market. An hour or so later Richard Whitney, a broker for Morgan's and vice-president of the Exchange, walked onto the floor to bid 205 for 25,000 shares of U.S. Steel, then available at 193½. For a moment, backed by the bankers' pool, stability seemed to return.

The next day came a torrent of reassuring statements — from bankers, from economists, from the Treasury Department, above all, from the White House itself. "The fundamental business of the country," said President Hoover, "that is, production and distribution of commodities, is on a sound and prosperous basis." And, as prices held for the rest of the week, the bankers quietly fed back into the market the stocks they had bought on Black Thursday, strengthening their own position against further storms. (Whitney had not even bought the U.S. Steel stock; the gesture of bidding was enough.)

The weekend gave the forces of fear and liquidation time to do their work. As the banks had protected themselves against the brokers, so the brokers now sought to protect themselves against their customers, and especially against those they were carrying on the margin. The result on Monday was a new outburst of forced sales, a new explosion of gloom and panic. On that day alone, General Motors stock lost nearly $2 billion in paper value. The market closed with foreboding. The next day the Exchange had barely opened when the rout began. Soon it was like an avalanche, vast numbers rushing to get out of the market with whatever could be salvaged from the general debacle. Brokers sold stock at any price they could get. By noon 8 million shares had changed hands; by closing time, the Exchange had broken all records with an unprecedented 16 million shares. During the day, the governors of the Exchange had called a meeting, crowding into a secluded office, sitting and standing on tables, lighting cigarettes and nervously discarding them till the room was stale with smoke. Most wanted to close the Exchange. But the governors decided that it must be kept open.

For a moment October 30 — Wednesday — brought new hope. The newspapers were once again plastered with optimism: Dr. Julius Klein, the President's personal economic soothsayer, John D. Rockefeller, John J. Raskob, all beamed with confidence about the future. As prices steadied, Richard Whitney took advantage of the interval of calm to announce that the Exchange would be open only briefly on Thursday and not at all for the rest of the week. But the flickering hope of stabilization turned out to be the final delusion. *Variety* summed it up in the headline of its issue on October 30: WALL ST. LAYS AN EGG.

When the Exchange reopened the next week, the downward grind resumed, leaving in its wake a trail of exploded values. By mid-November the financial community began to survey the wreckage. In a few incredible weeks, the stocks listed on the New York exchange had fallen over 40 per cent in value — a loss on paper of $26 billion. The New Era had come to its dismaying end.[6]

IV

As perspective has enabled economists to disentangle the causes of the collapse, the following points have come to seem most crucial:

1) Management's disposition to maintain prices and inflate profits while holding down wages and raw material prices meant that workers and farmers were denied the benefits of increases in their own productivity. The consequence was the relative decline of mass

purchasing power. As goods flowed out of the expanding capital plant in ever greater quantities, there was proportionately less and less cash in the hands of buyers to carry the goods off the market. The pattern of income distribution, in short, was incapable of long maintaining prosperity.

2) Seven years of fixed capital investment at high rates had "over-built" productive capacity (in terms of existing capacity to consume) and had thus saturated the economy. The slackening of the automotive and building industries was symptomatic. The existing rate of capital formation could not be sustained without different governmental policies — policies aimed not at helping those who had money to accumulate more but at transferring money from those who were letting it stagnate in savings to those who would spend it.

3) The sucking off into profits and dividends of the gains of technology meant the tendency to use excess money for speculation, transforming the Stock Exchange from a securities market into a gaming-house.

4) The stock market crash completed the debacle. After Black Thursday, what rule was safe except *Sauve qui peut?* And businessmen, in trying to save themselves, could only wreck their system; in trying to avoid the worst, they rendered the worst inevitable. By shattering confidence, the crash knocked out any hope of automatic recovery.

5) In sum, the federal government had encouraged tax policies that contributed to oversaving, monetary policies that were expansive when prices were rising and deflationary when prices began to fall, tariff policies that left foreign loans as the only prop for the export trade, and policies toward monopoly which fostered economic concentration, introduced rigidity into the markets and anaesthetized the price system. Representing the businessmen, the federal government had ignored the dangerous imbalance between farm and business income, between the increase in wages and the increase in productivity. Representing the financiers, it had ignored irresponsible practices in the securities market. Representing the bankers, it had ignored the weight of private debt and the profound structural weaknesses in the banking and financial system. Seeing all problems from the viewpoint of business, it had mistaken the class interest for the national interest. The result was both class and national disaster.

20. The New Era at Bay

FOR EIGHT and a half years, first as Secretary of Commerce, then as President, Herbert Hoover had a unique opportunity to study the workings and influence the policies of the American business system. No one was better placed to anticipate catastrophe. And, unless it was to be assumed that depression was inevitable under capitalism, one must assume that the depression of 1929 could have been averted by wise national policy. But if in these eight and a half years Hoover was concerned about the lag of purchasing power, about inadequate returns to farmers and workers, about regressive tax policies, about reckless stock market practices, about the piling up of private debt, about the defects of the banking system, then his concern never impelled him to effective action. And in many fields in which he did act — such as the expansion of foreign loans, the promotion of installment purchase at home, the support of economic concentration, the opposition to farm relief — his action accelerated the tendencies that caused the disaster.

Yet the fault was not Hoover's. He remained the most high-minded of the New Era leaders in the age of business. A handful of businessmen, it is true, had mumbled doubts. Paul Warburg had issued warnings. Charles G. Dawes, Vice-President under Coolidge, noted in his diary after the crash, "To me it seems that the signs of the coming of the present catastrophe were more pronounced than those of any other through which the United States had passed." [1] But such men were in the minority. Even men like Lamont of · Morgan's believed their own propaganda about the New Era.

Democratic businessmen were as fallible as Republican. In the spring of 1929 Bernard Baruch assured the readers of the *American Magazine* that they need no longer worry about the business cycle. Through the summer and fall hardly a week passed without some new dose of optimism from the chairman of the Democratic National Committee. Some obstinate dissenters had private doubts; but in the age of confidence doubt had to be phrased with caution. Thus in August 1929, Franklin D. Roosevelt, with a skeptical glance at "those business circles which can only see a fifty per cent. increase in prosperity and values for every year that goes by between now and the year 2000," warily asked a banker friend, "Do you still feel as I do that there may be a limit to the increase of security values?" 2 But Roosevelt assigned no date for the leveling-off. Even the radicals, confident of the collapse of capitalism in some far-off millennium, had no suspicion that depression might be just around the corner.

Nor, indeed, did many recognize the dimensions of the catastrophe. Andrew Mellon, who had little use for New York banks, said concisely to Hoover, "They deserved it." These "recent fluctuations," said Robert P. Lamont, Hoover's successor in the Commerce Department, would only "curtail the buying power, especially of luxuries, of those who suffered losses in the market crash. There are present today," Lamont added reassuringly, "*none* of the underlying factors which have been associated with or have preceded the declines in business in the past." Even the liberal publicist Stuart Chase regarded the stock market decline as a wholesome shakedown of inflated values. "We probably have three more years of prosperity ahead of us," said Chase, "before we enter the cyclic tailspin." 3

The businessmen of the nation agreed. Nor did the fall in employment in November and December seem any particular ground for alarm.

Things are better today [November 4, 1929] than they were yesterday.
— *Henry Ford*

Never before has American business been as firmly entrenched for prosperity as it is today [December 10, 1929].
— *Charles M. Schwab, Chairman of the Board, Bethlehem Steel*

Viewed in the longer perspective, the collapse of the inflated
price structure may be correctly regarded as a favorable
development from the point of view of general business.

> — *Editor of the* Guaranty Survey *of the*
> Guaranty Trust Company *of New York*

There are no great business failures, nor are there likely to
be. . . . Conditions are more favorable for permanent prosperity than they have been in the past year.

> — *George E. Roberts, Vice-President,*
> *National City Bank of New York*

I can observe little on the horizon today to give us undue or
great concern.

> — *John E. Edgerton, President, National*
> *Association of Manufacturers* [4]

II

But the President was somewhat more apprehensive. He feared
that the crash might induce a general wave of contraction and panic;
and he conceived it his duty to assume leadership in checking downward tendencies. "Liquidate labor, liquidate stocks, liquidate the
farmers, liquidate real estate," the Secretary of the Treasury had
said; his only cure was to let economic forces run their downward
course as they had in '73.[5] But Hoover, convinced that the economy was basically sound, saw no reason for bringing misery to every
sector of society. Where laissez-faire policy would call for putting
the whole structure of prices and costs through the wringer, the
New Era philosophy called for the maintenance of price levels and
of spending. If this could be done, Hoover reasoned, then the stock
market crash could be contained.

He unfolded his program in a series of conferences with business
and community leaders in the next weeks. Through voluntary
pledges from industry, he hoped to maintain wage rates and sta-
bilize industrial prices. Through understandings with industry and
local governments, he hoped to continue capital expansion and
public building at a normal pace. Through Federal Reserve policy,
he planned to make credit abundant for business borrowers.
Through the Federal Farm Board, he aimed to prop up the agri-

cultural sector. Through an upward revision of the tariff, he could protect American industry against foreign competition. And, with these policies under way, he hoped through persuasive exhortation and wise counsel to restore business confidence.

Of these policies, only tariff revision required new legislation. The special session of 1929 having failed on the tariff, the preparation of a new bill became the main business of Congress in the months immediately after the crash. The task was in the charge of two fervent protectionists, Senator Reed Smoot of Utah and Congressman Willis C. Hawley of Oregon, determined to attain for the United States "a high degree of self-sufficiency" (Smoot), to make the nation "self-contained and self-sustaining" (Hawley). In many respects, it was an audacious effort. When Paul Douglas drafted a statement denouncing the bill, he was able to obtain the signatures of a thousand members of the American Economic Association in ten days. But academic disapproval could not embarrass the protectionist faith. "If this bill is passed," said the Republican leader of the Senate, Jim Watson of Indiana, "this nation will be on the upgrade, financially, economically and commercially within thirty days, and within a year from this date we shall have regained the peak of prosperity." When Congress enacted the Smoot-Hawley law, President Hoover signed it with six gold pens, saying that "nothing" would so retard business recovery as continued agitation over the tariff.[6]

III

As the first months passed after the crash, the administration viewed the future without visible alarm. At the turn of the year Secretary Mellon observed, "I see nothing in the present situation that is either menacing or warrants pessimism." In late January President Hoover announced that the unemployment trend had already been reversed; and early in February Secretary Lamont said that production and distribution were at normal levels; "there is nothing in the situation to be disturbed about." At the same time the Employment Service declared that "within the next sixty or ninety days the country will be on a normal employment basis," and Dr. Julius Klein exulted in the *American Magazine*, "It's Great

To Be a Young Man Today." On March 4 Lamont, in a meteorological mood, was certain that "as weather conditions moderate, we are likely to find the country as a whole enjoying its wonted state of prosperity." On March 7, in his most detailed statement on the economic situation, the President declared that unemployment, such as it was, was concentrated in twelve states; that "employment had been slowly increasing" since the low point in December; that business and the state governments were spending more for construction even than in 1929. "*All* the evidences," he said, "indicate that the worst effects of the crash upon unemployment will have been passed during the next sixty days." [7]

Hoover's position was not an easy one. He had rightly decided he could not indulge in a public pessimism that would only feed the panic. His fault lay not in taking an optimistic line, but in bending the facts to sustain his optimism,[8] and then in believing his own conclusions. For, despite the presidential exhortations, private spending was simply not maintaining 1929 levels. Despite the presidential cheer, unemployment was increasing. The leaders of business, for all their pledges, were finding it impossible to collaborate in pegging the economy. The solemn meetings of the fall, with their professions of common purpose, had turned out to be exercises in ceremonial — "no-business meetings," in J. K. Galbraith's phrase. "There has been more 'optimism' talked and less practiced," said Will Rogers, "than at any time during our history." Some Republican leaders even began to scent conspiracy in business reactions. "Every time an administration official gives out an optimistic statement about business conditions," complained Senator Simeon Fess of Ohio, chairman of the Republican National Committee, "the market immediately drops." [9]

The crucial period when a small amount of spending might have checked the cumulative forces of breakdown had already slipped by. But Hoover found in pledges an acceptable substitute for actions; assurances given took the place of dollars spent. "Our joint undertaking," he said, on May 1, 1930, before the United States Chamber of Commerce, "has succeeded to a remarkable degree." The intensity of the slump "has been greatly diminished." "I am convinced," Hoover said, "we have now passed the worst and with continued unity of effort we shall rapidly recover." [10]

21. The Contagion of Fear

ON THE DAY before President Hoover said that all the evidence promised substantial recovery in sixty days, a group of unemployed men and women, organized by the Communist party, staged a demonstration before the White House. For a moment the President stared curiously through the window. Later the police, blackjacks in their hands, routed the crowd with tear-gas bombs. In New York City on the same day 35,000 men and women gathered to hear Communist orators in Union Square. When the Communist leader William Z. Foster called for a march on City Hall, the Police Commissioner issued sharp orders. Hundreds of policemen and detectives, swinging nightsticks, blackjacks, and bare fists, charged the crowd. The scene resounded, the *New York Times* reported, with "screams of women and cries of men with bloody heads and faces. A score of men were sprawled over the square, with policemen pummeling them." One cop, in civilian clothes, wearing a sheepskin coat and carrying a long yellow nightstick, ran wildly through the square, striking out in all directions. Two policemen pinioned a girl by the arms and smashed her face with clubs. A woman wailed, "Cossacks, murderous Cossacks." [1]

March 6 was, by Communist decree, International Unemployment Day. The purpose of the demonstrations was to provoke police violence. In one city after another they achieved this purpose. But Communist agitation alone could not explain the impact of the riots. When else in America had Communists ever attracted crowds of 35,000? A gap was opening between the official mood in Washington and the human reality in city streets and in the countryside — between the presidential vision of accelerating private construction, declining unemployment, mounting confidence, and the actuality of privation and fear.

By the spring of 1930 at least 4,000,000 Americans were unemployed. Breadlines began to reappear in large cities for the first time since 1921 — lines of embarrassed men, shuffling patiently forward for a chance at a piece of bread and a cup of coffee. In New York City it was reported in March that the number of families on relief had increased 200 per cent since the crash in October. The municipal lodging houses were now crowded; nearly half of the first 14,000 admitted were first-timers; and the city was letting homeless men sleep on the municipal barge as it tied up at the dock at night, where the icy wind whipped across the East River. In Detroit, said William Green of the A.F. of L., "the men are sitting in the parks all day long and all night long, hundreds and thousands of them, muttering to themselves, out of work, seeking work." [2]

II

Across the country the dismal process was beginning, ushering in a new life for millions of Americans. In the twenties wage earners in general had found ample employment, satisfaction in life, hope for the future. Now came the slowdown — only three days of work a week, then perhaps two, then the layoff. And then the search for a new job — at first vigorous and hopeful; then sober; then desperate; the long lines before the employment offices, the eyes straining for words of hope on the chalked boards, the unending walk from one plant to the next, the all-night wait to be first for possible work in the morning. And the inexorable news, brusque impersonality concealing fear: "No help wanted here" . . . "We don't need nobody" . . . "Move along, Mac, move along."

And so the search continued, as clothes began to wear out and shoes to fall to pieces. Newspapers under the shirt would temper the winter cold, pasteboard would provide new inner soles, cotton in the heels of the shoe would absorb the pounding on the pavement, gunny sacks wrapped around the feet would mitigate the long hours in the frozen fields outside the factory gates. And in the meantime savings were trickling away. By now the terror began to infect the family. Father, no longer cheery, now at home for long hours, irritable, guilty, a little frightened. Sometimes the mother looked for work as domestic, chambermaid or charwoman; or the children worked for pennies after school, not understanding the fear that was touching them, knowing that they must do what they could to help buy bread and coffee.

As savings end, borrowing begins. If there is life insurance, borrowing on that, until it lapses; then loans from relatives and from friends; then the life of credit, from the landlord, from the corner grocer, until the lines of friendship and compassion are snapped. Meat vanishes from the table; lard replaces butter; father goes out less often, is terribly quiet; the children begin to lack shoes, their clothes are ragged, their mothers are ashamed to send them to school. Wedding rings are pawned, furniture is sold, the family moves into ever cheaper, damper, dirtier rooms. In a Philadelphia settlement house a little boy of three cried constantly in the spring of 1930; the doctor examined him and found that he was slowly starving. One woman complained that when she had food her two small children could barely eat; they had become accustomed to so little, she said, that their stomachs had shrunk. In November the apple peddlers began to appear on cold street corners, their threadbare clothes brushed and neat, their forlorn pluckiness emphasizing the anguish of being out of work. And every night that fall hundreds of men gathered on the lower level of Wacker Drive in Chicago, feeding fires with stray pieces of wood, their coat collars turned up against the cold, their caps pulled down over their ears, staring without expression at the black river, while above the automobiles sped comfortably along, bearing well-fed men to warm and well-lit homes. In the mining areas families lived on beans, without salt or fat. And every week, every day, more workers joined the procession of despair. The shadows deepened in the dark cold rooms, with the father angry and helpless and ashamed, the distraught children too often hungry or sick, and the mother, so resolute by day, so often, when the room was finally still, lying awake in bed at night, softly crying.[3]

III

This was 1930; it was, in Elmer Davis's phrase, the Second Year of the Abolition of Poverty. And it introduced thousands of Americans to a new and humiliating mode of existence — life on the relief rolls. Most of the unemployed held out as long as they could. But, with savings gone, credit exhausted, work unobtainable, there seemed no alternative save to subdue pride and face reality.

The system was, in the main, one of local poor relief, supplemented by the resources of private welfare agencies. Even in 1929 public funds paid three-quarters of the nation's relief bill; by 1932, the proportion rose to four-fifths. In larger cities, the social workers had had some success in improving standards of relief care, replacing the old "overseers of the poor" by public welfare departments. But in smaller communities, there was often no alternative to the poorhouse. And the whole patchwork system had an underlying futility: it was addressed to the care of unemployables — those who could not work in any condition — and not at all to the relief of mass unemployment.[4]

No other modern nation had in 1930 such feeble and confused provisions for the jobless. But the President had no doubt about the adequacy of the system for the winter of 1930–31. He told the American Federal of Labor in October that his antidepression policies had had astonishing success, and that workingmen should find inspiration in the devotion "of our great manufacturers, our railways, utilities, business houses, and public officials." Later in the month, rebuking those who were demanding a special session of Congress, the President reaffirmed his confidence that the nation's "sense of voluntary organization and community service" could take care of the unemployed.[5]

Yet, a week before, he had appointed an Emergency Committee for Employment under the direction of Colonel Arthur Woods, who had been active in the relief field during the depression of 1921. Hoover was reluctant to do even this, fearing that such action would magnify the emergency; and he informed the Committee that unemployment was strictly a local responsibility.[6] The Committee's function in consequence became that of advice and exhortation. Colonel Woods, a man of vigor, wanted to do more.

He submitted to the President a draft message to Congress calling for a public works program, including slum clearance, low-cost housing, and rural electrification. Woods and his Committee also favored Senator Robert F. Wagner's bills proposing the advance planning of public works and setting up a national employment service. But the President, rejecting the Woods program, addressed Congress with his usual optimism. Getting nowhere, Woods saw the Committee through the winter and resigned in April 1931.[7]

Other events began to define the President's position. In the summer of 1930 a prolonged drought killed cattle and crops throughout the Southwest. This was Hoover's sort of problem — Belgium all over again, so much more concrete than the irritating and intangible issues of depression. "To overcoming the drought," reported Mark Sullivan, Hoover's intimate among the newspapermen, "President Hoover turned with something like a sense of relief, almost of pleasure." [8] With echoes of his old confidence, he organized a program of assistance and asked Congress to appropriate money for government loans to enable farmers to buy seed, fertilizer, and cattle feed.

Democratic senators promptly sought to apply the Hoover program to human beings as well as livestock. Thus the old Wilsonian, William G. McAdoo, now senator from California, suggested that wheat purchased by the Farm Board be distributed to the unemployed. But Hoover reaffirmed his unwavering opposition to such proposals. The opposition, fighting back, taunted the President without mercy. He considered it wise to feed starving cattle, they said, but wicked to feed starving men, women, and children. He had fed the Belgians and the Germans, but would not feed his own countrymen. Hurt and distressed, the President, in February 1931, issued a deeply felt statement. If America meant anything, he suggested, it meant the principles of individual and local responsibility and mutual self-help. If we break down these principles, we "have struck at the roots of self-government." Should federal aid be the only alternative to starvation, then federal aid we must have; but "I have faith in the American people that such a day shall not come." [9]

IV

And so the nation staggered into the second winter of the depression, and unemployment began to settle into a way of life.
The weather was glorious much of the winter — clear, light air,
brilliant sunlight, dry, frosty snow. But the cold was bitter in un-
heated tenements, in the flophouses smelling of sweat and Lysol,
in the parks, in empty freight cars, along the windy waterfronts.
With no money left for rent, unemployed men and their entire
families began to build shacks where they could find unoccupied
land. Along the railroad embankment, beside the garbage incin-
erator, in the city dumps, there appeared towns of tarpaper and
tin, old packing boxes and old car bodies. Some shanties were
neat and scrubbed; cleanliness at least was free; but others were
squalid beyond belief, with the smell of decay and surrender. Symbols of the New Era, these communities quickly received their
sardonic name: they were called Hoovervilles. And, indeed, it was
in many cases only the fortunate who could find Hoovervilles. The
unfortunate spent their nights huddled together in doorways, in
empty packing cases, in boxcars.

At the breadlines and soup kitchens, hours of waiting would
produce a bowl of mush, often without milk or sugar, and a tin
cup of coffee. The vapors from the huge steam cookers mingling
with the stench of wet clothes and sweating bodies made the air
foul. But waiting in the soup kitchen was better than the scaveng-
ing in the dump. Citizens of Chicago, in this second winter,
could be seen digging into heaps of refuse with sticks and hands
as soon as the garbage trucks pulled out. On June 30, 1931, the
Pennsylvania Department of Labor and Industry reported that
nearly one-quarter of the labor force of the state was out of work.
Clarence Pickett of the Friends found schools where 85, 90, even
99 per cent of the children were underweight, and, in consequence,
drowsy and lethargic. "Have you ever heard a hungry child cry?"
asked Lillian Wald of Henry Street. "Have you seen the uncontrollable trembling of parents who have gone half starved for
weeks so that the children may have food?" [10]

And still unemployment grew — from 4,000,000 in March 1930
to 8,000,000 in March 1931. And, more and more, the community

found the relief problem beyond its capacity to handle. Local fiscal sources were drying up; local credit was vanishing; towns and counties found they could tax or borrow less and less. Some states had constitutional prohibitions against the use of state funds for home relief. And states too were on the verge of exhausting their tax possibilities; the general property tax had almost reached its limit, and, as income fell, the income tax, for the few states that had it, brought in declining amounts.

The burdens of private charity were meanwhile falling ever more heavily on the poor themselves. Emergency relief committees talked virtuously of the staggering of work and the "sharing" of jobs. But men working a day less a week to provide jobs for other workers were obviously contributing a portion of their own meager wages to relief while their employers contributed nothing. And, even when employers joined in company campaigns of voluntary donations, it was too often under the principle used in the Insull group, by which all, whether top executives or unskilled workers, threw in one days pay a month. The real recipients of the dole, wrote Professor Sumner H. Slichter of Harvard, were not the men lining up to receive a nickel from the Franciscan Fathers, but "the great industries of America," paying part of their labor overhead by taxing the wages of their employees.[11]

As the number of unemployed grew, the standards of relief care declined. More and more it seemed as if the burden was too great for individual communities to carry longer. In the fall of 1931 Governor Franklin D. Roosevelt of New York established a state emergency relief administration; other states followed this example. Effective relief, said William Allen White in September 1931, would be "the only way to keep down barricades in the streets this winter and the use of force which will brutalize labor and impregnate it with revolution in America for a generation." [12]

v

But President Hoover announced that a nation-wide survey had convinced him that state and local organizations could meet relief needs in the coming winter. Giving ground slightly, he then appointed a new committee to supersede the old Woods committee.

This was the President's Organization on Unemployment Relief, headed by Walter S. Gifford, president of the American Telephone and Telegraph Company. Gifford accepted the thesis of local responsibility with far more enthusiasm than Woods; and his main contribution was an advertising campaign designed to stimulate private charity. "Between October 18 and November 25," said Gifford and Owen D. Young in a joint statement, "America will feel the thrill of a great spiritual experience." Charity, the campaign hopefully suggested, could even inspire a new love between husband and wife.

On matters which might have fallen more directly within his responsibility, Gifford displayed indifference. Early in January 1932, after nearly five months in office, Gifford appeared before a committee of the Senate. There, under the incredulous questions of Robert M. La Follette, Jr., of Wisconsin and Edward P. Costigan of Colorado, Gifford disclosed imperturbably that he did not know how many people were idle, that he did not know how many were receiving aid, that he did not know what the standards of assistance were in the various states, that he did not know how much money had been raised in his own campaign, that he knew nothing of the ability of local communities to raise relief funds either through borrowing or taxation, that he did not know what relief needs were either in urban or rural areas, that he did not consider most of this information as of much importance to his job; but that, just the same, he had no question in his mind as to the capacity of the communities to meet the relief problem. "I hope you are not criticizing me for looking at life optimistically," he said plaintively. And, when Costigan asked him to supply the committee with the reports on which his optimism was based, Gifford replied, "I have none, Senator."

But on one question Gifford was clear: he was against federal aid. Should we not be concerned, asked La Follette, if the people in Philadelphia were receiving inadequate aid? As human beings, yes, said Gifford, adding incoherently, "but whether we should be concerned in the Federal Government officially with it, unless it is so bad it is obviously scandalous, and even then we would not be obliged to be concerned. I think there is grave danger in taking the determination of these things into the Federal Government."

Federal aid, he said, would lessen the sense of local responsibility; it would reduce the size of private charity. His "sober and considered judgment" was that federal aid would be a "disservice" to the jobless; "the net result might well be that the unemployed who are in need would be worse instead of better off." [13]

And so, through the winter of 1931–32, the third winter of the depression, relief resources, public and private, dwindled toward the vanishing point. In few cities was there any longer pretense of meeting minimum budgetary standards. Little money was available for shoes or clothing, for medical or dental care, for gas or electricity. In New York City entire families were getting an average of $2.39 a week for relief. In Toledo the municipal commissary could allow only 2.14 cents per meal per person per day. In vast rural areas there was no relief coverage at all. "I don't want to steal," a Pennsylvania man wrote Governor Pinchot, "but I won't let my wife and boy cry for something to eat. . . . How long is this going to keep up? I cannot stand it any longer. . . . O, if God would only open a way." [14]

VI

The shadow fell over the cities and towns; it fell as heavily over the countryside. Farmers had already drawn extensively on their savings before 1929. The Wall Street explosion only made their situation worse by diminishing even more the demand for farm products. And, where industry could protect its price structure by meeting reduced demand with reduced output, farmers, unable to control output, saw no way to maintain income except to increase planting. Total crop acreage actually rose in 1930 and showed no significant decline in 1931.

The burden of agricultural adjustment thus fell not on production but on price. The figures were dramatic. Between 1929 and 1934 agricultural production declined 15 per cent in volume, 40 per cent in price; industrial production 42 per cent in volume, 15 per cent in price.[15] The relative stability of industrial prices worsened the farmers' terms of trade; the ratio of the prices the farmer received to the prices he paid plunged from 109 in 1919 (in terms of 1910–14 prices) and 89 in 1929 to 64 in 1931.[16] Corn slid down to 15 cents, cotton and wool to 5 cents, hogs and sugar to 3 cents, and beef to 2.5 cents. A farmer who chewed one thick plug of Drummond a day required almost a bushel of wheat a day to keep him in chewing tobacco. It took 16 bushels of wheat — more than the average yield of a whole acre — to buy one of his children a pair of $4 shoes. Net farm income in 1932 was $1.8 billion — less than one-third what it had been three years earlier. So appalling a slump left many farm families with little income, and many with no income at all.

The farmer's obligations — his taxes and his debts — had been calculated in terms of the much higher price levels of the twenties. A cotton farmer who borrowed $800 when cotton was 16 cents a pound borrowed the equivalent of 5000 pounds of cotton; now, with cotton moving toward 5 cents, he must pay back the debt with over 15,000 pounds of cotton. And, while the farmer's income fell by 64 per cent, his burden of indebtedness fell a mere 7 per cent.[17] In the meantime, fences were standing in disrepair, crops were rotting, livestock was not worth the freight to market, farm machinery was wearing out. Some found it cheaper to burn their corn than to sell it and buy coal. On every side, notices of mortgage foreclosures and tax sales were going up on gate posts and in county courthouses. William Allen White summed it up: "Every farmer, whether his farm is under mortgage or not, knows that with farm products priced as they are today, sooner or later he must go down." [18]

The southwestern drought only intensified the sense of grievance. In January 1931, several hundred tenant farmers presented themselves at the Red Cross in England, Arkansas, and asked for food. They included whites and Negroes, and some carried rifles. When the Red Cross administrator said that his supply of requisition blanks had been exhausted, the mob marched on the stores and seized their own flour and lard. "Paul Revere just woke up Concord," said Will Rogers, "these birds woke up America." (A New York Communist wrote a short story based on newspaper reports of the incident. Lincoln Steffens, reading Whittaker Chambers's "Can You Hear Their Voices?" wrote the young author, "Whenever I hear people talking about 'proletarian art and literature,' I'm going to ask them to . . . look at you.") [19]

A. N. Young, president of the Wisconsin Farmers' Union, warned the Senate Agriculture Committee early in 1932: "The farmer is naturally a conservative individual, but you cannot find a conservative farmer today. He is not to be found. I am as conservative as any man could be, but any economic system that has it in its power to set me and my wife in the streets, at my age — what else could I see but red."

"The fact is today," Young told the Committee, "that there are more actual reds among the farmers in Wisconsin than you could dream about. . . . They are just ready to do anything to get even with the situation. I almost hate to express it, but I honestly believe that if some of them could buy airplanes, they would come down here to Washington to blow you fellows all up." [20]

VII

In country and city alike, anger was spreading. Edward F. McGrady, the conservative representative of the conservative American Federation of Labor, was testifying before a Senate committee in the spring of 1932. "The leaders of our organization," said Ed McGrady bitterly, "have been preaching patience." But preaching could not take the place of bread. "I say to you gentlemen, advisedly, that if something is not done and starvation is going to continue the doors of revolt in this country are going to be thrown open." Let the administration stop crying to the world that the most important thing to be done is to balance the budget. "There are another two B's besides balancing the Budget, and that is to provide bread and butter."

If the administration, said Ed McGrady, refused "to allow Congress to provide food for these people until they do secure work, as far as I am personally concerned, I would do nothing to close the doors of revolt if it starts.

"I say that as a man, as a citizen of the United States.

"It would not be a revolt against the Government but against the administration." [21]

22. Business at the Great Divide

It was a business country, Calvin Coolidge had said, and it wanted a business government. And the men of business, who in the twenties had been the men of power, could not believe that their age was over. With tedious regularity, they predicted economic revival. "Recognizing the presence of some unfavorable elements, and the necessity of a little time for needed readjustments . . . by early spring there should be definite signs of a turn. . . . 1930 will stand out as a year of unusual stability. . . . Renewed business expansion may be anticipated during the second half. . . . The last half should be marked by rapid recovery in every direction." In the spring Charles M. Schwab, the steel manufacturer, observed that business was "a lot healthier today" than it had been six or nine months earlier, and that "all present indications are that 1930, in broad perspective, will prove to be a year of normal business progress." In September, the president of the National Association of Manufacturers agreed with President Hoover that "the overshadowing problem of all problems is crime, which bestrides our nation like a colossus." Dr. Julius Klein, after conducting a poll of bank directors, announced that two-thirds had picked October as the turning point, and the rest had set the time as the following January. "The peak of the depression passed thirty days ago," said James A. Farrell of U.S. Steel in January 1931.[1]

After all, businessmen reasoned, the economy had survived depression before. "There is nothing very unnatural about conditions that now exist," said the president of the N.A.M.; "we have had at least seventeen of these cycles of depressions in the last 120 years," said the president of the United States Chamber of Commerce. "So long as we live under a system of individual liberty," said Charles E. Mitchell of the National City Bank, "we are bound to have fluctuations in business." "I think the best way to get rid of business cycles," wrote the wise Dwight Morrow, "would be to prove that they are inevitable." "You are always going to have, once in so many years, difficulties in business, times that are prosperous and times that are not prosperous," said Albert H. Wiggin of the Chase. "There is no commission or any brain in the world that can prevent it." Senator La Follette, startled, asked Wiggin whether he thought the capacity for human suffering to be unlimited. "I think so," the banker replied.[2]

If depression was inherent in the system, then so was recovery. "The fact that we have let nature take its course," said Richard Whitney of the Stock Exchange, "may augur well for the ultimate prosperity of the country." And, if recovery were inevitable, then the state must take care to do nothing which might hold it back. Government, as Henry Ford put it, should "stick to the strict function of governing. That is a big enough job. Let them let business alone." Little could be worse than trying to meet an economic crisis by passing laws. "Lifting the individual's economic responsibility by legislation," said the president of the N.A.M., "is to promote the very habits of thriftlessness in his life which produce his dependency upon such a process." Indeed, government had already acquired far too large a role in economic life. "Either state enterprise must give ground," said Merle Thorpe of *Nation's Business* in 1931, "or private enterprise must succumb." For Congressman James M. Beck the issue was resolved by 1932. "Few states are more socialistic" than the United States, Beck glumly concluded; "Russia is not more bureaucratic than America." [3]

II

Of all the threatened forms of governmental interference, the most sinister, in the judgment of many businessmen, was the dole for the jobless. Some businessmen, indeed, still regarded unemployment as a form of malingering. "Many of those who are most boisterous now in clamor for work," said the president of the

N.A.M., "have either struck on the jobs they had or don't want to work at all, and are utilizing the occasion to swell the communistic chorus." [4] But most contributed with admirable generosity to their community drives. Many also astutely backed the share-the-work plans; and even the publicity-shy J. P. Morgan was induced to make a radio speech supporting the block-aid campaign, by which workers pledged small weekly contributions to the unemployed. "We must all do our bit," said Morgan, as his two butlers listened at a receiver in a back room.[5]

Some devised even more unusual schemes to supplement local relief. Thus John B. Nichlos of the Oklahoma Gas Utilities Company wrote his friend Patrick J. Hurley, the Secretary of War, about an idea that he was trying out in Chickasha, Oklahoma. By the Nichlos plan, restaurants were asked to dump food left on plates into five-gallon containers; the unemployed could then qualify for these scraps by chopping wood donated by farmers. "We expect a little trouble now and then from those who are not worthy of the support of the citizens," wrote Nichlos philosophically, "but we must contend with such cases in order to take care of those who are worthy." Hurley was sufficiently impressed by the plan of feeding garbage to the jobless that he personally urged it on Colonel Woods.[6]

Anything was better than the dole, a word invested with every ominous significance. Newspapers printed photographs showing British families, wan and despairing, eking out miserable existences "on the dole." The impression grew that it was the dole itself which was responsible for the British depression. In 1930 Winston Churchill defended the British system in a message to American business. "I do not sympathize," Churchill wrote, "with those who think that this process of compulsory mass saving will sap the virility and self-reliance of our race. There will be quite enough grind-stone in human life to keep us keen." But to no avail. It was better, said Calvin Coolidge philosophically, "to let those who have made losses bear them than to try to shift them onto someone else." Unemployment insurance, said Henry Ford, would only insure that we always have unemployment. If this country ever voted a dole, said Silas Strawn, now head of the United States Chamber of Commerce, "we've hit the toboggan as a nation." [7]

The terms of the great dole debate remained perplexing. By 1931 few objected any longer to private charity or local relief for the unemployed; and few businessmen objected to federal aid to business. Yet many conservatives affected to regard federal aid to idle men and women as spelling the end of the republic. They generally invoked moral considerations to justify this viewpoint, citing the corrupting effects of government handouts, though it is possible that the prospect of federal relief raised the specter of British taxation as well as that of British decadence.

In the meantime, they continued to exhort about the need for abstinence, self-reliance, and hope. "Recovery," said Dwight Morrow, "is going to be brought about by the man who earns a modest living and spends just a little less than he earns." The president of the American Bankers Association endorsed the doctrine that salvation lay in reducing spending and announced a campaign "to induce our people to be economical and thrifty." "Just grin, keep on working," said Charles M. Schwab. "Stop worrying about the future, and go ahead as best we can." "What we must have is faith, hope and charity," said Walter S. Gifford, "and perhaps some day we shall not need charity." "Out of the depression we have been going through," said Myron C. Taylor of United States Steel, "we shall have learned something of high importance." Then he added: "It is too soon to say just what we are learning." [8]

Taylor's anticlimax was all too characteristic; it betrayed the bafflement with which men, so recently infallible, were viewing the breakdown. Some, no doubt, remained victims of their own homilies; but the more thoughtful and the more candid were shaken. Someone asked Sewell Avery of Montgomery Ward to explain the economic collapse. "To describe the causes of this situation," said Avery unhappily, "is rather beyond my capacity. I am unfortunate in having no friends that seem able to explain it clearly to me." Each new failure came to Dwight Morrow as a personal shock. When Kidder, Peabody went into reorganization, he was shaken; when Britain went off the gold standard, he was aghast; in the summer of 1931, he suffered from constant headaches and insomnia, spending sleepless nights on a study of unemployment until his death in October.

It was left to Daniel Willard of the Baltimore and Ohio to blurt out underlying fears. Throughout his seventy years he had never questioned the capitalist order. Yet a system that denied millions of men work and relief, he had come to feel, could not "be said to be perfect or even satisfactory." The problems of unemployment and the distribution of wealth were forcing him to doubt "the very foundations of our political and economic system." For himself, he continued, "I would steal before I would starve." [9]

III

Even old friends of business were becoming critical. President Nicholas Murray Butler of Columbia University denounced in the summer of 1931 the "easy diagnosis" and "smug prophecies" of the business leaders who said that we would come automatically through the depression. Planning was essential, said Butler, adding, "Gentlemen, if we wait too long, somebody will come forward with a solution that we may not like." "The danger in our situation," said Wallace B. Donham, dean of the Harvard Business School, "lies not in radical propaganda, but in lack of effective business leadership." The example of the Soviet Union, Donham suggested, showed the value and necessity of "a general plan for American business." "Unemployment," said Cardinal O'Connell of Boston, "is a ghastly failure of industrial leadership. . . . What is the flaw in the capitalist system which has governed industry for a couple of centuries that it creates and cannot resolve this paradox?" [10]

Thoughtful businessmen began to see the point. "The tragic lack of planning that characterizes the capitalistic system," wrote Paul Mazur of Lehman Brothers gloomily in 1931, "is a reflection upon the intelligence of everyone participating in the system." Bernard Baruch, moved by memories of the War Industries Board, soon asked for the suspension of antitrust laws to permit "industrial self-government under governmental sanction." William G. McAdoo, also recollecting the past, talked of a Peace Industries Board. Walter C. Teagle of Standard Oil of New Jersey wanted a revision of the antitrust laws to authorize "curtailment of production to reasonable market demand." Myron Taylor could not see how "cooperative plans sincerely undertaken by a basic industry for rationally adjusting production to demand" could be regarded as in restraint of trade. Rudolph Spreckels, an old T.R. Progressive, now president of the Sugar Institute, called for allocation by the government to each company of its proper share of the existing demand.[11]

But the first comprehensive plan came in September 1931 from Gerard Swope, a veteran of Hull-House and the War Industries Board, now president of General Electric. Swope's idea was the organization into trade associations of all firms with more than 50 employees engaged in interstate business. These trade associations would be self-governing units with responsibility for "coordinating" production and consumption and "stabilizing" prices; to accomplish this coordination, there would have to be uniform accounting practices and access to company books. The companies would further adopt pension and unemployment insurance systems, to be paid for and managed by both employers and employees. On top of the cluster of trade associations would be a national economic council. In short, in exchange for the cartelization of a substantial part of American industry, Swope proposed to guarantee to labor a high degree of employment or, that failing, unemployment insurance.[12]

In the meantime, Henry I. Harriman of the New England Power Company, who was elected president of the United States Chamber of Commerce in 1932, was thinking along similar lines. "We have left the period of extreme individualism," he wrote in his report as chairman of the Chamber's Committee on the Continuity of Business and Employment. "Business prosperity and employment will be best maintained by an intelligently planned business structure." But the antitrust laws, "suitable as they may have been for economic conditions of another day," stood in the way of collective action. They must accordingly be modified to permit companies to share the market, though, to protect the public, the government must have power to disallow excessive prices. The generality of business should be organized through trade associations, Harriman continued, leading up to a national advisory economic council at the summit. What of a recalcitrant minority? "They'll be treated like any maverick," said Harriman, remembering his Montana ranches. "They'll be roped, branded, and made to run with the herd." But, if business were to be given this power, added Harriman, it must accept the responsibility of setting up reserves to assure men against economic want because of sickness, unemployment, or old age. In the fall of 1931, a significant majority of the membership of the Chamber endorsed these proposals.[13]

By 1932 the American business community — or, at least, powerful elements in it — was moving fast toward ideas of central economic planning. The nation, said a Vermonter, Ralph E. Flanders of the Jones and Lamson Machine Company, was approaching a new stage in human development — "the self-conscious direction of the mechanism of economic and social life to ends of general well-being. The eye that has caught this vision," Flanders added, "is satisfied with no other." American business, as Henry I. Harriman summed it up, was coming to accept "the philosophy of a planned economy." [14]

23. The Agenda of Reform

IN THEIR WAY, the critics of American business were caught almost as short by the depression as was American business itself. The traditional concern of the liberal reformers had been with welfare and with freedom, of the labor leaders with wages and working conditions. Depression confronted both groups with a radically new challenge. Assuming the inevitability of economic growth, they failed to anticipate economic collapse. Few among them were ready with either diagnosis or cure.

The labor movement was particularly slow in response. William Green's editorials in the *American Federationist* hardly acknowledged the existence of mass unemployment until the middle of 1930. The A.F. of L. convention that year was notable chiefly for the violence with which the leadership repulsed the idea of unemployment insurance, Green warning, with all the zeal of a Henry Ford, that the dole would turn the worker into "a ward of the state." As the depression deepened, however, even the A.F. of L. had to recognize its existence. By March 1931, Green was calling for "sustained, coordinated planning" within industries and "integrated cooperation" among them; and in July he declared to President Hoover that unless American employers made a "collective guaranty of work security" they faced "the inevitable enactment of unemployment-insurance legislation which in effect will fasten a dole upon American industry."

When the Federation held its 1931 convention at Vancouver, Green was in a mood of unwonted ferocity. "I warn the people who are exploiting the workers," he said, "that they can drive them only so far before they will turn on them and destroy them. They are taking no account of the history of nations in which governments have been overturned. Revolutions grow out of the depths of hunger." [1] The militance was largely verbal, but it enabled the leadership to avert the endorsement of compulsory unemployment insurance which Dan Tobin of the Teamsters and other bolder leaders were demanding from the floor.

The leading railroad unions echoed this new bellicosity. In the spring of 1932, their leaders, including A. F. Whitney and D. B. Robertson, called on President Hoover. "Mr. President," they said, "we have come here to tell you that unless something is done to provide employment and relieve distress among the families of the unemployed . . . we will refuse to take the responsibility for the disorder which is sure to arise." It is our duty, they continued, "to give the constitutional government of the United States full warning. . . . There is a growing demand that the entire business and social structure be changed because of the general dissatisfaction with the present system." [2]

II

But rhetoric was no substitute for action; and the leadership of organized labor was notably wanting in concrete proposals, beyond the 30-hour week. All Matthew Woll's talk about "national planning that shall conceive of the economic activity of the Nation as a whole" could not conceal the lack of specifics. Only two important leaders seemed ready to get down to details — in each case because his own experience had prepared him to think in terms of planning.

One was Lewis of the United Mine Workers. For the coal miners, depression was no novelty; and Lewis had long since backed proposals for planning in his own sick industry. Now he suggested that stabilization planning be generalized for all industry under a national economic council. We must cast aside, Lewis said, the treasured old phrases, like "laissez faire," "competition," "rugged individualism." He yielded to no one, he hastened to explain, in opposition to subversive movements. "My sympathies have always been against all un-American and anti-American activities. On the other hand, I realize that we must face the facts today and that we must not seek to ignore the tremendous economic changes and tendencies of our own time." [3]

Like Lewis, Sidney Hillman of the Amalgamated Clothing Workers represented an industry which had been ruined by cut-throat competition and could be saved only by industry-wide cooperation. "Really to control unemployment," said Hillman, "we must think and act in terms of economic planning"; and experience had shown that "voluntary cooperation in economic planning is not enough." In his version, the national economic council, to be established under a national house of industrial representatives, including both labor and management, would be given "the authority to work out salvation and the power to carry plans into effect." [4]

Lewis and Hillman, in the end, differed little from Gerard Swope and Henry I. Harriman. But the invocation of "planning" created problems of its own. How under planning were prices to be set? Resources allocated? Wages determined? When such questions were asked, an enormous vagueness tended to set in. The hard choices, it seemed, were to be postponed for the hypothetical economic council.

III

Nor were the professional economists much help in filling the technical gap. The grand academic figures — Taussig, Ely, Commons, Mitchell, Seligman — were hardly more prepared for depression than the leaders of business and labor. But the economic heretics of the twenties found stimulus, some even vindication, in depression. And, of all the economists of the day, none was quicker in regaining his feet after the crash than William T. Foster of the old team of Foster and Catchings. For the crash, after all, turned out to have been predictable in terms of the Foster system; and, if he knew the causes of depression, he also conceived he knew the cure.

As he looked back on the twenties, Foster had no doubt about tracing the breakdown, not, in the orthodox manner, to extravagance, but to thrift. "Far from having been profligate, the nation wasted its substance in riotous saving." Why had industry stopped making goods and hiring labor? "Solely because it cannot sell the goods." "We shall not restore good times," Foster emphasized, "*no matter what else we do*, until we spend more." "The only sound way speedily to stop the depression is to increase total pay-rolls."

But purchasing power would not revive, Foster said, of its own accord. "For three years we have waited, in vain, for private enterprise to put the necessary currency and credit into circulation." It was folly, he liked to say, to turn the job over to the "lazy fairies." "When private enterprise fails, public enterprise is our only resource. We can restore consumer purchasing power by collective action, and in no other way. Collective action means, necessarily, action by the Federal Government."

The first step should be the increase of the national debt "as far as is necessary to restore employment and production." There was no point in worrying about the size of the debt; once national income began to rise, "then the repayment of the indebtedness of the Federal Government becomes a simple matter." The government should spend freely — for roads, for slum clearance, for all forms of public works. At the same time, tax reduction could release more money for spending. If nothing else were possible, then pay the bonus; "it is the one way — though a poor one — of conscripting some of the slacker dollars." In every way it could, the government must put dollars into the hands of those who would spend them. "If that is inflation," said Foster, "there is nothing the country needs right now so much as inflation."

But more was necessary, Foster added, than emergency action. Steep taxes on incomes, profits, and inheritances would keep savings from collecting again in stagnant pools in the future. "It is impossible, as this country has demonstrated again and again, for the rich to save as much as they have been trying to save, and save anything that is worth saving." In their own interest, "we should take from them a sufficient amount of their surplus to enable consumers to consume and business to operate at a profit. This is not 'soaking the rich'; it is saving the rich." In addition, Foster wanted compulsory unemployment and health insurance, the guarantee of bank deposits and rigorous regulation of the security exchanges and stock issues.

Foster had long since lost his illusions about Hoover. The administration seemed to have committed itself to "the economics of original sin"; it had acted as if misery were foreordained and nothing could be done about it. Instead of action, the nation got exhortation. "M. Coué seemed to have become our Minister of Finance." And yet recovery could be so easy! "If anyone still doubts that our economic troubles are mainly mental, let him consider what would happen if the United States declare war today." Congress would appropriate billions of dollars; orders would go forth to factory and farm; prosperity would return. "Some day," said Foster, "we shall realize that if money is available for a blood-and-bullets war, just as much money is available for a food-and-famine war." [5]

IV

Foster's views found support chiefly among other heretics. The Englishman John A. Hobson had developed independently an underconsumptionist analysis of stagnation. Where Foster explained the failure of demand by stressing the leakages from buying power in the processes of business saving and financing, Hobson gave attention to the lopsided structure of wealth distribution, which put income in the hands of the wealthy, who would save it, rather than of the poor, who would spend it. He was also more pessimistic about the possibilities of correcting the tendencies toward oversaving without a revision of the capitalist system. If his analysis was more sustained and sophisticated, his recommendations — deficit spending and progressive taxation — coincided with those of Foster. His writings were not without influence in America. [6]

The publication in 1930 of John Maynard Keynes's *Treatise on Money* carried a far more accomplished English economist to the side of the underconsumptionists. To the new doctrines, Keynes brought a rigor of logic, a subtlety of analysis, and a brilliance of exposition which in the end converted them into a new orthodoxy. "This is not a crisis of poverty," Keynes told America in 1932, "but a crisis of abundance." Some voices insisted that escape lay in retrenchment and economy, "in refraining, wherever possible, from utilizing the world's potential production." These, said Keynes, with contempt, were "the voices of fools and madmen." It was inconceivable to him the rubbish men had to utter in the United States if they were to keep respectable. Sensible bankers "have to go about assuring the world of their conviction that there is no serious risk of inflation, when what they really mean is that they cannot yet see good enough grounds for daring to hope for it." So long as this mood persisted, Keynes said he could imagine no course of events that could restore American prosperity in the near future.[7]

In America, Foster and the underconsumptionists had many readers but few followers. A consulting engineer named David Cushman Coyle, whose specialty was structural design, developed somewhat similar views of economic policy. "The higher incomes are not being expended automatically at a sufficient rate to make the country run," Coyle said, "and that is why the Federal Government has to take these surplus incomes and expend them." But the most powerful of Foster's disciples was Marriner Eccles, a Utah banker, who read Foster with care, reinterpreted underconsumption in terms of his own experience as a businessman, and came up with recommendations that surpassed Foster in concreteness and trenchancy.

The problem, as Eccles defined it, was to use government to bring about an increase of purchasing power. The answer, in his view, was government spending — for public works; for relief ("we shall either adopt a plan which will meet this situation under capitalism, or a plan will be adopted for us which will operate without capitalism"); for the domestic allotment plan in agriculture; for any other measures which would get money into circulation. The age of uncontrolled individualism, said Eccles, was over; the economy could survive only "under a modified capitalistic system controlled and regulated from the top by government." [8]

V

For Foster the depression was "exclusively a monetary phenomenon" and hence to be solved "solely by monetary measures." [9] Actually his monetary measures, as they unfolded, would require a considerable set of institutional readjustments; and in Eccles the need for institutional reform was frankly conceded. Yet both

Foster and Eccles began with the problem of purchasing power and moved on to the problem of structure. Another school of economists — the institutional school, which found its inspiration in Veblen, Patten, and Commons — took structural reform as its starting point.

The more cautious institutionalists made their headquarters at the National Bureau of Economic Research and concentrated on working out statistical pictures of economic development. But another group in the institutionalist tradition, centering at Columbia University, addressed itself to policy issues. Two economists — Gardiner C. Means and Rexford G. Tugwell — and a lawyer — Adolf A. Berle, Jr. — combined in these years to build a fresh and arresting theory of the American economy.

Means, the youngest of the three (he was thirty-six in 1932), had long been exploring the area where economics intersected with law and where institutions thus set the pattern of economic development. With James C. Bonbright, he published *The Holding Company* in 1932, a first attempt at letting light into the mysteries of corporate structure; and the same year, with Adolf Berle, Means collaborated in producing one of the most influential economic treatises of the time, *The Modern Corporation and Private Property*. Berle, in the years after the disillusion at Paris, had turned to the practice and teaching of law. To their collaboration Means brought an original and capacious economic intelligence; Berle, a few months the senior of the pair, both the finicky precision of a legal technician and the broad perspectives of a social prophet. Each felt that the rise of the modern corporation had revolutionized the economy — and each concluded that it consequently had to revolutionize ways of thinking about public policy. Means developed the implications of this revolution for economic theory, Berle for law and for politics.

In 1930, according to *The Modern Corporation*, the 200 largest nonbanking corporations controlled nearly one-half of the non-banking corporate wealth of the nation and almost one-quarter of the total national wealth. Half the steel industry was in the hands of two companies, half the copper industry of four companies; half the anthracite coal was mined by four companies; nickel and aluminum were virtual monopolies. Three groups of companies controlled more than half the electric power industry; two companies made nearly two-thirds of the automobiles; three companies controlled 70 per cent of the cigarette trade; one company made half the agricultural machinery — and so it went, from industry to industry. By 1932, according to Berle's calculations, 65 per cent of American industry was owned by about 600 corporations. This meant that some 6000 men, as directors of these corporations, virtually controlled American economic life; "eliminating the inactive directors, the number of men is reduced to not more than two thousand." If the rate of growth were to continue, 70 per cent of all corporate activity would be conducted by 200 corporations in 1950. "Mr. Brandeis struggled to turn the clock backward in 1915; Professor Felix Frankfurter is inclined to believe even now that it cannot last"; but the process could not be reversed. Where society had once been dominated by a feudal system, so now there was evolving a "corporate system" controlled by a handful of industrial barons.

VI

From this situation Means drew daring conclusions for economic theory. Classical economics had presupposed a vast number of small business units equalizing supply and demand through free competition in the market. Monopoly was a deviation, to be summarily dealt with in the footnotes. But what had once been the deviation was now surely becoming itself the norm. "The individualism of Adam Smith's private enterprise," Means wrote, "has in large measure given way to the collective activity of the modern corporation, and economic theory must shift its emphasis from analysis in terms of competition to analysis in terms of control."

The decisive change was from what Means called the "trading market" — the free market of the classicists — to the "administered market." The modern corporation, he suggested, by bringing so large a part of economic life within the administrative control of single units, had altered the character of the economy. As fixed prices replaced flexible prices, the market no longer had an inherent tendency toward equilibrium. In the classical model, an excess of supply over demand would cause a fall in prices until demand caught up; but in the administered market such an excess was likely instead to cause a fall in production. The free market remained dominant only in agriculture; and Means pointed out that the disparity between the agricultural sector, where in depression prices fell and production was maintained, and the industrial sector, where production fell and prices were maintained, was a further source of economic instability.

While Means examined the economics of the corporate revolution, Berle looked at its social implications. The increase in size and the diffusion of ownership caused, it was obvious, an increasing separation between ownership and control. The spread of stockholding, which to Herbert Hoover meant that everybody owned American business, meant to Berle that no one owned it. "Property that you can see means one thing in your life; the property which is only a piece of paper in your safety deposit vault means quite something else." The "owner" was helpless to do anything with this "property," except to sell it for what the security markets would let him have. It was hardly too much to say, observed Berle, that in the corporate system the old idea of private property was slowly losing its grip.

With the separation of ownership and control, the profit motive also began to wane. Those who controlled the great corporations, Berle said, had other interests beside paying dividends to stockholders. Their organizations were becoming social institutions. Modern industrial managers would have to function "more as princes and ministers than as promoters or merchants." One could understand more about them by studying Alexander the Great, seeking new worlds to conquer, than by remembering Adam Smith's petty tradesmen.

Public policy, Berle and Means contended, must aim now at "a unified, controlled, sensible operation" of the new corporate system. This might come about, Berle thought, through the gradual growth by business into responsibility, as "group after group of men who operate the system realize that their first job is to make the system work; and that if this involves their working together instead of working at cross-purposes, then work together they must." So, over generations, a responsible banking community had arisen in Britain; so too, the United States might build "a purely neutral technocracy," running "a collectivism without communism, a common action based on a common responsibility for the result." As against communism, such a collectivism would allow "a complete intellectual freedom; men can discuss and differ." As against laissez-faire capitalism, it would allow men to work "in terms of the national life as a whole, and not in terms of profit." There must be, in addition, a series of immediate reforms; the support of demand through government spending; the reorganization of the stock market and the federal control of security issues; the centralization of the banking system; the revision of antitrust laws to permit consolidation and even monopoly, along with detailed regulation of all concentrated industries; old age, sickness, and unemployment insurance.

"Is this suggestion of a responsible business community," Berle asked wistfully, "merely a dream?" Business leadership, he wrote in 1932, was still characterized by "seizure of power without recognition of responsibility — ambition without courage." The industrial directors "assume little responsibilities to the community, to their customers or to their labor; have no cohesion; fight among themselves." The way things were, Berle gloomily concluded, "the American and the Russian systems will look very much alike within a comparatively short period — say twenty years. There is no great difference between having all industry run by a committee of Commissars and by a small group of Directors." [10]

VII

Rexford G. Tugwell of the economics department at Columbia simplified certain panels of the institutionalist design with deft and audacious brush strokes. He wholly accepted the analysis of *The Modern Corporation;* but where Berle and Means concentrated on industry, Tugwell extended his interest to agriculture; and where Berle and Means tended to be cautious in recommendations, Tugwell speculated on far frontiers both of individual psychology and social planning.

Born in Chautauqua County in western New York, Tugwell was forty years old in 1931. He had studied with Simon Patten and Scott Nearing at the Wharton School and had vibrated to the excitement of the progressive era. As a youth, he turned to Whitmanesque verse, proclaiming himself big and well made, muscled, lean, and nervous, sick of a nation's stenches, sick of propertied czars:

> We begin to see richness as poorness; we begin to dignify toil.
> I have dreamed my great dreams of their passing,
> I have gathered my tools and my charts;
> My plans are fashioned and practical;
> I shall roll up my sleeves — make America over!

He went into the twenties an apostle of economic unorthodoxy and social reform. He had learned from Patten the economics of abundance and the theory of national planning. From Veblen he took the idea that the domination of "industry" by "business" condemned mankind to the age of scarcity. From Dewey he derived the instrumentalist conviction that reason was the tool with which to shape the future. And in the work of Frederick Winslow Taylor, the father of scientific management, Tugwell found the techniques by which society might achieve the ends proposed by Patten, Veblen, and Dewey. The greatest economic event of the nineteenth century, Tugwell liked to say, was when Taylor first held his stopwatch on a group of shovelers in the Midvale Steel plant. Only Taylor had not gone far enough. Tugwell believed that the logic of scientific management required the extension of planning from the single factory to the industry and then to the entire economy. "We needed a Taylor now for the economic system as a whole."

He had no use for the classical theory of the free market. "There is no invisible hand," he said, adding characteristically, "There never was." But the search for "a real and visible guiding hand to do the task which that mythical, non-existent, invisible agency was supposed to perform" met more than the opposition of business. It also met the opposition of old-style antimonopoly progressivism. More polemical than Berle and Means, Tugwell attacked trust busting as a "demagogic stereotype," an obsolescent cliché, a hopeless and disastrous error. The policy of the "pulverization of business" meant that government was pitting itself against "inevitable, unconquerable industrial forces." It branded as legally wrong what was economically necessary. Rural progressivism was "reactionary," Wilson's New Freedom "anachronistic." While Tugwell had little regard for Theodore Roosevelt and seems not to have been influenced by Croly, he endorsed their preference in the old American antithesis: "Hamilton, far more than Jefferson, had divined what was going on in the economic world and what needed to be done about it."

If any one characteristic was clear to Tugwell about the economic system, it was unity. The greatest need was therefore coordination. This had been achieved once — by the War Industries Board, "America's war-time socialism." The war, said Tugwell enviously, was "an industrial engineer's Utopia. . . . Only the Armistice prevented a great experiment in control of production, control of price, and control of consumption." But the attempt would be surely made soon again. "Ours is a society struggling to become cooperative," he wrote. "All the technical forces tend to produce a collectivistic society; all the thwarted motives of men cry aloud for it. But the way is blocked by the ideologies of the past, buttressed by those who have grown strong in its favors." [11]

VIII

In 1927, Tugwell percipiently called attention to the fact that the increase in labor productivity was outstripping the increase in wages. But business, he commented in *Industry's Coming of Age,* was not likely to pass on the gains of productivity on its own accord. And there was neither the public demand nor the technical knowledge to make planning possible in the industrial sector. On the other hand, both these conditions, he began to think, might exist for agriculture. The farmers were seeking a national agricultural policy; and the Farm Extension Service not only supplied information for forecasting but itself constituted a rudimentary apparatus for control. Thus concern with planning led Tugwell into agricultural economics; and his concern with agricultural economics soon brought him to the attention of former Governor Frank Lowden of Illinois and, in 1928, into the Al Smith campaign.

The depression intensified Tugwell's interest in planning. Speaking in the winter of 1931 before the American Economic Association, he tried to confront his audience with the full meaning of a planned economy. A national council with advisory powers, of the kind proposed by Swope or Harriman, could not, Tugwell said, do the job. People might try to distinguish between partial and total planning; but "they all come to the same thing — or will not work." The logic of planning amounted in the end, practically, "to the abolition of 'business.' " Profits would have to be limited and their uses regulated, prices controlled, speculative gains eliminated. There would be constitutional changes too, "the laying of rough, unholy hands on many a sacred precedent, doubtless calling on an enlarged and nationalized police power for enforcement."

"When industry is government and government is industry," Tugwell concluded, "the dual conflict deepest in our modern institutions will be abated. This is one of the basic reasons why the prospect of a planned economy is so congenial to every other hope and belief I have." And, let no one be deceived, the situation in America was getting explosive. For "the future is becoming visible in Russia; the present is bitterly in contrast; politicians, theorists, and vested interests seem to conspire ideally for the provocation to violence of a long-patient people." [12]

This was Tugwell's most radical pronouncement, and it was a little hard to gauge its intent. Three years later he claimed before a Senate committee that in tracing out the logic of a planned economy he "was trying to show that it would not work." [13] But these phrases of 1934 were uttered by a government official whose first obligation, as he saw it, was to protect the President who had appointed him. His argument of 1931 could perhaps be fairly read as an expression of Tugwell's cocky desire to shock an audience with the implications of its too glib slogans. In the same period, he was working out a more sober solution in a book, much revised and finally published in 1933, *The Industrial Discipline and the Governmental Arts.*

The spirit of the American Economic Association address had been defiant, doctrinaire, all-or-nothing. In *The Industrial Discipline* Tugwell affirmed the feasibility of a middle way, asserting his faith in what he elsewhere called "the possibilities of a managed society." [14] "We can experiment now," he said, "and we ought to do it before it is too late. Otherwise we are surely committed to revolution." And he made it clear that he did not want revolution. "Liberals would like to rebuild the station while the trains are running; radicals prefer to blow up the station and forego service until the new structure is built." The ultimate objectives might not be so very different, "but there is all the difference in the world in the ways of achieving what is hoped for." Somewhere between stubborn privilege on one side and "dark destructive intention" on the other, liberalism had to accomplish a democratic reconstruction of economic institutions.

Tugwell's own program now bore a strange resemblance to the plans of Harriman and Swope which had so recently roused him to such sardonic reflections. He called for the organization of industries in self-governing associations, building up to an Industrial Integration Board with industrial and public representatives. The central board would coordinate the industry plans with the overall government plan. One ingenious suggestion was a tax on undistributed corporate surpluses in order to force investment funds into the open market and thus to subject plans for capital expansion to external control.[15]

While Tugwell went beyond Harriman or Swope in giving his central board enforcement powers, he obviously did not feel that his managed society threatened essential freedoms. The contrast between *The Industrial Discipline* and the drastic alternatives he had presented to the American Economic Association suggested the conflict within him between the theorist, given to dashing and ominous generalization, and the activist, with a pragmatic sense of reality. For Tugwell's doctrine was always — nearly always — redeemed by his deepest commitment, which was to experimentalism as a social method. He distrusted sacred dogmas and ultimate ends. When Professor George S. Counts dared the schoolteachers to recruit their pupils in the building of a new social order, Tugwell observed, "In this I disagree with Mr. Counts as fundamentally as it is possible to disagree with any one on anything." For Tugwell, education properly aimed at teaching methods, not goals.

His faith in experiment determined Tugwell's attitude toward communism. The future was becoming visible for him in Russia in only a technical sense; the fixed ideology of Marxism, the "vast human sufferings," the "repression, spying and violence" repelled him. "The point at issue," he remarked, "is whether it is better to have social management or not to have it. The answer seems to depend on whether management involves suppression of competing ideas." If the only alternatives were communism and laissez faire "an experimentalist might as well retire from the scene. Fortunately they are not."

With all his zest for institutional reform, he also understood as an experimentalist that there were other things to be done — perhaps, indeed, to be done first. In almost the tones of William T. Foster, he wrote in the winter of 1931, that the support of purchasing power was "a first and most essential task of any plan which was expected to work" and "the point of attack which has most possibilities." [16]

IX

Within the broad range from monetary policy to institutional reform, other liberal economists made contributions. Paul H. Douglas of the University of Chicago brought to the task a resourceful grasp of theory and a powerful personality. He agreed with Foster and Eccles — and with Berle and Tugwell — on the need for government action in support of purchasing power. He argued cogently for unemployment insurance and other forms of social security. But his special contribution was his belief that the crisis required new political instruments.

In 1928 Douglas had seen little choice between Smith and Hoover; and, after the crash, the League for Independent Political Action, which he had organized in 1929, conceived itself increasingly as the nucleus for a new radical party. John Dewey served as the LIPA's chairman; Howard Y. Williams, a former Social Gospel preacher, as executive secretary; and the national committee consisted of a mixture of liberals, like Stuart Chase, Oswald Garrison Villard, and Morris Ernst, with Socialists like Norman Thomas, Harry Laidler, and Reinhold Niebuhr. Douglas, outlining the LIPA philosophy, dismissed both major parties as "primarily business parties."

A few weeks after the election of 1930, Dewey asked George W. Norris to head a new party based on the principles of planning and control. The weary veteran, who had now left the Republican party and called himself an independent, declined. "There is no hope," he told Dewey and Williams in his Senate office. He added, in a letter, "Experience has shown that the people will not respond to a demand for a new party except in case of a great emergency, when there is practically a political revolution."

But Douglas, continuing his efforts, published in the spring of 1932 a book entitled *The Coming of a New Party*. He reaffirmed his rejection of the major parties; the Democratic party was not only reactionary in the South and corrupt in the great cities but was "largely maintained by the business interests as a combined lightning rod and lifeboat." No doubt Governor Roosevelt of New York had liberal qualities; but he could not be expected to transform his party. "There is indeed nothing," Douglas said, "that liberals need to rid themselves of more than the infantile notion that a president can by himself greatly change things." Americans must look forward to the day when "the Democratic party will ultimately go down before the rise of a vigorous party of the farmers and workers in much the same way as the Liberal party in England has dwindled as the Labour party has grown."

For 1932, Douglas favored Norman Thomas and the Socialists. "A truly planned economy," he believed, "is almost impossible under capitalism and only practical under socialism." But Douglas remained nondoctrinaire; in the United States, he felt, the question of socialization would be settled not by a categorical answer to the general proposition but by a series of experiments. The Four-Year Plan, presented by LIPA in January 1932, called for piecemeal measures — federal relief, public works, social security, tariff reduction — and envisaged public ownership only for the utilities.

Douglas's Soviet journey had given him, as it had given Tugwell, a new sense of the feasibility of planning. It had also pointed up new perils. "Power," said Douglas in 1929, "is as subtly corrupting as wealth"; the "almost inevitable consequence" of the Soviet system seemed the creation of a hierarchy "which, in its pride and callousness, would bear little resemblance to those self-sacrificing spirits who initiated it." The problem for the United States as Douglas now saw it, was to achieve full employment while avoiding the "severe dictatorship and the denial of democracy which unfortunately is also a feature of the Russian program." And he was clear that it was impossible to work with the American Communists in this enterprise. "They are in fact," he said, "determined to discredit all bodies which have other aims or methods than their own." [17]

<h2 style="text-align:center">X</h2>

In one form or another, liberal pragmatism was seeking means of attaining a stable economy within a framework of free institutions. George Soule of the *New Republic,* invoking F. W. Taylor, Veblen, and the War Industries Board, sketched his economic design in *A Planned Society* in 1932. Soule contended that the stimulation of effective demand must be "the main objective of any national economic policy" and called for deficit spending as the best means of achieving this objective; at the same time, he proposed a National Planning Board to serve as a center for production planning. "Every step in the direction of planning for social ends," he wrote, "must be a step away from capitalism." But his appeal was for gradual change rather than revolution; and he rejected the view that capitalism was on the edge of collapse.[18]

Charles A. Beard was even more vehement in his rejection of totalitarianism. The Communists, ruling "by tyranny and terror, with secret police, espionage, and arbitrary executions," had no lessons for a free society. As for the laissez-faire myth, "The cold truth is that the individualist creed of everybody for himself and the devil take the hindmost is principally responsible for the distress in which Western civilization finds itself." America must renounce the philosophy of the antitrust laws and accept the inevitability of integration. Beard's own solution, outlined as a Five-Year Plan in the summer of 1931, called for a system of cartels in the basic industries, to be controlled by a National Economic Council, representing business, labor, and agriculture.[19]

New proposals began to crowd the magazines. The institutionalist economist Walton H. Hamilton, dismissing the antitrust laws as the "common sense of another age," wanted "central direction" of the economy extending certainly to capacity, probably to output and possibly to price. John T. Flynn, the financial journalist, declared that "the one great possible hope for the survival of capitalism" lay in the replacement of the individual investor by investment pools, operating under government supervision; if this wouldn't work, he said, "then capitalism is doomed." [20]

XI

But perhaps the most widely read of liberal economists was Stuart Chase. Genially eclectic in his views, Chase had a tart and ingratiating style, an uncommon talent for lucidity in exposition, and an unlimited curiosity about all aspects of the system. He had sat at Veblen's feet in the early twenties; and Veblen remained his intellectual mentor; but he also read Taylor and Keynes, production theorists and monetary theorists, conservatives and cranks, and stirred them all together to brew his own effervescent concoctions. He returned from his trip to the Soviet Union with Tugwell and Douglas in 1927 enormously excited by the Gosplan and, unlike his friend Roger Baldwin, not at all perturbed by the GPU. "Russia is no dream," he wrote in 1931. "Day by day, her shadow falls sharper, bolder, upon the face of the world." But he regarded the Communist model as hopelessly committed to dogma; and he felt that violent revolution would be disastrous in a modern technical society like the United States.

The problem of production, Chase believed, was solved, and the world was ready to move into the age of distribution. This change threw the spotlight on two figures hitherto unappreciated in the economic drama: the technician, whom Chase called "the modern Prometheus in chains"; and the consumer. Give the technician his head, and abundance for all could be guaranteed. But technological development must be guided by planning, not by profit. Chase had almost a Luddite fear of the "anarchic momentum" of free-enterprise capitalism. His suggestion of 1932 for a ten-year moratorium on invention seemed only half jocular; it came after the publication of a book describing the satisfactions of the static economy of rural Mexico.

Once technical progress was under control, then the consumer would come into his own. To the consumers' organization and enlightenment (particularly through Consumers' Research laboratory, with its monthly reports on the quality of merchandise) Chase gave an important share of his energy. The age of consumption, he felt, shifted the whole focus of social discussion, rendering, not only capitalism, but also Communism obsolete. The basic question was no longer who owned what, but what method moved most goods with least social disruption.

In certain moods Chase regarded the future as requiring a sharp break with capitalism. Thus he once dismissed the proposals of Keynes as having the "fatal defect" of seeking to repair the prevailing system — "only patches on a boiler which is destined ultimately to explode." But for all the extravagance of his rhetoric, his own proposals usually turned out to be patches on the same boiler. Thus, in other moods, he contended that the restoration of purchasing power was "the key to the enigma." To this end, he called for a "stiff dose of inflation" as well as for redistributive taxation and public works. He proposed a system of "planned production," through revision of the antitrust laws, with industry organized through trade associations under a Peace Industries Board, and a universal system of minimum wages and maximum hours. "What American industry needs above all else, in my opinion," he wrote in the fall of 1931, "is coordination — an integration of supply to demand, and an end to the crucifying wastes and leakages of free competition. The more promptly a given industry acts as an intelligent unit instead of a mob of maniacs, the better I shall be pleased." His *New Republic* series and book of 1932, *A New Deal*, summed up his program in insouciant language, concluding characteristically: "Why should Russians have all the fun of remaking a world?" [21]

XII

The liberal economic thought of the early depression thus tended to converge on two practical programs. One, stemming from Keynes, Foster, and Eccles, approached the crisis from the viewpoint of the failure of demand and proposed to revive purchasing power through government spending. The other, stemming from Veblen and Patten, Berle and Means and Tugwell, approached the crisis from the viewpoint of the misworking of the institutional framework and called for economic integration through structural reform. And whether spenders or planners, these men were all pragmatists rather than dogmatists. They were united by a determination to work within the existing system, to proceed by reason and consent and to preserve the living continuities of free society.

Mr. Justice Brandeis supplied them with their charter in an eloquent moment in March 1932. Mr. Justice Sutherland, for the Supreme Court majority, had ruled that the depression did not justify the state of Oklahoma in declaring the manufacture of ice a public utility. No matter how desperate the crisis, the Supreme Court said, freedom of enterprise, as protected in the Fourteenth Amendment, was not to be tampered with "in the interest of experiments." Brandeis, his black-robed arms moving in expressive gestures, read a dissent with deep emotion in the crowded courtroom. He sharply denied that the Fourteenth Amendment intended to leave the people helpless before economic disorder. This was, he said, "an emergency more serious than war." It threatened "even the stability of the capitalistic system." In times like these, could the Court assume the responsibility for staying the course of social experiment? "There must be power in the States and the Nation," he said, "to remould through experimentation, our economic practices and institutions to meet changing social and economic needs. . . . Denial of the right to experiment may be fraught with serious consequences to the Nation." [22]

Faith in experiment implied belief in a middle way. The pragmatic approach rejected equally those who would make no change at all in the social order and those who demanded total change. It sought increased government management of the economy but stopped short of government planning of all economic decisions. John Maynard Keynes spoke for the pragmatic reformers in his *Saturday Evening Post* article of 1930. "I predict," he wrote, "that both of the two opposed errors of pessimism which now make so much noise in the world will be proved wrong in our own time — the pessimism of the revolutionaries who think that things are so bad that nothing can save us but violent change, and the pessimism of the reactionaries who consider the balance of our economic and social life so precarious that we must risk no experiments."

"If we would be guided by the light of reason," said Mr. Justice Brandeis, "we must let our minds be bold." [23]

24. Farewell to Reform

WILL ROGERS, watching, as he said, the first nation in history to go to the poorhouse in an automobile, uttered a warning early in 1931. "You let this country go hungry," he said, "and they are going to eat, no matter what happens to Budgets, Income Taxes or Wall Street values. Washington mustn't forget who rules when it comes to a showdown." In June 1931, a man driving a large car through the outskirts of Gary, Indiana, came to a sudden halt when a brick crashed through the window. "What's the big idea?" he called into the darkness. Out of the night came the reply, in a surprisingly level tone: "All rich guys ought to be strung up." "Who are you?" asked the driver. "We're the fellows that'll do the stringing." "Their patience is at an end," said the hotel clerk later that night. "Another four years of Hoover and . . ."

In September 1931, the American Legion resolved that the crisis could not be "promptly and efficiently met by existing political methods." In the same month Nicholas Murray Butler welcomed the new freshman class at Columbia with the odd remark that totalitarian systems brought forward "men of far greater intelligence, far stronger character and far more courage than the system of elections." In October, when Ambassador Charles G. Dawes heard that the British Broadcasting Corporation was planning to transmit Liberal and Labour election speeches to the United States, he killed the idea on the ground that such incendiary talk would dangerously inflame public feeling in America. And in Mississippi a veteran politician from the piny woods told an interviewer: "Folks are restless. Communism is gaining a foothold. Right here in Mississippi some people are about ready to lead a mob. In fact, I'm getting a little pink myself." His name was Theodore G. Bilbo.[1]

A malaise was seizing many Americans, a sense, at once depressing and exhilarating, that capitalism itself was finished. Some felt it dumbly on the breadlines or in the piny woods; but intellectuals, denied by the materialism of the twenties a sense of function in American society, were particularly vulnerable to this malady. Mencken had armed them with contempt for American culture, Veblen had exposed the economic system for them, Beard had exhibited the sordid motives beneath official ideals. And depression now liquidated their margin of emotional security. The intellectuals, like the brokers, suddenly found that they too had been living beyond their means. The "utter confidence" which, in Scott Fitzgerald's words, was the "essential prop" of the Jazz Age was gone; the borrowed time was running out. As Robert E. Sherwood wrote in 1931 in an apologetic introduction to *Reunion in Vienna,* a frivolous play about another world, the whole generation seemed to occupy a shell-torn no man's land, a "limbo-like interlude between one age and another." Ahead lay only "black doubt, punctured by brief flashes of ominous light, whose revelations are not comforting. Behind . . . nothing but the ghastly wreckage of burned bridges."

The lost generation seemed more lost than ever. Forced now to confront political and economic reality, its members demanded something more apocalyptic than theories about purchasing power or the domestic allotment plan. Half measures were no longer enough; this was a time of catastrophe. To compromise with privilege and with stupidity was to lose the battle before it had begun. Fitzgerald, recalling the radical enthusiasm of 1919, lightheartedly portrayed his contemporaries in 1931, "rummaging around in our trunks wondering where in hell we left the liberty cap — 'I know I *had* it' — and the moujik blouse." But by the summer of 1932, Fitzgerald himself, remote from Long Island and Deauville, was reading Marx and writing, "To bring on the revolution, it may be necessary to work inside the communist party." [2]

Younger people in particular resented the prospect of being cast adrift in a world they never made. "To us," wrote Eric Sevareid of the University of Minnesota, "it was all a mess. We refused to accept it as inevitable, untouchable. Men were *not*, regardless of

all the determinists, the helpless victims of uncontrollable forces. . . .
Men could take hold of the system and direct it." [3] Many, young
and old, began to dream of the possibility of a new turning in history which would abolish unemployment and distress and assure
mankind the decent life for which it yearned.

II

There was no older American dream. The millennial hope had
brought so many to the new continent. It had helped create the
passion for independence. In the early nineteenth century, it had
sprinkled the country with utopian communities. In the eighties it
had produced the vision of the cooperative commonwealth. By the
1930's radicals had been singing for a generation of how fair the
world would seem,

> When each man can live his life secure and free;
> When the earth is owned by Labor
> And there'll be joy and peace for all,
> In the Commonwealth of Toil that is to be.

Now depression was offering radicalism its long awaited chance.
And, at this moment of opportunity, the Socialist party seemed in
some respects the first claimant for the support of the disinherited.
It was the strongest of the radical parties. It had an established
name and an experienced leadership. In some localities it had a
traditional voting strength. While it had wilted under prosperity,
polling fewer votes in 1928 than in any presidential election since
1900, it had still done five times as well that year as the Communists.

Its very age and dignity conferred disadvantages. The men in
control of the party machinery — a group of New York Socialists,
largely European born, headed by Morris Hillquit — had fought
for too many years along accustomed lines. Yet, despite the Old
Guard, changes had come. In 1928, when the party nominated
Norman Thomas for President, it even eliminated the affirmation
of the "class struggle" as a condition for membership. Thomas, a
product of the Social Gospel, deeply influenced by Walter Rausch-

enbusch, had forsaken the Presbyterian pulpit for Socialist politics. He brought a liberating impulse into the party; and his unexpectedly good run in the New York City mayoralty election of 1929, coming a few days after the stock market crash, seemed to open the hope of a Socialist resurgence. But when it was proposed that Socialists take the initiative in persuading trade unions to join in setting up something like the British Labour party, Hillquit made the characteristic reply: "Why should we go out of our way to seek them out? Let them come to us." [4]

The Thomas group, essentially non-Marxist, middle class, college-educated, wanted closer relations with labor and with organizations like the League for Independent Political Action. As the depression deepened, a new faction arose, the Militants, led by Paul Blanshard and others, demanding that the party revive the class struggle and work for the achievement of socialism "in our life-time." The Militants also wanted a more sympathetic attitude toward the Soviet Union. But Hillquit and the Old Guard beat off the factional challenges and retained an uneasy control.

Paralyzed by internal squabbles, the Socialist party did not take effective advantage of the depression. Where the Communists courted the unemployed by mass meetings and riots, the Old Guard Socialists shrank from provocative methods. The party concentrated instead on research, education, and persuasion. In Thomas it had an unusually attractive and vigorous orator; but, while Thomas dared fearlessly to affirm labor's right to organize under the eyes of the company police, his most successful appeal was not to workers but to middle-class audiences in the colleges and the churches. Between 1928 and 1932, the Socialist party hardly more than doubled its tiny membership — from about 7000 to 15,000.[5]

In votes, the Socialist party continued to hold by far the largest following among the Marxist parties. But the Socialist appeal lacked qualitative intensity. It might be all right for ministers and social workers; but many intellectuals disdained this mixture of the Social Gospel, the scholastic orthodoxy of the Old Guard, and the "sewer socialism" of Milwaukee, Reading, and Bridgeport. Radicals liked to quote Trotsky's supposed remark about the Socialists as a party of dentists. The crisis called for more, as Granville Hicks put it, than hopeful reasonableness. "I should think," wrote John Dos

Passos, "that becoming a socialist right now would have just the same effect on anybody as drinking a bottle of near-beer." [6]

III

Socialism, in short, had been contaminated too; it had become something indistinguishable from social reform. And reform, many people began to feel in 1931, was not enough. In that year Lincoln Steffens published his *Autobiography*. The veteran reporter was now sixty-five years old. No American of the time seemed to have known so many famous people, asked so many searching questions, covered so many crises, or written so vividly about so much of the twentieth century. And no American had so tirelessly assayed the possibilities of liberalism. Steffens's life appeared to sum up a generation of the reformist hope.

When a bishop once challenged Steffens to explain the source of evil, he had replied that some people blamed Adam; Adam blamed Eve; Eve blamed the serpent, "and that's where you clergy have stuck ever since. You blame that serpent, Satan. Now I come and I am trying to show you that it was, it is, the apple." This, as he saw it, was the heart of the matter. The failure of the muckrakers taught him that so long as private property kept its power government had to be a system of bribery; corruption became "the very essence of the life of a state." Because reform aimed to change everything except this essence, it was futile. By 1912 Steffens decided that "nothing but revolution could change the system."

In the second and third decades of the century, he became a camp follower of revolutions, first in Mexico, then Russia, then Italy. He knew Carranza and Lenin and Mussolini, as he had known T.R. and La Follette and Wilson; and he found that he preferred the frank dictators to the democratic demogogues, as he had preferred the ward boss to the goo-goo. The Bullitt mission and Versailles completed his disillusion with democratic statesmanship; Italy in the twenties gave him a new sense of the totalitarian virtues. Liberty? Yes, Lenin had abolished it; so had Mussolini; but so had Wilson and Lloyd George in the emergency of war. "Don't we always abolish liberty when we are afraid or in trouble? Isn't liberty a psychological matter? Isn't it something that depends, not upon laws and constitutions, but upon our state of mind? Isn't liberty a measure of our sense of security and nothing else? Like democracy, like peace, liberty has to be founded in economic arrangements that abolish fear."

In the end, he concluded, the solution was to do what only the Communists had done: destroy the source of corruption by taking over the system of business which, in private hands, bred graft, thievery, and war. Russia had shown the way; but even in America, while the preparation for the future was not so purposeful, the trend was evident. America was moving, he wrote, unconsciously but "with mighty momentum" on a course that seemed likely to carry it to an ultimate meeting place with the Soviet Union.[7]

The response to the *Autobiography* was tremendous. Steffens was "the total American to date," said the New Era prophet Garet Garrett; and, in telling the story of his life, he was only making audible "the mind and conscience of a race." John Reed, the American Communist, had observed fifteen years before that being with Steffens was like watching flashes of clear light. Now, in the most striking of his flashes, Steffens seemed to be offering, as Newton Arvin said in the *Nation*, "the obituary of American reformism."[8]

The new generation, in particular, found in the book the quality of revelation. Thousands of letters poured into Steffens's cottage at Carmel, California. And Steffens, heartened by the response, pressed home what he felt to be the lesson of his life. The Russians, he would say with smiling confidence, had made "the great turning"; nobody else in the world had anything basic or real to propose. At a San Francisco meeting, he said that the Russian Revolution was the work of less than fifteen thousand people; pausing dramatically, he added: "Well, there are nearly fifteen thousand people in this hall." The old skepticism had disappeared. He had no more questions to ask. The long quest was over. "All roads in our day," he concluded, "lead to Moscow."[9]

IV

The following year an influential book by a much younger man generalized Steffens's indictment. Its title made the essential point — *Farewell to Reform: Being a History of the Rise, Life and Decay of the Progressive Mind In America.* Its author, John Chamberlain, twenty-nine years old, seven years out of Yale, expressed the new generation's impatience with the pragmatic heritage. The book offered a lively picture of the progressive heroes — T.R., Wilson, La Follette, Croly. But, in Chamberlain's view, their whole effort was a study in futility; pragmatic liberalism just could not stand the gaff. Harold Stearns had been right in isolating "the technique of liberal failure." Reliance on reform, said Chamberlain, could only prepare "the ground for an American Fascism." "The situation, looked upon with intelligence and considered as a long-range proposition," he concluded, "can lead to but one of two personal conclusions: it can make one either a cynic or a revolutionist." [10]

Steffens and Chamberlain had prepared the way: what was needed now was a persuasive account of the world beyond the revolution. This came early in 1933 with the American publication of John Strachey's *The Coming Struggle for Power.* Here at last, a single work, wide in its sweep, relentless in its logic, compelling in its faith, told the whole story. For a generation of British Socialists Strachey's book had come, in the words of Richard Crossman, as "a blinding illumination"; and for many disturbed Americans its impact was no less strong. Depression, as Strachey saw it, was the result of the betrayal of history by capitalism. "There is literally nothing," said Strachey, "to prevent the American people from producing and distributing *from to-morrow* sufficient goods and services to secure for every one of them an ample and secure standard of life; or rather there is nothing except the vile tangle of worn-out social relations." In the crisis, Communism offered "the one method by which human civilization can be maintained." For Strachey, the Soviet Union was capable of anything, even of "the indefinite postponement of death." "To travel from the capitalist world into Soviet territory," he wrote, "is to pass from death to birth." [11]

This millennial ecstasy was symptomatic. "If it be permissible to speak of Jesus as the Christ of dream," wrote one overwrought American intellectual in 1931, "it is equally profound to speak of Lenin as the Christ of reality." The Russian Revolution had opened a new era in the life of man — "death's dominance fading out of life's new dawn, life flowing lustily through the minds of

men, in red exultation . . . the young red dawn . . . the rebirth of
life, creation crying to be born again." The poet Kenneth Patchen
even sketched a new Mariolatry:

> In the Kremlin lamp of her eyes. . . .
> With the lightning Beauty of Revolution. . . .
> Comrades, the Red Woman!
> She is dream's image made real.
> She is the timeless Bride of all our loving.[12]

v

Was not Communism indeed "dream's image made real" — the
dream of collectivism which had so enchanted the liberalism of
the twenties? "The people will rule," Dewey had said, "when they
have power, and they will have power in the degree they own and
control the lands, banks, the producing and distributing agencies of
the nation. Ravings about Bolshevism, communism, socialism are
irrelevant to the axiomatic truth of this statement." [13] Dewey, like
Beard, might now back away from the logic of his own analysis;
like Beard, he might now criticize Soviet Russia and reject the
American Communists. But their followers well knew the phenomenon of the "lost leader"; after all, both Dewey and Beard had succumbed to the war fever in 1917. The young radicals had learned
their lesson from Harold Stearns; they would not stop analysis just
because the process was becoming painful. They were tired of experiment, of pragmatism, of piecemeal reform. They wanted
change, and they wanted certitude.

And little in what they had learned from Dewey, Beard, and
Veblen equipped them to resist the Soviet Union. Dewey, Beard,
and, no doubt, Veblen cared deeply about individual freedom
(though if Veblen did, he never wrote much about it); but this
faith in freedom was more a personal conviction than an organic
part of their political thought. They had made an implicit assumption of freedom when what they needed was an explicit theory of
the conditions which made freedom possible. Their writings about
the planned economy, for example, never explained realistically
how political opposition was to be maintained against an all-power-

ful state. When Dewey and Beard now criticized Russia, the criticism did not always seem to emerge squarely from their own premises. The Soviet Union continued to appear to some of their disciples as the exemplification of their own planning thesis of the twenties.

The heritage of the Social Gospel reinforced this impression; for the Social Gospel, in its long preoccupation with the fact that freedom in capitalist society often produced injustice, left too little room for liberty as a value requiring specific protection of its own. Seeing freedom as a threat to individuality rather than as the indispensable defense for the individual, the devotees of the social passion were no more equipped than the exponents of the planned economy to identify the perils of Communism. In 1932, the Federal Council of Churches pronounced the principle of competition as "nothing more than a partly conventionalized embodiment of primeval selfishness." The "Christian ideal," in contrast, demanded "hearty support of a planned economic system." [14] The Council did not mention Russia. But the *World Tomorrow*, the magazine of Protestant radicalism, had noted as early as 1930 that the Communists might soon discover, for all their atheism, that by establishing a thoroughgoing collective life they were laying "the foundations for a living Kingdom of God." The significance of the Soviet Union, said the Reverend Harry F. Ward in 1933, was "that it gives the masses that which our liberals are so afraid of, that which life has not had since the break-up of the Middle Ages — a central purpose." "Russia seems so fast to be developing a real human brotherhood under the name of social justice," wrote the Reverend Lyman P. Powell, "that we Christian nations may one day find ourselves obliged to learn anew at Russia's feet the deeper meaning of the social teachings of Jesus." [15]

The image of Russia thus became an image of intelligent planning and of unifying faith. Here at last was "a government acting directly for public ends and not for the protection of private interest" (Robert Morss Lovett). Here was "the only nation in the world today that has vanquished unemployment" (Maxwell S. Stewart). No doubt there was repression and control; but a nation at war, a social system in danger, inevitably exercised censorship; had the Soviet Union "committed any worse blunders than were committed by the United States during the World War" (Edmund Wilson)?

"Those Rascals in Russia along with all their Cuckoo stuff," said Will Rogers, "have got some mighty good ideas. . . . Just think of everybody in a Country going to work." Lecturers discussed the Communist experiment before enthralled audiences. Businessmen, seeking new markets, began to agitate for recognition of the Soviet regime. Ray Long, the editor of Hearst's *Cosmopolitan,* traveled to Moscow to sign up Russian writers and feted Boris Pilnyak, president of the All-Russian Writers' Union, at the Metropolitan Club in New York. William Allen White called Russia "the most interesting place on the planet," and the Book-of-the-Month Club distributed *New Russia's Primer,* with its graphic contrast between planned Russia and chaotic America. By 1931, as capitalism sank deeper in depression, Amtorg, the Soviet trading corporation in New York, was receiving about 350 applications a day from Americans wanting jobs in the Soviet Union.[16]

VI

The Communist certitudes challenged the self-doubt, the guilty conscience, the limited objectives of liberalism. At Columbia in these years many students read Strachey's *Coming Struggle* along with Lippmann's *Preface to Morals.* The contrast between Lippmann and Strachey, wrote James Wechsler, looking back at his undergraduate days, was that of "the solitary man futilely contemplating the spectacle of the West's decline arrayed against the man of the future." And Marxism supplied not only struggle and faith; it supplied, even more important, understanding. "It was the supreme logic of Marxism," recalled Stewart Alsop of his undergraduate days at Yale, "which made everything in contemporary history so luminously clear. . . . It [did] your thinking for you." [17]

The impression was spreading that the old progressivism was played out. Edmund Wilson wrote early in 1931 in Herbert Croly's magazine that he could not see how people of Croly's general persuasion could still bet on liberalism. "If the American radicals and progressives who repudiate the Marxist dogma and the strategy of the Communist party hope to accomplish anything valuable," Wilson said, "they must take Communism away from the Communists, and take it without ambiguities or reservations, asserting emphatically that their ultimate goal is the ownership of the means of production by the government." For all its defects, Wilson later added, the Soviet Union remained "the moral top of the world where the light never really goes out." [18]

To some the middle class itself was beginning to seem obsolete. Leading novelists registered the shift from older values. Theodore Dreiser, the specialist in American tragedy, began to discover a new hope in Communism. Sherwood Anderson, with his conviction that "the desire for money and position poisons all life," believed too for a moment in 1932 that Communism held the solution. "The world is in crisis," said Waldo Frank *and there is no time to lose.* The revolutionary tomorrow must be prepared today. Otherwise, it may come too late — too late to save mankind from the destruction of capitalistic war, and (still worse) from the moral siphilis [sic] of capitalistic peace." Dos Passos, completing his trilogy *U.S.A.*, summed up his impression of American society in the title of his last volume *The Big Money.* With the middle class in moral decay, the future, as Wilson said, lay with the workers, with "young men who start their careers as convinced and cool-headed revolutionists," looking to Russia "as a model of what a state should be" and seeking "a working-class dictatorship" for the United States.[19]

The next step was to regard art itself as a weapon in the struggle. The Communist Michael Gold opened the controversy with a violent attack on Thornton Wilder as the "prophet of the genteel Christ." Wilder's penetrating moral fantasies, set deceptively in other climes and ages, seemed to Gold the culmination of the hypocrisy of the bourgeoisie. He quoted Wilder with derision: "For there is a land of the living and a land of the dead, and the bridge is love, the only survival, the only meaning." "And nobody works in a Ford plant," Mike Gold continued "and nobody starves looking for work, and there is nothing but Love in God's ancient Peru, Italy, Greece, if not in God's capitalist America 1931!" Wilder's glitter and nostalgia were all an attempt to cover up the "billions wrung from American workers and foreign peasants and coolies." [20]

Archibald MacLeish, a lawyer turned poet, who had served his time with the lost generation in France, emerged as the chief defender of the old-fashioned theory that art was not a weapon. "A poem," he had written in 1925, "should not mean / But be." Persisting in this faith, he abominated what he called "the social cant"; there was, he said, too much sun on the lids of his eyes to be listening. In a notable work of 1932, "Invocation to the Social Muse," MacLeish stated with precision the issue between himself and Gold.

Does the lady suggest we should writhe it out in The Word?
Does Madame recall our responsibilities? We are
Whores, Fräulein: poets, Fräulein, are persons of

Known vocation following troops: they must sleep with
Stragglers from either prince and of both views.
The rules permit them to further the business of neither.

It is also strictly forbidden to mix in maneuvers.
Those that infringe are inflated with praise on the plazas —
Their bones are resultantly afterwards found under newspapers. . . .

There is nothing worse for our trade than to be in style. . . .

I remind you, Barinya, the life of the poet is hard —
A hardy life with a boot as quick as a fiver:

Is it just to demand of us also to bear arms?

Gold replied by charging that "Hitler's program, somewhat veiled in cauls and mysteries of the poetic womb," could be discerned in MacLeish's "Frescoes for Mr. Rockefeller's City." [21] The controversy sputtered out but the conscience of the times was drifting toward Gold. Later in the decade it seemed as if the new mood was almost converting MacLeish.

VII

If the artist's duty was not to portray the world but to change it, then the artist's goal must be to sharpen the worker's own understanding of the class struggle. A new school of "proletarian literature" began to be erected on this theory. The first impulse behind proletarian writing was doubtless a response to depression, a reaching out for new themes and techniques to replace the supposedly exhausted forms of the twenties and to express the new emotions of poverty and despair. But the Communist party was quick to provide the new movement with its marching orders. As Mike Gold said, the Revolution, "in its secular manifestations of strike, boycott, mass-meeting, imprisonment, sacrifice, agitation, martyrdom, organization," was a theme worthy of the "religious devotion" of the artist.[22]

The cult of proletarianism could not destroy all talent. Robert Cantwell's *The Land of Plenty*, a novel of 1934, opened with the failure of power in a lumber mill at night. The darkened plant, where no one could move without danger from the machines, with tension mounting among the workers and distant cries of *Yahoo! Yahoo!* echoing through the black, became for a moment a symbol for the stricken system. Darkness was the book's binding theme; at the end, after the brutal smashing of the inevitable strike, the fleeing strike leaders, at last aware of the dimensions of the struggle, sit helplessly in the brush by the beach, "waiting for the darkness to come like a friend and set them free." [23]

But Communist literary dictation reduced most of the novels to a recipe: aching oppression, intolerable provocation, the strike ("not like love, cloying, fearful, heartrending; it was fresh, clear, like cold air in her lungs, it was overwhelming, pitiless, like the triumphant march of an unvanquished army, like the rise to crescendo of drums and bagpipes; it was vast, it was as dazzlingly bright as the pain had been dark, it was the one word: STRIKE"), the workers' solidarity, the strike leaders coming to see that their local fight was part of a world-wide class struggle, the hard, selfless, farseeing Communists, and the final dedication to the time when "all the people would come out of the factories, singing in the streets." [24]

In a time of crisis, the very ruthlessness of the Communist

formula carried an appeal. No doubt, toughness and intransigence were distasteful. Yet was not one's very recoil from hardness a sign of bourgeois weakness? "God knows it makes my heart sick at times," a friend wrote to Granville Hicks in the summer of 1932; "from one angle, it seems nothing but grime and stink and sweat and obscene noises and the language of the beasts. But surely this is what *history* is. It just is not made by gentlemen and scholars, and 'made' only in the bad sense by the Norman Thomases and the Devere Allens and the John Deweys. Lenin must have been (from a conceivable point of view) a dreadful man; so must . . . all the others who have destroyed and built up. So will our contemporaries in the American movement be."

Some intellectuals thus were at once drawn and repelled by Communism; and even what repelled them eased their bad consciences. "Let's salvage as much as we can of the rather abstract things we care for," said Hicks's friend, "but golly, let's realize that there are far more basic and primitive things that have to be taken care of first (as long as men are starving and exploited), and do absolutely nothing, at any moment, to impede the work of the men who are fighting what is really our battle *for us*." [25]

VIII

The American Communist leaders in 1930 were the survivors of the series of sanguinary feuds that had been going on since the founding of the party in 1919. It was not indeed until 1923 that the American party achieved even the semblance of unity. As Moscow gradually consolidated its control in the next years, the American comrades found themselves increasingly involved in the struggles around the grave of Lenin. American leaders, attaching themselves to Stalin, Trotsky, Bukharin, or Zinoviev, rose and set in the reflected light of their Russian models. With the fall of Trotsky, James P. Cannon and Max Shachtman dropped out of the American constellation; with the fall of Bukharin went Jay Lovestone and Ben Gitlow. There remained in 1930 as the general secretary of the party a soft-spoken and tractable Kansan named Earl Browder, and, as the party's grand old man, the veteran labor organizer William Z. Foster.

Foster, who was fifty years old in 1931, had a notable past in the history of American labor. He had been active twenty years before in the IWW; he had been for a time a leading American exponent of French doctrines of anarchosyndicalism; and he had led the great steel strike in 1919. Indeed, he had kept his party membership secret for a period lest it handicap his work in the labor movement. By the middle twenties, however, he came into the open, and in 1928 he became the party's presidential nominee. In the intra-party battles, he had affiliated himself with the Stalinist faction, and he had reason for the highest anticipation when Stalin decided to reconstruct the American party in 1929. But, the anarchosyndicalist fervor with which he had conducted factional fights apparently raised suspicions in Moscow. To Foster's discomfiture, the inconspicuous but faithful Browder received the post of party leader.

But Foster remained the best-known party spokesman. In 1930 a committee of the House of Representatives, under the chairmanship of Hamilton Fish of New York, set out to investigate Communist activities. Fish, who twenty years before had been captain of the Harvard football team for which John Reed was cheerleader, summoned Foster as a leading witness. It was a striking contrast — the arrogant Hudson River aristocrat and the blue-eyed worker, with his nervous mouth, his long bony jaw, and his Irish charm.

"The workers in this country look upon the Soviet Union as their country, is that right?" demanded Fish. "The more advanced workers do." "Look upon the Soviet Union as their country?" "Yes." "They look upon the Soviet flag as their flag?" "The workers of this country," replied Foster, "have only one flag and that is the red flag." Fish went on: "If they had to choose between the red flag and the American flag, I take it from you that you would choose the red flag; is that correct?" Said Foster: "I have stated my answer." What about socialism? "The socialist," said Foster, "is a fascist."

Watching the show, Edmund Wilson could not help being impressed. The Communists obviously had the great advantage of knowing exactly what they wanted and how they proposed to get it. This uncompromising quality, Wilson suggested, gave them "a kind of strength which perhaps no other group in America, conservative or radical possessed." There might be real reason, after all, for Fish's fear of them: "they are people who are willing to die for a religion." [26]

Foster tried to communicate the same sense of absolute determination, without sentimentality or subterfuge, in his book of 1932, *Toward Soviet America*. The only escape for the workers, he wrote, was "the revolutionary way." Lest his meaning be mistaken, Foster took care to add that by "abolition" of capitalism, he meant "its overthrow in open struggle" by "the revolutionary proletariat in arms." The proletarian dictatorship would then organize the United Soviet States of America. "Under the dictatorship," Foster added coldly, "all the capitalist parties — Republican, Democratic, Progressive, Socialist, etc. — will be liquidated." [27]

IX

In this spirit, the party set out to take advantage of the depression. Party organizers, hatless young men in imitation leather jackets, went to the factories and to the breadlines. Some even ventured, with considerable personal courage, into the semifeudal counties of rural America — into the coal fields of Pennsylvania, into Williamson and Franklin Counties in Illinois, into Harlan County, Kentucky (where a miner told John Dos Passos in the fall of 1931, "By God, if they won't let us march under the American flag, we'll march under the red flag," and where Louis Stark described the situation to the *New York Times* as ripe for "revolution and a seizure of the reins of government").[28]

They directed their most spectacular efforts at the jobless. Unemployed Councils, set up by the Communist party, agitated, often to good effect, for better conditions in relief centers, for the stopping of eviction, for unemployment insurance. The party workers made a lot of noise, and they won credit for much that could more soberly be ascribed to conditions than to agitation. From the towns and cities they tried to move on to the nation. In December 1931, they staged a National Hunger March on Washington. Singing "The Red Flag" and "Solidarity Forever," a bedraggled procession shuffled through the winter sunlight of early

December, carrying angry banners: IN THE LAST WAR WE FOUGHT FOR THE BOSSES: IN THE NEXT WAR WE'LL FIGHT FOR THE WORKERS. On the ramps leading to the central portico of the Capitol the marchers met policemen, standing silently with rifles, riot guns, and shiny new tear-gas pistols; in the stonework above the steps were machine gun nests. A few days later, the national secretary of the Unemployed Councils told a Senate committee, "We intend to go forward on a struggle to organize the unemployed, to make them fight upon the streets of the cities." 29

The incessant activity had some effect. Charles Rumford Walker heard a talk on the Soviet Union at a meeting of unemployed workers in Detroit. A little man behind him shouted, "They've got a better system than we've got." "Are you a Communist?" Walker asked. "Hell, no," the man replied, "I'm a Roman Catholic; how can I be a Communist? But they've got a better system than we've got. . . . Work?" he added. "I've been out fifteen months. I've got four children, and I'll fight before I'll see 'em starve." 30 Yet these were exceptions. The bulk of people who shouted at Communist-staged demonstrations knew nothing about Communism; and very little rubbed off on them. "There have been sporadic uprisings in a number of our industrial cities in the past six months," Ed McGrady of the A.F. of L. told a Senate committee in the spring of 1932, "and in almost every case they passed it off or tossed it aside by saying that it was led by Communists. There may have been Communists in those uprisings, but as a matter of fact the great bulk of those people know nothing about Communism. They wanted bread." 31

Communism had a less enduring impact on the unemployed than it had on the conscience-stricken fugitives from the intellectual and professional classes. Yet even these, in joining the movement, were not, on the whole, making a deliberate choice between the Soviet Union and the United States, or even between free society and totalitarianism. They were responding, rather, to complex emotions of guilt and aspiration. As Whittaker Chambers described it, the power of Communism lay in the fact that it offered "what nothing else in the dying world had power to offer at the same intensity — faith and a vision." It demanded "those things which have always stirred what is best in men — courage, poverty, self-sacrifice, discipline, intelligence, my life, and, at need, my death." [32]

Some joined the party because they craved a faith; the party consecrated them to a living religion. Some sought power; the party promised them the future. Some were idealists; the party offered them a crusade. Some had a grudge against society; the party transformed the grudge into a philosophy. Some were lonely; the party gave them friends. Some were afraid; the party guaranteed them victory. "I was on the side of history," wrote J. B. Matthews, "where I could look across and view with sincere pity the floundering liberals and the obstructing capitalists. History would crush them like a juggernaut."

Capitalism, they believed, meant poverty and unemployment; Communism meant jobs and security. Capitalism meant imperialism and war; Communism meant freedom and peace. Capitalism was the past in the last stages of decay; Communism the hope that men could rebuild their lives according to their own design — that they could change the world. "Intoxication with a feeling of power," J. B. Matthews called it. Others experienced it more impersonally as contact less with power than with history. John Dos Passos, sitting in 1932 in the crowded Madison Square Garden, heard the chairman of a Communist meeting announce that the German comrades had won two million votes in the election. He felt within him, as he wrote, that "tremendous intoxication with history that is the great achievement of Communist solidarity." [33]

In the end, Communism became for some the whole of life, charging every moment with urgency and purpose. The long-time party member lost all other motivation. "The Party," said Ben Gitlow, "winds him up and keeps him going." "I should rather die than give up my active work with the Party," cried Mother Bloor. "— to give it up *would* be death. I have been so much a part of the Party that I cannot conceive of living in any sense without it." And for most of these the harsh party discipline, far from an obstacle, was an indispensable part of the appeal — the outward symbol of the inner passion.[34]

X

But Communism became the whole of life for very few Americans. In 1930 the party claimed only six thousand members; by 1932, after two years of furious agitation in the midst of economic collapse, only a meager twelve thousand.[35] Many more signed membership cards in these years; but most passed through the party as through a revolving door, finding the discipline unbearable, the dialectic meaningless, and the vocabulary incomprehensible. Some left the party for the same reason they entered it — because they cared deeply about democracy and freedom. The Communist vision had been enticing; but the facts, even after three years of capitalist decay, remained dull — a clique of dreary fanatics and seedy functionaries, talking to themselves in an unintelligible idiom, ignored by the working class, dedicating their main efforts to witch hunts against liberals and Socialists. The party was sodden, contentious, bureaucratic, and feeble.

A sense of wasted opportunity hung over all. The *Party Organizer* spent issue after issue brooding over the defects in organizing methods. Moscow issued periodic bulls castigating the American party. Yet somehow Communism would not click in the American scene. Lauren Gilfillan, going to "pit college" in a Pennsylvania mining town, found ample evidence of Communist activity; but, in a moment of stress, a young miner, the unit treasurer of the Young Communist League, told her: "Oh, to hell with Communism! They're a lot of stupid lummoxes. Real miners ain't Communists. The Communists've allus been in Avelonia and they allus will be. They just make a lotta noise." An economist, informed that the son of a prominent banker had become a Communist, replied that he would be more impressed if the son of a prominent worker had become a Communist. Perhaps the columnist, and Socialist, Heywood Broun — another of John Reed's classmates — best expressed the average reaction. "The club is against God because he doesn't exist," said Broun, "and against Norman Thomas because he does. The whole movement leaves me a little wistful. Not even Princeton itself has produced so many sophomores as the Communist Party." [36]

There remained a significance in the Communist vogue. The

intellectuals, like the canaries that miners used to carry with them in the shafts, could feel danger from afar. "Antennae of the race," Ezra Pound called them. If the pragmatic liberals were to fail, Communism would infallibly draw more and more men behind it on the fatal journey.

25. Climax in Washington

HERBERT HOOVER had brought with him in 1929 sizable majorities in both houses of the Congress. The Republicans had 17 more senators than the Democrats in the 71st Congress and 100 more representatives. But in the congressional election of 1930, the Democrats took the House, gaining over 50 seats; and the administration barely maintained a 48–47 plurality in the Senate — a meaningless margin, since the single Independent, Norris of Nebraska, and the minority bloc of progressive Republicans opposed the Hoover policies. The Democrats also did well in the states. Franklin D. Roosevelt won re-election as governor of New York; and the success of public power advocates in a series of state elections where private utilities were key issues — in Pennsylvania, where Gifford Pinchot became governor, in Wisconsin which brought in old Bob La Follette's younger son, Phil, in Oregon, in Washington, in Connecticut, in Maine, in Alabama — suggested a gathering revolt against business leadership. The 72nd Congress, when it convened in December 1931, faced a rising national demand for action.

Few of its members, though, were ready to meet the demand with constructive ideas. In the Senate only one man had shown a consistent preoccupation with the business cycle, the labor movement, and other issues of industrial society. This was Robert F. Wagner of New York. Remote now from his immigrant origins, save for a love of partridge smothered in sauerkraut and a taste for Wagnerian opera, Wagner in his middle fifties was the best-dressed man in the Senate. He was prosy on the floor and earnest in the hearing room; but his persistence had impact; and from his arrival in Washington in 1927 he had talked steadily about government's role in stabilizing the economy.

Depression gave this concern a new urgency. Unemployment seemed to him "a by-product of capitalism"; and any system which permitted men to go cold and hungry while warehouses bulged with clothes and food "must be radically wrong in some particulars." He was still sure that capitalism could be reformed, but not by repeating old incantations about rugged individualism. The only hope was federal action. By 1931 he was advancing a program of his own. His proposals started with $2 billion for public works. He wanted in addition a Federal Employment Stabilization Board for the advance planning of public works, an effective federal employment service, a system of collecting unemployment statistics, and a federal system of unemployment insurance.

But he could hardly have conceived measures more objectionable to Hoover. They cost too much money and gave too much power to government. The President accordingly vetoed Wagner's public works program, emasculated the Stabilization Board, vetoed the employment service (it would have been, Hoover gravely said, "a serious blow to labor"), and declined to request adequate appropriations for unemployment statistics. As for unemployment insurance, this measure even in the third winter of the depression seemed too radical for congressional consideration.[1]

Wagner's efforts in the stabilization field were paralleled by those of Robert M. La Follette, Jr., of Wisconsin in the field of relief. La Follette, who had succeeded to his father's seat in 1925 at the age of thirty, was square and stocky, with round face and black hair parted down the middle; he was a thoughtful student of economic affairs, a collected speaker, and a skilled parliamentarian. If he lacked his father's majestic vehemence, he still struck home almost as effectively with cool, sober, almost metallic understatement. And in Senator Edward P. Costigan of Colorado, La Follette found the ideal partner with whom to investigate the relief situation. Twenty years older than La Follette, born to wealth, a Harvard graduate, Costigan had come to the Senate in 1930. He was an arresting figure, with his hatchet face and his leathery skin, casual in manner, imperturbable and cutting in debate. During the relief hearings of the Committee on Manufactures, La Follette's intelligent persistence alternated murderously with Costigan's fast, sardonic incredulity.

A survey of municipal officials and social workers in 1931 convinced La Follette and Costigan that local relief could no longer do the job. "Nothing short of Federal assistance," said Costigan, "early provided and efficiently and constructively extended, can possibly satisfy the conscience and heart and safeguard the good name of America." In February 1932, the two men proposed a bill calling for a modest federal grant of $375 million to states for relief purposes. The Hoover administration succeeded in beating the first La Follette-Costigan measure. But La Follette and Costigan kept up their relief fight through the spring; and, in the same session, the battle expanded on the public works front, with Senators Wagner, Hugo Black of Alabama, and Bronson Cutting of New Mexico offering programs ranging from one to five billion dollars in magnitude.[2]

There was much talent in Senate opposition. Mr. Justice Brandeis noted that it was "very ably led and has proved very effective." He named Norris, La Follette, Black, and Borah and might have added Wagner, Cutting, Costigan, Hiram Johnson, Wheeler, and Gerald Nye. But, while the group could stir issues, it could rarely carry them. Much of the time it was not a group at all, but a congeries of righteous men, each proceeding to his own objective along his own path. All their efforts could not force powers on the administration which Hoover did not want, nor overcome instinctive congressional repugnance toward enlarging the role of the federal government or increasing the national debt. Many members of Congress seemed to doubt whether Congress could do anything in the crisis. Senator Gore of Oklahoma probably spoke a general sentiment when he said dourly in 1931 that you could no more relieve depression by laws "than you can pass a resolution to prevent disease. This is an economic disease. You might just as well try to prevent the human race from having a disease as to prevent economic grief of this sort." [3]

II

The situation in the House of Representatives was even more confused. That swirling body, bearing a fresh mandate from the people after 1930, contained men of all views. But its dominant figure, especially when he became Speaker in the 72nd Congress, was John Nance Garner. With his bright, ruddy face, short-cropped white hair, cold blue eyes, and tight small mouth, Garner presented at once the appearance of an infinitely experienced sage and of a newborn baby. Through persistence, through seniority, above all, through unlimited parliamentary astuteness, he had risen steadily to the leadership of the House Democrats. Now he had before him an unparalleled opportunity to make a national impression.

Garner was born in Red River County, Texas, in 1868. Fearing tuberculosis as a young man, he moved in 1893 to the little town of Uvalde, reputed in Texas to have the driest climate between Clarksville and the setting sun. In a decade he had become a leading citizen of Uvalde, a property owner on the way to his first fifty thousand dollars, and a member of the Texas legislature. As chairman of the committee on redistricting, Garner soon brought in a bill to provide himself with a congressional district; and in 1903 he arrived in Washington.

He was accompanied by his hard-working wife, who served as his secretary through most of his career. They lived a quiet life in respectable boardinghouses around Capitol Hill, rising at six, breakfasting on lamb chops and fruit, working hard during the day, visiting perhaps in the early evening with other congressional families, retiring regularly at nine. On warm spring afternoons he sometimes took the streetcar out to the zoo to feed the elephants and monkeys; and on occasional evenings, he relaxed around the card table, with the click of poker chips, the fragrance of cigars, the sips of bourbon and branch water. It was an old-fashioned life, self-respecting and self-contained. To the end Garner always remained "Mr. Garner" to his wife and son.

Garner made few speeches and offered few bills in the House, though he fought hard for the graduated income tax and for the Federal Reserve Act. Yet his combination of wiliness and integrity commanded the confidence of politicians. By the time of the First World War, he was recognized as a leading House Democrat. When Claude Kitchin's opposition to the war disqualified him as administration leader, Wilson made Garner his confidential representative in the House.

Garner maintained his equable course through the twenties. He was now the richest man in Uvalde, the owner of banks, stores, residences, farms, and ranches, of pecan orchards and beehives, of sheep, cattle, and mohair goats. In Washington he lived the agreeable life of a political pro, trading public gibes and private drinks with his opposite number and good friend, Nicholas Longworth of Ohio, the Republican Speaker. At the end of the day, Democratic members liked to gather in Garner's office to outline party strategy and to strike a blow for liberty.

In his politics, Garner remained stoutly Jeffersonian. "The great trouble today," he said as late as 1931, "is that we have too many laws. I believe that primarily a government has but two functions — to protect the lives and property rights of citizens. When it goes further than that it becomes a burden." But he was also Jeffersonian in his hostility toward big finance — a hostility strengthened by a country banker's natural hatred of Wall Street. In this spirit, he assailed the domination of government by business, led the fight against Mellon's tax reduction program, denounced the private utilities and supported government operation of Muscle Shoals. He also opposed the Ku Klux Klan in Texas and secured House endorsement for the Norris lameduck amendment.

He finally became the official Democratic leader in the 71st Congress. While he voted against the Smoot-Hawley bill, he saw to it that the goat's-hair and Bermuda onions from the Fifteenth District of Texas received their due protection. (Cordell Hull, the Tennessee free trader, believed that Garner was "at heart as much a high-tariff man as Smoot or Hawley.") Essentially Garner, with his collection of Jeffersonian maxims, was baffled by the depression. When he was elected Speaker in the 72nd Congress, he vacillated between cooperation and obstruction in his attitude toward the administration. Yet, whatever he did, he generally carried his well-disciplined followers with him. "This isn't a session of Congress," the progressive Republican from New York City, Fiorello H. La

Guardia, said one day; "this is a kissing bee." Some began to see Garner as a presidential possibility; perhaps a Texas Coolidge was what the nation needed. Soon Washington newspapermen were inventing names for him far more colorful than anything anyone had ever called him at home — "Cactus Jack" or "Chaparral Jack," or even the "Texas Tiger."

In February 1932 Garner formed a Democratic Economy Committee, charged with doing everything possible to balance the budget, including even the enactment of a sales tax. But this proposal went too far, and Democrats began to defy their leader. Reluctantly Garner threw himself into the fight. Applauded by conservative Democrats, like Representative Lewis W. Douglas of Arizona, Garner left the Speaker's chair, walked to the well of the House, and made a dramatic appeal for the sales tax. In his climax, he asked every member of the House who would pledge himself to a balanced budget to rise in his seat. Nearly the whole House stood in a moment of revivalist fervor. But the spell could not last. Under La Guardia's fiery leadership, the sales tax was knocked out of the bill. For a moment, Garner's prestige was in jeopardy. Still, rarely at a political loss, the Speaker now tried the opposite tack. Only a few weeks after his budget-balancing exhortation, he coolly sponsored a new bill, this one an omnibus public works measure, calling for about $2.5 billion of federal spending.[4]

Garner's turnabout on the budget suggested the depths of intellectual confusion among the parties. "The issues between them," wrote Senator Reed of Pennsylvania in 1931, "are very faint at the moment." There was a meaningful division within each party between the budget balancers and the expansionists; but their debates only led the men in the middle, like Garner, to seesaw back and forth from one to the other. The world of politics, said Anne O'Hare McCormick in the *New York Times,* was lost in its own fog. Capitol Hill had become a place "where everything is expressed and nothing is felt, a place where all the emotions are vicarious emotions, a place where all thoughts are clichés." [5]

III

The American system remained essentially a presidential system: in the end, all things came to the man in the White House. "His is the vital place of action in the system, whether he accept it or not," Woodrow Wilson once wrote, "and the office is the measure of the man — of his wisdom as well as of his force." And Herbert Hoover, as President, had far more definite ideas than most members of Congress about the cause and the cure of the economic crisis.

The depression was caused, Hoover said repeatedly in 1929 and 1930, by uncontrolled speculation in the securities market leading to an "inevitable crash." Still, if the crash was inevitable, the securities speculation, in Hoover's view, was not. It had been a gratuitous indulgence by an economy of whose "fundamental correctness" Hoover remained as convinced as on the day of his acceptance address in 1928. If the system of production and distribution was sound, then there was obviously no point in basic reform. The need, as he first saw it, was simply to seal off the rest of the economy from the shock effects of the Wall Street crash. The problem was, not to reorganize a defective structure, but to protect a healthy one.[6]

Hence his program of 1929: the support of purchasing power through attempts to peg wage rates and farm prices; the stimulus of credit through Federal Reserve open-market operations and the reduction of the discount rate; and, most important of all, the expansion of private and public construction. This, the President said, was the "greatest tool which our economic system affords for the establishment of stability"; and he placed the responsibility for its use on government at all levels, as well as on private industry. Appealing in late 1929 to governors to increase state programs, Hoover pledged that "the Federal Government will exert itself to the utmost within its own province."[7]

For months the verbal encouragement of public works remained Hoover's chief weapon. In January 1930, he said that total construction spending for the year would be larger than in the boom year of 1929. In May he said that the acceleration of the construction program had been "successful beyond our hopes." But, while the President and other officials were making their cheerful forecasts, private outlays for construction actually fell off in 1930 by over $2 billion, and public outlays rose by a bare $400 million. In 1931 private outlays declined another $2 billion; by 1932, they were down almost to one-quarter of what they had been in 1926. And, while the federal contribution to construction expenditures steadily increased, reaching half a billion dollars in 1932, the total of public construction steadily declined, as state and local governments ran out of money. In 1932 total public construction was nearly a billion dollars less than it had been in 1930.[8]

There were several reasons for the collapse of the public works effort. Despite all the talk about the "construction reserve" ever since the Unemployment Conference of 1922, nothing had been done, in Hoover's Department of Commerce or elsewhere, to establish a reserve fund or to work out a shelf of projects. Nor was there now the executive energy in the administration to push a public works program through. Mellon had always scoffed at the idea, and Hoover himself became at crucial moments a victim of his own optimism. In June 1930, a delegation headed by Dr. John A. Ryan of the National Catholic Welfare Council and Amos Pinchot urged on the President immediate expansion of federal public works. Hoover, listening with the exasperation of a man who knew the situation far better than his visitors, told the group that the interview was unnecessary. The tide had turned. Unemployment was declining. Business was expanding its activities. The government had the situation fully under control. Public works? "Gentlemen," the President said, "you have come sixty days too late. The depression is over." [9]

IV

Most important, the public works theory was fighting a losing battle in Hoover's mind against his mounting concern for the budget. For a time, this internal debate led to a dizzying alternation between presidential statements calling for more public works and presidential statements warning against more public expenditures. But as national income continued to sink through 1930, so did tax collections. Though the Treasury could still report a surplus of nearly $200 million for 1930, it was evident that the nation was headed for a deficit in 1931. As the deficit came nearer, Hoover became increasingly preoccupied with what he actually defined as "the primary duty of the Government, that is, to hold expenditures within our income." More and more, the growing federal debt seemed the primary threat to recovery. "For the Government to finance by bond issues," Hoover declared in December 1930, "deprives industry and agriculture of just that much capital for its own use and for employment. Prosperity cannot be restored by raids upon the public Treasury."

Tax revenues continued to fall in 1931; and the federal deficit that year was almost a billion dollars — the largest peacetime deficit in American history. With national income still going down, the prospect for 1932 was even more dismal; the deficit might well end up three times as great. Hoover now redoubled his efforts. He demanded the most rigid retrenchment in government. He called for an increase in taxes. He denounced proposals for public spending. "Nothing," he said flatly in November 1931, "will contribute more to the return of prosperity than to maintain the sound fiscal position of the Federal Government." In December 1931 he formally repudiated the contention, once his own, that further expansion of public works would aid recovery.[10]

Fear of the deficit became an obsession in 1932. When Wagner and Garner urged Congress to increase public spending, Hoover harshly questioned their motives and assailed their programs — "the most gigantic pork barrel ever proposed to the American Congress," "an unexampled raid on the public Treasury." Vetoing the Garner-Wagner relief bill, he wrote, "Never before has so dangerous a suggestion been seriously made to our country." Others pointed out that his own policy of raising taxes and cutting government spending could only reduce purchasing power still further; but the President replied in a crescendo of statements — twenty of them from December to May alone — reiterating what was becoming his single theme. "The absolute necessity of a balanced budget" (March 25) was "the most essential factor to economic recovery" (May 5), "the imperative and immediate step" (May 13), "indispensable" (May 21), "the first necessity of the Nation" (August 11), "the foundation of all public and private financial stability" (August 11).[11]

V

The infatuation with the balanced budget thus destroyed the major plank of Hoover's first antidepression program — the expansion of public works.[12] In the meantime, the President was moving toward a radically new diagnosis of the depression. The theory of 1929 — that the breakdown was the inevitable result of uncontrolled domestic speculation — was perhaps coming to seem irksome, possibly because it fixed responsibility too squarely on the American business community. In October 1930, Hoover suddenly discovered that the roots of the depression lay "only partly in the United States." The major cause, he now felt, had been the overproduction of raw materials abroad, leading to lower prices and reduced buying power in foreign countries and thus to reduced foreign purchases in America. The actual decline of the foreign trade balance in 1930 was less than $60 million, a sum which hardly explained the collapse of the American economy; but, despite statistics, the President grew rapidly more confident of his new thesis. In December he said that "the major forces of the depression now lie outside of the United States," and by June 1931, that "the main causes . . . came not from within but from outside the United States." [13]

Events in Europe soon gave a touch of plausibility to the new Hoover line. The failure of the Kreditanstalt in Vienna in June 1931 put the international gold standard under intense strain. Hoover's debt moratorium that summer was no more than a palliative, and in September it became evident that the City of London could no longer defend the pound. By January 1932 about forty nations — though not America or France — had gone off gold. The world financial crisis increased the pressure on the American economy.

For Hoover the restoration of the gold standard now became almost as indispensable as balancing the budget. Gold, he said, was a metal "enshrined in human instincts for over 10,000 years," and he did not mean to abandon it. John Maynard Keynes predicted that the curse of Midas would fall on the countries which clung to gold — that they would suffer the disadvantages of costs fixed in terms of gold, while their competitors in the world market could enjoy the benefits of devaluation. The United States, said

Keynes, was setting "the rest of us the problem of finding some way to do without her wheat, her copper, her cotton and her motor-cars"; it was willing the destruction of its own export industries. But Hoover identified America's economic future with gold. Indeed, he later claimed that the nation had been within two weeks of being driven off the gold standard early in 1932 when it was saved from incalculable disaster by the swift action of his administration. "Never," he subsequently recalled — perhaps a strong word for a century and a half of American history — "was our nation in greater peril." [14]

There remained crucial contradictions in Hoover's new internationalism. His attitude toward foreign debts and convertibility showed a genuine concern for the world financial community. But the world financial community seemed to him somehow separate from the world trading community. He never quite put the two ideas together. Even when he spoke, in the same sentence, of the American economy both as "self-contained" and as vulnerable to "shocks and setbacks from abroad," he apparently saw no inconsistencies. The result was that his gold and tariff policies worked at cross-purposes. While with one hand he tried to maintain convertibility, with the other he raised American tariffs, evidently not understanding that exchange depreciation and import duties might be alternative means of achieving the same end.

The gold standard which Hoover sought so earnestly to protect in 1932 he had in fact already gravely wounded when he signed the tariff of 1930. Denied the opportunity to earn dollars in the American market, many nations had no choice but to protect themselves against American exports. Thus Italy, Spain, France, Britain, Canada were quick to raise barriers against American goods. The drift toward economic nationalism threatened not only the world trading community but the world financial community as well. Yet 1932 found Hoover combining his international theory of depression with a stout defense of protective tariffs. The suggestion of reciprocal trade agreements he rejected as "a violation of American principles." [15]

VI

By 1932 Hoover had moved from the New Era philosophy, with its emphasis on maintaining purchasing power in the American economy, toward something much closer to old-fashioned laissez faire, where faith in a balanced budget and the gold standard was tempered only by a commitment to protectionism. This evolution was assisted by the growing influence of the Undersecretary of the Treasury, Ogden L. Mills of New York, who became Secretary in February 1932, when Hoover finally induced Mellon to go to London as Ambassador. But it was evident to Hoover and Mills that the balanced budget and the gold standard, while primary, were not enough by themselves. Something also had to be done to protect the business of the nation against threatening bankruptcy and liquidation.

One possible approach was that suggested by Gerard Swope and H. I. Harriman. There were reasons for supposing that the President might look with favor on industrial planning. After all, no one had done more in the twenties to foster the trade association and to advocate self-government in industry than Hoover, and few men had seemed to care less about the Sherman Act. Even as President, he had questioned "destructive competition," suggested the revision of the antitrust laws, and called for "the development of cooperative spirit and responsibility in the American business world . . . such that the business of the country itself could and should assume the responsibility for the mobilization of the industrial and commercial agencies." "Self-government outside of political government," he told the American Banking Association in 1930, "is the truest form of self-government." But perhaps the Swope and Harriman proposals implied too much in the way of reorganizing the fundamentally sound economic system. In any case, he dismissed the Swope plan as "the most gigantic proposal of monopoly ever made in history" and the Chamber of Commerce plan as "sheer fascism." [16] Evidently self-government outside of political government could be carried too far.

If the structure of business was not to be reorganized, the alternative was to guarantee the existing structure. The President was disappointed in his early hope that the New York banking community might bolster the credit system on its own, as it had in previous crises. Only twice during the depression, as he saw it, had the New York bankers come together for organized cooperation in an important way — once to save the reichsmark, once to save the pound. Counting on similar action in support of American business, Hoover summoned leading bankers to secret meetings in the fall of 1931, and invited them to pool their funds in order to provide a credit reserve for their weaker brethren. To his chagrin, most of the group insisted that this was the government's responsibility. "I returned to the White House after midnight," Hoover later wrote, "more depressed than ever before." After consideration, the bankers did agree to try the National Credit Association idea. But their hearts were not in it; and a few weeks later the project was an evident failure.[17]

In the meantime, Eugene Meyer, whom Hoover had appointed governor of the Federal Reserve Board in 1930, had been advocating a new plan. Meyer wanted to revive his old War Finance Corporation in the guise of a Reconstruction Finance Corporation, empowered to make loans to banks, railroads, and insurance companies. With the National Credit Association fiasco behind him, Hoover now reluctantly accepted the Meyer proposal. He still objected to an ambitious lending program, but he hoped that the passage of the legislation would by itself reassure the credit system and restore confidence. "I look upon it," Ogden Mills said of the RFC, "as an insurance measure more than anything else. I think its very existence will have a great effect psychologically, and the sooner it is created, the less use we will have to make of it." [18]

VII

The RFC thus became in 1932 the administration's new weapon against the depression. It faced an increasingly critical situation. Banks were closing their doors — nearly 2300 suspended in 1931 alone, and anxious depositors were beginning to withdraw their savings from banks that were still open. In the meantime, the flight of gold from the country, as foreign investors threw their American securities on the market and took gold in exchange, drew further on the metallic reserve. When the RFC went into operation in

February 1932, the total reserves of the Federal Reserve member banks had fallen to within $50 million of the lowest amount allowed by law.[19]

But the RFC leadership — Eugene Meyer as chairman, Charles G. Dawes as president — were not ready for vigorous action. During the year, the agency succeeded in disbursing only about $1.5 billion of its $2 billion, and the great bulk of this money went to banks and trust companies. Even this transfusion was not as effective as it should have been; for the RFC was authorized only to make loans to banks, not to purchase their stock; and the great need for banks was not more indebtedness but more capital. "For a fatal year and a half," Russell Leffingwell of Morgan's later observed, "the Reconstruction Finance Corporation continued to lend money to the banks on adequate collateral security and gradually bankrupted them in the effort to save them." [20]

For the first five months, RFC operations were kept secret — to some extent, even from the Democrats whom the RFC law required to be appointed to the board of directors. "Several months passed," Jesse Jones of Texas, the dominant Democrat in RFC, wrote later, "before Chairman Meyer and Secretary Mills seemed to think it necessary to regard the Democratic directors as their equals. . . . Apparently they expected us blindly to do their bidding." And, if it was bad to tell things to the Democratic directors, it was even worse to tell them to the people. In particular, Hoover objected to the publication of RFC loans on the ground that publicity might invite the very disasters — the run on the bank, for example — which the loans were intended to prevent. Jones, however, received this argument with skepticism. And the President did not strengthen his case by using secrecy to obscure the character of RFC loan policy.

In signing the bill, Hoover had declared that RFC was "not created for the aid of big industries or big banks." Statements issued in the first months of operation conveyed the impression that the agency was concentrating on help for the little fellow. But in July 1932, John Garner secured the passage of an amendment compelling the RFC to report its loans to Congress. An analysis of the loans outstanding now put a different face on the official statements. Thus Hoover's claim in April that the RFC had loaned $126 million to banks in 45 states took on a less virtuous aspect when it was discovered that over half this sum had gone to three large banks.

Charges of favoritism in the distribution of loans increased criticism of the RFC. In June Dawes suddenly resigned, announcing that he must return to Chicago to take charge of the affairs of the Central Republic Bank. A few weeks later the RFC loaned Dawes's bank $90 million; this was at a time when its total deposits amounted to only $95 million. Even this loan could not save the bank, which soon was forced into reorganization, though in time, and after litigation, the loan was repaid to the RFC. The circumstances by which Dawes's bank received prompt assistance from the agency he had just left while the unemployed were denied federal aid roused natural speculation. So too did the disclosure that Atlee Pomerene, Dawes's successor, had authorized a loan of $12 million to a Cleveland bank of which he was director. When John T. Flynn published these facts early in 1933, President Hoover's secrecy policy seemed to many wholly disreputable. And, to support this impression, the loans to big banks were tapered off as soon as the secrecy provisions were ended.[21]

VIII

The administration's special concern for business was natural enough. "The sole function of government," Hoover said in the fall of 1931, "is to bring about a condition of affairs favorable to the beneficial development of private enterprise." Let business recover, Hoover believed, and recovery for the rest of the nation — the worker, the farmer, the unemployed — would come in due course.

Thus the plight of labor received little direct attention. By September 1931 the President was forced to abandon his early effort to maintain wage rates. When the Norris–La Guardia bill outlawing yellow-dog contracts came up in 1932, the administration greeted it without enthusiasm. Republicans denounced it in Congress; and Hoover's Secretary of Labor, in a meeting with the counsel of the National Association of Manufacturers, even offered Donald Richberg a federal judgeship if he would abandon support of the measure. Richberg spurned the suggestion, and Congress finally passed the bill, Hoover appending a glum signature. In August 1932, when Hoover called together Business and Industrial Committees from the twelve Federal Reserve Districts to organize "a concerted program of action along the whole economic front," he did not think to ask labor representatives.[22]

At the start, the farmers received somewhat more attention. Depression suddenly brought into prominence what had been a peripheral part of the original Farm Board program — that is, the stabilization corporations, designed to support farm prices by holding temporary crop surpluses off the market. This stabilization system, however, had been intended as a means of ironing out minor crop variations, not of dealing with major surpluses. Any effect the Board's purchases of wheat and cotton had in maintaining prices in 1930 was quickly offset by the encouragement stiffening prices offered to new production, as well as by the continuing decline in demand. It became rapidly clear that price support could not work without production control.

In January 1930 the Board began to warn that it could not "protect farmers when they deliberately over-plant." By midsummer Alex Legge, president of International Harvester, whom Hoover had made chairman of the Board, and Secretary of Agriculture Arthur Hyde launched a campaign for voluntary acreage reduction. To cotton farmers, the Board suggested that they plow up every third row. To wheat farmers, it urged reduced sowing. But most farmers, having no assurance that their neighbors would reduce their planting, or perhaps thinking that they would, went on producing in the hope of cashing in on prospective higher prices.

"I believe," said Hyde, "in controlled production." But, he hastily added, "such control, in my judgment, must come about by voluntary action of the farmers themselves, and not by mandate of law." Yet in a few months the Board itself conceded that voluntary methods would not work because of the "individualistic character" of the American farmer. "While there are still a few of the agricultural leaders who lower their voices when they speak of production control," Legge told Hoover, "yet practically all of them have accepted the principle as essential."

But the President hated the idea of federal surplus control. He disliked almost as much the tentative experiments in stabilization permitted under his act of 1929. "Even indirect purchase and sale of commodities," he said, "is [sic] absolutely opposed to my theory of government." And so the Hoover farm policy declined into self-inflicted impotence. By mid-1931, the Board abandoned its price support efforts and devoted itself to the task of disposing of its holdings. Thereafter the administration watched farm prices fall with helpless defeatism.[23]

IX

The same belief that government should concentrate on aid to business led the President to continue to resist proposals for federal action on behalf of the unemployed. As the third winter of the depression approached, Hoover's principle began to receive new challenges. "We shall help the railroad; we shall help the financial institutions; and I agree that we should," said Senator Wagner. "But is there any reason why we should not likewise extend a helping hand to that forlorn American, in every village and every city of the United States, who has been without wages since 1929? Must he alone carry the cross of individual responsibility?" Nor was the argument that relief was a local problem as persuasive as it had been in 1929 or 1930. The administration did not tell General Dawes, noted Edith Abbott, the social worker, that he should seek assistance for his bank from the Chicago city council.[24]

The La Follette–Costigan bill, with its provisions for federal grants to states for relief purposes, was beaten in February 1932. But Senator Wagner and Congressman Henry T. Rainey, the Democratic leader in the House, began a new fight in the spring for alternative forms of federal aid. When Joseph T. Robinson of Arkansas, the Democratic leader in the Senate, proposed in May a federal bond issue of over $2 billion to subsidize self-liquidating public works, and Al Smith, Bernard Baruch, and Owen D. Young promptly backed the project, Hoover, his hand forced, came up with a counterproposal of his own, making the RFC the instru-mentality of federal assistance.[25]

The first result of the jockeying between the Democrats and

White House was the passage of the Wagner–Garner bill, which added to its spending proposals a provision enlarging the lending authority of the RFC by $300 million for loans to supplement local relief in needy states. Though Hoover favored this provision, as well as a provision enabling the RFC to undertake a program of self-liquidating loans, he objected to other aspects of the bill and vetoed it. When these provisions were enacted in a slightly different form a week later, the President accepted them, thereby approving the Emergency Relief Act of 1932. The use of loans, repayable with interest in July 1935, maintained to his satisfaction the pretense of local responsibility. It was evident in any case that the administration proposed to construe its new powers as narrowly as possible.

"These loans," the President said, "are to be based upon absolute need and evidence of financial exhaustion. I do not expect any state to resort to it except as a last extremity." From the White House viewpoint, the RFC was to discharge a banking function. When Governor Pinchot of Pennsylvania, pointing out that the expenditure of $60 million among the more than one million jobless in his state would give each of them only 13 cents worth of food per day for a year, applied for the sum of $45 million, the RFC, after due deliberation, made about $11 million available. By the end of the year, only $30 million of the $300 million was allotted for relief, and even less for public works.[26]

x

The President stood manfully by his principles. But it remains unclear both from his statements at the time and from his subsequent recollections what his actual picture was of the state of his nation. Years later he wrote, "Many persons left their jobs for the more profitable one of selling apples." This sentence perhaps epitomized the presidential incredulity before the depression. If people sold apples on the street corners, it must have been because they could make more money doing that than doing something else. What jobs there were which offered even less security than apple-selling did not rouse his curiosity.

From time to time, the President produced letters from his Surgeon-General affecting to show that the state of public health was better in depression than it had been in prosperity; "no greater proof could be adduced," he liked to say, "that our people have been protected from hunger and cold." When the United Hospital Fund of New York City replied with statistics showing an "abnormal and progressive" increase in sickness, when the Pennsylvania Secretary of Public Health reported alarming increases in malnutrition and tuberculosis, when the daily newspaper contained items demonstrating the effects of privation, the President brusquely rejected them. "Nobody is actually starving," he told newspapermen. "The hoboes, for example, are better fed than they have ever been. One hobo in New York got ten meals in one day." [27]

As there could be nothing basically wrong with conditions, so there could be nothing basically wrong with the economic mechanism. The problems thus lay in the area of psychology, not economics. As Ogden Mills put it, "There is more to fear from frozen minds than from frozen assets." Something of this feeling undoubtedly lay behind the optimistic exhortations of 1930. When the economy failed to respond to pep talks, the President looked for other stimulants. "What the country needs," he told Raymond Clapper in February 1931, "is a good, big laugh. There seems to be a condition of hysteria. If someone could get off a good joke every ten days, I think our troubles would be over." He said the same thing to Weber and Fields. In 1932 he asked Will Rogers to think up a joke that would stop hoarding. To Rudy Vallee, the crooner, he said, "If you can sing a song that would make people forget their troubles and the Depression, I'll give you a medal." And to Christopher Morley: "Perhaps what this country needs is a great poem. . . . I keep looking for it, but I don't see it. Sometimes a great poem can do more than legislation." [28]

No President ever worked harder. Up at six, he threw on old clothes for his only bout of exercise — his seven-o'clock session with his "medicine ball cabinet." For thirty or forty minutes he fired the ball hard back and forth with a group of friends; then breakfast; and he was in his office by eight-thirty. It was characteristic that he was the first President to have a phone on his desk. From breakfast until bedtime at eleven, he labored without stint, smoking long, thick cigars as worry etched new lines into his gray face and his eyes became strained and bloodshot. "I am so tired," he sometimes said, "that every bone in my body aches." His manner grew increasingly preoccupied and dour. As he walked about the White House, he rarely spoke to the servants; "never a good-morning or even a nod of the head," said Ike Hoover, the White House usher. If someone addressed him, a low murmur came in reply, almost as if dragged out by force. He rarely looked at people in conversation, instead shuffling papers on his desk and doodling on blank sheets. He had no capacity for relaxation and was irritated by interruption. "There was always a frown on his face and a look of worry," said Ike Hoover; he "never laughed aloud." One of his secretaries remonstrated with him over his lack of small talk. Said the President sternly, "I have other things to do when a nation is on fire." [29]

XI

Hoover was, as William Allen White said, "constitutionally gloomy, a congenital pessimist who always saw the doleful side of any situation." "He worried more than any President," said Ike Hoover. The Secretary of State, Henry L. Stimson, regretted his chief's fatal preference for "seeing the dark side first." Stimson, noting "the ever present feeling of gloom that pervades everything connected with the administration," could not remember a single joke cracked in a year and a half of Cabinet meetings. One private session with the President seemed to the Secretary of State "like sitting in a bath of ink." [30]

Friends urged him to be more of a public leader. "I can't be a Theodore Roosevelt," the President would say with sadness; or, "I have no Wilsonian qualities." And the strain of maintaining his principles in the face of the accumulating evidences of human need doubtless led both to anxiety and to self-righteousness. Said Esmé Howard, the genial British Ambassador, "I found him, without exception, the most difficult American to know whom I have ever met." "Of all the administrations," said Ike Hoover, who served for forty-two years at the White House, "the hardest one to work for was that of President Hoover," adding that whenever the Hoovers left the White House, the employees were "glad when they were gone." H. G. Wells had visited the White House twice before when he came to call on Hoover. In the days of Theodore Roosevelt, it had been like any comfortable, free-talking country house. Calling on Harding had been like attending a politician's reception, all loud geniality and handshaking. But his visit with Hoover, Wells felt, had been an intrusion on a "sickly, overworked and overwhelmed" man, with distraught officials appearing and disappearing through unexpected doors. Hoover could not converse, but delivered a discourse on American economic self-sufficiency, intended, Wells felt, for Pierre Laval, who had left Washington a few days before. "I did not find it interesting." [31]

All the official optimism could not conceal the underlying strain. The newspapermen were perhaps first to sense the situation. There was much about the Hoover regime they had disliked — the evident pleasure in ceremonial trappings, the company of Marines on guard at the summer camp, the buglers at official dinners, the Secret Service men stationed in odd corners of the White House. But the President's attitude in press conferences aroused more serious concern. He played favorites (Mark Sullivan and William Hard, for example, were in the medicine-ball group) and complained to publishers of reporters whose stories he did not like. Gradually he began to cancel his press conferences. In his last two years, he held hardly more than one a month. The conferences themselves consisted increasingly of official handouts. Bumbling attempts by White House secretaries to withhold news and to control the writing of stories only aggravated the situation. The President's relations with the press, Paul Y. Anderson of the St. Louis *Post-Dispatch* reported in 1931, had reached "a stage of unpleasantness without parallel during the present century. They are characterized by mutual dislike, unconcealed suspicion, and downright bitterness." [32]

XII

The gloom and insecurity communicated itself to the nation. A people looking for leadership could not but respond with resentment. Hoover became the butt of a thousand bitter jokes. One told of Hoover's request to Mellon for the loan of a nickel to call up a friend, and of the Mellon reply: "Here's a dime, call up all your friends." Another asserted that there was no question about Hoover's being the world's greatest engineer: "in a little more than two years, he has drained, ditched and damned the United States." Vaudeville comedians, on being told that business was turning up, asked, "Is Hoover dead?"

Furtive books began to appear, investigating Hoover's years in the Far East and in high finance, accusing him of crimes ranging from British citizenship to cheating the Chinese government, oppressing coolie labor, engaging in the slave trade, making money out of Belgian relief, and even bringing about the execution of Edith Cavell. The very word "Hoover" became a prefix charged with hate: not only "Hoovervilles," but "Hoover blankets" (newspapers wrapped around for warmth), "Hoover wagons" (broken-down automobiles hauled by mules), "Hoover flags" (empty pockets turned inside out), "Hoover hogs" (jackrabbits).

The sense of popular hatred wounded the President. "It is a cruel world," he remarked at one point; and, again, "My men are dropping around me." And it also, perhaps, helped confirm his intellectual rigidities. The White House usher noted that, where Theodore Roosevelt and Wilson liked to send for people who took views different from their own, Hoover preferred to discuss matters with people whom he knew in advance would agree with him. Looking back twenty years later in his *Memoirs*, Hoover himself could see no mistakes committed during his presidency, no opportunities missed, no wrong guesses, nothing to regret. And at the time, criticism began to seem to him, not just the give-and-take of politics, but a dangerous threat to the American way of life. "He regarded some of it," Theodore Joslin, his faithful secretary, said, "as unpatriotic." He felt himself fighting, not just for the established order, but for the survival of American institutions.[33]

The ideological issue emerged with increasing clarity in the second half of his administration. He felt, no doubt, genuine indignation at the behavior of leading businessmen. William Allen White reported that in private he grumbled at their perfidy and complained of their greed. "But also," White added, "because he had worked for thirty years with men of wealth, he could not publicly scold a million dollars, much less a hundred million." This was the America he respected, whatever its faults, and this America had to be preserved. His anger was directed rather at those who threatened to change this America, especially by enlarging the power of the federal government.

Hoover had, he admitted, "no taste" for emergency powers. To avoid the drift toward a superstate, he wanted "to solve great problems outside of Government action." Victory over depression must be won "by the resolution of our people to fight their own battles in their own communities." For the federal government to assume what had been local obligations would be to undermine "the very basis of self-government." The question for the future, he believed, was whether history should be written in terms of individual responsibility or of the "futile attempt to cure poverty by the enactment of law." Depression, he said, could not be ended "by legislative action or executive pronouncement. Economic wounds must be healed by the action of the cells of the economic body." [34]

Yet the same man who could invoke the healing processes of nature and warn with passion against centralization could also, in another mood, boast of "the most gigantic program of economic defense and counterattack ever evolved in the history of the Republic." For all his faith in individualism, he brought great areas of the economy — the banks, the railroads, the insurance companies, the farmers, even, toward the end, the unemployed — into the orbit of national action. No doubt, he entered on these programs grudgingly, and did as little as he could to develop their possibilities. Yet he breached the walls of local responsibility as had no President in American history.

How could he be so certain where the exact line of demarcation was drawn between beneficent intervention and limitless evil? Senator Norris's project for the government ownership and operation of Muscle Shoals seemed to him, for example, "the negation of the ideals upon which our civilization has been based." [35] Yet his own projects seemed equally Bolshevistic, for example, to James M. Beck. In the end, Hoover, dragged despairingly along by events, decided that wherever he finally dug in constituted the limits of the permissible. Doctrinaire by temperament, he tended to make every difference in degree a difference in kind and to transform questions of tactics into questions of principles.

As his term wore on, the ideological obsession grew. He had himself done unprecedented things to show the potentialities of national action; but anyone who went a step beyond transgressed the invisible line and menaced the American way of life. His was the tragedy of a man of high ideals whose intelligence froze into inflexibility and whose dedication was smitten by self-righteousness.

26. The Crisis of 1932

AND THE economic decline continued. National income, which had been $87.4 billion in 1929, fell with the value of the dollar to $41.7 billion in 1932. Unemployment rose: 4 million in 1930, 8 million in 1931, 12 million in 1932 — nearly one out of every four workers in the nation seeking a job. Net investment in 1931 was minus $358 million (in 1929 prices); the next year it fell to a disheartening minus $5.8 billion. The Federal Reserve Board index of manufacturing production went down from 110 in 1929 to 57 in 1932; wage payments from $50 billion to $30 billion. And, as prices and income fell, the burdens of indebtedness — farm mortgages, railroad bonds, municipal and state debts — became insupportable.

The decline described a jagged rather than a straight line, and occasional halts gave the administration flashes of hope that the worst might be over. In time, President Hoover was to claim that the depression had been twice licked: first in 1931, until the financial collapse in Central Europe checked recovery in America; again in 1932, until the prospect of unsound Democratic policies shattered business confidence. But, in fact, the slight upturn of January–March 1931 had ceased many weeks before the Kreditanstalt closed its doors in Vienna. And the slight upturn in the last five months of 1932 seems mainly to have been the consequence of the federal deficit of $2.9 billion — a deficit which Hoover wholly deplored and did his best to erase.[1] No basic attempts were made to tackle the structural difficulties in the economy — the fatal imbalance between business and agriculture, or the jerry-built banking system, or the unreliable security exchanges — nor was there sustained public effort to increase purchasing power. Until these things were done, there could be no alternative to the downward spiral.

Statistics reflected only dimly the human reality. The year 1932 brought new anguish. By spring, when United States Steel made its second large wage slash, the attempt to maintain pay scales had pretty well foundered. By the end of the year, the weekly wage in iron and steel averaged 63 per cent less than in 1929. The Pennsylvania Department of Labor reported in July 1932, that wages had fallen to 5 cents an hour in sawmills, 6 cents in brick and tile manufacturing, 7.5 cents in general contracting. In Malvern, Arkansas, lumber workers received 10 cents an hour; women in Tennessee mills were paid as little as $2.39 for a 50-hour week. In lighter industries, conditions were even worse. The Connecticut Commissioner of Labor recorded in the summer of 1932 the existence of over one hundred sweatshops hiring young girls for as little as 60 cents to $1.10 for a 55-hour week. A family of six, including four children, were found stringing safety pins on wires late into the night for four or five dollars a week. And it was increasingly hard for decent employers to continue paying 1929 wages while competitors were cutting their labor costs in half. The entire wage structure was apparently condemned to disintegration.[2]

II

But a job, even in sweatshops, was still better than unemployment; for the patchwork of relief was visibly collapsing. The need had never been greater. New people were crowding the offices, God-fearing members of the middle class who had not dreamed that they would one day stand drearily in line for a handout. As the applicants increased and the resources diminished, standards of assistance went down. By 1932 only about one-quarter of the unemployed were actually receiving relief, limited in the main to food, with sometimes a little fuel. Voluntary funds had almost given out; 90 per cent of relief came from public funds; and these funds too were diminishing. RFC aid was too meager and unreliable for advance planning. As a consequence, the administration of relief was on a disaster basis. "We of the cities have done our best," said the mayor of Toledo in the spring of 1932, but "we have failed miserably."

In New York City, those lucky enough to get on the rolls at all were averaging $2.39 per family per week; and the city's relief fund could take care of only about half the unemployed heads of families. A group of Latin Americans and Portuguese Negroes found refuge in a deserted Armour packing plant on West 30th Street, climbing to the top floor at night by rope ladder. Other unemployed built shacks in the bed of the abandoned reservoir in Central Park. They called it Hoover Valley and scavenged for a living almost under the shadow of the glittering, half-empty sky-scrapers on their southern horizon.

In Chicago, one out of every two workers was without a job. Municipal employees went for months without pay. From May 1931, the Chicago Public Library could not afford a single new book. Socialists and Communists organized demonstrations among the 700,000 unemployed. It might be better for Washington to send $150 million to Chicago now, Mayor Anton Cermak vainly suggested in June 1932, than to send federal troops later. (It was the same month as the loan to Dawes's bank.)

The Philadelphia Community Council described its situation in July 1932 as one of "slow starvation and progressive disintegration of family life." In the Pennsylvania coal fields, miners kept up a subdued battle against starvation, freezing in rickety one-room houses, subsisting on wild weed-roots and dandelions, struggling for life in black and blasted valleys. In Kentucky they ate violet tops, wild onions, and the weeds which cows would eat (one wrote, "as cows won't eat a poison weeds"), while wan children attended school without coats, shoes, or underclothes. In Logan and Mingo Counties of West Virginia, according to Clarence Pickett's testimony before a House committee, people were breaking into store-houses and stealing supplies. "I would steal before I would starve," interjected Congressman Kent Keller of Illinois. "I think all of us would probably," replied the Quaker official, adding hastily: "I don't know whether you want that in the record."

In Oakland, California, four-year-old Narcisson Sandoval, who had been living on refuse, died of starvation, while her brothers and sisters were rushed to a hospital on the verge of death. In

Northampton, Massachusetts, Anthony Prasol, the father of eight
children, killed himself because he had no hope of work or assistance. Faith in life itself seemed to be ebbing away: the national
birthrate for 1931 was 17 per cent below 1921 and 10 per cent
below 1926.[3]

III

In some localities discontent found constructive expression. In
Seattle the Unemployed Citizens' League was formed to permit
unemployed men and women to pool their services and products.
Shoemakers, carpenters, tailors, laborers practiced their trades,
drawing in return surplus wood, fish, apples, and potatoes. Soon
the League was organized in 22 districts and included 13,000
families, with almost 40,000 persons dependent on its self-help
programs. In Yellow Springs, Ohio, Arthur E. Morgan, president
of Antioch College, founded the Midwest Exchange. Similar projects sprang up in other parts of the country. By the end of 1932,
there were probably well over 100 self-help and barter organizations in nearly 30 states, many of them developing their own systems of scrip. As the national economy ran down, the unemployed
sought a form of security by setting up enclaves of their own.[4]

Still others, driven by remnants of an old questing hope,
abandoned their homes and took to the roads. No one knew for
sure how many there were — a million and a half or two million
on the move in 1932 was a plausible estimate. They rode the rods
or cadged rides from motorists, slept in flophouses or hobo jungles,
fled railroad detectives and evaded local police, wandering the
country in an aimless search for the America of better days. For
a moment, the two or three hundred thousand young people among
them seemed the *bezprizorni* of America, the wild boys of the road;
but they were mostly restless American youths (one out of twenty
a girl) sure that change could not be for the worse, always seeking
something, whether in the shanty towns near the big cities, or in
the sandstone caves along the Mississippi, under bridges or in
crowded boxcars. "I've seen a lot of the country in the last year,
and I'm glad I've seen it," one of them told Thomas Minehan,
"but if a guy travels too much he becomes a bum, *and I don't want
to be a bum.*"[5]

Yet for all this, the predominant mood after the third winter of depression was less one of revolt than of apathy. Too much had happened too quickly to too many for the implications to be fully absorbed. Life, as the song hit of this third winter had it, was just a bowl of cherries; don't take it serious — it's too mysterious. People were sullen rather than bitter, despairing rather than violent. Instead of fuming with resentment and rushing to the barricades, they sat at home, rocked dispiritedly in their chairs, and blamed "conditions." Miserable Hoovervilles grew up next to luxury flats; people went hungry within sight of elevators bursting with grain. A stunned population seemed to have lost the traditional American talent for direct action.[6]

IV

But 1932 was bringing signs of a new resentment. For the first time, a bitterness was beginning to rise against the rich and respectable. As yet, the bitterness was scattered and fragmentary. But it might foreshadow a deeper change in the popular mood.

It took its start perhaps in the battle against federal relief. The respectable classes had long claimed to oppose federal relief out of their concern for the moral health of the recipients. But this explanation was in 1932 decreasingly convincing. Many now found the realistic thesis advanced by Gifford Pinchot more impressive. "Local relief means making the poor man pay," Pinchot said. ". . . The force behind the stubborn opposition to federal relief is fear lest taxes to provide that relief be levied on concentrated wealth."

Even more important was a spreading impression that the rich were trying to contract out of what was, after all, a national crisis. The impression was in considerable measure unjust. Yet too many of the well-to-do seemed only to think of themselves and their fortunes. When Britain went off gold in September 1931, many businessmen, in a rush to put their money in Swiss francs or Dutch florins, converted American securities to gold and shipped the gold out of the country. This flight from the dollar, which early in 1932 reached the rate of $100 million a week and, according to Hoover, nearly forced the nation off the gold standard, was largely

produced by the waning faith of the rich in Mr. Hoover's administration.[7]

Even more irritating was the ingenuity with which some avoided
the payment of taxes. In Chicago, for example, where there was
hardly enough money for basic municipal services, large property
owners organized an open tax boycott; some of them were delin-
quent on real estate taxes as far back as 1929. Colonel Robert R.
McCormick, whose *Chicago Tribune* called on citizens to pay their
full taxes, listed the total of his own personal property, including
securities, at only $25,250, which called for a tax of $1515. Other
wealthy men, on their own representation, had even less taxable
property. Thus Silas Strawn of the United States Chamber of
Commerce could discover personal property holdings to an amount
requiring a tax of only $120, Louis Florsheim of the shoe company
$90, and the apparently semi-indigent S. J. T. Straus, chairman of
S. W. Straus investment banking firm, $18.[8]

Tax abatements continued. Even the high-minded Ogden Mills,
as Secretary of the Treasury, granted abatements and refunds in
the amount of $6 million to the estate of his father, of which he
was executor and beneficiary — an action unfortunately liable to
misunderstanding in the atmosphere of 1932. And more singular,
though the facts were not disclosed till the congressional investigations of 1933, was the systematic avoidance of federal income tax
by the very rich. J. P. Morgan, who appealed to workers to give of
their meager wages for the block-aid campaign ("we must all do
our bit"), paid not one cent of federal income tax himself in 1930,
1931, or 1932; nor, in the latter two years, did any of his partners.
Thomas W. Lamont's son, Thomas S. Lamont, by wash sales of
securities to his wife in exchange for money he had loaned her to
buy the stock, was able to claim a technical loss of $114,000 on
the transaction; a month after the tax returns were filed, he re-
purchased the stock from his wife at the same price she had paid
him. According to their tax returns, the Morgan partners, for all
their accumulation of town houses and limousines, yachts in Long
Island Sound and shooting boxes in Scotland, had virtually no taxable income at all in the depression years. What they did was
perfectly legal, but it was hardly calculated to win respect for their
civic spirit. Nor were these representations questioned by the

Bureau of Internal Revenue in the age of Mellon and Mills. One agent approved a Morgan partner tax form with the respectful comment: "Returned without examination for the reason that the return was prepared in the office of J. P. Morgan and Company and it has been our experience that any schedule made by that office is correct." [9]

But the Morgans at least remained within the technical limits of law. On March 12, 1932, Ivar Kreuger, the Swedish financier, alone in his luxurious Paris apartment, unbuttoned his waistcoat, indulged perhaps in a moment of gloomy retrospection, pressed a revolver against his chest, and put a bullet into his heart. The suicide two days later of George Eastman, the Rochester millionaire ("My work is done. Why wait?"), increased the conviction that the financiers of the world were operating under some obscure but intolerable strain. Eastman's death, it turned out, signified no financial irregularities. But the gradual unfolding of the Kreuger story put on display a record of international buccaneering which seemed to convict half the world of finance of inexhaustible criminality and the other half of abysmal stupidity. Kreuger, who had once sold real estate in Illinois, and built buildings in New York, was well known in America. He had been reverently interviewed by the *Saturday Evening Post* and canonized as a Titan (higher even than a Tycoon) by *Time*. Only two months before the moment of truth in Paris, he had personally assured President Hoover that the American people had no need to "become hysterical" about the problems of Europe. His death had been followed by tributes of a kind ordinarily reserved for college presidents or for eminent vestrymen. Now he was revealed as a swindler, forger, and cheat, and the American bankers who had accepted his pretensions as a pack of fools.[10]

v

If Kreuger, the Match King, was a gigantic thief, what Titan — or even Tycoon — could be trusted in the future? In Chicago, investors were already haunting the offices of Samuel Insull, demanding that he make good on his worthless stock. Protected night and day by thirty-six personal bodyguards, Insull, who believed in his own magic, tried to save his crumbling estate through new loans and new manipulations. But his fantastic improvisation was slowly dematerializing before everyone's eyes. When he abruptly departed for Europe in 1932, having resigned his eighty-five directorships, his sixty-five chairmanships, and his eleven presidencies, the *New York Times* wrote, "Mr. Insull fell, not because his ideals were wrong, but because of his persistent optimism. . . . He stands withal as one of the foremost and greatest builders of American industrial empires."

Yet by September it seemed possible that the great industrial builder was guilty of more than optimism; in the next months a Cook County grand jury indicted him for embezzlement. Soon his lawyers were sending him coded telegrams advising him to seek refuge beyond extradition in Greece. The old man, sitting disconsolately in European exile, could not understand what had happened. "Why am I not more popular in the United States?" he said. "What have I done that every banker and business magnate has not done in the course of business?" And Donald Richberg, Insull's old enemy in Chicago, voiced the popular verdict: "The true significance of the career of Samuel Insull lies in the fact that his sins were *not* exceptional, save in the sweep of his ambitions and the extent of the injuries he inflicted." [11]

Business had insisted on all credit for prosperity. Now it could hardly escape blame for adversity. "If the responsibility for the present crisis can be laid at anyone's door," said Newton D. Baker, himself a wealthy corporation lawyer, "surely Big Business is the most likely doorstep." And what the Dean of the Harvard Business School called "the failure of business leadership" was compounded by multiplying evidence of the failure of business morality — the misrepresentations uttered, the bonds forged, the taxes avoided, the confidence betrayed, the responsibilities rejected.[12]

And so the New Era faded away. Detroit, the home of Henry Ford, the New Era's prophet, was desolate in 1932; half the existing automotive capacity, it seemed, could make all the cars America would need for years to come. Even the best efforts of Detroit's resourceful and dedicated mayor, Frank Murphy, could not take care of the growing mass of unemployed. On March 7, 1932, in zero weather, a procession of jobless, perhaps three thousand in

number, marched with police permission from downtown Detroit
toward Henry Ford's River Rouge plant in Dearborn. When they
reached the city line, the Dearborn police ordered them to turn
back. But the marchers pressed on, demanding to present a peti-
tion at the Ford plant, their leaders cautioning them to maintain
"proletarian discipline." The police responded with tear-gas
bombs, the crowd with rocks and slag and chunks of frozen mud.
The Ford fire department poured freezing water on the marchers
through firehoses; then the police opened fire, first with guns and
revolvers, later with a machine gun. The crowd finally broke ranks
under the shower of bullets. A few tried to carry off the injured;
the rest fled down the road, leaving four dead and several wounded
behind. Out of the windows over Gate Four of the plant, some
Russian technicians, learning Ford's production methods, watched
the spectacle. . . . The bodies lay in state two days later under a
huge red banner bearing a picture of Lenin and the motto "Ford
Gave Bullets for Bread." The band played the Russian funeral
march of 1905, and thousands of Detroit workers followed the
coffins, as the dying afternoon sun glinted on the tall silvered
smokestacks of River Rouge.[13]

The administration took notice of the new restiveness. In 1931
it opposed the reduction of the Army ground forces because it would
"lessen our means of maintaining domestic peace and order."
When Congress voted a 10 per cent pay decrease for government
employees in 1932, Hoover sent a secret message urging the Senate
to make an exception for Army and Navy enlisted personnel because, in case of internal trouble, he did not want to have to rely
on troops disgruntled over pay cuts.[14] The national mood was
perhaps passing from numbness to exasperation. What had first
seemed listlessness now seemed the sign of some deeper gathering by
the people into themselves. The feeling was spreading that they had
somehow been let down, cheated, betrayed. The atmosphere was
one of overcast sultriness before a storm.

VI

Early in May 1932, some World War veterans in Portland, Oregon, contemplated the fact that the one nest egg they had left was the

government's promise of payment on their "adjusted compensation certificates" — the bonus for their wartime service, due them, by act of Congress, in the year 1945. If the money was really theirs, why should they not have it when they needed it? Tired of watching their children grow pale on a diet of stale doughnuts and black coffee, tired of community neglect, tired of official gabble, tired, above all, of waiting, the men in Portland decided to bring their plight home to the country by marching on Washington. They chose as leader an unemployed cannery superintendent and former World War sergeant named Walter W. Waters. Waters, who had a wife and two little girls, had not worked for eighteen months. Under his command, the group set out, riding the rods and living on handouts along the way. Its principles were "no panhandling, no drinking, no radicalism"; and it restricted its ranks to authentic veterans.

On May 21 they reached East St. Louis. When railroad officials tried to prevent their boarding a Baltimore and Ohio freight train east, they began to uncouple cars and soap rails in the marshaling yard. Soon units of the Illinois National Guard arrived to disperse them. In the end, the Bonus Expeditionary Force, as the Portland group derisively called itself, was sent out of the state by trucks. But the "Battle of the B & O" was now a front-page story.

Other veterans began to hit the road to Washington. Marching replaced for a moment the loneliness of unemployment; it renewed the comradely emotions of the doughboy army fifteen years before. By the time Waters arrived in Washington, his group had grown to a thousand; and, in the next weeks, dusty new contingents converged on the District of Columbia. The Congress, now debating Representative Wright Patman's bill for the immediate payment of the bonus, was confronted by a new kind of lobby, not men with cigars drinking rye and water at the Mayflower, but men in old army caps bivouacking on the marshy flats across the Anacostia River. Their demeanor remained respectful, their behavior disciplined. But their very presence contained a threat. On June 15 the House passed the Patman bill.

The Superintendent of Metropolitan Police was a retired army officer named Pelham D. Glassford, who had been the youngest brigadier-general in the AEF in France. He helped the veterans find billets, fed them from Army field kitchens, ordered the police to leave them alone, kidded and joshed them, and did all he could to keep up their morale. His patient amiability, as he rode around on his big blue motorcycle, soothed angry spirits. Moreover, once there, most of the veterans themselves hardly knew why they had come. They felt only a vague restlessness over conditions at home and a vague hope that their appearance might stir the government to action.

On June 17, as the bonus bill came for vote before the Senate, the veterans began to gather on Capitol Hill. The administration wanted to bring out the machine guns with which it had greeted the Communist hunger marchers in the previous December; but Glassford argued against a display of force. The men crowding the plaza before the Capitol felt that their bill was doomed. Still, their bitter wisecracks, as they lay in shirtsleeves on the green grass or sat on the marble steps, could not conceal remnants of hope. Waiting through the long afternoon into the soft Washington twilight, they talked, griped, dozed, sang war songs, sat on in silence.

Inside, the Senate was moving toward a vote. The mutterings from the crowd began to swell into a rumble. Waters himself, looking a little alarmed, persuaded the men to sing again. Then Senator Elmer Thomas of Oklahoma, a friend of the bonus, appeared beside Waters and whispered to him. In a moment, Waters walked to the top of the steps and spread out his arms. It took minutes for the noise to die down. At last, Waters spoke, his voice low and tired. "Comrades!" A shout from the crowd; then silence again. "Comrades, I have bad news." The bonus bill, he said, was dead. The men in the square rustled with uncertainty. There was a scattering of boos. "Comrades . . ." Waters called, "let us show them that we can take it on the chin. Let us show them that we are patriotic Americans. I call on you to sing 'America.'" The song completed, military shouts began to ring out across the plaza: "California — over here," "New Yorkers — fall in here." Quietly the men, now nearly twenty thousand, formed their platoons, about-faced, and marched back to the camp on the mud flats. In thirty minutes the great square was empty.

Some veterans, discouraged, now left Washington. But others

remained — "Stay till 1945" became their watchword. Life was settling into a kind of order at Anacostia Flats. The veterans built shacks out of lumber, packing boxes, scrap tin, and strips of canvas. Some lived in secondhand Army pup tents, provided by General Glassford. Falling back on basic training, half remembered from those springtime days fifteen years earlier, they held formation, waited in chow lines, organized baseball games, dug latrines (known as "Hoover villas") and rose and slept by bugle call. Wives and children began to join husbands, piecing together family life in the swampy land under the steaming sun. One problem was food, always of poor quality and in short supply; another, increasingly, was sickness. Heat and moisture bred disease out of half-buried garbage; flies swarmed in the tents; the Potomac bathed the north edge of the cantonment with the capital's sewage. The rancid odor of decaying food, sweat, chloride, and urine began to settle over the flats.

VII

And still the men waited, fifteen thousand or more of them, women and children now beside them, wanly hoping that the Congress might recur to the bonus before adjournment. Factional quarrels, begotten by heat and fatigue and irritability, began to disturb the B.E.F. Commander Waters, his ambitions whetted by authority, sought to increase his power. One day late in June he instituted a system of rigorous military discipline. "I'll do what I want whether you like it or not," he shouted to a group of dissenters, "and those that don't can get the hell out of the B.E.F. I'm going to be hardboiled!" He was already beginning to glimpse larger possibilities. He told Gardner Jackson that he was an ex-Socialist, that the bonus was only a pretext, that the B.E.F. was the vanguard of a general rising of the unemployed. Why should there not be a national organization, fighting the battle of all suffering Americans? "It would cry to high heaven," said Waters, "that, while there were billions for the bankers, there was nothing for the poor. It would tell the world that the vaunted democracy of America had become a sordid scheme of special privilege." Such an organization, Waters mused, thinking of Mussolini and Hitler, might well be called the Khaki Shirts.

Most of the men regarded Waters with weary indifference. His chief enemy was the Communist group, a puny minority making tardy attempts to clamber onto the B.E.F. bandwagon. The Communists wanted violence; and they angrily condemned the B.E.F. leadership for cooperating with Glassford in maintaining order. But the curses at Anacostia, as one observer commented, were directed impartially at the bankers and the Communists; and B.E.F. leaders were tireless in denouncing Communist activity, destroying their leaflets and throwing their leaders out of the camps. A kangaroo court of veterans sentenced Communist agitators to fifteen lashes across the back with a belt. As the *B.E.F. News* emphasized, while warning that the attitude of the rich was "making it easier for the Reds to add to their ranks," Communist principles ran counter to B.E.F. plans: "Eyes front — not left! " [15]

And so the days dragged on through July, with the men festering in the heat, wives gossiping, children playing, babies squalling (some, like Bernard Myers, were born at Anacostia), and Glassford presiding benevolently over all. When food grew short, he bought nearly a thousand dollars worth of supplies with his own money: "Why some of those boys soldiered for me; they're my boys." When John T. Pace, the Communist leader, was about to be mobbed by indignant veterans, Glassford told the crowd, "Pace has just as much right to speak here as anyone. Any of you who disagree with him and don't want to listen, go to some other part of the camp and play baseball." When whites and Negroes, exasperated by heat and boredom, fought on the dusty ground, Glassford, pushing them apart with bare hands, said, "We're all veterans together and there'll be no fighting among veterans."

The administration, in the meantime, viewed the Bonus Army as a local problem, the concern of the District Commissioners, but surely not of the President. By mid-July the veterans had been in Washington for two months. In all this period, not a word had come to them from the White House; not an administration official offered them sympathy or even bothered to tell them why their pleas had to be rejected. The President himself had ample time in these weeks to receive Jim Londos, the heavyweight wrestling champion, delegations from the Eta Upsilon Gamma Sorority and from the Baraca Philathea Union, adolescent winners of essay contests and other dignitaries; but audiences were denied to the leaders of the B.E.F. "Mr. Hoover does not shrink from holding conferences and issuing statements," said Walter Lippmann. "How can he justify the fact that he never took the trouble to confer with the bonus marchers?" His single act was to obtain passage of a bill lending money to veterans willing to return home, the loan to be deducted from the bonus due them in 1945.

VIII

As Congress moved toward adjournment, tension increased. "A dog in the gutter will fight to feed its pups," the *B.E.F. News* told the veterans, but for three years "you have cringed and fawned and begged for crumbs. . . . Why stand you thus, when all is within your power? Are you truly curs and cowards? Or are you men?" Underneath the presidential indifference, there were mounting signs of concern. The guard at the White House was increased; from time to time, especially when pickets appeared before the White House, the iron gates were chained, and the lawns swarmed with Secret Service men. Three hundred armed troopers secretly assembled in the Munitions Building nearby to be ready for any contingency. The *B.E.F. News* continued to lash its readers. They had waited like dumb oxen on street corners, it said, while their children starved; they were "yellow cowards" with "the guts of a louse."

On the last day of Congress, the veterans once again crowded into the Capitol plaza. "Comrades . . ." Waters shouted to them from the portico, "you've got to keep a lane open for the white collar birds inside so they won't rub into us lousy rats. We're going to stay here until I see Hoover." The President had announced that he would make the traditional visit to the Capitol for the adjournment ceremonies. But the limousine waited for two hours at the White House door, and in the end, for whatever reason, the President chose not to go. Once again the crowd on Capitol Hill returned harmlessly to its encampments.

Glassford planned to evacuate the remnants of the Bonus Marchers to a camp in the country, where he hoped they might try small manufacturing and subsistence farming. More veterans were departing every day. But the President and the District of Columbia Commissioners were growing increasingly anxious. On July 26 Secretary of War Hurley said that the B.E.F. had been a problem because it was so law-abiding and musingly considered the advantages of an incident that might justify the declaration of martial law. On July 28 the District police were ordered to clear a group of veterans out of some abandoned buildings along Pennsylvania Avenue into which they had settled. Waters advised the men to leave peaceably. But the Communist group, whose leader, Pace, had been arrested a few days before, saw its chance. They rushed the police line, threw bricks, and provoked a brief riot. Two hours later, police entered a second partially demolished building where two planks had been laid to take the place of missing steps. A policeman slipped between the planks; jittery and frightened, he turned, drew his gun and fired repeatedly into a crowd of veterans. One man, standing quietly by with his coat over his arm, fell dead. Other policemen started firing; a second man was hit fatally, others were wounded; then the voice of Glassford was heard — "Stop that shooting" — and again all was quiet.

Here was Secretary Hurley's incident. The Commissioners now resolved to ask for federal troops. The request went to the White House, where it was received with relief; and Secretary Hurley transmitted the orders to General Douglas MacArthur. MacArthur summoned his aide, Major Dwight D. Eisenhower, seized his riding crop, mounted his horse, and took personal command.

IX

They arrived late in the afternoon, four troops of cavalry clattering by with drawn sabers, followed by six tanks, with machine guns hooded, and a column of infantry, with fixed bayonets, steel helmets, gas masks and at their belts, blue tear-gas bombs. First, the soldiers cleared the downtown buildings with bayonets and gas. Then, as evening fell, they moved into Anacostia, turning out the inhabitants with military dispatch. They paused for an hour to permit evacuation. Then they moved ahead, tossing gas bombs into little groups of defiant veterans, setting fire along the way to the shacks and barracks lest the inhabitants return. (Secretary Hurley later denied that this had been done, but the firsthand evidence of newspaper reporters — and of photographs — left no question on this point.) Soon the veterans began to fire their own huts as they fled.

Women and children, their eyes streaming with tears, ran frantically from their dwellings, without time to gather their pathetic belongings. Young Eugene King, seven years old, turned back to his tent to get his pet rabbit. A soldier said, "Get out of here, you little son-of-a-bitch," and bayoneted him in the leg. Joe Angelo, a veteran from Camden, New Jersey, watched a self-confident cavalry officer lead soldiers with drawn bayonets against his Anacostia shack; suddenly he recognized the officer as George S. Patton, Jr., whose life he had saved in France fourteen years earlier, for which exploit he had received the Distinguished Service Cross ("undoubtedly the man saved my life," the dashing Patton told the press sourly later, "but his several accounts of the incident vary from the true facts").

Already the sputtering torches were lighting up the flats with bright orange flames. Behind, the great dome of the Capitol was silhouetted in the glare. Coughing, choking, vomiting, the Bonus Army fled the sickly-sweet odor of tear gas along Good Hope Hill and straggled into Maryland and safety. When the gray mists rose from the river in the morning, blue-white smoke was drifting over the smoldering ruins . . . Little Bernard Myers, the bonus baby, eleven weeks old, was dying in the hospital. The *B.E.F. News* suggested the epitaph: "Here lies Bernard Myers, aged three months, gassed to death by order of President Hoover."

The lines in the first issue of the *B.E.F. News* now seemed almost prophetic:

> Oh, Christ, who died for all,
> Will you return again?
> Or do you also feel
> Your work on earth in vain.
>
> You tried to teach men love.
> Lip-service many give,
> Look down, oh Lord, and see
> Yourself the lives we live.

This was one view. Douglas MacArthur had another. The "mob," he said, was animated by "the essence of revolution." "Beyond the shadow of a doubt," it was about to seize control of the government. "The President played it pretty fine in waiting to the last minute; but he didn't have much margin." The victory over the B.E.F. seemed one more triumph in a long military career. "I have released in my day," the General said, "more than one community which had been held in the grip of a foreign enemy"; but never, even when villages had lain for years under foreign military occupation, had he seen greater gratitude among a distressed populace.

The administration, so long so silent on the B.E.F., now issued a series of statements asserting that the Army was composed, in the main, of criminals and Communists, and a grand jury was set up to provide the proof. But, even though an obedient presiding justice instructed the grand jury to make the desired findings, the jury itself declined to mention Communists at all in its report and instead indicted three men, all of whom had been wounded overseas during the war. And the Attorney-General's charges against the Bonus Army, based on an inquiry started after the Army had dispersed, were not sustained by the more careful investigations of the Veterans Bureau or of the Welfare Department of the state of Pennsylvania.

Yet the administration remained unforgiving. When a group of writers, headed by Sherwood Anderson and Waldo Frank, called at the White House to protest the use of troops against unarmed civilians, they were told that the President was too busy to see them. Leaving, they heard a chorus of childish voices singing "Happy Birthday to You" across the White House lawn, as a delegation of schoolchildren offered Mr. Hoover a birthday cake. And, by October, General Glassford had been forced out of office.

The bonus issue was itself complex. Many Americans resented the pressure tactics of the veterans and felt, in addition, that the payment of the bonus would be an economic disaster. A few, like William Trufant Foster and Wright Patman, favored any expedient which would put money into the hands of spenders, even the bonus. But the merits of the argument faded before the national dismay over what appeared the President's indifference toward the men on Anacostia Flats. There seemed no excuse for his refusal to see their leaders; no excuse for resorting to arms when the B.E.F. was breaking up of its own accord; no excuse for forcing pell-mell evacuation in the dead of night; no excuse for failing to provide camp sites outside the District. "What a pitiful spectacle," said the Washington *News*, "is that of the great American Government, mightiest in the world, chasing unarmed men, women and children with Army tanks. . . . If the Army must be called out to make war on unarmed citizens, this is no longer America."

Yet the veterans had, on the whole, submitted quietly. The B.E.F. had had no arms; the soldiers had fired no shots; and what might have been in other lands a rebellion turned out instead a disorderly midnight rout of bewildered men and women. The nation's apathy was dented by the incident, but not broken.[16]

x

Still, the summer's testing had hardly begun. In Washington, the leaders of the farmers' organizations were speaking with a new desperation. The selection of Ed O'Neal, an Alabama planter, as president of the Farm Bureau in 1931 had fulfilled the old plan of Henry Wallace and Chester Davis for a marriage of corn and cotton. Tall, well dressed, ruddy, with thinning white hair and a hearty laugh that could be either disarming or menacing, O'Neal gave the Farm Bureau vigorous leadership. In the same year the National Farmers' Union also acquired a new chief — John A. Simpson, who had built the Farmers' Union of Oklahoma into a powerful organization. Taciturn and unyielding, he had the old Populist hatred for international bankers ("the worst criminals in this country") and a conviction that inflation through the re-monetization of silver was the best means of assuring the farmer the cost of production plus a reasonable profit in the Farmers' Union platform. In the long run, Simpson looked to the establishment of a cooperative commonwealth. "I feel the capitalistic system is doomed. It has as its foundation the principles of brutality, dishonesty and avarice." [17]

O'Neal and Simpson urged the farmers' case before congressional committees. But it looked as if pressure in Washington would avail little so long as the administration regarded the farm problem as insoluble. In 1931 a new farm leader appeared in Iowa to demand local action — Milo Reno, former president of the Iowa Farmers' Union. Nearly sixty-five years old, Reno was a big, slow-spoken, friendly man with a great upthrust thatch of tousled black hair, keen, deep-set eyes, and a five-gallon Stetson hat. He had fought the farmers' battle since the days of the Populists; he had been president of the Farmers' Union Life Insurance Company from its start; and he was one of the original champions of the "cost of production" thesis.

As early as 1927, Reno, as a member of a Farmers' Union committee, had suggested that if justice could not be obtained by legislation, no other course might remain than "organized refusal to deliver the products of the farm at less than production costs." Depression gave this notion of a farmers' strike new cogency. By the spring of 1932, it began to seem to some the only way of stemming the price collapse. Under Reno's leadership the Farmers' Holiday Association was formed — "holiday" was a sardonic reference to the "bank holiday" so affably proposed for the business community.

XI

The soil was rich and purple-black in Iowa; the red barns stood large and foursquare behind the comfortable white farmhouses with their ample lawns and swaying cottonwoods; the country teemed with abundance. But the buildings needed paint, the overalls of the farmer were patched and ragged, corn stood uncut in the field, parched by the sun. Along the roads near Sioux City in August 1932, sunburned farmers in ten-cent straw hats, carrying clubs, sticks, or pitchforks in their hands, were laying spiked logs and threshing-machine cables with loving care across the road. Their mood was jocular as they searched trucks for farm products and by one means or another persuaded those bound for market to think again and turn back. They waited in the sun and lay in the tall grass and made wisecracks and cursed a bit about the "international bankers" and slept in tents along the road — and the Ladies' Aid brought them basket suppers.

Independent of the Holiday movement but parallel with it arose a strike of the dairy farmers. Receiving two cents a quart for milk sold by distributors for eight cents in Sioux City, Woodbury County farmers declared an embargo on the entry of milk into the city (except for hospitals). All ten highways into town were under farmers' patrol; and the movement spread fast to Council Bluffs, to other Iowa communities, and into neighboring states. But with milk it was more than a matter of turning trucks back. The strikers ripped open the cans and poured them onto the road, the fresh milk forming a white river, drying and curdling on the cement, trickling into the drainage ditch. Around Council Bluffs the sheriff armed citizens with baseball bats and ordered them to clear the roads; then he arrested sixty of the pickets, until the threat of a mass march on the jail forced their release.

New faces were appearing on the picket lines, unfamiliar faces, city faces. From Des Moines came youths in brown shirts — members of the recently formed Khaki Shirts organization, some of them veterans of the Battle of Anacostia Flats, others idlers spoiling for a fight. And in New York City the Central Committee of the Communist party weighed the press reports from Iowa. Once again, as in the case of the B.E.F., the party had missed an opportunity. But it made the belated decision to send Ella Reeve Bloor, the veteran party worker, and her son Harold Ware west. Ware, the party's agricultural specialist, had lived on a Soviet collective farm, brought back $25,000 from Moscow to liberate the American peasant, and had only recently resigned as a consultant for Herbert Hoover's Department of Agriculture.

Reno and other Holiday leaders were meanwhile becoming a little frightened by what they might unleash. "You can no more stop this movement than you could stop the revolution; I mean the Revolution of 1776," said Reno, with mingled joy and apprehension. "I couldn't stop it if I tried." After a midnight shotgun attack on an encampment of farmers near Cherokee, Iowa, Reno used the projected conference of midwestern governors for Sioux City in September as the pretext to call off the strike. Hal Ware did what he could to keep the agitation alive by drafting resolutions for a farmers' mass meeting at Sioux City. But the farmers were growing bored; and as fall began, the presidential campaign, offering prospects of change, reduced the pressure for immediate action.

The Holiday movement made little economic sense. If mass withholding from the market might temporarily keep prices up, then release of the withheld produce would drive them down again. And only a minority of farmers, in any case, were prepared to take part in the movement. What the farm strike did was to throw into sharp relief the dilemma of a system incapable of using the plenty it produced, condemning millions to hunger because it lacked the wit or will to bring together the abundance and the need.[18]

XII

And so, as the third summer of the depression began to move into the fourth winter, the time of patience was running out. Virgil Jordan, the conservative economist of McGraw-Hill and the National Industrial Conference Board, reported after the 1931 meeting of the United States Chamber of Commerce that businessmen had lost faith in their leaders; they were ready to shoot the works. "An economic Mussolini, before many months have passed," said Jordan, "could have them parading in red, white and blue shirts, and saluting some new symbol."

A speaker, tall, vehement, arose in the House of Representatives early in 1932. "I am trying to provide security for human beings which they are not getting," said Congressman Hamilton Fish, Jr., of New York. "If we don't give it under the existing system, the people will change the system. Make no mistake about that." And, in three more months, Senator David A. Reed of Pennsylvania: "I do not often envy other countries their governments, but I say that if this country ever needed a Mussolini, it needs one now." In June the magazine *Vanity Fair* (among its editors, Clare Boothe Brokaw): "Appoint a dictator!" And in *Liberty* on June 25, Bernarr Macfadden: "What we need now is martial law; there is no time for civil law. The President should have dictatorial powers." By July, Henry Hazlitt was proposing in *Scribner's* a fundamental reorganization and unification of the American government.[19]

These were not representative voices. But they were symptomatic voices. They were not representative because the political system held out one more opportunity for change. Nineteen-thirty-two was the presidential year. So much had happened since the people had stood within sight of the day when poverty would be banished from the nation! The election in the fall would determine whether democracy could restore the confidence and loyalty of its people, or whether the years ahead would breed more embattled farmers and more B.E.F.'s, more Khaki Shirts and more Communists. Nineteen-thirty and 1931 had been years of economics; 1932 was providing a last chance for politics.

V

The Politics of Depression

27. The Democrats Prepare

THE ELECTION of 1928 had shown that despite the harmony at Houston, the split of 1924 was not yet mended in the Democratic party. The revolt of the South against Smith was in part the revolt of the old Bryan supporters who had backed McAdoo in 1924 — men who distrusted big business, disliked the cities, believed in the Eighteenth Amendment, and read the Bible. The essence of the Democratic problem was to bring these rural Democrats back into the party.

But the situation was complicated by the financial position of the National Committee. After the 1928 election, the party had an outstanding debt of $1,600,000. Two of the leading creditors, John J. Raskob and Bernard Baruch, were philanthropic Democratic millionaires, prepared to help carry the party along until 1932. But in exchange for their benevolence they naturally expected influence in shaping the party's organization and policy. Their influence, however — and most especially Raskob's influence — was not well calculated to recapture Democratic agrarianism.

Raskob once confessed that he found politics "difficult and unattractive." But he stayed on as national chairman, and he was determined that the National Committee should not relapse into its usual lethargy. Between 1924 and 1928, for example, the party did not even have a national headquarters. In 1929, 1930, and 1931, Raskob loaned the Committee $370,000 to keep it in active operation; less than $25,000 was repaid in that period. He hired as full-time director Jouett Shouse, a dapper Democratic politician, shrewd and effective for all his spats and walking sticks; and

Shouse, completing a revolution in party management, hired as full-time publicity director a veteran newspaper reporter named Charles Michelson.

"Who in hell is Charley Michelson?" asked Raskob — a query amply disclosing his political inexperience. Michelson, who had worked for Hearst in San Francisco in the great days of Ambrose Bierce and Fremont Older, had been for a dozen years head of the Washington bureau of the New York *World*. A hard-bitten cynic with a wintry, satanic smile and a dry humor, who had seen everything and lost all illusions, he brought a new professionalism to political publicity. While Shouse toured the country, making addresses and trying to revive local organization, Michelson turned out an uninterrupted stream of interviews, statements, and speeches in Washington. These releases — over 500 in the first two years, signed indifferently by leading Democrats in the House or Senate — poured ridicule on the Hoover administration. Michelson himself, playing interminable bridge or dominoes with newspapermen at the Press Club, saw to it that his best wisecracks received full circulation. This barrage undoubtedly had something to do with fixing the depression image of the Hoover administration, though not nearly so much as myth would later suggest. Actually Michelson issued more releases on the tariff than on any other topic and did not concentrate particularly on class issues. After all, he was working for Raskob. In any case, it was Hoover's response to the depression, and not the publicity about it, which created the image in the first place.[1]

II

Bernard Baruch did not differ profoundly from Raskob on policy matters. But this tall white-haired man, with his finely chiseled features and courtly manners, was infinitely more skilled in political operations. His success at the War Industries Board and his intimacy with Wilson constituted one reason for his influence in the Democratic party; his money was another (an unknown number of Democratic senators and congressmen were believed to campaign on his largesse); but the enduring reason was the widespread confidence in his sagacity. No one had more of that confidence than Baruch himself. His unaffected satisfaction with his accomplishments had an impersonal quality that removed it from mere egotism. It was as if his career, his success, his wisdom were a kind of national monument — a tribute to the possibilities American life opened up to a bright young Jew from South Carolina.

Wall Street and Washington had given Baruch a conviction that he had seen men under stress and knew the limits of human nature. His counsel tended to be short, stark, and intuitive. Some thought he infallibly cut through to the heart of issues, while others found him annoyingly dogmatic in face of social or human complexity. His hunches were by no means infallible — he had endorsed permanent prosperity in the spring of 1929 — but his reputation, his presence, and above all his public relations, so smoothly managed by Herbert Bayard Swope, preserved the hits and obliterated the errors. And there remained beneath the somewhat complacent realism and the instinct for power a deep, if rarely acknowledged, vein of idealism. America had touched it, Wilson had touched it, the Democratic party had touched it. He told Josephus Daniels in the twenties with utmost sincerity, "The world must decide between the constructive radicalism of Woodrow Wilson or the destructive radicalism of Lenin." [2]

Baruch's attitude toward the depression was fluctuating. When he talked to businessmen, he emphasized the need for government planning along the lines of the old War Industries Board. When talking to men he considered perilously progressive, he emphasized patience and orthodoxy. The Republican party, he thus wrote to Governor Roosevelt of New York in the fall of 1930, had enough trouble, what with hard times and the twelve million people who owned securities, each one representing not less than two votes. "Don't you help them by having them point at us," Baruch scrawled. "The economic body needs rest — not any more operations until it is stronger." [3] But while tending toward conservatism, Baruch, unlike Raskob, had no intention of binding himself irrevocably to a particular program or candidate. He wished to hoard his influence rather than expend it vainly. For him survival was more important than success. He would remain active in the struggles against radicalism within the Democratic party. But he did not plan to be caught on the losing side.

III

The policy initiative thus fell to Raskob; and Raskob had several clear objectives in the economic field. His fear was positive government. The continuation of the Republican tendency "to centralize greater and greater power in Washington," he said, might well result in a revolution that would divide the United States into two or three independent republics. The best Democratic hope, he thought, was to continue the strategy of 1928. "It is not the duty of the Democratic party," he said, "to engage in attacks upon business. . . . We should attempt to do everything to take the government out of business and relieve trade from unnecessary and unreasonable government restriction." He wanted to commit the party to the protective tariff, and he proposed that the Federal Trade Commission be given authority to suspend the antitrust laws.

To the Democrats of the South and the West, such a course seemed a betrayal of the party's dearest traditions. The old Wilsonian, George Creel of California, thought Raskob was destroying "every real distinction between Democracy and Republicanism." His leadership, Creel said, was providing the singular spectacle "of a party of opposition deliberately modeling itself along the lines laid down by its conservative opponents." Under this dispensation the rural Democrats, the dry Democrats, the antimonopoly Democrats, the progressive Democrats, the heirs of Bryan and Populism, were growing increasingly restive.

One of the most restive was Cordell Hull of Tennessee, who had moved from the House to the Senate in 1930. A passionate low-tariff advocate, Hull had been distressed by Smith's protectionism in 1928, but he had loyally gone down the line for the ticket. In 1929, however, he decided that the time had come for a fight against what he called "the unconditional surrender of the Democratic Party to the forces of high-tariff greed and privilege." In the next three years, Hull pressed that fight at every opportunity. And his natural ally was the one northeasterner who had consistently understood the old Bryan-McAdoo wing of the party — Franklin D. Roosevelt.[4]

Roosevelt considered an alliance between country and city Democrats wholly feasible. But he was certain that this alliance could work only on the basis of liberalism — in terms, that is, of opposition to business rule, not, as Raskob proposed, of bidding for business support. Early in 1931 Roosevelt expressed to Senator Copeland of New York his concern "lest our Party be misled along conservative or reactionary paths by those who fatuously believe that we can successfully compete with our Republican friends for the support of certain interests. It is silly," he added, "to imagine that this group will ever accept an invitation from us when they already own the original article, and they certainly have owned the Republican organization for many years." To another friend he wrote that the Democratic party must not yield to those who would "make our party a party of high tariffs and a friend to those vested interests which have so completely dominated the Republican organization for so many years. If we win, we must win because we are progressive." [5]

The debate between the liberals and conservatives was overlaid by the better publicized debate over prohibition repeal. There was, of course, an abundance of honest feelings on each side about prohibition. But, to a degree, the conservatives, like Raskob, hoped to make the issue prohibition in order to avoid making it business supremacy; while those who wished to bypass a party fight over repeal, like Roosevelt, did so because they wanted nothing to distract the old Bryan group from a fight against business rule.

And even more, by 1931, the liberal-conservative conflict was complicated by the problem of the presidential nomination. For by the spring of 1931 Roosevelt was drawing clearly ahead as the candidate for 1932, and Roosevelt's candidacy was aggressively identified with the liberal wing of the Democratic party.

IV

The first Democrat of national reputation to come out for Roosevelt's nomination was Burt Wheeler of Montana, La Follette's running mate in 1924. "I have always thought of you as one of the real leaders of progressive thought and action in this country," Roosevelt wrote in grateful response in the spring of 1930. "Therefore to be considered as [a] real progressive by you means something to me." And Wheeler quickly replied, "You more nearly typify the progressive thought of the Nation than anyone else." [6]

In March 1931, La Follette, Norris, Costigan, Cutting, and Wheeler issued a call for a Progressive conference in Washington. The militants of reform were in attendance, not only old faces, like Ickes, Hillman, Richberg, Charles Beard, Florence Kelley, and Lillian Wald, but some new ones, like Mayor Murphy of Detroit. Robert P. Scripps of the Scripps-Howard papers phrased the challenge: if wealth were not soon better distributed, he said, "the alternative is the goose step, one way or another, and Lenin or Mussolini makes mighty little difference." The conference drew up a program to achieve Scripps's goal. But George Norris, warning against overoptimism, said that the nation would not get really progressive legislation until it got a progressive President, "another Roosevelt." The conference loudly cheered this not very enigmatic reference.[7]

Roosevelt's record in Albany on public power, on unemployment relief, on labor legislation, on conservation and resources obviously commended him to the progressives. Many others had long thought of Franklin Roosevelt as a presidential candidate — his mother perhaps since 1882, his associate Louis Howe certainly since 1912, others when he ran with Cox in 1920, many more after his speeches nominating Smith in 1924 and 1928. But his campaign did not begin in earnest until his re-election as governor in 1930 with an unprecedented plurality of nearly three-quarters of a million votes. As the returns came in, James A. Farley, as state chairman, issued a statement that he and Howe had drafted with care and some apprehension. "I do not see," Farley declared, "how Mr. Roosevelt can escape becoming the next presidential nominee of his party, even if no one should raise a finger to bring it about." Farley, who had never discussed the Presidency with Roosevelt, read the Governor the statement over the phone after it had been released. Roosevelt laughed and replied, "Whatever you said, Jim, is all right with me."

A few days later, Roosevelt called to the gubernatorial mansion his most trusted adviser among the professional politicians, the urbane Edward J. Flynn of the Bronx. The Governor, Louis Howe, and Flynn chatted aimlessly through the dinner. Later, in the library, Roosevelt turned to Flynn and said briefly, "Eddie, my reason for asking you to stay overnight is that I believe I can be nominated for the Presidency in 1932." [8]

V

Roosevelt had many obvious assets — a familiar name, a charming personality, demonstrated political popularity, an impressive executive record in Albany, a dramatic personal victory over illness, a wide and well-cultivated acquaintance across the country. He had in Howe, moreover, an astute political confidante and in Flynn a crafty adviser. Yet Roosevelt alone among them had national political experience and instinct; he alone had political contacts in the South and West; and, in the end, he himself would have to make the basic decisions of the campaign.

Evidently he had already reached one decision — that is, to start lining up delegates as soon as possible. This decision had its dangers. By definition the front runner provided a target on which all others could concentrate their fire. In such conditions the obvious "stop Roosevelt" strategy would be to tie up so many votes in favorite son candidacies that he could not get the two-thirds vote required by Democratic conventions. Yet, weighing the risks, Roosevelt characteristically decided that activity was the best policy. To Flynn he now urged the importance of trips through the country, sounding out leaders, renewing Roosevelt's old political friendships and organizing for the 1932 convention. Flynn demurred. He was, he explained, no greeter or backslapper; he would be more effective in the background. Together Flynn and Roosevelt concluded that Jim Farley would be the ideal Roosevelt envoy.[9]

Farley was even less acquainted with the national picture than Howe or Flynn. He had worked his way up in the state organization from the town chairmanship of Stony Point through the county chairmanship to the state Assembly and the state chairmanship. But his engaging and imperturbable geniality, his orderly administrative habits, his known integrity, his exact and capacious memory, his modest and decent life — he was a devoted family man, who neither drank nor smoked and who faithfully attended Sunday mass — all these had made their mark in the state. His personal qualities could be relied on, Roosevelt felt, to disarm people in the hinterland who might otherwise be mistrustful of a big, bald, glad-handing Irish Catholic politician from New York. "You have done a wonderful piece of work," Roosevelt had written Farley after the 1930 campaign, "and I don't need to tell you how very appreciative and grateful I am. . . . I have an idea that you and I make a combination which has not existed since Cleveland and Lamont" [10] — a combination, Roosevelt might have added, that had propelled the earlier New York Democratic governor into the White House.

The next step was money. In March 1931, Henry Morgenthau, Sr., who had been Wilson's Ambassador to Turkey, Frank C. Walker, a New York lawyer, and William H. Woodin, president of the American Car and Foundry Company, contributed $5000 each. Others who gave to the Roosevelt campaign in the course of the next twelve months included Herbert H. Lehman, Lieutenant-Governor of New York, Flynn, Jesse Straus of Macy's, Robert W. Bingham of the Louisville *Courier-Journal,* James W. Gerard, Wilson's Ambassador to Germany, Colonel House, Dave Hennen Morris and Laurence A. Steinhardt, both New York lawyers, and a few others. In the spring of 1931, Howe and Farley set up headquarters at 331 Madison Avenue, New York City. Howe's dark inside office, the desk piled high with a clutter of letters, papers, and memos and dusted with a coating of cigarette ash, became the clearinghouse of the Roosevelt campaign.

VI

In June 1931 the annual Governors' Conference gave Roosevelt an opportunity to speak on national issues. He was assigned the relatively impenetrable topic "Land Utilization and State Planning." But he seized the occasion to offer views on the depression sharply different not only from those of the Hoover administration but from those of the Raskob wing of the Democratic party. People were rightly asking, Roosevelt told the governors, "why Government cannot and should not act to protect its citizens from disaster." Government must act, he said; it must undertake "the better planning of our social and economic life" — sickness and unemployment insurance, taxation, the tariff, land utilization and population redistribution. He emphasized the virtues of the states as the units for planning — "48 laboratories" for social experimentation — and he concluded with emphasis, "State and national planning is an essential to the future prosperity, happiness and the very existence of the American people." [11]

This call for positive government sharpened the ideological conflict within the Democratic party. And, soon after his return to Albany, Roosevelt proceeded to sharpen the political conflict. The Grand Lodge Convention of the Elks was to take place in Seattle, Washington, early in July; and Jim Farley, an enthusiastic Elk, was planning as usual to attend. Howe considered this fraternal mission a heaven-sent opportunity to take political soundings. Roosevelt agreed. On a warm June day, Farley descended on Hyde Park with a briefcase full of railroad timetables, a Rand McNally atlas and a list of national committeemen and state chairmen. By the end of the afternoon Roosevelt had worked out a detailed itinerary, by which Farley could cover eighteen states in nineteen days.

Farley set out on June 29. The next three weeks were a whirl of handshakes, luncheons, dinners, conferences in hotel rooms, sleeper jumps through the sweltering heat, names and faces meticulously registered in memory, reports sent back to New York by special delivery, sweat mopped off the big man's streaming face, new hands to shake, new people to meet, new names to remember.

Farley's method was adroit and tactful. There were three potential candidates from New York, he might first suggest — Roosevelt, Smith, and Owen D. Young. Then he would lead the conversation along designed lines, until he could see whether it was appropriate to get down to business. His letters home were sanguine and cheerful. "There apparently is a unanimity of sentiment for you . . . the organization in every instance is for you wholeheartedly. . . . I am satisfied, Governor, that the leaders want to be on the bandwagon. . . . If I continue to find the same sentiment . . . I will probably reach New York so enthusiastic that I will make a statement and those who read it will believe I am a fit candidate for an insane asylum."

Farley met 1100 local Democratic leaders in his nineteen days as "a travelling Elk on a tour." In the next few weeks he sent each one a personal letter, the signature genially inscribed in green ink. In the fall he continued incessant activity, meeting with Cordell Hull and Burt Wheeler in Washington, talking to national committeemen, and maintaining a network of contacts across the country by long-distance telephone. And in the fall Mary W. Dewson, the tall, rangy social worker who had been a leading figure in the Consumers' League and had worked in the Smith campaign, joined the headquarters to begin the job of corralling the women's vote. In December Molly Dewson followed Farley and made a useful trip across the country. (When she returned, she submitted so incredibly low an expense account that Roosevelt teased her about the entertainment she must have received from male Democrats along the way.) [12]

VII

Chairman Raskob watched the Roosevelt enthusiasm with growing irritation. When Charley Michelson suggested that the National Committee, to show its impartiality, might distribute the speeches of Roosevelt as well as those of other Democratic leaders, Raskob curtly rebuffed him.[13] In an effort to recall the party to what he conceived (forgetting Bryan and Wilson) to be traditional Democratic states rights doctrine, Raskob now called on the three living Democratic presidential candidates to reaffirm Jeffersonian orthodoxies at the Jackson Day dinner in Washington in January 1932. James M. Cox attacked the Republicans for advocating spending and centralization. John W. Davis denounced the whole theory of affirmative government. Then Al Smith proposed a program of federal public works to be financed by a government bond issue. This was the one spending issue on which most conservative Democrats agreed with the liberals; Baruch, Owen D. Young, and Joe Robinson endorsed versions of the Smith plan in the next month, though always in a context of budget balancing, government economy, and noninterference with business.[14]

Smith still remained Raskob's favorite candidate even if for the moment the chairman smiled on all candidates who might stop Franklin D. Roosevelt. Smith had, after all, been a great governor of New York; he had put on a notable campaign in 1928; he was only fifty-nine years old; and he retained a fanatical following in the country. True, he had seemed to flinch for a moment from the thought of another bitter national fight. As he said to another Irish Democrat, Arthur Mullen of Nebraska, in 1930, "There's no chance for a Catholic to be President. Not in my lifetime or in yours. . . . I can't win against bigots." When Ed Flynn told Smith in 1931 that he was going for Roosevelt, Smith said that nothing would induce him to enter the political arena again. Spreading a sheaf of papers on his desk, he said, "Ed, these are all debts that I must clear up. Financially, I am in an extremely bad position." He told the same thing to Herbert Lehman. On February 1, 1932, Farley went to see him, partly to explain his activities on behalf of Roosevelt, partly to feel out Smith; Smith was, Farley remembers, "extremely cordial," but remained inscrutable about his own intentions. (Later Smith told Congresswoman Mary T. Norton of New Jersey, "Farley betrayed me. Wait and see him betray Roosevelt.") [15]

Yet the presidential virus was hard to throw off. As election year came on him, Smith's resolve began visibly to weaken. His old scorn for Roosevelt came into the open. In the fall of 1931 Smith opposed a reforestation amendment to the state constitution demanded by Roosevelt; the decision of New York voters to ratify the amendment could only have deepened Smith's rancor. Meanwhile Roosevelt declined to take up his own aspirations with Smith, on the ground that Smith was the party's titular leader and had a right to express his own views in his own time, while Smith, for his part, grew increasingly incensed over Roosevelt's failure to talk over his candidacy. In early 1932, Smith told James M. Cox that by all the rules of the political game he was entitled to renomination.[16]

Always a practical man, responsive to concrete pressures, Smith had seemed a progressive when challenged by the needs of state government in a conservative period. But he had never developed a progressive philosophy. Now, plunged into a world of business against which he had no intellectual defense, he rapidly absorbed the Raskob point of view. "After I left Albany," he said in 1933, "after living in a mansion for six years I couldn't see First Avenue very well, so I went over on Fifth Avenue. I signed a lease for

$10,000 a year." [17] He was now president of the Empire State Building, a director of banks and insurance companies, a friend of the rich, driving around with his own chauffeur in his own limousine. The call for a public works program was a last fling for the old Al Smith. The bulk of his pronouncements in 1931 and 1932 were for rigid government economy, for a balanced budget, for reduction of the tax burden on business, and for a sales tax. He was the spokesman of northern business in the Democratic party. When Roosevelt finally made a formal announcement of his candidacy on January 21, 1932, Smith was quick to follow two weeks later.

VIII

Wherever it could, the National Committee encouraged local candidates. Maryland, for example, offered the vastly admired Governor Albert Ritchie. Now fifty-six years old, Ritchie had once been Bernard Baruch's general counsel in the War Industries Board and had been governor of Maryland since 1920. He was bland, elegant, self-contained, ornately handsome with his white hair and coal-black eyebrows; and he was the beau ideal in the politics of such other urbane and civilized Marylanders as H. L. Mencken, Gerald W. Johnson, and the young lawyer Dean Acheson.

In political philosophy, Ritchie was a literal Jeffersonian. Outside of Italy and Russia, he felt, the American people were already the most regimented in the Western world: "inspectors and spies and official regulators follow the one-hundred-percent American from the day he draws his first nourishment from his inspected mother's breast." In 1930 he contended that under Hoover "centralization of power has proceeded at a pace that would have appalled even [Alexander Hamilton's] most ardent followers"; the overriding issue, he said, was "State existence against Federal transgressions." A sensitive and candid gentleman, moved by the human tragedy of depression, Ritchie recognized mass unemployment as "the greatest challenge to our social order and the strongest argument in favor of Communism"; but all he advocated in the way of a solution was letting "natural forces take their course, as free and untrammeled as possible." In the impressive hunch of Bernard

Baruch, the "finger of fate" pointed to Ritchie as a possibility for the White House. Early in January 1932, the Maryland governor frankly said that he would like to be President ("Of course, I would. Who wouldn't?"), denounced unemployment insurance, and assailed the "appalling extension of government into almost every field of private enterprise." [18]

Another governor who the National Committee hoped might tie up some western delegations was W. H. Murray of Oklahoma. Alfalfa Bill was a figure out of an earlier America, tall and raw-boned, with wavy gray hair, a gaunt and weathered face, and seedy mustachios. He wore an old dirty frock coat over unpressed trousers that showed a shank of thin hairy leg, with wrinkled white socks hanging over the top of his shoes. He was a creation of America's last frontier, "born in a cotton patch during a November snowstorm," as he used to say of himself; "rocked in the cradle of adversity; chastened by hardship and poverty." As a young man, he had been attorney for the Chickasaw Nation; he served two terms in Congress after the Indian Territory became a state; then, after the First World War, restless in a search for new frontiers, he moved on to South America. He stayed in Bolivia for most of a decade, returned to Oklahoma two months before the Wall Street crash, and six months later was campaigning — successfully — for the governorship.

As governor, he ruled like a South American dictator. He freely employed the state militia, declared martial law in the oil fields, sneered at higher education, ridiculed farm conservation practices, and announced that certain crops grew best if planted when the moon was right. Slumped at the end of his spine in the governor's office, an old sweat-stained felt hat on his head, he greeted visitors with a snarling "What do you want?" A bouncer was always present to throw out unwelcome guests. Yet Murray himself was no illiterate. He was proud of his library and his erudition. In conversation, he mixed uncouth references to "varmints" and "polecats" with citations from Lycurgus and Quintilian. Sixty-two years old when the campaign began, he presented himself under the slogan of "Bread, Butter, Bacon, Beans." His candidacy, it was hoped, would split Roosevelt's following in the South and West.[19]

But the rural Democrats were soon offered a far more formidable possibility in John Garner. William Randolph Hearst was the active agent in promoting the Garner boom. For a time, Hearst had played with the idea of backing Roosevelt. But, though he endorsed Roosevelt's power and conservation policies, he came to detect in him sinister streaks of internationalism. Then Garner assured a Hearst emissary of his opposition to all foreign entanglement as well as his devotion to economy and thrift. On a New Year's broadcast in 1932, Hearst accordingly dismissed Roosevelt, Smith, Ritchie, Owen, D. Young, Newton D. Baker — "all good men in their way, but all internationalists" — and settled on Garner, "another Champ Clark," the one candidate whose motto would be "America First." [20]

McAdoo cheerfully accepted Garner as his heir. He had never forgiven Al Smith, of course, for the fight in 1924; and he had an obscure grudge against Roosevelt, with whom he had once been allied in New York politics. He tried to warn Dan Roper against Roosevelt: "Don't you know that he'll Tammanyize the United States?" ("I don't," Roper replied.) To Arthur Mullen, McAdoo whispered about Roosevelt's ill health and his inability to go through a campaign: "We don't want a dead man on the ticket, Arthur." ("We won't have one," said Mullen.) [21]

IX

With this bustling collection of aspirants, a deadlocked convention seemed likely. But deadlock might well open the way for a dark horse — for a man with few or no delegates in the early ballots — as it had in 1924. Roosevelt believed that the Raskob group were really keeping Owen D. Young in reserve, awaiting the moment of exhaustion; but Young, it was reported, had declined to run. The next conservative choice was evidently Newton D. Baker of Ohio.

Baker would indeed be a popular name to produce in the declining moments of a tired convention. This small man, with his quiet intensity and his startling capacity for oratory, had something for every camp. Progressives recalled him as a reform mayor of Cleveland, following in the footsteps of Tom Johnson. Idealists admired his long fight for the League of Nations, culminating in his eloquence in the 1924 convention. Realists remembered him as a distinguished Secretary of War. Conservatives knew him as one of the most prosperous corporation lawyers in the nation, with the Van Sweringen syndicate and Electric Bond and Share among his clients. In his literacy, his scholarship, and his high principles, he seemed in the tradition of Wilson and John W. Davis.

Baker refused to sanction any attempts to pledge delegates on his behalf. Four years before, he had actually pleaded a heart ailment to Roosevelt as a reason for political inactivity. Yet, after reiterating in January 1932 his familiar view that the United States should join the League, Baker abruptly reversed himself twelve days later. "I would not take the United States into the League, if I had the power to do so," he now said, "until there is an informed and convinced majority sentiment in favor of that action. . . . I am not in favor of a plank in the Democratic national platform urging our joining the League." [22] It seemed a long time since he had sworn that obligation to the dead to lift his voice, in season and out, by day and by night, in church, in political meeting and in the market place, until their sacrifice had been perfected.

Baker, in fact, had not only become expedient on international issues but had long ceased to be progressive on economic issues. As mayor of Cleveland, he had sponsored a municipal electric plant; as public utilities lawyer, he sponsored a pamphlet urging that the same municipal plant be shut down. He had signed newspaper advertisements demanding the open shop for Cleveland. Roosevelt's spuriously regretful writing off of Baker to Baker's wartime colleague Josephus Daniels had evident plausibility.

He labors under very definite political handicaps. Because of, or rather in spite of, his perfectly legitimate law practice he is labeled by many progressives as the attorney for J. P. Morgan and the Van Schweringens [sic]; he is opposed by Labor; he would be opposed by the German-Americans; and also by the bulk of the Irish because of his consistent League of Nations attitude up to this year. As they say, "them are the sad facts"! All this seems a pity because New would make a better President than I would!

Yet the Baker enthusiasm, warmed by commentators like Walter Lippmann, continued to bubble beneath the surface. "As nearly as I can gather," Norman H. Davis, who had been Assistant Secretary of the Treasury under Wilson, wrote in an insinuating letter to Baker, "there is no genuine enthusiasm for Roosevelt on the part of any of the more important men who have come out for him." Baker must have received many such letters; and some men, like Carter Glass of Virginia, were going to Chicago determined to make him the nominee.[23]

Bernard Baruch, it was whispered, was for Baker too — though no one really knew whom Baruch might be for: others thought it was Young, others Ritchie. It seemed clear only that he was opposed to Roosevelt. At a meeting of the Woodrow Wilson Foundation early in 1931, Henry Morgenthau, Sr., noting on the wall a picture of Roosevelt in the campaign of 1920, had said, "That's my candidate." Silence followed. Then Baruch spoke up: "Uncle Henry, if Frank is nominated, I won't give one cent to the Democratic party." "But, Bernie," said the old man, "hasn't he been a good governor?" "Yes," said Baruch, "but he's so wishy-washy."

Still, even in the case of Roosevelt, Baruch kept his opposition discreet. When Ernest K. Lindley, a newspaperman close to Roosevelt, suggested in the New York *Herald Tribune* that Baruch had joined the Raskob-Smith combine, Baruch protested to Roosevelt, "I am not interested in any candidate for the nomination." Roosevelt, who enjoyed this kind of game, replied in kind. "In regard to the national political situation," he wrote, "I am much in the position of one who sits on the sidelines and has little personal interest." But the Governor no doubt knew that Baruch's hostility would never become implacable so long as he sensed power behind the Roosevelt door; and he consequently kept the door open, occasionally inviting Baruch to Hyde Park with flattering phrases — "you have such clear thinking processes and such a fund of information that I should much like to get your slant on things." The process deceived neither man, and neither liked the other much, but each respected a realist.[24]

X

By February 1932, the crisscross of maneuver was becoming more intense than ever. Roosevelt's strategy was clear. It was to keep his lines open to the old Bryan-McAdoo wing of the party, now partly committed to the Garner candidacy, and to dissuade the Garner group from reaching an agreement with Smith. He was assisted in this project by the ancient hatreds that still divided Smith from McAdoo and from Hearst, as well as by the natural distaste of southern and western agrarians for eastern business. And he resolved now to take further steps to propitiate Hearst as the moving force behind the Garner movement. Baker's repudiation of the League had left Roosevelt exposed as the most internationalist of the candidates. Colonel House tried to persuade Hearst privately that there was no reason to worry about Roosevelt's views on foreign policy, but Hearst demanded a public statement. Early in February, Roosevelt accordingly declared that the League was no longer the League conceived by Woodrow Wilson; it might have been had the United States joined, but "the fact remains that we did not join." In present circumstances, he said, "I do not favor American participation." [25]

For the rest, Roosevelt continued to pound home his social and economic views. In a radio speech early in April he renewed his call for planning. In a slap at the Smith-Baruch enthusiasm for public works, Roosevelt said that, even if billions could be raised and useful works could be found, public works could only be a stopgap. "A real economic cure must go to the killing of the bacteria in the system rather than to the treatment of external symptoms." A first necessity, he said, was to restore purchasing power to the farming half of the country. Then there must be a program of saving farms and homes from mortgage foreclosure; the government could "provide at least as much assistance to the little fellow as it is now giving to the large banks and corporations." Another need was tariff revision "on the basis of a reciprocal exchange," allowing other nations to pay for our goods by sending us their goods. The government must begin to think in terms of "the forgotten man at the bottom of the economic pyramid."

The reference to the "forgotten man" struck an immediate response. A few days later, speaking at a Jefferson Day dinner in St. Paul, he expanded on the dangers of class government. He cited the electric power field where, as a "result of our blindness, of our failure to regulate, and of our failure to say that if private capital will not operate for a reasonable profit, Government will have to operate itself," Americans must pay "vastly more for that very necessary part of our modern life — electricity — than they should be paying." Not only must states reassert the public authority over private interests, but the country must recognize that the economic problem was national in scope and could be solved "only by the firm establishment of national control." What the nation needed, said Roosevelt, was "imaginative and purposeful planning," based on the "national community of interest" — "economic planning, not for this period alone but for our needs for a long time to come."

The next month, at Oglethorpe University in Georgia, Roosevelt affirmed once more the necessity for social planning in the interest of all: "we cannot allow our economic life to be controlled by that small group of men whose chief outlook upon the social welfare is tinctured by the fact that they can make huge profits from the lending of money and the marketing of securities." Must the country remain hungry and jobless while raw materials stand unused and factories idle? The trouble, said Roosevelt, lay not in an insufficiency of capital; if anything, the physical plant was overexpanded. The trouble lay in an insufficiency of buying power. "I believe," he said, "that we are at the threshold of a fundamental change in our popular economic thought. . . . We need to correct, by drastic means if necessary, the faults in our economic system from which we now suffer. . . . The country needs and, unless I mistake its temper, the country demands bold, persistent experimentation. . . . Above all, try something." [26]

XI

There could be little question about the meaning of the Roosevelt campaign. The New York governor was the only presidential candidate in either major party who consistently criticized business leadership, who demanded drastic (if unspecified) changes in the economic system, who called for bold experimentation and comprehensive planning. Though his prescriptions remained vague, the impulse behind his remarks was novel and, to some, menacing.

Among Roosevelt's enemies, a few consoled themselves by thinking that he did not really mean what he was saying: he was, as Baruch had said, too wishy-washy. Commentators both to the left and to the right of Roosevelt took this view, citing particularly his evasions in face of the corruptions of the Tammany regime in New York City. Thus the *New Republic* in 1931 termed him "a liberal-minded man, of excellent intentions," but "not a man of great intellectual force or supreme moral stamina." Oswald Garrison Villard of the *Nation* suggested that if the nomination were to be awarded "on the grounds of great intellectual capacity, of proved boldness in grasping issues and problems, of courage and originality in finding solutions," it would never go to Roosevelt. Heywood Broun poured brutal ridicule upon him, and Elmer Davis defined him as "a man who thinks that the shortest distance between two points is not a straight line but a corkscrew."

No one was more measured in his dismissal than Walter Lippmann. Early in January 1932, Lippmann warned the West and South against taking Roosevelt's progressivism seriously. He was, said Lippmann, "an amiable man with many philanthropic impulses, but he is not the dangerous enemy of anything. He is too eager to please." A highly impressionable person, without a firm grasp of public affairs and without very strong convictions, "Franklin D. Roosevelt is no crusader. He is no tribune of the people. He is no enemy of entrenched privilege. He is a pleasant man who, without any important qualifications for the office, would very much like to be President." ("In spite of his brilliance," Roosevelt wrote of Lippmann a few days later, "it is very clear that he has never let his mind travel west of the Hudson or north of the Harlem!") The Scripps-Howard press, coming out for Al Smith, summed up the case in a front-page editorial in June. "As Roosevelt generalizes, Smith is specific. As Roosevelt loves to delay, Smith loves action. Irresolution is ingrained in one, boldness in the other. . . . In Franklin Roosevelt," the editorial cruelly concluded, "we have another Hoover."

But Raskob and the National Committee could not accept so

consoling an interpretation of the Roosevelt campaign. Whether he meant what he said or not, he was stirring up dangerous emotions. He was frightening away business support. He was threatening to commit the party to radical programs. In April the National Committee planned a Jefferson Day celebration where once again the party leadership might administer a massed rebuke to Roosevelt. Everyone was to be on the dais — Al Smith, John W. Davis, James M. Cox, Newton Baker, Garner, Joe Robinson of Arkansas, Harry Byrd of Virginia — nearly every leading Democrat except the Governor of New York.[27]

Smith dominated the occasion. Speaking in his best style, crisp, candid, and hard-hitting, he sought to indict Roosevelt as both superficial and demagogic. "The country is sick and tired of listening to political campaign orators who tell us what is the matter with us," he said. "Few, if any, of them know what the cure is." We were told that we must restore the purchasing power of the farmer. "Fine! Of course we must. But how are we going to do it?" We were told that public works is a stopgap. "Whoever said it was anything else? It is at least better than nothing and infinitely better than a continuance of the disguised dole."

"Oratory puts nobody to work," said Smith; and appeals to "the forgotten man" were even worse. "At a time like this, when millions of men and women and children are starving throughout the land, there is always the temptation to stir up class prejudice, to stir up the bitterness of the rich against the poor, and of the poor against the rich." Such demagoguery, Smith said, was intolerable. "I protest against the endeavor to delude the poor people of this country to their ruin by trying to make them believe that they can get employment before the people who would ordinarily employ them are also again restored to conditions of normal prosperity."

His face red, his voice harsh and defiant, he pressed on. He had stated, he continued, that he would not be for or against any candidate. "I announce tonight an exception to that statement." The audience waited expectantly. "I will take off my coat and fight to the end against any candidate who persists in any demagogic appeal to the masses of the working people of this country to destroy themselves by setting class against class and rich against poor!" . . .

But reporters noticed that, even before this audience, his denunciation received but five brief seconds of applause.[28]

XII

In the meantime, the scramble was going on for delegates. Some delegations were already committed to Roosevelt: when he had received a wire of provisional notification from the Alabama delegation in December 1931, he scrawled his cheerful reply on the yellow message — "As T.R. would have said quote Delighted end quote F.D.R."[29] The first serious primary contest came in New Hampshire in March. Smith was the favorite in the press; but Roosevelt, backed by the state organization, won almost two to one and captured the entire delegation. A week later, Roosevelt beat Alfalfa Bill Murray in North Dakota, deflating the Murray boom. In the next weeks, Georgia, Iowa, Maine, Wisconsin, Nebraska, Michigan, and Kentucky swept into the Roosevelt camp.

Late in April came the primary in Massachusetts. Here, at last, Smith enjoyed organization support; both Governor Joseph B. Ely and Senator David I. Walsh were behind him. When Roosevelt, misled by the assurances of his son James, then resident in Boston, and of Mayor James M. Curley, imprudently entered the contest, Smith won by a vote of three to one, taking the entire delegation. Two days later, Smith showed surprising strength in Pennsylvania, though Roosevelt carried a majority of the delegates. And early in May, Garner won the California primary, with Roosevelt a poor second and Smith a strong third. W. G. McAdoo said jubilantly: "It is a serious and perhaps irreparable blow to the Roosevelt candidacy." But Roosevelt noted cheerfully to Josephus Daniels that if the California and Texas delegations could be won over this "would cinch the matter" of the nomination.[30]

Roosevelt was still in the lead, so far as delegates were concerned, but within a fortnight his bandwagon momentum had been stopped. Massachusetts, Pennsylvania, and California, wrote Walter Lippmann, were the only real tests; and in all these Roosevelt had made a poor showing. "When one remembers that he has been in sight of the nomination for months, that he alone among the candidates has a nation-wide organization, that his name is

Roosevelt, that he has sought to identify himself with the discontent of the people, his failure to show popular strength is remarkable." The professionals, Lippmann added, had come to realize that if Roosevelt were nominated his weaknesses would develop so rapidly during the campaign that he would surely be defeated. "The truth is that he has not a good enough grasp of issues nor the power of quick and firm decision to withstand the withering fire which the Republicans would subject him to." [31]

Yet the Roosevelt movement, though set back, was not checked. Steadily Arizona, Wyoming, West Virginia, Kansas, New Mexico, Montana, South Carolina, Vermont, Tennessee, Oregon, Nevada, Delaware, Colorado, Utah, Mississippi, Florida, Idaho, North Carolina moved into the Roosevelt camp. As the convention approached, it was apparent that the New York governor had nearly a majority of delegates, and that none of his rivals had the one-third necessary for a sure veto. Roosevelt was on the brink. But Chicago lay grimly ahead.

28. Decision in Chicago

ON JUNE 14, 1932, the Republicans gathered in Chicago to nominate their candidate for President. No one doubted how the delegates would vote. A springtime movement among New York businessmen for Calvin Coolidge had long since been snuffed out by the methodical Hoover organization. Yet newspapermen noticed the absence of Hoover banners, buttons or enthusiasm. The only picture of Hoover that Walter Lippmann could find was an oil painting in the back of a shop window on Michigan Boulevard.

The jobless men on West Madison Street watched impassively as the taxis and limousines decanted their passengers into the stadium. Everything moved along according to plan. The platform, which had been written in Washington and brought to Chicago by Ogden Mills, was routine: it opposed government spending, opposed direct federal relief, demanded the extension of the tariff, denounced crime and narcotics, approved Indians, Negroes, and children, endorsed the Hoover policies to the last detail. The delegates listened to an endless recitation of planks and accepted them largely without discussion. The depression elicited neither a fresh idea nor even a fresh word. Only one issue pierced the lethargy — this was prohibition; and here feelings ran strong. In the end, after a flare-up of debate, the convention adopted an unintelligible straddle which angered the dries without pleasing the wets. The Chicago *Tribune* denounced the plank as a "flagrant fraud."

Nominations came on the third day. Joseph Scott of California named the President in an old-fashioned speech: one who . . . one who . . . one who "has stood at the helm as the captain of our ship of state and has steered the vessel safely through fog and hurricane and passed the terrors of the lee shore . . . that glorious Californian, HERBERT HOOVER!" Toy balloons dropped from the ceiling, tin trumpets sounded, and the organ played "Over There." When a delegate from Oregon later came to the platform to nominate Dr. Joseph I. France of Maryland, something went conveniently wrong with the microphone; and Dr. France himself, who had proposed to stampede the convention by nominating Calvin Coolidge, was thrown out of the convention hall by the police. Such tactics were hardly necessary: the ticket of Hoover and Curtis was handily renominated.

The veteran Republican, President Butler of Columbia, declared in disgust that he had attended his last Republican convention. "I have seen many conventions," reported H. L. Mencken with a connoisseur's admiration, "but this one is the worst. It is both the stupidest and the most dishonest." [1]

II

Now the Democrats swarmed noisily into Chicago — goateed statesmen from the South, cowboys and oilmen from Texas, young men from the West, Tammany braves from New York. They filled to overflow the hotels, the committee rooms, and the convention halls so recently abandoned by the cheerless Republicans. Newspapermen noted that they tended to be younger than the Republicans; that they had fewer bald heads; that they were dressier; that they spent more money; that they were having more fun. "To the Republicans politics is a business," wrote Anne O'Hare McCormick in the *New York Times,* "while to the Democrats it's a pleasure." [2]

The party leaders had begun to gather the week before. On Monday, June 20, a week before the convention, the *New York Times* survey showed 566 votes pledged to Roosevelt or instructed for him. The rock-bottom Roosevelt strength on the first ballot, by this calculation, was barely less than a majority, but 200 votes short of the necessary two-thirds. Uneasily aware of their inexperience in national politics, Jim Farley and Ed Flynn set out for

Chicago to open the Roosevelt headquarters at the Congress Hotel. Louis Howe, staying behind in New York to clean up last-minute details, planned to join them in a few days.

On Tuesday, June 21, Garner arrived in Chicago with a declaration on policy. He came out for repeal, called for a one-third reduction in the cost of government, and denounced "the constantly increasing tendency toward socialism and communism" as "the gravest possible menace" to the republic. Farley, alert to the importance of keeping on good terms with anyone who might in time have delegates to release, promptly praised the Garner credo.

Chairman Raskob, arriving the same day, solemnly declared prohibition the greatest economic and social question before the country. (Cordell Hull replied for the Roosevelt forces, "It would be a damnable outrage bordering on treason, if this Democratic convention, like the recent Republican National Convention, should meet and adjourn without serious thought or mention of the unprecedented panic." Any delegate who failed to recognize depression as the key issue, Hull said, should be kicked into Lake Michigan.) Getting down to immediate business, Raskob added confidently that there would be no abrogation of the two-thirds rule, and that Jouett Shouse would be elected permanent chairman of the convention. In hazarding these predictions, Raskob identified the two preliminary issues of controversy. For many Roosevelt supporters wanted to get rid of the device by which a minority of delegates — one more than one-third — could veto the candidate supported by the majority of the convention. And there was active opposition to Shouse as permanent chairman.

In April, at a stormy meeting of the National Committee, the Roosevelt leaders had forced through the selection of Senator Alben Barkley of Kentucky as keynoter and temporary chairman. To achieve this, they had agreed that the Committee, having recommended Barkley as temporary chairman, should recommend Shouse as permanent chairman. Shouse said he would go along, provided Roosevelt would give the formula personal approval. When Farley read the resolution to Roosevelt over the phone, Roosevelt pointed out that the Committee, in recommending a permanent chairman, was usurping the authority of the convention. But, he added, if the Committee cared to "commend" Shouse to the convention, he

had no objection to that. The Raskob group immediately interpreted this as an ironclad commitment on Roosevelt's part; the
Roosevelt forces interpreted it as meaning nothing. Early in June
a meeting of Roosevelt leaders in Hyde Park decided to go for
Senator Thomas J. Walsh of Montana, who had presided through
the endless sessions in 1924, as permanent chairman.

As discussion went on behind the scenes, as old friends who had
not seen each other since Houston in '28 or Madison Square Garden in '24 pumped hands and slapped backs in the lobbies, the
leaders continued to arrive. Al Smith came in on Wednesday,
ruddy and cheerful, dressed in a blue suit and wearing a white
straw hat. Thousands crowded the La Salle Street Station to give
him a tumultuous reception. He had not come to lead a stop-Roose-
velt movement, he told a press conference: "I am here to get myself
nominated." On Thursday, Smith had a long conference with his
old enemy McAdoo, now acting as the Garner leader. After the
conference, they were photographed in an amiable handshake. But
the meeting had ambiguous overtones. As representatives of the city
and the countryside, the two men had nearly broken up the Democratic party eight years before. Now they were meeting to stop the
presidential drive of a younger man whom, in years past, both had
befriended, and who in 1932 was seeking to bring country and city
together. The Smith camp later claimed that he and McAdoo had
agreed that neither would release delegates until he consulted with
the other.

III

It was Smith who dominated the anti-Roosevelt coalition. His
supporter Mayor Frank Hague of Jersey City, the tyrannical boss
whose high stiff collar held his neck erect as a ramrod, broke on
Thursday the truce that had thus far kept public peace among the
candidates. "Roosevelt, if nominated, has no chance of winning,"
Hague angrily asserted. ". . . He cannot carry a single state east of
the Mississippi and very few in the Far West. . . . Why consider
the one man who is weakest?" Hull replied that the "old wrecking
crew," which had nearly ruined the party before, was at work again.
A. Mitchell Palmer, Wilson's Attorney-General, who had come to
Chicago as a Roosevelt delegate from the District of Columbia,

dismissed the Hague statement as "the wail of the lost." Roosevelt himself, not wanting to risk further divisions in the party, dictated from Albany a mild disclaimer to be issued in Farley's name: "Governor Roosevelt's friends have not come to Chicago to criticize, cry down, or defame any Democrat."

But many of the delegates crowding into the first meeting of the Roosevelt forces that afternoon were furious at Hague. Huey Long, voicing the militant sentiment, wanted the Roosevelt leaders to begin by an attack on the two-thirds rule. Farley demurred, knowing well that not all delegates who were for Roosevelt were against the rule, and fearing that a defeat on this issue might set back the whole Roosevelt drive. But Burt Wheeler, Cordell Hull, Josephus Daniels, and Homer Cummings all backed Long's motion. As the enthusiasm spread, Farley appeared visibly to be losing his grip on the meeting. "He looked bewildered, confused and pathetic," Molly Dewson recalled, "like a terrier pup who is being reproached for knocking over a table holding a vase of flowers." Before he knew it, the Roosevelt forces were pledged to a fight for a majority rule.

"The incident," Farley wrote later, "hit me like a blow on the nose." Southern radicals, like John Rankin of Mississippi, who called the two-thirds rule "a powerful weapon in the hands of the Wall Street element," might want abolition. But southern conservatives, like Senator Pat Harrison, working hard to keep Mississippi in line for Roosevelt, regarded abolition, with its renunciation of the minority veto, as a betrayal of the South. Badly worried, Farley tried to reach Roosevelt. A storm had downed wires in upstate New York; and it took some time to make a connection. Roosevelt, when reached, told Farley not to worry; a way would be found out of the mess. In the meantime, the anti-Roosevelt leaders wasted no time in exploiting their unexpected opportunity. The three living presidential candidates — Smith, Davis, and Cox — affirmed the sacredness of the rule. Carter Glass called the movement for abolition a "gambler's trick." Newton D. Baker in Cleveland virtuously said, "Sensitive men would find it difficult to defend a candidate who started out with a moral flaw in his title." Sam Rayburn and McAdoo said that rules should not be changed in the middle of the game.

And new candidates continued to arrive — the courtly Ritchie, losing a shoe in the crush of welcome at the Baltimore and Ohio station, riding to the hotel in a shower of confetti and ticker tape; Alfalfa Bill Murray, shabby and unkempt, a scarf wound tight around his neck despite the heat, discoursing in his headquarters before admiring crowds on monetary reform while he sipped black coffee and chewed on cigar butts. They too threw themselves into the fight to retain the two-thirds rule.

When Louis Howe reached Chicago the next morning, the Roosevelt ranks were crumbling on the issue, even in northern states like Pennsylvania. The New York delegation voted 67–25 to keep the rule — an indication that Tammany would go against Roosevelt at the showdown. Howe told Farley and Flynn that the only hope was to withdraw as gracefully as possible. On Monday, Roosevelt issued a statement from Albany abandoning the fight. "While about it," remarked the *New York Times* editorially, "it is rather a wonder that he did not abandon Chairman Farley [too]. . . . It was almost the crowning mismanagement of his mismanaged campaign." It seemed a trifle hard to call a campaign mismanaged which still looked likely to produce a majority of delegates on the first ballot. Yet there could be no question that Roosevelt had received a setback. "Farley and I took a lesson in national politics," Flynn wrote later. James Hagerty reported to the *Times*, "Newton D. Baker loomed tonight as the most probable dark horse."

IV

But Howe, Farley, and Flynn had by no means lost their nerve. They maintained three suites of rooms in the Congress, where they entertained delegates, meditated strategy, and kept in touch with the Governor at Albany. Howe, trusting nobody, had brought along Louise Hackmeister, his trusted telephone operator from New York, to run a special switchboard. An amplifier was attached to the direct wire to Albany; and Farley shepherded groups of delegates to the suite where they could chat with the candidate eight hundred miles away. This became a much sought diversion, and delegations complained when they thought they were being neglected. The Roosevelt charm, little diluted over the telephone cables, strengthened his cause.

Farley worked away among the delegates. Unhurried and tireless, his pink bald head gleaming, his hand forever outstretched, the correct name always on his lips, he greeted men and women he had met on his trip a year earlier, cheered the pessimistic, soothed the angry, and exuded an atmosphere of smiling confidence. A vast map dominated his headquarters, with each candidate's states in a separate splash of color. No one could miss the great stretches sewed up for Roosevelt. ("Lots of area," snorted Al Smith, but not "lots of delegates.") Howe's corner suite on the seventeenth floor, with the phone ringing and the radio blaring away and the little man, skinnier and whiter than ever, prowling and wheezing in his usual mess of untidiness and cigarette ash, remained the Chicago center for the Roosevelt strategy. But in the end the big decisions were passed on to Albany. "In most matters," said Ed Flynn, "we found it wise to get Roosevelt's judgment. We did nothing without first consulting him."

On Monday, Alben Barkley, the matchless Kentucky orator, delivered the keynote address, holding the audience for two hours with a rousing and witty indictment of Republican rule. The serious business began the next morning with the problem of contested delegations from Louisiana and Minnesota. Huey Long impressed the convention with an unexpectedly reasonable presentation of his case. His pro-Roosevelt delegation was seated. Then the convention seated the Roosevelt delegation from Minnesota.

But the larger test was the permanent chairmanship. Clarence Dill and James F. Byrnes urged the nomination of Tom Walsh. John W. Davis spoke eloquently for Shouse. As the teller called the roll, Jim Farley nervously jotted down the tally on long sheets of brown note paper. But the Roosevelt lines held firm; Walsh won by nearly one hundred votes. The pipe organ played "Happy Days Are Here Again"; the new chairman, dignified in white trousers, blue coat, and bow tie, his spectacles dangling from a black cord, was escorted to the platform. Farley breathed a heavy sigh of relief.

On Wednesday the convention awaited the platform. On the whole, the draft was little changed from the concise text A. Mitchell Palmer had prepared with Cordell Hull in Washington. The document blamed the depression on the "disastrous policies" pursued by Republican administrations — the economic isolationism, the encouragement of monopoly, the inflation of credit. Proclaiming itself as a "covenant with the people to be faithfully kept by the party," the platform pledged a 25 per cent reduction of federal expenditures, an annually balanced budget, a sound currency "to be preserved at all hazards," a "competitive tariff for revenue," and the "removal of government from all fields of private enterprise" except public works and conservation. At the same time, the platform called for federal public works and unemployment relief, state unemployment and old-age insurance, "effective control of crop surpluses" and other aid for farmers, the strengthening of the antitrust laws, regulation of holding companies and of the security exchanges, and "continuous responsibility of government for human welfare."

Despite these gestures to progressive sentiment, the platform on the whole favored retrenchment and laissez faire rather than expansion and planning; it was the expression of the right wing of the Roosevelt following, of the old Wilsonians — Hull, Palmer, Colonel House. The convention received it with genuine enthusiasm. "The resolutions committee," wrote Walter Lippmann, "has done the best job in any national convention for at least twenty years." But the greatest applause was reserved for the sentence, "We advocate the repeal of the Eighteenth Amendment." At this, pandemonium. For twenty-five minutes, everything stopped.

V

Farley and Howe had long since abandoned hope of rest. Snatching sandwiches off trays, napping a few moments in the hour before dawn, endlessly talking, endlessly phoning, endlessly scheming, they were devoting themselves to the last-minute drive for delegates. The Roosevelt strength was ostensibly unimpaired by the developments of the week. Yet, more and more, as the first ballot approached, the name of Newton Baker began to be whispered in the corridors and the lobbies. Farley redoubled his efforts to hold Mississippi and to win over Indiana and Ohio — all states where a Baker breakaway might be expected.

On Thursday, the nominations. Roosevelt's old friend, John E. Mack of Dutchess County, placed his name before the convention in an uninspired address. As he concluded, the first of the demonstrations began: the organ blared "Anchors Aweigh," the banners rose, the delegates marched and cheered, the chairman vainly pounded his gavel. Louis Howe, doubled up with asthma on his bed at the Congress, suddenly felt he could stand the naval song no more. "For God's sake, tell 'em to play something else," he said, between hacking coughs, to Ed Flynn. "Tell 'em; oh, tell 'em to play 'Happy Days Are Here Again.' " The order was quickly transmitted to Arthur Mullen, and Franklin D. Roosevelt was given a new anthem.[3]

As the Roosevelt nomination was seconded — most effectively by Homer Cummings of Connecticut — discontent and jeering were evident in the galleries. Al Smith, dressed in evening clothes, bustled along the runway into the convention floor; as he heard the name Franklin Delano Roosevelt he stopped and his face darkened. Turning on his heel, he muttered to a newspaperman standing next to him. "I can go back to the hotel and listen to that over the radio."

The other candidates followed along: Tom Connally nominating Garner; then Governor Ely of Massachusetts nominating Smith. Ely's was perhaps the most effective speech. Smith himself called it "the best speech I have ever heard in any convention since the days of Bourke Cockran." (Cockran had nominated him at San Francisco in 1920; Smith said nothing of the man who nominated him in 1924 and 1928.) And the demonstration that followed Ely was the longest, noisiest, and most genuine of the convention. The galleries joined in with adoring enthusiasm, waving handkerchiefs and showering confetti on the delegates marching below.

It was a moving moment. Yet the experts sensed the chill of defeat about the Smith effort. It had been rumored for days that he planned to take the rostrum and destroy Roosevelt in a single speech; but somehow the Happy Warrior had lost his touch. "Smith hates Roosevelt," said William Allen White, "and is afraid, for some queer reason, to put his wrath behind the punch." "The Al of today," wrote Mencken, "is no longer a politician of the first chop. His association with the rich has apparently wobbled him and changed him. He has become a golf player. . . . It is a sad spectacle."

VI

The Roosevelt strategy was clearly to detach the Garner movement from the anti-Roosevelt line-up. But the first ballot was on hand, and the Garner vote remained intact. If Garner continued immovable, there seemed every prospect of a repetition of 1924; and more and more it looked to the experts as if Newton Baker would emerge as the John W. Davis of 1932. On Thursday, indeed, Colonel Leonard P. Ayres of Cleveland opened a Baker headquarters. Delegates were beginning to receive wires urging Baker's nomination. Some discerned the hand of Bernard Baruch in this flurry. Others attributed it to Baker's good friends among the utilities. Yet the very evidence of Baker activity had the ironic effect of strengthening Farley in his dealings with the Garner leaders; for of all the possible candidates, Baker, so profoundly identified despite himself with the League, was the most objectionable to William Randolph Hearst. Throughout the week, one call after another went to San Simeon — from Farley, from Joseph P. Kennedy, from James M. Curley, from many others — warning Hearst that a deadlock would probably nominate the candidate he detested most.

At the same time, Daniel C. Roper of Washington, D.C., who had been Commissioner of Internal Revenue under Wilson and was now a Roosevelt enthusiast, kept in close touch with his old friend McAdoo. And early in the week Senator Harry Hawes of Missouri had phoned Roosevelt in Albany to see whether Garner would be acceptable as a running mate. When Roosevelt said fine, Hawes gave the press the impression that Garner also accepted the idea. Garner, angry at what seemed a premature surrender of his own candidacy, scolded Hawes in an indignant phone conversation. But Farley, stimulated by the Hawes initiative, now put on new pressure in Chicago, promising Sam Rayburn he would do all he could to win Garner the vice-presidential nomination. "We have come to Chicago to nominate Speaker Jack Garner," Rayburn enigmatically replied. ". . . But we don't intend to make it another Madison Square Garden." (Garner had already told a newspaper friend in absolute confidence a few days before the convention, "I am not going to deadlock the convention against the leader.")

Farley explored other possibilities. He offered the vice-presidential nomination to Ritchie and to Harry Byrd if they would give up their own candidacies and switch to Roosevelt. And before the first ballot, Farley had one more conference with Rayburn. Let Texas vote for Garner on the first ballot, Farley suggested, but then switch to Roosevelt before the result was announced; this would start the stampede. Rayburn was unimpressed. It would not be fair, he said, to pull out Garner until he had had a run for his money. How many ballots, he asked Farley, can you hold your lines without breaking? "Three ballots," Farley finally said, "four ballots, and maybe five." "Well," said Rayburn, "we just must let the convention go for a while, even if we are interested in the Vice-Presidency, and I'm not saying that we are."

VII

After the dinner recess on Thursday, delegates began to flock wearily back to their places. It was a sultry night. Dazzling lights, playing over the crowded hall for the newsreel cameras, increased both the heat and the drama. With an evening of nominating speeches still to come, might it not be better to postpone the first ballot till the next day? Farley, lying exhausted on a cot in the small gallery headquarters, called a council of Roosevelt leaders. Most agreed that delay would be dangerous — better to ballot that evening. Farley phoned the Governor in Albany. Roosevelt said by all means to go ahead. But the seconding speeches continued for hours, while the delegates sat on wearily in rumpled clothes and sweat-stained shirts amidst the litter of sandwiches, Coca-Cola bottles, and cigar butts, with the klieg lights sizzling and crackling overhead. Outside the windows the black sky was shaken by thunder and lightning around three; then slowly it began to lighten into faint streaks of gray and pink.

At 4.28 A.M. Chairman Walsh pounded for order and called for the first vote. As one delegation after another challenged the count and demanded a poll, the time stretched out still farther. It was nearly two hours later, with the morning sun beginning to shine through the haze, that the first ballot was completed. Roosevelt had 661¼ votes — one hundred short of two-thirds. Smith received

201¾, Garner 90¼, and seven others trailed distantly in the rear. Beaming, Farley waited for someone to announce a switch to Roosevelt. This, he thought, would set the bandwagon in motion. But no one arose. The convention floor presented a picture of confusion.

Roper now reported that California would not change without a caucus. Farley, hurrying to the floor, appealed to Mayor Anton Cermak of Chicago to deliver Illinois to Roosevelt; but Cermak, who could have done so, delayed. By now, in the commotion, the second ballot had started. Arthur Mullen meanwhile talked earnestly to Tom Connally of the Texas delegation. "If Garner will take the vice-presidential nomination," Mullen said, "an arrangement can be made to have him get it." Connally thought a moment and then said the matter required exploration; "let's adjourn, and see what we can do." And, on the phone to Albany, Huey Long pleaded with Roosevelt to come out for the immediate payment of the bonus. Roosevelt, interrupted as he was trying to draft a peroration for his acceptance address, replied that he couldn't; he wasn't in favor of the bonus. "Well," said Long, "you are a gone goose." In his shirtsleeves, chainsmoking cigarettes, occasionally talking over the phone by his side, Roosevelt had sat through the night by the radio in the small sitting room of the Executive Mansion.

Farley had held a few votes in reserve for the second ballot, knowing the importance of showing an increase each time round. But the results showed no conclusive change — Roosevelt up 16½ votes, Smith down 7½ votes, Garner holding firm. Arthur Mullen was quickly on his feet, calling for adjournment.

This time the anti-Roosevelt leaders protested. The Roosevelt drive had bogged down; now was the moment to set it in reverse. "We have been held here all night at great inconvenience," said Dudley Field Malone of New York, "and we are prepared to stay here all day." Farley muttered to a friend on the platform, "Watch this one closely. It will show whether I can ever go back to New York or not." Wearily, the convention pulled itself into a semblance of order and began the third ballot.

The Roosevelt lines were showing the strain. Mississippi, held by a single vote under the unit rule, was beginning to slip; and, if Mississippi went, Arkansas would go too. The defection of Arkansas, coming at the top of the alphabet, might start a flight away from Roosevelt on the next ballot. The Mississippi delegates were already arguing bitterly among themselves, when the Roosevelt leaders assigned Huey Long of Louisiana the job of keeping both states in line. Long, in a wilting pongee suit, sweat pouring down his face, descended like a host upon the delegation. He lectured, cajoled, pleaded, threatened, shook his fist in the face of senators, employed all his arts of upcountry eloquence. The line held: when the third ballot ended, as sunlight began to flood through the eastern windows of the stadium, Roosevelt had gained another 5 votes. Smith had lost another 4, Garner had gained 11. Exhausted, the convention gratefully accepted McAdoo's motion for adjournment. It was now 9.15 on Friday morning.

VIII

The next few hours were crucial. Mullen had already renewed his talks with Connally, repeating his pledge that he would do everything "humanly posible" to make Garner Vice-President. Connally responded with interest. And in the meantime Dan Roper, accompanied by Cordell Hull, had made an appeal along slightly different lines to McAdoo. He asked the Californian to consider the opportunity he had to promote the Wilsonian policies. Might not he himself be interested, Roper continued, wholly without authorization, in being Secretary of State? "No," said McAdoo. "No personal advantage must accrue to me." But McAdoo continued, "If I can get a recess of the convention, so I can take a poll of our California delegation, I'll endeavor to get them behind Roosevelt, and that will mean Texas too." Roosevelt, however, must agree to take Garner as the vice-presidential candidate, and to consult about federal patronage in California and about appointments to the Treasury and the State Departments. He added that Hearst's representatives were insisting that Texas cast at least seven ballots for Garner. That, Roper replied, would mean Smith or Baker; "I am told there are a hundred votes pledged to Baker as a second choice."

But Hearst already had read the portents. After the third ballot, he held a phone conversation with Colonel Joseph Willicombe, his representative in Chicago; and Willicombe promptly transmitted Hearst's decision to George Rothwell Brown in Washington. "Mr. Hearst is fearful," the message went, "that when Roosevelt's strength crumbles it will bring about either the election of Smith or Baker. Either would be disastrous." Tell Garner that the Chief believes "nothing can now save the country but for him to throw his delegates to Governor Roosevelt."

At eleven on Friday morning Brown met Garner in the Speaker's private room in the southeast corner of the Capitol. Garner seemed to know what was coming. For a moment they looked together in silence out on the green lawns around the Capitol. Then Brown repeated Hearst's message. Garner listened, his puckered face expressionless behind his shaggy eyebrows. Finally he said, "Say to Mr. Hearst that I fully agree with him. He is right. Tell him I will carry out his suggestion and release my delegates to Roosevelt."

IX

In the meantime, the Roosevelt leaders were engaged in anxious talk in Louis Howe's suite at the Congress. Howe was prostrate on the floor, his tie off, his shirt open at the throat, his head on a pillow, two electric fans trained on his face to bring relief from heat and asthma. Farley squatted heavily on the carpet to whisper in his ear: "Texas is our only chance." Howe feebly agreed.

Pat Harrison, who despaired of holding Mississippi for many more ballots, was already trying to set up a conference for Farley with Sam Rayburn. Farley, arriving first in Harrison's apartment, collapsed into a chair and fell dead asleep. When Rayburn entered, Farley roused himself and once again stated the case for an immediate decision. Rayburn, as he stood to go, said, "We'll see what can be done." The conference lasted only a few moments. Nothing was said about the Vice-Presidency. Farley reported back to Howe: "It's in the bag. Texas is with us." Howe, impassive at the climax of twenty years of effort, said only, "Jim, that is fine."

As Farley stumbled off to bed for a couple of hours nap, Howe continued to ride herd on the situation. Dan Roper rushed in to tell him about his talk with McAdoo. Howe then put Roper through to Albany and, in Roper's recollection, Roosevelt told him to give McAdoo the required assurances. This would seem to include the promise of the Vice-Presidency to Garner; but Flynn recalls telephone conversations with Roosevelt discussing other vice-presidential possibilities. Since there is no evidence that the rest of McAdoo's stipulations were respected, it seems probable that Roper's memory was at fault. Certainly Flynn strongly urged on Roosevelt that Garner's nomination would be an error, arguing that it would only further alienate the Catholic Democrats of the North whom it would be so necessary to conciliate after Smith's defeat. But Roosevelt decided that nonetheless Garner would be the best choice.

For a time Garner remained silent in Washington, eating his midday lunch, refusing frenzied calls from Smith leaders. Finally at 3 P.M. Chicago time, he put in a call to Rayburn in Chicago. "Sam," he said, "I think it is time to break this thing up. Roosevelt is the choice of the convention." Rayburn promptly announced a 6 P.M. meeting of the Texas delegation, now hopelessly scattered in hotel bedrooms and speakeasies through town. Even Garner's own decision, it developed, could not shake his bitter-end supporters. When Rayburn tried to rally Texas for Roosevelt at six, the caucus fell into contention. Some delegates continued to shout for Garner, women wept, people screamed angrily at each other. Finally Rayburn forced a vote: by a close 54–51 Texas decided to back Roosevelt on the fourth ballot.

Unaware of these developments, the anti-Roosevelt leaders looked ahead with increasing confidence. Mississippi seemed to have crumbled, for all Huey Long's efforts. Heywood Broun had just contemptuously dismissed Roosevelt as the "corkscrew candidate of a convoluting convention." There was more talk than ever about Baker. In any case, Roosevelt was surely through. . . . Once again the clerk began the interminable roll: "Alabama, 24 votes for Roosevelt." Arizona, Arkansas — the Roosevelt ranks were still holding. Then came California; and the lean, straight, spry figure of William Gibbs McAdoo rose to seek unanimous consent for the purpose of explaining the California vote to the convention.

A hush fell over the Stadium as McAdoo made his way to the platform. He was erect and smiling, his voice firm, his manner confident and graceful. "California came here to nominate a President of the United States," he said. "She did not come here to deadlock this convention or to engage in another disastrous contest like that of 1924." There was a premonitory stir among the delegates, a premonitory rumble in the galleries. We believe, McAdoo continued, that California must take a stand tonight that will bring this contest to a swift and satisfactory conclusion — "a stand prompted by our belief that when any man comes into a Democratic National Convention with the popular will behind him to the extent of almost seven hundred votes. . . ."

X

It was all clear now, and suddenly delegates were on their feet, clambering up on their seats, shouting, cheering, waving the pine poles to which their state banners were attached. The spontaneous emotion, so absent from the earlier Roosevelt demonstration, came in a rush as it became evident that he was to be nominated. But, even as the roar of approval surged up from the floor, another roar — hostile, menacing, angry — swept down from the galleries. McAdoo had heard this cry before, eight years earlier, from the Tammany hoodlums in Madison Square Garden. Now he flung back his head with disdain as boos and hisses showered down once again from the city mob. Then it had denied him the nomination. Today he would destroy Al Smith, as Smith and his followers had destroyed him. His lips were pursed with satisfaction, as he waited for the uproar to subside. Tom Walsh, in the meantime, his face red and his eyes snapping, pounded his gavel. But he could not still the crowd in the galleries. Finally he beckoned to Mayor Cermak, who appealed successfully for order.

"I want to thank the galleries for the compliment they have paid me," said McAdoo sardonically. " . . . I intend to say what I propose to say without regard to what the galleries or anybody else think." He paused, enjoying a moment of memory. "I want to cause no wounds. Those of 1924 were created against my wish. I should like to see Democrats fight Republicans instead of Democrats." And, in a moment, the conclusion: "California casts forty-four votes for Franklin D. Roosevelt." Again, the organ pealed and the stadium shook with applause. . . . F.D.R., at his radio many miles away, leaned back and grinned, "Good old McAdoo." His wife, tying up the flowing sleeves of her dress, went into the kitchen to cook bacon and eggs. And in Washington, John Garner, pacing the roof garden of the Washington Hotel, talked briefly to a newspaperman. "You've gone to Roosevelt?" the reporter said. Garner's cigar glowed in the night as he looked over at the dark bulk of the Treasury Department and the shining White House beyond. "That's right, son," he said at last, flicking away ashes. " . . . I'm a little older than you are, son. And politics is funny."

In Chicago every major candidate finally broke to Roosevelt except Smith. But Smith still polled 190½ votes at the end, and the nomination was never made unanimous. Smith himself left the hall with bitterness on his face. When asked if he would support the ticket, he chewed harshly on his cigar and replied, "I have no comment." Ritchie strode out stiffly. Nearly all the traditional leaders of the party — Davis, Cox, Baker, Jim Reed, all but Mc-Adoo — had fought Roosevelt and were dismayed by his victory. Tom Walsh, casting about for a note of harmony, spied Reed sitting on the platform. When Walsh asked him to speak, Reed refused. Then Arthur Mullen came up. "We're all Democrats, Jim," he said. "We are — yet," said Reed. But he rose and walked to the rostrum to remind his party of the old faith.

> It is the highest duty of the Democratic Party to get back the old principles and old methods. There has been no improvement on the policies of George Washington in regard to international affairs, and there never will be an improvement. There has been no improvement on the philosophy of Thomas Jefferson, and there never will be an improvement. There has been no improvement on the philosophy — the economic philosophy — of John Stuart Mill, and there never will be an improvement.

But the chairman's next announcement heralded a new dispensation: it was a wire from Franklin Roosevelt saying that he wished to fly to Chicago the next day to accept the nomination. That night Smith irreconcilables ripped posters of Roosevelt to pieces in the hotels.

XI

In Albany all was excitement. In abandoning the tradition by which acceptance took place in a formal ceremony some weeks after the convention, Roosevelt was responding to what he perceived as a passionate popular hope for a bolder temper in national affairs. The trimotored plane warming up under bleak skies at the Albany airport was itself a symbol of the new spirit of decision demanded by troubled times. Early Saturday morning Roosevelt and his party climbed aboard for the flight to Chicago.

The plane headed into squalls and bumpy air. It landed twice for refueling — at Buffalo and at Cleveland (where Newton Baker declined to join an official welcoming party). In the meantime, unmindful of the swaying ship, Roosevelt worked away at his acceptance speech with Samuel I. Rosenman, his counsel in Albany, cutting it, polishing it, putting it into final shape. . . . In Chicago delegates slept late, then went to the convention hall, where entertainers played and sang while the crowd waited for their nominee. Al Smith and his friends prepared to go home. Someone asked John J. Raskob whether he would support Roosevelt; Raskob curtly dismissed the question and, turning to one of his associates, asked how the stock market was doing. But Bernard Baruch, bland and unperturbed, appeared at the Roosevelt headquarters, politely inquired whether Ritchie might be considered for the Vice-Presidency, and asked to see a copy of the acceptance speech.

Around four-thirty in the afternoon, a good two hours late, the plane circled down out of low-hanging clouds and settled on the long runways of the Chicago airport. The crowd surged forward to greet the candidate. Roosevelt, with a broad smile, seized Farley's hand: "Jim, old pal — put it right there — great work." He drove through cheering streets to the Congress Hotel, where another throng had gathered to salute him. Al Smith had already left the hotel by a side door, departing more than an hour before train time in order to make sure he would not meet the victor. For a few moments Roosevelt rested in his room. At one point Louis Howe brought in Charley Michelson, who had bade farewell to Raskob and Shouse and moved over to Roosevelt headquarters. Roosevelt grinned. "Glad to see you aboard the ship."

The convention's long day reached its climax around six. The delegates had named John Garner for Vice-President by acclamation. Then at last, their presidential candidate appeared, dressed in a blue suit with a red rose in his lapel, his eyes shining, his head held high; and the convention rose, the cheers drowning out the boos which still came down from pockets of diehards in the galleries. "I regret that I am late," Roosevelt said, "but I have no control over the winds of Heaven and could only be thankful for my Navy training." The audience howled with pleasure.

His decision to come to Chicago, he said, might have been "unprecedented and unusual, but these are unprecedented and unusual times," and there were "absurd traditions" to be broken. "Let it be from now on the task of our Party to break foolish traditions." For the Democratic party was by the continuing logic of history "the bearer of liberalism and of progress." The theory of government that helps a favored few "and hopes that some of their prosperity will leak through, to labor, to the farmer, to the small business man" had been discredited. There was no alternative but to move ahead. "I warn those nominal Democrats who squint at the future with their faces turned toward the past, and who feel no responsibility to the demands of the new time," said Roosevelt, "that they are out of step with their Party." (Applause and cheering.) "Ours must be a party of liberal thought, of planned action, of enlightened international outlook, and of the greatest good to the greatest number of our citizens."

With dispatch he turned to the depression, pointing out that the enormous increases in productivity in the twenties had gone neither to lower prices or higher wages or even adequately to dividends or to taxes, but had gone instead into speculation and into "new and unnecessary plants which now stand stark and idle." What to do now? First, relief to all groups, whether at the top or the bottom of the pyramid; then retrenchment and economy in Washington, so that an example of solvency would be set for all levels of government; then prohibition repeal; securities legislation; public works; a shorter workweek; reforestation; planning of agricultural production; reduction of the interest rate; reduction of the tariff.

"What do the people of America want more than anything else?" Roosevelt asked. ". . . Work and security. . . . They are the spiritual values, the true goal toward which our efforts of reconstruction should lead." Today, Roosevelt said, out of the "era of selfishness" — an era for which we all must "blame ourselves in equal share" — there was emerging the hope of salvation.

"I pledge you," Franklin D. Roosevelt cried, "I pledge myself, to a new deal for the American people."

And the roar of the organ; the glare and sputter of the lights; the shouts and the cheers; the men standing on chairs and the women crying; the sweat and stench of the convention hall; the stale sandwiches and the empty bottles; the dead cigars and the abandoned badges and the litter of paper. And the men outside waiting in parks and hovels and along the side of roads; the hunger and the fear; the vague awakening of hope; and always the cheap song of the organ drowning out the bad times, casting out the sad times . . . HAPPY DAYS ARE HERE AGAIN! [4]

VI

The Happy Warrior

29. Childhood on the Hudson

FOR FRANKLIN DELANO ROOSEVELT, the first memories were life at Hyde Park along the Hudson. From the nursery on the third floor, he looked out on the fields and woods which lay between the great house and the river. Days and months had the rhythm of nature — winter, with a white blanket of snow settling over the ground, and sometimes ice for skating or ice boating on the river; the fresh fragrant gusts of spring; the hard, brilliant light and the vivid yellows and scarlets of fall; and the little boy driving with his father behind Josie, the mare, the last survivor of the trotting stable. Hyde Park meant dogs — Budgy, the white Spitz, and Boatswain, the big black Newfoundland. It meant the boy's pony in the stable. It meant books read aloud after tea or pored over by the fire at night — Randolph Caldecott's *Come Lasses and Lads* ("my Mother read these to me before I could read") or Eugene Field's *Songs of Childhood* ("my Mother's book from which she played and sang to me when I was a child") or Samuel W. Baker's *Cast Up by the Sea* ("one of my favorite boyhood books — read it over three times"). Above all, there were Father, calm and warm, and Mother, beautiful and adoring, and an enveloping sense of security and love. "In thinking back to my earliest days," he wrote many years later, "I am impressed by the peacefulness and regularity of things both in respect to places and people." [1]

The "River families" were born to this spacious sense of tradition and of leisure. Their world opened up before them, a solid and pleasant place, in which their task was to carry on and fortify standards they inherited from their fathers. They moved with as-

surance in the world outside as well. The boy's father, James
Roosevelt, had known Sam Houston and marched with Garibaldi.
After graduating from Union College and Harvard Law School,
he had made astute investments in railroads and in coal — enough
to keep his hand in the business world, though not enough to interfere with the more abiding pleasures of life. He regularly visited the watering places of Germany and the country houses of
England; he bred trotters on his Hyde Park estate until he felt
that it was no longer a sport for gentlemen; he smoked cheroots;
he always kept five hundred dollars in gold by his side; he had a
private railroad car and a place at the balls and cotillions of
New York. He was tall, with dark, muttonchop side whiskers,
agreeable blue eyes, and a distinguished manner. Only one thing
marked him among country squires: after the Civil War, James
Roosevelt, almost alone among Roosevelts, had returned to the
traditional family affiliation with the Democratic party.

James Roosevelt's first wife died, leaving him with one son,
James Roosevelt Roosevelt, known as "Rosy." In the spring of
1880, at a dinner party at Theodore Roosevelt's on Madison
Avenue, the elder James Roosevelt met a tall, handsome girl named
Sara Delano. Sallie Delano had been born in Newburgh, not far
from Hyde Park. Her father was an old friend of James Roosevelt's; and she had grown up in much the same world. When she
was eight, her mother had taken her on a clipper ship to China;
she had traveled extensively in Europe; and she was now a young
lady of aristocratic grace. James Roosevelt was fifty-two years old,
Sallie Delano only twenty-six, the same age as his son; but they
fell in love, were married in the fall, and James Roosevelt brought
his young bride back past the ivied stone columns and the broad
lawns down the long drive through the magnificent trees to his
comfortable country house at Hyde Park.

Life was pleasant for the Roosevelts — walking about the farm,
riding in the woods, rowing on the river, dinners and dances at
the houses of neighbors, cut-glass goblets glittering in candlelight.
Two years passed in unhurried comfort. New Year's Day 1882
found Hyde Park deep in snow. James and Sallie Roosevelt loved
to skim along the frosty white roads in the small Russian sleigh
(built originally for Napoleon III and brought back by James

from the Paris Exposition of 1872), Sallie deep in the red velvet
upholstery, with tall plumes waving from the check-hook and bells
jingling as they went. But soon this had to stop. On Monday,
January 30, 1882, James Roosevelt noted in his diary: "At quarter
to nine my Sallie had a splendid large baby boy. He weighs
10 lbs., without clothes." [2]

II

They named him Franklin Delano Roosevelt and lavished on
him the adoration which an only child could hardly escape. He
grew up a pleasant, lively boy, spirited but not obstinate, with a
will of his own but also with a desire to please his beloved parents.
He generally obeyed his mother, yet insisted that she cut off his
curls and revolted against the velvet Lord Fauntleroy suits. He
was an avid reader and a passionate collector, starting a stamp
collection at the age of nine.

During fall and winter he fished, hunted, skated, built rafts,
dug snow tunnels. In summer, the family fled the stifling heat
which came down over the Hudson, generally to Campobello, an
island off the New Brunswick coast, where the boy learned to handle boats in blue water. Or sometimes they went to the Delano
house at Fairhaven, Massachusetts, where he sat on the stringpiece
of his grandfather's stone wharf, watching a whaleship ride at
anchor in the stream, while over on the New Bedford shore, near
the winding wooden bridge, a dozen masts gleamed over the
granite warehouses. Fading glories, perhaps; but on rainy days he
revived them from the bound volumes of woodcuts of the great
whaling fleets of the fifties, or from old logbooks, buried in attic
trunks.[3]

The winter of 1887 they spent in Washington. President Cleveland had wanted to send the elder Roosevelt abroad in a diplomatic
post; but James refused, though Rosy Roosevelt was made First Secretary of the Legation in Vienna. Just before they left Washington,
Roosevelt took young Franklin over to the White House on a farewell call. The careworn President put his hand on the little boy's
head as the Roosevelts rose to go. "My little man," he said (as the
family remembered the story), "I am making a strange wish for

you. It is that you may never be President of the United States." [4]

And so the years passed. In 1896, at the age of fourteen, he spent the summer — one of many — in Germany, bicycling through the Black Forest with a tutor. This memory lingered — the little spotted German deer, and lunching off the trout caught in the brook behind the inn, and, behind the jolliness, an uncomfortable sense of national arrogance. For periods in the nineties he even attended village schools at Bad Nauheim. But his main education these years came from a succession of tutors at Hyde Park, especially from a Frenchwoman named Jeanne Rosat-Sandoz, who gave him strict but loving instruction in history and languages and taught him to cherish humane values. Years later Roosevelt wrote her, "I have often thought that it was you, more than anyone else, who laid the foundation for my education." [5]

III

When he returned from Europe in 1896, a new phase of his life opened. He was now to continue his education away from home; and his parents had long since entered him in the school established a dozen years before at Groton, Massachusetts, by the Reverend Endicott Peabody. In that excited autumn, while William Jennings Bryan tried to rally the working classes against crucifixion on a cross of gold, Franklin Delano Roosevelt, scared and stoical, set off for the most exclusive school in America.

Groton had been founded on the British model, entering its boys in forms, with seniority maintained through a system of student prefects. The students lived in tiny cubicles, took a cold shower every morning, washed in black soapstone sinks and tin basins, put on white shirts and black pumps for supper, and, after the evening study period, shook hands each night with the Rector and his wife before filing off to bed. The curriculum was classical, taught always with efficiency and sometimes with devotion. But it was above all the Rector who put his stamp upon the school, infusing the routine and the discipline with an awful moral significance.

Endicott Peabody was a big, clean-cut, broad-shouldered, handsome man, dedicated with passion to the idea of Groton School as a community — if not, indeed, as a family — that would produce Christians and gentlemen, men of high character and sound learning. In any situation, he would have seemed larger than life; and to the boys at Groton, he seemed larger than ever — his voice more booming, his anger more formidable, his love deeper, than that of anyone they had ever known. He liked to say that a headmaster had to be "a bit of a bully"; and he followed his boys, during their Groton days and after, with remorseless concern. But his solicitude, in the end, seemed genuine and disinterested. The remark ascribed to another young Grotonian, Averell Harriman, made the point: "You know he would be an awful bully," Harriman said to his father, "if he weren't such a terrible Christian."

So dominating a man and environment provided a stern testing. And the boys themselves, drawn in the main from a narrow social circle, contributed to the pervading pressure toward a somewhat snobbish conformity. A few were broken by the experience and ended, in the listing of one old Grotonian, as "cheats, drunkards, lechers, panhandlers, suicides." But some — the tougher ones — were braced by their years at Groton even while they suffered under the system. They were strengthened by the intellectual training, inspired by the moral purpose, and sent into the world with a high sense of their duties as Christian gentlemen. To survive unhappiness at Groton was to be capable of anything.

The Rector appreciated these too; perhaps he liked them more than he did some of the others; and they appreciated him. The influence of Mr. and Mrs. Peabody, Franklin Roosevelt said a third of a century later, meant more to him than that of any other people, "next to my father and mother." "More than forty years ago," he wrote to the old Rector in 1940, "you said, in a sermon in the old Chapel, something about not losing boyhood ideals in later life. Those were Groton ideals — taught by you — I try not to forget — and your words are still with me and with the hundreds of others of 'us boys.' " 6 Among the other boys at Groton before the First World War who retained the words were Averell Harriman, Dean Acheson, Francis and George Biddle, Sumner Welles, Bronson M. Cutting, Joseph C. Grew, William Phillips.

For young Franklin Roosevelt, Groton was a mixed experience. There was much excitement in the world: the Spanish-American

War in 1898, to which for a delirious moment he planned to run away as a volunteer; the Boer War in South Africa ("I cannot help feeling convinced that the Boers have the side of right"); the election of Cousin Teddy as governor of New York ("we were all wild with delight"); dances and girls during the Christmas holidays ("How about Teddy Robinson and Eleanor Roosevelt? They would go well and help to fill out chinks").

Within the school, he seemed friendly, adaptable, and inconspicuous, ending up modestly as manager of the baseball team, winner of the Latin and Punctuality Prizes, a dormitory prefect, and a member of the Debating Society (where, in January 1898, while arguing an assigned brief against the annexation of Hawaii, he said, "It is not generally known that Pearl Harbor, a port in one of the islands, belongs to the United States"). He responded earnestly to the Rector's social teachings, spending part of the summer of 1900 at a camp maintained by the school for poor boys from the city. Looking back thirty years later, Peabody recalled him as "a quiet satisfactory boy of more than ordinary intelligence, taking a good position in his Form but not brilliant. . . . We all liked him. So far as I know that is true of the masters and boys alike."

Yet this very inconspicuousness may have been in part protective coloration. Entering two years after the rest of his form, without experience of organized schooling, he was forced to learn the art of reserve behind the mask of geniality. Inevitably he was a bit set apart from the other boys. "He knew things they didn't; they knew things he didn't," said Eleanor Roosevelt half a century later. "He felt left out. It gave him sympathy for people who are left out." [7]

IV

He entered Harvard in the fall of 1900. In the meantime, his father, now seventy-two years old, fell ill. In late November the old man, frail and tired-looking in his velvet coat, began to decline. On December 7 he seemed better and, for a moment, Sallie could leave his bedside. But he quickly lapsed. The next day she wrote sadly in her diary: "All is over. At 2:20 he merely slept away."

After New Year's Franklin went back to college. He was still something of an outsider, so far as his own circle was concerned.

His smart friends tended to regard him as overmuch of an intellectual, and the girls of his own set called him "the featherduster" because of supposedly shallow and priggish qualities. In self-defense, perhaps, he affected a cockiness which to some appeared conceit. He was not taken for some reason into Porcellian, where Roosevelts were ordinarily welcome, and had to accept a lesser club. The failure to make Porcellian was a dismaying experience. But Roosevelt's lack of popularity should not be exaggerated. His energy and high spirits won him many friends. And life in Cambridge had its abundant compensations: the luxurious three-room suite he shared with Lathrop Brown in Westmorly Court in the center Gold Coast; the sharp tang of autumn air as the football crowds streamed across the river on the way to Soldiers Field; sleighrides in winter; and, on spring afternoons, with the sun sparkling off the water, stroking a boating club crew through the sharp, choppy Charles; or excursions to the North Shore to rest by "the sad sea waves." On evenings he played billiards at Sanborn's on Massachusetts Avenue or dined in style at the Touraine or Somerset in Boston. As librarian for his clubs — Fly and Hasty Pudding — he haunted dusty secondhand bookshops on Cornhill and laid the foundation for his own collections of naval books and prints.

He did more than adequately in his studies. Indeed, with his Groton preparation and President Eliot's enlightened "anticipation" plan, Roosevelt was able to take his A.B. degree in three years. He listened to many of Harvard's best — Edward Channing and Frederick Jackson Turner in history, William Z. Ripley and O. M. W. Sprague in economics, Josiah Royce in philosophy, A. Lawrence Lowell in government. And he wrote a good deal, especially for George Pierce Baker and Charles Townsend Copeland. One essay was an appeal to southern colleges to follow the example of Harvard and admit Negro students. Another considered the decline of the famous Dutch families of New York, so many with nothing left today but their name — "they are few in numbers, they lack progressiveness and a true democratic spirit." But the Roosevelts, the young man suggested, were different.

One reason, — perhaps the chief — of the virility of the Roosevelts is this very democratic spirit. They have never felt that

because they were born in a good position they could put their hands in their pockets and succeed. They have felt, rather, that being born in a good position, there was no excuse for them if they did not do their duty by the community, and it is because this idea was instilled into them from their birth that they have in nearly every case proved good citizens.

The Rector would have liked that.

Still none of his classes succeeded in really striking sparks in him. It was rather his extracurricular activities by which he grew. His interest in politics expanded. In 1900, attracted by Cousin Teddy's appearance on the Republican ticket, he became a card-holding member of the Harvard Republican Club, even putting on a red cap and gown to walk through a drizzle in the Republican torch-light parade before the election. In two years, he was less happy about Cousin Teddy — "His tendency to make the executive power stronger than the Houses of Congress," said the young man sententiously, "is bound to be a bad thing" — and in another year he went home to New York to vote for the first time, shouting with facetious enthusiasm: "Hooray for the Dimocrats of Hoide Park!" But he was loyal again to Cousin Teddy in 1904 and cast his first ballot in a presidential election for a Republican.

Most important of all to him was the *Crimson,* the undergraduate newspaper. He had won election to the editorial board as a freshman, and he decided to spend a fourth year in Cambridge in order to serve as editor-in-chief. His editorial range was wholly conventional, displaying the earnest senior's concern for the football team, the Harvard cheering section, boardwalks in the Yard in winter, and more fire extinguishers in the dormitories. But success on the *Crimson* crowned his Harvard career and no doubt strengthened his easy confidence in his own future.[8]

Before his Harvard years were over, he manifested this confidence even more decisively. An adored only son, Franklin well knew that he was the center of his widowed mother's life. In his sophomore and junior years, she had even taken a house in Boston to be near him. For imperious Sara Roosevelt, the relationship with her son must have seemed all either would ever want. Yet, at Fairhaven, on Thanksgiving, 1903, she was compelled to note in her diary,

"Franklin gave me quite a startling announcement." "Unknown to any of us," as she described it many years later, Franklin had fallen in love with Anna Eleanor Roosevelt, a fifth cousin once removed, nineteen years old. Now he firmly notified his mother of his desire for an early marriage.

Back in Cambridge after the ordeal, Franklin could write, almost gaily, "Dearest Mama — I know what pain I must have caused you and you know I wouldn't do it if I really could have helped it — *mais tu sais, me voilá!* . . . I am the happiest man just now in the world; likewise the luckiest." His mother responded, "I know that in the future I shall be glad and I shall love Eleanor and adopt her fully when the right time comes. Only have patience dear Franklin, don't let this new happiness make you lose interest in work or home."

Sara also received a touching letter from Eleanor: "I know just how you feel & how hard it must be, but I do so want you to learn to love me a little. You must know that I will always try to do what you wish. . . . It is impossible for me to tell you how I feel toward Franklin. I can only say that my one great wish is always to prove worthy of him." [9]

v

For Eleanor Roosevelt, her engagement was almost the first act of affirmation in a sorrowful life; the sadness of her childhood was bound to make her tentative, even toward the man she had agreed to marry. As a little girl, solemn and shy, she was torn between her father, Elliott Roosevelt, charming, good-looking, and weak, "the love of my life for many years after he died," and her mother, Anna Hall, "one of the most beautiful women I have ever seen." Elliott loved his daughter, and he dominated her fantasy life. "Somehow it was always he and I. . . . I wished to be left alone in a dream world in which I was the heroine and my father the hero." Anna was cold and often severe; and Elliott, perhaps under the strain of marriage to so austere a woman, was beginning to take to drink. By the time Eleanor was six, he was living apart from his family.

Anna Hall Roosevelt suffered from strains too. Severe headaches afflicted her, and for hours the little girl sat on the bed, stroking her mother's brow. But, in other moods, Anna held her daughter to standards so unrelenting that the child's confidence in herself was gradually undermined. Her mother called Eleanor "Granny," explaining to visitors, while the little girl shrank with shame, "She is such a funny child, so old-fashioned." Anna's manifest concern over her daughter's lack of beauty gave Eleanor a permanent conviction that she was unattractive. She punished Eleanor severely for minor lapses. "I was always disgracing my mother."

In 1892, when Eleanor was eight, her mother died of diphtheria. "One fact wiped out everything else — my father was back and I would see him very soon." But Anna had her last revenge: the children were left under the guardianship of their grandmother. And two years later, in the summer of 1894, Eleanor received word that her father had died. Inconsolable, she lived on with her grandmother until 1899, when an aunt took her to England. There she entered a French school run by a remarkable woman named Marie Souvestre. For the first time in years, Eleanor had a taste of happiness and a renewal of confidence.

But when she returned to America at the age of eighteen, it was to plunge once again into tense family relationships. Living at her grandmother's estate at Tivoli on the Hudson, Eleanor saw two uncles succumb, like her father, to drink and self-indulgence. And when she moved to New York City to live with her gay Aunt Pussie, she encountered new intimidations — above all, New York society. "I knew I was the first girl in my mother's family who was not a belle." Still, a warm friendship with an older friend, Bob Ferguson, gave her solace. And her interests began to diversify: she worked with Mary Harriman in the early stages of the Junior League; she joined the Consumers' League; she taught calisthenics and fancy dancing at the Rivington Street Settlement House. Sometime in this period, as Bob Ferguson became increasingly absorbed in Eleanor's friend Isabella Selmes, Eleanor started to see her cousin, now in college at Cambridge, Franklin Roosevelt.

If a loving childhood gave Franklin Roosevelt the confidence to surmount disappointment, so insecurity, in its way, prepared Eleanor Roosevelt for the ordeals of life. As she put it later, it "hardened me in much the way that steel is tempered." To avoid breakdown in the face of a barrage of emotional crises, she had to learn self-discipline. The example of her father and uncles showed what happened to those who lost the power of self-control. There thus developed in her, she later wrote, "an almost exaggerated idea of the necessity of keeping all of one's desires under complete subjugation." And to this desire to subordinate herself she joined a passion to help others. Convinced that she was unloved and unwanted, she believed that she could best win affection from those around her as she could minister to them. "The feeling that I was useful was perhaps the greatest joy I experienced."

Lonely, awkward, tense, Eleanor Roosevelt now found in her fiancé and his robust, extroverted family "a sense of security which I never had known before." As for Franklin, who was probably the partner more specifically in love, he sensed perhaps in Eleanor a person with his own mixed attitude toward the world in which they had both been reared; he admired her intelligence, integrity, and sympathy; and doubtless he was captivated by her lustrous eyes, her vivid smile, and her willowy grace — for contemporary portraits suggest that Eleanor Roosevelt was more attractive than she would admit in her own recollections. Indeed, at the time friends wondered why she was throwing herself away on the "featherduster." Certainly Franklin's determination to marry her was concrete and unshakable; it nerved him, an only child, twenty-two years old and still in college, to face down with relative equanimity the deep opposition of the mother to whom he was so attached and who was so dependent on him.

Sara Roosevelt, while having nothing against Eleanor, could not bear to lose Franklin. She reminded him that her own father had not married till he was thirty-three; she pleaded with him to complete his education; in a desperate move, she took him on a cruise to the West Indies. But to no avail: the Dutch stubbornness that was ordinarily so well hidden behind fluent affability had secured Franklin's decision.

VI

In the autumn of 1904 Franklin entered the Columbia Law School. In December the engagement was finally announced, and the wedding was scheduled for March 17, 1905. "We are greatly rejoiced over the good news," the President of the United States wrote Franklin. "I am as fond of Eleanor as if she were my daughter; and I like you, and trust you, and believe in you. No other success in life — not the Presidency, or anything else — begins to compare with the joy and happiness that come in and from the love of the true man and the true woman. . . . You and Eleanor are true and brave, and I believe you love each other unselfishly; and golden years open before you."

The date approached in a whirl of excitement and confusion. The bridesmaids helped Eleanor write notes of thanks for the wedding presents. One day it was discovered that Isabella Selmes, who suddenly married Bob Ferguson four months after Franklin Roosevelt's marriage, was writing, "Franklin and I are so pleased with your gift" and unconsciously signing her own name. Endicott Peabody came down from Groton to perform the ceremony, and Theodore Roosevelt came up from Washington to give away the bride. ("Well, Franklin," said Cousin Teddy after the ceremony, "there's nothing like keeping the name in the family.") The words were pronounced under a great bouquet of pink roses; groom kissed bride, and the party moved on to the wedding reception, where the guests clustered around the President in one room, leaving Franklin and Eleanor by themselves in another.[10]

At the Columbia Law School, Roosevelt was a dutiful rather than an enthusiastic student. He did his work faithfully and on the whole received adequate grades. But for a mind that proceeded from the particular to the general, the abstractions of the law tended to be tedious. "He will not find himself altogether happy with the law he is studying at Columbia," said Eleanor, "unless he is able to get a broad human contact through it." In the spring of 1907, he passed the New York Bar Examinations. Once this was out of the way, he did not bother to finish his degree. This was not an uncommon practice. A young Kentuckian named Stanley Reed, two years after Roosevelt in the Columbia Law School and a far better student, did the same thing.

After the end of the academic year, the young couple took a belated honeymoon in Europe, wandering through the palazzos of Venice, mountain climbing in the Dolomites, visiting the great country houses of Britain. They crossed the Atlantic with six Japanese naval officers, with whom the bridegroom sought to strike up conversation on naval topics: "I find myself giving out more information than I receive." In Paris a fortuneteller told Franklin that he was to be "President of the U.S. or the Equitable, I couldn't make out which!" In Scotland, Sidney and Beatrice Webb came to lunch; Franklin discussed Harvard with the husband while Eleanor talked over the servant problem with the wife. When they returned to New York in the fall, they moved into a house on East 36th Street which Sara had procured, furnished, and staffed in their absence.

Eleanor, recoiling from her years of premature responsibility, now bearing her first child, fell without conscious protest into a new role. "I was growing very dependent on my mother-in-law, requiring her help on almost every subject, and never thought of asking for anything which I felt would not meet with her approval." Her first baby — a daughter, Anna — was born in May 1906; there were five more (one of whom died in infancy) in the next ten years. As the family grew, Sara decided that the 36th Street house was too small. Buying a plot of land on East 65th Street, she built two connected houses, one for herself, one for her son and his family. Eleanor, unconsulted, continued to submit, though even her self-abnegation had its limits. One day, after they moved, Franklin found his wife distraught before her dressing table, sobbing that she did not like to live in a house that was in no way hers and did not represent the way she wanted to live. In the face of such outbursts, Franklin, committed to both wife and mother, preferred practical compromise to basic diagnosis. He developed a jovial obliviousness that would help in dealing with other tense human relationships in later periods of his life.[11]

VII

In the meantime, he was tackling the law as a junior clerk at Carter, Ledyard and Milburn, a Wall Street firm largely dedicated to thwarting the antitrust act. For Roosevelt the intricacies of corporate briefs had little attraction; but he liked nothing better than to leave his old roll-top desk and try a case in the municipal

courts, collecting witnesses, arguing points with sharp, small-time
lawyers, mixing happily in the rough and tumble of the courtroom.
It thrust him among people he had never met at Groton or the
Hasty Pudding. It taught him to deal with a variety of classes and
races; and it gave him his first intimate contact with the problems
of the poor, weak, and defenseless.

But practice in the municipal courts could hardly be a career.
Roosevelt was not much of a lawyer, and his mind was drifting
beyond the law. One day in 1907, as the clerks were chatting about
their ambitions, Roosevelt explained "with engaging frankness"
(as recalled by his fellow clerk, Grenville Clark) that he planned
to run for political office at the first opportunity and that he
wanted to be President. Cousin Teddy supplied the model: first
the state Assembly, then Assistant Secretary of the Navy, then
Governor of New York. "Anyone who is governor of New York,"
Clark recalls Franklin Roosevelt saying, "has a good chance to be
President with any luck." [12]

Theodore Roosevelt's example was bound to be infectious. He
had always been a vivid figure in Franklin's life, from those days
at Oyster Bay when he used to line up the children at the top of
steep dunes and rush down with them, pell-mell, the sand sinking
under their feet, to the beach below.[13] Indeed, T.R. dramatized
for the whole generation the image of the gentleman in public life.
For F.D.R., he gave excitement to the ideals of community service,
bred so deep in the squires along the Hudson, with their town
boards and fire companies and local charities, and to the conceptions of Christian duty made so compelling by Endicott Peabody
at Groton.

Nonetheless T.R.'s example was not enough to sway F.D.R. from
traditional Democratic affiliations. And upstate the Democratic
organization often sought out country gentlemen who had money
to spend in politics and might appeal to the independent vote.
John E. Mack, the Democratic district-attorney of Dutchess County,
spoke to Roosevelt early in 1910 about the possibility of running
for the state Senate. F.D.R. listened with interest, reflected, and
checked with T.R. (who told his sister, "Franklin ought to go in
politics without the least regard as to where I speak or don't speak.
. . . He is a fine fellow; but I wish he had Joe's [Alsop] political

views"). Soon Roosevelt was attending a political picnic at Pough-keepsie, redolent with beer and clams and sauerkraut, and he finally decided to go ahead.

It was a fundamental decision. For twenty-eight years, he had lived an upper-class life of suitable affability, conventionality, and vacancy. But somehow it had not come off. He had tried to play by the book, but his performance was not convincing. "Everybody called him 'Franklin,'" an acquaintance said, "and regarded him as a harmless bust." It all bored him too much — the chatter, the snobbery, the pomposity, the absorption in money. "He had the soul and instincts of a journalist, but he was in a social stratum where one must be ordinary, industrious, unread and inarticulate or else be branded as a smarty." Fortunately he had a way of escape. He was a Democrat, and politics offered an outlet for his ambition, his high spirits, his idealism and his realism. It allowed him at last to be himself. Still, the habit of masquerade remained. The public face could never be relied on to express the private man.[14]

VIII

It looked at first like a hopeless prospect. Only once since the Civil War had a Democrat carried the senatorial district. But F.D.R., his mind made up, campaigned aggressively. As twenty-two years later he would charter a plane to fly from Albany to Chicago, so in 1910 he broke precedent and hired an automobile to cover the outer reaches of his district. The two-cylinder red Maxwell, without windshield or top, bedecked with American flags, wheezed along at the perilous speed of twenty miles an hour, coming to a politic halt every time a team of horses hove in sight. The campaign had an autumnal gaiety of its own — the early morning departure from Hyde Park, the burst of dust along the winding roads, the speeches at country stores or grange halls or to curious groups of farmers at crossroads, lunch at small country hotels, and occasional stops at cider mills for cooling mugs of fresh sweet cider.

The young candidate was by no means a skilled orator. He talked with such terrifying pauses that his wife worried for fear he would never go on. But his quick charm, grace, and straightfor-

wardness pleased his audiences. The statue carved of him by
Prince Paul Troubetzkoy the next year — a sitting figure, without
legs — showed him handsome and manly. Assurance gradually
increased. Soon, after introduction, F.D.R. could smile and say,
"I'm not Teddy." When the crowd laughed, he would continue,
"A little shaver said to me the other day that he knew I wasn't
Teddy — I asked him 'why' and he replied: 'Because you don't
show your teeth.' "

The emergence of a bright new personality with a magic name,
even if he did not show his teeth, was one asset. Another was the
widening split in the Republican party, as Theodore Roosevelt
forced the gubernatorial nomination of a grave and able young
lawyer, Henry L. Stimson, against the wishes of the party bosses.
Rain on election Tuesday kept many normally Republican farmers
away from the polls. It was in any case a Democratic day across
the nation, and it was particularly a Democratic day in Dutchess
County, where Franklin D. Roosevelt, running well ahead of the
rest of the ticket, defeated his Republican opponent by over one
thousand votes. If T.R. had launched his political career in the
state Assembly, F.D.R. would launch his in the state Senate.[15]

The young senator moved to Albany in style, renting a spacious
brownstone house on State Street. His Hyde Park Fife and Drum
Corps appeared for the inauguration, drowning out the bishop's
prayer with its cacophony. In the afternoon, Eleanor and his
mother served sandwiches, beer, and cigars to Hyde Parkers crowding into the new Roosevelt home. That night the new Democratic
governor, John A. Dix, asked the young Roosevelts over to the
Executive Mansion for "a little informal dancing."

But the new life was not all frolic, and Roosevelt entered with
equal enthusiasm into the business of politics. He seconded the
nomination of Robert F. Wagner as president pro tem of the
Senate on behalf of the new and of the upstate senators. "Wagner
will be fairly good I think," Roosevelt noted in his diary. "He has
good intentions; the only obstacle is the pressure of his own machine." (At the same time, another competent New York City
Democrat, Alfred E. Smith, was made majority leader of the
Assembly.) But a more difficult question lay immediately ahead:
who should be sent to the United States Senate as successor to the
retiring Republican, Chauncey M. Depew? [16]

IX

The favored candidate was known to be William F. Sheehan, a wealthy businessman, the law partner of Alton B. Parker, the conservative Democrat whom F.D.R. had declined to support for the Presidency in 1904. Sheehan was now sponsored for the Senate by Boss Charles F. Murphy of Tammany Hall as well as by the utilities and railroad interests with which he had been so long associated. For young Roosevelt, the choice of Blue-eyed Billy Sheehan seemed a betrayal of his party's supposed dedication to progressive government. "The Democratic party is on trial," he said on New Year's Day, "and having been given the control of the government chiefly through up-State vote, cannot afford to surrender its control to the organization in New York City." Other young Democrats had similar doubts. As the time approached for a party caucus, the anti-Sheehan forces coalesced. Selecting Roosevelt as their chairman, they formed a bloc which declared it would not be bound by the Democratic caucus and which, with the Republicans, would have enough votes to stop Sheehan.

In the following weeks, the tall, thin, intense young man with a high collar and gold-bowed pince-nez emerged increasingly as the spokesman for the insurgents. "There is nothing I love as much as a good fight," he told the *New York Times* with true Rooseveltian gusto. "I never had as much fun in my life as I am having right now." His name and his easy accessibility captured the press, and his reputation began for the first time to spread beyond New York. The issue, he told the *Times,* was "bossism"; or, as he restated it for the Toledo *News-Bee* (which described him as Frederick D. Roosevelt), "Business must get out of politics. The people must make a stand against it. The Murphys, who represent business, must be cleaned out."

Actually Roosevelt himself had no compunction about consorting with Wall Street attorneys in the fight against Sheehan. "All Wall Street is not bad," he observed privately to one of them, "as a residence here of four years has shown me." Nonetheless, the words helped create the symbol. Letters poured in congratulating him. Thus one from James Forrestal, the Matteawan lumber contractor: "When I voted for you I was sure of your sterling qualities and sound judgment. Your actions prove I was right." (Forrestal's

ambitious son, James Vincent Forrestal, working on a Poughkeepsie paper, was one of Roosevelt's strong supporters.) And, best of
all, an accolade from Sagamore Hill: "Just a line to say that we
are all really proud of the way you have handled yourself. . . .
Give my love to dear Eleanor." — a longhand scrawl, signed Theodore Roosevelt. The Cleveland *Plain Dealer* speculated that if
none of T.R.'s sons turned out to be fit objects for popular adoration, "may it not be possible that this rising star may continue the
Roosevelt dynasty?" [17]

For ten weeks the bitter struggle continued. Boss Murphy, whose
commitment to Sheehan was perhaps only halfhearted, soon began
to explore the possibilities of compromise; and in time the unity
of the insurgents began to crumble away. Though they stopped
Sheehan, they reluctantly accepted as a substitute Justice James A.
O'Gorman, a former Grand Sachem of Tammany, far more identified with Murphy than Sheehan had ever been. Bob Wagner and
Al Smith promised the rebels that there would be no reprisals, and
Roosevelt and his associates were restored to the party. Both sides
claimed victory.

                                    X

With melodrama over and the foundation for a reputation laid,
F.D.R. settled down to the tedious work of a state legislator. His
opposition — qualified — to bossism had defined one part of his
developing political philosophy. Now other issues, particularly
those coming to him as chairman of the Forest, Fish and Game
Committee, were forcing him to think through his other positions.
His preliminary orientation had been vague enough. The ideal
candidate, he had blandly explained in February 1911, should be
"conservative in regard to business interests, and yet a man whose
position can never be questioned by the radical element of society."
But within this unbeatable framework, his social views, under the
pressure of immediate problems, began to gain new concreteness.

The central theme in Roosevelt's emerging philosophy was the
conservation of natural resources. This derived both from his own
preoccupations and from his admiration for his cousin Theodore.
From childhood, F.D.R. had cared deeply about nature — about

land, water, and trees. With maturity this concern was becoming more systematic. Thus around 1912 he began to plant one to four thousand trees every year at Hyde Park, filling the steep slopes between the mansion and the river with new growths of yellow poplar and white pine. As chairman of the Forest, Fish and Game Committee, he now seized the opportunity to press within the state the conservation crusade which T.R. had launched so brilliantly in the nation.

To start it off, he invited Gifford Pinchot, T.R.'s intimate friend and Chief Forester of the United States, to come to Albany for a lecture in the Assembly Chamber. Pinchot threw two pictures on the screen. One was an old Chinese painting, showing a green valley in the year 1500, in a corner of which could be dimly discerned a logging chute. The other was a photograph of the same valley four centuries later, parched and deserted, the bare rocks reflecting the glare of the sun. This disaster was the result, Pinchot suggested, of the greed for profit through logging. It was this lesson Roosevelt hoped to imprint on the state of New York.

For F.D.R., conservation was a natural enough extension of the Hudson River tradition, with its patrician sense of responsibility for the land. But he soon discovered that proposals to save the land roused the bitter hostility of the lumber magnates and other businessmen. "It is an extraordinary thing to me," he once exploded, "that people who are financially interested should not be able to see more than about six inches in front of their noses." Could these people not understand that it was far better to preserve forests and watersheds in the long-run interest of all than to destroy them for a few to make a quick dollar? [18]

From timber and wild life, he proceeded naturally enough to water and the protection of power sites. Roosevelt fought hard for a bill providing for the state construction, ownership, and operation of hydroelectric plants and their transmission lines; here he felt for the first time the formidable pressure of the utility companies. And from resources planning it was but a short step to the notion of planning in the cities as well as on the countryside. Thus, when Roosevelt's uncle, Frederic A. Delano, talked to him in 1912 about the new City Plan of Chicago, Roosevelt, as he later wrote, became from that moment "interested in not the mere planning of a single city but in the larger aspects of planning. It is the way of the future."

Similarly, belief in the conservation of natural resources might well lead to beliefs in the conservation of human resources. Roosevelt's initial interest in labor legislation had been tepid. But he soon became a sponsor of the Association for Labor Legislation; and by 1912 he was taking a fairly active part in support of labor measures. That year he received the cordial endorsement of the state Federation of Labor. While Roosevelt was by no means so responsive to industrial issues as city politicians like Smith and Wagner, it was more remarkable that this upstate aristocrat from a rural district should have bothered himself with such questions at all.[19]

XI

The conservation battle thus helped shape in Roosevelt's mind a broad conception of the public welfare as something that had to be vigilantly protected against private greed. He concluded that the community must itself be prepared to undertake measures of regulation and planning to keep the scramble for profit from wrecking the system. With F.D.R. as with T.R., the philosophy of conservation led straight to a belief in government intervention in the economy as the means of protecting the public interest.

In a speech at Troy in March 1912, young Roosevelt propounded his new philosophy of government. The basic impulse of modern history, he suggested, had been the struggle for individual liberty. But individualism had now created its own set of problems. "Conditions of civilization that come with individual freedom are inevitably bound to bring up many questions that mere individual liberty cannot solve." What could solve these questions? Only a new social theory; and "to put it in the simplest and fewest words," said Roosevelt, "I have called this new theory the struggle for the liberty of the community rather than the liberty of the individual." Every beneficial measure advanced in the last fifty years, he added, came under this definition, from conservation and antitrust action to state regulation of common carriers and commission government — "they are all steps in the evolution of the new theory of the liberty of the community."

What did this new theory imply for the ancient struggle for the liberty of the individual? "If we use the word 'liberty' in conjunction with the word 'community,'" Roosevelt said, "we necessarily give to that word 'liberty' a higher and nobler meaning than where the same word was applied to the individual." In other words, in cases of conflict, the liberty of the community must take precedence, which meant that "the right of any one individual to work or not as he sees fit, to live to a great extent where and how he sees fit, is not sufficient" and may indeed harm the well-being of the majority.

"To put it another way," he continued, "competition has been shown to be useful up to a certain point and no further. Co-operation must begin where competition leaves off and co-operation is as good a word for the new theory as any other." This meant in practice, for example, that an individual could not be permitted to cut his own trees from his own land, if stripping the soil of its protective cover endangered the water supply and thus the health of the community. Gifford Pinchot's Chinese lantern slides showed the consequences of indulging the unbridled pursuit of private profit. "Every man five hundred years ago did as he pleased with his own property. . . . And the sad part of it is that there are to-day men of the State who for the sake of lining their pockets during their own life-time are willing to cause the same thing that happened in China."

But conservation was only "the first lesson that points to the necessity for seeking community freedom."

> If we can prophesy today that the state (or in other words the people as a whole) will shortly tell a man how many trees he must cut, then why can we not, without being radical, predict that the state will compel every farmer to till his land or raise beef, or horses? . . . If we call the method regulation, people hold up their hands in horror and say "Unamerican" or "dangerous." But if we call the same identical process co-operation these same old fogies will cry out "well done."

In light of the new principle, he concluded, the old problems — trusts, rebating, control of common carriers — faded into minor issues. "Co-operation makes monopoly out of date, and we are coming to understand that the mere size of a trust is not of necessity its evil. A trust is evil if it monopolizes for the benefit of a few and contrary to the interests of the community."

This was the year of the New Nationalism, but few Americans, even T.R. himself, gave the new doctrines of public supremacy so trenchant a statement as the thirty-year-old state senator from Dutchess County.[20]

XII

As his experience in the state Senate ripened his political philosophy, so it also improved his technique as a politician. At the start, he was a far from popular figure in Albany. His great height, his haughty Groton-Harvard manner, his habit of throwing up his head so as to give the appearance of looking down his nose, his pince-nez — all this, combined with his leadership in the anti-Sheehan fight, stamped him as a snob and branded his ideas, in the outraged language of one regular Democrat, as "the silly conceits of a political prig." Frances Perkins, in Albany as representative of the Consumers' League, could remember young Roosevelt standing back of the brass rail arguing with two or three of his Democratic colleagues, his small mouth pursed up, his nostrils distended, his head in the air, and his cool, distant voice saying, "No, no, I won't hear of it!" "Awful, arrogant fellow, that Roosevelt," said the affable Big Tim Sullivan of Tammany Hall; and even Smith and Wagner thought him impossible. Once, after a highhanded Roosevelt intervention in a debate, Wagner said coldly, "Senator Roosevelt has gained his point. What he wants is a headline in the newspapers. Let us proceed to our business."

But in time the organization began reluctantly to accept him as a Democrat, even if a perverse one. And Roosevelt in time began to understand the city Democrats, and even to learn from them. Over a quarter of a century later, discussing an immigration problem with Frances Perkins, he suddenly remarked, "Tim Sullivan used to say that the America of the future would be made out of the people who had come over in steerage and who knew in their own hearts and lives the difference between being despised and being accepted and liked." Then he added, "Poor old Tim Sullivan never understood about modern politics, but he was right about the human heart." Looking back at himself in his early years, Roosevelt could say, "You know, I was an awfully mean cuss when I first went into politics." [21]

Yet, though the gap narrowed, Roosevelt remained an outsider. Tammany smelled to him corrupt and conservative. A fervent Democrat, Roosevelt was not to be tempted by Cousin Teddy's progressive Republicanism; but, in his own way a fervent progressive, Roosevelt was certain that the Democratic party required liberal leadership. By the end of 1911, he decided that such leadership might best come from the neighboring state of New Jersey. He soon made a pilgrimage to Trenton to meet Governor Woodrow Wilson, and by the spring, in open defiance of Boss Murphy, he was busy trying to build a Wilson movement in association with other New York political leaders, among them William Gibbs McAdoo.

Though not a member of the New York delegation, Roosevelt went to the Baltimore convention in order to shout for Wilson. This first brush with national Democratic politics was an exciting experience. The national committeeman from Wisconsin, Joseph E. Davies, gave him credentials; he met such southern Democrats as Josephus Daniels of North Carolina and Cordell Hull of Tennessee; and he had the time of his life amidst the parading and the balloting. When Wilson finally won the nomination, Roosevelt, in a state of pleasurable exhaustion, wired his wife in Campobello: ALL MY PLANS VAGUE SPLENDID TRIUMPH.[22]

F.D.R. seized the moment of Murphy's discomfiture to set up an organization of anti-Tammany, pro-Wilson Democrats in New York. But, shortly before the Democratic state convention, he fell ill of typhoid fever, and Murphy reasserted his control over the party without too much trouble. Roosevelt, helpless in New York City, was now faced with the problem of his own campaign for re-election in Dutchess County. At this moment, there came to mind a reporter he had known at Albany as correspondent of the New York *Herald* — Louis McHenry Howe.

XIII

Howe, forty-one years old in 1912, was a veteran newspaperman, with a hopeless addiction to politics and a cynical view of human nature. Born in Indiana, he had moved as a child to Saratoga Springs, where his father ran the local newspaper and dabbled in Democratic party affairs. Louis was frail as a boy, the victim of asthma, bronchitis, and a persistent heart murmur. But he was sharp, humorous, hard-working, and uncomplaining. As a reporter on his father's paper, he frequented the ornate Edwardian hotels of Saratoga Springs crowded with sportsmen, gamblers, and politicians; to the end of his life, he conveyed the atmosphere of this racy era before the First World War.

He was an unprepossessing man, short, thin, and generally dirty, his face pitted with small dark scars from a youthful bicycle accident, his nose big and ugly, tremendous ears sprouting from his high stiff collar, a Sweet Caporal cigarette perpetually stuck into his small mouth, his nervous fingers yellow with tobacco, his dark clothes baggy and unpressed. The extra-size collar, usually sweat-stained and wilted, was worn to conceal a neck Howe regarded as inordinately long and swanlike. He took a belligerent pride in his appearance, portraying himself to an observer as "one of the four ugliest men, if what is left of me can be dignified by the name of man, in the State of New York. I am wizened in the Dickens' manner. My eyes protrude because of so much looking. Children take one look at me on the street and run." One reporter called him a "medieval gnome," and Howe accepted the designation with relish. His manner was abrupt and unpredictable, complicated by a dry, owlish humor and seasoned with unlikely oaths ("Mein Gawd" was his favorite). He was secretive by nature, delighting in mystery and intrigue. Yet beneath the seamed and creased face, the sarcastic twist of the mouth, and the disillusioned banter, there was a genuinely sensitive spirit. It occasionally found unexpected reflection in his expressive brown eyes; or in his surprising artistic pleasures — his water colors, his etchings, his penchant for amateur theatricals and for elaborate birthday celebrations.

Howe had watched Roosevelt's fight against Sheehan from the Albany press gallery, first with skepticism, then with mounting admiration and ardor. What solace the wrinkled little reporter must have found in the sight of the tall, clear-skinned young aristocrat. If Howe could not have this careless magnificence himself, then at least he could identify himself with a man whose qualities he so much prized. Carlyle was his favorite historian; and he knew the need for heroes and for hero worship. On a winter day in 1911 he entered the paneled library of the Albany house with the coat of arms over the fireplace to interview Roosevelt for his paper. Seated in a huge armchair, he watched F.D.R. striding the room before the leaping fire, explaining his determination to stop Sheehan. "Almost at that very first meeting," Howe later said, "I made up my mind that . . . nothing but an accident could keep him from becoming President."

In the spring of 1912, when Roosevelt organized independent Democrats for Wilson, Howe came along to do the publicity. By June, when F.D.R. was at the Baltimore convention, Howe could begin a letter to him with the only half-sardonic salutation "Beloved and Revered Future President" (followed by "This is a line to remind you that you have a date with me to go in swimming"). Now in the fall Roosevelt, flat on his back with typhoid, asked Howe to take over the campaign he could not make himself. With a resort to publicity methods new to Dutchess County, Howe flooded the district with multigraphed "personal" letters, posters, and newspaper advertisements setting forth the case for Roosevelt ("NEEDED IN THE FIGHT FOR CONSERVATION. . . . ONE OF LABOR'S BEST FRIENDS IN ALBANY"). Once again the normally Republican district sent its young Democratic senator to Albany.

Victory in 1912 sealed a political partnership. Howe's welcome in the Roosevelt household was not total. Eleanor Roosevelt disliked the "dirty little man" with his untidy clothes, his racking cough, and his perpetual cigarette. But F.D.R. found in Howe an astuteness in political operation which supplemented his own inexperience, and an astringent attitude toward life, which stimulated his own high spirits. Howe was indifferent to political ideology, beyond a commitment to the Democratic party and a newspaperman's contempt for stuffed shirts; but he was a master of political technique, and here Roosevelt needed assistance. Ac-

tually Howe, for all his skill at deflation, had also a weakness for
gimmicks and experiments not unlike Roosevelt's own; but they
rarely succumbed at the same time, and each delighted in serving
as a restraint on the other. Roosevelt took on a new dimension in
politics when he joined Howe to his person, and Howe found all
the fulfillment he ever wanted in life in merging his identity with
that of Roosevelt.[23]

XIV

Victory in 1912 opened new doors. Roosevelt's re-election in
Dutchess County was part of a broad Democratic sweep. Governor
Woodrow Wilson of New Jersey was now the President-elect; for
the first time in sixteen years, Democrats were in power in Washington. F.D.R., returning to Albany for his second term, had a
briefcase full of bills he wished to push through the new legislature.
Yet in January he conferred at Trenton with Governor Wilson,
who had already asked Frank Cobb and Herbert Bayard Swope of
the New York *World* to suggest a good upstate New York Democrat
for Assistant Secretary of the Navy and had received in response
the name of Franklin Roosevelt.

No one knows what happened at the Trenton meeting. A few
days before inauguration F.D.R. went to Washington. There
McAdoo, soon to take over as Secretary of the Treasury, offered him
an Assistant Secretaryship or the Collectorship of the Port of New
York. F.D.R. refused. On the night before inauguration, he told
Josephus Daniels of North Carolina, who was scheduled to be
Secretary of the Navy, that "if he served in any place in the administration he preferred to be in the Navy Department." Daniels,
who had had Roosevelt in his mind ever since they first met at the
Baltimore convention, kept his counsel. But the next morning in
the lobby of the Willard Hotel he ran again into the New Yorker.
When Roosevelt offered his congratulations at Daniels's appointment, Daniels now responded: "How would you like to come with
me as Assistant Secretary of the Navy?" Roosevelt's face beamed
with pleasure: "How would I like it? How would I like it? I'd
rather have that place than any other position in public life."
Daniels, well pleased, cleared the appointment with Wilson, who

said "Capital," and then consulted the senators from Roosevelt's home state.

Senator O'Gorman said that Roosevelt would be acceptable. The second New York senator was the Republican Elihu Root. When Daniels told Root what he intended, a queer look crept over Root's face.

"You know the Roosevelts, don't you?" Root asked skeptically.

"Whenever a Roosevelt rides," Root said, "he wishes to ride in front." [24]

30. Testing in Washington

"IT IS INTERESTING to see that you are in another place which I myself once held," wrote Theodore Roosevelt. Josephus Daniels found it interesting too, noting in his diary: "His distinguished cousin TR went from the place to the Presidency. May history repeat itself." [1] It was doubtless also interesting for the same reason to young F.D.R. But there were other reasons why Franklin was drawn to the Navy. From his childhood he had loved ships and open water. From his early teens he had read Admiral Mahan and acquired a strong belief in the influence of sea power on history. No branch of the national government so excited his imagination.

As for Daniels, he wanted Roosevelt in part because he felt that his Assistant Secretary should come from the Northeast. But his more important reason, as Josephus Daniels's son Jonathan later suggested, was something else. It was that Roosevelt symbolized the kind of young man that Democratic old-timers like Daniels wanted to attach to the new liberal administration. Daniels was nearly fifty-one years old in 1913. He was an old-fashioned figure — old-fashioned in his dress, with his pleated linen shirts, his black string ties, and his thick hunting-case watch; old-fashioned in the simplehearted moral indignation that occasionally blazed through his blue eyes; old-fashioned in his generous, innocent, almost mystical faith in the people. He had given head and heart to William Jennings Bryan in 1896, the same year that young Franklin Roosevelt set off for Groton; and he had fought beside Bryan ever since to make the Democratic party the champion of the oppressed. The Wilson administration could succeed, he devoutly believed, only as it renewed the dedication of the honorable young men of the nation — men like Franklin Roosevelt — to the democratic faith.

For Roosevelt, Daniels was a new experience. At first the young New Yorker saw only an editor from the provinces — "the funniest looking hillbilly I had ever seen" — who could not tell a hatch from a halyard. For a time, the smooth young Assistant Secretary convulsed his friends at the Metropolitan Club with imitations of his rustic chief. One day Franklin Lane, the Secretary of the Interior, told Roosevelt that he should be ashamed of himself — either show Daniels loyalty, or resign his office. And in time Roosevelt himself began to discover that he had much to learn from Josephus Daniels.[2]

The Secretary may have seemed a landlubber, if not a fool, to the regular Navy, and the admirals may have given the Assistant Secretary the pleasant feeling that he alone understood their problems; but might their attention not also be, perhaps, because they thought they could get from him things they could not get from his boss? Flattered at first by their solicitude, Roosevelt gradually developed a wariness about their motives. While he still prided himself on his success in working with the admirals, he could not but see that Daniels was more successful in working with the admirals' masters, the Congress of the United States. In his cagey, country-editor way, Daniels could persuade congressional committees. This was a new world for Roosevelt, and he admired those who succeeded where he sometimes failed.

II

His chief job as Assistant Secretary was to supervise the business affairs of the Navy. He brought Louis Howe to Washington with him, and together they nervously faced up to the problems of dealing with labor and with business. Howe, eager at the prospect of a new constituency, urged Roosevelt to take on labor relations as a personal responsibility. Roosevelt, always ready for new experience, kept his office door open to labor leaders, sought an understanding of their problems, won their personal friendship, and strove, with success, for an enlightened labor policy in the Navy yards. In the end, he could legitimately (with Howe) claim credit for the fact that there was no major strike in any U.S. Navy yard.

Daniels educated Roosevelt; so did labor; so too did business. Daniels approached the businessmen who sought contracts with the suspicion of a Bryanite agrarian, convinced that monopoly was a menace to the country; Howe approached them with the cynicism of a newspaperman, sure that everyone had his angle; Roosevelt, with the determination of a big Navy man who wanted every dollar he could get from the Congress to go as far as possible in building the fighting strength of the Navy. Whatever the difference in approach, the conclusion was the same: businessmen should not be allowed to make excessive profits out of national defense. The Assistant Secretary became particularly embroiled in efforts to stop collusive bidding among steel and coal companies. Too many businessmen seemed intent only on making all the money they could out of the nation's security. The result was perhaps to make him wonder when private enterprise ever willingly served the public welfare.

Other departmental responsibilities contributed to his education. Chronic disorder in the Caribbean had long concerned the Navy; and in 1915, after an outburst of revolutionary violence in Haiti, American Marines took over control of the Haitian government. Early in 1917 Roosevelt inspected the Navy Department's new dependency. Observing the theory of Haitian independence with exquisite courtesy, he made an agreeable personal impression on the natives; and, in company with Major-General Smedley D. Butler, he toured the island and approvingly noted the benefits of occupation. While he did not draft the Haitian constitution, as he carelessly claimed a few years later, he went away from Haiti with a sense of personal proprietorship which stood him in good stead and bad in the years ahead.[3]

III

But the Navy did not take him away from politics. There was always the problem of safeguarding his lines of communication with New York. He and Howe found an ally in Daniel C. Roper, the First Assistant Postmaster-General, when it came to allotting federal jobs. But Tammany viewed with mounting suspicion what seemed to be Roosevelt's attempt to build an organization of his own; and suspicion increased when it looked as if the Assistant Secretary were eying the gubernatorial or the senatorial nomination for 1914. In time, as organization Democrats complained of Roosevelt, Wilson inserted himself into the picture, said soothing words to Tammany, and, by implication, disowned the Roosevelt activities.

Nonetheless, in August 1914 Roosevelt, apparently at the behest of McAdoo, who had his own quarrel with Tammany, agreed to enter the senatorial race. F.D.R. himself seemed to have had doubts about his hasty decision: "my senses have not yet left me," he wired Howe. The step was taken against the advice of Daniels, without consultation with Howe and without the knowledge of major party leaders (though McAdoo seems to have given Roosevelt the erroneous impression that Wilson favored the decision). After some delay, Boss Murphy replied by proposing as the organization candidate James W. Gerard, Wilson's Ambassador to Germany. When Gerard cabled the State Department from Berlin that he would run only if the President approved, Bryan, noting his own feeling that "Roosevelt would be the best man," asked Wilson whether to call off Gerard. But Wilson elected not to interfere.

Roosevelt thus found himself in an impossible campaign against an impeccable and invisible candidate. He stumped the state for three weeks, denouncing Murphy and Tammany and eulogizing the New Freedom. But Gerard, never stirring from Germany, swept the primary by a margin considerably greater than two to one. Roosevelt, rather jaunty in defeat, took pleasure in the fact that he had carried a good many rural counties. Gerard was himself badly beaten in the election.

It was an instructive experience all around. Roosevelt understood from it the power of Boss Murphy's machine in the primaries, while Murphy, after Gerard's later collapse, may have understood better the importance of an "independent" candidate in the general election. During the campaign Howe had suggested to F.D.R. that it might be "the right time to show you don't hate all Tammany." This was also plainly the Wilson policy. By 1915 Roosevelt evidently made up his mind to abandon his efforts to build an upstate anti-Tammany movement. That year he endorsed his Albany friend Al Smith, who was Tammany's candidate for sheriff in New York, declaring him worthy "of any gift in the

power of the people of the State"; and in 1916 he helped get Bob
Wagner the offer of the postmastership of New York City. For his
part, Murphy likewise began to acknowledge the distasteful necessity, if he were to attract the independent vote, of working with
men like McAdoo and Roosevelt. By 1917 Roosevelt and Murphy
were photographed together at Tammany's annual Fourth of July
celebration. (A speaker on the occasion was Representative Martin
Dies, Sr., of Texas, a notable foe of foreigners and radicals; whether
his tall young son, Martin, Jr., accompanied him, is not recorded.)
As a practical politician, Roosevelt was learning a good deal —
about patronage, about party organization, about working with
congressmen, about living with bosses.[4]

IV

But it was above all the Navy itself that absorbed him. He
adored his new life — the seventeen guns and four ruffles when he
visited the fleet, the blueprints and the charts and the battle plans,
the officers, old and young, and the ships. "I now find my vocation
combined with my avocation in the most delightful ways." Among
the younger officers whom he knew as aides or as commanders were
William D. Leahy, William F. Halsey, Harold R. Stark, Emory S.
Land, Husband E. Kimmel. He would know them again. And
his relations with his chief became more relaxed. A memorandum
of 1915 suggests a new tone. F.D.R.:

Secnav
1. I beg to report
(a) That I have just signed a requisition (with four copies
attached) calling for purchase of eight carpet tacks.
                                                                ASTNAV
And Daniels's scribbled reply:

Why this wanton extravagance. I am sure that two would
suffice.

                                                                J.D.[5]

Yet issues still divided them — less manners now than policy.
Moments of tension with Mexico and with Japan in 1913 and 1914

made it clear that F.D.R. stood with the big-navy forces in the Department. In the case of Mexico, he publicly remarked in good T.R. style, "I do not want war, but I do not see how we can avoid it. Sooner or later, it seems, the United States must go down there and clean up the Mexican political mess." The Japanese threat disturbed him even more; and he became especially exercised over the possibility of a surprise Japanese attack on a United States Fleet weakened by division between the two oceans. "I do not anticipate trouble with Japan, but it may come," wrote Theodore Roosevelt to his young kinsman, adding prophetically, "and if it does it will come suddenly." Keep the fleet together, T.R. warned. Admiral Mahan sent letters to similar effect, saying, "I wrote to you because I know of no one else in the Administration to whom I should care to write." (In the autumn of 1914 Mahan, tired and old, called at the Assistant Secretary's office in the hope of finding Roosevelt, whom he had never met. But Roosevelt was out; and a few days later, taken suddenly sick, the great Admiral was dead.)[6]

Mexico and Japan constituted only the prelude. In the early summer of 1914 Archduke Franz Ferdinand was shot at Sarajevo, and in the next weeks the balance of Europe began to totter. Franklin Roosevelt had no illusions about the meaning of the ultimatums and mobilizations of late July. "A complete smash up is inevitable," he wrote Eleanor, as he hurried back to Washington. ". . . It will be the greatest war in the world's history." But on arrival, he found everyone "utterly oblivious to the fact that the most terrible drama in history was about to be enacted." Daniels seemed sad that his faith in human nature and civilization "and similar idealistic nonsense" had received such a rude shock. "These dear good people like W.J.B. and J.D. have as much conception of what a general European war means," he wrote, "as Elliott [not quite four years old] has of higher mathematics." Nor was Roosevelt impressed by the assurances of businessmen that no nation could afford modern war. "History shows that money in spite of what the bankers say is not an essential to the conduct of war by a determined nation." [7]

There now began a quiet duel in the Navy Department between the Secretary and his activist aide. Daniels shared with Bryan the old-fashioned isolationism which feared lest militarism and foreign entanglement corrupt the unique destiny of America. But Roosevelt, reared in the tradition of Mahan and T.R., saw the war as a practical exercise in protecting the physical security of the nation; if security required bigger ships, more men under arms, or even military action itself, so much, perhaps, the better for the people. Where war was for Daniels, as for Bryan and (for the moment) Wilson, a problem in ideology and morals, it was for Roosevelt a problem in defense.[8]

F.D.R. became more than ever an advocate of preparedness. He even leaked information concerning the inadequate state of national defense to Republican critics. He rejoiced at Bryan's resignation in 1915, chafed under Daniels's refusal to face up to what he himself saw as the logic of the American position, and came very near the thin edge of insubordination. "I have gone ahead and pulled the trigger myself," he wrote of one decision he took without clearance with his chief. "I suppose the bullet may bounce back on me." And again, "I just *know* I shall do some awful unneutral thing before I get through!"[9] But, with an exact sense of what he could get away with, he always stopped short of the action that even the tolerant Daniels would not forgive.

When Wilson finally decided in 1915 to adopt a preparedness program, Roosevelt, remaining a few steps ahead, now began to agitate for industrial mobilization under a Council of National Defense and for universal military training. He quieted down somewhat in 1916, perhaps because it was an election year. Now, always the politician, he tended to deplore criticism. "How would you expect the public to be convinced that a dangerous fire was in progress, requiring every citizen's aid for its extinguishment," he asked in one speech, "if they saw the members of the volunteer fire department stop in their headlong rush toward the conflagration and indulge in a slanging match as to who was responsible for the rotten hose?"[10] (The firehose, stored away in the recesses of memory, would be uncoiled again to put out other fires.)

v

The election reawakened his dormant progressivism. He threw himself wholeheartedly into the campaign and exulted in its startling denouement. On election night, when he left a party given by Henry Morgenthau, Sr., at the Biltmore in New York to take the sleeper to Washington, he shared the general belief that Wilson had been defeated. The next day altered matters — "the most extraordinary day of my life," he wrote Eleanor; and, after another day "of the most wild uncertainty," it appeared that Wilson had won. The election, said Roosevelt, was "the debacle of plutocracy." To his wife he added a poignant line: "I hope to God I don't grow reactionary with advancing years." [11]

Politics could only be an interlude in the drama across the Atlantic. By the fall of 1916, Roosevelt seems to have felt that American involvement was inescapable: "We've got to get into this war," he said to Daniels. A few months later President Wilson came to similar conclusions; but he feared far more than his impetuous subordinate to take on himself the responsibility for American entrance. When F.D.R. as Acting Secretary of the Navy proposed a fleet movement in March 1917, Wilson vetoed it, explaining he would do nothing that might allow future historians to say that the United States had committed the act of aggression.[12] . . . In another time, an older Roosevelt would better appreciate the presidential hesitation.

Franklin and Eleanor Roosevelt sat in the Capitol when Wilson told Congress that war would help make the world safe for democracy. "I went and listened breathlessly and returned home still half dazed," said Eleanor. As for Franklin, his boldness was at last finding outlet in the task of mobilizing the United States Navy for the greatest war in American history. If he were not so daring as he sometimes liked to think ("from Feb. 6 to March 4," he later said of the prewar period, "we in the navy committed acts for which we could be, and may be yet sent to jail for 999 years"), he had no compunctions about cutting corners, spending money, stimulating new naval construction, proposing new ideas, and unmercifully prodding his more cautious chief. From the start, he centered on German submarine warfare as the main threat; and he favored all-out cooperation with the Allies as the best way of employing American resources.

His fight for the North Sea mine barrage illustrated his performance at its best. Against the opposition of the British Admiralty and of Admiral Sims, the American naval liaison officer in London, Roosevelt argued that a mine net might go far to close the passage between Scotland and Norway to German submarines. In time he won over Daniels and Wilson and even Sims and the Admiralty; and, though the long debate had delayed the decision, the barrage did come into play in time to trap a few submarines before the war came to an end.[13]

Politics receded to the background. For a moment in 1918, he considered Boss Murphy's suggestion that he be the Democratic candidate for Governor in New York. Though Wilson thought he ought to run, Roosevelt said to the President that he could not be asked to "give up war work for what is frankly very much of a local political job in these times." Later F.D.R. remembered that he had suggested Al Smith to Wilson as an alternative; but his recollection appears confused.[14] Certainly his main concern was with the war; the New York gubernatorial negotiations were a minor incident at a time when he was planning a trip to Europe to inspect American naval operations.

VI

War administration gave him not only invaluable training but a sense of developing personal powers. He negotiated contracts with dispatch, speeded up procurement, and backed the proposal for a war labor board made by Felix Frankfurter of the War Department. He put his fingers in everything that concerned the Navy, generally (though not always) contributed clarity and speed, and achieved a reputation as a decisive executive. He had changed markedly from the priggish young man of Albany. Josephus Daniels, looking back years later, exclaimed, "How young and debonair, striding and strong he had been!" Bainbridge Colby thought him "the handsomest and most attractive man in Washington"; the Britisher Nigel Law found him "the most attractive man whom it was my good fortune to meet during my four years in America"; even Walter Camp, the Yale football coach, called him "a beautifully built man, with the long muscles of the athlete."

But questions remained about his thoroughness and depth. On Sunday afternoons Franklin sometimes joined other bright young

men at the house of Justice Oliver Wendell Holmes; years later
Holmes recalled Roosevelt as "a good fellow with rather a soft
edge." This summed up a current impression of a certain shallow-
ness and frivolity, once people looked beyond the physical magnetism and the administrative vigor. "He was likable and attractive," recalled his friend William Phillips, the Assistant Secretary
of State, "but not a heavyweight, brilliant but not particularly
steady in his views. He could charm anybody but lacked great-
ness. He had tremendous vitality, an eagerness and interest in
everything; and he certainly made a very efficient Assistant Secretary of the Navy. He was always amusing, always the life of the
party, but he did not seem fully mature."

The Roosevelts had rented a house on N Street owned by T.R.'s
sister. T.R. himself had occupied it in the first days of his Presidency while he waited for Mrs. McKinley to quit the White House.
Summers, of course, the family went to Campobello, Franklin
joining Eleanor and the children when he could. (In the summer
of 1916, there was a polio epidemic. Roosevelt, abnormally apprehensive, did not permit the children to return until September
and then insisted that his mother fumigate everything at Hyde
Park, where the coachman's child had been stricken.) But the
house on N Street was now the center of their life. Eleanor, on
her own at last, made it a place of friendly hospitality.

She had never before lived so busy a life — official luncheons,
formal calls in the afternoon, state dinners, hideously correct and
ruled by protocol. But Washington under the Democrats had its
relaxed side — baseball or hare-and-hounds with the children in
Rock Creek Park, tennis and golf at the Chevy Chase Club, gay
parties on summer evenings under the rose arbor behind the
N Street house, Sunday suppers, with Eleanor scrambling eggs at
the table in a chafing dish. William and Caroline Phillips were
special friends; the two young couples, along with Secretary of the
Interior Franklin K. Lane and Adolph Miller of the Federal Reserve Board and their wives, dined together regularly throughout
the Wilson administration.

Occasionally Henry Adams asked them for lunch at his house
on Lafayette Square. Once, when F.D.R. expressed worry about a
government decision, Adams looked at him fiercely and said,

"Young man, I have lived in this house many years and seen the occupants of the White House across the square come and go, and nothing that you minor officials or the occupant of that house can do will affect the history of the world for long!" But Eleanor, who remembered Mr. Adams as an old gentleman frisking with her children in his victoria outside the house on N Street, was never able to regard him as quite the cynic he was supposed to be.

The new life was accelerating the drift from the old values. It all somewhat alarmed Sara Delano Roosevelt, watching her children now from afar. "I am sorry to feel that Franklin is tired and that my views are not his," she wrote on one occasion, "but perhaps dear Franklin you may on second thoughts or third thoughts see that I am not so far wrong." The issue remains obscure in the letter, but no one could doubt Sara Roosevelt's dismay at her son's increasing heterodoxy. "What with the trend to 'shirt sleeves,' and the ideas of what men should do in always being all things to all men and striving to give up the old fashioned traditions of family life, simple home pleasures and refinements, and the traditions some of us love best," she wrote emotionally if incoherently, "of what use is it to keep up things, to hold on to dignity and all I stood up for this evening." One could be "as democratic as one likes," she concluded, but she would stick by her " 'old fashioned' theories."

In some respects, the drift from the old values had perhaps gone farther than Sara knew or than Franklin intended. In 1914 Eleanor had employed as social secretary Lucy Mercer, a young Virginia girl of impeccable background. In the next years Roosevelt himself developed a friendly affection for her. She was a sweet, womanly person, somewhat old-fashioned in manner but gay and outgoing; and Roosevelt must have found in her relief from the tensions of work and war. Sometimes she joined him and other friends on a cruise down the Potomac; always her presence was relaxing. Eleanor may have sensed something that summer. Certainly, she delayed her departure to Campobello, and, after she finally left in July, her husband wrote, "You were a goosy girl to think or even to pretend to think that I don't want you here *all* the summer, because you know I do! But honestly *you* ought to have six weeks straight at Campo." He added, "As you know I am unreasonable and touchy now." A few days later he wrote her carelessly of another Potomac cruise; Lucy was in the company; "such a funny party," he noted, "but it worked out *wonderfully!*" It was evidently the enchantment of summer, later fading away.[15]

VII

Franklin had other reasons to be disturbed in 1917. His name, he was told, was on a list for elimination by German agents, and the Secret Service recommended that he carry a revolver as he walked to and from his office. He did so for a few days, until the silliness of it overcame him and he put the gun away. Still, the revolver symbolized the problem of fighting the war in Washington while other men of his generation were dying in trenches. T.R., who had been forty when he left the Navy Department for Cuba in 1898, urged Franklin, who was thirty-five in 1917, to resign and enlist, and Franklin needed no urging. But Josephus Daniels, General Leonard Wood, and Wilson all told him flatly he was more useful where he was. "Neither you nor I nor Franklin Roosevelt," Wilson said to Daniels, "has the right to select the place of service to which our country has assigned us." [16]

Yet safety rankled. Rebuffed in his attempts to resign, he maneuvered for foreign duty in his civilian status. In the spring of 1918 he finally persuaded Daniels that he was now more needed — for a time, at least — in Europe than in Washington. Disdaining the comparative safety of a transport, he elected to cross on a newly commissioned destroyer taking its shakedown cruise as escort for a convoy.

He reveled in every moment of the trip and recorded it all faithfully in his diary — the transports, great black lightless masses, silhouetted astern in the west; the gun drills; the submarine alerts (as Roosevelt retold the story through the years, the German U-boat reported in their vicinity at the Azores came closer every time until he had almost seen it submerge himself). Then to England: he met Lloyd George ("I had a very good time") and George V ("a delightfully easy person to talk to"), consulted with his British opposite members, spent a weekend with Lady Astor at Cliveden, and spoke at a banquet at Gray's Inn, in honor of the ministers responsible for the fighting forces. He told the group at Gray's Inn that his trip to Europe had brought home to him "the necessity for more of this intimate personal relationship" if coalition warfare was to work. One member of his audience should have been listening harder: he was a sturdy, tough, and brilliant Englishman, forty-four years old; his name was Winston Spencer Churchill. Churchill later forgot the meeting, then in his memoirs summoned up a memory of Roosevelt's "magnificent presence in all his youth and strength."

On to France, landing at Dunkirk, driving to Paris (at the Saint Inglebert air base Roosevelt found young Robert A. Lovett in command — "he seems like an awfully nice boy"), calling on Clemenceau ("the wonderful old man"), talking with Marshal Joffre ("his face had a gray look"), and then, in his compulsive search for action, to the front. Furious at the naval attaché who had tried to set up a safe-and-sane tour, Roosevelt pushed himself as near to actual fighting as he could go. He saw Château-Thierry and Belleau Wood and Verdun, was under enemy fire ("the long whining whistle . . . followed by the dull boom and puff of smoke"), and came within a mile of the German lines.

War now had a face for him: the brown earth churned by shells and churned again, the shell holes filled with water, the farmhouses spattered with machine gun shots, the smell of dead horses, the rusty bayonets, broken guns, discarded overcoats, rain-stained love letters, crawling lines of ants; and the many little mounds, some unmarked, some with a bayonet stuck in the earth, some with a helmet, and some, too, with a whittled cross and a tag of wood or wrapping paper and in a pencil scrawl an American name. He took away an indelible impression of it all — the chaos, the waste, the fatigue, "the darkness and constant fighting without rest or sleep." He saw war, and exulted in it, and hated it.

Then Italy (at Turin he met Captain Fiorello H. La Guardia of the Air Corps and at Rome Captain Charles E. Merriam of the Committee on Public Information); back to France; back to England. When he finally returned to New York in September, he was carried ashore on a stretcher, dangerously ill with double pneumonia. A letter from Theodore Roosevelt cheered his convalescence: "We are *very* proud of you." But this was still not enough; his passion was to get into uniform. Restored to health, F.D.R. took his plea once again to the President. Wilson told him that he was too late — he had received the first suggestions of an armistice from Prince Max of Baden and the war would soon be over.[17]

Roosevelt went to Europe again as Assistant Secretary — in 1919, when he was sent to dismantle the naval establishment in Europe. This time Eleanor accompanied him, and they heard the news of Theodore Roosevelt's death in the mid-Atlantic. "I cannot help think that he himself would have had it this way," mused F.D.R., "and that he had been spared a lingering illness of perhaps years." Once in France, the work of naval demobilization went swiftly enough. Most of it was done by Roosevelt's aide, Commander John M. Hancock, who had been head of Navy Purchasing during the war. The Roosevelts meanwhile established themselves at the Ritz in Paris and listened in on the edges of the peace conference. In February they returned with the Wilsons on the *George Washington*. At lunch one day Wilson spoke with fervor of the League. "The United States must go in," he told the Roosevelts, "or it will break the heart of the world, for she is the only nation that all feel is disinterested and all trust." Enthusiastic crowds greeted the President on his arrival in Boston. At lunch the Roosevelts met Governor Calvin Coolidge; Eleanor learned before the rest of the country "how silent the gentleman could be!" On the train to Washington, more crowds cheered the President at every station.[18] It was early 1919, and the world was full of hope.

VIII

The war brought to life the principles of strategy Roosevelt had absorbed from Mahan. It taught him about the requirements of logistics in global war and about problems of coalition diplomacy. In foreign affairs, he now felt that America had "taken on for all time a new relationship" to the world; it would commit a grievous wrong to itself and to all mankind "if it were even to attempt to go backwards towards an old Chinese wall policy of isolation." And, on the domestic side, he ascribed the success of the war effort to the mobilization plan devised by Wilson and Secretary of War

Newton D. Baker: "the conception of the War Industries Board and the control from Washington of every industrial and transportation facility originated in the White House." In other words, he emphasized, "the American organization for war was created *from the top down, not from the bottom up.* This is most important." [19]

The mobilization experience turned his thought to issues of government administration. He felt, for example, that the relationship between foreign policy and military strategy was so close that there must be a mechanism for regular consultation among the State, War, and Navy Departments. In April 1919, he proposed the establishment of a Joint Plan-Making Body, made up of representatives of all three departments and charged with the job of defining American objectives and capabilities. Roosevelt sent this rudimentary sketch for what would later be the National Security Council to the State Department, but never received an acknowledgement. His letter, misdirected to the Division of Latin American Affairs, ended up unread in the State Department archives. [20]

His crusade for efficiency extended also to domestic concerns. He continued his campaign for "some form of universal training for the youth of the country." He had ideas on labor policy: on the one hand, "a larger share of the profits" for labor; on the other, no work stoppages in essential industries ("we can't stand for any small group in a community holding up a community"), with strikes to be prevented by a system of labor courts. He called for the establishment of a federal budget system and severely criticized the functioning of the federal government. "The government of the United States, on the whole, is the least efficient administrative body that we have in the United States," he said early in 1920, adding that "unless we set our own house in order, and, by American constitutional means, make our government as efficient as we would conduct our own private individual businesses . . . it will simply mean the spread of doctrines which seek to effect a change by unconstitutional means." In general, he advocated an increase in executive authority and responsibility and a simplification and speeding-up in the processes of the Congress. [21]

Above all, he took away an exalted conception of the President as *the* leader of the nation. Woodrow Wilson had completed the lesson he had first learned from T.R. As F.D.R. put it in 1920:

Most of our great deeds have been brought about by Executive Leaders, by the Presidents who were not tools of Congress but were true leaders of the Nation, who so truly interpreted the needs and wishes of the people that they were supported in their great tasks. Washington would not have led us to victory in the Revolution if he had merely followed the actions or lack of action of the Continental Congress. Lincoln would not have issued the Emancipation Proclamation if he had heeded the leaders of the Senate. Cleveland would not have maintained the Monroe Doctrine in the Venezuela affair if he had first asked the advice of mere party leaders. Roosevelt would not have kept the Government out of the clutches of predatory interests if he had bowed to Mark Hanna and Foraker and Boss Platt. Wilson's administration would not have been successful in the War if he had not adopted the policy of calling in the experts of the Nation, without regard to party affiliations, in order to create and send across the seas that great Army in record-breaking time.[22]

IX

But as 1919 progressed, the first flush of postwar hope began to fade. In the Navy Department Roosevelt found himself engaged in a discouraging series of controversies — with Admiral Sims over the conduct of the Department; with Captain Joseph K. Taussig over the Daniels-Roosevelt attempt to reform the Navy's prison system; with Procurement over an oil scheme palmed off on Roosevelt and Howe by the high-pressure Yankee promoter, Arthur P. Homer. One result of these disputes was to align him more decisively than ever before with Secretary Daniels as against the admirals. Another was to make him feel more than ever the defects of federal control. In general, he commenced to favor the return of government functions to private industry. "Competitive genius," he said in 1919, "is the key to the manufacturing world; stifled by over-regulation, or confiscated by law, industry dies. . . . In Heaven's name, do not brain industry with the club of politics." The great exception was the radio field, where Roosevelt warmly backed Daniels's project of a government monopoly.[23]

Nor could he escape the nightmares of the year. Attorney-General A. Mitchell Palmer lived across the street; and Franklin and Eleanor Roosevelt returned to their home on a June evening moments after a bomb had blasted in the front of the Palmer house and blown up the man who had planted it. Alice Longworth, arriving on the scene, wrote later that it was "difficult to avoid stepping on bloody chunks of human being," adding, "It was curiously without horror." Still, if Mrs. Longworth remained calm, the rest of the country didn't. In speeches Roosevelt conscientiously warned against the threat of Bolshevism. Yet he by no means enlisted in the Palmer crusade. When the commandant of the Boston Navy Yard fired some machinists as of doubtful loyalty, Roosevelt, discovering that three were Socialists, wrote, at the height of an uproar which was to drive Socialists from the New York Legislature: "Now, my dear Admiral, neither you nor I can fire a man because he happens to be a Socialist." Roosevelt added that the machinist who had circulated Communist literature in the shops should be discharged. "This," Roosevelt said, "is a very different thing from being merely a Socialist." [24]

Nineteen-twenty did not begin happily. Roosevelt was ill again; he had his tonsils out; he looked poorly. The children were sick. He was in trouble with Daniels, who suspected him (not altogether unjustly, in these early stages) of disloyalty in the fight with Sims. He was in trouble with Wilson too; at least on February 22 Daniels noted in his diary, "FDR persona non grata with W." It remains unclear what had disturbed the ailing and irritable President or how long the feeling lasted; another diary entry suggests at least through July. And early in February Lucy Mercer became the second wife of the much older widower Winthrop Rutherfurd. Yet Roosevelt was too resilient to stay down long. The development of the Sims fight soon brought him into closer relations than ever with Daniels. And the approach of the election of 1920 revived his interest in politics.[25]

X

He had signaled his political availability the year before when he spoke before the Democratic National Committee at Chicago, denouncing the Republicans as the party of reaction and hailing the Democrats as the party of progress. In the spring of 1920, Roosevelt and Howe now drew up a series of platform recommendations. The general tone was strongly progressive. One item even called for government borrowing as a means of financing public works in hard times — "we believe such policy," they said, "to be the constructive preventive for acute depression." In the meantime, Roosevelt was mentioned as a possible candidate for the Senate in New York, or, if Al Smith chose not to run, for the governorship, or even for the Vice-Presidency. By June the third possibility had caused enough talk for Roosevelt to complain, not too hard, to his law partner, "I am wondering who started this fool Vice-Presidential boom." As delegates began to converge on San Francisco in late June for the convention, F.D.R. might have had hopes, though, knowing as he did the uncertainties of politics, he could not have had expectations.[26]

From the start, when he wrested the New York standard from the sullen New York delegation to join in the Wilson parade, Roosevelt was an active figure at San Francisco. After Bourke Cockran nominated Smith, Roosevelt made a graceful seconding speech. For the first seven ballots, along with the rest of the New York delegation, he voted for Smith. But Smith was soon outdistanced by McAdoo, the heir of the administration (though not of the President, who wanted a third term for himself), and by James M. Cox, a progressive governor of Ohio who was the candidate of the city machines as well as of those who regarded too close association with the Wilson administration as a liability. When Smith dropped out, Roosevelt voted mostly for McAdoo (though he seems to have cherished dark-horse hopes for John W. Davis), while Boss Murphy and most of the New York delegation went for Cox.

Evidently Murphy, in a last-minute effort to put Cox over, promised without much enthusiasm that he would support Roosevelt for the Vice-Presidency. But, as is usual in such cases, a number of people had the same idea at the same time. Roosevelt's friends had already been active in his behalf; and Cox himself recalls that when his manager asked him his preference for the second place on the ticket, he proposed Roosevelt, whom he did not know but who seemed to meet the requirements of geographical and political balance. Judge Timothy T. Ansberry of Ohio, close to Cox, was also a Roosevelt supporter and eventually put his name in nomination. As for Roosevelt, he took part in none of the decisive conferences and could only have known vaguely what was going on. Indeed, he was chatting idly back of the speakers' platform when Ansberry told him that they were about to make the nominating speeches and that he had better leave the hall.

Al Smith seconded Roosevelt; so did Joe Davies of Wisconsin; and the convention took the idea up with enthusiasm. In a few moments, the other candidates had withdrawn and the nomination was his by acclamation. It was a popular choice. As Walter Lippmann promptly wired Roosevelt, "When cynics ask what is the use we can answer that when parties can pick a man like Frank Roosevelt there is a decent future in politics." Other congratulations tumbled in. Herbert Hoover wrote that he considered it a contribution to the good of the country, adding that it would bring the merit of a great public servant to the front. From New York the chairman of the Rockland County Democratic Committee sent in his congratulations; James A. Farley had not yet begun to sign his name in green ink. Robert H. Jackson of Jamestown wrote that the nomination "renews my interest in politics, which for the last few years has considerably waned." But Roosevelt's Groton schoolmate and onetime friend Colonel Robert R. McCormick of the Chicago *Tribune* thought differently. "He is to put the honey of a name on the trap of a ticket," said the *Tribune* with scorn. "Franklin is as much like Theodore as a clam is like a bear cat. . . . If he is Theodore Roosevelt, Elihu Root is Gene Debs, and Bryan is a brewer." [27]

XI

The political outlook was dim for the Democrats, and they knew it. But for Roosevelt personally the opportunity of a national campaign, winning him the acquaintance of local leaders, establishing him as a national figure, was an exciting prospect. It was also one more fulfillment of the parallel with T.R., who had been forty-two years old — four years older than F.D.R. — when he had been nominated for the Vice-Presidency twenty years earlier. F.D.R. flung himself into the campaign with high spirits. Returning from San Francisco, he began to sense that the League of Nations was a popular issue; and, when he stopped to confer with Cox at Columbus, he told a press conference that he regarded the League as "the dominant issue of the campaign." Refurbishing a favorite metaphor, he later spoke of it as a fire department which would prevent the spreading of fire from a neighbor's house to one's own. Cox and Roosevelt hit it off pleasantly, though the presidential candidate briskly slapped down a characteristic suggestion from his running mate that the Vice-President be promised a seat in cabinet meetings.

A few days later the two men made a pilgrimage to Washington to see the President. They found Wilson in a wheelchair on the White House portico, his face gaunt and sunken, a shawl concealing his paralyzed left arm. He said, in a weak voice, "Thank you for coming. I am very glad you came." The warmhearted Cox was much moved; Roosevelt noticed his glasses mist up with tears. Later Cox said, "Mr. President, we are going to be a million per cent with you, and your Administration, and that means the League." [28]

There remained only the farewell to the Navy. It was a gala occasion: organized labor presented him with a loving cup; loyal employees filed in to shake him by the hand. Roosevelt, reviewing his years in Washington, saw things now in mellow perspective. "No words I write will make you know better than you know now how much our association has meant," he told Josephus Daniels in a longhand note. "All my life I shall look back — not only on the *work* of the place — but mostly on the wonderful way in which you and I have gone through these nearly eight years *together*. You have taught me so wisely and kept my feet on the ground when I was about to skyrocket — and in it all there has never been a real dispute or antagonism or distrust."

"Please let me keep on coming to you," F.D.R. concluded, "to get your fine inspiration of real idealism and right living and good Americanism."

Daniels replied. "We will be brothers in all things that make for the good of our country." [29]

Then to Hyde Park, for the official ceremonies of notification. The local committee was under the chairmanship of a Dutchess County neighbor, Henry Morgenthau, Jr.; and the happy crowd filled the lawns before his mother's house, while he delivered his acceptance address from the front porch. He had worked hard on the speech, and it summed up the campaign as he saw it. Two issues stood out: the need for an affirmative policy in foreign affairs and the "pressing need of organized progress at home." He defended the League as the road to peace. He called for the improvement of working conditions, for the reorganization of government (including the Congress), for resources development according to "a continuing plan." The hope for "normal conditions" he dismissed as a foolish dream. "We can never go back. The 'good old days' are gone past forever; we have no regrets. . . . We must go forward or flounder. . . . We oppose a mere period of coma in our national life." [30]

XII

Roosevelt planned an extensive campaign. Howe could not join him at first because of unfinished business at the Navy Department; but he borrowed Stephen Early, whom they had known as the Associated Press man at the Navy Department, to serve as advance man, and took another veteran newspaperman, Marvin McIntyre, from naval public relations to travel on the special train. Charles McCarthy, still another member of F.D.R.'s Navy team, remained behind to backstop operations in New York. McCarthy's secretary, Marguerite LeHand, was a handsome blue-eyed, black-haired girl of great efficiency and calm.

For Roosevelt's party the campaign was the best of fun. They went merrily from place to place, greeting politicians and the press, addressing party rallies, relaxing at midnight over cards. Steve Early later told Harold Ickes that Roosevelt did not take life seriously enough in 1920, that he was just a playboy, preferring poker to speech conferences. Yet he spoke with vigor and effect, until campaigning exuberance led him to claim one day in Montana that he had written the constitution of Haiti, and that the Central American republics would automatically vote with the

United States if the United States entered the League. This intrusion of rather crass realism, compounded by Roosevelt's extravagant version of his own role, invited Republican attack. Harding called the Roosevelt statement "the most shocking assertion that ever emanated from a responsible member of the government of the United States." In the end Roosevelt made the politician's false claim that he had been misquoted, but the damage had been done and Roosevelt's rash boast haunted him for years to come.

In the Northwest he spoke with eloquence of resources development. "Where we have spent a hundred millions up to now," he said of reclamation projects, "we must spend ten times that figure in the immediate future. . . . I look for the day, and that at no distant time, when every gallon of water in our streams will be used for practical purposes, instead of allowing it to run to waste." He denounced Harding as "evasive, indefinite, weak, reactionary." And, in Centralia, Washington, where Legionnaires and Wobblies had murdered each other, he described his visit as a pilgrimage to the graves "of the martyred members of the American Legion who here gave their lives in the sacred cause of Americanism" and pledged his determination to rid the land of those "who seek by violence to destroy the Constitution and Institutions of America." [31]

He was apparently effective enough in his appeal to Progressive Republicans to make the Republican National Committee send Theodore Roosevelt, Jr., west after him. "He is a maverick," said young Theodore of Franklin in what he conceived to be the patois of Wyoming. "He does not have the brand of our family." But F.D.R. was not deterred by Oyster Bay superciliousness. His mother always used to say, when asked why the other Roosevelts disliked them, "Perhaps it's because we are so much better looking." He kept up the pace through September and October, speaking until his voice grew raw, giving almost a thousand speeches in all. He appeared to radiate confidence, but, when McIntyre once quietly asked him if he had any illusions that he might be elected, he replied, "Nary an illusion." To an English friend he wrote early in October, "We are cutting down our opponents' lead. . . . Whatever the result may be, it will have been a most interesting experience." [32]

XIII

Harding's victory came as no surprise. Roosevelt interpreted it as the inevitable result of the "tidal flow of discontent and destructive criticism" following the war. "Every war brings after it a period of materialism and conservatism; people tire quickly of ideals and we are now repeating history." When he wrote this, he perhaps had in mind a remark Wilson had made to him. "It is only once in a generation that a people can be lifted above material things," Wilson had said. "That is why conservative government is in the saddle two-thirds of the time."

In a post-election meeting with Cox, Roosevelt predicted that the Democrats would not elect a President until a fairly serious depression had occurred. All that could be hoped for, Roosevelt told friends abroad, was that the new administration would not be "so tremendously reactionary as to fan the flames of Radicalism." He gave his campaign associates initialed gold cuff links and arranged for annual reunions where they might look ahead as well as back. "Thank the Lord we are both comparatively youthful!" he wrote Steve Early.

In Washington Josephus Daniels, the retiring Secretary of the Navy, informed Admiral Taylor, whom he considered the ablest officer in the Department, that Theodore Roosevelt, Jr., was slated as Assistant Secretary in the new administration. The Admiral wearily shook his head. "I have had to stand two Roosevelts," he said. "I cannot try another." [33]

After a decade, Franklin Roosevelt was a private citizen once more. He returned without enthusiasm to his rather sedate law partnership but also entered with somewhat more interest into a new job — vice-president in charge of the New York office of the Fidelity and Deposit Company of Maryland, a surety bonding firm. Finance appealed to him more than the law. In addition, he undertook varied civic and charitable activities. It was an exhausting year, culminating in an unpleasant if ineffective attempt by the Republican majority of a Senate investigating committee to smear him with old Navy Department scandals. When Van-Lear Black, the Fidelity and Deposit's president, offered in August to take him to Campobello on his yacht, Roosevelt accepted with gratitude.

XIV

They ran into rough weather in the Bay of Fundy, and Roosevelt, who alone knew the waters, had to stand long hours at the wheel until the boat was safely in harbor. The next day, they fished for cod from a small boat. As he was preparing bait, he suddenly slipped overboard. "I never felt anything so cold as that water!" he later said. ". . . so cold it seemed paralyzing." On the following day, August 10, 1921, as he cruised with his family near Campobello, they saw a blue haze rising over an island nearby. In the air was the pungent smell of burning spruce. Roosevelt quickly rallied his children to fight the forest fire. Armed with evergreen boughs, they beat the roaring flames until the fire was under control. "Our eyes were bleary with smoke; we were begrimed, smarting with spark-burns, exhausted." With characteristic energy, Roosevelt now decreed a two-mile dogtrot across Campobello Island, a fresh-water swim, and a dip in the freezing waters of the bay. This accomplished, they ran back in their bathing suits along hot, dusty roads to the house.

The mail had just arrived. Roosevelt felt a chill, but he could not wait to get the latest news. He sat on in his wet bathing suit, opening letters and papers, until he suddenly felt too tired to dress. "I'd never felt quite that way before," he later remembered. The next morning when he swung out of bed, his left leg dragged behind. He told himself that it was some muscular quirk, or perhaps a touch of lumbago. But he was running a fever and beginning to ache. Presently he had no reactions in the left leg at all, then none in the other.[34]

31. Trial by Fire

THERE BEGAN a grim period of uncertainty. Doctors were summoned. One, misinterpreting the symptoms, prescribed massage. Louis Howe arrived. He sat on Roosevelt's bed, rubbing his feet and back, while Roosevelt said again and again, "I don't know what is the matter with me, Louis. I just don't know." Then a specialist made a definite diagnosis of acute anterior poliomyelitis, stopped massage, and recommended hot baths and patience. Howe, along with Roosevelt's uncle, Frederic A. Delano, arranged for transportation to New York, Howe keeping the story from the press as long as possible in order to minimize the damage to Roosevelt's political future. They carried him by stretcher down to the beach, onto a motorboat, up a steep gangway, and passed him through a window into the special train. Franklin, Jr., remembers seeing his father: "he managed to wave to me, and his whole face burst into a tremendous sunny smile. So I decided he couldn't be so sick after all."

But he was sicker than even the doctors at first suspected. At Presbyterian Hospital in New York specialists became pessimistic, afraid that he might never sit up again. As for Roosevelt himself, who had lived by his exuberance of physical vitality, now struck down at the top of his life, no one knows what went through his mind those days. He would not let others see his own fears. "He is very cheerful and hopeful," reported his doctor in New York, "and has made up his mind that he is going to go out of the hospital in the course of two or three weeks on crutches." But good cheer was doubtless therapy, aimed as much at convincing himself as others. Lying awake in the dark of night, broken and helpless, brooding on the brilliance of the past and the bleakness of the future, choking down the fury and the despair, he must have gone through agony. He later used to claim Henley's "Invictus" as his favorite poem.[1]

II

In the meantime, a tense battle was taking place over his future. Sara Roosevelt felt with all her pent-up maternal passion that Franklin should resign himself to invalidism, retire to Hyde Park, and live the life of a country gentleman. Illness was offering her the opportunity, as one of her grandchildren later put it, "to reassume complete domination of her son's life." But everyone else — Roosevelt, his doctors, Louis Howe, above all, Eleanor Roosevelt — felt that he must return to normal activity as soon as he could.

Eleanor Roosevelt was no longer the timid girl who had unquestioningly accepted her mother-in-law's control fifteen years earlier. Washington had given her a measure of liberation, the consequence partly of separation, partly of the active life thrust upon her by war and by her work in hospitals and canteens. As late as 1920 she still sometimes felt herself awkward and uncertain. Once that year, she left a dinner party to tuck the children in bed and hear their prayers. Her husband finally went upstairs to see why she was gone so long. "I just can't stand to greet all those people," she said in tears. "I know they all think I am dull and unattractive. I just want to hide up here."

Still the campaign helped, particularly by bringing her close for the first time to Louis Howe. In Albany and Washington she had resented Howe's intimacy with her husband. But on the campaign train Howe made special efforts to reassure her, asking her opinion of speeches and assisting her through her moments of shyness. The new friendship became crucially important after her husband's illness. Howe was more than ever ready to devote his life to getting Roosevelt to the White House. Polio might make the job more difficult; "but, by gad, legs or no legs, Franklin will be President." He counted on Eleanor to keep Franklin in touch with people and with politics.

The winter after Campobello was hard in the overcrowded house in New York. It was, said Eleanor Roosevelt, "the most trying winter of my entire life." Sara felt that her daughter-in-law and Howe were tiring Franklin; the discussions over his care often became acrimonious. Regarding Howe as the source of the trouble, Sara launched a drive to get him out of the house, urging on fifteen-year-old Anna that it was grossly unfair for Howe to have a large front bedroom while she had a tiny top-floor bedroom in the back of the house. At her grandmother's instigation, Anna went to her mother and demanded a switch. Scenes followed. On occasions, temper flared at the dinner table and Anna, bursting into tears, retired sobbing to her room. Once while reading to the youngest boys Eleanor herself dissolved into a flood of uncontrollable tears and could not stop.

Yet, under Howe's prodding, she continued her program of self-assertion. She learned to swim and to drive a car. She began to mix in public affairs. Even before her husband's illness, she had done some work for the League of Women Voters. This had brought her into touch with able, social-minded professional women who greatly enlarged her horizons. Through Rose Schneiderman, she became interested in the Women's Trade Union League. Lillian Wald and Mary Simkhovitch brought her into social work circles. Marion Dickerman and Nancy Cook involved her in the Women's Division of the Democratic State Committee. She became concerned with party organization, started a paper for the Women's Division, and began to make regular political tours through the state, talking with local leaders. The worst hurdle of all was public speaking. When she was frightened, her voice became high and shrill and tended to break into a nervous giggle. "You were terrible," Howe would say afterward in his gruff-sweet manner. "There was nothing funny — why did you laugh? . . . Keep your voice down, and for Heaven's sake stop that silly giggling." Eleanor swallowed and learned, took voice lessons, gained skill and gained confidence. She ignored the latest fashions, wore her watch pinned on her bosom, and remained a stern prohibitionist; but she had made herself an able executive and a forceful and charming personality.[2]

III

As for Roosevelt, he leaned heavily on her. But he fought the essential battle — the interior battle — himself. His public mask was never more effective. Only once did she hear him say anything even bordering on discouragement. That had been a casual observation that they might as well spend money on a houseboat on the chance that it might help him be less useless in the future — a mild enough remark after so grim an ordeal. Grace Tully, who worked with him from 1928 to his death, wrote that he "never indulged in self-pity or otherwise gave outward indication that he felt annoyance at the restrictions caused by his illness." Dr. Ross McIntire, later his White House physician, said, "No one ever saw him indulge in so much as a moment of self-pity."

There were, of course, silent indications. Roosevelt had loved golf, but, after his illness, Eleanor never heard him mention golf again (though he did mention it to others); nor did he return to his once loved Campobello for a dozen years. But after the first rush of despair, as he told McIntire, he resolved to give everything he had to licking the disease. He knew that this would require the most extraordinary will, but he did not falter. "Since the beginning," wrote Louis Howe, "I do not remember one complaint, one objection to the terrific discipline which he imposed upon himself." Almost fiercely, he looked forward rather than back, dedicating himself to the task of reconquering health and activity.

It was hard, at first. It was even hard to restore a sense of normality in the household. He tried to remove the sadness and the strangeness for his children by showing them his legs and identifying the muscles; he shouted with glee over a quiver in a muscle that had been dormant. Gradually his ability to poke fun at himself as he learned to move around broke the tension. He exercised on a set of bars in the Hyde Park garden; or walked with painful slowness on crutches along the driveway, beads of perspiration forming on his forehead; or crawled to the edge of the swimming pool and let himself down, saying wryly, the Bay of Fundy in his mind, "Water got me into this fix, water will get me out again!" Soon he began to see people again. When Josephus Daniels made his first visit, Roosevelt, from his bed, fetched him a blow that nearly made him lose balance. "You thought you were coming to see an invalid," F.D.R. said, "but I can knock you out in any bout." All that was wrong was that he had lost power in his leg muscles. "I am determined to have this power brought back and then I can outrun you." [3]

He worked at his stamp collection, built model boats at a workbench and sailed them with Howe in the Hudson, edited records of the town of Hyde Park, negotiated with Famous Players–Lasky over a screen play based on the life of John Paul Jones, pored over catalogues to order naval prints, and talked eagerly with friends and visitors. He read endlessly: history and local documents, Hoover's *American Individualism* ("I have taken great pleasure in reading it"), and the brash new weekly launched that year by Henry R. Luce ("My only criticism is that occasionally, in the need of being brief, TIME has made statements in regard to events which are not wholly fact").

After a while, leaning on crutches, with his legs stiffened by heavy iron braces, he returned to work at the Fidelity and Deposit, and on occasion he took houseboat cruises in Florida waters or rented cottages in New England. One friend recalls Howe's offering breakfast at a small house in Marion, Massachusetts: "This is to make you strong. I will see that you become President of the United States."

And all the time Roosevelt worked away, exercising endlessly, watching patiently and without complaint for signs of life in his dead limbs. The process both generated optimism and was lubricated by it. He could not go on without hope: 1921 (to Richard E. Byrd) — "By next Autumn I will be ready to chase the nimble moose with you!"; 1922 (to Leonard Wood, describing the condition of his muscles) — "They are all coming back"; 1923, finally abandoning active membership in the local country club — I "cannot possibly play golf for a year or two"; 1924 (to General Richman P. Davis) — "Just as soon as that day comes I shall try my hand at golf again"; 1925 (to Joe Tumulty) — "I am keeping everlastingly at it, and hope to be able to walk by this time next year." [4]

He found swimming the best exercise because the water removed weight from his legs. In the summer of 1924, George Foster Peabody, an old friend, wrote him about the therapeutic values of the natural springs at a ramshackle health resort he owned in western Georgia called Warm Springs. Roosevelt, eager to try anything, inquired further, and that fall he rented one of the cottages around the rambling old wooden hotel. In a pool nearby the water had a temperature of 89 degrees in addition to an unusually high specific gravity; its warmth and buoyancy were ideally adapted to exercising paralyzed muscles. Feeling immediate improvement, he decided to come back in the spring.

A newspaper story about Roosevelt's "swimming himself back to health" attracted national attention, and other paralytics started to come to Warm Springs the next year. Roosevelt himself, in the absence of medical supervision, took charge. He helped his fellow sufferers in their exercises and, with his cheerfulness, lifted their spirits and gave them hope. As patients continued to arrive, he began to import doctors. But it became clear that some more organized solution was necessary. In 1926 Roosevelt persuaded a committee of orthopedists to investigate the medical possibilities of Warm Springs. Following their favorable report, he bought the springs and facilities from Peabody in 1927, vesting title in the Warm Springs Foundation. The Foundation proceeded to transform the resort into a center for the treatment of polio victims. Roosevelt assumed personal financial responsibility, staking over two hundred thousand dollars, perhaps two-thirds of his fortune, on the venture. He did it with unquenchable enthusiasm. He owed much to Warm Springs — for the challenge to his executive energies as well as for the buoyancy of its waters. He built a cottage of his own, where neighbors began to leave small gifts of flowers, strawberries, or honey on the doorstep. There, on Pine Mountain, amidst the peach blossoms and the azaleas, under the blazing Georgia sun, he found his second home.[5]

IV

As vitality returned, he began to resume his business and political activities. Howe, now irrevocably attached to him, was his diligent aide in both fields. Marguerite LeHand, staying on from the 1920 campaign, took over the duties of a confidential secretary. "Missy," as she was known in the family, was lovely, composed, stylish, intelligent, and absolutely loyal; far more than a secretary, she became for him a gracious presence and an ever loving friend. Eleanor Roosevelt was each day a more valuable member of the team. Roosevelt depended most on her for reports of the outside world. His searching questions about what she had seen trained her faculties of observation until she learned to miss nothing and to remember everything.

The Fidelity and Deposit Company provided him with a foothold downtown. His law partnership with Langdon Marvin, which he had begun after his election to the state Senate in 1910 and had re-entered in 1920, did not fit his new life. This was partly because of the physical difficulty of climbing the stairs to his old office, but more because of the type of business — "mostly estates, wills etc.," said Roosevelt, "all of which bore me to death." In 1924 he severed his connection with Emmet, Marvin and Roosevelt, and a few months later entered a new partnership with a shrewd, salty Irishman named Basil O'Connor. With O'Connor, he found himself in faster legal company; and the new practice, which roamed in a venturesome way into the corporate field, was much more congenial.[6]

He seemed to get his greatest excitement, however, out of a miscellany of business promotions and speculations along the way. He had a gambler's zest for new ideas, and, while he never gambled very much on any single one of them, he examined every new scheme with preliminary enthusiasm. Many ingenious ideas flitted through that resourceful mind: the use of marks to buy corporate stock during the German inflation; the establishment of commercial dirigible lines in the United States: the selling of advertising space in taxis; the development of automatic vending machines and of quarter-in-the-slot cameras; the prospect of cornering the lobster market.[7]

This was Roosevelt's restless share in the intoxication of the New Era. More serious was his presidency of the American Construction Council, the trade association for the building industry, founded in 1922 on the inspiration, in part, of Secretary of Commerce Hoover. Roosevelt was concerned here not only with fighting the business cycle by leveling out the construction curve but with encouraging industrial self-government as an alternative to government intervention. "Government regulation," he said in 1922, "is not feasible. It is unwieldy, it is expensive." Yet, citing Hoover, he argued that the trend was toward public control. "Unless we control ourselves, the Government is undoubtedly going to step in, in some form, in the coming years."

Industrial self-government required information, however; and, when he proposed to Hoover that the Commerce Department cooperate by developing a building index, Hoover sternly rebuked him for inviting government interference. In the end, the Council never received adequate support from industry or government. Roosevelt maintained his connection until 1928 but finally felt that it would take the shock of depression to bring about reorganization in the industry.[8]

Yet, even while law and business absorbed time and energy, politics remained his abiding preoccupation. Materialism might dominate the age, and even Roosevelt's private business life, but it was not to dominate the Democratic party. In a message to a Jackson Day dinner a few months after his illness, he proclaimed the necessity of keeping "the control of our government out of the hands of professional money-makers" and denounced the Republicans for their belief that laws "designed to make men very rich without regard to the rest of the nation can bring about a prosperous and happy country." If he could not travel, he could at least write letters. With Howe's aid, he began a farflung correspondence with Democratic politicians across the land. The theme was constantly repeated — the party must reconsecrate itself "to the principles of progressive democracy," though with an effort to avoid "the more radical views, such as those of the non-partisan league."

He bobbed back swiftly into state politics. When Al Smith was reluctant to run for Governor again in 1922, Roosevelt played a leading role in inducing him to accept the nomination. He continued a wary process of reconciliation with Tammany, supporting Dr. Royal S. Copeland, the Tammany candidate for Senator in 1922, and publicly lamenting in 1924 the death of his old enemy Boss Murphy — "the strongest and wisest Leader" the New York City organization had had in generations. When the dashing

Jimmy Walker was elected mayor in 1925, Roosevelt wrote him a trifle optimistically, "I know that you will make good 100 per cent."

As the 1924 election approached, Roosevelt pressed his efforts to make the Democrats the party of liberalism. "It seems to me that we have got to nominate a really progressive, if not a radical Democrat," he told one correspondent, adding, ". . . if I did not still have these crutches I should throw my own hat in the ring." He might not wish to throw his hat in the ring then, but Howe, in a series of confidential conversations in 1923 and 1924, did his best to keep Roosevelt's name alive. (Among those with whom Howe consulted on Roosevelt's behalf was Lewis Green Stevenson of Illinois, son of one Adlai Stevenson and father of another.) Some even suggested F.D.R. for the Vice-Presidency; but he responded, "I do not want to be Vice-President. To have to preside over the United States Senate, as at present constituted, for four whole years would be a thankless, disagreeable and perfectly futile task."

v

Initially he looked with favor on McAdoo for 1924. But the setback to the McAdoo campaign, following the disclosure of Mc-Adoo's acceptance of a retainer from Doheny, inclined him toward Smith. He continued to fear that Smith was not enough of a national figure, and Howe predicted that McAdoo, if he could not win, would at least have enough delegates to block Smith. But Smith, anxious to open contact with western and southern leaders, invited Roosevelt to be his nominal campaign manager; and Roosevelt, who knew that the party required both its agrarian and its urban wings, accepted.

He was almost alone in emerging with distinction from the harrowing days at Madison Square Garden. Roosevelt, said the *Herald Tribune*, was "the one man whose name would stampede the convention"; he was, said the *World*, "the real hero . . . the one leader commanding the respect and admiration of delegations from all sections." Harry Byrd of Virginia wrote that Roosevelt was "the most popular figure in the convention" and that he hoped the time would come when he could support his presidential candidacy. Another delegate quoted Tom Pendergast of Kansas City as saying of Roosevelt, "the most magnetic personality of any individual I have ever met, and I predict he will be the candidate on the Democratic ticket in 1928." [9]

After the convention, Roosevelt rebuffed any suggestion that he might be a candidate for Governor. Warm Springs was now on his agenda, and he played little part in the campaign. In October he told Eleanor that he was philosophic enough to think that if Coolidge were elected, "we shall be so darned sick of conservatism of the old money-controlled crowd in four years that we [will] get a real progressive landslide in 1928." After the election he was more pessimistic. "Much as we Democrats may be the party of honesty and progress," he wrote, "the people will not turn out the Republicans while wages are good and markets are booming. . . . I only wish that the Democrats throughout the country could unite more closely, get rid of their factionalism and their localism, get a better hearing from the press and put their national organization on a sound financial basis."

This last sentiment led to his circular letter of December 1924 with his proposals for reorganizing the party machinery. Though this project fizzled out, the effort helped re-establish Roosevelt as a national leader. In letter after letter, he warned the party against dissipating its energy in sectional quarrels or in premature battles over personalities. There had been enough of "this unspeakable groping about in the darkness"; the need was for unity and affirmation: "There is one common ground — Progressive Democracy — on which we can all agree." This did not mean ultraradicalism; "to rush blindly along paths proclaimed as highways to Utopia by some of our friends would be to find ourselves hopelessly mired in the quicksands of untried political theories"; but it did mean steady progress — not "Conservatism with a move on" but "Progressivism with a brake on." There were too many progressives at present in the Republican party, too many conservatives in the Democratic: "I cannot help feeling that a realignment will come." [10]

But in what direction should the party move? Roosevelt was beginning to formulate tentative ideas. He was troubled by the belief of many Democrats that "we should have *less* governing from Washington with a decrease in the existing functions of the national government." Such a program overlooked the hard fact that "the complexities of modern civilization and the breaking down of state boundaries in such agencies as public utilities, interstate commerce and the kind of selling of commodities through country-wide large corporations, seem in many cases to demand some form of government requisition to prevent abuses or extortion." In his address as temporary chairman of the Democratic state convention in 1926, Roosevelt gave concise expression to his developing view of the responsibilities of government. It represented a sharp break from the party's traditional Jeffersonianism.

If we accept the phrase "the best government is the least government" we must understand that it applies to the simplification of governmental machinery, and to the prevention of improper interference with the legitimate private acts of the citizens, but a nation or a State which is unwilling by governmental action to tackle the new problems, caused by immense increase of population and by the astounding strides of modern science, is headed for decline and ultimate death.

He continued to see little hope in the age of "gross materialism"; "the stone wall which we all face at the present moment is, of course, the complacency of the multitude of voters." Yet "in spite of what our bank friends say, the country cannot keep going industrially at 100 % forever." And beneath the absorption in the money game he discerned other qualities in the people. "Our public men are, at this moment, politically afraid of idealism, but it doesn't change the fact that the country still is willing to listen to things other than materialistic." Yet it would take time. Nineteen-twenty-eight might well be too soon. "Frankly," Roosevelt wrote one correspondent, "I do not look for a Democratic president until after the 1932 election." [11]

VI

In the meantime, there were politics in New York. Smith and others tried to draft Roosevelt for the Senate in 1926. He turned them down. This was partly because he did not want to interrupt his exercises: "if I devote another two years to them I shall be on my feet again without my braces." But it was partly too because he could not endure the thought of life in the Senate. "I like administrative or executive work, but do not want to have my hands and feet tied and my wings clipped for six long years. . . . My explosions would come at too frequent intervals to be effective."

In other respects, however, he faithfully followed the Smith lead in New York. Indeed, when Louis Howe heard in 1927 that a group of southern drys, headed by Carter Glass, were about to propose that Smith withdraw as a presidential possibility in Roosevelt's favor, Howe feared that the Smith forces would resent this as an independent Roosevelt bid for the nomination. "I threw enough cold water on the idea," Howe wrote Roosevelt, "to extinguish the Woolworth Building." Roosevelt later wrote to Josephus Daniels arguing against a compromise choice, such as himself, for the presidential nomination, and making out a strong case for Smith. "Strictly between ourselves," he added, "I am very doubtful whether any Democrat can win in 1928." [12]

Roosevelt genuinely admired Smith's administrative intelligence and drive. He regarded him with personal affection, and he thought he would make an excellent candidate. In a long letter to Smith in 1926, he outlined in masterly fashion the tactics Smith should follow if he wanted the nomination in 1928. But Roosevelt was not a member of the Smith inner circle; and Smith seems to have looked on him as a dilettante, useful as window dressing for the party but not to be taken too seriously. Even in this period there was minor friction between them. As chairman of the Taconic State Park Commission, Roosevelt sent Smith a letter criticizing him for yielding to Robert Moses and canceling a through parkway in Dutchess County. "I know of no man I have met in my whole public career who I have any stronger affection for than yourself," Smith characteristically replied. "Therefore, you can find as much fault with me as you like. I will not get into a fight with you for anything or for anybody. But that does not stop me from giving you a little tip and the tip is don't be so sure about things that you have not the personal handling of yourself." [13]

This flare-up did not, however, disturb a basically cordial relationship. As the 1928 convention approached, Roosevelt worked ever more actively for Smith. For Vice-President, Roosevelt favored Cordell Hull of Tennessee: "I am old-fashioned enough to believe that the nominee for Vice-President should be chosen with the thought that the Almighty might call on him to succeed to the presidency, and Hull would make a fine President." So far as platform was concerned, Roosevelt plugged his familiar issues: agriculture, government reorganization, "preservation of national resources, particularly water power, in the ultimate ownership of the people," internationalism in foreign policy, and "substitution of a Democratic Government of practical idealism in the place of an Oligarchy of gross materialism." He tried to educate Smith on issues like foreign affairs and farm policy about which the New York governor, even as a potential presidential nominee, was ignorant. The hostility to Smith as a Roman Catholic particularly enraged Roosevelt: It "makes my blood boil," he wrote to Daniels, "as a Protestant of a long line of wholly Protestant ancestry." His indignation over religious issues grew steadily more intense, until he ended by denouncing what he called "a very un-American, a very disgraceful and a very vile campaign." [14]

At the Houston convention in June he sustained the striking impression he had made at Madison Square Garden four years earlier. His movement around the floor, no longer on crutches, but with his legs locked in braces, leaning on a cane and the arm of a son, gave a plausible picture of physical near-recovery. He served as Smith's floor manager, nominated him, and was an important element of harmony in a notably harmonious gathering. But Smith, still looking on Roosevelt as a handsome façade rather than as a serious politician, paid little attention to his ideas about the campaign. He rejected Roosevelt's doubts about Raskob as national chairman and his arguments against the strategy of competing for big business support. By August Roosevelt was complaining that he rarely could get in to see the candidate, even to discuss so important a problem as persuading McAdoo to come out for him. In the meantime, Roosevelt worked away as head of the Businessmen's Division at national headquarters. His wife, whose work in New York had won the respect of the party professionals, was in charge of the Women's Division.

VII

In September Roosevelt went to Warm Springs. During the summer much pressure had been brought on him to accept the nomination for Governor in New York. But he was more determined than ever to let nothing stand in the way of complete physical recovery. Almost as important, 1928 looked neither to him nor to Howe a Democratic year. The pressure continued, however, and, when the Democrats convened in Rochester late in September, the leaders were agreed that Roosevelt's presence on the state ticket, by carrying New York for the Democrats, might make the difference between national victory and defeat for Smith. Howe, anticipating a squeeze play against Roosevelt, warned him by telegraph: THE WAY THINGS ARE RUNNING HERE MY CONVICTION THAT YOU SHOULD NOT RUN IS STRONGER THAN EVER AND ELEANOR AGREES. But the only excuse that would be accepted, he added, was the health plea. ANY OTHER REASON WILL BE OVERRULED BY THE GOVERNOR HIMSELF.

For several days telegraph and telephone wires hummed between Warm Springs and the North. IF THEY ARE LOOKING FOR GOAT WHY DONT WAGNER SACRIFICE HIMSELF, wired Howe sourly on the 26th. Hoping to end the boom, Roosevelt issued a definite refusal to the press. When Smith called him personally (Howe: GOVERNOR TRYING TO REACH YOU . . . BEWARE OF GREEKS BEARING GIFTS), Roosevelt said that his chances for walking again depended on keeping up his regimen at Warm Springs: "As I am only 46 years of age, I feel that I owe it to my family and myself to give the present constant improvement a chance to continue." His daughter wired: GO AHEAD AND TAKE IT; Roosevelt replied, YOU OUGHT TO BE SPANKED. MUCH LOVE. PA. Smith enlisted others in the attempt to change Roosevelt's mind. Ed Flynn, boss of the Bronx, called; Roosevelt now mentioned not only his health but his financial responsibilities to the Warm Springs Foundation. When Flynn suggested to Smith that Roosevelt might run if Warm Springs were taken care of, Smith confidently replied, "Tell him that it will be all right. I don't know how the hell we are going to do it, but we'll do it some way." Soon Raskob agreed to underwrite Roosevelt's Warm Springs obligations.

At this point Eleanor Roosevelt arrived in Rochester, and efforts were made to add her to the claque. She refused to argue with her husband; but Flynn, at least, and Raskob, received the impression that she hoped he would run, and she finally consented to try and get him on the phone. Roosevelt, who had already started to evade phone calls, had now left Warm Springs for the day, with no word where he could be reached. Eleanor's call finally caught up with him when he was addressing a Democratic rally a few miles from Warm Springs. Eventually, after spinning out the speech from sheer perversity, he took the call in a drugstore phone booth. His wife, who had to catch the sleeper to New York, handed the phone over to Smith, then vanished. She was not to know how the conversation came out until she bought a paper in New York the next day.

Smith found a nightmare of static on the line; no one could hear anything. The operator suggested they try again when Roosevelt got back to Warm Springs. This time the connection was clear. Raskob gave his assurances about the Foundation; Smith set forth the political arguments; Herbert H. Lehman, a New York banker of known executive competence, came on to say that he was prepared to run for Lieutenant-Governor and relieve Roosevelt whenever he wanted to leave the state. Smith, desperate, returned to plead with Roosevelt to accept as a personal favor to him. Roosevelt, with Missy LeHand by his side crying "Don't you dare — don't you dare," remained negative. Finally Smith asked whether, if nominated, he would refuse to run. Roosevelt slowly replied that he did not know. That was all that was necessary.

The next morning the convention nominated Roosevelt by acclamation. Howe, throwing up his hands, wired: MESS IS NO NAME FOR IT. . . . FOR ONCE I HAVE NO ADVICE TO GIVE. And, again: TELL MISSY YOUR MISSUS AND MYSELF ARE JUST AS PLEASED AS SHE IS. Though his wife later expressed doubt whether he would ever have walked again in any case, there can be no question that Roosevelt himself felt he was surrendering his last chance for total recovery. "I never knew a man to make greater sacrifice than you did," wrote Raskob, "in coming to the aid of our Party." As for Warm Springs, Roosevelt did not accept Raskob's proffered loan of $350,000, but Raskob in the next years was a generous supporter of the Foundation. Years later Roosevelt told Emil Ludwig, "I didn't want it," smiting himself on the knee; "I wanted, much more, to get my right leg to move! . . . But the moral pressure was too strong." [15]

VIII

The Republican press was quick to picture the crippled Roosevelt as the pathetic victim of Smith's insensate ambition. Smith cracked back, "A Governor does not have to be an acrobat. We do not elect him for his ability to do a double back-flip." And Roosevelt soon added that, since he was obviously not in condition to "run" for office, he was counting on his friends to make it possible for him to walk in.

The campaign began in earnest in the middle of October. F.D.R. had, once again, an effective team. Louis Howe was in command at headquarters. Henry Morgenthau, Jr., the Dutchess County neighbor with whom Roosevelt had become increasingly friendly during the twenties and whose agricultural interests gave him a wide acquaintance in farm areas, was advance man. Missy LeHand was sick in Warm Springs; so Grace Tully, a pretty and intelligent girl who had been working for Mrs. Roosevelt in national headquarters, was brought in to serve as secretary. And Samuel I. Rosenman, a young lawyer, was added to brief the candidate on state problems.

Rosenman, a serious and systematic man, had organized the issues of the campaign in a series of large red manila envelopes, each carefully labeled by subject matter. As a devoted Smith follower, he noted with skepticism the candidate's soft collar, the loose tweed suit, the battered felt hat, the patrician carelessness of dress and manner. Yet he could not quite feel that Roosevelt was entirely the lightweight he had heard about in Smith circles. "The broad jaw and upthrust chin, the piercing, flashing eyes, the firm hands," he wrote later, " — they did not fit the description." Indeed, he was disconcertingly impressive. "He was friendly, but there was about his bearing an unspoken dignity which held off any undue familiarity."

When Roosevelt set off on his upstate tour, speaking extemporaneously from the back of a Buick, he first concentrated on national issues, especially religious bigotry. But he soon had to talk on state problems, and now he turned to the young lawyer for assistance. They quickly devised a method of work on speeches: a first draft from Rosenman, on the basis of which Roosevelt dictated a new version to a stenographer; then the reworking of the new draft in conference, until at last it was time to type the reading copy. Roosevelt was much impressed by the orderly character of Rosenman's mind, the fluency of his writing, and the levelheadedness of his judgment. For his part, Rosenman was fascinated by Roosevelt's skill as an editor — his capacity to take a page of dull copy and, through cuts and rearrangements and insertions, bring it to life and give it the stamp of his own personality.

The Roosevelt campaign offered a vigorous defense of the Smith administration. As F.D.R. stated his position on Smith's ideal of welfare government:

> If his program for the reduction of hours of women and children is Socialistic, we are all Socialists; and if his program for public improvements for the hospitals of the State and the prisons of the State is Socialistic, we are all Socialists. And if his program for bettering health in this State, for his great aid to the educational program of this State, if they are Socialistic, we are Socialists and we are proud of the name. . . .
>
> Anybody in public life who goes ahead and advocates improvements is called a radical. The Democratic Party in this state has gone on and advocated improvements, and it has put them through, and it has been called radical and everything else, and it is keeping on winning, and the Democratic Party in this State will keep on winning as long as it goes ahead with a program of progress.

Campaigning sometimes presented difficulties. On one occasion there was no ground-floor side entrance to the stage. Not wanting to seem to be seeking sympathy by taking the long walk up the center aisle, Roosevelt elected to climb the fire escape. Using his strong arms and shoulders, he painfully lifted himself up the steep ladder, pausing occasionally for breath, making jokes to relieve the tension, then resuming, until his face was streaming with sweat and his white shirt was wringing wet. Once up, he had time only to mop his face before he had to walk out on the stage. But no one in the audience guessed what he had been through.

It was a triumphant personal campaign, and it bore up Democratic hopes in a new surge of optimism. On election night at the Biltmore, however, the Democrats watched the returns with mounting gloom. It was soon clear that Smith was beaten; even in his own state, he was falling hopelessly behind. From early returns, it looked as if Roosevelt was beaten too. Then the candidate, noticing unusual delays in reports from upstate, began to wonder whether local officials were slowing up the count in order to be in a position to alter the returns, if that should prove necessary to elect a Republican governor. Picking up the phone, he called sheriffs in upstate counties: "I want you personally to see that the ballots are not tampered with." The maneuver worked, and the returns began to come in more rapidly.

By morning they knew that, while Smith had lost not only much of the Solid South but also his own state, and by 100,000 votes, Roosevelt had carried New York by 25,000. "The one bright spot on this extremely dark horizon," wrote Sumner Welles to Roosevelt, surveying the Democratic collapse, "is the fact that you have been elected Governor of New York." "You are," said Harry Byrd, "the hope of the Democratic party." [16]

32. Responsibility in Albany

So ONE MORE ITEM in the timetable he had outlined to Grenville Clark twenty-one years earlier was achieved. Once more he sat in Theodore Roosevelt's chair. And, like Theodore Roosevelt, he proposed to run his own administration. "I've *got* to be Governor of the State of New York," he told Frances Perkins, "and I have got to be it MYSELF."

The emphasis was necessary. Al Smith had been a great governor. Now, denied the Presidency, he seemed disinclined to relinquish the governorship. His motives were doubtless mixed. A sincere concern for Roosevelt's health and for the state's welfare mingled with a reluctance to yield power. Basically perhaps he had little respect for Roosevelt's strength, intellectual, moral, or even physical. A friend told Roosevelt that Smith had said of him, "He won't live for a year." In any case, Smith informed Roosevelt that Belle Moskowitz was ready to start work on the inaugural address and the message to the legislature. Smith also suggested that Mrs. Moskowitz be appointed the Governor's secretary and that Robert Moses be kept on as Secretary of State. And he reserved for himself a suite at the DeWitt Clinton Hotel in Albany to help on the big decisions.

But Roosevelt's amiable patrician exterior was deceptive. The new Governor was no longer a playboy in politics. Inside he had become a calculating and tough operator. His role in the twenties — the systematic correspondence with politicians through the nation, the effort to hold a balance between the city and country wings of the party — had been carefully designed to foster his own posi-

tion. He liked power too much to surrender it. To Smith's proposals for him, Roosevelt blandly replied that the inaugural address and the message were nearly finished, but that he would be
glad to show them to Mrs. Moskowitz and to Smith when he got
to Albany. This he "forgot" to do. Smith soon began to realize
that neither Mrs. Moskowitz nor Moses was to be retained. As
Roosevelt coolly remarked to Sam Rosenman, whom he had in
mind for Governor's Counsel, "I do not expect to continue to call
on these people whom Al has been using."

Roosevelt had no wish for an open break. Indeed, he kept on
nearly all the department heads from the Smith administration.
But the bare assertion of independence was enough to incite Smith's
suspicion. Al later claimed that he was convinced, from this moment, that Roosevelt planned to seek the presidential nomination.
And Al himself was beginning to change. Financial success dazzled
the boy from the Fulton Fish Market, as it ultimately bored the
Hudson River squire. They had never been really close; and increasingly they were bound to drift apart. In 1931 Smith remarked
that he and Roosevelt had remained friends socially and that Roosevelt had gone out of his way to be agreeable to the Smith family,
"but" — then he rose, stamped his foot, and said — "do you know,
by God, that he has never consulted me about a damn thing since he
has been Governor." [1]

II

As Roosevelt began to build his own administration, he found
an increasingly valuable assistant in Sam Rosenman. The young
lawyer with his composed intelligence, his imperturbable manner,
and his talent for self-effacement soon made himself indispensable
— enough so as to arouse Louis Howe's jealous resentment. Rosenman used to warn new Roosevelt associates, "Louis'll 'give you the
foot' if you don't watch out." [2] Howe, of course, took over most
of the confidential duties which Smith had intended for Belle Moskowitz; and her work as social welfare adviser was given to Frances
Perkins, whom Roosevelt named Industrial Commissioner. Henry
Morgenthau, Jr., first received Roosevelt's old seat on the Taconic
State Park Commission, later became chairman of the Agricultural

Advisory Commission and, after that, Commissioner of Conservation. For Secretary of State, to replace Moses, Roosevelt sought out Edward J. Flynn, whom he liked best among the professional politicians of the state.

Flynn, who came from a well-to-do Irish family, had graduated from Fordham Law School and served in the state Assembly. In the early twenties, by cool political maneuvering, he had won Charles F. Murphy's blessing and become Democratic leader in the Bronx. Immaculate in dress, a fresh carnation always in his buttonhole, Flynn was courteous and cultivated in social relationships, tough and utterly realistic in politics. Graft to him was worse than immoral; it was stupid. With standards, if without illusions, he sought to keep his own machine honest and responsive to community needs. "Bosses are inevitable under our system of government," he liked to say, "bad bosses are not."

Flynn was a man of uncertain moods, sometimes succumbing to gusts of black pessimism. Still, crisis generally found him calm and resourceful. His very financial independence — especially his flourishing law practices — gave him power. "I've had a lot of fun with politics and loved it," he once said, "but I've always been in the position where, if anything happened, it wouldn't make a damn bit of difference to me." Roosevelt found Flynn socially agreeable and politically astute. He regarded him, moreover, as his only ally in New York City, where Tammany still was filled with old suspicions. At first reluctant to come to Albany, Flynn eventually capitulated to the Roosevelt charm.[3]

Roosevelt himself settled down with enormous zest in the large Victorian Executive Mansion, now overflowing in Roosevelt fashion with children, guests, and politicians. Warm Springs did somewhat recede, as he had feared: instead of spending three months a year there, he now considered himself lucky to get away for six weeks. Mrs. Roosevelt continued her busy life, teaching three days every week at the Todhunter School in New York City, then returning to Albany to resume her duties as hostess at the Executive Mansion. When someone asked her whether housekeeping bothered her much, she could reply, "I rarely devote more than fifteen minutes a day to it."[4]

III

The broad lines of Roosevelt's policies had been solidly laid down in the Smith administration. But he was temperamentally incapable of marking time. Without hesitation, he soon began to strike out in directions of his own, first in public power and conservation, and later, after the depression had started, in relief and social security.

His concern with cheaper electric power dated from his service in the state Senate nearly twenty years before. Nor had his interest lapsed in the years between. As early as 1921 he began to talk about harnessing the high tides of Passamaquoddy Bay, near Campobello, for hydroelectric use; and during the Mississippi floods of 1927, when he told Smith that the solution of the flood problem was to store water on the higher reaches of the tributary rivers, he emphasized that this should be done in conjunction with a program to "develop hydro-electric power for the benefit of the people of the United States." [5]

The fight for cheaper power, as he saw it, had two aspects: the promotion of public power, plus the effective regulation of the private utility companies. He had his own ideas on the problem, but he also called on outside advice. As he had twenty years before, he turned to Gifford Pinchot, now Governor of Pennsylvania. He brought Morris Llewellyn Cooke, a Philadelphia management engineer and power expert, into the New York picture; and he appointed the economist Leland Olds to a top staff position in the New York State Power Authority. He pressed ahead with Smith's program for public power development on the St. Lawrence. But he went further than Smith when he said that the state should build its own transmission lines if utilities buying state power would not accept contracts designed to cheapen rates to consumers. One condition on which Roosevelt insisted was the abandonment of the reproduction-cost theory of valuation as a rate base. Roosevelt favored instead the prudent-investment theory, which by basing rates on the original cost of facilities rather than on the current cost of replacement, better prevented the increase of rates through stock-watering and other forms of fictitious capitalization.

Still larger issues seemed to him at stake in the water power debate. The St. Lawrence River, Muscle Shoals, and Boulder Dam, he said in 1929, were the last three great natural power sites still owned by the people. Let them therefore be developed by public authority so that they could "remain forever as a yardstick with which to measure the cost of producing and transmitting electricity." And let government improve the regulation of utilities: "if we in the United States virtually give up the control over the utilities of the nation, attacks on other liberties will follow." Through such statements he began to win national attention as a leader in the fight for public power.[6]

The battle for better conservation and land policies also meant a return to familiar battlefields in Albany. Roosevelt liked nothing better than to introduce himself as a farmer. This self-identification was genuine enough. But it also enabled him to operate, both in state and national politics, as a mediator between the city and country wings of the Democratic party. And it marked another way in which he diverged from Smith, who dismissed the farmer in 1929 as "inherently a Republican," adding snappishly, "I never made any impression on any considerable number of them." [7]

Roosevelt looked to regional planning as the way of improving the farm situation. This meant the withdrawal of submarginal land, reforestation, and related land use and conservation measures. His constitutional amendment of 1931 authorizing the state to buy up abandoned farms for reforestation, though denounced by Smith, was sustained by the people. "What a queer thing that was for Al to fight so bitterly," Roosevelt said. ". . . I cannot help remembering the fact that while he was Governor I agreed with almost all the policies he recommended but I was against one or two during these eight years. However, for the sake of party solidarity, I kept my mouth shut." [8]

IV

But conservation had come to mean more to Roosevelt than simply planning for land and resource use. "Broadly speaking," he said in 1931, "its implications of saving and protecting what we own that is of genuine worth, whether of wealth, of health or of happiness, is inclusive enough to take in all the functions of government." [9] After the Wall Street crash in October 1929, while President Hoover was assuring visitors in Washington that the depression was over, Governor Roosevelt was considering a variety of plans designed to salvage its victims.

One scheme derived from his own nostalgia for country life. People living on farms, he felt, at least had no fear of starvation or of losing their jobs. Government might therefore do more to "plan a better distribution of our population as between the larger city and the smaller country communities." There would be no point in doing this, of course, if the only result was to increase the number of people in commercial farming. But Roosevelt wanted to combine rural living with industry. With improved transportation, the worker no longer needed to live next to the factory; indeed, with hydroelectric power, why should not factories themselves move into the countryside? "Industry of its own volition," Roosevelt suggested, "is likely to seek decentralization." All this might enable the worker to till his own plot of land for subsistence farming and thus enjoy the "opportunities for healthful and natural living" in the country, while still retaining his job in industry.[10]

On welfare issues, Roosevelt's extension of his conservationist faith found ready support in the social work approach of Frances Perkins. Even before the depression, Roosevelt and Miss Perkins had begun to move toward a system of old-age pensions in New York. After unemployment began, their first effort was to make people understand the magnitude of the crisis. When Hoover announced in late January 1930 that employment had started to increase, Frances Perkins promptly showed on the basis of Labor Department statistics that the situation was getting worse. By March, while the reality of the downturn was still scarcely acknowledged in Washington, Roosevelt appointed a Commission on the Stabilization of Employment in New York. Soon, at the Governor's Conference at Salt Lake City, he endorsed the principle of unemployment insurance.

But unemployment insurance was a long-range program; something more immediate was needed to fight the hunger and cold of a depression winter. Watching the gradual breakdown of local relief, Roosevelt called in August 1931 for the establishment by

New York State of a Temporary Emergency Relief Administration. He delivered the message in person to the legislature, emphasizing that "modern society, acting through its Government, owes the definite obligation to prevent the starvation or dire waste of any of its fellow men and women who try to maintain themselves but cannot." Aid to jobless citizens, Roosevelt said, "must be extended by Government, not as a matter of charity, but as a matter of social duty"; "the State accepts the task cheerfully because it believes that it will help restore that close relationship with its people which is necessary to preserve our democratic form of government." [11]

Study with Simon Patten had given Miss Perkins ideas about larger economic issues. "Scientific analysis and planning," she told a Senate committee in 1930, "will, I believe, reduce the unemployment problem so as to make it practically negligible"; and she supported the movement toward planning through industrial self-government. [12] While Roosevelt was less specific about methods, he too began to talk increasingly of the importance of planning. "Real planning is needed for the complex future," he said in the summer of 1931. "It is time we experimented. . . . I believe that the coming winter is going to bring forth a great many suggestions for experimenting with our economic system. . . . Please do not dismiss these ideas with the word radical. Remember the radical of yesterday is almost [always] the reactionary of today." [13]

Roosevelt was the first governor to call for state aid for relief; and the New York TERA was the first state relief agency to go into action. Its executive director was a lively and fast-moving social worker from New York City named Harry L. Hopkins. At the same time, Roosevelt found work for the unemployed on state conservation projects, setting up work camps, planting trees, and reclaiming the land. And he seized upon his assigned topic at the Governors' Conference in 1931 — "Land Utilization and State Planning" — to make a national appeal for experiment. He still was inclined to insist, both on this occasion and elsewhere, on the advantages of planning on the state level. This was partly because of the emphasis on the states as laboratories for social experiment which he retained from a talk with Lord Bryce many years before; partly because he feared that the "rich and powerful industrial interests of the East" would control federal planning; more seriously, no doubt, because, like any active executive, he tended to favor the concentration of power on whatever level he happened to find himself. In such moods, he warned piously against the steady process in Washington "of building commissions and regulatory bodies and special legislation like huge inverted pyramids over every one of the simple Constitutional provisions"; states rights, he said, had to be jealously guarded against the "doctrine of regulation and legislation by 'master minds' " in Washington.

But the scope of planning was less important in the baffled years of 1930 and 1931 than the liberating emphasis on the idea itself, with its implication that men through government could do something to extricate themselves from their misery. It was the prevalent economic fatalism which exasperated Roosevelt as much as anything. When an orthodox economist told him that the only hope was to let the system strike bottom, he said to the man, a look of disgust on his face, "People aren't cattle, you know!" [14]

v

No governor in the nation was more responsive to the challenge of the depression. And he combined executive decision with political address. He faced a Republican legislature, hostile to public power, labor, conservation, and social reform. Yet his use of the radio to rouse the folks at home often forced legislators to accept measures they originally opposed ("it seems to me," Roosevelt said in 1929, "that radio is gradually bringing to the ears of our people matters of interest concerning their country which they refused to consider in the daily press with their eyes"); and, in the end, the Governor got a good deal of his program through. As William Green of the A.F. of L. wrote Roosevelt, "Labor has very seldom secured the enactment of so many measures which so favorably affect their economic, social and industrial welfare during a single session of a legislative body." [15]

The first term provided him with another kind of political testing. With Ed Flynn's assistance, Roosevelt had started out to do his best to live equably with his old foe, Tammany Hall. But Tammany, it developed, could hardly live equably within itself.

The sachems were quarreling inside the wigwam; and inquisitive outsiders raised increasingly searching questions about James J. Walker as mayor of New York. It became evident that Walker, with all his Broadway insouciance, could no longer wisecrack away the corruption flourishing so luxuriantly in his administration. Roosevelt at first tried to ignore the whole business, pleading (correctly but inadequately) that the Governor had no right to investigate the affairs of municipalities. Later he developed a technique of seeming to intervene just enough to quiet the reformers without intervening so much as to alienate the Tammany leaders. As time passed, the balancing act became increasingly difficult.

In the meantime, the Republicans counted on making Tammany an issue in the state campaign of 1930. The Governor tried to dismiss New York City corruption as a "local" issue and stood instead on the liberalism of his program. When the Hoover administration sent in Secretary of State Henry L. Stimson, Secretary of War Patrick J. Hurley, and Undersecretary of the Treasury Ogden Mills, Roosevelt ridiculed this invasion in a sharp, satirical speech. In November 1930, the voters of New York returned him to Albany for a second term by a plurality of 725,000, unprecedented in the history of the state. It was then that Jim Farley issued the statement about Roosevelt and the Presidency.

In the new session the Republicans promptly proposed a legislative investigation of New York City. Roosevelt now acquiesced, and the inquiry was soon under way, directed by Judge Samuel Seabury, an anti-Tammany Democrat whom Roosevelt had appointed to investigate the New York City Magistrates Court the year before. Roosevelt's cooperation with Seabury became close enough for a time to enrage the Tammany leaders. Following a report from Seabury late in 1931, Roosevelt even removed the sheriff of New York County. But Seabury and Roosevelt soon became uneasy partners. Seabury, who opposed Roosevelt's presidential candidacy, was thought to be cherishing presidential aspirations of his own. His determination to make a case against Walker — a case completed only a few weeks before the Democratic convention — may have been strengthened by a desire to force Roosevelt to choose at the worst possible moment between breaking with Tammany and capitulating to it.

Nothing damaged Roosevelt's reputation more than his handling of the New York scandals. The reformers — in New York State and outside — felt him to be afraid of Tammany, or else hopelessly muddled; the organization politicians — in New York State and outside — felt him to be hostile to Tammany, or else hopelessly weak; and nowhere could he find footing solid enough to support a standard to which his own adherents could repair. Since the Seabury inquiry was far more dramatic than the Power Authority or the Temporary Emergency Relief Administration, the image of Roosevelt which increasingly emerged from the headlines of 1931 and 1932 was that of a vacillating politician rather than a hard-hitting and creative governor. And he did not help himself by succumbing to moments of irritability, particularly toward the reformers. "This fellow Seabury," Roosevelt said to Colonel House a few weeks before the Democratic convention, "is merely trying to perpetuate another political play to embarrass me."

Many observers agreed with Walter Lippmann's judgment of June 1932: "This squalid mess is due to nothing but Governor Roosevelt's own weakness and timidity. . . . The trouble with Franklin D. Roosevelt is that his mind is not very clear, his purposes are not simple, and his methods are not direct." [16] There were issues on which Roosevelt as governor was clear, simple, and direct; and they were conceivably more significant than the New York City scandals. But they received less notice at the time. The reputation of his governorship never wholly escaped the blight of evasion and indecision which his maneuvering before the Tammany affair cast on it.

VI

If the Walker case overshadowed F.D.R.'s reform program in his second term, his developing presidential candidacy overshadowed it even more. State issues had absorbed him since 1928. Now it seemed time for him to turn his attention once again to the nation. He had, of course, a mind well stocked with a variety of ideas and opinions on national questions. Still, his interest in both the American past and the present had tended to be practical and specific rather than reflective. He thought he loved history;

but serious history — analytical history — really bored him. What he really loved were books of travel or adventure, or antiquarian reconstructions of the nautical or Hudson River past. He had no sustained interest in political philosophy or in economic theory.[17]

There remained, however, a framework of general ideas in terms of which he approached contemporary issues. Whiling away time during his convalescence, he had embarked on the composition of a history of the United States. All that remains — probably all that was written — is the introduction, a bold sketch of the historical background of the age of discovery. But the terms of his approach were significant. Mechanical change, he felt, had brought about "a clear division of humanity into classes," where "a mere handful, certainly less than one in a hundred, owned and controlled the very lives and fortunes of the other ninety-nine." In such terms — technological progress and social conflict — he portrayed the decline of feudalism, the quickening of commerce, the rise of the middle class, and the expansion of Europe to the West.[18]

He recurred to themes of change and conflict when he lectured at Milton Academy in 1926. History, he declared, remembering Endicott Peabody, had followed a series of up-and-down curves, but the up-curves were always the longer. Change was inevitable in any society; unrest was "a healthy sign"; and social disorder was caused "as much by those who fear change as by those who seek revolution." Let not modern Rip Van Winkles seek "to justify conservatism by calling all who seek new things heretics or anarchists." Our national danger lay not in radicalism but in "too long a period of the do-nothing or reactionary standards." Science had transformed the conditions of existence. "No person who truly visualizes the future doubts that we are at the threshold of an era of cooperative endeavor between peoples and continents." As yet, we still suffered "from an ancient disease known as 'class consciousness.'" We talked of service; but "true service will not come until all the world recognizes all the rest of the world as one big family." [19]

The challenge to American leadership, as he saw it in 1928, was to fit together "an old political order fashioned by a pastoral civilization and a new social order fashioned by a technical civilization." This required, he told the Harvard Phi Beta Kappa Society in 1929, a new recognition of society's obligations to the sick, the poor, and the helpless. "What used to be the privilege of the few," he said, "has come to be the accepted heritage of the many." [20]

His conception of what he called at Harvard "The Age of Social Consciousness" drew strength, of course, from his conservationist's theory of government as trustee for the people, obligated to preserve and develop the nation's inheritance. It represented more broadly the welling up of the old emotions of the New Nationalism and the New Freedom — a tough grasp on central ideas of justice and welfare based on a profound commitment to old American dreams of progress. He believed in an ascertainable public interest and considered it worth fighting for.

One other strain entered in: that was his country squire's scorn for the rich who lacked a sense of social responsibility. This clearly ran through Franklin Roosevelt, even if he never articulated it so dramatically as did his Hudson River neighbor, Herbert Claiborne Pell of Hopewell Junction. Pell, who had grown up in Tuxedo and Newport in more splendid days and served as Democratic state chairman in New York for a time in the twenties, had no use for the businessmen who took over after the war. "The destinies of the world were handed them on a plate in 1920. Their piglike rush for immediate profits knocked over the whole feast in nine years. These are the people, who with an ignorance equalled only by their impudence, set themselves up as the proper leaders of the country." He considered both aristocrat and bourgeois totally selfish, but the aristocrat at least thought of the interests of his grandson, while the bourgeois thought only of himself. By 1931, Pell disgustedly instructed the managers of his property not to invest a dollar in any American corporation. The country was doomed, he said, until it could liberate itself from the rich. "They have shown no realization that what they call free enterprise means anything but greed." Don't fool yourself, he warned his own class: the masses "will overwhelm us or protect us according to whether they have been cheated or treated fairly."

Pell's words were too biting for Roosevelt's more politic temperament. But Roosevelt combined a similar sense of *noblesse oblige* and community responsibility with a landed gentleman's disdain for trade and an aristocrat's lightheartedness and complacency. His long acquaintance with the rich gave him advantages in dealing with them. "Wilson thought that the rich were villains," said an old friend of Roosevelt's; "Mr. Roosevelt knew they were foolish and ignorant." He had no respect for their judgment or their aspirations. "We may well ask," he said in a Fourth of July speech in 1929, "are we in danger of a new caveman's club, of a new feudal system, of the creation of such a highly centralized industrial control that we may have to bring forth a new Declaration of Independence?" The crash destroyed no illusions for him. It only confirmed his sense of the greed and stupidity of business leadership.[21]

VII

Still, he could cope with the crash emotionally better than he could intellectually. All he could recall of the classical economics he had learned at Harvard now seemed irrelevant. "Our professors" — he would describe a circle on the desk — "taught us: this sector of the circle is wealth, this sector here is empty, and so on. All gone!" [22]

Sam Rosenman was no better prepared to deal with the economics of depression. "If you were to be nominated tomorrow and had to start a campaign trip within ten days," he told Roosevelt in March 1932, "we'd be in an awful fix." Broad impressions were not enough; somewhere there had to be specific ideas. Whom should we consult? Roosevelt asked. Not businessmen nor politicians, said Rosenman; they had had their chance and fallen on their faces. "I think we ought to steer clear of all those. . . . My idea is this: Why not go to the universities of the country? You have been having some good experiences with college professors. I think they wouldn't be afraid to strike out on new paths just because the paths are new."

Roosevelt puffed on his cigarette. The idea could hardly have been new to him: he had been calling on college professors ever since the beginning of his governorship. Two months before, at lunch with Professor Raymond Moley of Columbia, he had made an apparently casual remark which Moley had interpreted as an invitation to help on the national campaign. Rosenman, acting independently, now proposed that Moley be made a key figure in the operation. Nodding, Roosevelt told Rosenman to go ahead.

Rosenman promptly called Moley to explain the importance of equipping the Governor with a corps of experts. "He made it easy for me to encourage the notion that he was the originator of this happy idea," Moley later wrote. "To have said that it had occupied my thoughts every waking hour [since the lunch with Roosevelt] would have been unkind and stupid." In any case, Moley responded gratefully. When he and Rosenman met a short time later with Basil O'Connor in New York, Moley had already drawn up a list of topics and of men who might deal with them.

For agriculture, Moley nominated his Claremont Avenue neighbor and Columbia colleague, Rexford G. Tugwell. For credit, he suggested Professor Adolf A. Berle, Jr., of the Columbia Law School. Other Columbia professors were proposed, some of whom contributed memoranda and joined the Albany discussions. But Moley, Tugwell, and Berle, along with Rosenman and O'Connor, were the most durable members of what was soon known as Roosevelt's brains (later brain) trust.[23]

Though Moley was not a man of the intellectual stature of Tugwell or Berle, he was unquestioningly accepted by them and by Roosevelt and Rosenman as leader of the group. A native of Ohio, forty-five years old in the spring of 1932, he was a political scientist whose specialty was the administration of criminal justice. He had been fired early by the reform ideals of Tom Johnson and Newton D. Baker in Cleveland and had dabbled in Ohio politics fifteen years before, even becoming mayor of the tiny village of Olmsted Falls. But he had decided to retain his academic base and in 1923 moved east to join the government department at Columbia. His interest in criminal justice brought him into contact with Louis Howe; and in the 1928 campaign Howe introduced him to Roosevelt. As governor, Roosevelt fell into the habit of calling on Moley for drafts of speeches and statements, first in the field of juridical reform, and then more generally.

Moley was a stocky, square-shouldered man, streaks of gray in his thinning dark hair, shrewd, affable, and engaging, with a well-organized mind and a flair for speech writing. His voice was low and drawling, his manner almost diffident; he constantly smoked a professor's heavy dark pipe; but he had a quiet persistence in pushing forward himself and his ideas. Among academicians, he played the role of the realist who understood practical politics, scoffed at idealism, and dismissed the higher fervor of reform with tolerant cynicism. "I feel no call to remedy evils," he liked to say. "I have not the slightest urge to be a reformer. Social workers make me very weary. . . . I am essentially a conservative fellow. I tilt at no windmills." As ringmaster of the experts, he was tactful and, as middleman for their ideas, judicious and sensible. Roosevelt found his efficiency of great value. But Moley also had his own interior stresses. He was emotional in his attachments and his jealousies; and his affability concealed anxieties that strain and time might bring to the surface.[24]

VIII

Tugwell and Berle had greater confidence than Moley in the field of ideas but much less in the field of politics. Each approached worldly affairs with a curious mixture of tentativeness and arrogance. Tugwell, with his bright eyes and handsome profile, his bold enthusiasms, and audacious ideas, liked to shock, and often succeeded. Berle, slight, erect, quick of motion and brilliant of tongue, had been a child prodigy, a Harvard A.B. at eighteen, with experience ranging from the Versailles Conference to the Henry Street Settlement with Lillian Wald. He was capable, if necessary, of diplomacy; but, with his edgy manner and his intolerance of fools, he sometimes exploded in sarcasm and disgust. He had been a Hoover man in 1928 and was inclining toward Baker in 1932. Both men were continuously fertile in ideas, and neither was constrained by the past or intimidated by the future. It was of Berle that H. G. Wells remarked, "He began to unfold a view of the world to me which seemed to contain all I had ever learnt and thought, but better arranged and closer to reality." [25]

Moley, Tugwell, and Berle agreed on the nature of the economic problem. For them all, bigness was inevitable in economic life; "competition, as such," as Moley put it, "was not inherently virtuous . . . [but] created as many abuses as it prevented." They all dismissed the Wilson-Brandeis program of breaking up big business as futile. The problem was not to atomize bigness but to place it under control — to end what Moley vividly called "the anarchy of concentrated economic power which, like a cannon loose on a frigate's deck, tore from one side to another, crushing those in its path." "We are no longer afraid of bigness," said Tugwell. ". . . We are resolved to recognize openly that competition in most of its forms is wasteful and costly; that larger combinations must in any modern society prevail. . . . Unrestricted individual competition is the death, not the life, of trade." [26]

This was the background of the ideas they brought to Albany, talking them over with the Governor on the broad, old-fashioned porch of the Executive Mansion or around the fireplace in his study. Tugwell was dubious on his first Albany trip, expecting to meet the evasive executive he had read about in the newspapers. Roosevelt was in his chair on the veranda. Tugwell was instantly struck by the smile, the tossed head, the gesture with the cigarette holder. "Everything I saw and heard was merged in an impression of vitality." Later they went into the sprawling Victorian house filled with overstuffed chairs. They dined, sitting around a table laden with a profusion of jellies, pickles, hot biscuits, and nuts. Roosevelt attacked the roast duck with gusto but commented that he preferred wild duck, "well-hung and chased over the fire," a sophisticated taste astonishing to Tugwell. Then they retired to the library for eager, probing talk.

There were many such evenings. Moley urbanely steering the discussion, Tugwell and Berle flashing ahead with their ideas, Rosenman acting the devil's advocate, O'Connor offering the realist's comment, and always Roosevelt, listening, interrupting, joking, needling, cross-examining, absorbing the ideas and turning them over in his mind. With his broad family humor, he called the group his "Privy Council," as he spoke of "Sammy the Rose" and "Henry the Morgue"; but no one could tell from his genial curiosity what he accepted from them, or what he rejected. "We could throw out pieces of theory," Tugwell wrote later, "and perhaps they would find a place in his scheme. We could suggest relations; and perhaps the inventiveness of the suggestion would attract his notice. But the tapestry of the policy he was weaving was guided by an artist's conception which was not made known to us."

IX

It was the economic crisis that dominated these evenings. The group rejected the latter-day Hoover thesis that the depression was international in origin. Tugwell expounded the underconsumptionist theory: the failure of business to pass on the gains of improved productivity either through higher wages or lower prices had caused a deficit of purchasing power which made depression inevitable. (The night after he had set this forth in Albany, a jobless man caught his sleeve on upper Broadway. Tugwell turned and said, "My friend, I did you a good turn last night." The panhandler stood openmouthed.) Roosevelt seemed to accept the underconsumptionist thesis as a matter of course. What should be done? Tugwell believed that prices of manufactured goods had to be forced down. "Why not raise wages too?" asked Roosevelt.

There were differences here. Tugwell, in his way, agreed with Mellon that the fever of the twenties had to run its course. The struggle to maintain the price structure, he feared, would hold back recovery. But Berle and Roosevelt had inflationist leanings. The price of deflation seemed to them too great. Yet they conceded that inflation might do nothing but perpetuate structural maladjustment. Whatever their differences on the price question, Tugwell and Berle agreed that some prices should go down, some up. One day in May, Roosevelt asked Tugwell about money as a means of raising the price level. Tugwell told him about the theory of the "commodity dollar" but tried to suggest that the purely monetary approach was inadequate. Roosevelt remained discontented; "he wanted something simpler than we could provide." [27]

When Roosevelt left for Warm Springs late in April 1932, he asked Moley and Rosenman to continue preparing memoranda "so I don't get too far behind on my homework." When Rosenman went down to visit Roosevelt three weeks later, he brought a great pile of documents, covering a variety of issues. By this time Roosevelt was scheduled to speak at Oglethorpe University. Ernest K. Lindley of the New York *Herald Tribune*, a sympathetic newspaperman who had absorbed many of Tugwell's and Berle's ideas, provided the Oglethorpe draft, with its emphasis on the need for planning and for bold, persistent experimentation. [28]

This was the last speech of the preconvention campaign. But there was no rest for the brain trusters. Some policy questions were proving harder to crack than others; in particular, the agricultural problem — Tugwell's special job — remained baffling and unsatisfactory. Tugwell, regarding his own thinking on the subject as stale, rather desperately decided to attend a meeting of farm economists held in Chicago shortly before the convention. From Beardsley Ruml in Washington he had heard hints of new developments in the domestic allotment plan; at Chicago he could talk with M. L. Wilson of Montana, who had become the plan's apostle. When he arrived in Chicago, he found not only Wilson, but Henry Wallace of Iowa. For several days they talked late into the night in the dormitory rooms at the University of Chicago where they were billeted. Tugwell was finally persuaded that he had found what he was seeking — a workable means of restricting agricultural production on which the farm leaders might agree.

But time was growing short. On Monday of convention week, Tugwell called Roosevelt and tried to unravel the intricacies of the plan. After half an hour, Roosevelt, finding he still did not get it, brought Rosenman to the phone. Rosenman could not get it either. Roosevelt laughed. "Well, Professor," he finally said to Tugwell, "put it in a telegram — two or three hundred words — and we'll work it into the speech. I'll take your word for it that it's the latest and most efficient model." [29]

Moley had completed the first draft of an acceptance speech by the third week in June. Then he went on to Chicago, where he joined Tugwell, while Roosevelt and Rosenman began the long vigil in Albany. The Moley draft was too long, and Roosevelt worked away at odd moments with Rosenman to cut it down. The speech also lacked a conclusion. After listening to the all-night balloting, Rosenman, nervous and restless, retired with hot dogs and a pot of coffee to try his hand at writing the peroration which he half thought would never be used. It was then that Rosenman, jogged perhaps by the title of a Stuart Chase article in the current *New Republic* ("A New Deal for America") but without noting any special significance (any more than Roosevelt did when he came to deliver the words), set down the sentence, "I pledge you, I pledge myself, to a new deal for the American people." [30]

X

The Roosevelt insiders at Chicago had meanwhile been worrying considerably in their separate ways over the acceptance speech. Louis Howe had written a draft of his own, which he made sure that Moley heard about but refused to let him see. Moley, upset by Howe's mysterious activity, grew frantic over the fate of his Albany draft. Tugwell and O'Connor, taking a fresh look at the Moley draft, worked twelve hours without stopping on a word-by-word rewrite which, with Moley's permission, they phoned back to Albany. After the nomination, Moley was greatly relieved to discover that the favored version in Albany still followed his original draft; but, when he showed the Albany text to Howe, the wizened little man, angry that anyone else should share the pinnacle with Roosevelt after his twenty-year dream, was furious. "Good God, do I have to do everything myself?" he said to Moley. "I see Sam Rosenman in every paragraph of this mess."

In the morning after the nomination, Moley sped back to Howe's suite. Howe now condescended to give Moley a vague account of his own draft. Just then Bernard Baruch entered, accompanied by General Hugh S. Johnson; Howe took them into an adjoining room. Moley, convinced that Baruch's arrival meant the beginning of a compromise with conservatism, stared gloomily out of the window. Suddenly Jesse Straus tapped him on the shoulder: "Can we let Baruch see the acceptance speech?" Moley, considering himself goaded beyond endurance, flung the manuscript at the bewildered Straus with the words: "Please do! . . . This happens to be what Franklin Roosevelt believes and wants to say. But I'm sure he wouldn't be the first man to cave in under pressure." Moley was soon appeased, however, when Baruch said that he preferred the Albany draft.

Roosevelt, meanwhile, had decided against the Tugwell-O'Connor redraft; and had decided too that the Albany text was still too long for delegates exhausted by days of convention excitement. On the plane to Chicago, he and Rosenman hacked away at the speech, reducing it by main force to manageable proportions. When they arrived in Chicago, however, Howe met them with his own draft — ten or twelve pages long, based on a review and amplification of the Democratic platform. Roosevelt demurred at being offered a speech which he had never seen before; but Howe was insistent. As they drove in through the crowded streets, Roosevelt, waving his hat and responding to the cheers, kept glancing at Howe's manuscript on his lap.

Moley and Tugwell pushed through the crowd at the Coliseum and stood in the center aisle when Roosevelt began to speak. For a moment they were stunned. The language was new to them; could Howe have won out in the end? But soon they began to hear the words they knew so well. Roosevelt, aware how much the occasion meant to his faithful friend, had taken Howe's first page; then reverted to the text he had brought from Albany. ("I have known him as well as a valet could," Howe said a few months later, "and he still remains a hero to me.") [31]

XI

It had been a long time since the youth had set out so gaily in the two-cylinder red Maxwell along the dusty back roads of Dutchess County; since Prince Troubetzkoy, with what fatal prescience, had cast the statue of the stalwart young man without legs; since the meeting with Howe in the paneled library in Albany ("Beloved and Revered Future President"); since Wilson and the war and the fight for the League in 1920; since that afternoon in Campobello when the flames of the forest fire had warmed his body and the chill of the icy waters had entered his legs, never to depart. Finally, he was at the climax and the boy had become a man, half a century old, his brown hair now tinged with gray, his face lined and troubled, yet resolutely hopeful in spirit about the possibilities of America and the possibilities of democracy.

Many men — and women too — had entered into the making of this man: Theodore Roosevelt and Woodrow Wilson, Louis Howe and Josephus Daniels, Sara Delano Roosevelt and Eleanor Roosevelt, Al Smith and Jim Farley and Sam Rosenman, Moley and Tugwell and Berle. Sickness had done much too, though his friends would forever dispute the extent to which the ordeal of the twenties had really changed him. Alben Barkley, who had known him in the Wilson administration, listed himself as "one of those who believe that F.D.R. would have been a great leader regardless of whether he had ever been stricken." But Eleanor Roosevelt felt that the struggle had given him a depth he did not have as a young man, and his uncle Frederic A. Delano wrote, "His severest test was the 'Polio,' and to my mind that is what really made him what he is, — a 'twice born man.' " Frances Perkins and Henry Morgenthau, Jr., similarly thought he underwent a "spiritual transformation," that suffering had purged him of frivolity and arrogance, enlarging his compassion and deepening his understanding. William Phillips, seeing him in the spring of 1932 for the first time in years, found him "a different person from the charming and at times irresponsible young man of the old Wilson days. The two-year fight against the dread disease had evidently given him new moral and physical strength." [32]

Yet it was not to be forgotten that before he was stricken Roosevelt had shown himself a man of sufficient capacity to help run the Navy Department in the greatest war in American history and to be nominated for the Vice-Presidency of the United States. Polio did not transform him so much as it developed in him latencies and potentialities that gave him a new power, a new sympathy, a new self-control, a new specific gravity. Both physically and morally, he seemed less superficial and complacent, more composed, more mature. He had learned much in the arts of patience and perspective. When asked in later years whether things ever worried him, he would reply: "If you had spent two years in bed trying to wiggle your big toe, after that anything else would seem easy!" Having met this challenge, he was able to surmount later crises, shaking off his cares and relaxing over his stamp collection or going to bed for eight hours of dreamless sleep. "I let Herbert do the worrying for me," he used to say as governor, referring to serious-minded Lieutenant-Governor Lehman. "When he was sick," reported Irvin McDuffie, his valet, "he didn't say a murmuring word. . . . He complained as little as any man I ever saw. . . . He could throw off anything."

The very sense of being a cripple began in time to recede from him; and others lost their consciousness of his infirmity. Only an aggravated fear of fire remained to mark his physical helplessness (though even this was not deep: he always insisted on wax tapers for the family Christmas tree). When stories tickled him, he could even exclaim, with no feeling of incongruity, "Really, it's as funny as a crutch"; or, when he wanted to end a visit, "I'm sorry, I have to run"; or, "I got out of bed on the wrong foot this morning." After so terrible a struggle, inner peace came naturally. "He had more serenity than any man I have ever seen," said Francis Biddle. "One felt that nothing ultimately would upset him." [33]

XII

The brush with death increased his joy in living; it added to his vitality a new dimension of gratitude for the wonder and variety of life. Humor was another way of lightening the burdens of helplessness, and his laugh boomed as never before, underlining his cheerful gibes at friends or at himself. He had always delighted in people. But now they were his vital links with life, and his extroverted Rooseveltian sociability was compounded by his invalid's compulsion to charm anyone who came to his bedside. He sought more intensely than ever to know people, to understand them, to win them to him. Sometimes he even blurred his own feelings in an excess of amiability. His smiles and his hearty "yes, yes, yes" generally meant only that he had heard what had been said and wanted the speaker to continue, not (as the speaker sometimes thought — and Roosevelt sometimes let him think) that Roosevelt agreed with him.[34]

The anxiety to please had other perils. Roosevelt found it hard, for example, to refuse people, to send them away, to hurt their feelings. But the desire to be liked also opened him up to their needs and fears. It explained in great part the genius for assimilation which was developing within him and which was giving him so extraordinary a receptivity. Invisible antennae stretched out, picking up with faultless precision the intangibles of human emotion. The individual case was for him the center of the learning experience; from it, he extrapolated with bold confidence to the nation and the world.

His intellectual processes had always been intuitive rather than logical. He often thought lazily and superficially. But he felt profoundly. His ratiocination annoyed some observers, who, missing the intermediate steps of the syllogism, condemned his oversimplifications and felt that portentous decisions were precariously reared on idiotic anecdotes about farmers whom Roosevelt knew down the way in Dutchess County. But the individual case was really more often the symbol than the source of his conclusion; it was the shortcut way of putting over a vast movement of feeling, imagination, and sympathy which Roosevelt himself could neither articulate nor understand but which had a plunging accuracy of its own.

This deep instinct emerged from and was fertilized by his capacious memory. Detail stuck in his mind like sand in honey. He remembered trees, rivers, mountains, landscapes, geographical locations, sea-level readings, ship tonnages, coins, stamps, business operations, political relationships, and above all, people. He admired men of encyclopedic mind: Jefferson, Franklin, Count Rumford, and Theodore Roosevelt seemed to him unique in possessing a many-sidedness which, as he liked to say, took in the whole sweep of civilization.

His own intellectual appetite was vast and tolerant, without much discrimination or taste. He was a skimmer rather than a reader, extracting the essence of articles or books with astonishing speed. Outside of the beauties of nature or architecture, he had little capacity for aesthetic appreciation. He rarely read novels or poetry or listened to music. When he looked at pictures, it was the subject, not the technique, which appealed to him; he disliked modern art and wanted painting to be healthy and "clean." [35]

Without transforming his intellect, illness gave it new power and penetration. Immobility forced him to focus his energy and will. Before, he had wavered among a thousand interests. As Louis Howe complained, "You couldn't pin him down." Now he learned to concentrate. He could shift from one subject to another, as if, in his wife's phrase, he were pulling down curtains in his mind. Flat on his back, he had had nothing to do but to think and read and talk. Someone later asked him how he knew so many things. "You fellows with two good legs spend your spare time playing golf, or shooting ducks and such things," he replied, without self-pity, "while I have had to get all my exercise out of a book." [36]

Above all else, perhaps, the victory over polio confirmed the

Rooseveltian inheritance of optimism. A cheerful strength radiated from him, which roused in others not pity but exhilaration and a sense of their own possibilities. He could communicate confidence by the intonation of his voice, the tilt of his head, the flourish of his cigarette holder. "In all the years of my husband's public life," said his wife, ". . . I never once heard him make a remark which indicated that any crisis could not be solved." [37] So robust a faith was the inevitable afterglow of a personal struggle during which he could never for a moment admit the possibility of defeat. He identified himself with fortune, and flinched from those who might rashly offend it. He could not bear the provocation involved in lighting three cigarettes on a match or having thirteen at table.

XIII

To many, the optimism was too good to be true. Roosevelt's apparent belief that every story had a happy ending gave him the aspect of a grown-up Boy Scout. He seemed, said Milton MacKaye, all light and no shadow, all bright hope and no black despair. Some found him smug, bland and superficial, without tension and without tragedy. Yet others, who knew him better, confessed a deeper bafflement. The public face, all grin and gusto, had been carefully cultivated from the first years at Groton and Harvard; illness had made it second nature. But behind the cordiality and exuberance there remained an impassable reserve which many reconnoitered but none could penetrate. The relentless buoyancy was less an impulse of the soul than a mask of cheer to the world, in part spontaneous enough, but more a defense against pity without and discouragement within. "In Roosevelt," said Felix Frankfurter, "optimism was not an anodyne, it was an energy." Beyond the screen, the real Roosevelt existed in mystery, even to himself. Even religion provided only conventional and unexamined consolation. He believed in being a good Episcopalian as he believed in being a good American; but he did not like to reflect on sin and salvation. As he once told Eleanor, "I think it is just as well not to think about things like that too much!"

Underneath there remained the other man — tougher than the public man, harder, more ambitious, more calculating, more petty, more puckish, more selfish, more malicious, more profound, more complex, more interesting. Only intimate friends saw Roosevelt in these aspects, and then in enigmatic and sometimes terrifying glimpses. The eyes, friendly but impenetrable, the smile, genial but noncommittal, the manner, open but inscrutable — all signified the inaccessibility within. He enjoyed people, but rarely gave himself to them. Detachment endowed him with a capacity for craftiness in politics and for calculation, sometimes even for cruelty, in human relations. Those who loved him best he teased most mercilessly. Nearly everybody was expendable. As he could be insouciant and shallow intellectually, so he could be tricky and evasive morally. He seemed soft and complaisant, but he was terribly hard inside. "It is the hard substance," as Harold Ickes said of him, "that can take the high polish!" But could public leaders afford private commitment? Noncommitment also gave him the inner independence which could free him for idealism as well as cynicism — and it freed him for both. Still, if noncommitment meant public liberation, it also meant private sadness. It condemned him to a final loneliness and melancholy, from which he recoiled in others but which he accepted in himself with serenity.

At bottom, Franklin Roosevelt was a man without illusions, clearheaded and compassionate, who had been close enough to death to understand the frailty of human striving, but who remained loyal enough to life to do his best in the sight of God.[38]

VII

The Darkling Plain

33. Campaign for America

THERE WAS no time to waste. "The campaign starts at ten o'clock tonight," Franklin D. Roosevelt told the Democratic National Committee the day after his nomination. In place of the already forgotten John J. Raskob, he made Jim Farley national chairman; and he told Ray Moley to continue in charge of speeches and issues. To each he made clear the separate nature of his responsibilities. "I'm interested in getting him the votes — nothing else," as Farley observed to Moley. "Issues aren't my business. They're yours and his. You keep out of mine, and I'll keep out of yours."

As for the strategy of the campaign, Roosevelt already had his own definite ideas. Democratic senators were unanimous in telling Farley that the candidate had best stay at home, stick mostly to radio, and confine himself to a few carefully staged rallies in the East. But Roosevelt, intent on presenting the electorate with a dynamic image of energy and decision as well as on dispelling doubts about his physical capacity, was determined on a cross-country campaign. This point accepted, he left Farley and Moley with their marching orders and prepared to relax with his sons on a sailboat off the Maine coast. Moley, Berle, and Tugwell remained behind in their disorderly suite in the Hotel Roosevelt to get material in shape for the fall tours.[1]

The brain trust had already begun to expand to meet its new responsibilities. The major addition was the gift from Bernard Baruch of his close associate General Hugh S. Johnson. Johnson, who was fifty years old in 1932, brought to the suite in the Roosevelt a far more varied experience than his academic associates. His

past stretched back to a small town in frontier days in the Indian
Territory. He had been a bright, cocky boy; neighbors still remembered his childhood chant — "Everybody in the world is a
rink-stink but Hughie Johnson and he's all right." He moved on
to the Cherokee Strip, then entered West Point in the same class
with Douglas MacArthur, took a commission in the Cavalry, and
served in Texas and the Philippines. He stayed on in the Army
in the dreary years before the First World War; but at the same
time, he wrote boys' books and studied law at the University of
California. After chasing Villa along the Mexican border (Johnson shared a tent with a fellow cavalry officer, George S. Patton, Jr.,
already known for his pearl-handled revolvers), Johnson was recalled to Washington; and, after the declaration of war in 1917,
he planned and then administered the draft, took over Army
Purchasing, and became the War Department's representative on
the War Industries Board.

He performed his war jobs, as he performed everything else,
with prodigious energy, drama, and dispatch. While so engaged,
he won the favorable attention of, among others, Baruch. Resigning from the service as a brigadier-general in 1919, he joined
George Peek at the Moline Plow Company, helped Peek develop
the McNary-Haugen plan, quarreled with Peek, joined Baruch in
business, worked for Al Smith in 1928, lost a fortune in the crash,
and then devoted himself to figuring out how to end the depression.
His personality was picturesque and irresistible. When they first
brought the General to Albany, he fascinated Roosevelt and the
entire company while he read aloud a vigorous indictment of the
Hoover administration — all except Moley, that is, who, having
heard it twice before, left the room in search of rest but still could
not escape the tremendous rumble of the General's voice on the
floor above. They had such a high time that night that they all
missed the train back to New York. (Roosevelt later said to Moley
of the Johnson document, "It's great stuff. Water it down 70 percent and make it into a speech.")

In his basic diagnosis, Johnson had many points of agreement
with the brain trust. Where he conspicuously differed lay in his
deep commitment to budget-balancing. As Johnson saw the situation, all the elements required for revival were there except one —

business confidence; and business confidence could best be regained through fiscal stability. So government economy was a central feature of his program.

But for the moment this was more a difference in priority than in substance; and, in any case, it seemed unimportant next to the zeal with which the General expounded the gospel of central economic coordination. He shared the brain trust's contempt for laissez faire. The War Industries Board had given him the conviction that it was possible for government to direct the national economy. On the problem of economic stability, he had long contended that "the first requisite for prosperity is consumption, and that requires purchasing power." If government direction could bring industry, agriculture, and the consuming groups into proper balance, the domestic market, he argued, could sustain national prosperity. In June 1932 Johnson had set forth his program in a slightly jazzed-up form as a proclamation by "Muscleinny, Dictator pro tem." "The sole cure," this remarkable document emphasized, *"was singleness of control and immediate action."* [2]

For Tugwell and Berle particularly, the campaign appeared a unique opportunity to put over precisely this point. Roosevelt's preconvention speeches, culminating with his address at Oglethorpe, had foreshadowed, unmistakably if vaguely, a conception of an organic economy in which government, accepting the drive of modern technology toward bigness, would seek to reorganize the chaotic business order into a system of national integration. Tugwell and Berle differed among themselves in emphasis — Tugwell leaning toward integration through an extension of governmental discipline, Berle hoping for repentance and responsibility among business leaders. But even Moley, though far less clear cut in his doctrine, wholly accepted the Van Hise thesis of "concentration and control" and went along a good deal of the way with Tugwell in the pursuit of conjuncture. Never before had there seemed such a chance to gain a clear mandate for national planning.[3]

II

But the brain trust was now less influential than it had been before Chicago. Nomination had shifted Roosevelt's base and con-

fronted him with new problems of conciliation and leadership. He
was now the candidate of the entire party, not just of its liberal
wing. The conservative Democrats, having lost the nomination,
were working overtime to win the nominee; and, if they began to
despair of converting Roosevelt, they could at least keep him from
excessive commitment. In their own public speeches, moreover,
they could identify the party as much as possible with orthodox
policies.

Conservative pressure began with his own running mate. Garner
made his position abundantly clear when he said, in accepting the
nomination, that nearly all the existing troubles were "the consequence of government's departure from its legitimate functions."
"Had it not been for the steady encroachment of the Federal Government on the rights and duties reserved for the States," Garner observed, "we perhaps would not have the present spectacle of the
people rushing to Washington to set right whatever goes wrong."
He phrased his beliefs more pungently when he gave Donald Richberg a message for Roosevelt. "Tell the Governor that he is the
boss and we will all follow him to hell if we have to," Garner said,
"but if he goes too far with some of these wild-eyed ideas we are
going to have the shit kicked out of us." To Roosevelt, Garner
argued vainly that extensive speaking tours would be unnecessary:
"All you have got to do is to stay alive until election day." [4]

Roosevelt's defeated rivals worked even harder to commit the
party to conservatism. "We should stop talking about the Forgotten
Man and about class distinctions," said Al Smith in October. ". . .
The Forgotten Man is a myth and the sooner he disappears from
the campaign the better." For Smith, the formula for recovery was
government retrenchment; and "the fairest and most intelligent"
way of meeting the need for current revenues — and of making
possible income tax reduction where it mattered, that is, in the
highest brackets — was to impose a sales tax. Governor Ritchie
declared that the Democratic party could be relied on to stop federal encroachment on states rights, to end government competition
with private enterprise, and to balance the budget. Carter Glass
inveighed against the Hoover policy by which "the minions of
Federal bureaucracy are given full sway to distribute huge sums of
money picked from the pockets of the American people." His

fellow Virginian Harry F. Byrd proposed an immediate decrease
of federal spending by a billion dollars. John W. Davis summed it
all up by denouncing Hoover for "following the road to socialism
at a rate never before equaled in time of peace by any of his
predecessors." [5]

<h3 style="text-align:center">III</h3>

Yet, if conservative Democrats were bent on moving Roosevelt
to the right, liberal Democrats were no less bent on moving him
toward the left. The left to which they mostly sought to commit
him was progressivism in the Bryan-Wilson tradition. This older
progressivism now existed in two forms — in the free-swinging
populism of western and southern radicals; and in the Brandeisian
economics of eastern lawyers and intellectuals.

The western and southern senators, favoring an old-style, rip-
roaring campaign against the interests, had strong claims on Roosevelt's attention. Some of them, like Wheeler of Montana, had been
among his earliest supporters. Others, like Hiram Johnson of
California, Bob La Follette of Wisconsin, and Bronson Cutting of
New Mexico, were the advance agents of what was hoped to be a
large-scale Republican defection. George Norris was, of course,
the grand old man of American progressivism.

The most vociferous, however, in pressing progressive views on
the candidate was Huey Long of Louisiana, who regarded himself
as the spokesman of radicals of both parties. One day in August at
Hyde Park, a phone call interrupted Roosevelt at lunch. The
receiver was brought to the table. Roosevelt grinning broadly, put
his hand over the mouthpiece, and said, "It's Huey." The guests
could dimly hear an angry voice ranting over a press report that
Roosevelt had entertained Owen D. Young at Hyde Park. These
were not the folks that had put him over at Chicago, Long told
Roosevelt; and, in a flood of profanity, Long warned against further association with Davis, Baker, Glass, and other conservatives.
Roosevelt took it lightly, but there could be no mistaking Long's
seriousness. When he finally hung up, Roosevelt remarked gravely,
"It has its funny side but actually Huey is one of the two most
dangerous men in the United States today. We shall have to do

something about him." (Rex Tugwell, who was present, later asked him who the other one was. Said Roosevelt, "Douglas MacArthur.")

One thing Roosevelt could do about Long was to invite him to Hyde Park too. Arriving for lunch in a loud suit, orchid-colored shirt, and watermelon-pink tie, the Louisiana senator was placed next to the candidate. Throughout the lunch Roosevelt and Long talked intently while the other guests chatted among themselves. Suddenly, during an unexpected lull, Sara Delano Roosevelt, who had been gazing incredulously at this apparition, whispered loudly, "Who is that AWFUL man sitting on my son's right?" [6]

Roosevelt was prepared to offer more than lunch to satisfy the Longs. For Long's position had respectable support, not only from serious progressives like Norris and La Follette, but from thoughtful conservative politicians over the country. Thus Governor O. Max Gardner of North Carolina, no radical, warned Roosevelt in July not to deceive himself about the demand for change or, if this demand were thwarted, the danger of "a violent social and political revolution." "The American people are against things as they are," said Gardner. "We are more than blind if we can think the American people will stand hitched to the *status quo*. . . . If I were Roosevelt, I would become more liberal. I would march with the crowd, because I tell you the masses are marching and if we are to save this Nation it has got to be saved by the liberal interpretations of the sentiments now ruling in the hearts of men." [7]

As for the Brandeis version of the progressive creed, it had the inestimable advantage of a persuasive spokesman at Roosevelt's elbow. This was Professor Felix Frankfurter of Harvard, whom the candidate had known since the time twenty-five years earlier when they were both young lawyers in New York City. Frankfurter, who was fifty years old in 1932, had come to the United States from Vienna at the age of twelve. After graduating from the College of the City of New York and the Harvard Law School, he became an aide to Henry L. Stimson when Stimson was United States Attorney in New York and then accompanied Stimson to the War Department. Later, as professor at the Harvard Law School, he worked with both Theodore Roosevelt and Wilson. In 1918 he returned to Washington, lived in the House of Truth, and served as chairman of the War Labor Policies Board, where he renewed his acquaintance with the young Assistant Secretary of the Navy. In the twenties he continued a distinguished teaching career in Cambridge while, on the side, he argued the constitutionality of welfare legislation in the Supreme Court for the Consumers' League, spoke up for Sacco and Vanzetti, and developed the case against the labor injunction. Small, quick, articulate, jaunty, Frankfurter was inexhaustible in his energy and his curiosity, giving off sparks like an overcharged electric battery. He loved people, loved conversation, loved influence, loved life. Beyond his sparkling personal qualities, he had an erudite and incisive legal intelligence, a resourceful approach to questions of public policy, and a passion for raising the standards of public service. And, to make these things effective, he had what Mr. Justice Holmes had not unkindly described in 1920 as "an unimaginable gift of wiggling in wherever he wants to."

On economic problems, Frankfurter, like Brandeis, distrusted the grandiose schemes of the social planners. He saw no inevitability in monopoly; and he favored a brisk and versatile strategy by which the federal government should use its power to reform the practices of competitive enterprise. He enchanted Roosevelt in his way as much as the brain trusters did in theirs. "Felix has more ideas per minute than any man of my acquaintance," Roosevelt once said. "He has a brilliant mind but it clicks so fast it makes my head fairly spin. I find him tremendously interesting and stimulating." Now, in inconspicuous visits to Albany and Hyde Park, Frankfurter urged on Roosevelt an up-to-date version of the Brandeis program by which government would reverse the trend toward economic concentration through rigorous regulation of investment banking and of the securities exchanges. Like western progressivism, this too would commit the candidate to a battle against the interests.[8]

From the viewpoint of Tugwell and Berle, progressivism in either the western or eastern form was as obsolete and almost as obnoxious as outright conservatism. As the brain trusters saw it, the old-fashioned progressives, instead of recognizing the organic character of the economy and the need for central direction, were keeping alive the fatal illusion that, if only big business were sufficiently denounced and divided, then the economy would run by itself.

But trust busting would make no contribution to recovery, and it would make planning impossible. The brain trust feared it as the dead end of liberal reform.

IV

Thus, with the campaign scarcely under way, the candidate found himself in the center of a triangle of advice: at one corner, integration and social planning; at another, retrenchment, budget balancing, and laissez faire; at a third, trust busting and government regulation.

Roosevelt, in the center, had few clear-cut ideas of his own with which to reduce the confusion. Such economic furniture as stocked his mind was most conventional: he had written in 1930 that competition could "almost be called a law of nature" and in 1931 that a government could not "keep running year after year if it spends more than it receives in taxes." But the seminars of the spring of 1932 had challenged his classical clichés, instructed him in the importance of purchasing power, and given him strong doubts concerning the self-recuperative powers of the system. In his first post-convention speech — a radio address on July 30 — he called for increased government intervention in the economy and even spoke of the "revision of some of our institutions" as necessary to recovery. Yet at the same time he said, "Stop the deficits. . . . Any Government, like any family, can for a year spend a little more than it earns. But you and I know that a continuation of that habit means the poorhouse."

He was learning a good many rather divergent things from the crossfire of advice centering on him. But he had the larger wisdom to resist consistency. More basic perhaps than anything else was his feeling that the economic crisis had outdistanced the economists, and therefore that the important thing was to keep options alive. Moley reinforced the candidate's dislike of dogmatism. "If we can't get a President with a fluid mind," he had said in the spring, "we shall have some bad times ahead." Tugwell, hoping for commitment, composed one speech straight out of the last chapter of The Industrial Discipline. Roosevelt listened, as he always did, and for a moment in conversation even elaborated the Tugwell ideas. "But I knew, when I thought it over," Tugwell later wrote, "that nothing would come out of it. . . . The candidate could preserve his freedom to improvise and that, he seemed to think, was essential." As Roosevelt finally said to Tugwell about planning, "That kind of thing would have to grow rather than be campaigned for." [9]

In addition, a hundred other things crowded the candidate's mind besides economics. There was the organization of the campaign itself. Jim Farley ran the headquarters with inexhaustible geniality and skill. He brought in such experienced politicians as Claude Swanson of Virginia, Joseph C. O'Mahoney of Wyoming, and Arthur J. Mullen of Nebraska to help overcome his own lack of national experience. To head the Women's Division, he called on Molly Dewson, who had switched from social work to politics following her effective labors in the campaigns of 1928 and 1930. Louis Johnson of West Virginia, a leading figure in the American Legion, ran the Veterans' Division; Dan Tobin of the Teamsters, the Labor Division. But there were difficulties. The alienation of the conservatives and talk of a "new deal" had made fund raising difficult. From time to time headquarters had no money at all; sometimes it had to pass the hat so the candidate could go on the air. Baruch, despite his earlier attitude, was the largest contributor; William Woodin, Vincent Astor, John J. Raskob, William Randolph Hearst, Pierre S. du Pont, James W. Gerard, Joseph P. Kennedy, and James M. Curley were other reliable donors.[10]

Roosevelt was much concerned too with campaign strategy — for example, with mobilizing dissident Republicans behind his candidacy. The remnants of the Progressive Republicans had made a last pathetic effort in their own party in the spring, when Harold Ickes, after failing to induce Hiram Johnson to try for the Republican nomination, agreed to solicit support for Gifford Pinchot. But it had all been unavailing: "we of the progressive faith," concluded George Norris, "have to look to the Democratic Party." Roosevelt told the Democratic National Committee in July that he expected many Republican votes; and he formulated his campaign indictments, not against the Republican party, but only against the Republican leadership. In September the National Progressive League was organized for Roosevelt, with Norris as chairman, Fred C. Howe as secretary, and Frankfurter, Ickes, Donald Richberg, and Henry Wallace on the national committee. As the campaign developed, the Progressive Republicans were assigned an increasingly important role in the winning of the West.[11]

Throughout the confusion the candidate, more experienced in national politics than any of his managers, had little choice but to run his own campaign. This he did with efficiency. "Roosevelt so ordered the various divisions of his political activity," Moley later testified, "so sharply delegated authority and so clearly maintained personal contact with each of us that there was never the semblance of conflict and never an overlapping of function." Louis Howe summed it up without too much exaggeration: "Never in forty years of experience have I known of a Presidential campaign being so completely controlled, dominated and directed . . . by the candidate himself." [12]

v

And beyond the campaign there remained in August the continuing irritation of Mayor Walker. The convention had only deferred what many voters throughout the country regarded as a critical moral test. "While many independents and Republicans are favorably inclined toward you," Harold Ickes had written in July to Roosevelt (whom he did not know), "I find that they are not prepared to make up their minds finally until after you have passed upon the case of Mayor Walker." The dapper mayor had become a national symbol for the evils of machine politics. "For every Tammany vote his acquittal brings you," warned a friend, "you will lose a dozen in the west."

It was a problem Roosevelt could not escape. Among other difficulties, he liked Walker personally. Once that summer he mused aloud, "How would it be if I let the little mayor off with a hell of a reprimand?" Then suddenly, as if answering himself, he said sharply, "No. That would be weak." From that moment Moley regarded Walker's removal as inevitable. Others were less certain: by Ed Flynn's testimony, he, Mrs. Roosevelt, and Louis Howe speculated many times as to what the Governor's intentions were.

In August Roosevelt called Walker to a series of hearings in

Albany. Handling the cross-examination himself, Roosevelt suddenly showed such poise and such mastery of a complex mass of intricate evidence as even to impress skeptics like Walter Lippmann. He remained inscrutable, however, on his final decision. On the evening of September 1, a group including Farley, Frank Walker, Rosenman, and Basil O'Connor talked over the Walker case with him. O'Connor was Walker's lawyer. Most of them advised letting him off with a reprimand. When the Governor seemed unresponsive, someone, after lighting a cigarette, flung the match at him with a derisive "So you'd rather be right than President!" Roosevelt said calmly, "Well, there may be something in what you say." Just then the phone rang with dramatic news. Walker had resigned. The denouement permitted Roosevelt to emerge from the situation with a minimum of political injury.[13]

VI

In the meantime, Roosevelt, opening the fall campaign, seemed to be moving toward the Brandeisian corner of his triangle of policy advice. Speaking in Columbus, Ohio, toward the end of August, he launched a scathing indictment of Hoover's economics; then set forth a program of his own, centering on federal regulation of security exchanges, holding companies, and banks. For Tugwell and Berle, such a regulatory program included useful minor reforms; but they did not feel a program designed to produce lasting recovery should concentrate on peripheral remedies. Instead of renewing his preconvention call for social planning, Roosevelt now seemed almost to criticize Hoover for having tried to plan so much. As Tugwell saw it, the little professor from the Harvard Law School had triumphed, with the support of Louis Howe, who hated investment bankers, and of Hugh Johnson, who loved the thought of cracking down on financial leaders. "On that day," Tugwell later wrote of Columbus, "we returned to trust-busting and began to abandon the struggle for conjuncture." [14]

Yet Tugwell surely overstated Roosevelt's finality of decision, as he perhaps underestimated the practical wisdom in the candidate's ambiguity. The next big economic speech was the farm address, delivered in Topeka in mid-September. Many hands contributed

to the final text. In July M. L. Wilson had come on to New York
and Albany with Mordecai Ezekiel to explain the domestic allotment plan. Wilson agreed to supply a draft for the farm speech;
after alarming delays and many telegrams and phone calls, it finally
arrived late in August, with accompanying material from Henry
Wallace. At the same time, Morgenthau prepared passages on land
use and on farm indebtedness; and Johnson, as an old agricultural
expert, wrote a draft of his own. Roosevelt, going over the mass of
material, added his ideas; so did Tugwell; and Moley finally sat
down to combine the various documents into a single text. The
result, with its discreet endorsement of the domestic allotment
plan, was plainly on the side of social management. "We must
have, I assert with all possible emphasis, national planning in
agriculture. . . . We need unity of planning, coherence in our Administration and emphasis upon cures rather than upon drugs." [15]

Three days later in Salt Lake City, Roosevelt presented a railroad
program as another contribution to "the reordering of economic
life." In Portland, on September 21 he discussed the power problem, calling for government regulation of public utility holding
companies and, in cases where the private utility supplied too little
power or charged too much for it, for public development. Four
great government power developments in the four corners of the
nation — the St. Lawrence River, Muscle Shoals, Boulder Dam,
and the Columbia River — could each serve, he said, as "a national
yardstick to prevent extortion against the public and to encourage
the wider use of that servant of the people — electric power." [16]

VII

As the candidate continued his pragmatic way, Berle and Tugwell, left behind in their suite at the Roosevelt in New York, worried increasingly about the intellectual consistency of the campaign.
Thus far F.D.R. had apparently taken, at one time or another, both
sides of the old liberal debate between the New Nationalism and
the New Freedom. Could these positions, in fact, be reconciled?
Or, if not reconcilable in their ultimate implications, could some
modus vivendi be constructed which would at least hold the campaign together? Berle, addressing himself to this problem, pro-

duced a draft that, with a minimum of change, Roosevelt delivered on September 23 to the Commonwealth Club in San Francisco.

None of Roosevelt's speeches caught up more poignantly the intellectual moods of the early depression than this one. After a brilliant historical account of the background of American democracy, Roosevelt suggested that the age of expansion had come to an end.

A glance at the situation today only too clearly indicates that equality of opportunity as we have known it no longer exists. Our industrial plant is built; the problem just now is whether under existing conditions it is not overbuilt. Our last frontier has long since been reached, and there is practically no more free land. More than half of our people do not live on the farms or on lands and cannot derive a living by cultivating their own property. There is no safety valve in the form of a Western prairie to which those thrown out of work by the Eastern economic machines can go for a new start. We are not able to invite the immigration from Europe to share our endless plenty. We are now providing a drab living for our own people. . . . The independent business man is running a losing race. . . . If the process of concentration goes on at the same rate, at the end of another century we shall have all American industry controlled by a dozen corporations, and run by perhaps a hundred men. But plainly, we are steering a steady course toward economic oligarchy, if we are not there already.

The time had come, Roosevelt said, for a reappraisal of values. "Our task now is not discovery or exploitation of natural resources, or necessarily producing more goods. It is the soberer, less dramatic business of administering resources and plants already in hand, of seeking to re-establish foreign markets for our surplus production, of meeting the problem of underconsumption, of adjusting production to consumption, of distributing wealth and products more equitably, of adapting existing economic organization to the service of the people." The problem of government was to further the development of an economic constitutional order — "a form of organization which will bring the scheme of things into balance, even though it may in some measure qualify the freedom of action of individual units within the business." Such an order, Roosevelt added, could not reject the gains of economic bigness, merely because some corporations abused their power.

Private economic power, he said, had now become a public trust. Businessmen had to assume the responsibility which went with power. And when they failed, then government must be swift to protect the public interest. "Government in this regard is the maintenance of a balance, within which every individual may have a place if he will take it; in which every individual may find safety if he wishes it; in which every individual may attain such power as his ability permits, consistent with his assuming the accompanying responsibility." [17]

It was a powerful speech, serenely philosophical in its acceptance of a transformed American destiny. But the speech reflected Berle more than it did Roosevelt. The candidate certainly honestly accepted it at the time as a convincing interpretation of the American dilemma. Yet his assent may have been more notional than real; the rhetoric at the beginning — "America is new. It is in the process of change and development. It has the great potentialities of youth" — seemed to express Roosevelt's *élan* more truly than the calm assertion later on that the age of expansion was over. Still, the Commonwealth Club address provided impressive reasons for enlarging the role of government. For Roosevelt, who was more interested in results than in systems, this was probably more important than the basic framework of interpretation.

VIII

As for the debate between the planners and the atomizers, the Commonwealth Club speech in a certain sense obscured the issues by transcending them. And, just as this was taking place, the third side of the triangular dialogue became more important. With the time approaching for a speech on the tariff, the old-style laissez-faire Democrats, who had suffered too long in the age of Fordney-McCumber and Smoot-Hawley, now concentrated on committing the candidate to something as near as possible to a free-trade position. The most influential champion of this view was Senator Cordell Hull of Tennessee.

In August Moley had asked Charles W. Taussig to consult with Hull on a tariff speech. Taussig, nephew of the Harvard economist, president of the American Molasses Company, and a marginal member of the brain trust, had free-trade views himself; and he returned from Tennessee with a draft bearing Hull's endorsement and calling for an across-the-board tariff cut of 10 per cent. Though Tugwell and Berle, at least, were far from economic isolationists, and though even Moley accepted the need for eventual tariff reduction, the planning philosophy implied a kind of economic nationalism, if one far less hostile to imports than Smoot-Hawleyism. To accept the Hull-Taussig draft, the planners felt, would be to concede too much to the theory that the depression was international in its origins. Moreover, they were convinced that indiscriminate tariff reductions would jeopardize schemes for national integration and obstruct urgently needed internal readjustments; and they feared that Hull's evident inclination to write off the war debts might only revive the disastrous experiment of the twenties, by which American loans artificially subsidized an American export trade. Moley and Tugwell favored instead a policy of tariff reduction through bilateral negotiation, under which foreign goods could be selectively admitted to the American market while the government still kept control of imports in its own hands. Hugh Johnson, who shared the general dislike of the Hull-Taussig draft, set immediately to work on an alternative, pacing up and down the suite at the Roosevelt before a relay of stenographers till the draft was completed. His proposal was that foreign markets be found for domestic surpluses by a series of "old-fashioned Yankee horsetrades" along bilateral lines: in this way, imports could be limited to those foreign goods which would least upset the domestic economy.

Moley turned the competing drafts over to Roosevelt. "He read the two through with seeming care," as Moley later described the episode. "And then he left me speechless by announcing that I had better 'weave the two together.'" When Moley demurred, Roosevelt suggested that they postpone the whole matter to the campaign train. In the next few days, M. L. Wilson sent Roosevelt a strong letter arguing that a call for horizontal reduction would be disastrous in the farm belt. This impressed Roosevelt, who now asked Moley to confer with Senators Tom Walsh and Key Pittman, both protectionists, in preparing a new version.

By this time, the train was in California. When Taussig now reappeared to help on the speech, Walsh, who had no patience for free traders, brusquely dismissed him. As Moley worked on with Walsh, the shadow of Cordell Hull, hurt and resentful, seemed to be riding with them in the swaying compartment on the train into Arizona. In time, Walsh's more extreme protectionist language was toned down. Finally the speech went to Roosevelt, who accepted it contentedly as "a compromise between the free traders and the protectionists."

For Moley, who believed no such compromise conceivable, this was an appalling performance. It is possible, however, that Moley oversimplified a complex situation. Roosevelt's personal tariff views were unquestionably internationalist. He told Anne O'Hare Mc-Cormick in October 1932 that the multiplying trade barriers were "symptoms of economic insanity." "If the present tariff war continues," he said, "the world will go back a thousand years." Yet, until the whole crazy system could be revised, he continued, was it not necessary to give the American economy emergency protection? At the bottom of a depression, a long-run internationalist might thus see no responsible alternative to short-run nationalism; this, in fact, was already the position of Keynes in England. No American government, Roosevelt felt, could leave the American people in misery until world recovery eventually began. The restoration of American prosperity through the re-establishment of national purchasing power would do more to bring about world recovery, he said, "than all of the promotional schemes of lending money to backward and crippled countries could do in generations. In this respect, I am for America first."

When Roosevelt discussed the tariff in the campaign, his first purpose was to maintain freedom of action — a purpose that corresponded to the intellectual realities and at the same time helped him escape the political consequences of taking too clear-cut a position. The result was the Sioux City speech, which grieved Cordell Hull without satisfying the protectionists and yet kept options open and gave both sides ground for hope.[18]

And so on October 3, Roosevelt, completing his swing through the West, returned to Albany. There had been so much movement, so much frenzy, so many hands shaken, people consulted, crowds charmed, flash bulbs exploded — with the telegraph poles racing by until the moment came for the candidate once again to put on the steel braces, lumber down the corridor to the back platform, introduce "my little boy, Jimmy" while the audience laughed at James Roosevelt's towering seventy-five inches, talk seriously for a moment, his hand on Jimmy's arm, then walk back to the compartment as the train began to pick up speed. Time never stopped on the train. There was always Moley, with a new speech draft, or the team of senators — Tom Walsh, Key Pittman, James F. Byrnes — on whose wisdom the candidate greatly counted. ("I have never traveled on a trip of the kind that was as happy and as successful," Pittman wrote Roosevelt after the western tour. "I have never had a candidate listen so patiently and attentively to advice and then so gently and kindly take the contrary view and do what he pleased, and, in your case, always right.") [19]

Great crowds turned out — at railroad stations, in packed auditoriums, and outdoors in open fields. People seemed, on the whole, serious and interested rather than demonstrative. "The country yearned for a Messiah," reported Ernest K. Lindley. "Mr. Roosevelt did not look or sound like a Messiah." Yet he remained "the one sure means of rebuking the party in power." If audiences did not succumb to ungovernable enthusiasm, at least they began to respond with increasing warmth to the candidate's confidence and hope. People began to look for the Roosevelt characteristics: the upthrust head; the confidential look with eyebrows arched when he let fly a gibe at the opposition, followed by the slow grin as the audience caught on; the sly mockery; the biting scorn; the righteous wrath.

For Roosevelt, the faces before him were an unforgettable experience — the great mass of Missourians under the lights before the Capitol at Jefferson City, the Kansans listening patiently in the hot sun at Topeka, the Nebraska farmers in the red glow of sunset at McCook, the stricken but dauntless miners of Butte. Sometimes voices rang out of the dark. At Bellefontaine, Ohio

— "You are not going to make them all lie down on park benches like Hoover." Others simply stared with quiet intensity.

"I have looked into the faces of thousands of Americans," Roosevelt told a friend. ". . . They have the frightened look of lost children." He had seen the same expressions in the crowds welcoming Wilson to Paris — the expression, above all, of yearning. "Then they were thinking of the war. Perhaps this man, their eyes were saying, can save our children from the horror and terror we have known. Now they are saying: 'We're caught in something we don't understand; perhaps this fellow can help us out.' " Sometimes the faces seemed to him "happy in a great hope." Roosevelt himself, endlessly watching out of train windows, from the back seat of automobiles, from the platform of the crowded auditoriums, smiling, waving his battered Italian felt hat, seemed to gather new strength from the people.[20]

x

It was now mid-October, with trees turning scarlet and gold and the premonitory chill of winter freshening the air. The campaign began to expand, voices became more shrill, the silent and the reluctant were drawn into the battle. John N. Garner, who hated speaking ("any set speeches from me will not get additional votes, and might give the opposition arguing material"), made his single campaign appearance and tried to reassure businessmen, concerned over his incendiary reputation, by recalling that he had opposed free silver in 1896. Roosevelt shook Al Smith's hand at the New York Democratic convention — and did not call him, as the press reported, "you old potato." Huey Long bubbled over to a reporter, "The great trouble with the Democrats is that we have all the votes and no money. In the present situation I believe the best thing we could do is to sell President Hoover a million votes for half what he is going to pay to try to get them. We can spare the votes and we could use the money." [21]

And the Republicans, now at last, were marching out to meet the enemy. It had taken Republican headquarters time to settle on its strategy. At first Hoover believed, for mysterious reasons, that Roosevelt would probably be (as he told Stimson) "the easiest man to beat." In this mood, Republican leaders contented themselves with sniping at the Democratic candidate as an irresponsible dilettante given to feckless experiment. When Roosevelt unveiled his pet project of large-scale reforestation, Secretary of Agriculture Hyde ridiculed the idea as "utterly visionary and chimerical." Ogden Mills, in an early attempt to set the tone of the campaign, said, "The Democrats seem willing to try anything, whereas the Republicans are firm in their belief that a violation of well-established, sound economic principles will not only defeat the purpose of the remedial measures proposed, but will, in fact, result in even greater disaster." In other moods, Republicans suggested that the supposedly radical Garner was the real threat. As Secretary of the Navy Charles Francis Adams asked ominously, "Would any President be able to control Garner?" [22]

Hoover himself had originally planned to give no more than three or four speeches. Early in July he told Stimson that, while Roosevelt might have some success among the radicals in the West and South, he was not a strong character. In four months of campaigning, Hoover said, Roosevelt would lose the confidence of the business elements in the East. This, the President seemed to imply, would insure his defeat. But by August Hoover's attitude began to change. Now he seemed both more fearful of Roosevelt's strength and more determined to do anything to stop his election. When Stimson cautioned him against using the recovery machinery in ways that might seem partisan, Hoover "broke out into a rather impassioned speech in which he said that even if the Democrats would go along with him, he was going to use all the machinery to win the election, for he felt that victory was necessary to the country." Stimson, shocked, replied that he could not believe that Hoover meant what he said. "I don't even now," Stimson later noted in his diary, "but he kept repeating it and it was only evidence to me how far he had been swung by his fatigue and the terrible strain he had been under." [23]

As reports of Roosevelt's September trip in the West began to come into Republican headquarters, pressure increased on Hoover to take the road. Few of the other Republican spellbinders were much help; some of the most influential — like Borah — were no help at all. It soon became all too apparent, in the words of the

President's secretary, "that he could not work through others, that he would have to bring about his re-election by his own efforts." The Democratic victory in Maine in September was particularly depressing. "It is a catastrophe for us," the President said. "It seems that we have got to fight to the limit." At the end of September, Hoover told Stimson that there was a feeling of "hatred" for him all through the West, that this could only be overcome by "fear," and that "the only possibility of winning the election, which is lost now, would be exciting a fear of what Roosevelt would do."

The first speech was scheduled for Des Moines in his native state. As the train made its way across the Middle West in early October the President, worn out from endless toil in Washington, found little to cheer him in the coldness of the crowds. Once, as he came in from the back platform, he said that it reminded him of traveling on the Harding funeral train. When he arrived in Des Moines, he was greeted by farmers parading the streets with banners saying, "In Hoover we trusted; now we are busted." But the Des Moines address itself put new heart into the Republicans. Speaking with force and feeling, Hoover proudly set forth the record of his administration and defended the gold standard, the protective tariff, and the drive for a balanced budget as the three keystones of Republican policy.[24]

Hoover now plunged into the campaign with a kind of furious desperation, going into Indiana and Maryland and West Virginia, into Ohio and Michigan. When he came to Detroit, a mass of people met him with boos and catcalls at the station. After the mounted police scattered the mob, Hoover and his party drove to the auditorium in limousines provided by Henry Ford (who had posted in his plants a meaningful notice: "To prevent times from getting worse and to help them get better, Persident Hoover must be elected"). Silent men and women lined the streets; occasionally there were jeers or signs with the stark message, DOWN WITH HOOVER. The President seemed bewildered and stricken. Rising to speak at the hall, his face ashen gray, his hands shaking, he invoked the name of Calvin Coolidge and pledged further reductions in government spending.[25]

XI

Roosevelt, in the meantime, pushed on with his summons to a New Deal. He promised that the federal government should assume responsibility for relief where local aid had broken down. He called for public works and for unemployment insurance. Early in October he proposed measures of "regularization and planning for balance among industries and for envisaging production as a national activity." Business "must think less of its own profit and more of the national function it performs. Each unit of it must think of itself as a part of a greater whole."

But the Hoover counterattack soon began to have its effect. For some time Baruch and Johnson had been urging a speech on the budget and government economy; and Louis Howe, enthusiastic over the idea, organized relays of senators to harass Roosevelt about it during the western trip, until the exasperated candidate finally told him to "hush up." When Roosevelt returned from the West, Johnson now descended on him with a speech calling for a 25 per cent reduction in government expenditures. Johnson read the draft aloud with such gusto that the brain trust, even Tugwell, succumbed. "It was," Tugwell said later, "a piece of unforgivable folly."

Though the speech, soon given at Pittsburgh, departed from Roosevelt's campaign policy of avoiding rigid commitments, there could be no doubt that it expressed his sincere views on fiscal policy. Innocently discussing the problems of national finance in terms of a family budget, the candidate denounced the Hoover administration for living beyond its means and for favoring the idea "that we ought to center control of everything in Washington as rapidly as possible." Government must retrench; only starvation could justify keeping the budget out of balance; but, in case of dire need, he said, he would run a deficit.

In the next weeks, Roosevelt reiterated his main campaign themes, speaking in Illinois, in Missouri, in Maryland. In Baltimore he roused a momentary Republican storm when he said that in 1929 the Republican party was in complete control of all the branches of the federal government — the executive, the legislative,

"and, I might add for good measure, the Supreme Court as well."
Under Hoover's sharp attack, he began to equivocate even more on
his already equivocal tariff position. When Republicans challenged
him to name the tariffs he wanted to lower, Roosevelt hastily said
that he would not withdraw protection against countries with lower
living standards (October 19), that he knew of no excessively high
duties on farm products (October 25), and that he favored "continued protection for American agriculture as well as American
industry" (October 31). But he remained essentially on the offensive, attacking Hoover as the spokesman of stagnation and despair.
Running safely ahead, Roosevelt diminished his militance in the
last days, concluding on notes of faith, resolution, and dignity.[26]

XII

Hoover, once warmed up, could not stop. For most of October
he concentrated on the tariff as the central issue, declaring repeatedly that there was "no measure in the whole economic gamut
more vital to the American workingman and the farmer today than
the maintenance of a protective tariff." Soon, as work and passion
wore him down, a new concern began to predominate. The more
he heard Roosevelt promise "a new deal," the more the promise
seemed to him to prefigure revolutionary social and economic
change. Others felt that he himself had created ample precedent
for positive government. "Between Mr. Hoover and Mr. Roosevelt,"
said Walter Lippmann, "there was, in 1932, no issue of fundamental
principle as to the responsibility of the modern state for the modern
economy." But for Hoover the fatal line always remained one step
beyond anything he was prepared to do himself.

On the last day in October, he made the traditional appearance
at Madison Square Garden. His first sentence set forth his keynote.
"This campaign is more than a contest between two men. It is
more than a contest between two parties. It is a contest between
two philosophies of government." Roosevelt, Hoover charged, was
"proposing changes and so-called new deals which would destroy
the very foundations of our American system." With contempt
Hoover called the roll of the revolutionists, the crowd booing each
name in response: Norris, La Follette, Cutting, Long, Wheeler,

Hearst — these men were "exponents of a social philosophy different from the traditional American one." If their candidate came to power, he would increase federal spending; he would inflate the currency; he would destroy the federal credit; he would reduce the tariff; he would put the federal government into the power business; he would undermine the Supreme Court; he would build a "bureaucracy such as we have never seen in our history."

The President's words were deeply felt; the sense of crisis had given him a somber eloquence. Sometimes he tumbled over the edge, as when he cried of the tariff, "The grass will grow in the streets of a hundred cities, a thousand towns; the weeds will overrun the fields of millions of farms if that protection be taken away." But he left no doubt about his basic fear. "This election," he concluded in New York, "is not a mere shift from the ins to the outs. It means deciding the direction our Nation will take over a century to come." [27]

XIII

Roosevelt, hearing the speech by radio through the half-open door of his room in a Boston hotel, said indignantly, "I simply will not let Hoover question my Americanism." But those to the left of Roosevelt felt that Hoover in his portrait of a revolutionary Roosevelt was paying the Democrat far too great a compliment. Men who believed that nothing short of revolution could meet the crisis were not impressed by vague talk of new deals from country gentlemen. To the real radicals Roosevelt seemed at best warmhearted but superficial, at worst glib and insincere, in any case hopelessly committed to the capitalist system. And the left-wing intellectuals knew, if they knew anything, that capitalism was dead. "Progressivism today, if we are to revaluate the term," wrote John Chamberlain in September, "must mean either Norman Thomas or William Z. Foster, ineffectual though one or both of them may be." [28]

For the sober, hopeful reformer of academic or social work background, the Socialist party remained the ideal outlet and Norman Thomas the predestined leader. His hoarse, rasping oratory had real impact in 1932 on the educated middle class — more than on the working classes; and for many this tall, lean, white-haired man seemed to be expressing the national conscience. The League for Independent Political Action, after due deliberation in Cleveland in July, voted to endorse Thomas. Paul Douglas, while admitting "a genuine liking" for Roosevelt because of his stand on public power and unemployment insurance, condemned the Democratic party as the chief obstacle in the way of a third party of farmers, wage earners and white-collar workers; "its destruction," said Douglas, "would be one of the best things that could happen in our political life." John Dewey, convinced that "a Raskob will dominate a Wheeler or a Walsh" in a Roosevelt administration, denounced the "suicidal character" of the policy of backing Roosevelt as a lesser evil. Many intellectuals, from Elmer Davis to Henry Hazlitt, from William Trufant Foster to Stuart Chase, from George S. Kaufman to Stephen Vincent Benét, from Morris Ernst to Reinhold Niebuhr, felt that the only intelligent vote was one for Thomas.[29]

But for the more romantic intellectuals, Thomas was hardly better than Roosevelt. "If I vote at all," said Lewis Mumford, "it will be for the Communists, in order to express as emphatically as possible the belief that our present crisis calls for a complete and drastic re-orientation." Others rejected the conditional mood. "As responsible intellectual workers," said a group of writers in a statement called *Culture and the Crisis* in October, "we have aligned ourselves with the frankly revolutionary Communist Party, the party of the workers." Republicanism, they said, was bankrupt; the Democratic party was "the demagogic face of Republicanism"; the Socialist party offered "mere reformism which builds up state capitalism and thus strengthens the capitalist state and potential Fascism." The Communist party alone proposed the real solution — "the overthrow of the system which is responsible for all crises." Here was an ideal worth fighting for, and "a practical and realizable ideal, as is being proved in the Soviet Union." "It is capitalism," the manifest concluded, "which is destructive of all culture and Communism which desires to save civilization and its cultural heritage from the abyss to which the world crisis is driving it." The signers included such leading novelists as Theodore Dreiser, Sherwood Anderson, John Dos Passos, Erskine Caldwell, and Waldo Frank; such critics as Edmund Wilson, Newton Arvin,

Malcolm Cowley, Granville Hicks; such professors as Sidney Hook and Frederick L. Schuman; such journalists as Lincoln Steffens, Matthew Josephson, and Ella Winter. It was an impressive evidence of the defection of intellectuals from the existing order.[30]

XIV

But, while certain intellectuals were thus rejecting Roosevelt as the prophet of pap, Herbert Hoover continued to see him as the precursor of revolution. The Democratic philosophy, he charged in early November, was "the same philosophy of government which has poisoned all Europe . . . the fumes of the witch's caldron which boiled in Russia."

He said this near the end of the campaign at St. Paul, and he went on to say that the Democrats had become "the party of the mob." When he added, "Thank God, we still have a government in Washington that knows how to deal with the mob," an angry murmur began to roll up from the audience. The President, white-faced, exhausted, stumbling in speech, repeatedly losing his place in his manuscript, swayed on the platform. Behind him a man gripped an empty chair to be shoved under him in case of collapse. Colonel Starling, chief of the Secret Service, broke into a cold sweat. After the speech a prominent Republican took Starling aside and said, "Why don't they make him quit? He's not doing himself or the party any good. It's turning into a farce. He is tired physically and mentally."

Now, at last, he was going home — back to Palo Alto to cast his vote. William Allen White visited him the evening before the election, as the President was preparing his final broadcast. The presidential train stood on a siding in the Nevada desert, where twilight outlined black masses of mountains in the far distance, across endless stretches of flat earth, white with alkali. Inside sat Hoover, his eyes lusterless and red-rimmed, his body slumped with fatigue. Summoning energy for this last effort, he warned the radio audience against "false gods arrayed in the rainbow colors of promises" and denounced "the destructive forces of sectional and group action of our opponents." The election, he said again, would affect the welfare of generations to come.

As he spoke, observed White, "his voice comes tired — how infinitely tired — and his words how hollow and how sad in disillusion." He was nearing the end of a bitter trail.[31]

XV

Across the continent Franklin D. Roosevelt, among friends and neighbors in Poughkeepsie, quietly summed up his surging memories of the campaign — the crowds, the faces, the scenes, the kaleidoscope of America. "You may not have universally agreed with me," he told the radio audience at the end, "but you have universally been kind and friendly to me. The great understanding and tolerance of America came out to meet me everywhere; for all this you have my heartfelt gratitude."

"Out of this unity that I have seen," he added, "we may build the strongest strand to lift ourselves out of this depression." [32]

And on the morrow America voted. The gamblers and the pollsters had little doubt of the outcome: the odds were strongly in favor of Roosevelt, and little Hoover money could be found. But the people were to make the decision, and they could not know the conclusion until they had performed the act. And so they streamed to the polls, voting their fears, voting their hopes. Three million more cast their ballots than four years before.

Franklin Roosevelt heard the returns in a small room off Democratic headquarters on the first floor of the Biltmore Hotel in New York. His family surrounded him, and a few friends: Ed Flynn, the O'Connors, the Rosenmans, Henry Morgenthau, Jr., Raymond Moley. Jim Farley dodged in and out, with late bulletins. Louis Howe, suddenly overcome with pessimism hid himself away in the cluttered office on Madison Avenue.

Early returns showed a clear Roosevelt trend. But Howe, deep in gloom, nervously lighting one Sweet Caporal after another, could only say, "Losers always have a big spurt at the start." Gradually the reports converted even Howe. Around eleven o'clock, Eleanor Roosevelt and Jim Farley came over to persuade him to come back to the main headquarters. Howe was delighted at the visit but preferred to congratulate Roosevelt over the phone, while he pored over the returns, as Farley said, like a miser inspecting his gold. In time the old man reached into the drawer of his desk and lifted out a bottle of sherry. He had put it away twenty years ago in Albany after the Sheehan fight; it was not to be opened until Franklin Roosevelt was elected President. Carefully Howe filled glasses, raised his own, and said, "To the next President of the United States!"

By eleven o'clock it was clearly all over. Shortly before midnight Roosevelt, smiling and happy, singled out Howe and Farley as the "two people in the United States, more than anybody else, who are responsible for the great victory." A quarter of an hour after midnight Herbert Hoover conceded defeat at Palo Alto. About one-forty Roosevelt finally left the Biltmore to go to East 65th Street. His mother, meeting him at the door, embraced him and said, "This is the greatest night of my life." [33]

34. A Nation Waits

FRANKLIN D. ROOSEVELT, surveying in post-election calm the conditions of the country, could not but have been awed by the responsibility he was about to inherit. At least thirteen million of his countrymen were walking cold streets in search of work. Everywhere the system of local relief was breaking down. The spurt in economic activity in the summer of 1932, as a result of the fillip administered by Hoover's involuntary excursion into deficit spending, had long since succumbed to the downward grind of deflation. As prices fell, the burden of debt incurred at higher price levels was becoming every day more intolerable. It was bankrupting the railroads, it was bankrupting local government, it was exerting an unendurable strain on the whole structure of banking and credit, it was goading the farmers into violence. A long winter stretched ahead, with nothing certain save discouragement and despair.

And there was to be no respite. He had so much mail to answer — McAdoo writing from California about "the eager and confiding look on the faces of thousands of people who were working and praying for your election, because they believe that you will . . . make it possible for them to secure employment and to *live* again"; William H. Woodin reporting that the feeling in Wall Street was "one of relief and almost enthusiasm"; Josephus Daniels trying to reverse titles and to address F.D.R. as Chief (to which Roosevelt replied, "My dear Chief: That title still stands and I am still Franklin to you"). There were so many people to see. Even a Communist group peremptorily demanded an audience in preparation for the National Hunger March on Washington the next

month. To their surprise, Roosevelt received them and listened
patiently to a Stalinist harangue. A member of the delegation
finally said, "We want you to tell President Hoover the Federal
Government must —" when Roosevelt interrupted tartly, "I can't
tell the President to do anything. I'm simply a private citizen so
far as the Federal Government is concerned." [1]

For a moment, the President-elect thought of making a visit to
Europe. William C. Bullitt, back from the Riviera, Vienna, and
the Bosporus, had bobbed up in Roosevelt's entourage. Now he
outlined possible itineraries, but Roosevelt soon decided that the
domestic crisis should take priority.[2] The administration, however,
remained loyal to the international theory of the depression.
Hoover's debt moratorium having expired, the next installment
of war debt payments would fall due on December 15. A few days
after the election, Roosevelt was astonished to receive from Hoover
a long telegram suggesting a conference on foreign debt policy.

II

The auspices for the meeting were not happy. Hoover had released his message to the press some hours before Roosevelt received it, an irritant to the recipient. Their relations, in any case,
had deteriorated a good deal since 1920, when Roosevelt had wanted
Hoover as a Democratic candidate for President, or even since 1928,
when Roosevelt refused to write an article criticizing Hoover on
the ground that the Republican candidate was "an old, personal
friend."

A curious episode in Hoover's administration had left uneasy
questions in at least Eleanor Roosevelt's mind. With the Governors' Conference scheduled nearby in Virginia, Hoover invited
the governors to a state dinner at the White House. Knowing that
guests had to stand in the East Room until received by the President
and his wife, Eleanor Roosevelt looked on the evening with preliminary alarm. Her alarm deepened when the Hoovers were an
extraordinary half-hour late in making their appearance. Roosevelt, tensely holding himself erect through sheer force of will, survived the ordeal and never seems to have mentioned it later; and it
is inconceivable that Hoover could have consciously subjected his

crippled rival to so cruel an experience. Nonetheless, an unfortunate impression remained. As Eleanor Roosevelt put it, "It seemed as though he were being deliberately put through an endurance test." [3]

There did not seem great likelihood of a meeting of minds on the issue Hoover had selected for the conference. Both Hoover and Roosevelt, it is true, opposed cancellation of the debts, and, in so doing, ranged themselves against the great majority of international bankers and of academic economists. But they differed sharply over the significance both of the debts themselves and of international economic relations in general. Hoover, who saw no further hope in domestic policy, was more than ever convinced that "the next great constructive step" in fighting the depression lay in the international field. The only remedy he could now see for the American price collapse was the re-establishment of the international gold standard. By this means, he earnestly assured the nation, "the tide of prices can be most surely and quickly turned and the tragic despair of unemployment, agriculture and business transformed to hope and confidence." If setting aside some part of the war debt payments would contribute to the stabilization of world currencies in terms of gold, Hoover was ready to readjust debt relationships. He continued to see no incompatibility between his faith in international financial action against the depression and his faith in high tariffs for the United States. [4]

But Roosevelt, and his advisers, believing the depression was primarily a domestic problem, thought that American recovery was to be achieved primarily through domestic means, and that there were many unexplored possibilities for domestic action. While they were prepared to go farther than Hoover in reducing trade barriers through reciprocal negotiations, they did not want to tie the American price level to world prices. The war debt problem therefore seemed to them more explosive politically than it was significant economically. They could see nothing the Europeans could trade for debt reduction which would justify a domestic uproar that might threaten the recovery program; they felt that the transfer problem — the inability of the debtor countries to make their payment in dollars — was exaggerated, since transfers were being made every day from Europe to New York to service private debts; and they greatly mistrusted the pressure for cancellation from Wall Street and the international banking community, since forgiveness of the war debts would have the obvious effect of making private debts more collectible. While in the long run something would have to be done about the debts, the problem thus occupied at the moment a low place on the Roosevelt agenda. It was not, in Roosevelt's view, the key to anything. Accordingly the President-elect not only opposed — as did Hoover — any move to postpone the payments due on December 15, but — unlike Hoover — opposed any action that would use a debt settlement to strengthen the international gold standard or would seem to give the international approach priority over the pressing domestic questions.[5]

Matters were not helped when a report reached New York from Sumner Welles that Ogden Mills had said, "We now have the fellow in a hole that he is not going to be able to get out of." [6] The debt talk began to take on the appearance of an attempt to commit the incoming administration in advance to the international theory of the depression and thus to sidetrack the New Deal. Roosevelt himself had no choice but to accept Hoover's invitation, and he wished to be helpful where he could. But he was deeply concerned not to be maneuvered into accepting after the election the programs he had presumably defeated during the campaign. It seemed obvious that he could not accept responsibility for public policy without the power to make it.

III

As for the President, even though he had initiated the meeting, he fully returned Roosevelt's suspicions about it. The election still hung heavily on him. Stimson, reflecting that he had served two of the three Republican Presidents ever to be rejected for second terms, could not help contrasting Taft and Hoover. Taft had been philosophical and almost relieved in defeat; but Hoover, Stimson observed, "had wrapped himself in the belief that the state of the country really depended upon his re-election. I really believe he believed it." Even after the vote, the President still had "the aroma of battle on him." "My chief fear," noted Stimson on the morning of the conference, "is the attitude in which Hoover is approaching the meeting. He has allowed himself to get so full of distrust of his rival that I think it will go far to prevent a profitable meeting." [7]

Both principals were visibly ill at ease on November 22, when Roosevelt stopped off in Washington on his way to Warm Springs — Roosevelt nervously smoothing disheveled hair after the drive from the station, Hoover grave, cold, and glum. In the context, Moley and Mills, who also attended the meeting, assumed somewhat the aspect of seconds in a duel. Roosevelt had known Mills since they were boys together along the Hudson, and for a moment they engaged in a passage of urbane banter about the campaign. But the atmosphere was strained as the four men settled themselves in the Red Room under portraits of Adams, Jefferson, Madison, and Grant. Hoover and Mills lit cigars, Roosevelt and Moley cigarettes, while pitchers of ice water and orangeade were brought to a convenient table.

Then Hoover began his presentation. Averting his eyes from Roosevelt, looking first at the great seal of the United States, woven in the carpet at his feet, and then at Moley, he set forth his views with cogency. From time to time, Roosevelt inserted questions, mostly prepared in advance by Moley after consultation with Berle and Tugwell. Finally the President suggested the reconstitution of the old Debt Commission and proposed that Roosevelt join with him in choosing the members. Roosevelt and Moley shied away from this, fearing both commitment to priorities they rejected and undue emphasis on what seemed to them a peripheral issue. By now it was dusk; the afternoon light was dim through the heavy red curtains.

Very little had flowed between the old President and the new. Hoover, passionately certain that he alone knew how to solve the crisis, could not make out his successor. "He did not get it at all," Hoover was heard to lament; they had spent their time, he later told Stimson, in educating a very ignorant and well-meaning young man. Yet Hoover also somewhat inconsistently believed that Roosevelt had agreed to his proposals. No doubt strings were left hanging: Roosevelt supposed he had assented to Hoover's broad principles, which he soon affirmed in a public statement, but he had no intention of accepting his immediate program, in which he had no confidence. The misunderstanding became evident the next day when Roosevelt resented what he regarded as Hoover's attempt to commit him to Hoover's prepared statement, while Hoover resented equally Roosevelt's refusal to underwrite the administration policies. The result of the meeting was thus aggravation of mistrust.[8]

IV

The November conversations did not end the matter. Hoover had spoken then of his hopes for the long meditated International Economic and Monetary Conference. In December Moley, catching a glimpse of a State Department report on the conference agenda, detected what he considered one more attempt to use international commitments to tie Roosevelt's hands in domestic reform. Moley and Tugwell promptly urged Roosevelt to speak to Edmund E. Day and John H. Williams, Hoover's representatives on the Preparatory Commission, before the agenda was frozen.

At the same time, Hoover put pressure on Roosevelt to join in a new effort at debt renegotiation before the Conference. But Roosevelt, consulting with Tugwell and Lewis Douglas, once again resisted what he regarded as an attempt to entangle him in responsibility for policies not his own (though Douglas's role remains ambiguous; a day or two later in Washington he gave Mills and Stimson the impression that he really agreed with them.)[9] Hoover then released the exchange of messages to the press as if finally washing his hands of an intolerable relationship.

At this point Stimson suddenly received a telephone call from his old friend Felix Frankfurter, who was staying the night with Roosevelt at Albany. Frankfurter reported Roosevelt as saying out of a clear sky, "Why doesn't Harry Stimson come up here and talk with me and settle this damn thing that nobody else seems to be able to?" Stimson, conveying the message to the President, found Hoover adamant against the idea. "You won't get anything," said the President bitterly, "you won't get anything. You can't trust him."

But Roosevelt soon renewed the invitation. As Stimson thought about it, it began to seem to him "incomprehensible that we should take a position which would deprive the incoming President of

the United States of important information about foreign affairs."
From the start, he had regretted "very strongly the situation which
has been produced by the suspicion which both Hoover and Mills
have of Roosevelt." Action on the basis of their "violent prejudice"
appeared to him "untenable"; "we should give this man as fair
a chance as possible." When Hoover returned to Washington after
the New Year, Stimson reopened the question. The President repeated that Roosevelt was a very dangerous and contrary man and
that he would never see him alone. But Stimson responded that
it was a ticklish responsibility to refuse information to the President-elect; even if Roosevelt were as bad as Hoover thought, it
would be worse to give him this grievance than anything he might
do in the way of treachery.

After twenty-four hours, Hoover finally gave grudging consent.
On January 9, a cold Monday morning, with rain turning to sleet
and then to snow, Henry L. Stimson, who had been defeated for
Governor of New York so many years before in the Democratic
surge that had first sent Franklin D. Roosevelt to the state Senate,
took a train to Hyde Park for his first meeting with Roosevelt.
They talked alone from eleven in the morning to five-thirty in
the afternoon.

Stimson later said he was "touched, overwhelmed by the kind-
ness he showed me." On Far Eastern policy, Roosevelt fully approved what Stimson had been doing; his only possible criticism
was that the administration had not begun its policy earlier. The
President-elect also endorsed the disarmament effort, continued
tepid about the Economic Conference, objected to Hoover's idea
of a commission to handle the war debts, and raised a number of
questions about Latin America. "I had never had a talk with him
before," Stimson wrote in his diary, "but we had no difficulty in
getting on. . . . I was very much pleased because none of the President's forebodings were realized." By the time they met again
later in the month, Roosevelt could remark, "We are getting so
that we do pretty good team-work, don't we?" Stimson laughed
and said, "Yes." [10]

V

As for the debt problem and the Economic Conference, Roosevelt sought late in December to convince Day and Williams at Hyde Park that the Conference should be postponed until his domestic program had a chance to take hold. But just before the New Year, Norman H. Davis, the veteran Democratic internationalist and currently the United States delegate to the Disarmament Conference at Geneva, returned from Europe to exert all his persuasiveness to get the Economic Conference back on schedule. Moley and Tugwell, representing the domestic priority, began to feel that a struggle was going on for Roosevelt's soul. Through January, their alarm increased as Roosevelt first saw Stimson alone, then publicly backed Stimson's view that the United States should take part in arms embargoes, and then endorsed the Stimson Doctrine, by which the United States refused to recognize the Japanese conquest of Manchuria.

This "made me feel better than I have for a long time," Stimson wrote in his diary; but it made Moley and Tugwell feel worse, and they harassed Roosevelt about it at the first opportunity. "I have always had the deepest sympathy for the Chinese," Roosevelt replied, recalling his ancestors in the China trade. "How could you expect me not to go along with Stimson on Japan?" Tugwell rejoined that he sympathized with the Chinese too, but that the Stimson policy could lead to war. Roosevelt conceded this possibility and said flatly, to Tugwell's horror that war with Japan might well be better now than later.[11]

After these events, the announcement that Roosevelt had agreed to discuss with Hoover the British request for a review of their debt situation distressed Moley and Tugwell even more. The domestic priority now seemed in acute jeopardy. Still, Roosevelt did ask Moley to accompany him to the meeting. But Norman Davis came to Washington too, though he was not meant to go with Roosevelt to the White House; and on the morning before the talk with Hoover, Davis had an impassioned argument with Moley and Tugwell over their desire to postpone debt negotiations till after March 4 and to keep these negotiations out of the Economic Conference. After this set-to, Davis asked Roosevelt whether he could come to the White House too. Roosevelt good-naturedly agreed.

Hoover began by presenting the need for immediate action in vigorous language. ("He seems to me close to death," Moley later told Tugwell. "He had the look of being done, but still of going on and on, driven by some damned duty.") Stimson, Mills, and even Davis joined in the barrage; Moley replied; and Roosevelt finally intervened to reaffirm his opposition both to negotiations before March 4 and to mixing debts with the other economic matters.

New confusion followed, however, when — as Moley and Tugwell saw it — Stimson attempted later in the day to obtain Roosevelt's agreement to a statement embodying the very proposals he had rejected that morning at the White House. Roosevelt, rushing for his train to Warm Springs, told Stimson to work it out with Moley. Moley and Tugwell then conferred with Stimson and his aides at the Department. When Tugwell re-explained the Roosevelt position, Stimson angrily accused him of trying to tear down everything he had been working for during his term as Secretary. Tugwell reddened, but held on to his temper. Eventually Stimson regained his good humor and referred ruefully to the problem of trying to be Secretary of State for two Presidents at once. The final text expressed the Moley-Tugwell interpretation of the Roosevelt position. Thereafter the debt controversy receded to the background of the international picture.[12]

VI

In the meantime, on December 5, 1932, the lameduck 72nd Congress convened for its final session. It met as if under siege; on the first day, a double line of policemen, armed with tear gas and riot guns, blocked the Capitol steps. A new army of Communist hunger marchers had moved into Washington, twelve hundred strong, in greasy gray caps and torn sweaters, chanting "Feed the hungry, tax the rich." The police (General Glassford had long since been forced out) roughly herded them into a detention "camp" — an exposed stretch along New York Avenue where they spent the night, sleeping in trucks or on the pavement, with no shelter against the freezing wind. The next day cops taunted them, denied them food, water, and medical attendance and, for a period, refused them permission to dig a latrine. In the end, members of Congress, who felt that even Communists retained certain rights as Americans, won them permission to parade. Under the escort of heavily armed police, the threadbare army marched to Capitol Hill, where the Red Front Band bravely played the thin strains of the "Internationale." [13]

In the White House, the President saw the short session as his last opportunity to push through his program. "To the extent that I am able," he told one of his secretaries, "I shall round out the record of the last four years before March 4th. I intend to bring that record to completion as nearly as I can." And conservative Democrats for their part saw a chance to set Roosevelt's policy for him. The important thing, they continued to believe, was to balance the budget, save the gold standard, and restore business confidence; and the quick way to do this was to enact a sales tax. The Democratic party, said Al Smith, now had an opportunity to purge itself of "the populists who blighted the party for so many years with their free-silver and other economic heresies . . . the mountebanks with their cloutish antics and their irresponsible ravings against millionaires and big business." [14] When Hoover proposed a sales tax, Garner and Joe Robinson, as Democratic leaders of House and Senate, acceded without bothering to consult the President-elect. They thought they were responding to a moral imperative; "we must balance the budget," Garner told the press. But Roosevelt, who had other views, promptly disavowed the proposal. Garner thereupon paid a personal call on Hoover to apologize for his failure to honor the agreement.

Yet Roosevelt and his advisers, while rejecting the sales tax as regressive, were hardly less anxious to raise new revenue. Even Tugwell and Berle, though not so fanatical about balanced budgets as the conservative Democrats, were far from being inflationists or deficit spenders. Concerned with the structure of the economy rather than with the volume of demand, they thought more along the lines of institutional reorganization than of monetary expansion. Tugwell found a kindred spirit in Bob La Follette; together they reasoned that government, by transferring income from the well-to-do to the impoverished, might generate enough buying power to keep the economy in motion. "Neither of us," Tugwell reflected later, "thought at that time that budgetary deficits would need to be resorted to." [15]

Only a few heretics questioned budget balancing. Some western Democrats and progressive Republicans, like Henry Wallace in Iowa, demanded one variety or another of inflation. Maynard Keynes condemned retrenchment as a beggar-my-neighbor enterprise. "One man's expenditure," he wrote, "is another man's income." Consequently the deferment of spending became an antisocial act; its logical conclusion would be to leave everyone flat on his back starving to death from his refusal to buy another's services. Must we wait, Keynes bitterly asked, for a war to renew public spending and thus end the depression? Was there nothing else for which even "the deadheads" might regard it as legitimate to run a deficit? William Trufant Foster continued similarly to call for government spending; and Stuart Chase contended, "Prosperity can never be restored by spending less but only by spending more. . . . A rigid programme of economy might so far shatter purchasing power and provoke unemployment that the dole, naked and wholesale, would be the only substitute for revolution."

But most bankers and economists, like most politicians, were haunted by images of a German inflation, with satchels stuffed with dollars to buy a loaf of bread. If inflation remained the threat, then retrenchment was the solution. It was in vain that Keynes wrote, "To bring up the bogy of inflation as an objection to expenditure is like warning a patient who is wasting away from emaciation of the dangers of excessive corpulence." [16]

VII

From all sides pressure thus played on the President-elect. Moley was now functioning more than ever as his alter ego — a whole cabinet rolled into one, trying to ride herd on all major issues of both domestic and foreign policy. The campaign brain trust had dissolved. Never again would Moley, Tugwell, Berle, and Johnson meet as a team. And Roosevelt was already displaying disconcerting new habits, especially of asking new people to do jobs which he neglected to tell anybody else about. The comparative order of the campaign had disappeared. "The informality of the whole performance," said Tugwell in retrospect, "gave it a certain nerve-wracking quality." This especially irritated Moley, who retained the nominal responsibility for coordination and now took out his exasperation in fits of temper.

Yet Moley found compensations. Thrust into the floodlight by the conference with Hoover, he was becoming an object of national attention. "I had a pleasant chat with Professor Moley," said the irrepressible Huey Long, "I told him that I knew he was a wise man, but that there never was a wise man who did not have to see someone wiser at some time and that I was available at any time he wanted to come. I added that I would not tell a soul about it except the newspapermen." Sam Rayburn of Texas, more direct in his approach, leaned across the aisle toward Moley on the train back from Warm Springs in December and whispered meaningfully, "I hope we don't have any god-damned Rasputin in this Administration." [17]

There was no god-damned Rasputin in the administration. This became evident late in January when Tugwell gave an interview to Forrest Davis of the New York *World-Telegram*, sensationally billed as an authoritative forecast of the New Deal. The Tugwell program included $5 billion for public works, with direct federal relief and an expansion of RFC activities; it also envisaged sound currency and a balanced budget, to be achieved through drastic increase of income and inheritance taxes and through borrowing. "If we lack purchasing power," said Tugwell, "we lack everything. . . . There is just one thing to do: Take incomes from where they are and place them where we need them." To save the country by saving the banks, he added, was like trying to revive a dying tree "by applying fertilizer to its branches instead of to its roots." The interview annoyed Roosevelt and caused the cancellation of Tugwell's scheduled visit to Warm Springs, as well as the postponement of the publication of *The Industrial Discipline*. ("After this," Tugwell wrote in his diary, "I shall never trust another reporter.") [18]

And there were other voices around the President-elect. Felix Frankfurter moved softly in and out of Albany, spreading the gospel

according to Justice Brandeis. Lewis Douglas, the able and attractive young congressman from Arizona, spoke of solutions in
rigorous governmental reorganization and retrenchment. For a
moment, Bernard Baruch thought his hour had arrived. "Apparently," he confided to a friend, "I am to be responsible for the
economic side of this whole thing." New ideas poured in every
day by letter and telegraph. And in the storm center remained
Roosevelt himself, open-minded, curious, experimental, sanguine,
genially keeping his own counsel.

Tom Connally of Texas, visiting Warm Springs in December,
was shocked to find Roosevelt talking of budget balancing and
stressing the constitutional limitations on government action. "If it
was constitutional to spend forty billion dollars in a war," the Texas
senator protested, "isn't it just as constitutional to spend a little
money to relieve the hunger and misery of our citizens?" But the
President-elect sat on in his shirtsleeves, smoked his cigarette, and
remained noncommittal — a performance possibly designed to induce Connally's reaction and thus to test the possibilities open to
him. The old Wilsonians Cordell Hull and Dan Roper became so
fearful of Roosevelt's apparent conservatism that they besought
Josephus Daniels to urge the President-elect to be more progressive.
"When I talk to him," complained Huey Long, "he says 'Fine!
Fine! Fine!' But Joe Robinson goes to see him the next day and
again he says 'Fine! Fine! Fine!' Maybe he says 'Fine!' to everybody." [19]

VIII

Yet, if Roosevelt was evasive about programs, he had a powerful instinct about direction and a considerable range of commitment to policies. It was perfectly clear from the campaign, for
example, that he believed in positive government as a means of
redressing the balance of the economic world; that he wanted
federal relief as well as old-age assistance and unemployment insurance; that he planned a program of public works; that he would
push the conservation of natural resources, including land utilization, reforestation and flood control; that he meant to tackle the
crop surplus problem and to restore agricultural purchasing power;

that he hoped to redistribute population between city and countryside; that he wished to regulate speculation and the security
exchanges.

The campaign as well as his governorship committed him to
sweeping action in the public power field; he had permitted a writer
in September 1932 to describe as his "minimum" program the passage of the Norris Muscle Shoals bill, the completion of the investigation of the power trust, and the enactment of legislation
regulating public utility holding companies.[20] For the economy
as a whole, he had spoken more vaguely in the campaign of establishing an economic constitutional order and of the national
planning of production. In the international field, he had espoused — if warily — the idea of tariff reduction through reciprocal
trade agreements. And his governorship indicated that he wanted
to improve wages and hours and to strengthen the trade union
movement. No one could seriously have supposed that Roosevelt
was planning a do-nothing administration. He had even once talked
in the campaign of revolution — "the right kind, the only kind
of revolution this nation can stand for — a revolution at the ballot
box." The only reassurance for conservatives had been his Pittsburgh pledge of government retrenchment and budget balancing
and his recurrent promise of sound money (though he had carefully refrained from defining this in terms of the existing gold
standard).[21]

A few days after the New Year, William Randolph Hearst sent
an emissary to the President-elect. Roosevelt told Hearst's agent
that he considered farm relief the first priority; then unemployment
relief and public works, though he described Hearst's five-billion-
dollar program as "too large at present." Conservation, reclamation,
reforestation, and subsistence farming, he thought, could mop up
surplus labor. Budget balancing was to be achieved by governmental economies, especially in veterans' pensions. "If the fall in
the price of commodities cannot be checked," Roosevelt added,
"we may be forced to an inflation of our currency. This may take
the form of using silver as a base, or decreasing the amount of
gold in the dollar. I have not decided how this inflation can be
best and most safely accomplished."

Roosevelt similarly assured George Creel that he was bent on

striking changes. The debacle of 1929, Roosevelt told Creel, marked
the end of an era. The old order of rugged individualism had
gone; interdependence was now the order of the day. What was
plain was that all business had come to be affected with a public
interest, and that business which could make a fair return only
by child labor, long hours, low wages, lying and cheating was not
business the country wanted. The new economic order would have
to enforce national standards, bringing great industries, such as
mining, milling, manufacturing, and agriculture, under central
control. Only by such means, he said, would it be possible for
men to go to sleep at night without fear of the morrow.[22]

IX

By late January, Washington observers began to note that liberals
making the pilgrimage to Warm Springs returned more cheerful
than conservatives. The visit of George Norris was perhaps especially significant. As early as December, Roosevelt had written
Norris that he was "particularly anxious" for his company on a
trip to Muscle Shoals. In mid-January, the two men stood together overlooking Wilson Dam, watching the thousands of gal-
lons of water, white and turbulent, plunge through the spillways.
Now, at least, the rushing water might light homes, turn wheels,
replenish the Valley. Roosevelt said to his companion: "This
should be a happy day for you, George." Norris, tears in his eyes,
responded slowly, "It is, Mr. President. I see my dreams come true."
Later, speaking from the portico of the State Capitol at Montgomery, Roosevelt made it clear that his interest went beyond the
narrow question of whether power should be public or private at
Muscle Shoals. "I am determined on two things," he said, "as a
result of what I have seen today. The first is to put Muscle Shoals
to work. The second is to make of Muscle Shoals a part of an
even greater development that will take in all of that magnificent
Tennessee River from the mountains of Virginia down to the Ohio
and the Gulf."

In a few days, seated before the fireplace at the Little White
House at Warm Springs, he unfolded before a group of newspapermen a broad vision of multi-purpose development throughout the

Tennessee Valley, linking water power, flood control, forestry, conservation, reclamation, agriculture, and industry in one vast experiment. "I think," he said, "the development will be the forerunner of similar projects in other parts of the country, such as in the watersheds of the Ohio, Missouri and Arkansas rivers and in the Columbia River in the Northwest." He recurred to his old conviction that the balance of population between city and farm would have to be readjusted. Even if 1929 levels of business activity could be restored, there would still be five million men out of work. "The normal trend now is a back-to-the-farm movement. . . . We have been going at these projects piecemeal ever since the days of Theodore Roosevelt and Gifford Pinchot. . . . I believe it is now time to tie up all these various developments into one great comprehensive plan within a given area." [23]

Roosevelt had other moments of concreteness, as when he outlined his plans for the reorganization of transportation at another press conference. But a vagueness remained — a vagueness perhaps inescapable in the void before responsibility. Always he talked — to himself as well as to the others, defining his direction, clarifying his tasks, but avoiding rigid commitment. "Let's concentrate upon one thing — " he told his old friend from Wilsonian days, Dan Roper, "save the people and the nation and, if we have to change our minds twice every day to accomplish that end, we should do it." And, when Tugwell once gloomily remarked that they were in for the worst economic difficulties the country had ever known, Roosevelt replied, with mingled dread and exhilaration, "Yes, I know it; but there is nothing to do but meet every day's troubles as they come. What terrible decisions we'll have to make! and sometimes we'll be wrong!" [24]

35. Confusion in the Void

IN THE MEANTIME, Congress struggled ineffectually with a series of legislative proposals, some coming from the retiring President, others from the President-elect. Hoover wanted government retrenchment, a sales tax, banking and bankruptcy legislation, and a general mortgage discount system. Roosevelt had his own version of the bankruptcy and mortgage relief measures, and added to the agenda such further items as repeal of the Eighteenth Amendment, legalization of beer, and a new farm policy. And some members of Congress, like Senator Black of Alabama with his thirty-hour law, had their own solutions for the crisis. But party discipline was nonexistent; tempers were everywhere short, nerves frayed. Huey Long was on a private rampage, filibustering Carter Glass's banking proposals. James E. Watson, Hoover's leader in the Senate, hoped by blocking legislation in January to force Roosevelt into a special session in March, presumably on the theory that the new President would be caught without a program. Hoover himself was saying by mid-session "I don't want them to do anything now." [1] Increasingly the session mirrored — and therefore intensified — the frustration of the country.

This was hiatus, the great void. The old regime's writ had run, while the new had no power to break through the stagnation. Hoover was a discredited failure, Roosevelt a vague and now fading hope; and, suspended between past and future, the nation drifted as on dark seas of unreality. It knew only a sense of premonition and of change; but the shape of the future was as baffling as the memory of the past. One figure, emerging inconspicuously out of a forgotten time, emphasized the transformation a few years had wrought. In New York on a cold winter day in December, Calvin Coolidge spent an afternoon in idle talk with an old friend. "We are in a new era to which I do not belong," he finally said, "and it would not be possible for me to adjust myself to it. These new ideas call for new men to develop them. That task is not for men who believe in the only kind of government I know anything about." In another three weeks Coolidge was dead.[2]

Much died with him — in particular the prestige of the business community to which he had consecrated himself with such bleak fanaticism. In January the Senate Banking and Currency Committee enlarged an investigation of practices in banking and on the stock exchange begun a year earlier. As newspapermen watched with astonishment, leading figures of the banking world shuffled to the stand, where, under the patient and ruthless questioning of Ferdinand Pecora, the new Committee counsel, they squirmed, fidgeted, and sweated, while reluctantly confessing to one breach after another both of normal ethics and of normal intelligence. Many idols began to crumble as the Pecora inquiry proceeded. But many more crumbled, almost as devastatingly, when the Senate Finance Committee in the last two weeks of February gave businessmen a rostrum from which they could offer their economic wisdom to the nation.

II

Senator Pat Harrison, a conservative Democrat, staged the show in an effort to head off racial ideas. In the end, he could hardly have offered a stronger invitation to radicalism. It was here that John W. Davis said he had nothing to offer, either of fact or theory; that General Atterbury of the Pennsylvania Railroad saw no solution except hitting the bottom; that Bernard Baruch insisted that the national credit was about to be exhausted and that the government could no longer borrow. "Balance budgets," said Baruch, "stop spending money we haven't got. Sacrifice for frugality and revenue. Cut government spending — cut it as rations are cut in a siege. Tax — tax everybody for everything."

On and on they came, in a melancholy parade. One senator asked

Jackson Reynolds of the First National Bank of New York whether he had a solution. "I have not," said Reynolds, "and I do not believe anybody else has." Myron C. Taylor of United States Steel? "I have no remedy in mind" beyond retrenchment and budget balancing. David F. Houston, Wilson's Secretary of Agriculture and of the Treasury, and now president of Mutual Life? "Avoid any unnecessary appropriations." Edward D. Duffield of the Prudential? "The thing of primary importance is the balancing of the Federal Budget." Paul Block of the Block papers? "First in importance is the balancing of our Budget." Nicholas Murray Butler? "Governmental economy and balanced budgets." Will Clayton of Clayton and Anderson? "Balance the Budget through a drastic reduction in the cost of Government." Ernest T. Weir of Weirton Steel? "The great necessity [is] for balancing our Budget."

A few heretics appeared. John L. Lewis of the United Mine Workers, in demanding national planning, said scornfully, "The balancing of the Budget will not in itself place a teaspoonful of milk in a hungry baby's stomach or remove the rags from its mother's back." William Randolph Hearst called for a sales tax but also, in a last hangover from his radical past, for the nationalization of the railroads. J. David Stern, publisher of the Philadelphia *Record,* denouncing budget-balancing, invoked the authority of John Maynard Keynes, "the greatest economist living today." "How can government meet this situation?" asked the economist Lawrence Dennis. "The first condition to be recognized is the need for more spending." Donald Richberg, the old Progressive, wanted a planned economy. But such off-key voices were drowned in the general clamor for government retrenchment.[3]

And so, in the fourth winter of the depression, American business seemed to plead not only financial but also intellectual bankruptcy. Richberg, in his appearance before the Senate Finance Committee, delivered a savage judgment.

> I submit that every conspicuous leader of affairs who has appeared before this committee and who has attempted to justify the continuance of the present political economic system unchanged, with its present control unreformed, is either too ignorant of facts, too stupid in comprehension, or too viciously

selfish in his short-sighted philosophy, to be worthy of any attention in this time of bitter need for honest, intelligent, and
public-spirited planning for the rehabilitation of our crumbling
civilization.

George Sokolsky, after a six-thousand-mile trip around the country
that winter, reached the same conclusion. "Confidence in the erst-
while leadership of this country is gone. Mention the name of any
of the great men of the Post-War era, and there is only derision. No
banker, no great industrialist, no college president commands the
respect of the American people." Joseph P. Kennedy, himself a
Wall Street speculator, wrote, "The belief that those in control of
the corporate life of America were motivated by honesty and ideals
of honorable conduct was completely shattered." "In the past five
years," Walter Lippmann said, "the industrial and financial leaders
of America have fallen from one of the highest positions of influence and power that they have ever occupied in our history to one
of the lowest." [4]

III

The mighty had fallen, but nothing had risen to take their places.
The people could only stir in impotent mistrust. The cities remained quiet in the winter of 1932–33, in spite of William Green's
brave talk in January before a Senate committee about "class war"
and "the language of force." But the countryside, still shaken by
the Farm Holiday agitation of the preceding summer, was finding
each new stage in direct action easier and more popular.

The debt situation was becoming increasingly critical. In Iowa,
the most heavily mortgaged state, nearly one-third of the value of
farms was in thrall, mainly to banks and insurance companies. Sinking farm prices made it harder than ever to pay interest or taxes
out of cash received for current production. With misfortune
striking down the industrious equally with the idle and incompetent,
farmers grew increasingly determined not to surrender without a
fight. They formed committees of action to resist tax sales and
mortgage foreclosures — unsmiling men, dressed in overalls or in
corduroy, wearing old red or green sweaters, carrying clubs.

At Storm Lake, Iowa, farmers flourished a rope and threatened to hang a lawyer who was about to conduct a foreclosure. In Van Buren County, Iowa, Mrs. Otto Nau forced Sheriff Bostock off her farm at the point of a rifle. At Le Mars, five hundred men gathered in a sullen mob to watch the farm of John A. Johnson go on auction; when the agent for the New York Life Insurance Company offered a sum less than the face value of the mortgage, people slapped and mauled him; a few shouted "Lynch him!" Outside of Pleasanton, Kansas, someone found the murdered body of a man who had just foreclosed on a five-hundred-acre farm. At Sidney, Nebraska, farm leaders threatened to march two hundred thousand debtors to the State Capitol at Lincoln and "tear it down" unless they got relief. At Malinta, Ohio, a noose hung ominously from Albert Roehl's barn to warn off outside bidders. In one bankruptcy proceeding after another, friends of the debtor, using unspoken intimidation to cut off other bids, bought back the property for a few cents and restored it to its owner.

The rumblings reached Washington. Ed O'Neal told Congress that unless something were done there would be revolution in the countryside in less than twelve months. "Gentlemen of the Committee," John A. Simpson of the Farmers' Union said before the Senate Agricultural Committee, "the biggest and finest crop of little revolutions I ever saw is ripe all over this country right now." And in New York, Mother Bloor, the veteran Communist agitator, back from the Middle West, said with professional admiration, "I never saw anything like the militancy of those farmers."

But it was not Bolshevism that was moving the men of the middle border. They were rather defending rights of property, especially the right of men to keep the homes they had carved out of the prairie by years of labor and self-denial — a right to be affirmed, by force if necessary, against all the banks and insurance companies in the world. Theirs, as they saw it, was the way not of revolution but of patriotism. The foreclosure riots at Primghar, Iowa, thus came to an end when a deputy sheriff sank to his knees before a crowd of angry farmers and obediently kissed the American flag.[5]

Yet such activity still represented a new conception of the rights of property and the duties of Americans. A cult of direct action was beginning to grow. Al Smith responded to it in another way early in February. Depression was equivalent to war, he said; indeed, things were already worse than they had been in 1918. "And what does a democracy do in war? It becomes a tyrant, a despot, a real monarch. In the World War we took our Constitution, wrapped it up and laid it on the shelf and left it there until it was over." So too Walter Lippmann, a few days later — give the President for a year the widest and fullest powers, limit congressional rights of debate and amendment, "the danger is not that we shall lose our liberties, but that we shall not be able to act with the necessary speed and comprehensiveness." [6] And in the distance, as Americans drifted in the great void, more ominous formations gathered — Minute Men and Silver Shirts, Khaki Shirts and White Shirts and American Nationalists. The nation was evidently on the brink of an abyss. The *Moody Bible Institute Monthly* even detected eschatological portents in the winter's tribulations: the last days might be on hand, the final crisis before the millennium.

IV

Perhaps nothing better evidenced the fear of the void than the strange excitement which flared so high that winter and then, with equal suddenness, died away. The excitement had a prophet: an eccentric New York engineer named Howard Scott. Scott's career went back to the exuberant hopes of 1919. He had known Veblen in New York, had absorbed (or, as his disciples later claimed, stimulated) Veblen's ideas about the future role of engineers in industrial society, and in 1920 had founded an organization called the Technical Alliance as a way of realizing Veblen's dream of a soviet of technicians; Stuart Chase was one of its members. For a time in these years, Scott served as a consultant for the IWW. In that period too he may have read articles in *Industrial Management,* in which W. H. Smith discussed a new idea of social organization called "technocracy."

In the twenties, Scott became a familiar character in Greenwich Village. On the side he ran a floor-wax business; but his dedication was to economics, and he talked away, confidently and vehemently, to all who would listen. *Wealth, Virtual Wealth and Debt* by Frederick Soddy, an Oxford professor who had won the Nobel prize in chemistry, fortified Scott's economic ideas when it was published in the United States in 1926. As Scott saw the future, the inexorable increase of productivity, far outstripping opportunities for employment or investment, must mean permanent and growing unemployment and permanent and growing debt, until capitalism itself collapsed under the double load. The industrial age had at last "turned upon its masters to destroy them." But, "in that moment of destruction [it] offers to the inhabitants of the American continent a security that they have never known." The hope was to give over control to the technicians, who (he was contending by 1932) could provide a standard of living ten times as great as 1929 on an average sixteen-hour work week. Everything in the technocratic utopia would be as scientific as the machine itself. "No political structure or political legerdemain has any use whatever in an energy state. In a technological administration controlling the continent, there would be no place for political action of any kind."

But, to achieve a full use of economic resources, the old price system would have to go. "Mass production, necessary to produce at lowest physical cost, must run at continuous full load," Scott said. "In order to maintain this rate of operation, there must be assigned mass purchasing power equal to the output of production. . . . The control of the rates of flow of goods and services cannot occur under a price system. . . . There must be an accurate measurement of all rates of flow, substituted for the process of evaluation now used in our currency and credit structure." Scott wanted to replace money based on gold by money based on ergs and joules — based, that is, on the measurement of energy. If goods were priced according to the amount of energy used in making them, then the total of prices would equal the total of kilowatt hours of labor. (Scott was never very clear about the measurement of services.) With the proper allocation of energy money, consumption would thus unfailingly balance production.

Depression at last provided Scott a hearing and an audience. In August 1932 New York newspapers broke the story of an energy survey of North America to be conducted at Columbia University by a group called Technocracy under Scott's direction. Suddenly the idea seized the popular imagination. Technocracy offered a plausible explanation for mass unemployment. Its diagnosis was cast in the authoritative language of science and engineering. Seeing the future in terms of technology rather than of politics or finance, it appealed to people who had lost faith in men and money but not in machines. "There are no physical factors in existence which would prevent the efficient operation of this continent on an energy basis," Scott said. "The only thing that does prevent it is our devotion to a shibboleth — price."

As a practical matter, the movement had obvious drawbacks. "Technocracy does not know how to get from here to there," Scott confessed. . . . It is not interested in political methods." Yet popular excitement rose amazingly around it. Bankers and industrialists flocked to hear Scott at banquets at the Metropolitan Club and the Pierre. Upton Sinclair, quivering with italics, called Technocracy *"the most important movement which has shown its head in our time."* Stuart Chase saw in it "perhaps the most arresting challenge which the American industrial system has ever faced." The *Nation* pronounced Technocracy "the first step toward a genuine revolutionary philosophy for America" and addressed an open letter to its prophet. Radio comedians made jokes about it; a new dance was named after it at Roseland; in Chicago (according to *Time*) the sponsors of the Anti-Rodeo League and the Mental Patients Defenders Association formed the Technocratic party of the United States.

Not everything, however, was acclaim. "Of all the sure-cures hawked since the depression began," said H. L. Mencken with scorn, "it is the worst. Communism, I think, is more rational." Archibald MacLeish, noting that the economic determinism of Marx was possibly giving way to the technological determinism of Scott, observed dryly, "One mechanistic nipple replaces another." Al Smith perhaps offered the definitive comment. "As for substituting engineers for political leaders in running the country," he said, "I cannot refrain from mentioning the fact that we have finished an era of government by engineers in Washington."

Howard Scott, in his engineer's leather coat, with red handkerchief and red necktie, gaunt and voluble, did his best by fast talking to maintain the atmosphere of impending revelation. But such statistics and charts as he did disclose were too obviously defective, and the great energy survey always remained for the indefinite fu-

ture. In the middle of January, Nicholas Murray Butler on behalf
of Columbia disclaimed any connection with Scott. A few days
later, the reputable members of the Committee on Technocracy —
including Professor Walter Rautenstrauch of Columbia and Leon
Henderson of the Russell Sage Foundation — denounced Scott and
resigned. Caught between ribaldry and irrelevance, the technocratic
dream faded as rapidly as it had arisen. Yet a residue remained:
a sense of infinite technological possibility; a susceptibility to new
approaches; a readiness to break with the past.[7]

The cracking and crumbling and the search for a savior might
well have chiliastic implications. Every day more of the nation
yearned to wrap up the Constitution and stake all on something
very like dictatorship. The system rested in the end on confidence,
on faith; and the very elements of confidence and faith were trickling
away. As the nation's banks staggered under the weight of debt,
men and women across the land, filled with vague disquiet, began
to go to the cashiers' windows and withdraw their savings. As withdrawals mounted in the first two weeks of February, a financial crisis
seemed inescapable. And leadership seemed more futile than ever:
Hoover, mute and helpless in Washington; Roosevelt, waiting affably but without authority in the wings, idly cruising, at the moment, in Vincent Astor's yacht *Nourmahal* off the Florida coast.

v

On February 14 the governor of Michigan decreed an eight-day
bank holiday, closing all the banks of the state. On the 15th, Roosevelt went ashore at Miami. A motorcade took the President-elect
to a reception at the Bay Front Park as dusk began to fall. (In a
car behind, Vincent Astor and Ray Moley academically discussed
the risks of assassination in crowded city streets.) Sitting on top of
the back seat of his open car, Roosevelt addressed the crowd. As he
finished, the newsreel people asked him to repeat his speech for them.
He courteously replied that he could not. Then he slid off the back
of his car into his seat.

Just then Mayor Cermak of Chicago came forward. (Cermak was
seeking political favors; he would never have had to go to Miami
on this mission, Jim Farley later wrote, if he had not stalled on de-

livering the Illinois delegation to Roosevelt after the first ballot in Chicago.) A man appeared with a long telegram and started to explain it to Roosevelt. The President-elect, leaning forward to listen, turned toward the left side of the car. Suddenly Roosevelt heard what he took to be the explosion of a firecracker; it was followed immediately by several more explosions. Blood mysteriously spurted on the hand of one of the Secret Service men. Roosevelt abruptly became aware in the half-light of a short, swarthy man standing on a small box thirty-five feet away, wildly spraying bullets in his direction. A roar of fear and horror began to rise from the crowd. In a moment Roosevelt's strong voice rang out above the panic, "I'm all right! I'm all right!"

Joe (or Giuseppe) Zangara was an unemployed bricklayer who had bought his revolver at a pawnshop on North Miami Avenue for eight dollars. Nagging pains in an ulcerated stomach filled him with deep hostility toward the world. "I have always hated the rich and powerful. . . . I hoped I would have better luck than I had ten years ago when in Italy I bought a pistol to kill King Emmanuel. . . . I sat there in the park waiting, and my stomach kept aching more than ever. . . . I do not hate Mr. Roosevelt personally, I hate all Presidents, no matter from what country they come, and I hate all officials and everybody who is rich." And so, his stomach blazing as if it were on fire, he poured his bullets toward the presidential car. Mayor Cermak, writhing in agony, fell to the ground; four others were wounded. Roosevelt motioned to have Cermak put in the back of his car and told the chauffeur to drive to the hospital. "Tony, keep quiet — don't move," he said. "It won't hurt if you keep quiet."

The events at Miami shocked the nation into reality. If the thin chance which had saved the people their President-elect was sobering, his own response was more than that — it was heartening and exhilarating. For Roosevelt, it was clear, really lacked physical fear, and an impulse of courage now flowed out to the nation against the backdrop of gunfire at Miami.

When John Garner warned him about the dangers of assassination in December, Roosevelt had reassuringly answered, "I remember T. R. saying to me 'The only real danger from an assassin is from one who does not care whether he loses his own life in the act or not. Most of the crazy ones can be spotted first.' " Nor did the actuality of the attempt now disturb him. "I have never in my life seen anything more magnificent," Moley later wrote, "than Roosevelt's calm that night on the *Nourmahal.*" His only concern was the condition of Cermak and the others who had been wounded. (Cermak died a few days later.) "He was a fatalist," reported McDuffie, his valet. "He believed what was to be would be. He laughed! He didn't take that very seriously. He wasn't a man to be in a very serious mood over a thing that's gone under the bridge. If it was over, it was over." The next morning, when McDuffie brought out the tie rack, Roosevelt reached for the same red tie he had worn the day before. As McDuffie remembered it: "I said, 'This morning we won't put the red tie on.' And he laughed and laughed. . . . That was the only time I ever selected his tie." [8]

(Fourteen months earlier, a British politician, crossing Fifth Avenue in New York between 76th and 77th Streets around ten-thirty at night, had looked in the wrong direction and was knocked down by an oncoming car — a moment, he later recalled, of a man aghast, a world aglare: "I do not understand why I was not broken like an eggshell or squashed like a gooseberry." Those who believe that personalities make no difference to history might well ponder whether the world would have been the same in the next two decades had Giuseppe Zangara's bullet killed Roosevelt at Miami in 1933 and had Mario Contasini's car killed Winston Churchill on Fifth Avenue in 1931.) [9]

VI

Miami, breaking the nation's mood, brought a new rush of faith in the President-elect. And, in the meantime, Roosevelt himself had been making gradual progress in setting up the new administration. As early as October he had told Farley that he wanted George Dern of Utah for Secretary of the Interior and Farley himself for Postmaster-General. For a period after the election, however, cabinet-making was held up by competing conservative and progressive pressures. Even his mother had suggestions. "I wonder who you will take to Washington," she wrote. "I should try Owen Young or Newton Baker." But by early January Roosevelt could assure William Randolph Hearst's emissary that it would be a "radical" cabinet; "there will be no one in it who knows the way to 23 Wall Street. No one who is linked in any way with the power trust or with the international bankers." Baker, Young, and John W. Davis, he said, were definitely out; and the Secretary of the Treasury would not be a banker.[10]

Roosevelt did not propose to let those who had lost at Chicago win in Washington. At the same time, he did not intend the cabinet to become a reward for past political support. When Howe, Farley, Flynn, and Walker formed an informal committee to take care of the FRBC — For Roosevelt Before Chicago — group, Roosevelt warned them off the cabinet. "I don't want anybody naming a single one of them, not even you, Louis," he told Howe, adding, with a flourish of his cigarette toward the other three, "and that goes for you and you and you." Thus Arthur Mullen of Nebraska, who had worked so hard for Roosevelt at the convention, had his heart set on the Attorney-Generalship; but Roosevelt decided by January that he wanted Senator Thomas J. Walsh of Montana. But Walsh, the great parliamentarian and investigator, was reluctant to leave the Senate. Finally, after almost a month of indecision, he surrendered to Roosevelt's insistence.[11]

The next place to be filled was the most important of all, the State Department. A year earlier, Roosevelt had told Dan Roper that he wanted Newton Baker for Secretary of State. Then events in the interval had eliminated Baker. The newspapers now mentioned Norman H. Davis. But Frankfurter and others urged on Roosevelt that Davis was disqualified by his dubious business career in Cuba before the First World War, when the United States Supreme Court affirmed a judgment against him as having violated a fiduciary relationship, taken secret profits, and defrauded his business associates.[12] While Roosevelt consulted Davis on foreign affairs in these weeks, there is no evidence that he considered him seriously for the State Department. Talking to Moley in late December, he narrowed his list down to three: Robert W. Bingham of Louisville, Owen D. Young, and Cordell Hull. Bingham, Roosevelt said, had been recommended by Colonel House (though House later claimed to Harold Ickes that he had recommended Hull), but Roosevelt did not know much about him. As for Young, while he was a man of intelligence and conscience, Roosevelt feared that his utility connections would disturb the progressives. On the other hand, Roosevelt greatly respected Hull's high-mindedness and dignity. He knew in addition that he was greatly in Hull's political debt. Louis Howe was also for Hull.

Soon after, Roosevelt asked Louis B. Wehle to sound out Hull. But the Tennesseean seemed at first constrained and resentful, finally telling Wehle that he had never received one word of recognition for all his labor on Roosevelt's behalf. Or so, at least, Wehle remembered it; Hull himself later recalled the first suggestion as coming directly from Roosevelt when the President-elect paused in Washington on his way to Warm Springs in mid-January. "I was really almost thunderstruck," Hull wrote later. ". . . No one had informed me I was under consideration." While Hull thought it over, five Democratic senators separately warned Moley (according to his recollection) that Hull was overidealistic on the subject of tariff reduction and that he could not handle men well. When Moley reported this, Roosevelt replied, "You tell the senators I'll be glad to have some fine idealism in the State Department." Hull's fear that he could not afford the social side of the job was met by the proposal that Roosevelt's old friend of Wilson days, William Phillips, be appointed Undersecretary and take over the responsibilities of official entertaining. In mid-February, after Miami, Hull notified Roosevelt of his acceptance.[13]

VII

For the Treasury, the first choice was inescapable. Ever since he had run the Treasury Department for Wilson, Carter Glass of Virginia had been the Democratic party's expert on public finance. On the same Washington visit that he offered State to Hull, Roosevelt offered Treasury to Glass. But Roosevelt may well have made this offer with misgivings, for Glass's sternly orthodox views on monetary matters would much limit the play of government policy. For his part, Glass sought explicit assurance that the administration would not launch a policy of inflation. When Moley, acting as Roosevelt's agent, passed this on, Roosevelt replied, "So far as inflation goes, you can say that *we're not going to throw ideas out of the window simply because they're labeled inflation.* If you feel that the old boy doesn't want to go along, don't press him." Adolf Berle later had the impression that Roosevelt wished Moley to handle the negotiations so that Glass would refuse; but Glass also feared for his health, and his family doctor pronounced strongly against his assuming administrative responsibilities. On February 7, Glass finally sent in a letter of declination.[14]

Moley now suggested William Woodin to Howe, and Howe quickly agreed. Woodin's business record would make him acceptable to the financial community, and he was more flexible on policy than Glass. But Baruch and others in the meantime persuaded Glass to reconsider. For another two weeks no decision was possible. Finally Glass reaffirmed the original refusal. Roosevelt promptly offered Woodin the job. Woodin at first demurred, until, after a long drive through Central Park, Basil O'Connor beat down his doubts.[15]

As for Agriculture, Henry Morgenthau, Jr., who had been Roosevelt's conservation commissioner in New York and publisher of *The American Agriculturist,* was a leading possibility. Roosevelt was fond of him, and his influential father, Henry Morgenthau, Sr., yearned to see his son in the cabinet. But Tugwell, who was Roosevelt's chief adviser on agricultural policy, ardently backed Henry A. Wallace of Iowa. According to Thomas H. Beck of the Crowell Publishing Company, Roosevelt asked Beck to collect opinion from farm leaders. The overwhelming majority preferred Wallace. Ed O'Neal of the Farm Bureau seems to have been particularly vehement in opposition to Morgenthau.

Wallace himself had recommended George Peek for the job. But Roosevelt, who liked what he had seen of Wallace and wanted a Progressive Republican in the cabinet, wrote him early in February offering the post. Following up the letter, Moley repeated the invitation to Wallace in Des Moines by telephone. Moley said impatiently, "Hello! Hello! What's the answer?" After another interval he heard Wallace's hesitant "Yes." "I will try to do my part in Washington," young Henry wrote in a last editorial for *Wallace's Farmer.* "No doubt I shall make many mistakes, but I hope it can always be said that I have done the best I knew." [16]

VIII

For Commerce, Roosevelt's first thought was evidently Jesse I.
Straus of R. H. Macy's in New York. But he faced mounting pressure to recognize the old Wilson-McAdoo group in the party. Mc-
Adoo, Josephus Daniels, Colonel House, and others pressed the
claims of Dan Roper, who had served ably in a number of posts for
Wilson and who had been a political ally of Roosevelt's fifteen
years before. Roosevelt, who had originally penciled in Roper as a
possible Comptroller of the Currency, now decided to promote him
to Secretary of Commerce. Unfortunately, in the confusion no one
spoke to Straus about the change of plan, until Henry Morgenthau,
Sr., assuaged his paternal disappointment over the Agriculture decision by taking it on himself to inform Straus that he was not to
be in the cabinet either. The manner of the communication infuri-
ated Straus even more than the fact communicated; but Roosevelt
in time smoothed it over and persuaded Straus to become Ambassador to France.[17]

The Labor Department presented fewer difficulties. Molly Dewson, missing no opportunity to advance the cause of her sex, organized a campaign of letters from people in the labor and social work
fields urging the appointment of Frances Perkins. Roosevelt, predisposed already in Miss Perkins's favor, was immensely impressed
by what he regarded as this spontaneous outpouring on her behalf.
The only dissenter, it seemed, was Miss Perkins herself. Scribbling
a longhand note to Roosevelt on February 1, she expressed hope
that rumors about her appointment were unfounded. "For your
own sake and that of the U.S.," she wrote, "I think that the appointment of someone straight from the ranks of some group of organized
workers should be appointed — to re-establish firmly the principle
that *labor is in the President's councils.*" Why not John Frey or
Ed McGrady of the A.F. of L.? "Whatever I might furnish in the
way of ideas etc. are yours at any time & ad lib. without the necessity
of appointing me to anything. I think you know that."

But Roosevelt remained unmoved. Calling Miss Perkins to his
65th Street house two weeks later, he told her that he wanted her as
Secretary of Labor. For a few moments Miss Perkins argued against
him, repeating that she was not a representative of organized labor,

and, when this failed to impress Roosevelt, that she could not consider the job unless he would back her in an extensive social program. Roosevelt replied that he liked her ideas and wanted her to go ahead. At that, Miss Perkins threw up her hands and accepted the job.[18]

Interior was not so simple. George Dern, who had been Roosevelt's first choice, roused opposition among conservationists and doubt among the supporters of public power. Roosevelt accordingly promised Dern a cabinet post in principle, but said he would let him know later which department it would be. Seeking elsewhere for a Secretary of the Interior, he looked particularly among the western Progressives in the Senate. But both Hiram Johnson of California and Bronson Cutting of New Mexico declined. In any case, feeling was growing that Roosevelt was going too far in stripping the Senate in order to adorn the cabinet.

About this time a new figure entered the race, Harold L. Ickes of Chicago. Ickes's original ambition had been to be Commissioner of Indian Affairs, but, on consideration, he had decided to shoot for the stars and seek the secretaryship. By early February, however, Ickes had pretty well abandoned hope even of the Indian Bureau. So far as he could tell, Roosevelt had never heard his name. Then Moley asked him to attend an economic meeting with Roosevelt as a representative of the Progressives. On his way to the meeting, Ickes ran into Arthur Mullen, who agreed to call Roosevelt and mention Ickes as a Progressive possibility for the Interior Department. Roosevelt asked Mullen what he knew about Ickes. Mullen replied that his appointment would be acceptable to Cutting and Johnson, but that he knew nothing about his personal record. Roosevelt said that he had no time for investigation; he had to appoint someone at once.

When the group filed in for the conference the next morning, Roosevelt asked, "Is Mr. Ickes here?" The meeting was brief; and, as it was breaking up, someone — whom Ickes later identified as Rex Tugwell — caught Ickes at the head of the stairs and said that Roosevelt wanted to see him. The President-elect wasted no time. "You and I have been speaking the same language for the past twenty years," he said, "and we have the same outlook. I am having difficulty finding a Secretary of the Interior. . . . I have about come to the conclusion that the man I want is Harold L. Ickes of Chicago." Telling Moley later in the day that he had found his Secretary of the Interior, Roosevelt explained with delight, "I liked the cut of his jib."

That night a man and a woman separately picked their way across the first floor of the East 65th Street house, littered with newspapers, rugs rolled up along the wall, trunks and boxes jammed into the corner. Then they waited together in the room outside Roosevelt's study on the second floor. Soon the man was ushered inside. As he left a few moments later, Roosevelt introduced him to the woman with a smile: "I would like to have the Secretary of the Interior meet the Secretary of Labor." [19]

IX

With Ickes in Interior, place had to be found somewhere for Dern; and this problem was quickly solved by the War Department. As for Navy, after Glass had turned down the Treasury, Roosevelt could now turn to Glass's senatorial colleague from Virginia, Claude A. Swanson. The appointment of Swanson gave the Navy an amiable chief and, at the same time, made room in the Senate for Roosevelt's old friend, to whom he now looked for support, former Governor Harry F. Byrd.

And so, in one way or another, the cabinet was constructed. Though the professionals had been ignored (Ickes correctly said that if Roosevelt had tried to clear his choice with Ed Kelly or Pat Nash, the Democratic leaders in Illinois, "they would have instantaneously passed beyond the help of a pulmotor"),[20] the result still conformed to normal political standards — three senators and a governor, along with representatives of farmers, businessmen, and reformers, of Wilsonians and professional politicians, with a due regional and political spread. Three members — Woodin, Wallace, and Ickes — were nominally Republicans, even though Ickes had voted the Republican presidential ticket only once in the last quarter-century, and Woodin and Wallace had both supported Smith in 1928. All, save for Wallace and Ickes, were old friends of the President, whose views he knew well from long acquaintance. Thus consideration of issues played little part in the selection, except in the negotiations with Glass. The outcome was a cabinet that would be reasonably good in its own work and reasonably strong on the Hill, with the Democratic party and with the independent liberals, but without being especially impressive to the nation.

There remained the brain trust itself. Roosevelt had relied on Moley, Tugwell, and Berle too much to wish to dispense with them now. "Your contribution of Ray and Rex," he wrote Sam Rosenman in March, "was probably the best that anyone made during the whole campaign." He planned to make Moley Assistant Secretary of State, a job whose freedom from statutory duties would permit its holder to work directly with the President; and he thought of Tugwell as Assistant Secretary of Commerce and Berle as a Federal Trade Commissioner. But Berle promptly declined a Washington appointment, and Tugwell intended to do likewise, until the choice of Wallace as Secretary of Agriculture altered his plans.

"We are in the course of making a friendship," Tugwell noted in his diary in early January when he and Wallace were working together on farm legislation "and are exploring each other's minds with a sort of delighted expectancy." When Wallace accepted the secretaryship, he proposed to Tugwell that he become Assistant Secretary, adding, with characteristic modesty, that he hesitated to make the suggestion, "for, Rex, I really ought to be working under you." Tugwell, who felt strongly the need for drastic reorganization in the Department, finally concluded that he might go there for a while to do Wallace's surgery for him.[21]

As for Moley, he looked upon his projected appointment with rising suspicion. He sharply disagreed with Hull's tariff views; and he feared that the new Secretary would not easily tolerate a subordinate closer to the President than he was himself. Accordingly, Moley pressed the President-elect for a precise definition of his own responsibilities and finally extracted a statement awarding him the foreign debts, the Economic Conference, and such additional duties as the President might direct. As newspaper stories continued to obscure the situation, Moley thought that the only hope lay in publishing the statement. "Do you not agree," Moley suggested to Louis Howe in the presence of Josephus Daniels, "that the President owes it to me to do this?" But Daniels firmly pointed out that the release of such a statement would undoubtedly make

Hull turn down the appointment, and Roosevelt soon told Moley that the statement was not for publication. At this, Moley privately decided to stay in Washington for only a month.[22]

X

In the meantime, the pressure was steadily building against the banking system. The disclosures of the Pecora investigation doubtless increased mistrust of bankers, as the publication in January of secret RFC loans had increased mistrust of banks. But the basic source of doubt went deeper. Even in the years of prosperity bank suspensions had averaged 634 per year (nearly twice as many in a single year as the *total* suspended in the dozen years after 1934). In 1931 Keynes had specifically warned that the position of the banks in the United States might be "the weakest element in the whole situation." (He warned also against placing confidence in the soundness of bankers. "A Bankers' Conspiracy! The idea is absurd! I only wish there were one! . . . A 'sound' banker, alas! is not one who foresees danger and avoids it, but one who, when he is ruined, is ruined in a conventional and orthodox way.")

In later years Hoover looked back at the banking system with bitterness, pronouncing it "inexpressibly feeble and badly organized" and "the weakest link in our whole economic system." But neither by words nor actions did he show such concern as President. He spoke with confidence of "the inherently sound condition of the banks" (November 15, 1929), "the strong position of the banks" (December 3, 1929), "the soundness of the credit system" (October 2, 1930), and "the strength of our banking system" (October 6, 1931). Though this satisfaction declined in the last years of his administration, he never proposed serious reform.[23]

Now years of negligence were having their consequences. The American people, having seen over five thousand banks suspend in three years, did not mean to wait around until the rest of their hard-earned savings blew away in one final explosion. They were beginning to understand that supervisors had permitted bankers to conceal the extremity of their condition by counting their bond holdings, including much uncollectible paper, at values long since rendered obsolete by the plunging market. A spreading conviction that devaluation was inevitable increased a tendency to exchange cash for gold. Everyone determined to play it safe — to place their money, if they had a little, in a sock, or if they had a lot, in a foreign country. Federal Reserve figures in February reflected the decline in gold reserves, the increase in hoarding and the accelerating flight from the dollar.

There had been bank holidays before — in Nevada in October 1932, and in Louisiana in early February 1933 — but, so far as most Americans were concerned, the banking crisis began in Michigan in mid-February. Here two bank holding companies dominated the state. One, the Union Guardian Trust, was already on the ropes and pleading for a $50 million RFC loan; if it went under, all Michigan banks would have to shut their doors. The administration first wanted to rush in RFC aid, until Senator James Couzens of Michigan, who saw no point in lending federal money to unsound banks, said he would denounce any RFC loan that exceeded the value of the collateral. Secretary of Commerce Roy D. Chapin and Undersecretary of the Treasury Arthur A. Ballantine then worked out an alternative plan that depended on Henry Ford's willingness to subordinate deposit liabilities due him from the Union Guardian Trust. In a dramatic interview, Chapin and Ballantine met with Ford at Dearborn on the morning of February 13 — the economic hero of the New Era confronting the representatives of the New Era's government while the structure of that dizzy dream was everywhere crumbling around them.

Ford, American individualist to the end, flatly refused to cooperate. He told Hoover's emissaries that the effort to bolster up the financial situation was wrong; that the RFC had probably been a mistake; and that the economy had to go through the wringer. So far as the Union Guardian Trust was concerned, he would not contribute a single dime because the principle was wrong; and, if it did not open the next day, he would withdraw the $25 million the Ford Company had on deposit with the First National, Detroit's largest bank — an act which all knew would seal the fate of the rest of Michigan's banks. If the government wanted to save the banks, let it act. If not, the fault was not — as Chapin and Ballantine seemed to be saying — his. "There isn't any reason why I, the largest individual taxpayer in the country, should bail the government out of its loans to banks." When Chapin and Ballantine persisted, Ford talked darkly of intrigue and conspiracy. When they tried to warn him of the probable consequences of his action, Ford repeated that the government was making its own decision. "All right, have it that way," Ford said, "I think that Senator Couzens was probably right in saying 'Let the crash come.' " [24]

It is doubtful whether fresh injections by the RFC could in any case have done much save prolong the agony. But Ford's attitude excluded even this. In Michigan there was nothing left save for the governor to proclaim a bank holiday. As Michigan banks closed, an infection of panic began to spread across the country. In Washington, three days after the Michigan proclamation, the President personally penned a long letter that was delivered the next day by the Secret Service to the President-elect in New York. In his agitation, the President even misspelled his successor's name on the envelope.

The letter set forth Hoover's familiar thesis that the crisis was essentially a crisis of confidence, not of national policy or of economic structure. He had had the depression beaten by the summer of 1932, Hoover suggested, until "interruptions to public confidence" — caused plainly by the Democrats — had dashed the cup from his lips. And now again in February the banking crisis was psychological, not economic; "the major difficulty is in the state of the public mind." If only popular attitudes could be improved — if only, as he wrote more candidly to other correspondents, "fear for the policies of the new administration" could be dispelled — then all might once again be well. "I am convinced," Hoover told Roosevelt, "that a very early statement by you upon two or three policies of your Administration would serve greatly to restore confidence and cause a resumption of the march of recovery." What policies? "It would steady the country greatly," the President informed the President-elect, "if there could be prompt assurance that there will be no tampering or inflation of the currency; that the budget will be unquestionably balanced, even if further taxation is necessary; that the Government credit will be maintained by refusal to exhaust it in the issue of securities."

In short, in the name of "cooperation" Hoover proposed that Roosevelt repudiate the New Deal and commit himself in advance to the essential policies of the Hoover administration. In a letter to Senator Fess of Ohio, Hoover spelled out the measures which Roosevelt must now disavow: "such proposals as the bills to assume Federal responsibility for billions of mortgages, loans to municipalities for public works, the Tennessee improvements and Muscle Shoals, are of this order"; equally the President-elect would have to disavow his opposition to the sales tax and to an increase in the tariff. Three days after his letter to Roosevelt, Hoover wrote frankly to Senator Reed of Pennsylvania, "I realize that if these declarations be made by the President-elect, he will have ratified the whole major program of the Republican Administration; that is, it means the abandonment of 90% of the so-called new deal." [25]

XI

In making these extraordinary suggestions, Hoover unquestionably wrote out of a righteous conviction that his own program constituted the only hope of saving the republic. It was a measure, indeed, of his passion that he thought Roosevelt might at his behest abandon 90 per cent of his own "so-called new deal" and adopt the program the people had already rejected in the election. To fall in with Hoover's plan, Roosevelt would have had to be far less principled even than Hoover supposed he was. Yet Hoover actually told Stimson on February 22, five days after he had sent his letter, that Roosevelt's refusal to do what Hoover had bidden was the act of "a madman."

Roosevelt, instantly perceiving its implications, had dismissed the Hoover letter as a "cheeky" document. His advisers regarded it almost with incredulity. Fear was the trouble, all right, but it was not, as they saw it, fear of the new administration: it was fear of the old system. People were not withdrawing their money because they were afraid of Roosevelt's policies but because they were afraid of the banks. Nor would optimistic declarations help. Reorganization and reform were required, not rhetoric. "I am equally concerned with you in regard to the gravity of the present banking situation — " Roosevelt finally replied to Hoover, "but my thought is that it is so very deep-seated that the fire is bound to spread in spite of anything that is done by way of mere statements."

By some mysterious chance, however — whether the product of Roosevelt's irritation or of carelessness in his office — the reply was held up for ten days and did not arrive at the White House until March 1.[26]

The banking community had its own ideas about what should be done. On February 27, Thomas W. Lamont informed Roosevelt that J. P. Morgan's believed "the emergency could not be greater." The solution favored at 23 Wall Street was to authorize the RFC to deposit money without security in all banks in need of help. Roosevelt watched not without amusement while the bankers who had so high-mindedly objected to federal assistance for farmers or the unemployed now demanded such assistance for themselves. He commented that he could see no reason for specially protecting this interest as against all others; it was more important, he said, to save the people.

The Roosevelt circle was thinking along quite different lines. Early in January Roosevelt had discussed the question whether it might not be possible to go off gold in international exchange so that money might be managed internally. As he told Tugwell, he understood that First World War laws authorizing the President to embargo gold exports by proclamation had never been repealed. Investigation soon showed that the Trading with the Enemy Act of 1917 had been several times amended; but conceivably the clauses which terminated part of its authority did not apply to the gold control provisions. This seemed a possible basis for action.[27]

In the meantime, the situation was becoming steadily worse. In Washington Pecora remorselessly interrogated Charles E. Mitchell of the National City Bank. Shaggy, broad-shouldered, red-faced, Mitchell dwindled under questioning, the arrogant banker becoming a stammering man in the dock, transfigured by confusion and guilt.[28] Before the nation, Mitchell now exposed one after another of the fantastic banking practices of the boom period, exposing at the same time the solicitude with which the bankers had always taken care of themselves first. In 1929, for example, he had avoided all income tax payments by selling stock at a "loss" to a relative from whom he subsequently bought it back. After the crash in 1929, he said, the National City Bank had made $2.4 million of the stockholders' money secretly available to the bank officers with or without collateral and without interest so they could stay in the market; no more than 5 per cent of the money had been repaid. When bankers complained that the Pecora investigations were wrecking confidence, they "should have thought of that," said Roosevelt, "when they did the things that are being exposed now." More and more the worry spread; more questions were asked, more rumors circulated, banklines began to displace breadlines. By March 2 nearly half the states were enacting or contemplating bank holidays. Where the bronze doors remained open, depositors stood in line hoping to draw out savings while there still was time.

The bolder spirits around Hoover were pressing for action. Ogden Mills, who had also unearthed the old Trading with the Enemy Act, urged the President to control gold on the international exchanges and limit gold withdrawals at home. But Hoover, faithful to his limited conception of presidential leadership, believed that the Federal Reserve Board rather than the President was the agency of decision; and he concentrated in his last week on asking the Board (in writing) what it thought of the federal guarantee of deposits or the use of clearinghouse scrip in areas affected by bank suspensions. When the Board lamely responded on March 2 that it had nothing to suggest, Mills once again urged the use of the war powers. But Attorney-General William D. Mitchell questioned the legality of these powers. Hoover accordingly decided to use them only with the concurrence of the President-elect.

XII

On the chilly afternoon of March 2, Franklin Delano Roosevelt and his party took the ferry across the Hudson and boarded the Baltimore and Ohio train to Washington. They had with them rough drafts of two presidential proclamations: one calling for a special session of Congress; the other invoking the Trading with the Enemy Act and declaring a bank holiday. Consultation was endless in the President's car as the train rolled south.

In a moment of quiet, Jim Farley dropped into the chair beside the President-elect. Roosevelt appeared deeply aware of the solemnity of the days ahead. Moreover, he was saddened by word of the unexpected death of Tom Walsh. In a last-minute decision, he asked the old Wilsonian Homer Cummings, who had been slated to be Governor-General of the Philippines, to be Attorney-General.

To Farley he now spoke sobering words. A thought about God, he said, was the way to start off his administration. His mind went back to his own religious training as a child. Religion, he told Farley, would be in the end the salvation of all peoples; "for ourselves it will be the means of bringing us out of the depths of despair into which so many have apparently fallen." [29]

By the time they arrived in Washington in the midst of sleet and rain, they found confusion, exhaustion, and alarm. Eugene Meyer of the Federal Reserve Board had swung over a majority of his Board in favor of absolute closing of the banks, and he was joined in this view by Mills and Ballantine at the Treasury. While Hoover continued to disapprove, he seemed to have lost command of his own administration; and Treasury and Federal Reserve Board representatives on their own initiative asked Will Woodin to get Roosevelt's assent to a bank holiday proclamation. About eleven on the night of March 2, Woodin reported that Roosevelt was steadfast in his refusal to take action until he had power; Hoover must do as he thought best on his own responsibility. When Hoover was informed of this exchange, he quickly disclaimed the Treasury–Federal Reserve proposal and said that a proclamation controlling exchange and hoarding would do the job. What would Roosevelt think of this? To this suggestion Roosevelt returned the same answer.

On the afternoon of Friday, March 3, Roosevelt took his family to the White House for tea with the retiring President — the Hoovers' reluctant substitute for the traditional dinner. A few moments later Moley, tossing on his bed at the Mayflower in an effort to catch up on sleep, received a call from Warren Robbins, a Roosevelt cousin, presently Chief of Protocol. Robbins reported that Ike Hoover, the White House usher, had warned Roosevelt that the President was planning to spring Mills and Meyer on the President-elect during the formal visit with new proposals on the crisis. Thus alerted, Moley appeared at the White House in time to second Roosevelt in the renewal of the talks.

But the discussions merely traversed familiar ground. Meyer once again urged a bank holiday; Hoover once again denied that a bank holiday was necessary and argued for a more limited procla-mation; Roosevelt once more repeated the messages he had sent through Woodin the night before. When Hoover said that he could not act by himself because his Attorney-General doubted the validity of the emergency powers under the Trading with the Enemy Act, Roosevelt replied that he believed the required powers were still valid, but that, in any case, he could not guarantee against future congressional disapproval of presidential action for Hoover, or, for that matter, for himself.

Roosevelt spent the evening before Inauguration Day in consultation with congressional leaders in his suite at the Mayflower. Hoover telephoned twice; witnesses differ as to what was said.[30] But the situation remained unchanged. And in the White House, at midnight: "We are at the end of our string. There is nothing more we can do."

In the Treasury, Hoover's officials, now joined by Woodin and Moley, still hung over long-distance phones as they checked on banking conditions through the nation. The only hope, in their view, lay in a national shutdown. They urged Governor Lehman to declare a banking holiday in New York; but New York bankers, led by Thomas W. Lamont, counted on an upsurge of confidence with the new administration, and were resistant. Finally, at 4.20 Saturday morning, Lehman issued his proclamation. Illinois followed his example. As dawn broke over America, the banks of the nation seemed in *rigor mortis*.

And Inauguration Day came, dull and dreary, skies dark and overcast, breaking on a people afraid, yet expectant.

> Plodding feet
> Tramp — tramp
> The Grand Old Party's
> Breaking camp.
> Blare of bugles
> Din — din
> The New Deal is moving in.

So Robert E. Sherwood in a sardonic poem, saturated with the national doubt. The new President radiated optimism. But what lay behind the mask of smiles?

> Are we sure that you have fixed your eyes on
> A goal beyond the politician's ken?

Have you the will to reach the far horizon
Where rest the hopes of men? [31]

XIII

As for Franklin Roosevelt, no one could tell what lay behind the
imperturbable composure. In part, no doubt, he knew that what
happened before inauguration would be blamed on his predecessor,
not on himself, and that the worse the crisis on March 4 the greater
the opportunity for reconstruction. Yet, beyond this, he had a deep
and unquestioning confidence in the energy and inventiveness of
free society. American democracy, he believed, had not had its fair
test. Now the Presidency itself seemed to offer the last hope for
national revival.

In his vice-presidential campaign a dozen years earlier Roosevelt
had set forth his conception of the President as the *leader* of the
nation, so truly interpreting the unspoken needs and wishes of the
people that he could count on their support in great tasks. Mus-
ing on these problems in 1928, he had noted, "There is no magic
in Democracy that does away with the need for leadership." His
own contact with dynamic Presidents had confirmed this faith in
presidential leadership.

There could be no doubt about the influence Theodore Roosevelt had on him, even if F.D.R. was sometimes irritated when people compared him to T.R.; nor could there be doubt about Wilson's impact, even if F.D.R. spoke more often in private of Cousin
Ted. Family attached him to one, party to the other. Each had
given him the conviction that the American people responded to
vision and moral purpose. And he found the contrast between
them instructive. As he once wrote:

Theodore Roosevelt lacked Woodrow Wilson's appeal to the
fundamental and failed to stir, as Wilson did, the truly profound moral and social convictions. Wilson, on the other hand,
failed where Theodore Roosevelt succeeded in stirring people
to enthusiasm over specific individual events, even though
these specific events may have been superficial in comparison
with the fundamentals.[32]

A President in a time of crisis, Franklin Roosevelt could well have thought, needed both the Wilsonian and the Rooseveltian qualities. He had to appeal to underlying convictions; he had to stir people over specific events; above all, he had to make government the affirmative instrument of the people.

Years before, when Franklin Roosevelt went to Washington as Assistant Secretary of the Navy, Theodore Roosevelt had outlined in his *Autobiography* two opposing theories of the Presidency. One, which he called the Buchanan-Taft school, took the view that the President could do nothing, no matter how necessary it was to act, unless the Constitution explicitly commanded the action. The other, which T.R. called the Jackson-Lincoln school, looked on the President as duty-bound to do everything that the needs of the nation demanded where the Constitution did not explicitly forbid him to render the service. "I believed in invoking the National power with absolute freedom for every National need," said Theodore Roosevelt; "and I believed that the Constitution should be treated as the greatest document ever devised by the wit of man to aid a people in exercising every power, necessary for its own betterment, and not as a straitjacket cunningly fashioned to strangle growth." And so too Woodrow Wilson: "The President is at liberty, both in law and conscience, to be as big a man as he can. His capacity will set the limit. . . . The Constitution bids him speak, and times of stress and change must more and more thrust upon him the attitude of originator of policies." [33]

XIV

These were "times of stress and change," and Roosevelt had thought much of the responsibilities of the Presidency in 1932. "The Presidency is not merely an administrative office," he told Anne O'Hare McCormick during the campaign. "That's the least of it. It is more than an engineering job, efficient or inefficient. It is pre-eminently a place of moral leadership. All our great Presidents were leaders of thought at times when certain historic ideas in the life of the nation had to be clarified." So Washington had personified the idea of federal union, Jefferson and Jackson the idea of democracy, Lincoln union and freedom, Cleveland rugged honesty.

"Isn't that what the office is — " he suggested, "a superb opportunity for reapplying, applying in new conditions, the simple rules of human conduct we always go back to? I stress the modern application, because we are always moving on; the technical and economic environment changes, and never so quickly as now. Without leadership alert and sensitive to change, we are bogged up or lose our way, as we have lost it in the past decade."

"The objective now, as I see it," Roosevelt emphasized, "is to put at the head of the nation someone whose interests are not special but general, someone who can understand and treat with the country as a whole. For as much as anything it needs to be reaffirmed at this juncture that the United States is one organic entity, that no interest, no class, no section, is either separate or supreme above the interests of all." Here spoke the spirit that animated both the New Nationalism and the New Freedom. Here too spoke the man who in the year before his inauguration visited forty-one of the states and traveled nearly thirty thousand miles across the land, a man who brought to the White House more extensive and intimate knowledge of his country and of his countrymen than almost any predecessor. His experience, as Felix Frankfurter wrote him after the election, equipped him well to be "the comprehending expression of the diverse interests, feelings, hopes and thought of the multiple forces which are unified into the nation." [34]

The American experiment in self-government was now facing what was, excepting the Civil War, its greatest test. Even more perhaps hung on the capacity to surmount crisis than in 1861. In 1933 the fate of the United States was involved with the fate of free men everywhere. And through the world the free way of life was already in retreat. Thirty-three days before, on January 30, 1933, while Franklin Roosevelt celebrated his fifty-first birthday at Warm Springs by cutting an eighty-pound cake for the patients and staff, one hundred thousand massed Storm Troopers and National Socialists marched through the darkened streets of Berlin under the flaring light of torches. Column after column, singing, chanting, waving swastika banners, pounded past the Brandenburg Gate and down Unter den Linden. President von Hindenburg, rigid and erect, watched out of a lighted window of the Chancellery, marking time to the martial music with a crooked stick. At another window, laughing, waving, bowing, flinging out his arm toward the marchers in staccato salutes, his whole figure ecstatic with anticipation, stood Germany's new Chancellor, Adolf Hitler.[35]

Many had deserted freedom, many more had lost their nerve. But Roosevelt, armored in some inner faith, remained calm and inscrutable, confident that American improvisation could meet the future on its own terms. And so on March 4, as he took the silent ride in the presidential limousine down the packed streets to the Capitol, he was grim but unafraid. Deep within, he seemed to know that the nation had resources beyond its banks and exchanges; that the collapse of the older order meant catharsis rather than catastrophe; that the common disaster could make the people see themselves for a season as a community, as a family; that catastrophe could provide the indispensable setting for democratic experiment and for presidential leadership. If this were so, then crisis could change from calamity to challenge. The only thing Americans had to fear was fear itself. And so he serenely awaited the morrow. The event was in the hand of God.

Notes

Notes

In order to avoid a hopelessly large number of notes, I have followed the practice of collecting the references necessary to a particular passage in a single note. The full citation of each title is to be found on the first mention in each chapter, with the exception of the following works, which receive abbreviated citation throughout:

Franklin D. Roosevelt, *Public Papers and Addresses*, S. I. Rosenman, comp. (New York, 1938–50), cited as F.D.R., *Public Papers*, with the year covered by the volume in parenthesis.

Franklin D. Roosevelt, *His Personal Letters: Early Years*, Elliott Roosevelt, ed. (New York, 1947); *His Personal Letters: 1905–1928*, Elliott Roosevelt, ed. (New York, 1948); *His Personal Letters: 1928–1945*, Elliott Roosevelt, ed. (2 vols., New York, 1950), cited as F.D.R., *Personal Letters*, I, II, III, IV.

Herbert Hoover, *State Papers and Other Public Writings*, W. S. Myers, ed., 2 vols. (New York, 1934), cited as Hoover, *State Papers*, I, II.

Herbert Hoover, *Memoirs . . . Years of Adventure, 1874–1920* (New York, 1951); *Memoirs . . . The Cabinet and the Presidency, 1920–1933* (New York, 1952); *Memoirs . . . The Great Depression, 1922–1941* (New York, 1952), cited as Hoover, *Memoirs*, I, II, III.

Bureau of the Census, *Historical Statistics of the United States, 1789–1945* (Washington, 1949), cited as *Historical Statistics*.

Franklin D. Roosevelt Collector, cited as *F.D.R. Coll.*

Of the manuscript collections cited, the following are at the Roosevelt Library at Hyde Park, New York: Franklin D. Roosevelt Papers; Louis M. Howe Papers; Mary W. Dewson Papers; Harry L. Hopkins Papers; Roosevelt Foundation Papers; Henry Morgenthau, Jr., Diary; Herbert Claiborne

Pell Papers. The Henry L. Stimson Diary is at the Sterling Library, Yale University. I consulted the Norman H. Davis Papers at the Council on Foreign Relations in New York City; they are now in the Library of Congress. The Adolf A. Berle, Jr., Papers, and the Rexford G. Tugwell Papers are in the personal possession of Mr. Berle and Mr. Tugwell. I am grateful to Anna Roosevelt Halsted for permission to consult certain family material cited as Roosevelt Family Papers. The Oral History Project is at Columbia University.

CHAPTER 1 *(Pages 1-8)*

1. T. G. Joslin, *Hoover Off the Record* (New York, 1934), 366, 180.
2. The account of the inauguration is based on a number of eyewitness accounts, particularly those of Edwin C. Hill in his vivid broadcast of March 6 (transcript in the Roosevelt Papers), Anne O'Hare McCormick ("The Nation Renews Its Faith," *New York Times Magazine,* March 19, 1933), Edmund Wilson ("Inaugural Parade," *New Republic,* March 22, 1933), and *Time,* March 13, 1933; also E. W. Starling, *Starling of the White House* (New York, 1946), 305-6; Henry L. Stimson, Diary, March 4, 1933.
3. Herbert Hoover, *Memoirs,* III, 344.
4. E. J. Flynn, *You're the Boss* (New York, 1947), 125; Grace Tully, *F. D. R., My Boss* (New York, 1949), 64; I. H. Hoover, *Forty-Two Years in the White House* (Boston, 1934), 227.
5. Tully, *F. D. R.,* 67-68.
6. For citations and further details see Chs. 19-22.
7. Senate Agriculture and Forestry Committee, *Agricultural Adjustment Relief Plan: Hearings,* 72 Cong., 2 Sess. (1933), 15; Senate Manufactures Committee, *Federal Aid for Unemployment Relief: Hearings,* 72 Cong., 2 Sess. (1933), 455; Senate Judiciary Committee, *Thirty-Hour Work Week: Hearings,* 72 Cong., 2 Sess. (1933), 21-22.
8. *Time,* Jan. 9, 16, 1933.
9. Elmer Davis, "The Collapse of Politics," *Harper's,* Sept. 1932; Cornelius Vanderbilt, Jr., "Do the American Bourbons Realize Their Fate?" *Liberty,* July 2, 1932; H. F. Pringle, "A Year Ago Today," *Red Book,* April 1934.
10. Senate Finance Committee, *Investigation of Economic Problems: Hearings,* 72 Cong., 2 Sess. (1933), 1060, 758, 5, 8; *Time,* March 6, 1933.
11. White to Walter Lippmann, April 19, 1932, in W. A. White, *Selected Letters . . . 1899-1943,* Walter Johnson, ed. (New York, 1947), 324; Reinhold Niebuhr "After Capitalism — What?" *World Tomorrow,* March 1, 1933; Hamilton Fish, Jr., to F.D.R., Feb. 24, 1933, Roosevelt Papers.
12. Hughes to F.D.R., Feb. 28, 1933, Roosevelt Papers.
13. For text (without the opening sentence), F.D.R., *Public Papers* (1933);

see also Roosevelt's own memorandum on the speech's composition, March 25, 1933, Roosevelt Papers; and S. I. Rosenman, *Working with Roosevelt* (New York, 1952), 89 ff.

CHAPTER 2 *(Pages 11–16)*

1. *Parliamentary Debates, House of Commons,* Nov. 11, 1918, quoted in R. H. Ferrell, *Peace in Their Time* (New Haven, 1952), 3.
2. S. J. Woolf, "Bullitt Looks at the European Scene," *New York Times Magazine,* Sept. 6, 1936; Jack Alexander, "He Rose from the Rich," *Saturday Evening Post,* March 11, 18, 1939; Janet Flanner's sketch in *An American in Paris* (New York, 1940); Ernesta Drinker Bullitt, *An Uncensored Diary from the Central Empires* (New York, 1917), 4.
3. Address to Congress, Jan. 8, 1918, Woodrow Wilson, *Messages and Papers,* Albert Shaw, ed. (New York, 1924), I, 466, 469.
4. Lincoln Steffens, *Autobiography* (New York, 1931), 791–92, 799; W. C. Bullitt, *The Bullitt Mission to Russia* (New York, 1919), 54.
5. Berle to Upton Sinclair, Dec. 27, 1939, Berle Papers. I should perhaps add that neither Professor Morison nor Governor Herter remembers the episode in quite the same way.
6. *Papers Relating to the Foreign Relations of the United States: The Paris Peace Conference* (Washington, 1942–47), XI, 570–74.
7. I follow here the account given by Mr. Hoover in *America's First Crusade* (New York, 1942), 50–51; in his *Memoirs* (I, 462) he says he met *both* Smuts and Keynes on his morning walk.
8. H. C. F. Bell, *Woodrow Wilson and the People* (New York, 1945), 342–44; Wilson, *Messages,* II, 810.
9. J. M. Keynes, *Economic Consequences of the Peace* (New York, 1920), 297.

CHAPTER 3 *(Pages 17–26)*

1. "The Great Decision," *New Republic,* April 7, 1917.
2. Edward Stanwood, *History of the Presidency* (Boston, 1898), 509–13; Richard Hofstadter, *The Age of Reform* (New York, 1955), Ch. 2.
3. Robert M. La Follette, *La Follette's Autobiography* (Madison, Wisc., 1913), 478, 479.
4. Theodore Roosevelt, *An Autobiography* (New York, 1913), 67; Roosevelt to F. S. Oliver, Aug. 9, 1906, in Theodore Roosevelt, *Letters,* E. E. Morison, ed., 8 vols. (Cambridge, 1951–54), V, 352; Roosevelt to Sir Edward Grey, Nov. 15, 1913, in Theodore Roosevelt, *Works* (Memorial ed.), XXIV, 409.
5. H. L. Stimson and McGeorge Bundy, *On Active Service in Peace and War* (New York, 1948), 63; Roosevelt to F. S. Oliver, Aug. 9, 1906, in Theodore Roosevelt, *Letters,* V, 351, to F. J. Turner, Nov. 4, 1896, I, 564, to W. H. Moody, Sept. 21, 1907, V, 803.

6. Stimson and Bundy, *On Active Service*, 60.
7. La Follette, *Autobiography*, 478, 686–87.
8. Herbert Croly, *The Promise of American Life* (New York, 1909), 12–13, 17, 20–21, 25, 169, 274.
9. G. W. Perkins, *Copartnership: Address . . . [before] the Canadian Club, Ottawa, February 4, 1911* (n.p., n.d. [1911]), 3; *Address . . . Before the Quill Club of New York, December 20, 1910* (n.p., n.d. [1911]), 5; "Business and Government," *Saturday Evening Post*, March 16, 1912; *Wanted — A Constructive National Policy: Address . . . [before] Michigan College of Mines . . . August 7, 1911* (n.p., n.d. [1911]), 12; *A Constructive Suggestion: Address . . . Youngstown, Ohio, December 4, 1911* (n.p., n.d. [1912]), 4–5, 9; *Copartnership*, 15; *Efficiency in Business and What It Must Stand For: Address . . . Before . . . the Massachusetts Institute of Technology, Boston, January 4, 1911* (n.p., n.d. [1911]), 15; *Modern Industrialism: Address . . . [before] Southern Commercial Congress, Atlanta, Georgia, March 8, 1911* (n.p., n.d. [1911]), 7.
10. C. R. Van Hise, *Concentration and Control* (New York, 1912), 278.
11. Theodore Roosevelt, Introduction to S. J. Duncan-Clark, *The Progressive Movement* (Boston, 1913), xix; Theodore Roosevelt, *The New Nationalism* (New York, 1910), 23–24.
12. Washington Gladden, *Social Salvation* (Boston, 1902), 229–30, 61; Walter Rauschenbusch, *Christianizing the Social Order* (New York, 1912), 449.
13. Frances Perkins, "A Method of Moral Progress," *New Republic*, June 8, 1953; Florence Kelley, *Minimum Wage Boards* (New York, [1911]); Lillian Wald, *Windows on Henry Street* (Boston, 1934), 45. See also the *Annual Reports* of the Consumers' League; Florence Kelley, "Twenty-five Years of the Consumers' League Movement," *Survey*, Nov. 27, 1915; Paul Kellogg, "Semi-Centennial of the Settlements," *Survey Graphic*, Jan. 1935; Josephine Goldmark, "50 Years — The National Consumers' League," *Survey*, Dec. 1949; speech by Paul H. Douglas at the Fiftieth Anniversary Dinner of the Consumers' League, Dec. 9, 1949; Jane Addams, *The Second Twenty Years at Hull-House* (New York, 1930); Josephine Goldmark, *Impatient Crusader: Florence Kelley's Life Story* (Urbana, Ill., 1953); R. L. Duffus, *Lillian Wald* (New York, 1938); Frances Perkins, *People at Work* (New York, 1934), Sec. II.
14. Theodore Roosevelt to Mrs. Frederick Nathan, Jan. 20, 1907, National Consumers' League, *Eighth Annual Report* ([New York, 1907]), 15; Addams, *Second Twenty Years*, 18–27; Roosevelt to G. W. Perkins, Aug. 23, 1913, in Theodore Roosevelt, *Letters*, VII, 742–43.

CHAPTER 4 *(Pages 27–31)*

1. Woodrow Wilson, *The New Freedom* (New York, 1913), 7–8, 55, 190, 198, 218, 221, 284; "Ideals of Public Life" (1907), quoted by A. S. Link,

Wilson: The Road to the White House (Princeton, 1947), 115; "The State and the Citizen's Relation to It" (1909) and "Spirit of Jefferson" (1906), quoted by William Diamond, *The Economic Thought of Woodrow Wilson* (Baltimore, 1943), 73, 78.

2. W. G. McAdoo, *Crowded Years* (Boston, 1931), 104–5; G. W. Perkins, *The Modern Corporation: Address . . . [at] Columbia University, February 7, 1908* (n.p., n.d. [1908]), 2; W. G. McAdoo, *Decent Treatment of the Public by Corporations and Regulation of Monopoly: A Speech . . . Before the Chamber of Commerce, Boston, Mass., January 30, 1911* (n.p., n.d.[1911]), 8, 9.

3. Senate Interstate Commerce Committee, *Control of Corporations, Persons and Firms . . . Hearings*, 62 Cong., 2 Sess. (1911), I, 1258, 1278; A. T. Mason, *Brandeis and the Modern State* (Princeton, 1933), 96; A. T. Mason, *Brandeis: A Free Man's Life* (New York, 1946), 585.

4. Link, *Wilson*, 492.

CHAPTER 5 *(Pages 32–36)*

1. Brandeis to Wilson, Sept. 30, 1912; A. S. Link, *Wilson: The Road to the White House* (Princeton, 1947), 492.

2. Herbert Croly, *Progressive Democracy* (New York, 1914), 16–17, 54; Charles A. Beard, "Jefferson and the New Freedom," *New Republic*, Nov. 4, 1914; Walter Lippmann, *Drift and Mastery* (New York, 1914), 136–37; George W. Perkins, *National Action and Industrial Growth* [New York], 1914, 9, address at Lincoln Day Dinner of the Progressive Party, Feb. 12, 1914.

3. Woodrow Wilson, *The New Freedom* (New York, 1913), 284.

4. It is an odd and stilted book. At one point Dru muses about Russia and wonders when her deliverance will come. "There was, he knew, great work for someone to do in that despotic land." As the book ends, Dru has resigned his dictatorship, learned "Slavic," and sailed with his preternaturally patient girl friend from San Francisco to an unknown destination, presumably to start the Russian revolution. See [E. M. House], *Philip Dru, Administrator* (New York, 1912). House's original version of the book, I am informed by B. W. Huebsch, its publisher, and Harry E. Maule, was rewritten by Mr. Maule in order to bring it up to minimum standards of readability. The revision had to do only with style, however, not with content or form. Colonel House was apparently unhappy about the changes and gave only grudging approval to the final version.

Students of the occult, noting the resemblance between some of Dru's domestic program and the New Deal, take pleasure in pointing out that the first two letters of Dru's names spell F [Ph] DR. Roosevelt actually called the novel to a friend's attention in 1932, shortly before the Democratic convention; and a year later, toward the end of the Hundred Days, Miss LeHand wrote Huebsch, "The President desires to obtain a copy of . . . 'Philip Dru, Administrator.' " (F.D.R. to W. H. MacMasters, June 8, 1932, M. A. LeHand to B. W. Huebsch, June 1, 1933, Roosevelt Papers)

5. F. K. Lane, *Letters,* A. W. Lane and L. H. Wall, eds. (Boston, 1922), 297.

6. A. S. Link, "The South and the 'New Freedom,'" *American Scholar,* Summer 1951.

7. Walter Lippmann, "The Case for Wilson," *New Republic,* Oct. 14, 1916; Herbert Croly, "The Two Parties in 1916," *New Republic,* Oct. 21, 1916; A. S. Link, *Woodrow Wilson and the Progressive Era* (New York, 1953).

8. H. L. Ickes, *Autobiography of a Curmudgeon* (New York, 1943), opposite 164, 217; Roosevelt's speech of March 28, 1918, in Theodore Roosevelt, *Letters,* E. E. Morison, ed., 8 vols. (Cambridge, 1951–54), VIII, 1294; Donald Richberg, *Tents of the Mighty* (Chicago, 1930), 97.

CHAPTER 6 *(Pages 37–45)*

1. Randolph Bourne, *Untimely Papers* (New York, 1919), 140.

2. Theodore Roosevelt, *The Foes of Our Own Household* (New York, 1917), 122; B. M. Baruch, *American Industry in the War* (New York, 1941), 29.

3. Baruch, *American Industry,* 104–7.

4. Baruch, *American Industry,* 29; "Morale," *New Republic,* April 21, 1917.

5. John Dewey, "What Are We Fighting For?" *Independent,* June 22, 1918, reprinted as "The Social Possibilities of War," in *Characters and Events* (New York, 1929), II, 552–57; see also Dewey, "The New Social Science," *New Republic,* April 6, 1918.

6. Donald Richberg, *Tents of the Mighty* (Chicago, 1930), 81–82; W. E. Weyl, *The End of the War* (New York, 1918), 303, 304; Arthur Pound and S. T. Moore, eds., *They Told Barron* (New York, 1930), 22.

7. Woodrow Wilson, *Messages and Papers,* Albert Shaw, ed. (New York, 1924), II, 673–74.

8. Mary Synon, *McAdoo* (Indianapolis, 1924), 187.

9. White to Bryce, Feb. 19, 1917, to Mark Sullivan, Jan. 28, 1918, to Paul Kellogg, Dec. 2, 1919, in W. A. White, *Selected Letters . . . 1899–1943,* Walter Johnson, ed. (New York, 1947), 177, 185, 203.

10. John Dos Passos, Introduction, *Three Soldiers* (Modern Lib., New York, 1932).

11. Richberg, *Tents of the Mighty,* 96–97.

12. Woodbury Willoughby, *The Capital Issues Committee and War Finance Corporation* (Baltimore, 1932).

13. A. M. Palmer, "The Case Against the 'Reds.'" *Forum,* Feb. 1920.

14. Zechariah Chafee, Jr., *Free Speech in the United States* (Cambridge,

1941), Ch. 5; Josephus Daniels, *The Wilson Era: Years of War and After, 1917–23* (Chapel Hill, 1946), 546.

15. Harold Stearns, *Liberalism in America* (New York, 1919), 110, 146–47.
16. F. C. Howe, *The Confessions of a Reformer* (New York, 1925), 279, 282; H. L. Ickes, *Autobiography of a Curmudgeon* (New York, 1943), 222. Ickes eventually decided that he had been right the first time.
17. Daniels, *Wilson Era*, 560.
18. [C. W. Gilbert], *The Mirrors of Washington* (Washington, 1921), 184.

CHAPTER 7 *(Pages 49–53)*

1. Arthur Pound and S. T. Moore, eds., *They Told Barron* (New York, 1930), 13–14.
2. For Harding see S. H. Adams, *The Incredible Era* (Boston, 1939); A. R. Longworth, *Crowded Hours* (New York, 1933), 324–25; [C. W. Gilbert], *The Mirrors of Washington* (Washington, 1921), 30.
3. David Karsner, *Talks with Debs in Terre Haute* (New York, 1922), 18.
4. Adams, *Incredible Era*, 7–8; W. A. White, *Autobiography* (New York, 1946), 619; W. A. White, *Masks in a Pageant* (New York, 1928), 431; N. M. Butler, *Across the Busy Years* (New York, 1939), I, 411.
5. H. M. Daugherty with Thomas Dixon, *The Inside Story of the Harding Tragedy* (New York, 1932), 134, 207, 214.
6. White, *Autobiography*, 619–20; E. W. McLean, *Father Struck It Rich* (Boston, 1936), 253.
7. Adams, *Incredible Era*, 371–78; Herbert Hoover, *Memoirs*, II, 49–52; Charles Michelson, *The Ghost Talks* (New York, 1944), 229.
8. McLean, *Father Struck It Rich*, 275; T. L. Stokes, *Chip Off My Shoulder* (Princeton, 1940), 127–28.

CHAPTER 8 *(Pages 54–60)*

1. W. A. White, *A Puritan in Babylon* (New York, 1938), 241–43.
2. F. L. Allen, *The Lords of Creation* (New York, 1935), 184.
3. H. L. Stimson, "Reminiscences" (Oral History Project, Sept. 1949), 4.
4. J. A. Garraty, *Henry Cabot Lodge* (New York, 1953), 421*n*, 394–96; Hoover to Fall, March 12, 1923, H. M. Daugherty with Thomas Dixon, *The Inside Story of the Harding Tragedy* (New York, 1932), 187–90; Taft to A. I. Vorys, June 10, 1923, to Horace Taft, Feb. 21, 1924, in H. F. Pringle, *Life and Times of William Howard Taft* (New York, 1939), II, 1022; Russell Lord, *The Wallaces of Iowa* (Boston, 1947); 227.
5. M. J. Pusey, *Charles Evans Hughes* (New York, 1951), II, 427, 428, 565; Herbert Hoover, " 'Coolidge Prosperity,' " *Collier's*, Oct. 6, 1951; in the second volume of his *Memoirs* (58), Hoover somewhat softened this characterization of Hughes.

6. Morrow to Lamont, May 25, 1920, Harold Nicolson, *Dwight Morrow* (New York, 1935), 233.
7. Esmé Howard, *Theatre of Life* (Boston, 1936), II, 491; A. H. Vandenberg, *The Trail of a Tradition* (New York, 1926), 396; Calvin Coolidge, *Foundations of the Republic* (New York, 1926), 41, 187, 201; Calvin Coolidge, *Have Faith in Massachusetts* (Boston, 1919), 14, 19; White to Ickes, March 18, 1926, in W. A. White, *Selected Letters . . . 1899–1943*, Walter Johnson, ed. (New York, 1947), 255; I. H. Hoover, *Forty-Two Years in the White House* (Boston, 1934), 233, 268; Calvin Coolidge, *Autobiography* (New York, 1929), 196; S. J. Woolf, *Drawn From Life* (New York, 1932), 45; Hoover, *Memoirs*, II, 55; J. E. Watson, *As I Knew Them* (Indianapolis, 1936), 248; W. H. Taft to Horace Taft, Sept. 29, 1923, in Pringle, *Taft*, II, 1019; see also biographies by W. A. White and C. M. Fuess.
8. Lodge to Roosevelt, Oct. 20, 1902, *Selections from the Correspondence of Theodore Roosevelt and Henry Cabot Lodge, 1889–1918*, 2 vols. (New York, 1925), 542. This is one of the passages that Lodge, editing the letters in 1924, chose *not* to strike out.
9. B. N. Timmons, *Portrait of . . . Charles G. Dawes* (New York, 1953), 238; Taft to I. M. Ullman, Nov. 12, 1924, in Pringle, *Taft*, II, 968.

CHAPTER 9 *(Pages 61–70)*

1. John Ihlder, "The Business Man's Responsibility," *Nation's Business,* Nov. 1925; J. W. Prothro, "Business Ideas and the American Tradition," *Journal of Politics*, Feb. 1953; *New York Times*, Oct. 24, 1924.
2. S. J. Woolf, *Drawn From Life* (New York, 1932), 223–29; Lucius Beebe, "Mellon—Croesus and Corinthian," *Outlook*, Feb. 4, 1931; E. G. Lowry, *Washington Close-Ups* (Boston, 1921), 154–56.
3. A. W. Mellon, *Taxation: The People's Business* (New York, 1924), 17, 18, 69, 80.
4. G. W. Norris, *Fighting Liberal* (New York, 1945), 288.
5. For Garner's speeches, with tables and statistics, see *Congressional Record*, 71 Cong., 2 Sess. (March 14, 1930), 5329, and 71 Cong., 3 Sess. (Dec. 16, 1930), 873–76.
6. W. A. White, *A Puritan in Babylon* (New York, 1938), 333; Herman Oliphant to Henry Morgenthau, Jr., March 29, 1937, Morgenthau Diary, LXI, 185 ff.; "Twelve Ways to Dodge the Income Tax," *New Republic,* May 29, 1935.
7. Mellon, *Taxation*, 20.
8. Woodrow Wilson, *Messages and Papers*, Albert Shaw, ed. (New York, 1924), II, 1227.
9. White, *Puritan in Babylon*, 279–81, 289.
10. E. P. Herring, "Politics, Personalities, and the Federal Trade Commission, II," *American Political Science Review*, Feb. 1935.

11. A. A. Berle, Jr., and G. C. Means, *The Modern Corporation and Private Property* (New York, 1932), 32, 40.

12. P. H. Douglas, "Purchasing Power of the Masses and Business Depressions," *Economic Essays in Honor of Wesley C. Mitchell* (New York. 1935), 125-26.

13. Maurice Leven, H. G. Moulton, and Clark Warburton, *America's Capacity to Consume* (Washington, 1934), 94.

14. White, *Puritan in Babylon*, 344.

15. National Bureau of Economic Research figures; cf. A. F. Burns, *Economic Research and the Keynesian Thinking of Our Times* (New York, 1946), 30, 32.

16. J. K. Galbraith, *The Great Crash* (Boston, 1955); *Historical Statistics,* Ser. N 221-23, N 228-32; George Soule, *Prosperity Decade* (New York, 1947), 295; A. L. Bernheim and M. G. Schneider, eds., *The Security Markets* (New York, 1935), 50, 53; Bureau of the Census, *Statistical Abstract of the United States: 1948* (Washington, 1948), 367.

17. S. E. Harris, *Twenty Years of Federal Reserve Policy* (Cambridge, 1933), II, especially pages 436-39; for a convenient tabulation of "Principal Policy Actions of Federal Reserve System," Joint Committee on the Economic Report (Patman Committee), *Monetary Policy and the Management of the Public Debt* (Sen. Doc. 123, 82 Cong., 2 Sess., 1952), Part I, 216-33.

18. White, *Puritan in Babylon*, 335-38. Ripley's *Main Street and Wall Street* came out in 1927.

19. *New York Times,* Jan. 7, 1928; H. P. Willis, "The Failure of the Federal Reserve," *North American Review,* May 1929.

CHAPTER 10 *(Pages 71-76)*

1. Julius Klein, "Business," in C. A. Beard, ed., *Whither Mankind* (New York, 1928), 95; Garet Garrett, *The American Omen* (New York, 1929), 149.

2. Bruce Barton, *The Man Nobody Knows* (New York, 1925), Introduction.

3. Eugene Lombard, "Where the Surplus Value Comes From," *American Industries,* Jan. 1920; cf. J. W. Prothro, "Business Ideas and the American Tradition," *Journal of Politics,* Feb. 1953; J. E. Edgerton, "The President's Annual Address," *American Industries,* Nov. 1925; J. M. Beck, *The Vanishing Rights of the States* (New York, 1926); *Congressional Record,* 69 Cong., 1 Sess. (April 5, 1926), 6924.

4. Owen D. Young, "What is Right in Business," *Review of Reviews,* March 1929.

5. See Harry Bennett, with Paul Marcus, *We Never Called Him Henry* (New York, 1951).

6. Ford in an interview with Samuel Crowther, Crowther, *A Basis for Stability* (Boston, 1932), 73.

7. E. A. Filene, *Successful Living in the Machine Age* (New York, 1933), 18; Garrett, *American Omen,* 79–80.

8. H. L. Mencken, *Prejudices: Third Series* (New York, 1922), 271.

9. White to R. S. Baker, Dec. 8, 1920, in W. A. White, *Selected Letters . . . 1899–1943,* Walter Johnson, ed. (New York, 1947), 213.

10. John Dos Passos, "Washington: The Big Tent," *New Republic,* March 14, 1934; Eastman to J. J. Storrow, Nov. 9, 1925, in C. M. Fuess, *Joseph B. Eastman* (New York, 1952), 338; D. C. Roper, *Fifty Years of Public Life* (Durham, N.C., 1941), 241–45; Alfred Lief, *Democracy's Norris* (New York, 1939), 226; Brandeis to Alfred Brandeis, April 10, 1921, in A. T. Mason, *Brandeis: A Free Man's Life* (New York, 1946), 530.

11. F. Scott Fitzgerald, "Echoes of the Jazz Age," *Scribner's,* Nov. 1931; see also for an account of Lindbergh's impact, W. T. Foster and Waddill Catchings, *The Road to Plenty* (Boston, 1928), 221.

CHAPTER 11 *(Pages 77–89)*

1. Mr. Hoover writes in the first volume of his *Memoirs* (120): "I joined the National Republican Club in 1909"; in the second volume (33): "In the Presidential campaign of 1912, I had enlisted under the standard of Theodore Roosevelt. That same year, I joined the National Republican Club." Similarly, in the first volume of his *Memoirs* (9), he writes, "There was only one Democrat in the village"; in *The New Day* (Stanford University, 1928), 49, he says, "there were two or three Democrats in the town."

2. Hoover, *Memoirs,* I, Chs. 1–12, especially pages 155, 124, 135; Will Irwin, *Herbert Hoover: A Reminiscent Biography* (New York, 1928), 59–60; "The President's Fortune," *Fortune,* Aug. 1932.

3. Hoover, *Memoirs,* I, Chs. 12–55, especially pages 140, 218, 287; Brandeis to Norman Hapgood, July 21, 1917, in A. T. Mason, *Brandeis: A Free Man's Life* (New York, 1946), 520; Josephus Daniels, *The Wilson Era: Years of War and After, 1917–1923* (Chapel Hill, 1946), 316; P. C. March, *The Nation at War* (New York, 1932), 73; J. M. Keynes, *The Economic Consequences of the Peace* (New York, 1920), 257; House to Wilson, July 30, 1919, in *Papers Relating to the Foreign Relations of the United States: The Paris Peace Conference* (Washington, 1942–47), XI, 623.

4. Brandeis to Norman Hapgood, Feb. 11, 1920, Mason, *Brandeis: A Free Man's Life,* 530.

5. F.D.R. to Hugh Gibson, Jan. 2, 1920, Roosevelt Papers. Hoover thirty years later had no recollection of political talks with Roosevelt, Hoover to Freidel, Oct. 11, 1951, Frank Freidel, *Franklin D. Roosevelt: The Ordeal* (Boston, 1954), cf. also 56–58; Milton MacKaye, "The Governor," *The New Yorker,* Aug. 22, 1931.

6. Quoted by T.R.B., *New Republic,* May 10, 1943.

7. Herbert Hoover, *American Individualism* (New York, 1922), 8, 19, 48, 36, 18, 68, 24, 8, 37, 29, 61, 17, 39, 44.
8. O. G. Villard, *Prophets True and False* (New York, 1928), 24.
9. Henry Hazlitt, "Salvation Through Charts," *Nation*, Aug. 23, 1933; for Hoover's continued use of this argument, see, e.g., *New Day*, 132–33.
10. Quoted by Julius Klein, "Business," in C. A. Beard, ed., *Whither Mankind* (New York, 1928), 104.
11. E. J. Howenstine, Jr., "Public Works Policy in the Twenties," *Social Research*, Dec. 1946; C. J. Anderson, "The Compensatory Theory of Public Works Expenditure," *Journal of Political Economy*, Sept. 1945; E. E. Hunt, "From 1921 Forward," *Survey Graphic*, April 1929; F.D.R. to R. H. Edmonds, June 20, 1923, Roosevelt Papers; C. J. Hynning, "Evolution of National Planning," *Plan Age*, June 1939; R. G. Tugwell and E. C. Banning, "Governmental Planning at Mid-Century," *Journal of Politics*, May 1951; O. T. Mallery, "Prosperity Reserves," *Survey Graphic*, April 1929; V. A. Mund, "Prosperity Reserves of Public Works," *Annals of the American Academy of Political and Social Sciences*, May 1930.
12. *New York Times*, Nov. 21, 1928; *Literary Digest*, Dec. 8, 1928; W. T. Foster and Waddill Catchings, "The New Attack on Poverty," *Review of Reviews*, April 1929; W. T. Foster and Waddill Catchings, "Better Jobs and More of Them," *Century*, July 1929; Howenstine, "Public Works Policy."
13. Walter Lippmann, "The Peculiar Weakness of Mr. Hoover," *Harper's*, June 1930.
14. W. A. White, *A Puritan in Babylon* (New York, 1938), 353.
15. S. J. Woolf, *Drawn from Life* (New York, 1924), 49; W. M. Jardine to W. A. White, Aug. 1936, in White, *Puritan in Babylon*, 400; J. E. Watson, *As I Knew Them* (Indianapolis, 1936), 255–56; I. H. Hoover, *Forty-Two Years in the White House* (Boston, 1934), 176–79; E. W. Starling, *Starling of the White House* (New York, 1946), 268–69.
16. Hoover, *New Day*, 12, 16, 22, 30, 120–21, 156, 174, 182, 214.

CHAPTER 12 *(Pages 93–104)*

1. F. K. Lane, *Letters*, A. W. Lane and L. H. Wall, eds. (Boston, 1922), 464–65.
2. A. T. Mason, *Brandeis: A Free Man's Life* (New York, 1946), 533–34; J. M. Blum, *Joe Tumulty and the Wilson Era* (Boston, 1951), 261–62.
3. Woodrow Wilson, "The Road Away from Revolution," *Atlantic*, Aug. 1923.
4. McAdoo to F.D.R., Dec. 15, 1922, Roosevelt Papers.
5. Frances Perkins, *The Roosevelt I Knew* (New York, 1946), 22; *Time*, July 11, 1949.

6. Alfred E. Smith, *Up to Now* (New York, 1929); H. F. Pringle, *Alfred E. Smith: A Critical Study* (New York, 1927); Norman Hapgood and Henry Moskowitz, *Up From the City Streets* (New York, 1927); F.D.R. to H. R. Micks, May 9, 1924, Roosevelt Papers; Felix Frankfurter, "Why I Am for Al Smith," *New Republic,* Oct. 31, 1928; W. A. White, *Masks in a Pageant* (New York, 1928), 463 ff.

7. *New York Times,* June 27, 1924; Lippmann to F.D.R., June 27, 1924, Roosevelt Papers; Paxton Hibben, *The Peerless Leader: William Jennings Bryan* (New York, 1929), 197.

8. *New York Times,* June 29, 1924.

9. *New York Times,* June 23, 29, 1924; D. C. Roper, *Fifty Years of Public Life* (Durham, N.C., 1941), 224-25.

10. Charles Michelson, *The Ghost Talks* (New York, 1944), 235.

11. T. A. Huntley, *Life of John W. Davis* (New York, 1924), 5, 274; Blum, *Tumulty,* 247.

12. E. N. Doan, *The La Follettes and the Wisconsin Idea* (New York, 1947), 103-4, 111-12.

13. *New York Times,* May 29, 1924; for La Follette on the Soviet Union see Lincoln Steffens, *Autobiography,* 2 vols. (New York, 1931), II, 806.

14. *Labor,* July 26, 1924; Donald Richberg, *Tents of the Mighty* (Chicago, 1930), 137-38; R. B. Nye, *Midwestern Progressive Politics* (East Lansing, Mich., 1951), 325-47.

15. B. C. Marsh, *Lobbyist for the People* (Washington, 1953), 6; Richberg, *Tents of the Mighty,* 138.

16. Walter Lippmann, *Men of Destiny* (New York, 1927), 6.

17. The text of this letter may be found in Carroll Kilpatrick, ed., *Roosevelt and Daniels: A Friendship in Politics* (Chapel Hill, 1952), 82-83.

18. Cummings to F.D.R., Dec. 12, 1924, Glass to F.D.R., Dec. 17, 1924, Rainey to F.D.R., Dec. 30, 1924, Roosevelt Papers.

19. F.D.R. to T. A. Adams, Nov. 4, 1925, to W. A. Oldfield, April 11, 1925, Roosevelt Papers; *New York World,* Dec. 3, 1925.

CHAPTER 13 *(Pages 105-110)*

1. *Historical Statistics,* Ser. E 72-75, E 76-87, E 88-104, E 244-55.

2. Arthur Capper, *The Agricultural Bloc* (New York, 1922), 107-8.

3. G. N. Peek and H. S. Johnson, *Equality for Agriculture* (Moline, Ill., 1922); G. N. Fite, *George N. Peek and the Fight for Farm Parity* (Norman, Okla., 1954); J. D. Black, *Agricultural Reform in the United States* (New York, 1929), Ch. 8; H. C. and A. D. Taylor, *The Story of Agricultural Economics in the United States, 1840-1932* (Ames, Iowa, 1952), xiii, 583-90; D. N. Kelley, "The McNary-Haugen Bills, 1924-1928," *Agricultural History,* Oct. 1940; M. R. Benedict, *Farm Policies of the United States, 1790-1950* (New York, 1953), 208 ff.

4. Capper, *Agricultural Bloc,* 9; Herbert Hoover, *American Individual-*

ism (New York, 1922), 173, 189, 190, etc.; *Wallace's Farmer,* April 23, 1920; Russell Lord, *The Wallaces of Iowa* (Boston, 1947), 214–15.

5. H. C. Taylor, "A Farm Economist in Washington, 1919–1935," MS; Lord, *Wallaces,* 251.

6. Black, *Agricultural Reform,* 248; Hoover, *Memoirs,* II, 174, 111; Lord, *Wallaces,* 257.

7. H. A. Wallace, *Agricultural Prices* (Des Moines, 1920), 8, 17–18.

8. Lord, *Wallaces,* 233–34; Wallace's first reference to the "ever-normal granary" came in *Wallace's Farmer,* March 3, 1922; see also H. A. Wallace, "Controlling Agricultural Output," *Journal of Farm Economics,* Jan. 1923; M. O. Sillars, "Henry A. Wallace's Editorials on Agricultural Discontent, 1921–1928," *Agricultural History,* Oct. 1952.

9. Lord, *Wallaces,* 256; O. M. Kile, *The Farm Bureau Through Three Decades* (Baltimore, 1948), 132.

10. Lord, *Wallaces,* 273.

11. Black, *Agricultural Reform,* Ch. 10; H. A. Wallace, *New Frontiers* (New York, 1934), 156–57; interview with John D. Black, Oct. 1955.

12. R. G. Tugwell, "Reflections on Farm Relief," *Political Science Quarterly,* Dec. 1928.

CHAPTER 14 *(Pages 111–116)*

1. *Historical Statistics,* Ser. D 77–89, D 117–20, D 121–33, D 134–44; "The Next Labor Offensive," *Fortune,* Jan. 1933; E. M. Hartl and E. G. Ernst, "The Steel Mills Today," *New Republic,* Feb. 19, 1930; G. S. and Broadus Mitchell, "The Plight of Cotton-Mill Labor," in J. B. S. Hardman, ed., *American Labor Dynamics* (New York, 1928), 206–7; J. E. Edgerton, "The President's Annual Address," *American Industries,* Nov. 1929.

2. Leo Wolman, *Ebb and Flow in Trade Unionism* (New York, 1936), 16.

3. Quoted by J. B. S. Hardman, "Fifty Years of American Labor," *New Republic,* Oct. 21, 1931.

4. Reinhold Niebuhr, *Leaves from the Notebook of a Tamed Cynic* (Chicago, 1929), 111.

5. W. H. Taft to Horace Taft, May 7, 1922, in H. F. Pringle, *Life and Times of William Howard Taft* (New York, 1939), II, 967.

6. *New York Times,* Sept. 19, Oct. 18, 1928.

7. H. W. Laidler and Norman Thomas, eds., *Prosperity?* (New York, 1927), 145–46.

8. G. W. Norris, *Fighting Liberal* (New York 1945), 241–43, Ch. 29.

9. Fred E. Beal, *Proletarian Journey* (New York, 1937), Bk. II; Margaret Larkin, "Ella May's Songs," *Nation,* Oct. 9, 1929.

CHAPTER 15 *(Pages 117–124)*

1. Theodore Roosevelt, *The New Nationalism* (New York, 1910), 22;

Gifford Pinchot, *The Fight for Conservation* (New York, 1910), 46, 38.

2. Gifford Pinchot, *Breaking New Ground* (New York, 1947), 333–39; Pinchot, *Fight for Conservation*, 83, 27–28.

3. Will Rogers, *The Autobiography of Will Rogers,* Donald Day, ed. (Boston, 1949), 373.

4. Ferdinand Pecora, *Wall Street Under Oath* (New York, 1939), 225–26; M. W. Childs, "Samuel Insull," *New Republic,* Sept. 21–Oct. 5, 1932; M. L. Ramsay, *Pyramids of Power* (Indianapolis, 1937); J. C. Bonbright and G. C. Means, *The Holding Company* (New York, 1932), 108–13.

5. For summaries of the Federal Trade Commission investigation of the utilities, from which this material is drawn, Ernest Gruening, *The Public Pays* (New York, 1931); C. D. Thompson, *Confessions of the Power Trust* (New York, 1932); Jack Levin, *Power Ethics* (New York, 1931).

6. Hoover before 48th Convention of the National Electric Light Association, June 1925; Amos Pinchot, "Hoover and Power," *Nation,* Aug. 5, 1931; Felix Frankfurter, *Law and Politics* (New York, 1939), 280–83.

7. Hoover, *Memoirs,* II, 174.

8. G. W. Norris, *Fighting Liberal* (New York, 1945), 11, 19.

9. Norris, *Fighting Liberal,* 19, 93.

10. R. L. Neuberger and S. B. Kahn, *Integrity: The Life of George W. Norris* (New York, 1937), 339, 187; M. W. Childs, *I Write from Washington* (New York, 1942), 37–41; Edmund Wilson, *The American Jitters* (New York, 1932), 105–6.

11. G. W. Norris, "The Power Trust in the Public Schools," *Nation,* Sept. 18, 1929; Norris, *Fighting Liberal,* 160–61, 171, 248. Neuberger and Kahn, *Integrity,* 176.

12. John Dewey, "The Need for a New Party," *New Republic,* March 25, 1931; Frankfurter to F.D.R., Jan. 5, 1929, Roosevelt Papers.

13. F.D.R. at Oswego, Oct. 24, 1928, speech draft, Roosevelt Papers.

CHAPTER 16 *(Pages 125–129)*

1. *New York Times,* June 28, 1928.

2. H. C. Pell to William Manice, Aug. 6, 1935, Pell Papers.

3. Louise Overacker, *Money in Elections* (New York, 1932), 75.

4. J. J. Raskob, with Samuel Crowther, "Everybody Ought to be Rich," *Ladies' Home Journal,* Aug. 1929; R. C. McManus, "Raskob," *North American Review,* Jan. 1931.

5. Milton to McAdoo, July 31, 1928, in Edmund A. Moore, *A Catholic Runs for President* (New York, 1928), 114; F.D.R. to G. L. Radcliffe, July 11, 1928, to V. L. Black, July 25, 1928, to Ward Melville, Sept. 21, 1928, Roosevelt Papers.

6. T. L. Stokes, *Chip off My Shoulder* (Princeton, 1940), 238–41; Bruce

Bliven, "Trouping with Al Smith," *New Republic*, Oct. 10, 1928; J. M. Proskauer, *A Segment of My Times* (New York, 1950), 61–62.

7. *New Republic*, Sept. 5, 1928.

8. Samuel Lubell, *The Future of American Politics* (New York, 1952), 34–41, 169; S. J. Eldersveld, "The Influence of Metropolitan Party Pluralities in Presidential Elections since 1920," *American Political Science Review*, Dec. 1949.

9. Davis to F.D.R., Jan. 29, 1929, Roosevelt Papers; Silas Bent, "Will the Democrats Follow the Whigs?" *Scribner's*, Nov. 1929.

CHAPTER 17 *(Pages 130–144)*

1. For a more extended discussion of this process, Arthur M. Schlesinger, Jr., "The Revaluation of Liberalism," in a forthcoming series of lectures at Barnard College, edited by Basil Rauch.

2. John Dewey, *Human Nature and Conduct* (Modern Lib.), 107.

3. John Dewey, *Individualism Old and New* (New York, 1929), 18, 33, 118, 155.

4. George Soule, "Herbert Croly's Liberalism, 1920–1928," *New Republic*, July 16, 1930; Edmund Wilson, " 'H. C.,' " *The Shores of Light* (New York, 1952), 476–84; Felix Frankfurter, "Herbert Croly and American Political Opinion," *New Republic*, July 16, 1930; George Soule, "Hard-boiled Radicalism," *New Republic*, Jan. 21, 1931.

5. C. A. Beard, ed., *Whither Mankind* (New York, 1928), 406, 19, 407.

6. C. A. Beard, *Toward Civilization* (New York, 1930), 299, 300–301, 303.

7. W. T. Foster and Waddill Catchings, *Business Without a Buyer* (Boston, 1927), 19, 85; W. T. Foster and Waddill Catchings, *The Road to Plenty* (Boston, 1928), 158, 194, 200.

8. Wallace's comment was on the paper jacket; Roosevelt made his in his copy of *The Road to Plenty*, now in the Roosevelt Library.

9. Foster and Catchings, *Road to Plenty*, 153–54.

10. Patten to F. H. Giddings, March 24, 1898, in Joseph Dorfman, *The Economic Mind in American Civilization* (New York, 1949), III, 188; S. N. Patten, "Extravagance as a Virtue," *Current Opinion*, Jan. 1913; S. N. Patten, *The New Basis of Civilization* (New York, 1907), 186; S. N. Patten, *Essays in Economic Theory*, R. G. Tugwell, ed. (New York, 1924), 255; R. G. Tugwell, "Some Formative Influences in the Life of Simon Nelson Patten," *American Economic Review*, Suppl., March 1923; R. G. Tugwell, "Notes on the Life and Work of Simon Nelson Patten," *Journal of Political Economy*, April 1923; R. G. Tugwell, "The New Deal: The Progressive Tradition," *Western Political Quarterly*, Sept. 1950; C. M. H. Lynch, "Frances Perkins," *Mount Holyoke Alumnae Quarterly*, April 1929.

11. Thorstein Veblen, *The Engineers and the Price System* (New York, 1921), 9, 104, 120–21, 146.

12. Herbert Hoover, *The New Day* (Stanford University, 1928), 110; S. H.

Strawn, "Problems of the Manufacturer," *American Industries*, Oct. 1929.
13. G. L. Joughin and E. M. Morgan, *The Legacy of Sacco and Vanzetti* (New York, 1948); Phil Stong, "The Last Days of Sacco and Vanzetti," in Isabel Leighton, ed., *The Aspirin Age, 1919–1941* (New York, 1949), 169 ff.; Malcolm Cowley, "Echoes of a Crime," *New Republic*, Aug. 28, 1935; Edmund Wilson, "The Consequences of the Crash," *Shores of Light*, 496–97; R. M. Lovett, *All Our Years* (New York, 1948), 190; John Dos Passos, *The Big Money* (New York, 1936), 462; Murray Kempton, *Part of Our Time* (New York, 1955), 45–50.
14. Douglas was notably more reserved. For Tugwell, Chase, and Douglas, see Stuart Chase, Robert Dunn, and R. G. Tugwell, eds., *Soviet Russia in the Second Decade* (New York, 1928); John Dewey, *Impressions of Soviet Russia* (New York, 1929), 121; R. G. Tugwell, "Experimental Control in Russian Industry," *Political Science Quarterly*, June 1928.
15. Lincoln Steffens, "Stop, Look, Listen!" *Survey Graphic*, March 1927.
16. Walter Lippmann, *Men of Destiny* (New York, 1928), 27; Steffens to Jo Davidson, Feb. 18, 1929, in Lincoln Steffens, *Letters*, Ella Winter and Granville Hicks, eds., 2 vols. (New York, 1938), II, 829–30.
17. F. C. Howe, *The Confessions of a Reformer* (New York, 1925), 195–96; "Where Are the Pre-War Radicals," *Survey*, Feb. 1, 1926; F. C. Howe, "Where Are the Pre-War Radicals," *Survey*, April 1, 1926; Donald Richberg, *Tents of the Mighty* (Chicago, 1930), 59; Steffens to Ella Winter, Aug. 2, 1929, in Steffens, *Letters*, II, 841; White to Brandeis, Jan. 12, 1929, in W. A. White, *Selected Letters . . . 1899–1943*, Walter Johnson, ed. (New York, 1947), 290.

CHAPTER 18 *(Pages 145–152)*

1. Scott Fitzgerald, *This Side of Paradise* (New York, 1920), 304; "Early Success," *The Crack-Up*, Edmund Wilson, ed. (New York, 1945), 87–90.
2. Scott Fitzgerald, "Echoes of the Jazz Age," *Scribner's*, Nov. 1931; G. J. Nathan, *The World of George Jean Nathan*, Charles Angoff, ed. (New York, 1952), 201; Malcolm Cowley, "Twenty Years of American Letters," *New Republic*, March 3, 1937; Louis Kronenberger, "H. L. Mencken," *New Republic*, Oct. 7, 1936.
3. Anderson to Waldo Frank, Oct. 29, 1917, in Sherwood Anderson, *Letters*, H. M. Jones and W. B. Rideout, eds. (Boston, 1953), 18; in *Vanity Fair*, 1923, quoted by Malcolm Cowley in *Exile's Return* (New York, 1934), 118.
4. Donald Richberg, *Tents of the Mighty* (Chicago, 1930), 25; Donald Richberg, *The Shadow Men* (Chicago, 1911); Donald Richberg, *A Man of Purpose* (New York, 1922), 301, 313, vi.
5. W. C. Bullitt, *It's Not Done* (New York, 1926), 340, 371; Francis Biddle, *The Llanfear Pattern* (New York, 1927), 252.

6. H. L. Mencken, *Notes on Democracy* (New York, 1926), 9, 22, 106–7, 126, 137, 176, 192; H. L. Mencken, *Prejudices: Second Series* (New York, 1920), 102, 117; H. L. Mencken, *Prejudices: Fifth Series* (New York, 1926), 70.

7. Irving Babbitt, *Democracy and Leadership* (Boston, 1924), 205, 214, 288, 312. One of Babbitt's darker warnings perhaps deserves repetition: if man "succeeds in releasing the stores of energy that are locked up in the atom — and this seems to be the most recent ambition of our physicists — his final exploit may be to blow himself off the planet." (*Democracy and Leadership*, 143)

8. T. S. Eliot, "The Waste Land," *Collected Poems, 1909–1935* (London, 1936), 61–77.

9. Walter Lippmann, *A Preface to Morals* (New York, 1929), 187, 229, 209, 329–30.

10. J. W. Krutch, *The Modern Temper* (New York, 1929), 9, 45, 183, 247, 249.

CHAPTER 19 *(Pages 155–160)*

1. Hoover, *State Papers*, I, 3–13; W. T. Foster and Waddill Catchings, "Mr. Hoover's Road to Prosperity," *Review of Reviews*, Jan. 1930.

2. R. L. Wilbur, "What About Our Public Lands?" *Review of Reviews*, Dec. 1929; Hoover to J. M. Dixon, Aug. 21, 1929, in Hoover, *State Papers*, I, 91–96; *Boston Globe*, Aug. 28, 1929; E. L. Peffer, *The Closing of the Public Domain* (Stanford University, 1951), Ch. 11.

3. Amos Pinchot, "Hoover and Power," *Nation*, Aug. 12, 1931; P. Y. Anderson, "Mr. Hoover's Last Mile," *Nation*, Nov. 9, 1932.

4. This was a minority view among reputable economists. Keynes, however, took the same position the next year, contending that the increase in the interest rate "played an essential part in bringing about the rapid collapse. For this punitive rate of interest could not be prevented from having its repercussions on the rate of new investment . . . and was bound, therefore, to prelude an era of falling prices and business losses everywhere." J. M. Keynes, *Treatise on Money* (New York, 1930), II, 296. But see Thomas Wilson, *Fluctuations in Income and Employment*, 3rd ed. (London, 1948), 147 ff.

5. J. M. Keynes, "Fluctuations in Net Investments in the United States," *Economic Journal*, Sept. 1936; Wilson, *Fluctuations*, 118.

6. J. K. Galbraith, *The Great Crash* (Boston, 1955); F. L. Allen, *Only Yesterday* (New York, 1931), Ch. 13; Burton Rascoe, "The Grim Anniversary," *New Republic*, Oct. 29, 1930; Irving Fisher, *The Stock Market Crash — and After* (New York, 1930); Matthew Josephson, "Groton, Harvard, Wall Street," *The New Yorker*, April 2, 1932.

CHAPTER 20 *(Pages 161-165)*

1. B. N. Timmons, *Portrait of . . . Charles G. Dawes* (New York, 1953), 286.
2. F.D.R. to J. Lionberger Davis, Aug. 5, 1929, Roosevelt Papers.
3. Hoover, *Memoirs,* II, 58; *New York Times,* Nov. 1, 4, 1929 (my italics added to the Lamont statement).
4. For compilations of business predictions, see *Review of Reviews,* Jan. and Feb. 1930 and *American Industries,* Jan. 1930; Edward Angly, ed., *Oh Yeah?* (New York, 1931).
5. Hoover, *Memoirs,* III, 30-31.
6. Reed Smoot, "Why a Protective Tariff?" *Saturday Evening Post,* Sept. 10, 1932; W. C. Hawley, "The New Tariff: A Defense," *Review of Reviews,* July 1934; statement of F. W. Fetter, *American Economic Review,* June 1942; D. C. Roper, *Fifty Years of Public Life* (Durham, N.C., 1941), 236; *Nation,* July 1, 1931; Hoover, *State Papers,* I, 318.
7. J. T. Adams, "Presidential Prosperity," *Harper's,* Aug. 1930; "The Hoover Happiness Boys," *Nation,* June 18, 1930; "Prophet Lamont," *New Republic,* Nov. 5, 1930; Julius Klein, "It's Great To Be a Young Man Today," *American Magazine,* Feb. 1930. For Hoover's March 7 statement (my italics) *New York Times,* March 8, 1930; this important statement is oddly not included in Hoover's collected *State Papers* nor mentioned in the other semiofficial accounts of the Hoover administration.
8. For example, in Aug. 1930, Professor Charles E. Persons resigned from the Census Bureau in protest against statistical techniques designed to minimize and obscure the number of unemployed. (*New York Times,* Aug. 16, 1930)
9. J. K. Galbraith, *The Great Crash* (Boston, 1955), 144; Will Rogers, *The Autobiography of Will Rogers,* Donald Day, ed. (Boston, 1949), 232; Gilbert Seldes, *The Years of the Locust* (Boston, 1933), 63.
10. Hoover, *State Papers,* I, 289-96.

CHAPTER 21 *(Pages 166-176)*

1. *New York Times,* March 7, 1930; J. N. Leonard, *Three Years Down* (New York, 1939), 123-25.
2. Bruce Bliven, "On the Bowery," *New Republic,* March 19, 1930; Green before the House Judiciary Committee, *Unemployment in the United States: Hearings,* 71 Cong., 2 Sess. (1930), 23.
3. See the various congressional hearings on unemployment and articles in the *Survey Graphic* and elsewhere; also Clinch Calkins, *Some Folks Won't Work* (New York, 1930); Bruce Bliven, "No Money, No Work," *New Republic,* Nov. 19, 1930.
4. J. C. Brown, *Public Relief, 1929-1939* (New York, 1940), 429.

5. Hoover, *State Papers*, I, 391, 395, 405.
6. For Hoover's reluctance, see "Formation of Committee," interview with E. P. Hayes and E. L. Bernays, Feb. 26, 1931, Hopkins Papers. The local theory of unemployment was carried to an absurd extent. On Aug. 25, 1931, T. T. Craven, the Chief Coordinator of the Federal Coordinating Service, sent a directive to All Area Coordinators, reminding them: "All reference to the Federal business associations, the Federal Coordinating Service and to the Federal Government should be avoided, both directly and by implication. As stated before, the problem of relief is local and personal and this service is being used as a channel of communication only." (Hopkins Papers)
7. E. P. Hayes, *Activities of the President's Emergency Committee for Employment* (Concord, N.H., 1936), 43, 141-44; H. L. Hopkins, *Spending to Save* (New York, 1936), 21-25.
8. Mark Sullivan, "The Case For the Administration," *Fortune*, July 1932.
9. Hoover, *State Papers*, I, 496-99.
10. Congressional hearings; Hugo Johanson, "Bread Line," *Atlantic*, Aug. 1936; Edmund Wilson, *Travels in Two Democracies* (New York, 1936), 30-31; C. R. Walker, "Relief and Revolution," *Forum*, Aug. 1932; R. L. Duffus, *Lillian Wald* (New York, 1938), 287-88, 349-50.
11. S. H. Slichter, "Doles for Employers," *New Republic*, Dec. 31, 1930.
12. White to William Green, Sept. 1, 1931, in W. A. White, *Selected Letters . . . 1899-1943*, Walter Johnson, ed. (New York, 1947), 317.
13. Senate Manufactures Committee, *Unemployment Relief: Hearings*, 72 Cong., 1 Sess. (1932), 311-31.
14. Senate Manufactures Committee, *Federal Cooperation in Unemployment Relief: Hearings*, 72 Cong., 1 Sess. (1932), especially 7, 136-37.
15. Federal Farm Board, *Second Annual Report*, Senate Agriculture and Forestry Committee, *Agricultural Conference and Farm Board Inquiry: Hearings*, 72 Cong., 1 Sess. (1931), 457-58; Wallace to F.D.R., Dec. 1, 1934, Roosevelt Papers.
16. *Historical Statistics*, Ser. E 88-104.
17. *Historical Statistics*, Ser. E 244-55; testimony of Ed O'Neal, Senate Banking and Currency Committee, *Refinancing Past Due Obligations on Farms and Homes: Hearings*, 72 Cong., 1 Sess. (1933), 174-76.
18. Sen. Banking Com., *Refinancing . . . Obligations*, 175; W. G. Clugston, "Thunder in the Wheat Belt," *Nation*, Aug. 5, 1931; L. A. Dahl, "Class War in the Corn Belt," *New Republic*, May 17, 1933; W. A. White, "The Farmer Takes His Holiday," *Saturday Evening Post*, Nov. 26, 1932.
19. *New York Herald Tribune*, Jan. 4, 1931; *New Republic*, Jan. 14, 1931; Leonard, *Three Years Down*, 163; Will Rogers, *The Autobiography of Will Rogers*, Donald Day, ed. (Boston, 1949), 237; Whittaker Chambers, "Can You Hear Their Voices?" *New Masses*, March 1931;

Steffens to Chambers, June 18, 1933, in Lincoln Steffens, *Letters,* Ella Winter and Granville Hicks, eds. (New York, 1938), II, 961; Edith Abbott, *Public Assistance* (Chicago, 1940), 705–6.

20. Senate Agriculture and Forestry Committee, *To Establish an Efficient Agricultural Credit System: Hearings,* 72 Cong., 1 Sess. (1932), 28.
21. Sen. Man. Com., *Unemployment Relief,* 214.

CHAPTER 22 *(Pages 177–183)*

1. Business litany compiled from forecasts of the Guardian Trust Company, Cleveland, Moody's Investment Service, Brookmire Economic Service, Standard Statistics Company, and McGraw-Hill; see *Review of Reviews,* Feb. and July 1930; J. E. Edgerton, "The Unemployment Situation and An Idea," *American Industries,* Sept. 1930; Julius Klein, "When Do We Come Out Of It?" *American Magazine,* Sept. 1930; *Time,* Jan. 14, 1935.
2. Edgerton, "Unemployment Situation"; S. H. Strawn, "The Need for Restored Confidence," *Nation's Business,* Jan. 1932; for Mitchell and Wiggin, Senate Manufactures Committee, *Establishment of a National Economic Council: Hearings,* 72 Cong., 1 Sess. (1931), 533, 373, 364; Morrow to Charles Burnett, May 7, 1931, in Harold Nicolson, *Dwight Morrow* (New York, 1935), 394.
3. *New York Times,* Sept. 16, 1931; Henry Ford, Associated Press interview, March 14, 1931; Sen. Man. Com., *Nat'l Economic Council,* 536; Edgerton, "Unemployment Situation"; Merle Thorpe, "Our Vanishing Economic Freedom," *Saturday Evening Post,* Oct. 3, 1931; J. M. Beck, *Our Wonderland of Bureaucracy* (New York, 1933), 85.
4. Edgerton, "Unemployment Situation."
5. *Time,* April 4, 1932.
6. Nichlos to Hurley, Jan. 9, 1931, Hurley to Woods, Jan. 13, 1931, Hopkins Papers; H. L. Hopkins, *Spending to Save* (New York, 1936), 26–28.
7. Winston S. Churchill, "The Dole," *Saturday Evening Post,* March 29, 1930; James C. Young, "Ford Scans the Economic Future," *New York Times Magazine,* May 24, 1931; Gilbert Seldes, *The Years of the Locust* (Boston, 1933), 101, 153–54; J. N. Leonard, *Three Years Down* (New York, 1939), 157–59.
8. J. C. Long, "Dwight W. Morrow," *Scribner's,* Sept. 1935; W. T. Foster and Waddill Catchings, "Must We Reduce Our Standard of Living?" *Forum,* Feb. 1931; Strawn, "Need for Restored Confidence"; Hopkins, *Spending to Save,* 41–42; W. S. Gifford, "Can Prosperity Be Managed?" *Saturday Evening Post,* Nov. 8, 1930; M. C. Taylor with Samuel Crowther, "Leisure and the Machine Age," *Saturday Evening Post,* March 28, 1931.
9. Senate Banking and Currency Committee, *Unemployment Relief: Hearings,* 72 Cong., 1 Sess. (1932), 184; J. C. Long, "Morrow";

Daniel Willard, "The Challenge to Capitalism," *Review of Reviews,* May 1931.

10. N. M. Butler, "A Planless World," in C. A. Beard, ed., *America Faces the Future* (Boston, 1932), 11, 19; Leonard, *Three Years Down,* 138; W. B. Donham, *Business Adrift* (New York, 1931), 33, 35–36, 141–42.

11. Paul Mazur, *New Roads to Prosperity* (New York, 1931), 95–96, 139; B. M. Baruch, "A Plan For the Regulation of Production," in J. G. Frederick, ed., *A Philosophy of Production* (New York, 1930), 93–103; W. L. White, *Bernard Baruch* (New York, 1950), 74; *New York Times,* June 5, 1931; Samuel Crowther, *A Basis for Stability* (Boston, 1932), 118, 59; *Nation,* Oct. 8, 1930; B. M. Baruch, "A Few Kind Words for Uncle Sam," *Saturday Evening Post,* April 5, 1930; B. M. Baruch, "Notes for Address to Ninth Reunion of the United States War Industries Board . . . November 11, 1931" (mimeographed).

12. Gerard Swope, *Stabilization of Industry* (New York, [1931]); Gerard Swope and Others, *Discussion of 'Stabilization of Industry'* (New York, [1931]); Sen. Man. Com., *Nat'l Economic Council,* 303–11.

13. J. H. Barnes, "Government and Business," *Harvard Business Review,* July 1932; H. I. Harriman, "American Business Turns a Page," *New York Times Magazine,* Dec. 2, 1933; H. I. Harriman, "The Stabilization of Business and Employment," *American Economic Review,* March 1932; Sen. Man. Com., *Nat'l Economic Council,* 167–68, 185–88; *Congressional Record,* 73 Cong., 1 Sess. (June 7, 1933), 5164.

14. Ralph E. Flanders, "Limitations and Possibilities of Economic Planning," *Annals of the American Academy of Political and Social Science,* July, 1932; Harriman, "American Business."

CHAPTER 23 *(Pages 184–203)*

1. Louis Stark, "Labor's Unemployment Program," *Survey,* Nov. 15, 1930; William Green, "The Way Forward," *American Federationist,* March 1931; Green to Hoover, July 24, 1931, in Senate Manufactures Committee, *Establishment of a National Economic Council: Hearings,* 72 Cong., 1 Sess. (1931), 604; *American Labor Year Book, 1931* (New York, 1931), 32–34; Louis Adamic, "The Collapse of Organized Labor," *Harper's,* Jan. 1932; Gilbert Seldes, *The Years of the Locust* (Boston, 1933), 205.

2. *New York Times,* May 14, 1932.

3. Senate Finance Committee, *Investigation of Economic Problems: Hearings,* 72 Cong., 2 Sess. (1933), 792; Sen. Man. Com., *Nat'l Economic Council,* 644–45.

4. Sidney Hillman, "Unemployment Reserves," *Atlantic,* Nov. 1931; Sidney Hillman, "Labor Leads Toward Planning," *Survey Graphic,* March 1932; Sen. Man. Com., *Nat'l Economic Council,* 435–36.

5. W. T. Foster, "Wizards with Boot-straps," *North American Review,*

April 1933; Senate Banking and Currency Committee, *Unemployment Relief: Hearings,* 72 Cong., 1 Sess. (1932), 63; W. T. Foster and Waddill Catchings, "Must We Reduce Our Standard of Living?" *Forum,* Feb. 1931; Sen. Finance Com., *Economic Problems,* 1152–53; W. T. Foster and Waddill Catchings, "'In the Day of Adversity,'" *Atlantic,* July 1931; W. T. Foster, "When a Horse Balks," *North American Review,* July 1932.

6. See J. A. Hobson, *Rationalization and Unemployment* (New York, 1930); J. A. Hobson, *Poverty in Plenty* (New York, 1931); J. A. Hobson, "The World's Economic Crisis," *Nation,* July 20, 1932.

7. J. M. Keynes, "The World's Economic Outlook," *Atlantic,* May 1932.

8. Senate Banking and Currency Committee, *Further Unemployment Relief Through the Reconstruction Finance Corporation: Hearings,* 72 Cong., 2 Sess. (1933), 129; Sen. Finance Com., *Economic Problems,* 713, 706.

9. Sen. Banking Com., *Unemployment Relief,* 57.

10. A. A. Berle, Jr., and G. C. Means, *The Modern Corporation and Private Property* (New York, 1932); G. C. Means, "The Growth in the Relative Importance of the Large Corporation in American Economic Life," *American Economic Review,* March 1931; G. C. Means, "The Separation of Ownership and Control in American Industry," *Quarterly Journal of Economics,* Nov. 1931; G. C. Means, "Who Controls Industry?" *Nation,* May 4, 1932; A. A. Berle, Jr., "For Whom Corporate Managers Are Trustees: A Note," *Harvard Law Review,* June 1932; A. A. Berle, Jr., and Louis Faulkner, "The Nature of the Difficulty" (May 1932), Berle Papers; A. A. Berle, Jr., "A High Road for Business," *Scribner's,* June 1933; A. A. Berle, Jr., "The Social Economics of the New Deal," *New York Times Magazine,* Oct. 29, 1933; A. A. Berle, Jr., "Private Business and Public Opinion," *Scribner's,* Feb. 1934; A. G. Gruchy, "The Administrative Economics of Gardiner C. Means," *Modern Economic Thought: The American Contribution* (New York, 1947), 473–540.

11. (R. G. Tugwell is the author of the works cited in the following unless otherwise stated.) "The Light of Other Days," Chs. 1–6, MS autobiography in the Tugwell Papers; "Government in a Changing World," *Review of Reviews,* Aug. 1933; "Social Objectives in Education" in R. G. Tugwell and Leon Keyserling, eds., *Redirecting Education* (New York, 1934), I, 55; "Experimental Economics," in R. G. Tugwell, ed., *The Trend of Economics* (New York, 1924), 384; "The New Deal: The Available Instruments of Governmental Power," *Western Political Quarterly,* Dec. 1949; R. G. Tugwell, Thomas Munro, and R. E. Stryker, *American Economic Life,* 3rd ed. (New York, 1930), 365; "The Progressive Tradition," *Western Political Quarterly,* Sept. 1950; "Governor or President?" *New Republic,* May 16, 1928; "After the New Deal: 'We Have Bought Ourselves Time to Think,'" *New Republic,*

July 26, 1939; "America's War-Time Socialism," *Nation*, April 6, 1927; *The Stricken Land* (New York, 1946), 436. See also "The Experimental Economics of Rexford G. Tugwell" in Gruchy, *Modern Economic Thought*, 405–70; Russell Lord, "Rural New Yorkers," *The New Yorker*, March 23, 30, 1935; [J. F. Carter], *The New Dealers* (New York, 1934), 92.

12. R. G. Tugwell, "The Principle of Planning and the Institution of Laissez-Faire," *American Economic Review*, Suppl., March 1932.

13. Senate Agriculture and Forestry Committee, *Confirmation of Rexford G. Tugwell: Hearing*, 73 Cong., 2 Sess. (1934), 11.

14. Tugwell and Keyserling, *Redirecting Education*, I, 64.

15. R. G. Tugwell, *The Industrial Discipline* (New York, 1933), 85, 87, 229, 207, 212–15.

16. Tugwell, Munroe, and Stryker, *American Economic Life*, 712; Tugwell and Keyserling, *Redirecting Education*, I, 68, 90, 105–6, 107; Tugwell, "Planning and . . . Laissez-Faire"; Tugwell, "Discourse in Depression," quoted in R. G. Tugwell, "The Progressive Orthodoxy of Franklin D. Roosevelt," *Ethics*, Oct. 1953.

17. (P. H. Douglas is the author of the first five following works.) "Money, Credit and the Depression," *World Tomorrow*, March 1932; "Connecting Men and Jobs," *Survey Graphic*, Dec. 1930; "The Prospects for a New Political Alignment," *American Political Science Review*, Nov. 1931; *The Coming of a New Party* (New York, 1932), 164, 171, 195, 96–97, 93, 215–16; "Lessons from the Last Decade," in H. W. Laidler and Norman Thomas, eds., *The Socialism of Our Times* (New York, 1929), 54. See also *American Labor Year Book, 1930* (New York, 1930), 126–30; *American Labor Year Book, 1931* (New York, 1931), 157–58; *American Labor Year Book, 1932* (New York, 1932), 100; Devere Allen, ed., *Adventurous Americans* (New York, 1932), 181–90; Norris to Dewey, Dec. 27, 1930, in R. L. Neuberger and S. B. Kahn, *Integrity: The Life of George W. Norris* (New York, 1937), 185–86; John Dewey, "The Need for a New Party," *New Republic*, March 18, 25, April 1, 8, 1931.

18. Sen. Man. Com., *Nat'l Economic Council*, 459–63; George Soule, *A Planned Society* (New York, 1932), 277; George Soule, "Hard-boiled Radicalism," *New Republic*, Jan. 21, 1931.

19. C. A. Beard, " 'A Five-Year Plan' for America," *Forum*, July 1931; C. A. Beard, "The Myth of Rugged American Individualism," *Harper's*, Dec. 1931; C. A. Beard, "The Rationality of Planned Economy" in C. A. Beard, ed., *America Faces the Future* (Boston, 1932), 400–401.

20. W. H. Hamilton, "The Control of Big Business," *Nation*, May 25, 1932; J. T. Flynn, "The Evil Influence of Wall Street," in S. D. Schmalhausen, ed., *Behold America!* (New York, 1931), 198; J. T. Flynn, "A Demand for State Action on a Security Wage," *Forum*, Oct. 1931.

21. (Stuart Chase is author of the following works.) "Harnessing the Wild

Horses of Industry," *Atlantic*, June 1931; "What Do the Liberals Hope For?" *New Republic*, Feb. 10, 1932; *Prosperity, Fact or Myth* (New York, 1929), 188; *A New Deal* (New York, 1932), 240, 86, 97, 252; "The Age of Distribution," *Nation*, July 25, 1934; "A New Deal for America: IV," *New Republic*, July 27, 1932; *The Nemesis of American Business* (New York, 1931), 95, 97; "Mergers Pfd.," *New Republic*, Oct. 14, 1931; "The Case for Inflation," *Harper's*, July 1932.

22. 285 U.S. at 280, 306, 307-8, 311; *Time*, April 4, 1932.
23. J. M. Keynes, "Economic Possibilities for our Grandchildren," *Saturday Evening Post*, Oct. 11, 1930; 285 U.S. at 311.

CHAPTER 24 *(Pages 204–223)*

1. Will Rogers, *The Autobiography of Will Rogers*, Donald Day, ed. (Boston, 1949), 237; Cornelius Vanderbilt, Jr., *Farewell to Fifth Avenue* (New York, 1935), 197–98; Walter Lippmann, *Interpretations, 1931–1932*, Allan Nevins, ed. (New York, 1932), 30; *New York Times*, Sept. 24, 1931; C. G. Dawes, *Journal As Ambassador to Great Britain* (New York, 1939), 404; Hilton Butler, "Bilbo — The Two-Edged Sword," *North American Review*, Dec. 1931.
2. R. E. Sherwood, *Reunion in Vienna* (New York, 1932), 7; Scott Fitzgerald, "Echoes of the Jazz Age," *Scribner's*, Nov. 1931; Scott Fitzgerald, *The Crack-Up*, Edmund Wilson, ed. (New York, 1945), 126; Arthur Mizener, *The Far Side of Paradise* (Boston, 1951), 225, 234.
3. Eric Sevareid, *Not So Wild a Dream* (New York, 1946), 56–57.
4. *New York Times*, Nov. 25, 1929.
5. Daniel Bell, "The Background and Development of Marxian Socialism in the United States," in D. D. Egbert and Stow Persons, eds., *Socialism and American Life* (Princeton, 1952), I, 369–70.
6. "Whither the American Writer," *Modern Quarterly*, Summer 1932.
7. Lincoln Steffens, *Autobiography* (New York, 1931), II, 706, 574, 631, 818, 832, 872.
8. Garet Garrett's comment on the book jacket of Steffen's *Autobiography;* John Reed, "Almost Thirty," *New Republic*, April 29, 1936; Newton Arvin, "Epitaph of a Generation," *Nation*, April 15, 1931.
9. Granville Hicks on Steffens in Malcolm Cowley and Bernard Smith, eds., *Books That Changed Our Minds* (New York, 1939), 12; Granville Hicks, "Lincoln Steffens: He Covered the Future," *Commentary*, Feb. 1952; Steffens to Ella Winter Steffens, Aug. 16, 1930, Feb. 7, 1933, to Sam Darcy, April 12, 1936, in Lincoln Steffens, *Letters*, Ella Winter and Granville Hicks, eds. (New York, 1938), II, 878, 949, 1020; Lillian Symes to the editors, *Modern Monthly*, Oct. 1934.
10. John Chamberlain, *Farewell to Reform* (New York, 1932), 305, 310, 323. Even while bidding reform farewell, Chamberlain announced that he thought redistributive taxation (190–91) or votes (309) might pro-

vide an alternative to violent revolution. But these notes of concession were drowned out in his general sounding of doom. See his "Votes Will Do," *Common Sense*, Feb. 16, 1933, for a first attempt to undo the effects of *Farewell to Reform*.

11. John Strachey, *The Coming Struggle for Power* (Modern Lib., New York, 1935), 358–60, xi, 406–7; Richard Crossman, "John Strachey and the Left Book Club," *New Statesman and Nation*, Jan. 7, 1956.

12. Schmalhausen, "An American vs. America," in S. D. Schmalhausen, ed., *Behold America!* (New York, 1931), 755; S. D. Schmalhausen, ed., *Recovery Through Revolution* (New York, 1933), 477; Kenneth Patchen, *Before the Brave* (New York, 1936), 49.

13. Dewey, "The Imperative Need for a New Radical Party," *Common Sense*, Sept. 1933.

14. J. H. Nichols, *Democracy and the Churches* (Philadelphia, 1951), 226–27.

15. *World Tomorrow*, Sept. 30, 1930; H. F. Ward, *In Place of Profit* (New York, 1933), 96–97; L. P. Powell, "A Clergyman Looks in on Russia," *Review of Reviews*, Oct. 1934.

16. R. M. Lovett, "The Degradation of American Politics," in Schmalhausen, *Behold America!* 43; M. S. Stewart, "Where Everyone Has a a Job," *Survey Graphic*, Aug. 1931; Edmund Wilson, "Art, the Proletariat and Marx," *New Republic*, Aug. 23, 1933; Rogers, *Autobiography*, 249; White to Ickes, Nov. 14, 1933, in W. A. White, *Selected Letters . . . 1899–1943*, Walter Johnson, ed. (New York, 1947), 337; Albert Parry, "A Gold Rush to Moscow," *Outlook*, July 15, 1931.

17. James Wechsler, *The Age of Suspicion* (New York, 1953), 37; Stewart Alsop, "Wanted: A Faith to Fight For," *Atlantic*, May 1941.

18. Edmund Wilson, "An Appeal to Progressives," *New Republic*, Jan. 14, 1931; Edmund Wilson, *Travels in Two Democracies* (New York, 1936), 321.

19. "Whither the American Writer," *Modern Quarterly*, Summer 1932; "How I Came to Communism," *New Masses*, Sept. 1932; Edmund Wilson, "What I Believe," *Nation*, Jan. 27, 1932.

20. Michael Gold, "Wilder: Prophet of the Genteel Christ," *New Republic*, Oct. 22, 1930.

21. Archibald MacLeish, "The Social Cant," *New Republic*, Dec. 21, 1932; Archibald MacLeish, "Ars Poetica" and "Invocation to the Social Muse," in *Collected Poems, 1917–1952* (Boston, 1952), 41, 94–95; Michael Gold, "Out of the Fascist Unconscious," *New Republic*, July 26, 1933.

22. Joseph Freeman, Introduction to Granville Hicks, *et al.*, eds., *Proletarian Literature in the United States* (New York, 1935), 11, 25.

23. Robert Cantwell, *The Land of Plenty* (New York, 1934), 369.

24. William Rollins, *The Shadow Before* (New York, 1934), 175; Cantwell, *Land of Plenty*, 301.

25. Granville Hicks, "Communism and the American Intellectual," in I. DeW. Talmadge, ed., *Whose Revolution?* (New York, 1941), 80, 84.

26. House Committee to Investigate Communist Activities, *Investigation of Communist Propaganda*, 71 Cong., 2 Sess. (1930), 348, 348–85; Edmund Wilson, "Foster and Fish," *New Republic*, Dec. 24, 1930.

27. W. Z. Foster, *Toward Soviet America* (New York, 1932), 212, 213, 275.

28. John Dos Passos, *The Theme is Freedom* (New York, 1956), 82; *New York Times*, Sept. 30, 1931.

29. John Dos Passos, "Red Day on Capitol Hill," *New Republic*, Dec. 23, 1931; J. N. Leonard, *Three Years Down* (New York, 1939), 204–6; Senate Manufactures Committee, *Unemployment Relief: Hearings*, 72 Cong., 1 Sess. (1932), 209; Ella Bloor, *We Are Many* (New York, 1940), 227–30; C. R. Walker, "Relief and Revolution," *Forum*, Sept. 1932; Nathaniel Weyl, "Organizing Hunger," *New Republic*, Dec. 14, 1932.

30. C. R. Walker, "Down and Out in Detroit," *Forum*, Sept. 1931.

31. Senate Manufactures Committee, *Federal Cooperation in Unemployment Relief: Hearings*, 72 Cong., 1 Sess. (1932), 36.

32. Whittaker Chambers, *Witness* (New York, 1952), 196.

33. J. B. Matthews, *Odyssey of a Fellow Traveler* (New York, 1938), 256; John Dos Passos, "Four Nights in a Garden," *Common Sense*, Dec. 5, 1932.

34. Matthews, *Odyssey*, 91; Benjamin Gitlow, *The Whole of Their Lives* (New York, 1948), 237; Bloor, *We Are Many*, 307.

35. J. B. S. Hardman, "Communism in America," *New Republic*, Aug. 27. 1930; Bell, "Marxian Socialism," 353.

36. Lauren Gilfillan, *I Went to Pit College* (New York, 1934), 359; "It Seems to Heywood Broun," *Nation*, March 26, 1930; George Soule, "Are We Going to Have a Revolution?" *Harper's*, Aug. 1932.

CHAPTER 25 *(Pages 224–247)*

1. S. J. Woolf, "Wagner Seeks Humanity in Government," *New York Times Magazine*, July 31, 1932; S. J. Woolf, "A Senator Asks Security for Workers," *New York Times Magazine*, Jan. 11, 1931; Senate Commerce Committee, *Unemployment in the United States: Hearings*, 72 Cong., 2 Sess. (1930), 8; H. F. Pringle, "The Janitor's Boy," *The New Yorker*, March 5, 1927; [J. F. Carter], *The New Dealers* (Washington, 1934), 56–57; Hoover, *State Papers*, I, 530–32.

2. Senate Manufactures Committee, *Unemployment Relief: Hearings*, 72 Cong., 1 Sess. (1932), 8; E. N. Doan, *The La Follettes and the Wisconsin Idea* (New York, 1947), 163–70; W. M. Raine, "Costigan of Colorado," *Nation*, Oct. 29, 1930; Edmund Wilson, *American Jitters* (New York, 1932), 114; H. L. Hopkins, *Spending to Save* (New York, 1936), 43–74.

3. A. T. Mason, *Brandeis: A Free Man's Life* (New York, 1946), 600–601; Senate Agriculture and Forestry Committee, *Agricultural Conference and Farm Board Inquiry: Hearings,* 72 Cong., 1 Sess. (1931), 135–36.

4. B. N. Timmons, *Garner of Texas* (New York, 1948); G. R. Brown, *The Speaker of the House* (New York, 1932); Tom Connally, *My Name Is Tom Connally* (New York, 1954), 91, 78; S. J. Woolf, "Garner Revives a Jacksonian Tradition," *New York Times Magazine,* Nov. 22, 1931; P. Y. Anderson, "Texas John Garner," *Nation,* April 20, 1932; R. S. Allen, "Texas Jack," *New Republic,* March 16, 1932; George Milburn, "The Statesmanship of Mr. Garner," *Harper's,* Nov. 1932; Raymond Moley, *27 Masters of Politics* (New York, 1949), 68–75; M. W. Childs, *I Write from Washington* (New York, 1942), 88–89; Cordell Hull, *Memoirs* (New York, 1948), I, 133.

5. D. A. Reed, "The Future of the Republican Party," *Atlantic,* March 1931; John Dewey, "The Need for a New Party," *New Republic,* March 25, 1931.

6. Hoover, *State Papers,* I, 145, 181, 290; Herbert Hoover, *The New Day* (Stanford University, 1928), 30.

7. Hoover, *State Papers,* I, 137, 182.

8. *Historical Statistics,* Ser. H 1–26, H 33–35.

9. Amos Pinchot, "We Met Mr. Hoover," *Nation,* Jan. 14, 1931; testimony of J. A. Ryan, Senate Banking and Currency Committee, *Further Unemployment Relief Through the Reconstruction Finance Corporation: Hearings,* 72 Cong., 2 Sess. (1933), 144; Mellon to W. L. Jones, June 18, 1929, in Federal Employment Stabilization Board Papers, National Archives; W. T. Foster, "The Bill for Hard Times," *Survey Graphic,* April 1936; Senate Education and Labor Committee, *Establishment of Administration of Public Works: Hearings,* 72 Cong., 1 Sess. (1932), especially 107–15.

10. Hoover, *State Papers,* I, 240, 578; II, 28, 459–60; W. S. Myers and W. H. Newton, *The Hoover Administration: A Documented Narrative* (New York, 1936), 156–57.

11. Hoover, *State Papers,* II, 106, 148, 149, 175, 189, 194, 196, 232.

12. The act setting up the Reconstruction Finance Corporation in 1932 authorized a new public works effort, based on self-liquidating loans; but the administration spent only a small portion of the sums available under the act. See page 241.

13. *Historical Statistics,* Ser. M 55; Hoover, *State Papers,* I, 376, 429, 574.

14. J. M. Keynes, *Essays on Persuasion* (London, 1931), 292–93; Herbert Hoover, *Addresses Upon the American Road, 1933–1938* (New York, 1938), 30. For the gold crisis controversy, see Myers and Newton, *Hoover Administration,* 79, 159–73, and Rixey Smith and Norman Beasley, *Carter Glass* (New York, 1939), 317–20.

15. Hoover, *State Papers,* II, 46, 397.

16. Hoover, *State Papers,* I, 136, 382, 394, 437; Hoover, *Memoirs,* III, 334, 420; Myers and Newton, *Hoover Administration,* 119, 155.

17. Mark Sullivan, "Storm Over Washington," *Saturday Evening Post*, April 1, 1933; Hoover, *Memoirs*, III, 84–88, 97.

18. Senate Banking and Currency Committee, *Creation of a Reconstruction Finance Corporation: Hearings*, 72 Cong., 1 Sess. (1932), 40.

19. J. H. Jones, *Fifty Billion Dollars* (New York, 1951), 14–15.

20. Leffingwell to Alexander Sachs, Jan. 4, 1935, Roosevelt Papers.

21. Hoover, *State Papers*, II, 106; Jones, *Fifty Billion*, 517, 72–83; J. T. Flynn, "Inside the RFC," *Harper's*, Jan. 1933.

22. Hoover, *State Papers*, II, 8–9; *New York Times*, Oct. 19, 20, 1932; Myers and Newton, *Hoover Administration*, 242.

23. Federal Farm Board, *Second Annual Report*, 492, 514, 526; Legge to Hoover, March 5, 1931, in Forrest Crissey, *Alexander Legge* (Chicago, 1936), 206; A. M. Hyde, "The Agricultural Teeter Board," *Review of Reviews*, Oct. 1931; Hoover, *State Papers*, II, 312; O. H. Kile, *The Farm Bureau Through Three Decades* (Baltimore, 1948), 166–68; Lawrence Sullivan, "The Curse of Plenty," *Outlook*, Sept. 3, 1930; Russell Lord, "The Forced March of the Farmers," *Survey Graphic*, April 1936; Theodore Norman, "The Federal Farm Board (Ph.D. Thesis, Harvard University).

24. Wagner in the Senate, *Congressional Record*, 72 Cong., I Sess. (Jan. 15, 1932); Edith Abbott, "The Fallacy of Local Relief," *New Republic*, Nov. 9, 1932.

25. *New York Times*, May 12, 13, 1932.

26. Hoover, *State Papers*, II, 236; Senate Banking and Currency Committee, *Unemployment Relief: Hearings*, 72 Cong., 1 Sess. (1932), 18; Alfred E. Smith, "The New Outlook," *New Outlook*, Oct. 1932; Abbott, "Fallacy of Local Relief"; J. C. Brown, *Public Relief, 1929–1939* (New York, 1940), 126.

27. Hoover, *Memoirs*, III, 195; Hoover, *State Papers*, I, 608, II, 45, 101; Sen. Man. Com., *Unemployment Relief*, 116–17; O. E. Clapper, *Washington Tapestry* (New York, 1946), 3–4.

28. S. J. Woolf, "Mills Weighs Our Problems," *New York Times Magazine*, Feb. 28, 1932; Clapper, *Washington Tapestry*, 3–4; Will Rogers, *The Autobiography of Will Rogers*, Donald Day, ed. (Boston, 1949), 275; *Time*, April 4, 1932; Christopher Morley, "What the President Reads," *Saturday Review of Literature*, Sept. 24, 1932.

29. T. G. Joslin, *Hoover Off the Record* (New York, 1934), 4, 6, 55, 318, 194; I. H. Hoover, *Forty-Two Years in the White House* (Boston, 1934), 184, 233, 250, 267, 323; Donald Richberg, *My Hero* (New York, 1954), 149–50.

30. W. A. White, *Autobiography* (New York, 1946), 515; Hoover, *Forty-Two Years*, 267; H. L. Stimson and McGeorge Bundy, *On Active Service in Peace and War* (New York, 1948), 196, 197, 205.

31. W. A. White, "Herbert Hoover," *Saturday Evening Post*, March 4, 1933; Esmé Howard, *Theatre of Life* (Boston, 1936), II, 569; Hoover,

Forty-Two Years, 184, 187; H. G. Wells, *Experiment in Autobiography* (New York, 1934), 679.

32. J. E. Pollard, *The Presidents and the Press* (New York, 1947), 737-70; P. Y. Anderson, "Hoover and the Press," *Nation*, Oct. 14, 1931; J. F. Essary, "The Presidency and the Press," *Scribner's*, May 1935; R. P. Brandt, "The President's Press Conference," *Survey Graphic*, July 1939.

33. Joslin, *Hoover*, 91, 182, 34; J. N. Leonard, *Three Years Down* (New York, 1939), 215-16; Hoover, *Forty-Two Years*, 232.

34. W. A. White, "Herbert Hoover," *Saturday Evening Post*, March 4, 1933; Hoover, *State Papers*, II, 189, I, 470, 502-3, 504, 582, II, 251, I, 430-431.

35. Hoover, *State Papers*, II, 249, I, 527; Alfred Lief, *Democracy's Norris* (New York, 1939), 395.

CHAPTER 26 *(Pages 248-269)*

1. *Historical Statistics*, A 117, A 118, J 30; A. F. Burns, *Economic Research and the Keynesian Thinking of Our Time* (New York, 1946), Appendix; Paul Webbink, "Unemployment in the United States," *American Economic Review*, Feb. 1941; Thomas Wilson, *Fluctuations in Income and Employment*, 3rd ed. (London, 1948), Ch. 17; J. T. Flynn, "Who But Hoover?" *New Republic*, Dec. 4, 1935; J. T. Flynn, "Hoover's Apologia: An Audacious Torturing of History," *Southern Review*, Spring 1936; George Soule, "This Recovery," *Harper's*, March 1937.

2. D. D. Bromley, "Vanishing Wages," *New Outlook*, April 1933; R. S. Halle, " 'Lucky' To Have a Job," *Scribner's*, April 1933; J. T. Flynn, "Starvation Wages," *Forum*, June 1933; "The Next Labor Offensive," *Fortune*, Jan. 1933; Frances Perkins, "The Cost of a Five-Dollar Dress," *Survey Graphic*, Feb. 1933.

3. " 'No One Has Starved,' " *Fortune*, Sept. 1932; H. L. Lurie, " 'Spreading Relief Thin,' " *Social Service Review*, June 1932; "Is It To Be Murder, Mr. Hoover?" *Nation*, Aug. 3, 1932; *Time*, March 14, 1932; *San Francisco Chronicle*, July 1, 1932; M. A. Hallgren, *Seeds of Revolt* (New York, 1933), Chs. 1, 7; testimony of H. L. Lurie, in Senate Manufactures Committee, *Federal Aid for Unemployment Relief: Hearings*, 72 Cong., 2 Sess. (1933), 74-77; J. L. Heffernan, "The Hungry City," *Atlantic*, May 1932; J. N. Leonard, *Three Years Down* (New York, 1939), 187-89, 266-79; Gilbert Seldes, *The Years of the Locust* (Boston, 1933), 208-10, 342; Lillian Symes, "Children *Are* Starving," *Common Sense*, Dec. 5, 1932; House Labor Committee, *Unemployment in the United States: Hearings*, 72 Cong., 1 Sess. (1932), 145-46.

4. Wayne Weishaar and W. W. Parrish, *Men Without Money* (New York, 1933); R. C. Hill, "Seattle's Jobless Enter Politics," *Nation*,

June 29, 1932; T. J. Parry, "The Republic of the Penniless," *Atlantic,* Oct. 1932; Malcolm Ross, "The Spread of Barter," *Nation,* March 1, 1933; Hallgren, *Seeds of Revolt,* 195–201; Leonard, *Three Years Down,* 288–90.

5. Thomas Minehan, *Boy and Girl Tramps of America* (New York, 1934), 20; L. A. Norris, "America's Homeless Army," *Scribner's,* May 1933; Leonard, *Three Years Down,* 272–76.

6. George Soule, "Are We Going to Have a Revolution?" *Harper's,* Aug. 1932; G. R. Clark, "Beckerstown: 1932," *Harper's,* Oct. 1932; Bernard DeVoto, "Notes on the American War," *Harper's,* May 1938; M. A. Hamilton, *In America Today* (London, 1932), 17.

7. Gifford Pinchot, "The Case for Federal Relief," *Survey Graphic,* Jan. 1932; Hoover, *Memoirs,* III, 116; Cornelius Vanderbilt, Jr., *Farewell to Fifth Avenue* (New York, 1935), 221–26.

8. Hallgren, *Seeds of Revolt,* 124–26.

9. *New York Times,* Jan. 6, 13, 1933; Ferdinand Pecora, *Wall Street Under Oath* (New York, 1939), Ch. 9.

10. *New York Times,* Jan. 8, March 13, 15, 1932; Leonard, *Three Years Down,* 226–30.

11. M. L. Ramsay, *Pyramids of Power* (Indianapolis, 1937); *New York Times,* June 12, 1932; *New York World-Telegram,* Dec. 9, 1933; Donald Richberg, "Gold-Plated Anarchy," *Nation,* April 5, 1933; Leonard, *Three Years Down,* 230–35; Stewart Holbrook, *The Age of the Moguls* (New York, 1953), 236–44.

12. N. D. Baker, "Human Factors in a Depression," *New Outlook,* Nov. 1932; W. B. Donham, "The Failure of Business Leadership and the Responsibility of the Universities," *Harvard Business Review,* July 1933.

13. Oakley Johnson, "After the Dearborn Massacre," *New Republic,* March 30, 1932; Hallgren, *Seeds of Revolt,* 172–74; Harry Bennett, with Paul Marcus, *We Never Called Him Henry* (New York, 1951), 91–94; Edmund Wilson, *American Jitters* (New York, 1932), 65.

14. Memorandum of the Meeting of the Technical Staff of the Delegation of the United States to the Disarmament Conference, Nov. 23, 1931. Norman H. Davis Papers; J. F. Byrnes to M. H. McIntyre, Oct. 6, 1936, Roosevelt Papers.

15. In 1949–51, especially during the MacArthur and McCarthy controversies, attempts were made to establish the thesis that the B.E.F. was the product of a Communist conspiracy.

Much of the case for alleged Communist control of the B.E.F. rests on testimony given by John T. Pace, the Communist leader at Anacostia, before the House Committee on Un-American Activities. Pace testified that there could not have been over 100 Communists in the B.E.F. and that "the active party group, party fraction, that we knew were reliable party members would number no more than 25"; but added that the Communists were about to seize control of the whole B.E.F. and, indeed, claimed in an interview that "we controlled every action" of the B.E.F. Pace's assertions of 1949 about Communist control are quite inconsistent with the amply attested facts of 1932. For Pace's testimony, see House Un-American Activities Committee, *Communist Tactics Among Veterans: Hearings*, 82 Cong., 1 Sess. (1951); and a three-part interview with Howard Rushmore, *New York Journal-American*, Aug. 28-30, 1949.

Benjamin Gitlow's similar assertions in *The Whole of Their Lives* (New York, 1948), 226-30, can be most easily refuted by citing the article, "A Labor Party for America," *Modern Monthly*, Sept. 1933. This article condemns the Communist and Socialist parties for failing to take advantage of revolutionary conditions in the United States. "The rebellious actions that did take place, as for example the farmers' strikes, the Veterans' Bonus March on Washington, etc., were of a spontaneous character and took place in spite of these two parties. They did not organize them. They had no leadership in these movements. When the Communist Party tried to inject itself into the Veterans' Bonus March, the mass of the veterans resented it as interference and looked upon the Communists as a foreign, hostile source." The author of this article was Benjamin Gitlow.

In sum, it may be said definitely that (a) the movement originated spontaneously and the Communists were latecomers in their effort to exploit it, (b) the B.E.F. leaders were openly and militantly anti-Communist, (c) the Communists at no time represented more than a minuscule and beleaguered minority, and (d) there would have been a Bonus March if there had been no Communist party in existence.

16. For the Bonus affair see, especially, the *B.E.F. News*, June-Sept. 1932; *New York Times* and *Time* for the relevant dates; W. W. Waters with W. C. White, *B.E.F.: The Whole Story of the Bonus Army* (New York, 1933); P. Y. Anderson, "Tear-Gas, Bayonets, and Votes," *Nation*, Aug. 17, 1932, and "Republican Handsprings," *Nation*, Aug. 31, 1932; John Forell, "The Bonus Crusade," *Virginia Quarterly Review*, Jan. 1933; F. C. Springer, "Glassford and the Siege of Washington," *Harper's*, Nov. 1932; Gardner Jackson, "Unknown Soldiers," *Survey Graphic*, Aug. 1932; Gertrude Springer, "What Became of the BEF," *Survey Graphic*, Dec. 1932; "The Summer of the BEF," *Washington News*, Nov. 23, 1946; H. W. Blakely, "When the Army Was Smeared," *Combat Forces Journal*, Feb. 1952; J. H. Bartlett, *The Bonus March and the New Deal* (Chicago, 1937); Jack Douglas, *Veterans on the March* (New York, 1934); Hoover, *Memoirs*, III, 225-32; T. G. Joslin, *Hoover Off the Record* (New York, 1934), Ch. 22; W. S. Myers and W. H. Newton, *The Hoover Administration* (New York, 1936), 498-501; Clark Lee and Richard Henschel, *Douglas MacArthur* (New York, 1952), 54-58; T. L. Stokes, *Chip Off My Shoulder* (Princeton, 1940),

301–4; John Dos Passos, "Washington and Chicago," *New Republic*, June 29, 1932; Walter Lippmann in *New York Herald Tribune*, Sept. 14, 1932; M. A. Hallgren, "The Bonus Army Scares Mr. Hoover," *Nation*, July 27, 1932; Slater Brown, "Anacostia Flats," *New Republic*, Aug. 17, 1932; Malcolm Cowley, "The Flight of the Bonus Army," *New Republic*, Aug. 17, 1932; Patrick J. Hurley to *McCall's*, in *McCall's*, Dec. 1949.

17. O. M. Kile, *The Farm Bureau Through Three Decades* (Baltimore, 1948), 172–73; J. A. Simpson, "A Farm Leader Speaks," *Common Sense*, May 11, 1933; "Bryan! Bryan!!" *Fortune*, Jan. 1934.

18. W. A. White, "The Farmer Takes His Holiday," *Saturday Evening Post*, Nov. 26, 1932; D. R. Murphy, "The Farmers Go On Strike," *New Republic*, Aug. 31, 1932; *New York Times*, Aug.–Sept. 1932; WPA Iowa Federal Writers' Project, *Woodbury County History* (Sioux City, 1942), 56; M. H. Vorse, "Rebellion in the Cornbelt," *Harper's*, Dec. 1932; Wayne Gard, "The Farmer's Rebellion," *Nation*, Sept. 7, 1932; William Hard, "Reno and Revolt in Iowa," *Today*, Nov. 11, 1933; Bruce Bliven, "Milo Reno and His Farmers," *New Republic*, Nov. 29, 1933; Theodore Saloutos and J. D. Hicks, *Agricultural Discontent in the Middle West, 1900–1939* (Madison, Wisc., 1951), Ch. 15; Ella Bloor; *We Are Many* (New York, 1940), 233–36; Whittaker Chambers, *Witness* (New York, 1952), 332–34.

19. Virgil Jordan, "Business Leadership Passes the Buck," *New Republic*, May 20, 1931; Hamilton Fish, quoted in *Labor*, Feb. 9, 1932; Reed in the Senate, *Congressional Record*, 72 Cong., I Sess. (May 15, 1932), 9644; *Vanity Fair*, June 1932; F. A. Ogg, "Does America Need a Dictator?" *Current History*, Sept. 1932.

CHAPTER 27 *(Pages 273–294)*

1. Charles Michelson, *The Ghost Talks* (New York, 1944), 15–16; Leslie Wallace, "The Kansas Optimist," *Outlook*, Jan. 27, 1932; T. S. Barclay, "The Bureau of Publicity of the Democratic National Committee, 1930–1932," *American Political Science Review*, Feb. 1933; Ray Tucker, "Presidential Publicist," *Today*, July 13, 1935.

2. [C. W. Gilbert], *The Mirrors of Washington* (Washington, 1921), 146–60; "No Climax," *Fortune*, Oct. 1933; Jonathan Daniels, *The End of Innocence* (Philadelphia, 1954), 326.

3. Baruch to F.D.R., Nov. 18, 1930, Roosevelt Papers.

4. George Creel, "Let's Have Another Party," *World's Work*, March 1930; "Goodbye to Mr. Raskob," *New Republic*, March 2, 1932; Cordell Hull, *Memoirs* (New York, 1948), I, 131, 140; *New York Times*, March 6, 1931.

5. F.D.R. to R. S. Copeland, Feb. 23, 1931, and to H. C. Nixon, Feb. 27, 1931, Roosevelt Papers; F.D.R. to Alfred E. Smith, Feb. 28, 1931, and

to Jouett Shouse, Feb. 28, 1931, in F.D.R., *Personal Letters*, III, 179.

6. F.D.R. to Wheeler, June 3, 1930, and Wheeler to F.D.R., June 10, 1930, Roosevelt Papers.

7. Brandeis to Norman Hapgood, May 29, 1930, in A. T. Mason, *Brandeis: A Free Man's Life* (New York, 1946), 600–601; Alfred Lief, *Democracy's Norris* (New York, 1939), 375–79; *New York Times*, March 12, 13, 1931.

8. J. A. Farley, *Behind the Ballots* (New York, 1938), 62; E. J. Flynn, *You're the Boss* (New York, 1947), 84.

9. Flynn, *You're the Boss*, 82–84.

10. F.D.R. to Farley, Nov. 21, 1930, J. A. Farley, *Jim Farley's Story* (New York, 1948), 7–8. This letter may have been prompted by a letter from Herbert Claiborne Pell, an old friend of Roosevelt's who had been state chairman in the twenties: "Send Farley a nice letter. I know that if the head of the ticket had at any time during the five years that I was Chairman, expressed a single word of gratitude for the work that I did, it would have been very much appreciated." (Pell to F.D.R., Nov. 10, 1930, Roosevelt Papers)
   Colonel House questioned the wisdom of sending Farley out of the state; but Howe stoutly defended Farley as an emissary to political organizations in the West, if not to independent voters or to the South; Howe to House, Aug. 17, 1931, Roosevelt Papers.

11. F.D.R., *Public Papers* (1928–32), 486, 487, 495.

12. Farley to F.D.R., July 6, July 11, 1931, Louis Howe Papers; Farley, *Behind the Ballots*, 81–89; note on 1931 expense account, Dewson Papers.

13. Michelson, *The Ghost Talks*, 35.

14. *New York Times*, Jan. 9, May 12, 1932.

15. A. F. Mullen, *Western Democrat* (New York, 1940), 260–61; Flynn, *You're the Boss*, 86; Farley, *Behind the Ballots*, 96; Mrs. Norton repeated Smith's remark to Molly Dewson on March 5, 1948, M. W. Dewson, "Farley from the Woman's Angle," in MS autobiography, "An Aid to the End," Dewson Papers.

16. Farley, *Behind the Ballots*, 95; J. M. Cox, *Journey Through My Years* (New York, 1946), 416.

17. Senate Finance Committee, *Investigation of Economic Problems: Hearings*, 72 Cong., 2 Sess. (1933), 853–54.

18. Ritchie before the Southern Society of New York, Dec. 10, 1924, Ritchie to F.D.R., Dec. 8, 1924, Roosevelt Papers; O. G. Villard, *Prophets True and False* (New York, 1928), 119–24; A. C. Ritchie, "Give Us Democracy," *North American Review*, Oct. 1930; "Roosevelt, Ritchie, and Pinchot," *Nation*, June 17, 1931; *New Republic*, Dec. 2, 1931; *New York Times*, Jan. 8, 1932.

19. Cora Miley, "'Alfalfa Bill,'" *New York Times Magazine*, Aug. 16, 1931; S. J. Woolf, "'Alfalfa Bill' Sizes Up Our Troubles," *New York*

Times Magazine, Jan. 31, 1932; Jack Spanner, " 'Alfalfa Bill,' " *North American Review,* April 1932; T. L. Stokes, *Chip Off My Shoulder* (Princeton, 1940), 318; *Time,* Feb. 29, 1932.

20. E. D. Coblentz, *William Randolph Hearst* (New York, 1952), 118–19, 126–29, 40; *New York Times,* Jan. 3, 1932.

21. D. C. Roper, *Fifty Years of Public Life* (Durham, N.C., 1941), 258; Mullen, *Western Democrat,* 262; *New York Times,* Feb. 19, 1932.

22. Baker to F.D.R., Nov. 6, 1928, Roosevelt Papers; *New York Times,* Jan. 15, 27, 1932; George Creel, "Newton D. Baker's Measure," *Collier's,* March 19, 1932; O. G. Villard, "Newton D. Baker — Just Another Politician," *Nation,* April 13, 1932; Katherine Palmer, "Newton D. Baker," *Review of Reviews,* April 1932.

23. Villard, "Baker"; F.D.R. to Daniels, May 14, 1932, in Carroll Kilpatrick, ed., *Roosevelt and Daniels* (Chapel Hill, 1952), 116; Davis to Baker, April 7, 1932, Norman H. Davis Papers; Rixey Smith and Norman Beasley, *Carter Glass* (New York, 1939), 308.

24. Memorandum by Sidney Hyman of interview with K. C. Blackburn, March 27, 1949, Roosevelt Foundation Papers; Baruch to F.D.R., Dec. 6, 1931, F.D.R. to Baruch, Dec. 19, 1931, and March 22, 1932, Roosevelt Papers.

25. *New York Times,* Feb. 2, 3, 1932; Coblentz, *Hearst,* 120–21.

26. F.D.R., *Public Papers,* I, 624–47.

27. "Is Roosevelt a Hero?" *New Republic,* April 1, 1931; O. G. Villard, "The Democratic Trough at Chicago," *Nation,* July 13, 1932; Elmer Davis, "The Collapse of Politics," *Harper's,* Sept. 1932; Walter Lippmann, *Interpretations, 1931–1932,* Allan Nevins, ed. (New York, 1932), 261, 262, 273; Walter Lippmann, "Today and Tomorrow," *New York Herald Tribune,* April 28, 1932; F.D.R. to M. L. Cooke, Jan. 18, 1932, Roosevelt Papers; *Time,* June 20, 1932.

28. *New York Times,* April 14, 1932.

29. F.D.R. to W. C. Fitts, Dec. 16, 1931, Roosevelt Papers.

30. *New York Times,* May 5, 1932; F.D.R. to Daniels, May 5, 1932, in Carroll Kilpatrick, ed., *Roosevelt and Daniels,* 115.

31. Walter Lippmann, "The Deflation of Franklin Roosevelt," *Review of Reviews,* June 1932.

CHAPTER 28 *(Pages 295–314)*

1. R. V. Peel and T. C. Donnelly, *The 1932 Campaign* (New York, 1935), Ch. 4; H. L. Mencken, *Making a President* (New York, 1932), 63; Walter Lippmann, *Interpretations, 1931–1932,* Allan Nevins, ed. (New York, 1932), 289; T. G. Joslin, *Hoover Off the Record* (New York, 1934), 226–27; *Time,* June 20, 27, 1932; R. M. Lovett, "Hoover in Excelsis," and John Dos Passos, "Spotlights and Microphones," *New*

Republic, June 29, 1932; N. M. Butler, *Across the Busy Years* (New York, 1939), 284.

2. Anne O'Hare McCormick, "The Two Conventions: Chicago Contrasts," *New York Times,* July 3, 1932.

3. At least this is Tugwell's recollection; Moley gives a similar account; but Ed Flynn recalls that he made the suggestion to Howe; and Lela Stiles, who was also present, gives a fourth account.

4. For the convention *New York Times,* June 20–July 4, 1932; *Official Report of the Proceedings of the Democratic National Convention* (n.p., n.d. [1932]); J. A. Farley, *Behind the Ballots* (New York, 1938), 102–54; E. J. Flynn, *You're the Boss* (New York, 1947), Ch. 9; A. F. Mullen, *Western Democrat* (New York, 1940), 251–80; Charles Michelson, *The Ghost Talks* (New York, 1944), 4–10; Cordell Hull, *Memoirs* (New York, 1948), I, Ch. 11; Mencken, *Making a President,* Chs. 11–20; B. N. Timmons, *Garner of Texas* (New York, 1948), Ch. 10; Raymond Moley, *After Seven Years* (New York, 1939) 27–34; J. A. Farley, *Jim Farley's Story* (New York, 1948), 19–26; S. I. Rosenman, *Working with Roosevelt* (New York, 1952), Ch. 6; Mary W. Dewson, "An Aid to the End," Vol. I, MS autobiography in the Dewson Papers; T. L. Stokes, *Chip Off My Shoulder* (Princeton, 1940), 314–23; E. D. Coblentz, *William Randolph Hearst* (New York, 1952), 130–39; Lela Stiles, *The Man Behind Roosevelt* (Cleveland, 1954), Ch. 10; Tom Connally, *My Name Is Tom Connally* (New York, 1954), Ch. 17; Grace Tully, *F. D. R., My Boss* (New York, 1949), 51–52; W. L. Cross, *Connecticut Yankee* (New Haven, 1943), 267–68; J. M. Proskauer, *A Segment of My Times* (New York, 1950), 71–72; J. F. Guffey, "Politics and Supreme Courts," *Vital Speeches,* Sept. 15, 1937; Joseph Alsop and Robert Kintner, "The Guffey," *Saturday Evening Post,* April 16, 1938; D. C. Roper, *Fifty Years of Public Life* (Durham, N.C., 1941), 259–61; R. G. Tugwell, "A New Deal Memoir: Early Days, 1932–1933," Ch. 1, MS in the Tugwell Papers; R. M. Lovett, "The Big Wind at Chicago," *New Republic,* July 13, 1932; John Dos Passos, "Out of the Red with Roosevelt," *New Republic,* July 13, 1932; Lippmann, *Interpretations,* 298–314; J. F. Dinneen, *The Purple Shamrock* (New York, 1949), 189–90; Eleanor Roosevelt and Lorena Hickok, *Ladies of Courage* (New York, 1954), 254–55; Jack Yellen and Milton Ager, "Happy Days Are Here Again" (Copyright 1929).

CHAPTER 29 *(Pages 317–343)*

1. F.D.R. book inscriptions, Roosevelt Papers; undated, untitled memorandum, Roosevelt Papers.

2. Joseph Alsop and Robert Kintner, "The Roosevelt Family," *Life,* Sept. 9, 1940; R. H. Kleeman, *Gracious Lady: The Life of Sara Delano Roosevelt* (New York, 1935), Chs. 1–7; Sara Delano Roosevelt, with

Isabel Leighton and Gabrielle Forbush, *My Boy Franklin* (New York, 1933), Part I; F.D.R., "History of the President's Estate at Hyde Park, New York, with Anecdotes," Roosevelt Papers; Eleanor Roosevelt, *Franklin D. Roosevelt and Hyde Park* (Washington, 1949); Clara and Hardy Steeholm, *The House at Hyde Park* (New York, 1950), Ch. 4; F.D.R. Press Conference #621, Feb. 5, 1940, Roosevelt Papers; F.D.R. to A. G. Schwarz, March 18, 1935, Roosevelt Papers; Frank Freidel, "Roosevelt's Father," *F.D.R. Coll.*, Nov. 1952.

3. F.D.R., Introduction to C. W. Ashley, *Whaleships of New Bedford* (Boston, 1929), iv, v; *Today*, Dec. 9, 1933.

4. Kleeman, *Gracious Lady*, 146; S. J. Woolf, *Here Am I* (New York, 1941), 200–201; A. C. Murray, *At Close Quarters* (London, 1946), 96.

5. F.D.R. to Jeanne Rosat-Sandoz, March 31, 1933, and see Constance Drexel to F.D.R., March 15, 1933, Roosevelt Papers; Constance Drexel, "Unpublished Letters of F.D.R. to His French Governess," *Parents' Magazine*, Sept. 1951; F.D.R. to A. C. Murray, March 4, 1940, in Murray, *At Close Quarters*, 86; Adolf A. Berle, Jr., Diary, May 2, 1942, Berle Papers; Press Conference #992, Feb. 23, 1945, Roosevelt Papers.

6. Though in 1933 Roosevelt ascribed the remark about boyhood ideals to Phillips Brooks, F.D.R., *Public Papers* (1933), 419.

7. F.D.R., *Personal Letters*, I, 29–413; F. D. Ashburn, *Peabody of Groton* (New York, 1944); George Biddle, *An American Artist's Story* (Boston, 1939), 50–66; F.D.R. to Endicott Peabody, April 25, 1940, Roosevelt Papers; S. D. Roosevelt, *et al.*, *My Boy Franklin*, 36–50; Frank Freidel, *Franklin D. Roosevelt: The Apprenticeship* (Boston, 1952), Ch. 3; John Gunther, *Roosevelt in Retrospect* (New York, 1950), 171–75; Eleanor Roosevelt on "Author Meets the Critics," Feb. 9, 1950.

8. F.D.R., *Personal Letters*, I, 417–534; Freidel, *Apprenticeship*, Ch. 4; Kleeman, *Gracious Lady*, 206–33; F.D.R., "The Roosevelt Family in New Amsterdam before the Revolution," Roosevelt Papers.

9. Kleeman, *Gracious Lady*, 233; S. D. Roosevelt, *et. al.*, *My Boy Franklin*, 62; F.D.R. to his mother, Dec. 4, 1903, Eleanor Roosevelt to Sara Roosevelt, Dec. 2, 1903, in F.D.R., *Personal Letters*, I, 518, 517; Sara Roosevelt to F.D.R., Dec. 6, 1903, Roosevelt Family Papers.

10. Eleanor Roosevelt, *This Is My Story* (New York, 1937), Chs. 1–5; Eleanor Roosevelt, "The Seven People Who Shaped My Life," *Look*, June 19, 1951; Kleeman, *Gracious Lady*, 233–44; Mildred Adams, "When T. R. Gave His Niece in Marriage," *New York Times Magazine*, March 17, 1935; Theodore Roosevelt to F.D.R., Nov. 29, 1904, Roosevelt Family Papers.

11. Earle Looker, *This Man Roosevelt* (New York, 1932), 47–48; F.D.R., *Personal Letters*, II, Ch. 1; Eleanor Roosevelt, *This Is My Story*, Chs. 5–7.

12. Grenville Clark, in *Harvard Alumni Bulletin*, April 28, 1945; Freidel, *Apprenticeship*, Ch. 5; "What's To Become of Us?" *Fortune*, Dec. 1933.

13. Press Conference #570, Aug. 8, 1939, Roosevelt Papers.
14. Theodore Roosevelt to Anna Roosevelt Cowles, Aug. 10, 1910, *Letters from Theodore Roosevelt to Anna Roosevelt Cowles, 1870–1918* (New York, 1924), 289; G. W. Martin, "Preface to the President's Autobiography," *Harper's*, Feb. 1944.
15. Freidel, *Apprenticeship*, Ch. 5; *Poughkeepsie News-Press*, Oct. 27, 1910; reminiscences of Harry T. Hawkey in Clara L. Dawson to Eleanor Roosevelt, Dec. 13, 1937, Roosevelt Papers; Eleanor Roosevelt, *This Is My Story*, 167; M. H. Hoyt, "Roosevelt Enters Politics," *F.D.R. Coll.*, May 1949; *F.D.R., Public Papers* (1933), 338–39.
16. F.D.R., Diary, Jan. 1–3, 1911, Roosevelt Papers.
17. F.D.R., Diary, Jan. 1, 1911, Roosevelt Papers; *New York Times*, Jan. 22, 1911; *Toledo News-Bee*, Jan. 23, 1911; F.D.R. to Chalmers Wood, Feb. 1, James Forrestal to F.D.R., Jan. 28, 1911, M. H. Hoyt to F.D.R., July 8, 1940, Theodore Roosevelt to F.D.R., Jan. 29, 1911, Roosevelt Papers; *Cleveland Plain Dealer*, Jan. 23, 1911; Freidel, *Apprenticeship*, Ch. 6; Vlastimil Kybal, "Senator Franklin D. Roosevelt, 1910–1913," *F.D.R. Coll.*, Nov. 1951.
18. F.D.R. to W. M. Taylor, Feb. 17, 1911, Roosevelt Papers; Nelson C. Brown, "Personal Reminiscences of Franklin D. Roosevelt," Roosevelt Papers; F.D.R., "A Debt We Owe," *Country Home*, June 1930; F.D.R., *Public Papers* (1935), 363–64; F.D.R. to Dexter Blagden, Feb. 21, 1912, Roosevelt Papers.
19. A. B. Rollins, Jr., "The Political Education of Franklin Roosevelt," Chs. 9–11, Ph.D. thesis, Harvard University; Freidel, *Apprenticeship*, Chs. 7–8; F.D.R., "Growing Up By Plan," *Survey Graphic*, Feb. 1932.
20. Speech put together from manuscript version in Roosevelt Papers, and from the *Troy Record*, March 4, 1912.
21. Frances Perkins, *The Roosevelt I Knew* (New York, 1946), 11–13; Freidel, *Apprenticeship*, Ch. 7; *New York Times*, Dec. 25, 1911; *New York Globe*, June 2, 1911.
22. F.D.R., *Personal Letters*, II, 192; Freidel, *Apprenticeship*, Ch. 8.
23. John Keller and Joe Boldt, "Franklin's On His Own Now," *Saturday Evening Post*, Oct. 12, 1940; Lela Stiles, *The Man Behind Roosevelt* (Cleveland, 1954), Chs. 1–2; S. J. Woolf, "As His Closest Friend Sees Roosevelt," *New York Times Magazine*, Nov. 27, 1932; Elliott Roosevelt, "The Most Unforgettable Character I've Met," *Reader's Digest*, Feb. 1953; Looker, *This Man Roosevelt*, 72; Raymond Moley, *27 Masters of Politics* (New York, 1949), 140; Rollins, "Political Education," Ch. 15; *Poughkeepsie Enquirer*, Nov. 3, 1912.
24. I am indebted to Mr. Arthur Walworth for citations from Daniels's manuscript diary, March 6, 9, 15, 1913; see also Josephus Daniels, *The Wilson Era: Years of Peace, 1910–1917* (Chapel Hill, 1944), 124–28; Josephus Daniels, "Franklin Roosevelt As I Know Him," *Saturday Evening Post*, Sept. 24, 1932; Josephus Daniels, "God Bless Franklin

Roosevelt," address at the Electoral College Banquet, Jan. 19, 1941; communication from Herbert Bayard Swope, Dec. 6, 1954; Jonathan Daniels, *The End of Innocence* (Philadelphia, 1954), 53–55. There are unimportant variations in Josephus Daniels's accounts of his talks with Roosevelt and Root.

The mistrust of Roosevelts had received a classic statement twenty-four years before when Cabot Lodge was trying to persuade James G. Blaine to make T.R. Assistant Secretary of State. "Mr. Roosevelt is amazingly quick in apprehension," Blaine wrote to Mrs. Lodge. "Is there not danger that he might be too quick in execution? . . . I do somehow fear that my sleep at Augusta or Bar Harbor would not be quite so easy and refreshing if so brilliant and aggressive a man had hold of the helm. Matters are constantly occurring which require the most thoughtful concentration and the most stubborn inaction. Do *you* think that Mr. T.R.'s temperament would give guaranty of that counsel?" (J. A. Garraty, *Henry Cabot Lodge,* New York, 1953, p. 104)

CHAPTER 30 *(Pages 344–367)*

1. T.R. to F.D.R., March 18, 1913, Roosevelt Papers; Jonathan Daniels, *The End of Innocence* (Philadelphia, 1954), 55.
2. William D. Hassett, "The President Was My Boss," *Saturday Evening Post,* Oct. 31, 1953.
3. Frank Freidel, *Franklin D. Roosevelt: The Apprenticeship* (Boston, 1952), Ch. 16.
4. For Roosevelt in the Navy Department, see especially the admirable account in Freidel, *Apprenticeship,* Chs. 9–12; also Daniels, *End of Innocence,* Ch. 3; Lela Stiles, *The Man Behind Roosevelt* (Cleveland, 1954), Chs. 3–4; F.D.R., *Personal Letters,* II, Chs. 5–7; Josephus Daniels, *The Wilson Era: Years of Peace, 1910–1917* (Chapel Hill, 1944), 131–32; A. B. Rollins, Jr., "The Political Education of Franklin Roosevelt," Chs. 17–19, Ph.D. thesis, Harvard University.
5. F.D.R., *Personal Letters,* II, 236, 299.
6. *Milwaukee Sentinel,* April 27, 1914; Freidel, *Apprenticeship,* 232; T.R. to F.D.R., May 10, 1913, and Mahan to F.D.R., Aug. 18, 1914, Roosevelt Papers.
7. F.D.R. to Eleanor Roosevelt, Aug. 1, Aug. 2, 1914, *Personal Letters,* II, 233, 238, 239–40.
8. F.D.R. speech at the Republican Club, Washington, Jan. 30, 1915, Roosevelt Papers.
9. F.D.R. to Eleanor Roosevelt, n.d. [1915], Sept. 2, 1915, *Personal Letters,* II, 291, 267.
10. F.D.R., speech before Navy League Convention, April 13, 1916, Roosevelt Papers.

11. F.D.R. to Eleanor Roosevelt, Nov. 8, Nov. 9, 1916, *Personal Letters,* II, 339; F.D.R. to David Gray, Nov. 24, 1916, Roosevelt Papers; Freidel, *Apprenticeship,* 267.

12. F.D.R., remarks at Roosevelt Library Dinner, Feb. 4, 1939, in F.D.R., *Public Papers* (1939), 117-18.

13. Eleanor Roosevelt, *This Is My Story* (New York, 1937), 245; Freidel, *Apprenticeship,* Chs. 17-19.

14. See his own conflicting accounts, F.D.R. to Wilson, July 8, 1918, F.D.R., "Memoranda of Trip to Europe, 1918," speech at Atlanta, Sept. 26, 1928, F.D.R. to Ray Stannard Baker, Oct. 21, 1938, Roosevelt Papers. Also Rollins, "Political Education," Ch. 20; Freidel, *Apprenticeship,* 339-43; Daniels, *End of Innocence,* 259-60.

15. Daniels, *End of Innocence,* 336, 159-60, 80-81, 201, 233-35; Natalie Sedgwick Colby, *Remembering* (New York, 1938), 196; Freidel, *Apprenticeship,* 321; Eleanor Roosevelt, *This Is My Story,* 236-37; Eleanor Roosevelt, *This I Remember* (New York, 1949), 53-54; O. W. Holmes to H. J. Laski, Nov. 23, 1932, M. DeW. Howe, ed., *Holmes-Laski Letters* (Cambridge, 1953), 1420; William Phillips, "Reminiscences" (Oral History Project, July 1951), 67; Sara Roosevelt to Franklin and Eleanor Roosevelt, Oct. 14, 1917, in F.D.R., *Personal Letters,* II, 274-75; Anna Roosevelt, "My Life with F.D.R.," *The Woman,* June 1949; Frances Parkinson Keyes, *Capital Kaleidoscope* (New York, 1937), 19; F.D.R. to Eleanor Roosevelt, July 17, 25, 1917, in F.D.R., *Personal Letters,* II, 347-52.

16. Josephus Daniels, address at Electoral College Banquet, Jan. 19, 1941, Roosevelt Papers; Daniels, *Wilson Era,* 130; Freidel, *Apprenticeship,* 301-2.

17. F.D.R., *Personal Letters,* II, Ch. 10; *The War Book of Gray's Inn* (London, 1921), 57; W. S. Churchill, *The Gathering Storm* (Boston, 1948), 440; T.R. to F.D.R., Sept. 23, 1918, Roosevelt Papers; F.D.R. to Daniels, Feb. 14, 1941, in Carroll Kilpatrick, ed., *Roosevelt and Daniels: A Friendship in Politics* (Chapel Hill, 1952), 220; Freidel, *Apprenticeship,* Chs. 20-21.

18. Eleanor Roosevelt, *This Is My Story,* 275, 292-293; F.D.R. to Daniels, Jan. 9, 1919, in Frank Freidel, *Franklin D. Roosevelt: The Ordeal* (Boston, 1954), Ch. 1.

19. F.D.R., speech at the Worcester Polytechnic Institute, June 25, 1919, and F.D.R., "Memorandum for Captain Thomas G. Frothingham" [n.d., ca. 1925], Roosevelt Papers; Freidel, *Apprenticeship,* 319.

20. E. R. May, "The Development of Political-Military Consultation in the United States," *Political Science Quarterly,* June 1955; Freidel, *Ordeal,* 20.

21. F.D.R., speech at the Worcester Polytechnic Institute and speech at the Harvard Union, Feb. 26, 1920, Roosevelt Papers; Freidel, *Ordeal,* Ch. 2; Rollins, "Political Education," Ch. 21.

22. F.D.R., speech at Manchester, N.H., Sept. 13, 1920, Roosevelt Papers.

23. *New York Times*, June 29, 1919; Freidel, *Ordeal*, Chs. 2-3.

24. Alice Roosevelt Longworth, *Crowded Hours* (New York, 1933), 283; F.D.R. to S. S. Robison, Dec. 30, 1919, in Freidel, *Ordeal*, 30-31.

25. Freidel, *Ordeal*, 58; Daniels, *End of Innocence*, 309-10, 316.

26. D. R. Fusfeld, *Economic Thought of Franklin D. Roosevelt* (New York, 1956), 74-75; F.D.R. to Langdon Marvin, June 17, 1920, Roosevelt Papers.

27. F.D.R. to T. B. Love, Jan. 26, 1938, Lippmann to F.D.R., July 8, 1920, Hoover to F.D.R., July 13, 1920, Farley to F.D.R., July 7, 1920, Jackson to F.D.R., July 7, 1920, Roosevelt Papers; J. M. Cox, *Journey Through My Years* (New York, 1946), Ch. 20; Rollins, "Political Education," Ch. 21; Freidel, *Ordeal*, Ch. 4-5; *Chicago Tribune*, Aug. 13, 1920.

28. Cox, *Journey*, 241-42; Emil Ludwig, *Roosevelt: A Study in Fortune and Power* (New York, 1938), 82.

29. F.D.R., *Personal Letters*, II, 489-91.

30. F.D.R., *Personal Letters*, II, 500-508.

31. H. L. Ickes, *The Secret Diary . . . The First Thousand Days, 1933-1936* (New York, 1953), 699; for Haiti episode, see excellent analysis in Freidel, *Ordeal*, 80-83; speeches in Spokane, Aug. 19, San Francisco, Aug. 23, Centralia, Aug. 21, 1920, Roosevelt Papers.

32. *New York Times*, Sept. 18, 1920; Daniels, *End of Innocence*, 321; F.D.R. to Arthur Murray, Oct. 9, 1920, and speech at Brooklyn, Sept. 6, 1920, Roosevelt Papers; Freidel, *Ordeal*, Ch. 5; Rollins, "Political Education," Ch. 22; Hassett, "The President Was My Boss."

33. F.D.R. to Anna Henderson, Nov. 9, 1920, to Willard Saulsbury, Dec. 9, 1924, to Robert W. Bingham, Sept. 29, 1931, to Key Pittman, Nov. 18, 1929, to Martin Archer-Shee, Nov. 9, 1920, to Stephen Early, Dec. 21, 1920, Roosevelt Papers; Daniels, *End of Innocence*, 323.

34. Earle Looker, *This Man Roosevelt* (New York, 1932), 111-12; Anna Roosevelt, "My Life with FDR," *The Woman*, July 1949.

CHAPTER 31 *(Pages 368-385)*

1. F.D.R. to Walter Williams, Oct. 31, 1929, Roosevelt Papers. The best account of Roosevelt's illness is in John Gunther, *Roosevelt in Retrospect* (New York, 1950), 221-27; see also F.D.R. to Dr. William Egleston, Oct. 11, 1924, in R. T. McIntire, *White House Physician* (New York, 1946), 31-34; Lela Stiles, *The Man Behind Roosevelt* (Cleveland, 1954), 76; Eleanor Roosevelt, *This Is My Story* (New York, 1937), Ch. 21; F.D.R., *Personal Letters*, II, Ch. 13. H. G. Wells, meeting Roosevelt in 1934, was physically reminded of Henley, *Experimenting in Autobiography* (New York, 1934), 680.

2. Elliott Roosevelt, "The Most Unforgettable Character I've Met," *Reader's Digest*, Feb. 1953; S. J. Woolf, *Here Am I* (New York, 1941),

195–96; Eleanor Roosevelt, *This Is My Story*, Ch. 21; Helena Huntington Smith, "Noblesse Oblige," *The New Yorker*, April 5, 1930; Eleanor Roosevelt and Lorena Hickok, *Ladies of Courage* (New York, 1954), 257–64; Kathleen McLaughlin in the *New York Times*, Oct. 8, 1944; S. J. Woolf in the *New York Times*, Sept. 23, 1945; Anna Roosevelt, "My Life with FDR," *The Woman*, July 1949; Eleanor Roosevelt, "The Seven People Who Shaped My Life," *Look*, July 19, 1951.

3. Eleanor Roosevelt, *This I Remember* (New York, 1949), 25; Grace Tully, *F. D. R., My Boss* (New York, 1949), 33; McIntire, *Physician*, 8, 5; Eleanor Roosevelt, Foreword, in F.D.R., *Personal Letters*, II, xviii; Louis Howe, "The Winner," *Saturday Evening Post*, Feb. 25, 1933; Anna Roosevelt, "My Life with FDR"; Gunther, *Roosevelt*, 228–32; Josephus Daniels, *The Wilson Era: Years of Peace, 1910–1917* (Chapel Hill, 1944), 131; Josephus Daniels, "Franklin Roosevelt As I Know Him," *Saturday Evening Post*, Sept. 24, 1932.

4. F.D.R. to L. A. Wilkinson, Jan. 18, 1923, to H. R. Luce, Aug. 13, 1923, Roosevelt Papers; D. S. Carmichael, "An Introduction to *The Log of the Larooco*," *F.D.R. Coll.*, Nov. 1948; F.D.R. to R. E. Byrd, Nov. 21, 1921, to Leonard Wood, May 2, 1922, to J. P. Adriance, Dec. 15, 1923, to R. P. Davis, Oct. 27, 1924, to J. P. Tumulty, Nov. 7, 1925, Roosevelt Papers.

5. An agreeable though fictionized account is Turnley Walker, *Roosevelt and the Warm Springs Story* (New York, 1953).

6. F.D.R. to Van-Lear Black, Sept. 24, 1924, to G. T. Emmett, Sept. 24, 1924, and to Langdon Marvin, Dec. 19, 1924, Roosevelt Papers.

7. Frank Freidel, *Franklin D. Roosevelt: The Ordeal* (Boston, 1954), Ch. 9; D. R. Fusfeld, *Economic Thought of Franklin D. Roosevelt* (New York, 1956), Ch. 7.

8. *New York Times*, June 4, 1922; *Constructor*, June 19, 1922; Hoover to F.D.R., June 12, 1923, F.D.R. to Johnson Heywood, Oct. 29, 1923, to C. F. Abbott, Oct. 24, 1925, to D. L. Hoopingarner, March 26, 1928, Roosevelt Papers.

9. F.D.R. to H. G. Starkweather, Dec. 27, 1921, to F. J. Rowan, Jan. 8, 1923, to Stephen Van Tassel, Nov. 13, 1922, to James J. Walker, Nov 8, 1925, to J. W. Jenkins, Aug. 20, 1923, to Stephen Demmon, July 18, 1923, Byrd to F.D.R., July 17, 1924, I. B. Dunlap to F.D.R., July 10, 1924, Roosevelt Papers; E. J. Flynn, *You're the Boss* (New York, 1947), 131; *New York Herald Tribune*, July 1, 1924; *New York World*, July 7, 1924; Freidel, *Ordeal*, Ch. 10.

10. F.D.R. to Eleanor Roosevelt [Oct. 1924], in F.D.R., *Personal Letters*, II, 566; F.D.R. to W. C. Martin, Dec. 9, 1925, to Willard Saulsbury, Dec. 9, 1924, to Russell Murphy, n.d. [March 26, 1926], to E. T. Meredith, March 17, 1925, to J. A. Edgerton, Jan. 27, 1925, to D. W. Thom, July 20, 1925, to E. N. Vallandigham, May 21, 1926, Roosevelt Papers.

11. F.D.R. to Winter Russell, April 16, 1925, speech at the Syracuse Con-

vention, Sept. 27, 1926, to T. A. Adams, Nov. 4, 1925, to H. C. Hansbrough, July 22, 1925, to J. W. Remick, Jan. 23, 1925, to Sidney Gunn, Dec. 29, 1925, Roosevelt Papers.

12. F.D.R. to Adolphus Ragan, Dec. 9, 1925, to George Foster Peabody, Dec. 11, 1925, Louis Howe to F.D.R., April 26, 1927, F.D.R. to Daniels, June 23, 1927, Roosevelt Papers.

13. F.D.R. to Smith, Sept. 17, 1926, F.D.R. to Smith, Jan. 30, 1928, Smith to F.D.R., Feb. 3, 1928, Roosevelt Papers.

14. F.D.R. to George Van Namee, March 26, 1928, to C. C. Donaugh, March 27, 1928, to Daniels, July 26, 1928, to Nicholas Roosevelt, Jan. 28, 1929, Roosevelt Papers.

15. E. K. Lindley, *Roosevelt* (New York, 1931), Ch. 1; Howe to F.D.R., Sept. 25, 26, 26, 28, 28, 28, Oct. 1, 2, 3, 1928, Roosevelt Papers; Eleanor Roosevelt, *This I Remember*, 44, 46; Flynn, *You're the Boss*, 67–70; Doris Fleeson, "Missy — To Do This — FDR," *Saturday Evening Post*, Jan. 8, 1938; Anna Roosevelt, "My Life with FDR," *The Woman*, Aug. 1949; Emil Ludwig, *Roosevelt: A Study in Fortune and Power* (New York, 1938), 119–20; Raskob to F.D.R., Dec. 3, 1928, M. H. McIntyre to G. M. Kimberly, Feb. 10, 1936, Roosevelt Papers; J. T. Flynn, *The Roosevelt Myth* (New York, 1948), 266–70; Freidel, *Ordeal*, Ch. 15.

16. Freidel, *Ordeal*, Ch. 16; S. I. Rosenman, *Working with Roosevelt* (New York, 1952), Ch. 2; F.D.R. speech at Flushing, Oct. 29, 1928, Welles to F.D.R., Nov. 10, 1928, Byrd to F.D.R., Jan. 9, 1929, Roosevelt Papers; Flynn, *You're the Boss*, 70–72; Anna Roosevelt, "My Life with FDR" (Aug. 1949). There are discrepancies between Rosenman's and Flynn's account of election night; the exchange of letters between John Godfrey Saxe and Roosevelt (Dec. 20, 27, 1940, Roosevelt Papers) suggests that Rosenman's account is the more accurate.

CHAPTER 32 *(Pages 386–410)*

1. Frances Perkins, *The Roosevelt I Knew* (New York, 1946), 52; S. I. Rosenman, *Working with Roosevelt* (New York, 1952), 30–31; Grace Tully, *F. D. R., My Boss* (New York, 1949), 45; Clark Howell to F.D.R., Dec. 2, 1931, in F.D.R., *Personal Letters*, III, 230–31; F.D.R. to Adolphus Ragan, April 6, 1938, Roosevelt Papers; Grace Tully to Lindsay Rogers, Aug. 27, 1948, Roosevelt Foundation Papers; J. M. Proskauer, *A Segment of My Times* (New York, 1950), 63–64; James Kieran, "Roosevelt and Smith," *New York Times Magazine*, June 28, 1936.

2. J. F. Carter, "Sire of the Secret Six," *Today*, Jan. 13, 1937; Raymond Moley, *After Seven Years* (New York, 1939), 7.

3. E. J. Flynn, *You're the Boss* (New York, 1947), 235, 74–78; Raymond Moley, *27 Masters of Politics* (New York, 1949), 118–27; E. J. Flynn,

"Reminiscences" (Oral History Project, March 1950), 12; "More Candor," *The New Yorker*, Aug. 30, 1947.
4. F.D.R. to Bruce Bliven, Aug. 6, 1931, Roosevelt Papers; Diana Rice, "Mrs. Roosevelt Takes On Another Task," *New York Times Magazine*, Dec. 2, 1928.
5. F.D.R. to G. Hall Roosevelt, May 20, 1921, and to Smith, May 20, 1927, Roosevelt Papers.
6. F.D.R., "The Real Meaning of the Power Problem," *Forum*, Dec. 1929; F.D.R. to F. A. Delano, Nov. 22, 1929, and to J. Lionberger Davis, Oct. 5, 1929, Henry Salant to F.D.R., April 11, 1931, Roosevelt Papers; S. I. Rosenman, "Governor Roosevelt's Power Program," *Nation*, Sept. 18, 1929; Langdon Post, "The Power Issue in Politics," *Outlook*, July 15, 1931; Judson King, "Roosevelt's Power Record," *New Republic*, Sept. 7, 1932; M. L. Cooke, "The Early Days of the Rural Electrification Idea: 1914–1936," *American Political Science Review*, June 1948.
7. Alfred E. Smith, *Up To Now* (New York, 1929), 314.
8. F.D.R. to J. G. Saxe, Nov. 5, 1931, Roosevelt Papers.
9. *Public Papers of Franklin D. Roosevelt, Forty-Eighth Governor of the State of New York . . . 1931* (Albany, 1937), 716.
10. F.D.R., *Public Papers* (1928–32), 143, 507–8, 509, 511; the second Ithaca speech appeared as "Back to the Land," *Review of Reviews*, Oct. 1931.
11. F.D.R., *Public Papers* (1928–32), 458, 459; F.D.R., *Government — Not Politics* (New York, 1932), 29.
12. Senate Commerce Committee, *Unemployment in the United States: Hearings*, 71 Cong., 2 Sess. (1930), 43–45; Frances Perkins, "Helping Industry to Help Itself," *Harper's*, Oct. 1930.
13. E. K. Lindley, *Roosevelt* (New York, 1931), 332.
14. F.D.R., *Public Papers* (1928–32), 498, 571–72, 573–74; Perkins, *Roosevelt I Knew*, 108; see also F.D.R. to Charles Perkins, Dec. 8, 1930, to Mrs. Caspar Whitney, Dec. 8, 1930, to Governor W. P. Hunt, Sept. 29, 1931, Roosevelt Papers.
15. F.D.R. to Atlee Pomerene, Feb. 5, 1929, Green to F.D.R., Aug. 22, 1930, Roosevelt Papers.
16. F.D.R. to House, June 4, 1932, Roosevelt Papers; Walter Lippmann, *Interpretations, 1931–1932*, Allan Nevins, ed. (New York, 1932), 250, 251.
17. F.D.R. to V. M. Beede, Aug. 10, 1922, Roosevelt Papers; H. W. Van Loon, "What Governor Roosevelt Reads," *Saturday Review of Literature*, Oct. 15, 1932; L. H. Robbins, "Roosevelt Seeks Guidance in History," *New York Times Magazine*, Jan. 28, 1934; John Valentine, "FDR, Book Collector," *F.D.R. Coll.*, May 1949.
18. F.D.R., *Personal Letters*, II, 545–52.
19. F.D.R., *Whither Bound?* (Boston, 1926), 6, 13, 16, 20, 31, 28.
20. F.D.R., memorandum on Leadership, July 6, 1928, Roosevelt Papers;

F.D.R., "The Age of Social Consciousness," *Harvard Graduates' Magazine*, Sept. 1929.

21. H. C. Pell to Mary Carter, May 25, 1943, to Hamilton Fish, Jan. 2, 1937, to John W. Davis, Dec. 10, 1931, Pell Papers; Pell to F.D.R., Jan. 4, 1929, F.D.R. to Pell, Jan. 28, 1929, Roosevelt Papers; H. C. Pell, "A Contented Bourgeois," *North American Review*, Summer 1938; H. C. Pell, "The Future of American Honesty," *North American Review*, March 1933; G. W. Martin, "Preface to the President's Autobiography," *Harper's*, Feb. 1944; *New York Times*, July 5, 1929.

22. Emil Ludwig, *Roosevelt: A Study in Fortune and Power* (New York, 1938), 161.

23. Rosenman, *Working with Roosevelt*, 56–59; Moley, *After Seven Years*, 1–9.

24. Moley, *After Seven Years*, 8–9; E. K. Lindley, *The Roosevelt Revolution* (New York, 1933), 298–302; *Time*, May 8, 1933; "A Brain Trust At Work," *Review of Reviews*, July 1933.

25. H. G. Wells, *Experiment in Autobiography* (New York, 1934), 672.

26. Moley, *After Seven Years*, 23–24; R. G. Tugwell, "The Ideas Behind the New Deal," *New York Times Magazine*, July 16, 1933.

27. R. G. Tugwell, "A New Deal Memoir: Early Days, 1932–1933," Ch. 1, MS in the Tugwell Papers; R. G. Tugwell, "The Preparation of a President," *Western Political Quarterly*, June 1948.

28. Moley, *After Seven Years*, 21–22; Rosenman, *Working with Roosevelt*, 64–66.

29. Tugwell, "New Deal Memoir," Ch. 1.

30. Moley had used the phrase in a memorandum sent down to Warm Springs in May: "Reaction is no barrier to the radical. It is a challenge and a provocation. It is not the pledge of a new deal; it is the reminder of broken promises." A little later Stuart Chase and Bruce Bliven hit upon "A New Deal for America" as the title for a series of articles in the *New Republic*, beginning June 29, 1932. It was not, of course, in any case a wildly original phrase. In Henry James's *The Princess Casamassima* (1886), the Princess said, "I'm one of those who believe that a great new deal is destined to take place. . . . I believe, in a word, in the action of the people for themselves — the others will never act for them; and I'm all ready to act *with* them — in any intelligent or intelligible way." Three years later, in Mark Twain's *A Connecticut Yankee in King Arthur's Court*, the Yankee described Arthurian Britain: "So to speak, I was become a stockholder in a corporation where nine hundred and ninety-four of the members furnished all the money and did all the work, and the other six elected themselves a permanent board of direction and took all the dividends. It seemed to me that what the nine hundred and ninety-four dupes needed was a new deal." In 1903, Brooks Adams wrote: "We must have a new deal, we must have new methods, we must

suppress the states, and have a centralized administration, or we shall wobble over." And doubtless thousands of others used the phrase in similar sense before the spring of 1932. Roosevelt almost certainly never read *The Princess Casamassima*, but Eleanor Roosevelt has written that *A Connecticut Yankee* was his favorite Mark Twain novel; and Cyril Clemens, an unreliable source, quotes Roosevelt as claiming to have "obtained the phrase" from the *Connecticut Yankee*. But there can be little doubt that Rosenman contributed the actual words; and that the press, so to speak, created the phrase "New Deal" by endowing the words with a significance that neither Roosevelt nor Rosenman intended. (Clark Clifford informs me that the phrase "fair deal" was launched with as little premeditation in the Truman administration.

See Rosenman, *Working with Roosevelt*, 71; Moley, *After Seven Years*, 23; Henry James, *The Princess Casamassima*, Ch. 34; Mark Twain, *A Connecticut Yankee in King Arthur's Court*, Ch. 13; Thornton Adams, *Brooks Adams: Constructive Conservative* (Ithaca, N. Y., 1951), 100; Cyril Clemens, *Mark Twain and Franklin D. Roosevelt*, foreword by Eleanor Roosevelt (Webster Groves, Mo., 1949), 11, 19.

31. Moley, *After Seven Years*, 27–34; Rosenman, *Working with Roosevelt*, 67–79; R. G. Tugwell, Diary, Dec. 31, 1932, Tugwell Papers; Tugwell, "New Deal Memoir," Ch. 1; F.D.R., memorandum, March 25, 1933, Roosevelt Papers; Lela Stiles, *The Man Behind Roosevelt* (Cleveland, 1954), 174–75, 192; S. J. Woolf, "As His Closest Friend Sees Roosevelt," *New York Times Magazine*, Nov. 27, 1932.

32. Alben W. Barkley, *That Reminds Me* — (New York, 1954), 140; Eleanor Roosevelt, Foreword, in F.D.R., *Personal Letters*, II, xviii; F. A. Delano to H. S. Hooker, Oct. 28, 1936, Roosevelt Papers; Perkins, *Roosevelt I Knew*, 29; Henry Morgenthau, Jr., interview, April 11, 1947; William Phillips, *Ventures in Diplomacy* (North Beverly, Mass., 1952), 154.

33. Herbert Lehman, *Congressional Record*, 84 Cong., 1 Sess. (April 13, 1955), 3635; M. F. Reilly with W. J. Slocum, *Reilly of the White House* (New York, 1947), 15; National Emergency Council, *Proceedings*, Dec. 20, 1934, National Archives; Tully, *F. D. R.*, 320; Rosenman, *Working with Roosevelt*, 37; Max Hall, "A Hero to His Valet," *Emory University Quarterly*, Oct. 1947; Francis Biddle, interview, July 20, 1953; Perkins, *Roosevelt I Knew*, 81.

34. Flynn, *You're the Boss*, 210; Earle Looker, *This Man Roosevelt* (New York, 1932), 13; Perkins, *Roosevelt I Knew*, 33.

35. F.D.R., Press Conference #597, Nov. 14, 1939, Roosevelt Papers; Walter Tittle, *Roosevelt As an Artist Saw Him* (New York, 1948), 136; Woolf, "As His Closest Friend Sees Roosevelt."

36. Stiles, *Man Behind Roosevelt*, 83; J. N. Rosenau, "Interviews with

Mrs. Franklin D. Roosevelt," 297, Roosevelt Papers; Charles Michelson, *The Ghost Talks* (New York, 1944), 51.

37. Eleanor Roosevelt, "My Day," *New York World-Telegram*, Feb. 19, 1946.

38. These judgments, necessarily subjective, derive from conversations with many members of the Roosevelt circle. The quotations are from Felix Frankfurter, "Franklin Delano Roosevelt," *Harvard Alumni Bulletin*, April 28, 1945, Eleanor Roosevelt, *This Is My Story*, 150, and Harold Ickes, "My Twelve Years with F.D.R.," *Saturday Evening Post*, July 24, 1948. See also for valuable insights: Milton MacKaye, "The Governor," *The New Yorker*, Aug. 22, 1931; Isaiah Berlin, "Mr. Churchill," *Atlantic*, Sept. 1949; Marquis W. Childs, "Mr. Roosevelt," *Survey Graphic*, May 1940; Sir Arthur Salter, *Personality in Politics* (London, 1947), 176-77, Anne O'Hare McCormick, "Roosevelt's View of the Big Job," *New York Times Magazine*, Sept. 11, 1932, and "Still 'A Little Left of Center,'" *New York Times Magazine*, June 21, 1936; as well as the books and articles by Sherwood, Perkins, Moley, Stimson and Bundy, Freidel, Rosenman, Gunther, Tugwell, Lindley, and others.

CHAPTER 33 *(Pages 413-439)*

1. *Proceedings of the Democratic National Committee, 1932*, 587; Raymond Moley, *After Seven Years* (New York, 1939), 35-36; *New York Times*, July 4, 1932; J. A. Farley, *Behind the Ballots* (New York, 1938), 163-64; Charles Michelson, *The Ghost Talks* (New York, 1944), 12.

2. H. S. Johnson, *The Blue Eagle from Egg to Earth* (New York, 1935), 93-94, 114, 116, 121, 123-32, 140; R. G. Tugwell, "A New Deal Memoir: Early Days, 1932-1933," Ch. 1, MS in the Tugwell Papers; Raymond Moley, "There Are Three Brain Trusts," *Today*, April 14, 1934; Raymond Moley, *27 Masters of Politics* (New York, 1949), 168.

3. R. G. Tugwell, "The Progressive Orthodoxy of Franklin D. Roosevelt," *Ethics*, Oct. 1953; R. G. Tugwell, "The Preparation of a President," *Western Political Quarterly*, June 1948; Tugwell, "New Deal Memoir," Ch. 1.

4. *New York Times*, Aug. 27, 1932; Donald Richberg, *My Hero* (New York, 1954), 155; B. N. Timmons, *Garner of Texas* (New York, 1948), 168. In the interests of historical authenticity, I am using the version of the Garner statement told me by Mr. Richberg in an interview on Jan. 3, 1947, rather than the more genteel version printed in the Richberg book; the unexpurgated statement better explains the embarrassment which his book reports Richberg felt on having to convey so blunt a message to the presidential candidate.

5. Alfred E. Smith, "The New Outlook," *New Outlook*, Oct., Nov. 1932; Alfred E. Smith, "They're Wasting Your Money," *Red Book*, Nov.

1932; testimony, Senate Finance Committee, *Investigation of Economic Problems*, 854–55; A. C. Ritchie, "The Democratic Case," *Saturday Evening Post*, Oct. 29, 1932; Rixey Smith and Norman Beasley, *Carter Glass* (New York, 1939), 472; H. F. Byrd, "Better Government at Lower Cost," *Yale Review*, Sept. 1932; J. W. Davis in the *New York Times*, Oct. 30, 1932.

6. Tugwell, "Progressive Orthodoxy"; R. G. Tugwell, interview, Jan. 22, 1952; Grace Tully, *F. D. R., My Boss* (New York, 1949), 324.

7. O. Max Gardner, *Public Papers and Letters . . . 1929–1933* (Raleigh, N.C., 1937), 623.

8. Holmes to Laski, July 30, 1920, in M. DeW. Howe, ed., *Holmes-Laski Letters* (Cambridge, 1953), 272; Tully, *F. D. R.*, 140; "Felix Frankfurter," *Fortune*, Jan. 1936; Archibald MacLeish, "Mr. Justice Frankfurter," *Life*, Feb. 12, 1940; Archibald MacLeish, Introduction in Felix Frankfurter, *Law and Politics*, MacLeish and E. F. Prichard, Jr., eds. (New York, 1939).

9. F.D.R. to D. W. Hovey, Oct. 2, 1930, to Gilbert Orlovitz, Dec. 7, 1931, Roosevelt Papers; F.D.R., *Public Papers* (1928–32), 662–63, 666; Moley, *After Seven Years*, 11; Tugwell, "New Deal Memoir," Ch. 1; Tugwell, "Progressive Orthodoxy."

10. *New York Times*, Jan. 5, 1933; Louise Overacker, "Campaign Funds in a Depression Year," *American Political Science Review*, Oct. 1933.

11. Alfred Lief, *Democracy's Norris* (New York, 1939), 388–94; H. L. Ickes, *Autobiography of a Curmudgeon* (New York, 1943), 253; *Proceedings of the Democratic National Committee*, 597; *New York Times*, Sept. 26, 1932; A. F. Mullen, *Western Democrat* (New York, 1940), 294–95; Richberg, *My Hero*, 156–57.

12. *New York Times*, Jan. 5, 1933; Moley, *27 Masters*, 37–38.

13. Ickes to F.D.R., July 8, 1932, Elizabeth Bass to F.D.R., July 19, 1932, Roosevelt Papers; Moley, *27 Masters*, 209–11; Gene Fowler, *Beau James* (New York, 1949), 327; E. J. Flynn, "Reminiscences" (Oral History Project, March 1950), 15; Walter Lippmann in the *New York Herald Tribune*, Oct. 7, 1932; Mullen, *Western Democrat*, 286–87; S. I. Rosenman, *Working with Roosevelt* (New York, 1952), 83.

14. Tugwell, "Progressive Orthodoxy."

15. F.D.R., *Public Papers* (1928–32), 699.

16. F.D.R., *Public Papers* (1928–32), 712, 740.

17. F.D.R., *Public Papers* (1928–32), 742–56.

18. Moley, *After Seven Years*, 47–52; Anne O'Hare McCormick, "The Two Men at the Big Moment," *New York Times Magazine*, Nov. 6, 1932; F.D.R., speech at Atlanta, Oct. 24, 1932, Roosevelt Papers; Tugwell, "New Deal Memoir," Ch. 1; Moley to F.D.R., Nov. 30, 1935, Roosevelt Papers.

19. T. L. Stokes, *Chip Off My Shoulder* (Princeton, 1940), especially 324;

Anna Roosevelt, "My Life with FDR," *The Woman,* Oct. 1949; Pittman to F.D.R., Oct. 4, 1932, Roosevelt Papers.

20. E. K. Lindley, *The Roosevelt Revolution* (New York, 1933), 4; F.D.R., address at Poughkeepsie, Nov. 7, 1932, Roosevelt Papers; H. M. Kannee, transcript of campaign speeches, Roosevelt Papers; McCormick, "Two Men at the Big Moment."

21. Garner to F.D.R., Oct. 3, 1932, Roosevelt Papers; Farley, *Behind the Ballots,* 176; Press Conference #578, Sept. 12, 1939, Roosevelt Papers; *New York Times,* Oct. 11, 1932; *New York Herald Tribune,* Oct. 13, 1932.

22. H. L. Stimson, Diary, June 27, 1932; Dolly Gann, *Dolly Gann's Book* (New York, 1933), 230; *New York Times,* July 5, 12, 1932; *New York Herald Tribune,* Oct. 11, 1932.

23. Stimson, Diary, July 5, Aug. 5, 1932.

24. T. G. Joslin, *Hoover Off the Record* (New York, 1934), 295, 296, 301; Stimson, Diary, Sept. 25, 1932; I. H. Hoover, "The Hospitable Hoovers," *Saturday Evening Post,* April 14, 1934; *New York Daily News,* Oct. 5, 1932; Hoover, *State Papers,* II, 302, 308.

25. Joslin, *Hoover,* Ch. 26; Stokes, *Chip Off My Shoulder,* 304-5; E. W. Starling, *Starling of the White House* (New York, 1946), 299; Edward Angly, "A Story Time Has Told," *New Outlook,* April 1934; Hoover, "Hospitable Hoovers."

26. F.D.R., *Public Papers* (1928-32), 784, 808, 835-837, 853; Moley, *After Seven Years,* 59, 64; Michelson, *The Ghost Talks,* 11; Tugwell, "New Deal Memoir," Ch. 1.

27. Hoover, *State Papers,* II, 351, 337, 408-28; *New York Times,* Nov. 1, 1932; Walter Lippmann, *The Method of Freedom* (New York, 1934), 32.

28. Moley, *After Seven Years,* 64; John Chamberlain, "A Hamiltonian Reformer," *New Republic,* Sept. 14, 1932.

29. Paul Douglas, "Who Are the Democrats?" *World Tomorrow,* Sept. 28, 1932; John Dewey, "The Need for a New Party," *New Republic,* March 18, 1931; John Dewey, "Prospects for a Third Party," *New Republic,* July 27, 1932; *New York Times,* Oct. 7, 1932; R. M. Lovett, "Progressives at Cleveland," *New Republic,* July 20, 1932.

30. "How I Shall Vote," *Forum,* Nov. 1932; *Culture and the Crisis* (New York, 1932), 3, 17, 20, 24, 18, 30.

31. Hoover, *State Papers,* II, 452-54, 477-79; *New York Herald Tribune,* Nov. 6, 1932; *New York Times,* Nov. 6, 1932; Starling, *Starling,* 300; W. A. White, "Herbert Hoover," *Saturday Evening Post,* March 4, 1933.

32. F.D.R., address at Poughkeepsie, Roosevelt Papers.

33. *New York Times,* Nov. 9, 1932; Lela Stiles, *The Man Behind Roosevelt* (Cleveland, 1954), 216; Farley, *Behind the Ballots,* 185-89.

CHAPTER 34 *(Pages 440-455)*

1. McAdoo to F.D.R., Nov. 22, 1932, Woodin to F.D.R., Nov. 15, 1932, Roosevelt Papers; Daniels to F.D.R., Nov. 9, 1932, F.D.R. to Daniels, Nov. 17, 1932, in Carroll Kilpatrick, ed., *Roosevelt and Daniels: A Friendship in Politics* (Chapel Hill, 1952), 122-24; Milton Stone to F.D.R., Nov. 14, 1932, Roosevelt Papers; *Time*, Nov. 28, 1932.
2. F.D.R. to Norman Davis, Nov. 26, 1932, Davis Papers; L. B. Wehle, *Hidden Threads of History* (New York, 1953), 120-21.
3. Sumner Welles to Norman Davis, Nov. 28, 1932, Davis Papers; F.D.R. to W. H. Mahony, May 22, 1928, Roosevelt Papers; Eleanor Roosevelt, *This I Remember* (New York, 1949), 61.
4. Hoover, *State Papers*, II, 587, 589, 592; Hoover, *Memoirs*, II, 179-80.
5. Raymond Moley, *After Seven Years* (New York, 1939), 68-79; R. G. Tugwell, Diary, Dec. 20, 1932, Jan. 14, 1933, Tugwell Papers; R. G. Tugwell, "A New Deal Memoir: Early Days, 1932-1933," Ch. 1, MS in the Tugwell Papers.
6. Welles to Davis, Nov. 28, 1932, Davis Papers.
7. H. L. Stimson, Diary, Nov. 14, 11, 22, 1932.
8. Moley, *After Seven Years*, 72-77; I. H. Hoover, *Forty-Two Years in the White House* (Boston, 1934), 222-23; Stimson, Diary, Nov. 22, 1932. Hoover's own recollections of this meeting are manifestly garbled. Thus he remembers Stimson as having been present at this conference, which Stimson was not. Evidently Hoover confused the November 22 conference with the later discussions in January. See Hoover, *Memoirs*, III, 179-84.
9. Tugwell, Diary, Dec. 20, 1932; Stimson, Diary, Dec. 21, 1932.
10. Stimson, Diary, Dec. 22, 23, 24, 27, 28, 1932, Jan. 3, 4, 6, 9, 19, 1933; H. L. Stimson, "Reminiscences" (Oral History Project, Sept. 1949), 20-21; H. L. Stimson and McGeorge Bundy, *On Active Service in Peace and War* (New York, 1948), 289-93; Stimson to F.D.R., Dec. 10, 1932, F.D.R. to Stimson, Dec. 24, 1932, Roosevelt Papers.
11. Stimson, Diary, Jan. 17, 1933; Tugwell, Diary, Jan. 17, 1933; Moley, *After Seven Years*, 94-95.
12. Tugwell, Diary, Jan. 22, 1933; Moley, *After Seven Years*, 94-105; R. G. Tugwell, "The Protagonists: Roosevelt and Hoover," *Antioch Review*, Dec. 1953. The documents, as reproduced in Stimson, Diary, Jan. 20, 1933, bear out Moley's claim that the original Stimson statement failed to contain the agreement reached at the conference concerning the separation of the debt and the economic discussions. On the other hand, it should be noted that Stimson received the clear impression on January 19 that Moley agreed with Davis and himself on this question: when Moley took the opposite position at the White House conference on January 20, it seemed to Stimson "such a reversal of Moley's attitude

of the evening before, where he had been helpful on the subject, that I could not understand it."

13. *New York Times*, Dec. 5, 6, 1932; J. N. Leonard, *Three Years Down* (New York, 1939), 298–300; M. A. Hallgren, *Seeds of Revolt* (New York, 1933), 184–85; Malcolm Cowley, "Red Day in Washington," *New Republic*, Dec. 21, 1932; Allen Chase, "Both Hungry and Marching," *Common Sense*, Dec. 29, 1932; Robert Cantwell, "The Hunger Marchers' Victory," *Common Sense*, Jan. 19, 1933.

14. T. G. Joslin, *Hoover Off the Record* (New York, 1934), 331; Alfred E. Smith, "Democratic Leadership at the Crossroads," *New Outlook*, March 1933.

15. B. N. Timmons, *Garner of Texas* (New York, 1948), 171–72; Rixey Smith and Norman Beasley, *Carter Glass* (New York, 1939), 323–24; Tugwell, Diary, Dec. 27, 1932; *New York Times*, Jan. 6, 7, 1933; Tugwell, "New Deal Memoir," Chs. 1, 4.

16. J. M. Keynes in Arthur Salter, *et. al., The World's Economic Crisis* (New York, 1932), 61; J. M. Keynes, "The Economy Report," *New Statesman*, Aug. 15, 1931; J. M. Keynes, *Essays in Persuasion* (London, 1931), 162; Stuart Chase, "Government Economy," *Scribner's*, Dec. 1932.

17. Tugwell, "New Deal Memoir," Ch. 1; *New York Herald Tribune*, Dec. 1, 1932; Raymond Moley, *27 Masters of Politics* (New York, 1949), 242.

18. Tugwell, "New Deal Memoir," Chs. 1, 4; Tugwell, Diary, Dec. 20, 1932, Jan. 14, 25, 29, 1933; *New York World-Telegram*, Jan. 26, 1933.

19. W. L. White, *Bernard Baruch* (New York, 1950), 78; Tom Connally, *My Name Is Tom Connally* (New York, 1954), 148; Cordell Hull, *Memoirs* (New York, 1948), I, 161–62; *Time*, Jan. 23, 1933.

20. Judson King, "Roosevelt's Power Record," *New Republic*, Sept. 7, 1932; Alfred Lief, *Democracy's Norris* (New York, 1939), 396.

21. A persistent myth is that New Deal policies came as a total surprise after Roosevelt's 1932 campaign. The fact is that nearly all the New Deal measures were foreshadowed in the campaign. As E. K. Lindley summed up the situation, "With one exception, every important venture of the New Deal was forecast in Mr. Roosevelt's campaign." Rosenman writes, "Except for the NRA . . . every major project of the first term, every important part of the New Deal program, was foreshadowed in one or more of the speeches — and the NRA was certainly "foreshadowed" in the speech of October 6 about planning and regularizing production. Cf. E. K. Lindley, *The Roosevelt Revolution* (New York, 1933), 3, 10, 34–41; S. I. Rosenman, *Working with Roosevelt* (New York, 1952), 85–86.

22. E. D. Coblentz, *William Randolph Hearst* (New York, 1952), 146–51; George Creel, *Rebel at Large* (New York, 1947), 270–73.

23. F.D.R. to Norris, Dec. 14, 1932, Roosevelt Papers; *New York Times*, Jan. 22, 23, Feb. 3, 1933; F.D.R., *Public Papers* (1928–32), 888.

24. D. C. Roper, "The New Deal Endorses Profits," *Forum*, Dec. 1934; Tugwell, "New Deal Memoir," Ch. 1.

CHAPTER 35 *(Pages 456–485)*

1. James E. Watson, *As I Knew Them* (Indianapolis, 1936), 305; T. G. Joslin, *Hoover Off the Record* (New York, 1934), 340.
2. *New York Sun*, Jan. 6, 1933; H. L. Stoddard, *It Costs To Be President* (New York, 1938), 142–46. I am indebted to Robert Roeder for the phrase "the great void" in this connection.
3. Senate Finance Committee, *Investigation of Economic Problems: Hearings*, 72 Cong., 2 Sess. (1933), 18, 204, 215, 219, 287, 249, 77, 798, 941, 827, 443, 446, 683, 690, 300, 741.
4. George Sokolsky, "The Temper of the People," *New Outlook*, April 1933; Walter Lippmann, "Big Business Men of Tomorrow," *American Magazine*, April 1934; Joseph P. Kennedy, *I'm for Roosevelt* (New York, 1936), 93.
5. Testimony of E. A. O'Neal, Senate Banking and Currency Committee, *Refinancing Past Due Obligations on Farms and Homes: Hearings*, 72 Cong., 1 Sess. (1933), 168–76, and Senate Agriculture and Forestry Committee, *Agricultural Adjustment Relief Plan: Hearings*, 72 Cong., 1 Sess. (1933), 15; testimony of J. A. Simpson, Sen. Agr. Com., *Agricultural Adjustment Relief Plan*, 27–28; *Time*, Jan. 16, 23, Feb. 13, 1933; *Literary Digest*, Jan. 21, Feb. 4, 11, 1933; M. H. Vorse, "The Farmers' Relief Conference," *New Republic*, Dec. 28, 1932; Lief Dahl, "Nebraska Farmers in Action," *New Republic*, Jan. 16, 1933; Ella Bloor, *We Are Many* (New York, 1940), 237; Karl Presthold, "Do Farmers 'Revolt'?" *North American Review*, July 1933; "Bryan! Bryan!!" *Fortune*, Jan. 1934.
6. *New York Times*, Feb. 8, 1933; *New York Herald Tribune*, Feb. 10, 17, 1933.
7. Howard Scott, "Technology Smashes the Price System," *Harper's*, Jan. 1933; Allen Raymond, *What Is Technocracy?* (New York, 1933), especially 96–97; Howard Scott, "Technocracy — 1933," *Common Sense*, Dec. 1933; Wayne Weishaar, "Technocracy: an Appraisal," *North American Review*, Feb. 1933; Stuart Chase, *Technocracy: An Interpretation* (New York, 1933); "Twenty-Five on Technocracy," *Common Sense*, Feb. 2, 1933; Archibald MacLeish, "Technocracy Speaks," *Saturday Review of Literature*, Jan. 28, 1933; Alfred E. Smith, "The New Outlook," *New Outlook*, Jan. 1933; *New York Times*, Aug. 21, 1932, Jan. 18, 24, 1933; Paul H. Douglas, "Technocracy," *World Tomorrow*, Jan. 18, 1933; Paul Blanshard, "The Gospel According to Technocracy," *World Tomorrow*, Feb. 22, 1933; George Soule, "Technocracy," *New Republic*, Dec. 28, 1932; Virgil Jordan, "Technocracy — Tempest on a Slide Rule," *Scribner's*, Feb. 1933; W. W. Parrish, "Technocracy's

Challenge," *New Outlook*, Jan. 1933; Broadus Mitchell, "A Test of Technocrats," *Virginia Quarterly Review*, April 1933; letter by W. H. Smyth, *Nation*, Dec. 28, 1932; *Time*, Jan. 23, 1933; Robert Roeder, "Utopianism's Effects on America During the Great Void," written in my Harvard seminar; J. S. Gambs, *The Decline of the I.W.W.* (New York, 1932), 156–62; Joseph Dorfman, *Thorstein Veblen and His America* (New York, 1934), Ch. 24.

8. M. F. Reilly, *Reilly of the White House* (New York, 1947), 48–52; *New York Herald Tribune*, Feb. 16, 1933; *New York Times*, Feb. 16, 17, 20, 1933; *New York World-Telegram*, Feb. 16, 1933; F.D.R. to Garner, Dec. 21, 1932, Roosevelt Papers; *Time*, Feb. 27, 1933; Max Hall, "A Hero to his Valet," *Emory University Quarterly*, Oct. 1947; Raymond Moley, *After Seven Years* (New York 1939), 138–39; J. A. Farley, *Jim Farley's Story* (New York, 1948), 22.

9. *New York Times*, Dec. 14–22, 1931; *New York Herald Tribune*, April 6, 1955; In justice to Mr. Contasini, I should add that Churchill freely conceded that he was to blame for the accident, offered Contasini a check — which Contasini, though unemployed, refused — and then gave him an autographed copy of *The Unknown War*.

10. Sara Roosevelt to F.D.R., Nov. 14, 1932, Roosevelt Family Papers; J. A. Farley, *Behind the Ballots* (New York, 1938), 183; E. D. Coblentz, *William Randolph Hearst* (New York, 1952), 147.

11. Lela Stiles, *The Man Behind Roosevelt* (Cleveland, 1954), 231; E. J. Flynn, *You're the Boss* (New York, 1947), 123; Moley, *After Seven Years*, 109, 123; A. F. Mullen, *Western Democrat* (New York, 1940), 305.

12. *Davis v. Las Ovas Co., Inc.*, 227 U.S. at 80.

13. Cordell Hull, *Memoirs* (New York, 1948), I, 156–59; L. B. Wehle, *Hidden Threads of History* (New York, 1953), 129; Moley, *After Seven Years*, 111–18; H. L. Ickes, *The Secret Diary . . . The First Thousand Days, 1933–1936* (New York, 1953), 110; Charles W. Ervin, *Homegrown Liberal* (New York, 1954), 203–4.

14. Moley, *After Seven Years*, 118–21; Rixey Smith and Norman Beasley, *Carter Glass* (New York, 1939), 330–34; A. A. Berle, Jr., Diary, May 10, 1939, Berle Papers; Glass to F.D.R., Feb. 7, 1933, Roosevelt Papers; Rixey Smith, who was Glass's secretary at the time, confirms Moley and casts doubt on the account given in Farley, *Behind the Ballots*, 202–3.

15. Moley, *After Seven Years*, 121–23; Farley, *Behind the Ballots*, 206.

16. Russell Lord, *The Wallaces of Iowa* (Boston, 1947), 322–24; Raymond Moley, "Gideon Goes to War," *Newsweek*, Jan. 12, 1948; Sidney Hyman, memorandum of talk with Thomas H. Beck, March 13, 1949, Roosevelt Foundation Papers; O. M. Kile, *The Farm Bureau Through Three Decades* (Baltimore, 1948), 194; Wallace to F.D.R., Nov. 17, 1932, in G. C. Fite, *George N. Peek and the Fight for Farm Parity* (Norman, Okla., 1954), 241–42.

17. D. C. Roper, *Fifty Years of Public Life* (Durham, N.C., 1941), 265–66; Moley, *After Seven Years*, 124–25; R. G. Tugwell, Diary, Feb. 26, 1933, Tugwell Papers.

18. Mary W. Dewson, "An Aid to the End," Ch. 1, MS autobiography, Dewson Papers; Frances Perkins to F.D.R., Feb. 1, 1933, Roosevelt Family Papers; Frances Perkins, "Eight Years as Madame Secretary," *Fortune*, Sept. 1941; Frances Perkins, *The Roosevelt I Knew* (New York, 1946), 150–52.

19. F.D.R. to Dern, Feb. 2, Dern to F.D.R., Feb. 12, 1933, M. N. Dana to F.D.R., Jan. 23, 1933, Roosevelt Papers; H. L. Ickes, *Autobiography of a Curmudgeon* (New York, 1943), 261–70; Perkins, *Roosevelt I Knew*, 150–51; Mullen, *Western Democrat*, 302–3; Ickes, *First Thousand Days*, 240, 631; Moley, *After Seven Years*, 126–27.

20. H. L. Ickes, "My Twelve Years with F.D.R.," *Saturday Evening Post*, June 5, 1948.

21. F.D.R. to Rosenman, March 9, 1933, Roosevelt Papers; Moley, *After Seven Years*, 81; Tugwell, Diary, Jan. 7, Feb. 10, 17, 18, 1933; Raymond Moley, *27 Masters of Politics* (New York, 1949), 81.

22. Moley, *After Seven Years*, 115–18; Daniels to F.D.R., July 18, 1939, Roosevelt Papers; Josephus Daniels, *Shirt-Sleeve Diplomat* (Chapel Hill, 1947), 18–19.

23. *Historical Statistics*, N 141–47; J. M. Keynes, *Essays in Persuasion* (London, 1931), 168–78; Hoover, *State Papers*, I, 133, 145, 375, II, 4.

24. Memorandum of talk with Henry Ford, Feb. 13, 1933, by R. D. Chapin and A. A. Ballantine, Office of the Comptroller of the Currency, Banking Emergency Records, National Archives; A. A. Ballantine, "When All the Banks Closed," *Harvard Business Review*, March 1948; testimony of Edsel Ford, A. A. Ballantine, and others, Senate Banking and Currency Committee, *Stock Exchange Practices: Hearings*, 73 Cong., 2 Sess. (1934), Parts X, XI.

25. Hoover to F.D.R., Feb. 17, 1933, Hoover to S. D. Fess, Feb. 21, 1933, Hoover to D. A. Reed, Feb. 20, 1933, in W. S. Myers and W. H. Newton, *The Hoover Administration: A Documented Narrative* (New York, 1936), 338–41, 351; Moley, *After Seven Years*, 140.

26. Stimson, Diary, Feb. 22, 1933; Grace Tully, *F. D. R., My Boss* (New York, 1949), 63; Myers and Newton, *Hoover Administration*, 344–45; Moley, *After Seven Years*, 141–42; R. G. Tugwell, "The Protagonists: Roosevelt and Hoover," *Antioch Review*, Dec. 1953.

27. Lamont to F.D.R., Feb. 27, 1933, Roosevelt Papers; Tugwell, Diary, Jan. 14, Feb. 18, 26, 1933; Moley, *After Seven Years*, 142–144; E. K. Lindley, *The Roosevelt Revolution* (New York, 1933), 77–78; R. G. Tugwell, "A New Deal Memoir: Early Days, 1932–1933," Ch. 1, MS in the Tugwell Papers.

28. Edmund Wilson, "Sunshine Charley," *Travels in Two Democracies* (New York, 1936), 55–62.

29. Tugwell, "New Deal Memoir," Ch. 1; Farley, *Behind the Ballots,* 207–8; Farley, *Jim Farley's Story,* 36.
30. Cf. Moley, *After Seven Years,* 146–47, footnote; Myers and Newton, *Hoover Administration,* 366; Smith and Beasley, *Glass,* 340–42.
31. R. E. Sherwood, "Inaugural Parade," *Saturday Review of Literature,* March 4, 1933.
32. F.D.R. "Memorandum on Leadership," July 6, 1928, F.D.R. to Ray Stannard Baker, March 20, 1935, Roosevelt Papers; for F.D.R. and T.R., see also Earle Looker, *This Man Roosevelt* (New York, 1932), 55; H. F. Pringle, "The President," *The New Yorker,* June 30, 1934; Perkins, *Roosevelt I Knew,* 46.
33. Theodore Roosevelt, *An Autobiography* (New York, 1913), 378–80, 400–401; Woodrow Wilson, *Constitutional Government* (New York, 1908), 70.
34. Anne O'Hare McCormick, "Roosevelt's View of the Big Job," *New York Times Magazine,* Sept. 11, 1932; Frankfurter to F.D.R., Nov. 10, 1932, Roosevelt Papers; Lindley, *Roosevelt Revolution,* 34.
35. *Times* (London), Jan. 31, 1933; *New York Times,* Jan. 31, 1933; Konrad Heiden, *Der Fuehrer* (Boston, 1944), 540.

Index

Index

ABOUT THE AUTHOR

Arthur M. Schlesinger, Jr., won the Pulitzer Prize for History in 1946 for *The Age of Jackson* and the Pulitzer Prize for Biography in 1966 for *A Thousand Days: JFK in the White House*. He is the Albert Schweitzer Professor in the Humanities at the City University of New York. A graduate of Harvard, Schlesinger also studied at Peterhouse, Cambridge, and has been a professor of history at Harvard. He lives in New York City.